Understanding Media in the Digital Age

Connections for Communication, Society, and Culture

Everette E. Dennis
Fordham University

Melvin L. DeFleur
Louisiana State University

Allyn & Bacon

New York   San Francisco   Boston   Upper Saddle River
London   Toronto   Sydney   Tokyo   Singapore   Madrid
Mexico City   Munich   Paris   Cape Town   Hong Kong   Montreal

Editor in Chief: Karon Bowers
Acquisitions Editor: Jeanne Zalesky
Executive Marketing Manager: Wendy Gordon
Development Manager: David Kear
Senior Development Editor: Carol Alper
Associate Development Editor: Angela Pickard
Assistant Editor: Megan Lentz
Production Supervisor: Liz Napolitano
Managing Editor: Michael Granger/Linda Mihatov Behrens
Associate Managing Editor: Bayani Mendoza de Leon
Project Manager: Raegan Keida Heerema
Production Management: Elm Street Publishing Services
Senior Operations Specialist: Nick Sklitsis
Operations Specialist: Joanne Sweeney/Mary Ann Gloriande
Art Director: Kristina Mose-Libon
Cover Photograph: © Christoph Wilhelm/Stone/Getty Images

Library of Congress Cataloging-in-Publication Data

Dennis, Everette E.
   Understanding media in the digital age : connections for communication, society and culture / Everette E. Dennis,
Melvin L. DeFleur.
      p. cm.
   ISBN 978-0-205-59582-2
   1. Digital media.   2. Digital communication.   I. DeFleur, Melvin L. (Melvin Lawrence), II. Title.
   QA76.76.I59D46 2010
   004.6—dc22

                                                                                                2009029945

10 9 8 7 6 5 4 3 2—QWV—13 12 11 10

Allyn & Bacon
is an imprint of

www.pearsonhighered.com

ISBN-13: 978-0-205-59582-2
ISBN-10:   0-205-59582-0

CONTENTS

SPECIAL FEATURES

MEDIA LEADERS INSIGHTS

BIG IDEAS: MEDIA THEORIES EXPLAINED

Understanding Media in the Digital Age: Connections for Communication, Society, and Culture is all about connections—making connections between different kinds of knowledge from different disciplines and traditions drawing on the realms of experience and systematic scholarship. The goal is one of truly understanding and navigating media and communication in this, the digital age. In this time of uncertainty almost anything written will be tempered by time and will require inevitable change. That's as it should be. This book offers a substantive template, integrating different ways of knowing into a narrative, buttressed by data and analysis that is meant to be the basis for integrating new information, against the backdrop of what's come before. As seductive as the challenges of what industry analysts call the distance between Web 2.0 and Web 3.0— one representing the current preoccupation with *interactivity*—social networks, wikis, online collaboration and sharing—and the other, *the future*—everything that will follow in a web-based environment, including the "next big thing" that will usher in a communication and media landscape, is yet unimagined.

It is important we believe, in studying the field of media and communication, to develop a capacity for *strategic thinking*—looking expansively and in a disciplined fashion across many dimensions of knowledge to achieve understanding. It is common these days to focus on *critical thinking* to study media to become media critics, rather than informed users or future employees—or even more thoughtful, discerning citizens. This is written as the very concept of *mass communication* is being challenged and reconsidered, even though schools and courses of study embrace it—and honor the name, while media industries still use the term to describe their activity. That makes this book, and the conversation begun here by the authors and joined by students and their professors, an exciting venture since collectively our thinking about the field we call mass communication, communication, journalism or media studies will be shaped in that process. As the thought leader Kenneth Boulding put it, life itself is a conversation— it begins before we arrive on the scene; we join it for awhile and know that it will continue long after we've gone. Yet in the midst of massive economic, technological and regulatory changes, mass communication as a field of study and as media and entertainment industries warrants attention and analysis as never before. Always important in the modern age, the media and the processes that drive and direct them have grown in influence as linchpins of an information society modified by *all things digital*. This has given the media greater cultural and social impact, vital to all institutions and to every individual in society today. It is a time marked by what business leaders call "ease of entry," not only into the media market for owners and investors to start new media firms, but also when almost any individual can create a web site (possibly a web business) and communicate far and wide. It is a time when any citizen can potentially have personal impact across time and distance, something that was once almost beyond human imagination and indisputable that exercising freedom of the press or media belonged only to those who owned a printing press or operated a TV station.

Understanding Media in the Digital Age is more than a guidebook, but a reminder to be acutely aware of the forces and factors that have and continue to shape our media scene as part of the larger society and culture. The book is a new formulation by the authors that draws on earlier work, including a longstanding text that served as a laboratory for what appears here. From its beginning our work together as authors has uniquely linked research and intellectual inquiry with industry and professional experience. We aim at producing more than a simplistic inventory of media industries and instead craft a portrait of the functions of human communication as well as their applications in and across several distinct media industries, often organized under large corporate umbrellas, that exist alongside smaller scale efforts, some by ordinary individuals who also live and work in the digital era, well outside the behemoths of big media companies.

This book takes up the basic functions of communication, most often described as *information, opinion, entertainment,* and *advertising/marketing* as they have evolved within different media over several generations while the differences made by digital integration. We look at mass communication as a system, both in the United States and on the global scene. Against a backdrop of historical development and attention to media economies, technology and policy, we treat the several distinct media industries—because that's the way they still exist—both as social institutions and as part of increasingly integrated multi-media enterprises, which they are as well.

What readers will find here is the result of a longstanding partnership between the authors that produced eight earlier books, an experience that has helped us better understand the media as we've integrated knowledge gained through scholarship with observations in and across media industries involving leaders, managers, and professional employees at all levels. We have also benefited from commentary and criticism from people inside and outside the media and the academy, including media critics, reporters, financial analysts, people from a variety of other fields, and most especially, our current and former students. Our work is based on experience both in the United States as well as in some fifty countries where we have lived, worked, researched and taught. While benefiting from these many interactions and connections, in producing this text we did more than synthesize and represent the work of others. Our own active scholarship can be found within the text including theoretical perspectives that draw from research we have commissioned and proprietary material from industry leaders with whom we have worked. Ultimately this book is about sharing—our own work with that of others, drawing on classic sources well fixed in the literature, as well as new studies only recently published. All this is part of an interactive mix which we hope provides a framework for understanding media by engaging the very connections to which we've referred here. To that end we hope our readers will begin a journey toward strategic understanding that is both satisfying and elevating.

APPROACH OF *UNDERSTANDING MEDIA IN THE DIGITAL AGE*

We were inspired in part while preparing this book by an executive steeped in the digital world who argues that the "only new discipline" offered to date to make sense of it all is "connections planning." Connections, as a concept and reality, explains both the theory and practice of the digital media/communications world whether that involves a rich yield from social networking for an individual or the operation of a media company aimed at producing a product. Thus, we've organized this book to make connections based on knowledge and experience.

Part One begins with **Connections for Communication,** in which we explore the communications process in the context of the rise of digital media. We follow that with consideration of what we call, *navigating change* wherein global challenges for media and society are explored. Beginning here and throughout the book, we integrate digital developments into the narrative as they connect with the realities of current or planned operations.

Part Two explores the broad field of **Publishing,** which began with early printing and continues today with both the old form and across digital channels and platforms too. Here we examine the *book publishing* field, the first and still the most respected medium. From there we travel to *newspapers and news media,* examining the work they do delivering information to individuals and society over a variety of increasingly segmented and refined channels. As always in the book, the history of the medium and its social development is in the forefront. On then to *magazines,* truly voices for many interests and the inventors of market segmentation and audience specialization. Laced throughout this part of the book is the incremental integration of online technologies and delivery systems and what they portend.

Part Three examines **Electronic and Visual Media**, beginning with *motion pictures,* an old industry tempered and redefined in the digital age, as it finds new outlets for its creative expression, including social networks and new style theaters, some of them in the home. We also treat *radio,* truly the most resilient of the media, that rose dramatically and dominated the media scene at one time, and later was almost made extinct by *television* before it redefined itself, as it is doing today with digital and satellite applications. Then, the box that changed everything: television. From its early post-radio beginnings through the several stages of *cable* to the introduction of digital TV, this medium has been the most influential for fifty years, but faces challenges in a web-based world.

Part Four examines **Media Audiences, Services and Support.** We begin with a look at *news, journalism and public affairs* as a media function and source of content. As journalism produced by professionals is being redefined by citizen journalists and file sharing of all kinds, we consider the standards, styles and trends affecting its practice and distribution. If journalism is mainly concerned with the *information* function of media, *popular culture* best describes that of *entertainment.* Here we consider entertainment fare and music in the context of taste cultures and styles that affect media behavior and content. Next comes the media's economic driver, *advertising*—a process, industry and societal force—being radically redefined by digitization. From old media stretching to adapt to new advertising networks that bypass both old media and the advertising agency, we examine this vital and changing field. Advertising is rightly closely connected to *public relations,* which is also a process, industry and social forces, in part because many public relations firms are owned by large advertising holding companies, also because they work hand in glove to advance social communication. Both are deeply affected by digital technologies, which they began using even before conventional media companies did.

In *Part Five* we step back and consider the larger forces that are drivers of change—**Media Issues and Influences**—we consider three interrelated social forces—those of *economics, technology* and *policy* development. These concepts and real life areas connect with (and sometimes against) each other as part of a continuing conflict from which media change evolves and develops. Those forces are usually examined through the prism of *media effects,* which explain the processes and influences of mass communication, drawing on early and contemporary media research. We conclude this section with a look at *ethics,* an articulation of that branch of philosophy concerned with moral choices, so important in this case to media operations. Assessing the content and behavior of the media truly helps us understand them individually and as a social force. From these five parts over fifteen chapters, layered with many sources and analytical perspectives, we believe that understanding media in a digital age can be continuously enhanced.

Special features in this book include our original *Curves of Adoption* that track how media reached their current state and penetration levels, charts and graphs with the latest available statistics—and some speculative ones from forecasting companies and other material aimed at enhancing the reader's experience with this book. We also offer original material in our *Media Leaders Insights,* especially arranged for this book based on personal relationships with those interviewed. Also integrated into the book are selected *Big Ideas: Media Effects Explained* boxes, which draw on the work of Professor Margaret DeFleur of Louisiana State University, and are used by permission. We also offer a *Media and Communications Digitology* with Web links on major sources of continuing information in a constantly changing world.

RESOURCES IN PRINT AND ONLINE

Name of Supplement	Available in Print	Available Online	Instructor or Student Supplement	Description
Instructor's Manual and Test Bank Available for download at www.pearsonhighered.com/irc		X	Instructor Supplement	This text-specific instructor resource prepared by Amy Lauters, Minnesota State University, Mankato, is organized into two parts:
				Part 1: Instructor's Manual contains sample syllabi, chapter summaries, chapter learning objectives, a lecture outline, activities for student-based learning, and discussion questions.
				Part 2: Test Bank contains numerous questions blending multiple-choice, true/false, short-answer, and essay, organized by chapter. Each question is referenced by page number.
MyTest Available at www.pearsonmytest.com		X	Instructor Supplement	This flexible, online test generating software includes all questions found in the Test Bank section of the Instructor's Manual and Test Bank.
PowerPoint™ Presentation Available for download at www.pearsonhighered.com/irc		X	Instructor Supplement	This text-specific presentation package provides a basis for your lecture with PowerPoint™ slides for each chapter of the book.
MyCommunicationKit™ for *Understanding Media in the Digital Age* (access code required)		X	Instructor and Student Supplement	Prepared by Amy Lauters, University of Minnesota, Mankato, the MyCommunicationKit for *Understanding Media in the Digital Age* is a book-specific, dynamic, interactive study tool for students. Offerings are organized by chapter and include practice exams (with page references), relevant media, learning objectives, and weblinks.
Become Media Literate! Projects and Worksheets for the Critical Consumer of Mass Media	X		Student Supplement	Prepared by Meredith Everson of the Annenberg School of Communication at the University of Pennsylvania, projects and worksheets guide students through various exercises designed to help students become more aware of media and how they use it in their lives.
Allyn & Bacon Mass Communication Study Site (Open Access)		X	Student Supplement	The Allyn & Bacon Introduction to Mass Communication Study Site features practice tests, weblinks, and flashcards of key terms. The site is organized around major topics in your introduction to mass communication textbook.

Name of Supplement	Available in Print	Available Online	Instructor or Student Supplement	Description
Allyn & Bacon Mass Communication Interactive Video Library	X		Instructor Supplement	The video library features series of news clips from contemporary sources including ABC news, Dateline, Nightline, and Good Morning America, which explore issues such as media ethics, technology, and the role of media in society. Each segment is followed by critical thinking questions.
Study Card for Introduction to Mass Communication	X		Student Supplement	Colorful, affordable, and packed with useful information, Pearson's Study Cards make studying easier, more efficient, and more enjoyable. Course information is distilled down to the basics, helping you quickly master the fundamentals, review a subject for understanding, or prepare for an exam. Because they're laminated for durability, you can keep these Study Cards for years to come and pull them out whenever you need a quick review.

ACKNOWLEDGMENTS

The authors are grateful to many people who have helped along the way, but most notably at Fordham University, Guia Santos who played an extraordinary role in manuscript preparation and picture research as well as coordinating with various editors and other staffers at Allyn & Bacon, and whose work is gratefully acknowledged. Thanks also to two research assistants at Fordham—Daniel Brooks and Gregory Bergida, both of whom helped ferret out new information and data essential to the book. We are also grateful to Mario Panlillio, Jr., for his help in the final stages of the book. We would also like to thank the reviewers who helped us with the development of this project including Donald Allport Bird, Long Island University; Leigh Browning, West Texas A&M University; Larry L. Burriss, Middle Tennessee State University; Judith Cramer, St. John's University; Lillie M. Fears, Arkansas State University, Jonesboro; Jason Genovese, Bloomsburg University; Kirk Hallahan, Colorado State University; Kirk Hazlett, Curry College; George C. Johnson, James Madison University; Amy Lauters, Minnesota State University, Mankato; Papa A. Mitchell, University of Cincinnati; Dr. Hanna E. Norton, Arkansas State University; Gregg Payne; Chapman University; Mary L. Rucker, Wright State University; Charles B. Scholz, New Mexico State University; Mike Sowell, Oklahoma State University; Candace Walton, University of South Dakota; and Dr. Michiko Yamada, Meredith College.

—Everette E. Dennis, New York City
—Melvin L. DeFleur, Baton Rouge, Louisiana

Understanding Communication Concepts in the Internet Age

Many people are impatient in this Internet age, when all things digital seem to suggest that everything is always changing and that understanding what is happening in and around media and communication simply means keeping up with new developments, forgetting about earlier ideas and outdated devices.

We disagree, and so do some of the most knowledgeable and thoughtful media professionals and observers. This chapter casts the traditional views of communication in the context of both old or traditional media as well as new, digital media, yet we argue that mapping the big ideas that explain all forms of communication is also essential to truly knowing the most advanced new media. One digital media leader, the Head of Internet Advertising Bureau, even goes so far as to say that communication theories promulgated in the 1940s are, in fact, the fathers (and mothers) of such contemporary social networking sites as Facebook and MySpace. Not to understand the basic building blocks of communication—the concepts, history, and voices of experience—is a ticket to ignorance and could mean passing up a chance to have a map for coping with communication and media, now and in the future. This chapter explains why this is true—and thus we respectfully counsel patience.

If we count a human generation as about thirty years on average, we need go back only about two thousand grandmothers ago to come to a time when our prehistoric ancestors did not use language as we know it. Early human beings, such as *Australopithecus*, *Homo habilis*, and *Homo erectus*, did not speak. In fact, they could not, because the structure of their voice boxes was like that of modern apes and chimpanzees.[1] The use of complex languages only began when our Cro-Magnon ancestors (*Homo sapiens sapiens*)

FIGURE 1.1
Significant Transitions in Human Communication

1. **The Development of Speech and Language**
   Between 90,000 and 35,000 B.C.

2. **The Invention of Writing**
   Starting about 2500 B.C.

3. **The Invention of the Printing Press**
   1455

4. **The Beginnings of Mass Newspapers**
   Early 1830s

5. **The Invention of the Electric Telegraph**
   1844

6. **The Introduction of Films**
   About 1900

7. **Beginnings of Home Radio**
   1920s

8. **Wide Adoption of Television**
   1950s

9. **Development of the Internet**
   1980s and 1990s

10. **The Invention of Smart Phones (VoIP)**
    2000s

appeared sometime around forty thousand years ago, give or take a few thousand years.[2] This was the first great communication revolution for our species.

The subsequent development of increasingly efficient and flexible systems for storing, recovering, and disseminating information through the use of various media provided additional revolutions. At first, each step took thousands of years. As Figure 1.1 shows, however, the time between revolutions has been substantially reduced.

Few people today are even aware of that long history or of the great breakthroughs that each step required—first language, then writing, the alphabet, portable media, books, print, newspapers, telegraph, film, radio, television in various forms, computers, and the Internet. With those media in place today, human beings can use language and media together to conquer time and distance in ways that would have defied even the wildest imagination of people only a few generations back.

As a student of mass communication, you will discover how deeply embedded the media are in modern life. Throughout this book, we consider how media content influences us both individually and collectively and whether the influences of mass communication are beneficial, harmless, or hazardous. We will discover who owns our media, how they operate, what influences they have on both children and adults, whether they are ethical and responsible in what they present, and how much control we as a society actually have over their content. You'll get the "big picture" of media and communication, as well as details about their various components.

STUDYING MEDIA STRATEGICALLY

For those interested in communications, media, journalism, and the various communicative arts, truly understanding the world of which they are a part is a deceptively complex challenge. On the one hand, everyone is bombarded by communications of all kinds, and almost everyone masters the digital media quickly—from programming an iPhone to downloading music, Twittering, or searching for facts on Google. For the consumer and citizen (and these are different roles, as we'll discuss later), using the traditional media has been second nature for generations. As one critic mused, "We don't need a manual to learn to read the newspaper." (Although another countered, "Not so fast, there is actually a guide to reading the *Wall Street Journal*.") Until recent times, most people were limited to consumer roles. The ability to create content and actually participate in making media was mostly reserved for professionals. Even efforts to "teach people to talk back to media" and engage in interactive feedback were largely futile.

On the other hand, truly understanding the world of communication and the role that communication plays in everyday life, public affairs, society, and culture requires some deeper thought. As a student of communication, you need to have a broad context, or the conceptual map, into which media fit. This involves knowing and understanding the role of politics and culture, economics, technology, and the legal-regulatory climate in what is now a global environment.

Two concepts from the world of business help to explain the two levels of understanding you need: *leadership* and *management.* Management expert John Kotter distinguished between the two in an article in the *Harvard Business Review.* He pointed out that the first, leadership, involves "coping with change"; the other, "coping with complexity."[3] Coping with complexity means knowing how things work, such as knowing how a newspaper is organized and produced, how a website functions, or how advertising

The mobile camera phone, with its capacity to capture and transmit images for personal use or for larger audiences, illustrates the need for a systematic approach to studying media and their impact on individuals, institutions and society.

Reporters covering an event at a news conference are one stage in the process of gathering information that leads to mass communication.

fuels both. But many commentators say that's not enough, that a simple descriptive inventory fosters a simple notion of what the media system is all about. In addition to this kind of *strategic thinking* and practical knowledge, one also needs *critical thinking* and a capacity to evaluate and make sense of the media world. You need to understand why it is the way it is. Media students also benefit from a behind-the-scenes look, a deep, analytical assessment, some of it critical and aimed at finding prescriptions for change.

Scholars and commentators have been trying to map and make sense of media and communication for nearly two centuries, seeking names to describe the media world and theories to explain its operations and realities. Wisely, the thinking says that we need different ways of knowing to really understand our media system. Communication theory derived from the social sciences is helpful and so is a historical perspective. And, assuredly, the voice of experience from people who lead, manage, and work in media enterprises is crucial.

The Big Picture: Communication Theory

To explain the processes and effects of communication, we introduce several **theories**, statements that describe and explain what events or factors bring about, result in, or cause certain consequences. Theories and knowledge derived from systematic research about media have understandably grown up around academic institutions. Schools of journalism, mass communication, media studies, and the like were organized in the twentieth century with two goals: (1) to prepare a workforce for media and (2) to provide general knowledge and understanding of what media and communication actually do.

In 2006 *Time* magazine named "You" as its person of the year to reflect the importance of user-generated Internet content as a driving force in the modern world.

These dual missions have led to some divisions among those in media fields. A journalism professor at Columbia University explained the gap by pointing out the distinction between studying "journalism" and studying "about journalism." As a practical trainer of journalists, he had little use for theory and criticism. He wanted to get on with what he regarded as the main show: doing the work of reporting and covering the news.

This seeming gap between knowledge and practice may be exaggerated, however. Theories are in many ways the *most practical of all forms of knowledge.* That is true whether one is dealing with the physical, biological, or social/cultural world. Each of us makes use of any kinds of theories that have provided practical solutions every day in a multitude of ways. If you drive a car, feel comfortable in an air-conditioned or centrally heated room, eat a meal without serious health consequences, read at night using electricity, go to a movie, watch television, take medication, use a computer, or engage in hundreds of other routine daily activities, you are receiving the benefits of theories. They were developed by a host of researchers and scientists who conducted systematic research to develop theories that explain how things work. It was only after research and

BIG IDEAS: MEDIA THEORIES EXPLAINED

The Nature and Uses of Theory

Theories are developed in all fields that seek to understand their subject matter so that the implications of what is being studied can be understood. Simply put, *theories explain how things work.*

Most people think of a theory as something developed in physics, chemistry, or the biological sciences. Obviously, those fields have made remarkable achievements. However, the methods and logic of scientific investigation are now being applied to the younger field of mass communication as well, and a number of important theories have been developed in recent decades. Thus, the logic and methods of science have been adapted to the study of the processes and effects of mass communication to develop theories explaining how consequences occur.

Theories are not just vague speculations. They are, first of all, systematic *descriptions* of what prior conditions bring about what consequences. Such a description usually consists of a set of *assumptions* about the relationships between clearly stated prior conditions and a "therefore" statement describing the process or effects that they bring about. In simpler terms, theories are precise sets of statements about what causes are assumed to bring about what outcomes.

Statements about what causes what provide *explanations.* Thus, theories explain why certain effects occur as a result of prior conditions that are both necessary and sufficient to bring about those consequences.

To learn how things work, scientists (including those who study the media) conduct careful and extensive research. In fact, theories are usually initially proposed when researchers think that, as a result of studies they have conducted, they have discovered some cause-effect connection between some set of prior conditions and some consequences. If that is the case, they put together an initial (tentative) version of a theory that might explain what they have uncovered. Thus, a third feature of theories is that they are *products of research* that uncover possible causal connections between prior conditions and their consequences.

When such potential relationships have been identified, the tentative theory is set forth as a set of statements or propositions that logically predict what effects should be observable *if the prior conditions actually do cause the consequences.* Thus, a fourth feature of a well-developed theory is that it provides a prediction of what should be found by further careful observation—assuming that the theory is a correct description of what prior conditions cause what consequences.

Such logical predictions are then checked by careful research to see if the theory's prediction is accurate or not. Thus, a fifth feature of a theory is that it provides *a guide for relevant research* to check whether it has made a valid logical prediction. If the research shows that the prediction is correct, the theory has received positive support. If not, it needs to be modified and tested again or even abandoned. Theories, then, have the following features and functions:

1. Theories are sets of *interrelated propositions,* derived from research, that provide descriptions about how things work.
2. Theories provide *explanations* about what prior conditions bring about what consequences.
3. Theories provide *logical predictions,* that is, guides to research, about what should be found by further careful observation.
4. Theories are supported when their predictions are found by research to be *accurate.* If not, they must be revised and retested or simply rejected.

theories provided explanations of causes and results that clever people invented ways to use that knowledge in practical ways.

Although mass communication is a young field that has conducted systematic research for less than a century, a number of theories have been developed to explain various aspects of the process and consequences of mass communication. We introduce you to many of these theories in the upcoming chapters of this book.

Historical Perspective

Just as the physical and biological sciences have developed understandings and explanations of the aspects of nature that they study, so have media researchers and scholars made discoveries in the study of mass communication. Theories are useful, but as biologists must study an entire ecosystem, we must consider social and cultural factors to complete our understanding of the media. Many of these factors can be discovered by looking at history to learn what was happening in the politics, law, and social arenas that contributed to the way media developed. To provide and use that understanding, this book considers three important questions:

1. *How were our present media shaped by the events, trends, policies, and characteristics of society?* That is, what took place in earlier years as these media were developing that structured them as they are today? Reviewing what took place in the past is the only way we can understand what we have at present in a time of globalization and digitization.
2. *How do our media select, process, and disseminate various categories of content?* Who makes the decisions, and why, concerning what is presented to audiences by those who design and transmit the content of books, newspapers, magazines, movies, radio and television programs, and what appears on the Internet?
3. *What assumptions and forecasts can we make about the media we will have in the future and what they will offer to their audiences in the years ahead?* Many of the factors that have already had an influence on our media in the past will continue to play a part in changing them in the future. As noted in our first question, understanding the past provides insight into the present. Understanding both the past and the present provides a basis for trying to look ahead into the future.

Voices of Experience

Ultimately communication is about people. Understanding the processes of communication and communication theory provides a conceptual map. The history of communication, notably the technologies and institutions that we chart to understand its development, are important, but they tell only part of the story. Much of what we need to know and understand about communication is in the voice of the communicators—the people who have invented, led, and operated various media from drawings on cave walls to the latest Facebook download on an iPhone. It is also vital to understand the individuals (citizens and consumers) who make up the audience.

The people who have shaped the media include the inventive folks who conceived and invented various technical platforms from the printing press forward as well as those who created organizations and institutions that nurtured and helped develop media as an extension of human experience and the human senses. Think of the ways that media such as movies, radio, television, and the Internet extend one's line of sight, enable people to hear voices thousands of miles away, and provide a visual experience that would otherwise be impossible for a solitary individual.

Media content—from words on paper to visual images and the messages in social networking sites—involves human beings and their transactions. It is important to remember that what we need to know and understand about media and communication is also the product of the experience of the people who have made our media, processed messages, distributed them, and allowed for response and feedback. At every stage of the communication process, people play a role in shaping the reality of communication and ultimately our capacity to use and benefit from it. And sometimes that also means erecting barriers to the most effective and efficient communication, by preferring old habits to new challenges or by regulating some media, thus slowing their ultimate development and use.

THE INTERPERSONAL COMMUNICATION PROCESS

Where does one begin when tracing the development of mass communication? One answer is to start by looking closely at communication as it takes place between human beings at the interpersonal level. **Mediated communication** is, after all, interpersonal communication aided by sophisticated media technology that conquers both time and distance. The **media** are simply devices that bring messages quickly from communicators to multitudes—rather than to an audience of a single person.

To understand that process more fully, we must first look at how communication takes place in the *absence* of media. That is, what are the fundamentals of face-to-face human communication? With that analysis as a basis for comparison, we will take a close look at mass communication. This, in turn, will permit a comparison of the two and a fuller understanding of the advantages, limitations, and effects of communicating using our contemporary media.

Sharing Meaning with Verbal and Nonverbal Symbols

As noted at the start of this chapter, our first great communication revolution as a species was the ability to speak. This soon led to the development of **language**, a learned system, shared by members a culture, of verbal and nonverbal symbols that have accumulated and grown increasingly complex over time. Two key aspects of language set us apart from other species. One is learning. Animals clearly do communicate with each other, sometimes in relatively sophisticated ways, but their signs and signals are, in most cases, part of behavior systems that are genetically inherited and have changed little since the dawn of their existence. Birds, for example, are born knowing their individual songs. Another defining aspect of human language is its relationship to **culture**, the set of shared beliefs, values and customs transmitted from generation to generation among communities. In spite of romantic ideas about whales, porpoises, and other animals that supposedly "talk," animals do not use languages based on culturally shared systems of symbols, grammar, and meanings.[4]

Language, as we've noted, is composed of symbols. A **symbol** is a word, an action, or an object that "stands for" and arouses standardized internal meanings in people within a given language community. By a well-established rule, or convention, each symbol—such as "dog," "child," or even complex terms like "carcinogen" and "biodegradable"—is supposed to arouse similar internal meanings in everyone who uses it. In a similar way, actions such as gestures and facial expressions can be governed by meaning conventions. The same is true of certain objects, such as a cross, a Star of David, or a wedding ring. In our current age of mass communications, we still communicate, whether face to face or through media, by using verbal and nonverbal symbols.

Facebook caught up with MySpace in 2009 as the premier social networking website. Started by 22-year-old Harvard dropout Mark Zuckerberg, the website is responsible for 1% of all Internet traffic and is the sixth-most-visited site in the United States.

INFOGRAPHICS: THE EARLY YEARS.

A Basic Model of Human Communication

While each of us converses with other people many times every day, few of us step back from the process and ask exactly how it works. It is only in recent years that this question has been addressed in a theoretical way. One of the earliest attempts to develop a **model** of human communication—that is, a simple but accurate representation with either graphics or verbal propositions—came from the laboratories of Bell Telephone Company. Claude E. Shannon, working with Warren Weaver, was faced with the task of trying to determine how to improve physical signals, carried by a medium such as a telephone line, so that there was less chance of error when the messages being transmitted were received. The theory developed by Shannon and Weaver was a complex mathematical formulation.[5] However, it contained some very basic ideas that were seen as helpful by scholars trying to portray the process of language communication. Using Shannon and Weaver's depiction of the communication process, they developed a model that gives us, in very simple and linear terms, a representation of the human communication process. This model is shown in Figure 1.2.

The simple and linear view of human communication that was developed from Shannon and Weaver's work became a fairly standard way of describing the process.[6] Many similar verbal and graphic versions of this basic formulation can be found in communication textbooks. What the basic linear model did not include was the idea that communication has an **effect**. That is, people transmit messages that have some influence when they are received and interpreted. The idea can be added, and the following list of stages describes, in a simple way, what happens when one person communicates a message to another:

1. The act of human communication begins with a **sender**, who decides to initiate a message that expresses a specific set of intended meanings.
2. That sender **encodes** the intended meanings by selecting specific words and gestures with conventionalized interpretations that the receiver will presumably understand.
3. The message is then **transmitted**, spoken or written so as to cross the space between sender and receiver as a signal of patterned information.
4. The **receiver**, the individual to whom the message is directed, attends to and perceives the incoming patterned information, identifying it as a specific language message.
5. The receiver then **decodes** the message by constructing his or her own interpretations of the conventionalized meanings of the symbols.
6. As a result of interpreting the message, the receiver is influenced in some way. That is, the communication has some *effect*, which can range from trivial to profound.

Common sense tells us that often meanings may not match. One person may fail to understand what another person is saying even with a simple message, because there are various sources of inaccuracy that are difficult to control. Thus, Shannon and Weaver were right in saying that *noise* can enter the process at virtually any stage. **Noise** results from any physical, psychological, social, or cultural condition that reduces similarities between the intended meanings of the sender and the interpreted meanings of the receiver. Noise can result from dim light, poor acoustics, disruptive sounds, or any other physical condition that interferes with the transfer of information. It can also result from memory failure, faulty perception, or unfamiliarity with the language.

FIGURE 1.2
Shannon-Weaver
Model of
Communication

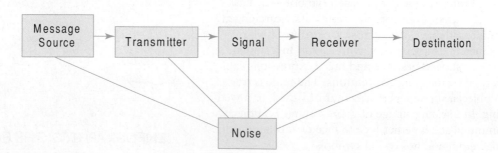

Noise can happen when the sender and receiver do not share the same cultural rules for the use of language, a common problem in a multicultural society. We normally put words together into sentences, paragraphs, and various constructions using accepted rules of *grammar,* functions for which classes of words (such as nouns or adjectives) can be used, and *syntax,* proper word order. These patterns themselves introduce meanings that go beyond those associated with each of the words used. For example, the pattern "The boy killed the snake" implies a meaning totally different from the pattern "The snake killed the boy," even though the words are identical. Usually, these patterns pose no serious problem in understanding human communication, because we learn the patterns and their associated meanings as part of our language, just as we learn the meanings of each word. When speakers of different languages converse, however, use of syntax and grammar can cause noise that interferes with true communication, even if both are using the same language.

This cartoon demonstrates the concept of noise when the sender and the receiver are not synchronized.

Almost all scholars today agree that this *basic linear model* of the human communication process greatly oversimplifies what actually takes place. *Linear* means following in a logical or progressive order such as watching a movie from beginning to end, rather than coming in and out. The human conversations that we engage in with people around us are **transactional,** rather than linear. People are not merely passive and linear senders and receivers. Each party encodes and decodes messages at the same time and is alert to all kinds of cues from the other person in a simultaneous back-and-forth, or *interactive,* process.[7] They respond to the content of others' meanings, ask for clarification, and indicate agreement. Thus, each person shifts roles to become a sender at one moment and a receiver at another.

In spite of its simplicity and obvious limitations, however, the basic linear model is useful for analyzing the communication process, allowing us to break it down into its distinct stages in order to understand what happens at each. This model simplifies the task of looking carefully at each separate stage of the process to see exactly how people use symbols and conventions of meaning to accomplish the act of human communication.

We can also use the linear model to look at the communication from a more complex, transactional view. The stages are at the heart of the transactions of any conversation. Even if both parties are simultaneously encoding, transmitting, and decoding, they are still serving as senders and receivers, initiating and receiving messages. In other words, the six stages noted above are embedded within the complexities of simultaneous transactional communication.

Communicating Accurately

As suggested above, the meanings intended by communicators and those interpreted by receivers may not be perfectly parallel. In that case, the communication has suffered a loss of **accuracy**. In fact, a perfect match between the meanings of both parties is unlikely, perhaps with the exception of trivial messages. In a commonsense way, then, loss of accuracy can be defined as any reduction in the correspondence between the details of the sender's intended message and those of the receiver's interpreted message.

THE ACCURACY PRINCIPLE.   There can be many causes of a loss of accuracy between meanings. Often accuracy suffers as a result of noise, as Shannon and Weaver's model shows. If accuracy is reduced, for whatever reasons, the communication will be less effective in achieving the goals of the communicator. That can be a problem in interpersonal communication, and, as will be made clear, it can be devastating in mass communication. This conclusion regarding accuracy and its consequences can be stated more formally as a rather commonsense generalization, which we call the **accuracy principle:**

> The lower the level of correspondence between the intended meanings of the sender and the interpreted meanings of the receiver, the less effective an act of communication will be in achieving either mutual understanding or an intended influence.

BIG IDEAS: MEDIA THEORIES EXPLAINED

Magic Bullet Theory

The earliest general theoretical perspective on the influence of mass communication was derived from the ideas of late nineteenth century social scientists and critics, who viewed the social order as a *mass society*. While its basic assumptions were widely shared when empirical research began, it was never developed formally as a specific set of propositions. But for several decades, scholars have referred to its essential ideas as the *magic bullet theory.*

Even though we realize today that it never matched reality, it was a beginning point for considering the process and effects of mass communication.

This theory also reflects Charles Darwin's evolutionary ideas. Before he published his *Origins of Species* (in 1859), conceptions of the nature of humankind emphasized *religious* origins. Human beings were said to be unique "rational" creatures created in the image of God. After Darwin, scientific thinking began to stress the importance of *genetic* and *biological* factors as causes of human behavior.

Influenced by this genetic perspective, social and behavioral scientists rejected "rational" views of human nature and stressed its *animal* side. They assumed that people were higher animals, and like other animals they inherited a set of *uniform inherited instincts* (derived from their evolutionary history). It was assumed, therefore, that human behavior was shaped by such biologically based "instincts," causing people to react more or less similarly to whatever "stimuli" (situations confronting them) came along. Thus, under this conception of human nature, responses made to stimuli were shaped either by "instincts" over which they lacked rational control or by other "unconscious" processes that were not guided by intellect.

This was a frightening view, and it had a strong influence on thinking about the power of mass communications. It portrayed human populations as composed of irrational creatures that could be swayed and controlled by cleverly designed mass communications "stimuli."

This theory led people, early in the century, to believe that those who controlled the media could control the public. Thus, the magic bullet theory implied that the media have direct, immediate, and powerful effects of a uniform nature on those who paid attention to their consent. This theory, summarized below, represented both popular and scientific thinking. It assumed that a media message reached every eye and ear in the same way, like a symbolic "bullet," bringing about the same changes of thought and behavior in the entire audience.

1. People in "mass" society lead *socially isolated* lives with limited social controls exerted over each other because they are from diverse origins and do not share a unifying set of norms, values, and beliefs.
2. Like all animals, human beings are endowed at birth with a *uniform set of instincts* that guide their ways of responding to the world around them.
3. Because people's actions are not influenced by social ties and are guided by uniform instincts, individuals attend to events (such as media messages) *in similar way*s.
4. People's inherited human nature and their isolated social condition lead them to *receive and interpret* media messages in a uniform way.
5. **Therefore**, media messages can be thought of as symbolic "bullets," striking every eye and ear among the members of their audience and resulting in effects on thought and behavior that are *direct, immediate, uniform,* and *powerful.*

Clearly, then, it is important for both the sender and the receiver to strive for accuracy if they are to achieve either goal of understanding or influence. But how, aside from careful selection of words and thoughtful organization of a message, can communication be made more accurate? Actually, in interpersonal communication, there are two very effective ways: one is by the receiver's providing *feedback,* and the other is by the sender's engaging in *role taking.* As we will see, these two ideas have profound implications for understanding the differences between face-to-face and mass communication.

THE FEEDBACK PRINCIPLE.   Usually, interpersonal communication is an ongoing process that goes back and forth between the parties. For example, you start to explain something to a friend and at some point your friend may frown or shrug as you are talking. Seeing this, you sense that he or she may not have understood very well. So you try to explain that point in a different way or provide a brief example as you continue with your account. Your friend then nods, and you conclude that you have clearly made your point. In such a face-to-face situation, the sender is ever alert to observable verbal and nonverbal signals coming back from the receiver. These cues provide **feedback**, a receiver's communication back to the communicator that indicates whether the message is getting through. In face-to-face communication, the receiver usually provides both verbal and nonverbal feedback on an ongoing basis to influence the communicator's selection of words, gestures, and meanings. Thus, the two parties alternately become both sender and receiver as the messages of one stimulates feedback from the other.

Feedback may be deliberate or not. In either event, the communicator takes feedback into account to try to increase communication accuracy. This is a very important idea. Stated simply, feedback leads to greater accuracy in communication. Conversely, without feedback, accuracy is likely to suffer. This can be stated as a second important generalization, which we call the **feedback principle**:

> If ongoing and immediate feedback is provided by the receiver, accuracy will be increased. That is, the intended meanings of the communicator have a better chance of being similar to those constructed by the receiver.

THE ROLE-TAKING PRINCIPLE.   When a sender correctly interprets feedback cues from the intended receiver and adjusts the message in order to increase accuracy, the communicator is figuratively placing himself or herself in the receiver's shoes; the sender tries, mentally, to be the receiver in order to understand how he or she is likely to respond to the message being transmitted. This process is called **role taking**, and it can be defined as the sender's use of feedback to judge which words and nonverbal cues will work best to arouse the intended meanings in the receiver.

Some people are better at role taking than others. Also, some situations are better suited for it than others. Role taking can be most effective in close, personal, and intimate situations where the communicating parties know each other well. It is most limited and ineffective in interpersonal situations where strangers are trying to communicate. These considerations lead to a third generalization, which we call the **role-taking principle**:

> In communication situations where the sender can engage in sensitive role taking, accuracy is increased. That is, meanings intended by the sender more closely match those constructed by the receiver.

In summary, these principles tell us that (1) face-to-face communication is accurate to the extent that adequate feedback cues are provided by the receiver and (2) accuracy depends on the extent to which the communicator uses role taking appropriately to formulate the message in terms that are likely to be well understood by the receiver. These principles governing the relationship among feedback, role taking, and accuracy in the case of interpersonal communication need to be kept in mind as we turn to and analyze the nature of mass communication. As will be discussed, it is with respect to these issues that the two kinds of communication differ considerably.

A production supervisor at *News 10 Now* in Syracuse, New York, works in the control room to get graphics ready for the twenty-four hour news channel's election night coverage.

THE "MASS" COMMUNICATION PROCESS

Communicating with media is not something new. Human beings have used various technologies to preserve messages in time or to send them over distances for thousands of years. In spite of their speed and audience size, today's mass media perform the same functions as their more primitive predecessors. Like the stone walls on which hieroglyphics were carved, the smoke signals of Native Americans, or the jungle drums of earlier times, modern media move information across either time or space. **Information** consists of a patterned physical signal corresponding to a message. Such information should not be confused with the *meaning* of the message. One example of information is the patterned sound waves we can hear when people speak to us. Both the speaker and the receiver must construct their own meanings of those physical signals, using memories of their shared language. In more complex and contemporary media, information is transmitted as particular patterns of electronic radiations, as in radio, or as in light waves, which we use to read, watch television, or view a movie. Only human beings can transform meanings in their heads into such signals, or as receivers, decode them back into a similar internal experience.[8]

Developing a Concise Definition

Using media that can reach huge audiences more or less simultaneously adds complexities. To discuss the *mass* nature of making use of such media, it will be helpful to develop a formal definition of mass communication. At first glance, this may seem unnecessary. After all, we are already familiar with such media as movies, newspapers, and television sets. But when senders use film, print, or mobile phones to communicate with large audiences, what is actually happening? Do all media operate according to the same underlying principles of communication, or is each medium unique in some way? And in what ways are the principles underlying mass communication different from those for a face-to-face conversation between two people? These questions are critical to understanding the nature of mass communication, and we will be exploring them throughout this book.

We cannot define mass communication in just a quick sentence or two because each medium includes its own special kinds of communicators, technologies, groups, content, audiences, and effects. To develop a good definition of mass communication, we must take all these aspects into account and proceed one step at time, describing each of the major features before pulling them together. In the sections that follow, that is exactly our strategy. We'll look at each "stage" in the mass communication process, then combine all the stages in an overall basic definition.

We can examine mass communication by using an expanded version of the same linear model that helps (at least in part) to explain face-to-face communication, a formulation that has its roots in Shannon and Weaver's information theory. While each progressive stage is far more complex, the basic stages are similar in many ways:

1. Mass communication begins with senders who are **professional communicators**. Professional communicators decide the nature and goals of a message to be presented to an audience via their particular medium. That message may be a news report, an advertising campaign, a movie, or an Internet report or podcast.
2. The intended meanings are *encoded* by production specialists, such as a news team, a film company, a magazine staff, or a digital media team.

3. The message is *transmitted* as information through the use of specialized media technologies to disseminate it, either as widely as possible or to a specified segment, or portion, of a general audience.

4. Large and diverse (mass) **audiences**, made up of individual receivers, attend to the media and perceive the incoming information, decoding it into a message of conventionalized verbal and nonverbal symbols.

5. Individual receivers selectively construct interpretations of the message in such a way that they experience subjective *meanings* that are, to at least some degree, parallel to those intended by the professional communicators.

6. As a result of experiencing these meanings, receivers are *influenced* in some way in their feelings, thoughts, or actions. That is, the communication has some effect.

These six stages provide not only a basic identification of what takes place in the process of mass communication but also a convenient framework for defining it carefully. Using these stages, we can formulate a definition of mass communication that enables us to separate it clearly from other forms:

> **Mass communication** is a process in which professional communicators design and use media to disseminate messages widely, rapidly, and continually in order to arouse intended meanings in large, diverse, and selectively attending audiences, in attempts to influence them in a variety of ways.

Which Media Are Mass Media?

With our definition of mass media in mind, we must ask which media really are (or are not) mass media. This is not an idle question because it sets boundaries on what needs to be studied under the general heading "mass communication."

One measure traditionally has been "household penetration," the percentages of households in a community or country that are reached. Typically a medium is regarded as especially important (and taken quite seriously) when it reaches 50% of households. Table 1.1 shows the number of years it took for various media and media technologies to reach a 50% penetration.

Is the telephone a mass medium? How about a fax machine or personal computers linked in a network? What about a large museum? Should we include rock concerts, theatrical performances, church services, or even parades in our study of mass communication? After all, each of these human activities is a form of communication. For our purposes, whether or not they are mass media depends on whether they can carry out the process of mass communication we have just defined.

TABLE 1.1

YEARS TAKEN TO REACH 50% OF U.S. HOUSEHOLDS

Newspapers	100+
Telephone	70
Phonograph	55
Electricity	43
Cable	39
FM Radio	30
Color Television	17
Personal Computer	17
Compact Disc Player	15
VCR	10
AM Radio	9
Black & White TV	8

Source: John Carey as compiled from Electronic Industry Assn., U.S. Department of Commerce, Dataquest.

To be true to our definition, we would have to conclude that talking on the telephone or sending an IM is *not* really mass communication because the audience is not large and diverse; usually there is only one person at each end of the communication. Furthermore, telephone users usually are not "professional communicators." The same is true of most emails while social networks can be mass communication, such as YouTube videos, (The Internet and the World Wide Web do, however, qualify as mass media for some other uses.) A museum does not participate in mass communication because it does not provide rapid dissemination with media though it may have a website. Neither does a rock concert qualify because it does not disseminate messages over a distance; it is a form of direct communication to audiences. Similarly, no situation in which live performers and an audience can see each other directly—in a theater, church, sports event, or parade—is usually mediated communication. Large-scale advertising by direct mail might qualify, except that it is not really continual. Thus, our definition turns out to be relatively rigorous. It enables us to set definite boundaries on what can be included and studied as a medium of mass communication. By definition, none of the activities listed above is such a medium, although all of them can arouse specific meanings and influence people.

Similarly, although people often speak of "the news media," this expression is misleading. News is a special form of *content* produced by media organizations that present their products to the public through the use of the same mass media that bring us communications about drama, music, and sports (as we will see in Chapter 4). Thus, we will treat the gathering and distribution of news not as a distinct mass medium in itself but as an important *process* dependent on the print, broadcast, and online media.

By exercising the criteria set forth in our definition, then, we can identify precisely what we consider to be mass media in the present text. The major mass media are as follows:

- *Publishing*—including books, magazines, and newspapers
- *Film*—principally commercial motion pictures
- *Electronic media*—mainly radio and television but also several associated forms such as cable television and DVDs

Although other kinds of media are worthy of study, the focus of our attention will be on those that closely fit our definition of mass communication. What about digital communications, involving the Internet, video-on-demand, or wireless devices? In Chapter 2, we'll see that digital communication sometimes functions as a mass medium that fits the above definition, and sometimes it does not.

COMPARING FACE-TO-FACE AND MASS COMMUNICATION

Having examined the nature of both face-to-face and mass communication, we can now ask how these two processes differ from each other. Our starting point is that mass communication (1) depends on mechanical or electronic media and (2) addresses a large, diverse audience. We can ask, then, do these two characteristics alter the communication process in some fundamental way? Or is mass communication just like any other form of human communication?

The Consequences of Using Any Medium

Human communication, whether with a medium or not, depends on verbal and nonverbal symbols and all the stages discussed in our basic linear model. Introducing a medium into communication between two people clearly alters the process, however. One major consequence is the *loss of direct and immediate feedback*. A second is *severe limitation on effective role taking* because of that loss.

LACK OF IMMEDIATE FEEDBACK.   As was suggested earlier, when we communicate with another person and we have a medium intervening between, we cannot perceive the rich nonverbal cues that are available when we converse face-to-face. Even when using the phone in direct interpersonal communication, we cannot detect visual, nonverbal messages such as a puzzled look, raised eyebrows, or a smile. Subtle tones of voice or small changes of pitch and emphasis may also be lost. Exchanges of text messages or email are even more limited. Phone and computer screens cannot show people's visual, nonverbal signs or signals (emoticons can only add limited approximations), and they both are unable to convey nuances of pronunciation and timing.

INABILITY TO ENGAGE IN EFFECTIVE ROLE TAKING.

Limitations on simultaneous feedback in virtually all mediated communication reduce our ability to understand how well our message is being understood by the person or persons toward whom it is directed.

Fans shouting at a TV set at a sports bar demonstrates one crude form of feedback.

LOSS OF ACCURACY.

Because of limitations in feedback and role taking, it is harder to attain accuracy when using a medium than in the direct, face-to-face, interpersonal mode. This, in turn, reduces communication effectiveness, a point that most people understand very well. Many of us have told a friend, "Let's not try to settle this over the telephone or through email. Let's get together and talk it over."

A more formal statement of the effects of mediated communication includes the following points:

1. The use of a medium *reduces the richness of feedback and limits the process of role taking.*
2. Both of these limitations *increase the possibility of similar meanings between senders and receivers.*
3. When meanings between sender and receiver are dissimilar, *accuracy is reduced and mutual understanding is limited.*
4. A decrease in the accuracy of communication *reduces the probability that the message will influence receivers.*

These limitations certainly apply to mass communication. Indeed they are even more important when communication takes place via a medium such as a newspaper, a movie, or television. In mass communication, a large, diverse audience is at the receiving end. There is no realistic way for the communicator to engage in any role taking during the process of transmitting a message or for the audience to provide immediate and ongoing feedback while transmission is taking place.

These limitations are well understood by professional communicators. TV anchors can never place themselves mentally in your personal shoes as you view the evening news. Thus, they are unable to understand and predict accurately how the audience will receive and interpret the broadcast. By extension, there is no way that such newscasters can modify their ongoing presentation on the basis of your feedback in order to make you understand more fully. The same stipulation applies to any professional communicator, whether the medium is a newspaper, a movie, a radio broadcast, and so on.

At the same time, professional communicators have some knowledge of the audience in a collective sense. Large communication corporations (for example, the major television networks) conduct extensive research on audience characteristics and behavior. The researchers study many categories of people to give an overall picture. The results of such research provide a form of "advance" feedback to communicators concerning the likely tastes and interests of at least the majority of their audience at a particular time.[9]

The information obtained from such research is the basis for certain necessary assumptions about audiences, assumptions that replace individual-by-individual role taking. However, that approach has serious limitations because assumptions can be inaccurate. The failure of hundreds of magazines, newspapers, films, and television programs over the years, despite extensive "market research," testifies to how imperfect such role-taking assumptions can be.

Feedback is similarly limited. Indeed, for all intents and purposes, it does not exist. Audience members cannot interrupt what they see as a confusing or infuriating television reporter or gain immediate access to a newspaper editorial writer. Even though mass media often emails or Twitters, this kind of reverse flow provides only delayed trickle of feedback from the few people who are motivated enough to go to the trouble.

Thus, by comparison with face-to-face communication, mass communication is essentially a *linear process*. Communicators try to guess how their messages will be received, mostly with indirect, delayed feedback in the form of advertising revenues, research findings, a few telephone calls, occasional letters, movie reviews, and box-office receipts. This delayed feedback may help them shape future communications, but it provides no basis for altering a message while it is being disseminated. As a consequence, accuracy and influence on any particular member of the audience are significantly limited compared with what can be accomplished in face-to-face communication. However, digital-tracking media can now provide much more precise feedback and interactive information than was formerly the case. With digital-tracking media, all digital messages essentially have their own DNA and can always be identified. In such a system, the communicator can keep track of all messages coming to a given individual. Thus media and advertisers learn a great deal about a person's media habits, consumer choices, attitudes, and much more. Sometimes this is coordinated with the consumer's age, income, education, race, and so on, thus offering a great deal of information about a given person or all persons who select a certain website or order online. This is, in effect, a window to the whole population that uses a particular medium or message. Previously, the main way advertisers and media organizations learned about people and audiences was through a sample of the whole population, such as the Nielsen ratings, which generalize from a small sample of the TV audience to make assumptions about program popularity and use.

The Consequences of Large, Diverse Audiences

Large and diverse media audiences are sometimes described as **aggregated** audiences because the total audience is composed of many distinct parts. An aggregated audience can pose additional significant limitation on the content, accuracy, and influences of the messages transmitted by a mass medium. Inevitably, much mass media content—perhaps most of it—is designed for the tastes and presumed intellectual level of "the average citizen" or, often, for the average member of a specialized category of people who are assumed to share some common taste or interest (for instance, all fishing enthusiasts, football fans, or fashion-conscious men). To form appropriate message content, communicators must make assumptions about their audiences. Most professional communicators tend to assume that the majority in their audiences:

Talk-show host Jerry Springer is a master at attracting a large diverse audience.

1. Has a *limited attention span.*
2. Prefers to be *entertained rather than enlightened.*
3. Quickly *loses interest in any subject that makes intellectual demands.*[10]

With no intention of being either critical or elitist, it seems clear that, in large part, these assumptions are correct. Well-educated people with sophisticated tastes and high intellectual capacity are a relatively minor part of the population. However, this is not really a problem in a profit-oriented media system.

The media in the United States, and many other countries, operate to make money for their owners. From the beginning, media evolved as a result of both a desire of people to communicate and a need to move goods and services. The earliest media needed financial resources to survive, and very soon their entrepreneurs recognized that they were dispensing a product that had value—and could make them a good living. Today, very large multinational media companies make very large amounts of money for their shareholders.

Most of today's media companies are not worried that cultivated citizens are in short supply, because these highbrow folks constitute only a very small segment of purchasing consumers. Professional communicators who prepare media content with a goal of maximizing profits can safely ignore them. It is much more profitable to reach the much larger numbers of *intellectually undemanding receivers whose aggregate purchasing power is immense.* In other words, as we will show in later chapters, reaching large numbers of exactly the right kind of people is critically important in the advertising-driven and profit-oriented American system of mass communication. Thus, all of the factors discussed above work together in a kind of system that encourages media content that is high in entertainment value and low in intellectual demand.

It is important to understand the conditions and principles that fit together to produce the above consequence, because they explain a great deal about why our media function as they do. Furthermore, we can then more readily understand why the media inevitably attract the attention of deeply concerned critics, who have generated a long list of charges and complaints supporting the idea that the media are both trivial and harmful in some way.[11]

The fact is that there is indeed much to criticize regarding what the system delivers. From the outset of mass communication, the content of American media has prompted thoughtful people to object to its generally shallow nature. We do not wish to imply that all media content is superficial or that is caters only to the interests of limited-capacity audiences. There certainly are books, newspaper analyses, magazines, radio programs, television shows, and Internet sites designed for educated and sophisticated audiences. Undeniably, however, most media content is of limited aesthetic or intellectual merit. Early in the twentieth century, critics focused on "yellow journalism," a term used to describe sensational news in the late nineteenth century and overemphasis on crime in newspapers. Today's lowbrow content includes forms that many people are concerned about such as violence, explicit sexual depictions, and vulgar language in the media.

The critics want different content. They urge the media to inform, enlighten, and uplift. They want media to provide in-depth information that will serve as a basis for intelligent political decision making, arts appreciation, and improvement in moral standards. These are commendable goals, which no thoughtful person can seriously dispute. At the same time, however, the environment in which the media operate makes it very unlikely that these goals will ever be fully achieved—not because greedy people will always control the media but because our society has mostly defined mass communication as part of the *private enterprise system,* organizations with the goal of making money for their owners.

The remaining chapters of this book address in some detail the many ways that society has shaped its media. The factors to be considered are the development of technology, the influence of a growing population with a multicultural composition, and the influences of political and economic systems. The chapters devoted to specific media focus on the unique features of each. They discuss the historical pattern of adoption of each and how each medium operates to disseminate its particular kind of information.

CHAPTER REVIEW

■ Communication has been an evolutionary process moving from nonverbal to verbal and then to complex messages and modes of expression along with the evolution of humans and their cultures.

■ Human communication differs sharply from the processes used by other species. It depends on systems of learned and shared verbal and nonverbal symbols, their meanings, and conventionalized rules for their use.

■ The basic act of human communication can be analyzed in terms of a linear model that includes six major steps: deciding on a message, encoding the message by linking symbols and meanings, transmitting information to span distance, perceiving the incoming information patterns, perceiving and constructing the message's meanings. As a result, receivers experience some effect.

■ In face-to-face communication, feedback and role taking are important principles related to accuracy.

■ Mass communication is also a linear process in which professional communicators encode and transmit various kinds of messages to present to different segments of the public for a variety of purposes. Through the use of mass media, those messages are disseminated to large and diverse audiences who attend to the messages in selective ways.

■ Members of the audience interpret the message selectively, and the meanings they construct may or may not parallel those intended by the communicator.

■ Mass communication and face-to-face communication differ in important ways. Because of feedback and role taking, interpersonal transactions can be flexible and influential. Mass communication lacks these features and is largely a one-way, relatively inflexible process.

■ In an advertising-driven and profit-oriented system, media content must be tailored to the majority, whose collective purchasing power is huge but whose intellectual level and tastes are not sophisticated. This tailoring of content results in many criticisms.

■ The study of mass communication must include attention to three broad sets of issues: (1) the many ways in which a society's history, values, and economic and political realities have influenced its media; (2) the unique features of each medium in the system that make it different from the other media; and (3) the kinds of influences that media have on us as individuals and on our society and culture.

STRATEGIC QUESTIONS

1. What, if any, value does communication theory have in understanding practical aspects of how individuals communicate?

2. How do the history of communication and the history of media technology contribute to understanding media in the digital age?

3. What's the relevance of the interpersonal communication process in mapping the way people communicate with others as well as their use of media?

4. What are the functions of communication, and how do they actually work in individual communication and mass communication?

5. How does charting the way people "adopt new technologies" help us understand the evolution of digital media?

6. Why would one want to compare face-to-face communication with mass communication? What value does such an exercise have?

KEY CONCEPTS & TERMS

Communication
  theory 4
Communications
  media 7
Language 2

Professional
  communicators 12
Symbols 7
Shannon and Weaver
  model 8

Accuracy principle 9
Feedback principle 11
Audiences 16

ENDNOTES

1. Philip Lieberman, "The Evolution of Human Speech: The Fossil Record," in *The Biology and Evolution of Language* (Cambridge, MA: Harvard University Press, 1984), pp. 287-329.

2. For a more detailed explanation of these and other changes in human communication, see Melvin L. DeFleur and Sandra Ball Rokeach, "A Theory of Transitions," in *Theories of Mass Communication,* 5th ed. (White Plains, NY: Longman, 1989), pp. 7-26

3. John P. Kotter, "What Leaders Really Do," in *Leadership Insights—Fifteen Unique Perspectives on Effective Leadership* (Boston: Harvard Business Review Publishing, 2002).

4. For an extended discussion of the basic nature of human face-to-face communication, see "Verbal Communication," in Melvin L. DeFleur, Patricia Kearney, and Timothy G. Plax, *Fundamentals of Human Communication* (New York: McGraw Hill, 2004).

5. Claude E. Shannon and Warren Weaver, *The Mathematical Theory of Communication* (Urbana, IL: University of Illinois Press, 1949).

6. Shannon and Weaver, *The Mathematical Theory.*

7. For a discussion of a simultaneous transactional model of human communication, see DeFleur, Kearney, and Plax, *Fundamentals of Human Communication.*

8. Everette E. Dennis, "The Two-Step Flow in the Internet Age," given at the Symposium Honoring Philip Meyer, University of North Carolina, March 21, 2008.

9. Edward Schiappa, *Beyond Representational Correctness: Rethinking Criticism of Popular Media* (New York: State University of New York Press, 2008).

10. Most news and entertainment writing texts caution their readers to write for ordinary persons, sometimes assuming the audience to be high school graduates with limited attention spans. They also suggest ways to capture reader and viewer attention with various devices.

11. Manuel Castells, *The Rise of the Network Society* (Malden, MA: Blackwell, 2000) and *The Network Society: A Cross-Cultural Perspective* (Cheltenham, U.K.: Edward Elgar Publishing, 2004); see also www.RandallRothenberg.com, "Facebook's Grandfathers (& MySpace's, Too!)," *I, A Bee,* Interactive Advertising Bureau, Nov. 11, 2007.

Navigating Change: The Rise of Digital and Global Media

Once upon a time, the **communication media**—sometimes called the **mass media** or **mass communication**—were relatively stable, with a few reliable TV networks, well-known newspapers and magazines, and other familiar players. One could have disappeared into the wilderness or gone to another planet for a few years, and upon returning not much would have been different. The same old, predictable media were there, looking pretty much the same as they had in earlier generations. There were always incremental changes, of course, but the structure and organization of the media, their economic underpinnings, their technologies, and the regulations that governed them rarely made dramatic shifts, lurches, or pendulum swings.

Beginning in the last years of the twentieth century, however, and accelerating to a dizzying pace in the first decade of the twenty-first century, we experienced a radical shift in the way that communication occurs among people and societies. This **digital revolution** came about thanks to the connectedness of a computer-driven, electronics-based system that makes possible the Internet and the World Wide Web. This revolution is regarded as a transformation almost as important in human history as the invention of the printing press and moveable type.

For much of human history, media also lived behind national boundaries, although there were always exceptions—early newsletters and newspapers traversing the oceans with international trade and books doing the same. Eventually movies, especially Hollywood films, were widely distributed in many places outside their country of origin. Much of that changed in the late twentieth century as old systems, like the former Soviet Union, collapsed and globalization occurred, driven by technology and economic forces. With the coming of communication satellites, national borders were crossed easily, and media such as television got greater reach. And, of course, global networks in what scholar Manuel Castells has called "the network society" allowed for true interactivity whereby people could communicate more easily across national boundaries and other barriers than ever before. For the media, this also meant the sharing of cultural products across many countries and societies. Some governments that do not want their citizens exposed to such intercultural influences have jammed broadcasts, controlled telecommunication systems, and restricted Internet distribution, efforts that sometimes prevent truly global communication. But now technology is more difficult to control, if not impossible.

As a result of globalization and the digital revolution, it now seems as if everything in the world of communication is constantly changing. The content of social networking sites, like MySpace, YouTube, and Facebook, and search engines, like Google, Yahoo!, and Ask.com, changes on a minute-by-minute basis. New video games make their way to the market daily or weekly. Familiar cable channels change their names as nearly all media and entertainment activities grow increasingly web-centric.[1] Indeed, a close look indicates that every medium of communication; the industry of which it is a part; as well as its content, audiences, and means of distribution are part of a dynamic process of change.[2]

If today's global, digital age is so radically different from everything that came before, truly expanding on and advancing all previous communication media and activities, why bother studying the old activities, trying to understand their origins and development? After all, one can live and work in the modern world without keen knowledge of ancient Egypt or the developments of the nineteenth century. One answer is because many of the so-called *legacy media* like books, magazines, and newspapers continue to exist side by side with newer media, as do radio, television, cable, motion pictures, and other players of the media family. Another answer is that many of the differences are derived from what came before. As one technology expert says, "To truly understand the nature of the Internet, you have to understand the history of radio." Even aspects that seem fundamentally different today were known, anticipated, and speculated about long ago. In this chapter, for example, we'll discover that many of the basic elements that you learned about in Chapter 1, of how human beings communicate among themselves—in groups, organizations, and even across societies—can be seen with great clarity in these first years of the digital age.

THE DAWN OF THE DIGITAL AGE

In the sweep of human history, there was in the beginning the *agrarian age,* when people were hunters and farmers, living in small villages in what was largely a feudal society. With the *industrial revolution* of the 1830s, we entered a world in which machines and manufacturing brought us cities, a system of transportation, and eventually innovations in communication, beginning with the telegraph, the first great challenge to time and distance and the forerunner of electronic communication and other media. The telegraph was followed by the advent of audio, visual, and electronic media, which lived alongside print, which dominated publishing media. A new *information age* began in the 1980s and 1990s, when more people were employed in the creation, development, and dissemination of information than in agriculture and manufacturing. This so-called information, or service, economy was made possible and spurred on by computers and ultimately an integrated networking society where digital communication dominated and ultimately changed everything. An **information society**, made possible by the digital revolution, has been credited with giving people everywhere greater access to information, thanks to cell phones and the Internet. With that access comes new freedom because of a greater capacity to communicate with one another. As L. Gordon Crovitz of the *Wall Street Journal* put it, "As information becomes accessible, individuals gain control."[3]

History of the Digital Revolution

In the 1960s, Canadian media guru Marshall McLuhan proclaimed the coming of "the global village."[4] His grand vision seemed, at the time, more of a global improbability, that *all* information and knowledge ever accumulated could be communicated interactively to *everyone* everywhere, who, by the way, could also communicate easily with each other. Every human being could potentially communicate freely with every other

Technology sometimes leapfrogs levels of social development from a primitive culture such as this one at a rural Peruvian village where a woman is accessing the Internet.

human being on the planet and would be both the recipient of and creator of information, messaging, and knowledge. With the coming of the personal computer, high-speed Internet access, and fiber optics networks and the rise of the World Wide Web, McLuhan's vision may seem to have been realized. But, as Figure 2.1 suggests, this is not quite the case. While there is Internet almost everywhere in the world, not everyone has it. In McLuhan's ideal world, everyone would be connected to a global network of interactive communication in which everyone can be a communicator, capable of originating, retrieving, storing, and disseminating messages. In reality there is no universal Internet penetration anywhere—yet. Some areas of the world have substantial access while others are wanting. As Figure 2.1 indicates, there is 73.6% penetration in North America compared with only 5.3% in Africa. In most developed societies, almost all individuals can get access to the Internet, if not at home then at public libraries and schools, but this is not generally true in developing or emerging nations. We live, one futurist says, in "the age

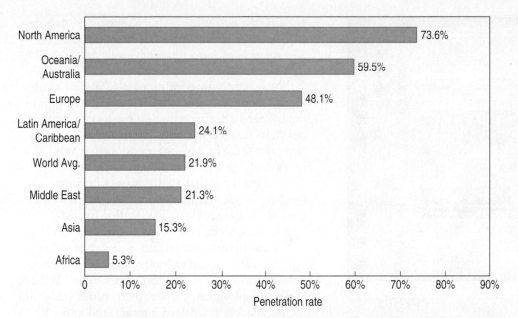

FIGURE 2.1
World Internet
Penetration Rates by
Geographic Regions

Source: Internet Wold Stats - www.internetworldstats.com/stats.htm. Penetration rates are based on a world population of 6,676,120,228 for mid-year 2008 and 1,463,632,361 estimated internet users. Copyright © 2008, Miniwatts Marketing Group

of improvisation,"[5] when people make their own messages and connect with their peers and others in a manner unprecedented in human history. How did we get here?

The digital revolution evolved incrementally but then swept onto the scene with great impact and force. We can identify three major phases in the development of new media:

- **The Early Days** During the 1970s and '80s, early renditions of the World Wide Web and the Internet were known and used almost exclusively in the military and educational institutions. Few other people knew about these massive information, storage, and retrieval networks, and those who did thought the general public would have little reason to ever use it.[6]

- **Boom and Bust** From 1994 onward, the new platform blossomed, as the personal computer won wide adoption, not just in offices and businesses but at home too. Around 1998 or 1999, an Internet business "bubble," or expansion, began. New businesses called *dot-coms** (named after the suffix in their web addresses) soared, as tens of thousands of websites blossomed and a powerful new media economy with billions of dollars at stake emerged. On paper, thousands of new multimillion-aires (many in their twenties) triumphed as they created a web industry attended by early search engines such as Ask.com (formerly Ask Jeeves) and social networking activities like simple Listservs. Big media entered the picture, creating new enter-prises, the most celebrated being the merger of TimeWarner, the publishing and electronic media company, with a relative newcomer, America Online (AOL).

   Overheated stock markets, slow-speed Internet, and other factors brought about a dot-com "crash," or widespread financial meltdown, in 2000 and 2001.[7] But the new platform and all that it represented was not to be counted out.

- **Reemergence** By 2002 and 2003, there was a comeback, with new media companies evolving, and old media, some that had not been involved in the dot-com revolution, cautiously entering the fray. High-speed Internet, flat-panel computer devices, cell phones, and other activity that connected old-line media with the new media of the Internet, broadband, wireless and satellite communication, and digital communication

---

* Dot-com (".com") refers to any commercial Internet address, just as ".edu" is for educational institutions and ".gov" is for government agencies.

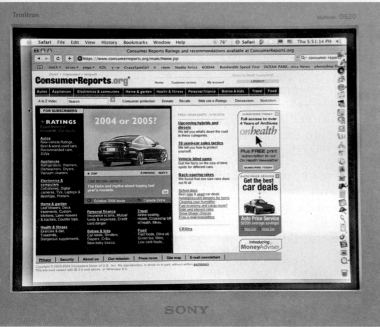

The evolution of digital communication on the Internet is demonstrated in these two screen shots that illustrate the difference between early simplified websites and today's more interactive ones.

got a new lease on life.[8] This happened in part due to relaxed government restrictions, including the deregulation of some old media industries.[9] And it should be noted that nothing is static.

New economic conditions also played a role. Once, daunting financial barriers to entry kept ordinary people from setting up media companies, but that changed with the Internet. And with the powerful force of new competition that was unleashed, the traditional media felt the bite. Many came to realize that their old business models, which depended on advertising and user fees, no longer sufficed. They called for new approaches, all driven by the digital revolution.

It was the connection and interplay of technology, government, and economic forces that led to a new era for digital media, sometimes called **Web 2.0**, which involves greater interactivity, better visual and audio capacity, high-speed Internet, and more. It's easy to see this radical change if one can compare websites and Internet media from the late 1990s to those of 2009 and beyond. And no doubt other changes will ensue, driven by the great social forces that guide, influence, and sometimes direct what happens to institutions, organizations, and individuals.

Thoughtful observers of media often wonder what big ideas today are going to shape the communication world of tomorrow, and whether digital media is yet another transition on the way to yet another new media revolution. History may help guide their speculations. Digital media, like all media, are both nurtured by and reflect powerful forces of their times:

■ *Economic* Some analysts say that the economy first and foremost creates a climate for innovation. It is important to consider not just the general economy but media economies as well. Sometimes old media strive to create impediments to change. For example, the newspaper industry was initially the greatest enemy of the telecommunication companies that ultimately helped harness the Internet for the use of ordinary people. Newspaper owners feared the death of their classified advertising, realizing that online ads with their interactive features would quickly render obsolete those printed in ink. Today, newspapers, although belatedly, embrace digital communication and have worked feverishly to implement it in their own enterprises.

■ *Technological innovation* New developments only occur when creative individuals have the ability and the need to invent new systems and devices.

■ *Government and legal* The regulatory hand of government can either encourage or erect barriers to the implementation and use of new media.

The Speed of Change in a Digital Age

The history of new media provides some idea of the speed at which the digital revolution has been taking place. Economic factors helped fuel this revolution. When first introduced, computers and newer devices such as cell phones, VCRs, DVDs, and flat-screen

TVs, were quite expensive and beyond reach of the average person. Earlier, radio and TV sets were expensive too. But very quickly prices went down, and the majority of households had these items. This same process has happened to a variety of media equipment throughout human history, but it is now happening faster than ever before.

Consider some traditional media. Bound books have been around since Roman times, and scrolls were in existence even before that. Newspapers and magazines, on the other hand, are much more recent developments; they were not possible until printing became available. As mass media, they came into their own during the 1800s, when steam presses made it possible to produce printed pages quickly and in large numbers. More modern and postmodern media—the movies, radio, television, and the Internet— were all developed during the 1900s. In each case, these media were introduced into the society as **innovations**, cultural items that had not been present earlier. None was instantly **adopted**—taken up to be used—by the majority of the population. In each case, a few people started using these media, and then their use became more common as they were adopted by larger and larger proportions of the population.

Social scientists Everett Rogers and F. Floyd Shoemaker have developed a very useful theory that describes and explains the process of the *adoption of innovation*.[10] It applies not only to the pattern by which a new medium of communication comes into use within a population but also to almost any kind of new cultural item that is either invented within the society or adopted from some outside source. The electric light, for example, as well as the pizza, the automobile, the refrigerator, the computer, the wristwatch, the cigarette, and the hamburger, are all examples of cultural items that followed a more or less similar **adoption curve**, the path toward widespread use. We summarized the adoption patterns of several technologies in Figure 2.2, and we will discuss adoption patterns of each of the major media in greater detail in the chapters that follow. Figure 2.2 compares the adoption curves of several digital communication innovations with those of earlier technologies. Notice that computers and the Internet were adopted by 50% of U.S. households within twenty years. This contrasts greatly with the telephone, which took seventy-five years to get to the same 50% penetration. If we rely on changing technology as an indicator, media adoption clearly is happening faster now than it was in earlier decades.

Defining Communication in a Digital Society

As we consider the role of media in a society dominated by digital influences, it is important to recognize that the technology driving so much of today does not operate in a vacuum, nor is it the only profound influence. Instead, technology is part of an amalgam of forces—cultural, social, political, and economic—that shape and influence all aspects of communication.

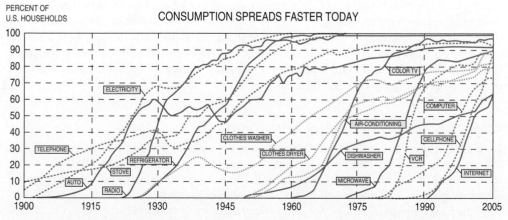

FIGURE 2.2

Consumer Adoption of New Technologies

Source: "Week in Review" *New York Times*, Feb. 10, 2008, p. 14; see also W. Michael Coz and Richard Alm, "You are What You Spend," also p. 14.

The complexity of modern communication includes the woman accessing information on a laptop computer and the man checking email on the cell phone.

Because we are in a period of great change, it is not surprising that we have difficulty finding the right term or phrase to describe what is a dynamic process and system of communication. **Mass communication**, as we discussed in Chapter 1, is a term invented to describe media organized to reach mass audiences, originally carried out by professionals and aimed at accumulated audiences in which it was impossible to truly identify an individual viewer or reader. The digital age and the Internet have, however, to some degree shaken this longstanding and settled definition of mass communication, because now anyone can become a communicator. In a digital world, when so-called *addressable* communication—by which a media message can reach a specific individual, rather than an entire audience or even a specific audience segment—is possible and where a person's specific interests and attributes can be tracked by advertisers, the term *mass* communication is in some dispute.

Some uses of digital communication technology are examples of mass communication, and others are not. Developing playlists of music, sending IMs or email, or creating Listservs or personal networks do not necessarily constitute mass communication any more than making phone calls did in the earlier times. In these cases, messages reach only a few people—though with highly sophisticated communication devices, such as Blackberry, iPhones, and various file-sharing methods—making these examples of **personal media**.

The capacity for interactivity and precise targeting of new recruits for one's personal communication space, or community, offered by many digital media can, however, provide the mechanism to move from personal to *intermediate* communication. **Intermediate communication** uses technology to create communities for like-minded people with similar interests or the same political or social views. These communities can be closed systems, such as a kind of virtual "private club" with an encoded website or a specific network in MySpace. Alternatively, they can be open systems, accessible to anyone who cares to connect with them, such as a political movement that uses new technologies to reach its followers and affords them a communicative role.

The methods of personal and intermediate communication are often employed by media industries, which transform them to mass media as they adopt their own digital strategies. It is also possible for an amateur developer of a website or new software system to create a global media enterprise (YouTube is an example), but these **personal media** quickly take on the characteristics of mass communication. They hire a staff, compete for advertising with traditional media, and even try to improve on the mass media model and accumulate audiences while they aggregate, or collect, content originally gathered by others, sometimes in the oldest media forms.

Concerns About the Digital Revolution

Like all changes, the information age has not been easily welcomed by everyone. Critics worried about the fast pace of what was happening from the mid-1990s forward: the array of new devices and systems available not just to the wealthy but also to ordinary people. On one hand, the increasingly widespread technology "leveled the playing field" by giving more people power to create and get information. On the other hand, the new approach required a shift in thinking as large as the shift that people in earlier centuries had to make to understand that the Earth was round. The collision of these two values, improved access with increased mental challenge, were summarized by journalist Thomas Friedman, who declared, "The world is flat."[11]

So even while we may celebrate the great human achievement of the digital age, where instantaneous communication is commonplace and the old barriers of time and distance are almost eliminated, digital communication also appears to have a darker side. We now face issues that include loss of privacy, cyber crime, and a seemingly inevitable decline of quality media that had evolved over two centuries.

Challenges of Media Study in a Digital Age

Once, the acquisition, processing, storage and dissemination, or spreading, of information was straightforwardly divided among different roles. A newspaper, for example, used reporters to gather news, staff to edit and print it, and carriers to distribute it. Today, however, there are almost an infinite number of channels for dissemination, as well as technological platforms to carry diverse content to individuals and audiences. Almost everyone is involved in acquiring information though emails, instant messages, and file sharing. Processing information is also done by ordinary individuals, as well as professional

The interactive nature of the Internet and its consequences are demonstrated in this whimsical treatment of a cyber-thief coming out of a computer screen.

communicators. Storage of news was almost nonexistent in past times, but today, news archives, film libraries, old TV programs, and other "digital assets" are valuated by investment bankers and given a sticker price. Dissemination involves not just the transmission of messages and feedback but also **repurposing** old content, repackaging it to use in a new way. The digital age has rendered obsolete the axiom that the only person who can truly communicate with others in society is one who owns a printing press—or TV station.

As many people know, graduate students tinkering with computers and software in garages have created world-renowned media enterprises, like Google and eBay, that now threaten the old, venerable players that have been in the communication business for centuries, such as newspapers. This is the challenge of the digital age. As confused and chaotic as the digital media world seems, there are natural pathways through the complexity that this book aims to join its readers in discovering.

Media scholar Harold D. Lasswell, for example, introduced back in the 1940s the idea of **media functions**, the purposes for which we use media. He argued that the functions of all media were:

- Surveillance of the environment.
- Correlation of the parts of society responding to the environment.
- Transmission of the social heritage from one generation to another.

To these, the media researcher Charles Wright added "entertainment," which he said involved "communicative acts, primarily intended for amusement," regardless of

A television weatherman, Steve Rambo, points to the sun on a map of the United States.

Famed CNN correspondent Christiane Amanpour covers a story in Jerusalem.

Latin American telenovelas such as the popular Mexican show Rosalinda carry out the function of entertainment.

other effects they may have. Lasswell almost certainly did not intend his theory to apply only to the media that existed during the 1940s, such as newsmagazines that delivered information to help people survey their environments. Instead, his list of purposes was part of a larger idea about the role of communication in society. Deeply imbedded in this explanation is the idea of *building community*, one of the driving forces of the digital age.

Today's media critics and practitioners have also listed the major goals of the media themselves, which are very similar to the functions for which audiences use media:

- **Informing**—through news, journalism, and public affairs information
- **Influencing**—through opinion media, editorials, and commentary
- **Entertaining**—through comedy shows and sites, fiction, dramas, film, and games
- **Providing a marketplace for goods and services**—through such methods as advertising and product placement

These media functions were never completely pure. Though newspaper stock tables, which list the prices of corporate stocks, came close to being pure information, and editorials of all types are nearly pure opinion, there was always blurring and merging. Traditionally, however, we identified *informing* with newspapers; *influencing* with opinion magazines or talk radio; *entertaining* with motion pictures and entertainment television; and providing a *marketplace* with advertising, commercial sponsorship, and the like. In the digital age, the functions of the majority of web-centric media—and others, such as video on demand (VOD) and wireless handheld devices (which we'll discuss later)—are blurred and merged together. Virtually all digital media are tied to advertising, marketing, and direct sales. Even Google, known mainly for offering information, also provides a marketplace by allowing some sponsored links that appear in searches. For example, if you put in the name of a major city, you'll be directed to an official website for travelers as well as lists of hotels and other services, all available for a price. Most search engine sites are similarly filled with commercial sources that will help you track a person who you are trying to find or some other information for a fee.

As we pointed out in Chapter 1 and earlier in this chapter, the media as they exist today have been shaped by a number of social, political, economic, and cultural influences from the past. Furthermore, the media will continue to be shaped not only by what they are today but by future social, political, economic, and cultural changes in our society as they continue to unfold. In later chapters, we will see how the present digital revolution is shaping the future of traditional media. The digital revolution is also exploding the scope of media, as we'll see next.

THE SPREAD OF GLOBAL MEDIA

As we mentioned earlier in this chapter, digital communication has vastly changed the reach of media and communication. It has erased the old barriers of time and distance, when it took weeks for a newspaper to be carried by ship across the ocean or when television networks had to send filmed news reports by airplane back to their home base for broadcast. With the advent of communication satellites, international

BIG IDEAS: MEDIA THEORIES EXPLAINED

Cultural Imperialism Theory

A theory associated with international or global communication is termed *cultural imperialism*. The basic idea is that the mass media, along with other industries in Western societies, follow a deliberate policy designed by powerful economic and political interests to *transform* and *dominate* the cultures of other people. This process is focused in particular, say those who oppose it, on developing countries' means—Africa, Latin America, and Asia.

This transformation is said to be displacing traditional values, beliefs, and other important features of the way of life in the receiving societies. It takes place, say those who subscribe to this theory, in spite of efforts on the part of the non-Western societies to resist such change.

At the heart of this process of domination are the Western mass media, which convey news and entertainment to people in many parts of the world. The content of these media, say the critics, emphasizes contemporary events in Western societies, secular beliefs and values, plus the material culture of both Europe and the United States.

The foundation of this theory came from three areas of scholarly concern about the role of the media in international communication. The first was a body of research and analysis from the 1950s and 1960s that led to the conclusion that mass media were a very important factor in *national development*. The media were found to be useful in bringing about rapid social change in those societies that valued this goal. The second was in often-heated debate within the United Nations agency UNESCO during the 1970s and 1980s protesting the domination by Western organizations of the *flow of news* all over the world, emphasizing the developed societies. Many leaders in developing countries resented this and fought for significant changes. The third is the current predominance in international markets of the products of American and European industries in an increasingly globalized society; these include digital technologies as well as digitized *films* and *television programs*.

These processes of global communication have come to be interpreted by critics as *imperialistic*. That is, American and European powers deliberately use the media to impose Western material culture and the many kinds of freedoms embodied in democracies on people who prefer to retain their traditional values, beliefs, political structures, and ways of life. This has been challenged in recent years as digital media have made end runs around the old means of communication, for they can be originated anywhere. Still stated formally, the theory of cultural imperialism assumes that:

1. The content of print and broadcast news, plus movies and television programming, produced by organizations in the United States and Europe is *widely distributed throughout the globe* to non-Western and so-called "developing" countries.
2. Citizens who live in such societies have only *limited choices* for media-provided information and entertainment outside those brought to them by Western global distribution systems. (Local systems lack the necessary resources to compete.)
3. Those in less-developed societies who receive the content distributed by Western global systems are exposed to what many in the audience perceive as *attractive alternatives* to their own material culture, values, and traditional ways of life.
4. Such audiences are led *to adopt, or want to adopt*, goods, services, values, and lifestyles that they see portrayed in the Western media, which creates both political unrest and markets for goods that can be exploited by Western powers.
5. **Therefore**, the developed societies *deliberately engage in cultural imperialism* by distributing media content that systematically undermines and replaces traditional beliefs, values, and lifestyles—leading people to prefer Western political systems, material goods, and perspectives.

Source: Herbert I. Schiller, *Communication and Cultural Domination* (New York: M.E. Sharpe, Inc., 1976); Julia Galeota, "Cultural Imperialism: An American Tradition," *The Humanist*, Vol. 64, May/June 2004.

Modern cell phones now deliver content in many forms including full motion video.

broadcasters could have a "footprint" that covered whole continents and regions. For example, MTV, once a single network available mostly in the United States, now has multiple networks and vast audiences in Asia and Latin America. The Internet, of course, has eased this process, as true global communication is now possible in a way that it once was not.

At one time when people talked about media systems or international communication, they meant a mostly self-contained national society and its media system—American, Russian, Chinese, Hungarian, and so on. Consider, for example, the Hungarian media system, which was for decades constrained by its connection to the former Soviet Union and by its own complex language. International communication most often meant the distribution of Western media and media products to developing nations in Africa, Asia, Latin America, and the Middle East, and rarely did media flow from those places back to the West.

Today, as many nations have increasingly well-developed and complex media systems and with the benefit of easy digital communication, media have become much more global in scope. While the movie industry of Hollywood still sends its products all over the world, motion picture studios in other countries are also exporting their products far and wide. For example, the massive Indian motion picture industry, usually called Bollywood, is especially potent. And Latin soap operas, called telenovelas, produced in such countries as Mexico, Venezuela, and Brazil find audiences among Spanish-speaking people in the United States and elsewhere. Music, of course, can and does go almost anywhere via the Internet and, in earlier times, in the mail, because its success is not blocked by language and is limited only by people's interest and taste.

One useful way to think about the globalization of the media and the spread of global media is to consider the "relative exportability" of different media services and products, in the words of media economist Robert Picard.[12] As Figure 2.3 demonstrates, newspapers have a "low" possibility to be exported while motion pictures have a "high" possibility. In effect, most newspapers were designed for local or national audiences. Few, if any, have a true world view or are globally oriented. Thus, with few exceptions, most newspapers traditionally stayed behind national borders and traveled abroad only occasionally by air mail. Now most newspapers have a web presence and are thus accessible to people anywhere. Still, most of their advertising and subscription business is local.

FIGURE 2.3
Relative Exportability of Different Media Products and Services

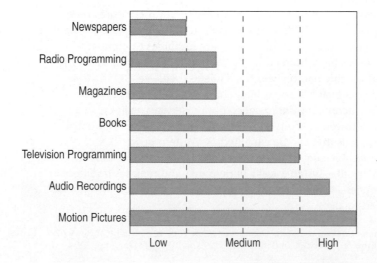

Radio programming, magazines, and books are regarded as more likely to have a global reach, impeded only by cost or local cultural interests. Television programming has been somewhat more successful crossing national boarders as have audio recordings.

Ultimately, Figure 2.3, which is mostly based on revenue trends in media industries, may change radically. To a limited degree there is a worldwide, niche audience of expatriates and tourists for almost any newspaper. The same can be said for magazines and books, especially if they are published digitally. Radio programs are already available on the Internet, as is some television programming. It is not yet clear whether the ease of access online will translate into profits for media companies whose content that is hard and expensive to produce is often found free on the Internet. One theory is that web visitors will drive advertising revenues that can be shaped by content producers.

Some countries have long championed their national media. The United Kingdom, for example has the iconic BBC, sometimes regarded as the best broadcaster in the world, which has bureaus the world over—and a global reach. CNN in the United States has a strong international service as well. Al Jazeera is an Arabic news network that disseminates its messages worldwide. Bloomberg media competes with the Associated Press and other news services such as Reuters to cover the news for audiences in many countries and regions of the world. Germany's Bertelsmann Corporation has media holdings in many countries based originally on its book publishing franchise. French firms like Hachette own magazines and book publishing houses, as do British firms like Thompson. Global media giants and their influence is seen in Figure 2.4 and Table 2.1.

Increasingly, media content drawn from many sources—Brazil's giant Globo television network and media company and Italy's RAI—become part of the media fare enjoyed by people in many countries.

While globalization of media and the rise of truly digital media, like MTV or VH1 music channels, has been strongly supported by the Internet and digital communication such as wireless and video-on-demand, it is stimulated by local interest and demand. Successful global media outlets and products are usually distinctive, if not unique. They are cost effective and usually have high production values, according to Robert Picard. But there are also barriers that block or slow global media, including various trade and regulatory rules—some countries extract local taxes or have rules that limit foreign media distribution. That's true in such countries as Canada and India, for example. Of course, there are language barriers too—a Japanese comic book will have limited appeal in the United States unless it is translated into English, and there are also cultural differences from one place to another than can be an impediment.

We should underscore that global media is a relatively new phenomenon—and it is growing. Once we could talk about comparative media, usually meaning a process by which we compared our media with those of another country to better understand our own, much like learning a foreign language improves one's understanding of his or her own language. Subsequently, critics and commentators talked about international communication, meaning an inventory of the different media and press systems of the rest of the world, region by region, country by country. Global media means that borders are porous and that most communication and media products can be accessed almost

The multiple functions of handheld digital devices like Apple's iPod includes downloading videos and television shows.

FIGURE 2.4
Global Media Giants

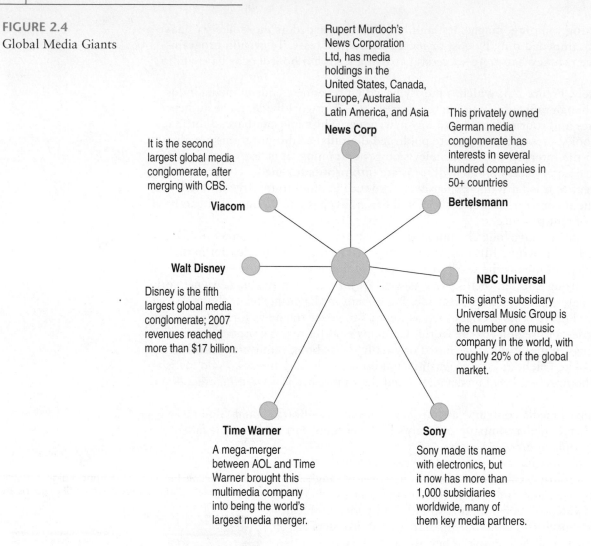

It is the second largest global media conglomerate, after merging with CBS.

Viacom

Rupert Murdoch's News Corporation Ltd, has media holdings in the United States, Canada, Europe, Australia Latin America, and Asia

News Corp

This privately owned German media conglomerate has interests in several hundred companies in 50+ countries

Bertelsmann

Walt Disney

Disney is the fifth largest global media conglomerate; 2007 revenues reached more than $17 billion.

NBC Universal

This giant's subsidiary Universal Music Group is the number one music company in the world, with roughly 20% of the global market.

Time Warner

A mega-merger between AOL and Time Warner brought this multimedia company into being the world's largest media merger.

Sony

Sony made its name with electronics, but it now has more than 1,000 subsidiaries worldwide, many of them key media partners.

Source: Modified from WGBH Educational Foundation, "Merchants of Cool: Media Giants."

everywhere. Add to this multimedia capacity and social networking, and the real possibilities of global media come into view, though they have not been fully realized yet.

TABLE 2.1

Top 25 Global Media Companies

	2007 Revenues (US$m)
1. Time Warner Inc.	$32.6
2. Vivendi (now NBC Universal)	29.6
3. The News Corporation Limited	28.6
4. Comcast Corporation	26.9
5. Bertelsmann AG	26.4
6. The Walt Disney Company	17.7
7. The DIRECTV Group, Inc.	17.2
8. Google Inc.	16.4
9. General Electric Company	15
10. CBS Corporation	14.1
11. Viacom Inc.	13.4

2007 Revenues (US$m)	
12. Omnicom Group Inc.	12.6
13. Thomson Reuters Corporation	12.5
14. WPP Group plc	12.3
15. Lagardere SCA	11.7
16. Cox Enterprises, Inc.	11.7
17. British Sky Broadcasting Group plc	9.9
18. Liberty Media Corporation	9.4
19. Reed Elsevier NV	9.2
20. Pearson plc	8.3
21. Gannett Co., Inc.	7.4
22. Yahoo! Inc.	6.9
23. The McGraw-Hill Companies, Inc.	6.8
24. Clear Channel Communications, Inc.	6.7
25. Dai Nippon Printing Co. Ltd.	5.7

Source: Datamonitor ComputerWire, "Top 25 Global Media Companies,"
http://www.computerwire.com/companies/lists/list/?listID=95032661-E4CB-4E36-B785-2EEF835DEFB1

CHAPTER REVIEW

- Communication and the development of media has been an evolutionary process moving from simple to complex messages and modes of expression and from the earliest times through the feudal, agrarian days to the industrial revolution and on to the digital age.
- The digital age is characterized by almost continuous and dizzying change as the methods of information storage and retrieval use new platforms, often employing the Internet and including social networking, search engines, and wireless communication.
- Through much of human history, communication and media have lived behind national borders with some exceptions, such as books and films.
- We are now in a network society in which people communicate more easily across national borders; this has resulted in the sharing of cultural products across many countries and societies.
- The digital age is radically different from anything that has come before, but legacy media—the old forms—both interact with new media and have themselves adopted digital means to maintain their place in industry and society.
- The information society, as opposed to industrial society, occurred when a majority of people were supported by an economy mostly concerned with the manipulation of language and symbols.
- The functions of the mass media are those of informing, influencing, entertaining, and providing a marketplace for a goods and services.
- The digital age has already had several stages—early days, boom and bust, reemergence, and the dawn of Web 2.0.
- Globalization has driven the spread of global media across the various regions and countries of the world, with an emphasis on media exports from developed information societies to developing countries.
- Many countries now participate in the export of media products and services including India, several Latin American nations, and others in Asia.
- One measure of globalization is the "relative exportability" of media products and services, but even this is changing in the digital age.
- Consumer adoption of new technologies and media has sped ahead in the digital age, and "curves of adoption" have accelerated.

STRATEGIC QUESTIONS

1. What are digital media, and how did they evolve?
2. Connect the mass communication process with your own use of media—which media do you use and rely on, and which media are less relevant to you?
3. Why, do you imagine, does it take so long for a new medium to reach 50% of the public?
4. What are digital media, and how do they help people navigate change?
5. What role does speed play in communication in the digital age?
6. Connect the drivers of globalization with digital media and communication.

KEY CONCEPTS & TERMS

Digital revolution   21
Information Age   22
Personal media   26
Adoption of innovation   25

Web 2.0   24
Media functions   27
Legacy media   21

Repurposing content   27
Dot-coms   23
Globalization   28

ENDNOTES

1. Walter S. Mossberg and Kara Swisher, "All Things Digital," *Wall Street Journal,* June 9, 2008, p. R1; Robert D. Hof, "Do We Have a Digital Revolution?," *BusinessWeek,* Feb. 2, 2004, p. 40; see also Everette E. Dennis Stephen Warley and James Sheridan, "Media Synergy: The Sequel," *Strategy + Business,* Issue No. 39, Spring 2005, pp. 3–4, published by Booz Allen Hamilton.

2. Everette E. Dennis and John C. Merrill, "Digital Strategies, the Internet and New Media," in *Media Debates, Great Issues of the Digital Age* (Belmont, CA: Thompson Wadsworth, 2006), p. 162–169.

3. L. Gordon Crovitz, "Optimism and the Digital World," *Wall Street Journal,* April 21, 2008, p. A15.

4. Harold D. Lasswell, "The Structure and Function of Communication in Society," in Lyman Bryson, ed., *The Communication of Ideas* (Institute for Religious and Social Studies, 1948), reprinted in *Sources: Notable Selections in Mass Media,* eds. Jarice Hanson and David J. Maxcy (Guilford, Connecticut, 1996), pp. 22–29.

5. Richard Tobaccowala, CIO, Publicis Groupe Media and CEO, DeNuo, at Monaco Media Forum, October 19, 2006, discussing "jazzy and improvisational" nature of digital media.

6. Katie Hafner and Matthew Lyon, *Where Wizards Stay Up Late* (New York: Simon & Schuster, 1996).

7. John Montavalli, *Bamboozled at the Revolution* (New York: Viking, 2002);

Everette E. Dennis and John C. Merrill, "Concentration of Media Ownership," in Dennis and Merrill, *Media Debates: Great Issues for the Digital Age* (Belmont, CA: Wadsworth 2006), pp. 44–53. Also see James M. Citrin, *Zoom, How 12 Exceptional Companies Are Navigating the Road to the Next Economy* (New York: Doubleday, 2002).

8. Gillian Doyle, *Understanding Media Economics* (London: Paul Chapman Pub., 2009) and Lawrence Lessig, *The Future of Ideas* (New York: Random House, 2001).

9. Louise Story, "$1 Billion Suit Aims to Counter Threat by YouTube," *New York Times,* March 19, 2007, p. C1. For an excellent treatment of mass media law, including new digital applicants, see Don R. Pember and Clay Calvert, *Mass Media Law* (New York: McGraw-Hill College, 2006) and T. Barton Carter, Juliet Lushbough Dee, and Harvey L. Zuckerman, *Communication Law in a Nutshell* (Saint Paul, MN: Thompson West, 2007).

10. Everett M. Rogers and F. Floyd Shoemaker, *Communication of Innovations: A Cross-Cultural Approach* (New York: The Free Press, 1971).

11. See Thomas Friedman, *The World Is Flat* [further updated and expanded, release 3.0] (New York: Farrar, Straus and Giroux, 2007).

12. Robert G. Picard, *The Economics and Financing of Media Companies* (New York: Fordham University Press, 2002).

Books: The First and Most Respected Mass Medium

If there is any medium of communication that is truly old school, it is books, the first and most venerable medium of all. Books came first among our current media, and they remain our choice for serious topics as well as for thoughtful entertainment. For more than a century, however, critics have been predicting the death of the book, if not the death of all print media. And for at least two decades, the electronic book, or e-book, has been touted as inevitable, a technology that would put an end to bulky hardcover and paperback books, bookstores, and the cumbersome process currently used to move an author's message from idea to finished product, displayed for sale.

Today, a number of technological futurists continue to claim that the days of the traditional book are numbered. They maintain that books will be obtained online to be read on a screen. As one such analyst put it:

> As a common item of communication . . . the physical object consisting of bound dead trees in a shiny wrapper is headed for the antique heap. Its replacement will be a lightning-quick injection of digital bits into a handheld device with an ultra-sharp display. Culture vultures and bookworms might cringe at the prospect, but it's as inevitable as page two's following page one. Books are goners, at least as far as being the dominant form of reading.[1]

Others are skeptical about such forecasts. Certainly, they feel, such changes may come, but they will not take place soon. It is difficult, they say, to curl up in bed with one's computer and read what is on the screen—having to restart the program after every interruption. Book enthusiasts also maintain that computer screens, at least in their present form, are inappropriate when one is sitting under a tree, on the patio, riding a bus or train to work, relaxing in a chair before the fireplace, or getting a tan at the beach. For a very long time, books printed on paper have been regularly read in such circumstances, and that is one of the great advantages that the traditional book has always enjoyed compared with more complex electronic media. At present, books printed on paper also have other advantages over existing forms of computerized reading devices: Books are simple, portable, relatively inexpensive, and permanent. They require no batteries or power supply, no complex software, no period of waiting until a machine warms up, and no special skills to open them or leaf through their pages. A book can be picked up or put down in an instant, or it can reside on a shelf unchanged for decades.

As technology advances, the advantages of the traditional book form may compare less favorably, although that remains to be seen. It does seem likely that advances in technology may ultimately challenge how we obtain and read lengthy documents. A more serious question might be not *whether* but *how soon* books in their traditional form will disappear.

The answer to that question depends on the time perspective one takes. As this chapter will explain, books have changed greatly at least three times over the centuries since they first appeared in the form of handwritten scrolls of papyrus or parchment. Because books are so commonly used in their present form, any radical transformation within a short time seems unlikely. But half a century or more from now, who knows? Certainly remarkable changes are already taking place in book retailing, and a new great transition—from traditional book to electronic form—appears to be beginning.

Whatever its physical form, the book is our oldest and most respected medium, without which civilization as we know it could not have developed. For hundreds of years, books in their traditional form have been the most important means by which we preserve our culture, transmit it to the next generation, and communicate important new ideas to millions of readers. For those reasons, whatever their future, books need to be understood in terms of where they came from, the form in which they exist today, and what they may be like in the decades ahead.

THE IMPORTANCE OF BOOKS AS A MASS MEDIUM

Because they are so common and familiar, it may be difficult for people today to appreciate the truly remarkable nature of books and to grasp easily the irreplaceable services they provide to individuals and society. Books represent an important and popular mass medium, widely used for a variety of purposes in contemporary society. The fact that they have not only survived for many centuries but also prospered in the face of increasingly sophisticated competing media is one indicator of their importance.

Books as a Mass Medium

Books as they exist today fit the definition of a mass medium that we developed in Chapter 1. Their "messages" are prepared and encoded by professional communicators and are normally transmitted to relatively large and diverse audiences. Like each of the mass media, they have distinctive characteristics that set them apart from the others:

- Because books (such as the textbook you're reading right now) often take a year or more to produce—even after the author gives the finished manuscript to the publisher—they are less timely than other print media, including newspapers and magazines.
- Books also differ from newspapers and magazines in that they are bound and covered and are consecutive from beginning to end.
- Books are made to last longer than any other print medium, and this feature lends itself to in-depth, durable exploration and development of topics or ideas.
- One obvious difference between books and other media—print and electronic—is that, like movies, they are not heavily supported by advertising. Books have to earn profits for their producers on the basis of their sale as content and as physical objects.

These characteristics suit the book for a special role among our contemporary media mix. Most books sell only a few thousand copies. Even a national runaway best seller will probably sell no more than 10 million copies over its effective years of life—less than the audience for some soap operas during a single day of television. Yet the social importance of books can hardly be overestimated. For one thing, many books are shared among several readers—whether formally through libraries or informally among friends and families—so books usually have readership far beyond their actual sales, which expands their reach.

In recent years, books have also received a paradoxical boost from the limitations and failures of other media. As print and electronic media seemed to many observers to "dumb down" their content in the early years of the twenty-first century, *Publishers Weekly,* the book-industry magazine, asked and answered this question: "Will books make the difference?" The authors asserted that, "As mainstream press falters, book publishing enjoys its status as the new Fourth Estate."[2] The Fourth Estate is a term attributed to the British statesman Edmund Burke who said, "There are three Estates in Parliament, but in the Reporters Gallery yonder there sat a Fourth Estate more important far than they all." Over the years the term has become synonymous with the news media, though generally not including the slow-paced book. Now, in a digital age, that is changing. The *Publisher's Weekly* editors were suggesting that, once, newspapers and then television were the vehicles for controversial material, but now major political stories or insider reports on the White House seem to be broken in books. Books thus set a substantive content standard for other media and can distribute their content widely and rapidly, thanks to digital media.

The Importance of Books

Even after a history that, as we will see, spans thousands of years, books today remain a medium of entertainment, the principal repository of our culture, guides to our technical knowledge, the source of teachings on many subjects, and our basic reference to religious doctrines.

In addition to serving as a major channel for transmitting our cultural heritage, books can promote powerful ideas and inspire great changes—even revolutions. They often persuade the influential, bringing new policies and solutions to problems.

One indicator of the power of books is the vigorous attempts made over the years to censor them. At first, books were not recognized as a political force. But as soon as those in authority realized that printing could be used to circulate ideas contrary to those of the ruling powers, presses came under strong regulation. In 1529, for example, Henry VIII of England established a list of prohibited books and a system of licensing printers.[3] The history of books is a fascinating story in itself, revealing how they have influenced, and been influenced by, cultures all over the world.

WHERE DID BOOKS COME FROM?

Most people realize that books have been around for a long time and that their development took place over an extended period. They also know that hand-lettered books were available long before the printing press became a reality. Perhaps less well understood is that extended book-like documents in the form of scrolls were produced before that. However, neither scrolls nor hand-copied books were a mass medium, easily acquired and read by many people. That transition would not take place until relatively modern times. How, then, did this medium become a part of our common culture? The sections that follow summarize the highlights in the development of the book throughout history into the form that we recognize today and the ways it may develop in the future. It is an incredible story that reveals how much we owe to a number of creative geniuses of earlier centuries.

These ancient cave drawings, our links to early civilizations, were found in Mali, West Africa.

The Evolution of Written Documents

The first step in understanding books and our other contemporary print media is to examine the origins of writing. The graphic representation of an idea, unlike speaking, required a *medium*. Thus, the development of writing and the evolution of media are part of the same process. A **medium** is a device by which a sender can move physical information (graphic symbols: sound, light, radio waves, etc.) through time or space in such a way that one or more people can receive the information and decipher the sender's intended meanings. A medium can be any object or arrangement of objects used to accomplish those goals so as to enable human beings to record, transmit, receive, and interpret messages. Media used in writing depend on some physical representation of thoughts and ideas, either by using pictures or other kinds of graphic symbols placed on a surface.

REPRESENTING IDEAS WITH GRAPHIC SYMBOLS.   The earliest known attempts to represent ideas with pictures—the first step toward the development of writing—were cave paintings, made fifteen thousand to twenty thousand years ago. Cave paintings are artistically very well respected, but, unfortunately, they are extremely limited as a way of communicating ideas. Their meanings to the people who made them and the reasons for which they were done remain unknown. Nevertheless, representing something graphically was a significant step beyond oral description of the objects and events being portrayed. Even if they were only *mnemonic devices*—serving as memory stimulators—depictions such as cave paintings could help a storyteller provide a more detailed and accurate account, compared with unaided recall.

In fact, this illustrates one major purpose of writing. In all its forms, writing is a tool for preserving ideas that were expressed earlier. In other words (to borrow from today's computer jargon), writing is a system for *information storage*. Just as we seek more and more storage capacity in computers, primitive people sought systems of graphic representation of ideas to free themselves from the limitations and inaccuracies of human memory.

Writing must also serve another purpose. Ideally, it permits people who did not record the idea originally to recover accurately the meanings and implications of those who did. In this sense (to borrow again from contemporary computer usage), writing is a means of *information exchange*. Thus, the development of picture drawing was not enough. Only the original artist could recall accurately what the intended meanings represented. The next step was to *standardize* both the depictions and the rules by which to interpret their meaning. That advance took more than ten thousand years.

STANDARDIZING MEANINGS WITH CULTURAL CONVENTIONS.   It was not until about six thousand years ago that people began to leave records in the form of codified writing that can be understood today. At some unknown point between 5000 and 4000 B.C., people in several areas of the Near East began to use drawings to represent ideas in a somewhat more uniform way.[4] Most were agricultural people, and their early attempts at writing grew out of their need to keep accurate accounts so as to record land ownership, boundaries, crop sales, and the like. Some were traders who needed reliable records of cargoes, profits, and commercial transactions.

Generally, these peoples' symbols were pictures of what they knew: birds, the sun, a bundle of grain, a boat, the head of a bull, or parts of the human body. True writing began to emerge when such graphic depictions came to represent *standardized meanings that were agreed upon by cultural conventions,* the rules for interpretation established among a given people. Because of the rule that assigned one and only one agreed-upon meaning to it, each symbol was understood by both senders and receivers in the same way. Thus, for those who understood the rules, a simplified drawing of a human form could mean "a man"; a crudely drawn rising sun might be "one day"; a stylized human foot, "walking"; and a wavy line, "water."

Such a system was called **ideographic**, or "thought writing," because it associated specific whole thoughts or meanings with pictures in a standardized way. It was also sometimes called **pictographic writing**. Well-known ideographic systems of writing were those developed independently by the early Egyptians, the Chinese, and the Mayans of the New World.

Ideographic writing works quite well—given enough ideographs. A separate picture is needed for each idea or thought that is to be recorded. One limitation is that, as a society and culture becomes increasingly complex, more new ideas or concepts need to have their own pictures, symbols, or characters. Eventually, in a truly complex society, the number of characters required in a system of ideographic writing can eventually become staggering. To illustrate this, the *hieroglyphic* (sacred carving) system used during the early Egyptian dynasties required only about seven hundred different ideographs. In a simple Chinese farming village today, only about fifteen hundred are needed. But, in contrast, highly educated Chinese literary scholars today may need to know up to fifty thousand different characters!

REPRESENTING SOUND IN WRITTEN FORM.   A much simpler system of writing is to link graphic symbols not to ideas or thoughts, but to *sounds*. Such a graphic symbol, linked to a specified sound by a cultural convention or rule that prevails among those who speak a particular language, is called a **phonogram**. The English **alphabet** that we use every day has twenty-six symbols, each linked to only a few variations of orally produced sounds. Our contemporary alphabet comes to us from ancient sources. It took more than two thousand years after the earliest attempts at writing to develop this incredibly efficient system. Even the alphabet's name reveals its origins—*alpha* and *beta* are the first two letters of the ancient Greek version.

The development of alphabets, like books and printing, ranks as one of the greatest human achievements. Alphabets made reading and writing—often a hideously complex activity with ideographic systems—literally "child's play." All of us, when we first tackled our ABCs as children, learned the consonant and vowel sounds uniquely linked to each of the twenty-six letters. Along with our numbers, plus a scattering of additional symbols representing punctuation, we can transform into spoken pronunciation virtually any set of written words that need to be orally expressed in our language (or vice versa).

Books as Scrolls: The First Transition

Throughout the time that writing and alphabets were being developed, societies themselves were undergoing great changes. Philosophers and scientists of the day asked questions and sought knowledge about the physical, social, and religious world. As answers accumulated, a need arose to record lengthy discussions and teachings. The rise of great religious systems also created a need to record lengthy sacred writings. The Old Testament of Judaism is an outstanding example of a long and complex set of ideas that could not have been passed on accurately in oral form over many generations. Later, Christians began to record the revelations, testimony, and injunctions of their scriptures. Islam soon followed with the teachings of the sacred Koran.

Great empires also rose as a result of military conquest. One of the great problems for all who governed was how to stabilize the social order and make it work more justly. Ancient codes of law were developed to provide formal guidelines for behavior and to specify punishments for deviance. A classic example is the system of 282 laws developed by the Babylonian King Hammurabi almost four thousand years ago. His laws covered everything from the regulation of commerce and military affairs to the practice of medicine and the treatment of children. In the absence of books, he had his laws carved on huge *stellae*—blocks of basalt stone, eight feet square—that he had set up in the center of each major city in his empire. But it was a terribly cumbersome system. Portable media were sorely needed.

The earliest portable media consisted of pads of wet clay, carried in boxes by the Sumerians–people who lived in the area that is now Iraq–between 3000 and 1800 years ago. Although the clay tablets of the Sumerians could be carried around, they were still heavy and bulky. As early as 3000 B.C., the Egyptians had developed a much lighter and easier-to-carry medium. **Papyrus** (from which, incidentally, we get our modern word "paper") is a paper-like surface made from pounding thin layers of reeds that grew by the Nile river.

Sheets of papyrus were sometimes joined together at the ends and rolled up on a stick to produce **scrolls**, extended documents that

Producing a *manu scriptus* was a demanding and laborious process carried out by monks in monasteries in which books were copied letter by letter on parchment or vellum. From the end of the Roman civilization until the fifteenth century, when printing was invented, this process preserved written records and human memory.

were in fact an early type of book. Thus, a first great transition in the form of books was from stone and clay to more portable media. Libraries in which these important documents could be stored were developed in Egypt, Rome, and Greece. Unfortunately, relatively few survived. Most ancient libraries were destroyed by invaders, or the scrolls did not withstand the ravages of time. But the few that remain, such as the famous Dead Sea Scrolls, provide insights of immense importance into the beliefs and cultures of earlier people.

Papyrus was a great technological solution. Because it was controlled by the Egyptians (and later the Romans), however, it was often difficult to obtain and was in perpetually short supply. As the use of writing spread, alternatives were devised, including **parchment** and **vellum**, both made from animal skins. These media were very expensive. An entire animal skin produced only a few pages. However, such skin surfaces were very durable, which helped some ancient scrolls survive into later centuries.

Books with Bound Pages: The Second Transition

With alphabetical writing well developed and with the availability of efficient portable media, such as papyrus, parchment, and vellum, it was not a difficult step for the Romans to move beyond the relatively cumbersome scroll to the more easily stored bound book with cut pages of uniform size. It was they who developed the book into the form that we know today.[5] They gave us pages with writing on both sides, bound at the edge between boards or covers.

A page from the Irish *Book of Kells,* an illuminating Latin manuscript from 800 AD known for its beautiful Celtic images, created by monks.

The Romans did far more that just develop the physical form of the medium. They also produced many innovations that shaped the *formats* we use in preparing books. For example, the Romans:

- Originated much of the grammatical structure of sentences that we follow today.
- Brought us the idea of paragraphs.
- Standardized systems of punctuation, much as we use them now.
- Created the forerunners of today's uppercase, or capital, and lowercase letters.

The Roman alphabet and the art of hand-lettered book production were all but lost as the Western world entered the so-called Dark Ages, which lasted for approximately seven centuries, from 476 A.D. until the 1200s. The precious knowledge of alphabetical writing was preserved mainly in Christian monasteries, where monks hand-copied thousands upon thousands of **manu scripti**, or hand-written books. (We still use the term *manuscript* to refer to an unpublished book.)[6] Most of the books produced in the monasteries were merely working documents used for practical purposes in churches and schools. However, some were exquisite works of art, "illuminated," or decorated, with elaborate letters and drawings.

PAPER BECOMES AVAILABLE.   One of the technologies that would become critically important in the development of all print media was the manufacture of *paper*, which became widespread in the twelfth and thirteenth centuries. The Chinese had developed paper and used it extensively as early as the second century A.D.[7] Later, during the middle of the eighth century, Persian soldiers captured a group of Chinese paper makers, who either taught the process to their captors or revealed it under torture (depending on whose version of the story one believes). In any case, the Islamic world had paper long before Europeans. It was brought to Spain by Moors in the twelfth century. The production and use of paper caught on quickly, and within a century it was being skillfully manufactured in all parts of Europe.

Printed Books: The Third Transition

The development of printing technology did not come out of nowhere. Many of the prerequisites—paper, literacy, the need for lengthy documents, and a sophisticated format for books—were already a part of Western culture. While all of these forerunners had been around for centuries, Johannes Gutenberg, a metalworker who lived in Mainz (now Germany), made a truly significant technological advance.

Around 1455, Gutenberg was the first to cast individual letters, made of metal, in such a way that, when the letters were inked and pressed to paper, they would print as clear and sharp as those on this page. The individual letters were known as **movable type**, because they could be arranged and rearranged, one letter at a time, into words and lines of print. Earlier printers had used letters carved into wood, but the durability of Gutenberg's metal type meant that the same set of letters could be used over and over without wearing out quickly.

It took Gutenberg about twenty years to develop just the right process for making the letters. He also invented a superior system for pressing the blank pages against the ink type—a screw-type press—and developed suitable inks.[8] Gutenberg's techniques were so simple and practical that they remained in use for hundreds of years.

The invention of a practical and efficient press marked one of those occasions when the ideas of a single person made a great difference. Once it became available, printing with movable type was immediately recognized as a truly extraordinary technological advance. The influence of that advance on Western civilization rivaled the influence of computers during the last decades of the twentieth century.

Some historians say the most significant development in modern human communication was the invention of movable type in 1455 by Johannes Gutenberg. He worked many years perfecting his invention, worrying that mechanical (rather than hand-copying) reproduction would never be accepted.

THE RAPID ADOPTION OF PRINTING. The number of books available simply exploded as the printing press quickly spread throughout Europe. Within a half century after Gutenberg's invention of movable type, a tidal wave of books were printed in the vernacular, or popular languages spoken by people outside of churches and universities. These books passed into the hands of increasingly eager populations. No one knows how many were published during the period, but estimates range between 8 million and 20 million copies.[9] (The average press run was only about five hundred copies per book, so these figures represent a very large number of titles.)

Because more and more of these books appeared in the vernacular, printing greatly accelerated developments in science, philosophy, and religion. Knowledge of many topics became available to almost anyone who was literate in a common language and had enough money to purchase a book. They were still expensive but much cheaper than the older *manu scripti*. It is very likely that even before Columbus's departure for the New World (about thirty-six years after Gutenberg's first press run), more books were printed than the accumulated total of all the *manu scripti* that had been copied during the previous thousand years since the fall of Rome. As presses and printing technology were improved during the 1600s and 1700s, and as paper became increasingly available, the number of books printed each year grew sharply.

The development of education in many countries contributed greatly to the growth in book publishing. More universities were established every year until, by the sixteenth century, they were common in all parts of western Europe. Religious changes (primarily the rise of Protestantism) brought a considerable demand for Bibles and other religious works. In addition, the Renaissance, with its expansion of art, science, philosophy, and literature, contributed to the demand for more and more books. Gutenberg had unleashed a powerful medium indeed.

THE DIGITAL FUTURE OF BOOKS: THE FOURTH TRANSITION

At this moment in time, the future looks quite bright for this venerable medium. There are, however, reasons to expect that, over the long term, another major transition will take place in the ways in which books are produced, stored, distributed, sold, and read. While it is unlikely that in the near future books printed on paper will become obsolete, the Internet and developing computer technology will introduce new ways for readers to obtain and read books and for vendors to sell them.

That transition is already starting, and we can use new technologies now available for publishing books, which may allow us to forecast what will happen to books over the decades ahead. Such predictions are difficult at best, but a number of recent developments provide some clues. Certainly interesting ways of *selling* books have been developed that were not a part of retailing even a decade or so ago. In addition, the ways in which books are transmitted from those who sell them to those who read them are already showing signs of change, as are the formats those readers are using. Specifically, the Internet is becoming a source for downloading books from vendors, and computer-like devices designed for reading books stored in digital files like the Sony Reader and Amazon Kindle are now selling well on the market.

Changes in Bookselling

The development of book retailing via the World Wide Web has already simplified book purchasing for those who are online. The Internet has long been a great bookseller, with Amazon.com being one of the first truly successful and profitable new media companies. With firms like Barnes & Noble and Borders, as well as Amazon, selling books online, purchasers no longer have to drive to a "brick-and-mortar" establishment, find a place to park, walk through the store, and search through the shelves hoping to find what they want. The computer literate can buy a book with a few clicks of a mouse, and within a short time it will be delivered to his or her home. Booksellers such as Amazon now strive to provide some of the "personal" services formerly offered in person in bookshops, such as reviews from readers and employee recommendations. Some, for example, offer shoppers messages telling them that "People who bought this book also bought...."

In addition to direct sales, the Internet has proven useful to publishers and authors, who were also quick to recognize its power as a promotional and marketing tool. A plethora of blogs allow readers to share reviews or even write "fan fiction" in the styles of their favorite authors. Authors (or their publishers) routinely maintain websites where readers can send emails to the authors, download podcasts of authors reading from their works, and link to other media that draw on books for content.[10]

Based on these current developments, can we predict that bookstores and libraries will all go out of business? At present, that does not seem likely in the foreseeable future. However, because of rising costs, online sales of conventional books to customers will continue to intrude upon retail marketing through traditional bookstores. Traditional retailers that do survive will be those that both operate stores with huge inventories of titles in hard copy and also develop effective online systems for selling books. The currently dominant product of booksellers, the ink-on-paper book, can also be expected to undergo some changes.

MEDIA LEADERS INSIGHTS: BOOK PUBLISHING

JONATHAN KARP

Publisher and Editor-in-Chief

Twelve

The Hachette Book Group

A high-profile and much respected editor, Jonathan Karp has acquired, edited, and guided some of America's most honored and successful works of fiction and nonfiction. A graduate of Brown University, Jonathan started his media career as a reporter for *The Providence* (RI) *Journal.* He began his editorial career at Random House, where he moved from editorial assistant to editor-in-chief.

In his present position, Jonathan works with leading authors to produce twelve high-quality books a year. Among books he's edited are *Seabiscuit*, *Shadow Divers*, *Thank You for Not Smoking*, and *The Last Don.* He edited best sellers by Senator John McCain, Senator Edward Kennedy, Donald Trump, Stephen Boshco, and others. Frequently quoted in the media as a cutting-edge editor, he has been praised for having a "great eye for great writing" and is said to work now only with "high-quality material."

1. When and under what circumstances did you first realize the import of New Media or the digital age?

   I started emailing with friends around 1987 and was introduced to computer-assisted research as a reporter at *The Providence Journal* the same year. Both were revelations. It was abundantly clear to me that the media environment would be changing, but the pace of change accelerated dramatically with the mass influence of search engines like Yahoo! and Google.

2. What impact did that experience have on you personally or professionally?

   Professionally, publishers have been able to track sales and distribute their books more effectively than ever before. When I entered the publishing business, authors used to express constant worry about their books not being available. The advent of Amazon and other online booksellers has diminished that concern considerably. Personally, I wonder whether digital media has shortened attention spans and created more emphasis on immediate events in the news culture and in our specific lives, through social networks.

3. How has it influenced the book publishing industry in the larger context of media and entertainment industries?

   More practical information is migrating online, where it can be searched more easily.

4. What is the greatest challenge or benefit of the digital revolution for book publishing? You've made some provocative comments about this in a *Washington Post* column.

   I believe the digital revolution will compel publishers to focus on what they do best: producing works of enduring quality that require years of research and reflection and distillation. With so many other media companies competing at a much faster pace, it makes sense for publishers to slow down and emphasize the authority and originality of their work. Those qualities can't easily be replicated by others in the media culture.

5. Are you optimistic about book publishing's future?

Yes. Some publishers will shrink or fade from prominence or be supplanted by upstarts, but there will always be a place in the culture for writers with interesting stories to tell and important ideas to convey.

6. What, if any, advice do you have for a person who aspires to a career in the book publishing industry?

Read widely. Follow your curiosity. Ask good questions.

Electronic Publishing and Reading

As was noted at the beginning of this chapter, pundits are predicting the death of books as they now exist—printed on paper, bound between covers, sold in bookstores, and stored on shelves in libraries. It would be much more efficient, such futurists maintain, to place books online, where users can download them from the Internet.

There are grounds for the belief that, in the truly long range, the nature of books will undergo some sort of transformation along those lines. *Books acquired on demand* and *books in digital form* downloaded from the Internet are already two visible ways in which this is beginning.

PRINTED BOOKS ON DEMAND.   For several years now, **books on demand** have been downloaded one at a time for individual customers as they buy them. Instead of a bookstore employee going to a shelf or to a stored inventory, the bookstore calls up from its central database on the Internet the title that the customer wishes to buy. A customer can either select the title while at the store or phone in the order form a different location. The book's content is swiftly downloaded at the store and printed on the spot for the customer. The resulting book is printed on paper, with a cover, and the customer reads it in that form.

This method of acquiring books represents only a tiny fraction of books sold, but some critics say change could come swiftly. Because books are the longest of long-form media, the storage capacity of digital communication is attractive to publishers. There are many advantages to electronic storage and distribution in an industry that is always worried about the bottom line and that carries huge inventories of books, many of which never sell.

- The massive costs of paper and printing are reduced to only what is needed for the books actually purchased.
- By simply maintaining an electronic database, rather than a warehouse of printed books, various so-called "middlemen" costs, including the warehouse itself and the expense of shipping books to retailers, are eliminated. Presumably, as these costs are reduced, the retail price of a book will also drop.
- Books no longer available in print can be stored in electronic form to be obtained in this way.
- Publishers would not need to absorb the costs of unsold books, as they currently do, through a widespread, but arcane, practice of **returns**—a system whereby booksellers send unsold inventories back to publishers with no penalty.

For these reasons, the book publishing industry truly welcomes technical innovation. In an on-demand printing system, the process of production, storage, and delivery of books has changed, but end use remains the same. Other models change the user experience.

DIRECT DOWNLOADING FROM THE INTERNET.   A somewhat different version of books via the Internet goes much further. In this system, book venders maintain no brick-and-mortar store nor even a warehouse in the usual sense. They only maintain a website and a server, via which they can be contacted directly by their customers. These online venders maintain a database of **e-books**, electronic book files that can be transmitted quickly and downloaded directly to the customer's computer and then, perhaps, to a **reader**, a dedicated device specially designed for reading these types of books.

There are already several online vendors that sell e-books, such as Powell's Books (www.powells.com). Currently, there is no single standard for reader devices or formats, so many e-book sellers supply files in a variety of formats to support a range of reading options, including the following:

- *Reading online.* Some companies, especially those that sell e-textbooks, such as eCampus (www.ecampus.com), sell access for a specified amount of time (most commonly a single semester or other school term) to books that users never actually download but must access at the vendor's website. These online texts are frequently enhanced with easy searching capabilities; audio, video, or animation clips; or the ability for users to write and store their own notes about the textbook.
- *Downloading, then reading from the computer.* Using software, such as Adobe's Digital Editions or Microsoft Reader, purchasers can download books onto their own computers and read their books from their computer screens at their leisure.
- *Downloading to another device.* Customers who want to read e-books on a device other than their computers generally must first download the book from the Internet to their computers, then download it again to the device via a connection cable. There are many options, including a variety of dedicated electronic readers, such as the Sony Reader. E-books can also be downloaded to Blackberry or other wireless "telephone" devices. One dedicated reader, Amazon's much-heralded Kindle, connects wirelessly with an e-book store on Amazon's website, where Amazon offers electronic books for less than half of the usual retail price for a paper-on-ink version. *Newsweek,* in an enthusiastic cover story titled "The Future of Reading," quoted Amazon founder Jeff Bezos as saying, "This is the most important thing we've ever done."[11]

For some years, e-books were tagged with complaints, that people don't like to read large amounts of text online and that they are put off by the horizontal (landscape) format of the typical computer. In response, many reader devices offer a vertical (or portrait) format that makers hope will satisfy the public. As this is written, the jury is out on the devices, but there is considerable optimism that books are finally catching up with the digital age. The Kindle, for example, holds large promise to provide instant books to readers at modest costs in a device that also searches the Web.

In an effort to promote the use of e-books, some companies offer free e-book software, and some vendors occasionally even offer free books as an inducement to purchase others later. Most, however, offer only a review of a sample chapter (usually the first one) or a "look inside the book" feature free online. As with similar features offered by online venders of traditional, paper books, the idea is to tease the site visitor into buying the whole book.

Although there are many improvements that still need to be made in both cost and ease of use, many observers see the potential for great advantages to the reading public from the spread of e-books:

- One vision for the future includes the idea that libraries and even large bookstores are replaced by large databases of electronic books. E-books could supplement the traditional books already in libraries, many of which have limited holdings or out-of-date materials, so that library users can have access to the most current of all forms of information. This would be a particular boon to many local school libraries, whose holdings are often hopelessly out of date.
- With rapid access to electronic books, people traveling on business or vacation need not lug along heavy hard copies in their luggage. They can get what they need at any time over almost any telephone line.
- In a very long-range sense, there is the tantalizing possibility that individuals in countries that have few libraries or a book publishing system can increase their level of literacy and cultural sophistication.

Predictions for the Fourth Transition

Generally, then, given the remarkable progress in computer systems that has taken place over the last twenty-five years, it seems likely that, at some point in the future, new technologies will be developed that will produce a fourth transition in the nature of books.[12]

However, even if all these technological changes take place, will bookstores and libraries all go out of business? At present, that does not seem likely. Books printed on paper will be with us for the foreseeable future. Their increasing use of digital platforms for distribution to readers is a promising development. However, it is likely that both systems—paper and electronic—will continue to coexist for some time, with businesses and libraries handling both forms. If that is the case, our current book publishing industry, described next, will undergo significant reconfiguration to produce and distribute e-books.

BETWEEN THE PAST AND THE FUTURE: BOOK PUBLISHING TODAY

Between the authors who prepare the content of a book and the public who reads it is the publishing company. The publisher's role is threefold: (1) to *select* and help shape what will be published; (2) to *produce* the book as a physical artifact; and (3) to *advertise and distribute* the book to receivers—which are usually retail book stores that sell it, in person or online, for a profit. In this section, we'll see how the publishing industry has evolved in America to perform those three functions as it does today. We'll also discover that, although authors prepare the actual content of a book, publishers take the risks involved in investing the money required to convert a manuscript into a book and to promote and distribute it to consumers. Because most publishers are privately owned businesses, they have a clear necessity to earn a profit. In recent years, the industry's changing economics have influenced the way publishers carry out their other roles.

A Short History of Book Publishing in America

Book publishing got off to a slow start during colonial days but picked up speed as education spread throughout the country. Developments throughout the nineteenth and twentieth centuries led to the practices that shape the flourishing book publishing industry of today.

BOOK PUBLISHING IN THE AMERICAN COLONIES.   Printing in the New World began very early. Approximately a century before the Pilgrims arrived at Plymouth Rock, Juan Pablo set up a press in Mexico City and, in 1539, printed the first book in the Americas, a religious work titled *Breve y Mass Compendiosa Doctrina Cristiana.*

Book publishing was slow to start in North America. The settlers who sailed on the Mayflower in 1620 were not avid readers, and the toil of settling a new land when they arrived left little time for reading. Most Pilgrims lived a life almost free of any form of communication other than talking.[13] Although reading was widespread in the Old World at this time, it was not until 1640 that the first book in New England was published, at the newly founded Harvard College in Cambridge, Massachusetts. It was a religious work titled the *Whole Booke of Psalmes* (most often called the *Bay Psalm Book*).

Horatio Alger's books for boys played a key role in American popular culture in the nineteenth century with their "rags to riches" and "poor boy makes good" tales.

The importance of books in American culture is transmitted from Europe where books sometimes celebrated in fine art such as Jan van Eyck's "St. Jerome in his study" displayed at the Detroit Institute of Art.

Book publishing on any scale continued to develop very slowly in the North American colonies, partly because of restrictions imposed by England, which governed the colonies. However, growing political dissent before the American Revolution stimulated all forms of publishing—books, early newspapers, and political pamphlets. These played a significant part in motivating the separation from England.

BOOKS AND LITERACY SPREAD IN THE NINETEENTH CENTURY.   In the decades following the Revolution, New York, Boston, and Philadelphia became established as centers of a budding publishing industry. Books published early in America's history included religious works and almanacs as well as political and social treatises. Before the 1800s, however, only a small proportion of the American population was able to read, so most of these works were intended for a fairly elite audience.

After the turn of the nineteenth century, the nation's early leaders believed that democracy required an informed citizenry if it was to survive as its architects had hoped. Following a plan devised in the 1830s by Horace Mann, of the Massachusetts legislature, tax-supported public schools were established to teach all children to read and write. Mann's plan made school attendance mandatory, and it was quickly adopted by other states.

By the 1840s, a growing audience for books existed in America. In addition to textbooks and scholarly and religious works, cheap paperback reprints of popular books appeared, including sensational fiction. By 1855 the United States far surpassed England in the number of books sold. That year saw the first publication of Whitman's *Leaves of Grass*, Longfellow's *Hiawatha*, and Bartlett's *Familiar Quotations*, which remains a basic reference source even today. Probably no other book in American history had as much impact on its time as one published during this period: Harriet Beecher Stowe's antislavery novel *Uncle Tom's Cabin*. Thus, as the nineteenth century progressed, book publishing in the United States became well established as a business, a mass medium, and a shaper of American culture.[14]

GROWING NUMBERS OF BOOKS PUBLISHED IN THE TWENTIETH CENTURY.   Figure 3.1 shows the changes in the output of book publishers in the United States during the twentieth century. Clearly, book publishing is a growing industry, with more titles being produced in recent years than at any time in our nation's history. There are two main reasons for this: 1) profit-seeking by increasingly sophisticated book publishers and 2) the continuing spread of education and literacy, leading to larger reading audiences.

FIGURE 3.1
Book Titles Published in the United States

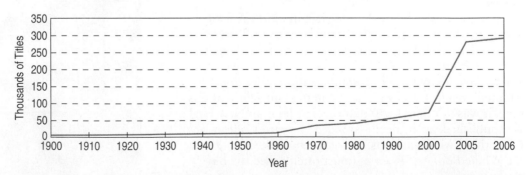

Source: U.S. Census Bureau Statistical Abstracts of the United States by year and http://www.bowker.com.

During the first half of the century, book publishing took an important turn toward commercialism. The titles and delivery methods that publishers offered the public became determined more and more by a sharp focus on profits. Many familiar features with today's book world were introduced during the twentieth century, as publishers sought ways to increase, and then satisfy, the American public's reading needs. These included:

- *Book clubs.* In the 1920s, the Book-of-the-Month Club and the Literary Guild were founded, expanding the market for novels and other works by reaching those who lived far from bookstores. Consumers subscribed to these services, and the "club" selected a new book from them every month.
- *Paperbacks.* One of the important innovations in book publishing in the United States was the introduction of the now-familiar small **paperback**. Even during the nineteenth century, following the development of cheap paper and high-speed presses, paperback "dime" novels were widely available and an important part of American publishing. However, until well into the twentieth century, more "serious" books were always published in hardcover. In Europe, less expensive paperbound books came into wide use well before World War II, but they did not catch on in the United States. However, when cheaper printing and binding were introduced during the 1950s, the small paperback format made it possible for all kinds of books to reach much larger audiences than ever before.

The continuing spread of education also fueled the rise of book publishing, particularly textbooks. Following World War II, more and more Americans pursued higher education. Demand for textbooks soared as returning veterans, helped by the GI Bill, filled colleges and universities. And, with the postwar baby boom, more children entered school than ever before. Today, the children of those baby boomers are overflowing primary and secondary schools and have already begun attending colleges and universities. Once again, the demand for textbooks is increasing.

The dollars Americans spent for books increased massively from the mid-twentieth century to the present. For example, total sales went from just over $435 million in 1947 to more than $23.6 billion in 2007. Even after taking inflation into account, that is a truly significant change.

Today's Book Publishing Process

Like movie producers or music moguls, publishers (to some extent, at least) have styles and reputations. In part, these come from how they organize the publishing process, how they deal with authors, and the physical appearance of their books. In spite of the press for profits, a few publishers are still known for their craftsmanship, producing books of high quality. The majority, however, produce books as quickly and cheaply as possible. A few publish "instant" books shortly after news events. During recent years, some books came on the market almost overnight on topics such as the 2008 election, the Olympics, or various natural disasters like the devastating Hurricane Katrina.

A more important consideration is content. That is, many companies focus on a general topic—for example, science, fiction, fine arts, medicine, law, or religion. There are other bases of specialization among publishers, such as nonfiction, high school texts, and so on. Table 3.1 shows a classification of types of books according to audience and function.

Books can also be classified in terms of their share of the market. As Figure 3.2 shows, trade books account for the largest share of books sold by publishers, making up nearly half of publishers' total sales—and that share is rising.[15]

Also regarded as "trade books" but sometimes categorized separately are books published by **university presses**, book publishers associated with and often subsidized by a particular educational institution. The output of university presses is a very small part of the overall business, but university presses are often far more important than their dollar sales would suggest because they reach an elite, influential audience and often are picked up and publicized by other media. Their books are aimed primarily

TABLE 3.1

TYPES OF BOOKS

Type	Description
Trade	Includes literature, biography, and all fiction and nonfiction books for general reading. These books are usually handled by retail bookstores.
Textbooks	Includes books for elementary and high schools, colleges, and universities. These books are usually sold through educational institutions or college bookstores, but publishers make their sales pitches to state or local school boards or faculty members.
Children's	Sold through bookstores or to schools and libraries.
Reference	Includes dictionaries, encyclopedias, atlases, and similar books. These require long and expensive preparation.
Technical and Scientific	Includes manuals, original research, and technical reports.
Law	Involves the codification of legal materials and constant updating.
Medical	Also requires frequent updating.

Source: Datus C. Smith Jr., *Guide to Book Publishing* (1989), pp. 128–129; used by permission of University of Washington Press.

at scholars and scientists. However, in recent years even many university presses have become more profit-oriented and have been expanding their lists to include topics of popular interest.

The processes involved in producing and distributing books are, however, similar among all types of publishing companies. Key people involved include authors, editors, book manufacturers, bookstores, and sales personnel. Naturally, many kinds of specialists and technicians have supporting roles. Today, publishers rely on nonemployees to do much of the work of developing a book, so to a great extent contemporary publishers have become orchestrators—hiring and coordinating the work of many outside suppliers.

FIGURE 3.2
End User Spending
on Books

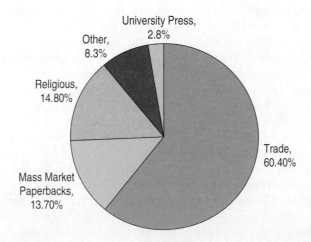

Source: Veronis Suhler Stevenson, Communication Industries Forecast, 2008–2012.

AUTHORS.   Since the time of Plato, whose *Republic* is the earliest surviving book-length work in philosophy, books have had their first stirrings of life as ideas in the heads of their authors. Nonetheless, because publishing is a competitive business, the author represents an important resource. Publishers must have a continuing flow of new manuscripts to process and sell, and, therefore, authors are key players in book publishing.

Becoming a trade-book author can be difficult. Beginning novelists may have a difficult time getting their works read by a publisher, but once a work is accepted, and especially if an author has previously produced successful works, things get better.

Authors are paid **royalties**, an agreed-upon small percentage of the publisher's earnings from selling books to retailers, rather than wages. The fiction author often receives a substantial **advance**, a payment that will be deducted from later royalties, from the publisher when the publisher accepts the manuscript for publication. Advances range from a few thousand dollars for a beginner up to millions for a well-known writer. If the book is successful, a novelist may receive huge additional income from paperback contracts and even movie or television rights.

On the textbook side, the relationship between publishers and authors is different. Publishers often seek out textbook authors and ask them to undertake a work that the publisher feels will sell. A publisher may offer a textbook author a contract before writing the book, on the basis of a detailed outline and perhaps a draft of a chapter, rather than an entire manuscript. However, textbook authors must be specialists in the field in which they are writing, and publishers carefully screen prospects. The financial incentives are also different. Although textbook authors are also paid via royalties, they usually command lower (or no) advances, compared with novelists or writers of other trade books. A good textbook can often go through several editions, however, providing a continuous, if modest, source of income for both the writer and the publisher.

AGENTS.   In the trade book world, authors normally work with **literary agents**. Agents perform many tasks. The agent:

- Ferrets out book ideas.
- Identifies authors whose works are likely to be of interest to publishers.
- Contacts publishing houses and particular editors who may be interested in a particular book or author.
- Represents the author in negotiating a contract with the publisher.

Agents are paid by authors. They receive a percentage (usually 15%) of the author's royalties.

EDITORS.   Either an author, an agent, or an editor may initiate the idea for a trade book. As publishers have increased their use of market research, the editor's role in initiating or reshaping the idea for a book has grown. For example, Time, Inc., sometimes sends prospective readers elaborate brochures describing a proposed book or series of books and eliciting responses. The replies received may lead editors to cancel the project or to change its proposed content, format, or promotion.

Once the publisher receives the author's original manuscript, several kinds of editors work on it:

- *Acquisitions editors* generate ideas for books and find able and willing authors. Acquisitions and other editors may also evaluate the quality of manuscripts and their sales potential.
- *Developmental editors* work directly with authors to organize the book effectively and help make it the most effective statement of its topic.
- *Copy editors'* main task is to check the spelling, syntax, grammar, actual language and expression of the manuscript and check "proofs" (preliminary printed versions of pages).

PRODUCTION STAFF.   To set the manuscript into a type for printing, publishers hire outside companies called **compositors**. Other specialists develop illustrations and design the print style, cover, and format of the book. As noted earlier, many of these tasks may be done by **freelancers**, people who are not employed by the publishing company but are hired for specific projects on a contract basis. The publisher also contracts with **printers** and **binders**. Generally, these are separate companies, often in other countries, that own the massive equipment needed to manipulate tons of blank paper into a finished book. These vendors can be almost anywhere. A publisher may be in New York and have its books printed, bound, and distributed in California or, for that matter, in Italy, for example.

SALES STAFF.   **Sales representatives** from the publishing company persuade **independent booksellers** to carry the company's books, school boards to adopt them, or college and university faculty members to assign them. A few publishers also run chains of bookstores of their own.

Thus, the publisher acts as a sort of impresario—a manager who brings together and coordinates a complex team including authors, editors, designers, compositors, printers, and booksellers. Through the various stages of bookmaking, publishers try to control the cost, schedule, and quality of the work. Their role, in the words of publishing executive Dan Lacy, is "somewhat analogous to that of a theater producer or an independent film producer."[16]

Book Publishing as a Business

Clearly, publishers are the risk takers. Editor Dan Lacy, commenting on the "essence of publishing as entrepreneurship," notes, "The publisher pays the costs and assumes the risks of issuing each book, and hence he occupies a highly speculative position."[17] Authors share this risk. Writing a successful novel or a complex textbook can take years. While the author may receive advances from the publisher before book publication, almost all the money will come much later from royalties. If the book does well, the author gets paid; if it does not, he or she has toiled a very long time for very little.

Just how big is this risk to authors and publishers? Substantial. Although it may seem surprising, many books—perhaps most—*never turn a profit!* It is very difficult to forecast whether a book will succeed, so the publishers are forced to gamble. However, publishers survive because the earnings for a really good seller can be high enough to pay for other books that lose money or barely break even. Moreover, if a book at least breaks even, it keeps a highly skilled staff in place and working until the real hot seller comes along, because when such a best seller does happen, the staff are sorely needed.

With every book a gamble, publishers try to take steps to improve their odds of "winning" financially. The pressure for profit that started back in the early twentieth century continues to fuel two trends that characterize today's book publishing business: 1) consolidation of ownership and 2) sophisticated marketing and selling techniques.

CONSOLIDATION OF OWNERSHIP.   Consolidation of ownership into the hands of just a few large companies is a factor common to all American media, including books.

Book publishing prior to World War II was always something of a dignified "gentlemen's" profession. It had not been the place to find either "big money" or shrewd business practices. Much of the industry had consisted of family owned enterprises passed on from one generation to the next. To take advantage of postwar opportunities for growth, however, publishers needed new resources, so they "went public." This means that they sold stock in their companies. That was an important turning point. Banks and other profit-oriented investors began to buy the stock. This increased the demand for a good return on investment. The bottom line, rather than the intellectual satisfaction of publishing important books, became the driving force, and it remains so today.

Public ownership paved the way for consolidation. Since the 1960s, and particularly in recent years, many publishers merged or were acquired by large communications corporations and conglomerates. Today, mergers and sales of companies continue to take place at a dizzying pace. As a result of such buyouts and consolidations, a small number of very large publishing firms gained financial resources, along with more sophisticated business and marketing skills.

Today, the mainstream of American publishing is found in the large publishing houses, many of which are located in New York City. Six large publishers dominate the market:

- Random House, Inc.
- Penguin Putnam, Inc.
- HarperCollins
- Holtzbrinck Publishing Holdings
- Time Warner
- Simon & Schuster

Some—like HarperCollins, owned by Rupert Murdoch's News Corp.; Random House, owned by the German giant Bertelsmann; and Time Warner—have other media properties that can help promote their books, as well as draw on the books as content for motion pictures, magazines, and other media. Today, just 2% of the nation's publishers account for about 75% of book sales.[18]

Although publishers gained financial backing and expertise through consolidation, many publishers also lost autonomy in decision making. More and more, they had to show constant profits for their stockholders and new owners. Publishing was no longer a dignified club but an objective business. Large publishing companies are now no different from other large businesses, being subject to buyouts, takeovers, and, above all, concern about annual earnings as opposed to producing a quality product that may sell in only modest amounts.

These economic changes forced publishers to alter the ways that they acquired, produced, and sold books. Now they conduct market research to make decisions about what to publish. As we have noted, most publishers now outsource much of what they once did "in house." They contract with freelancers outside the company to design the appearance of the book, edit the manuscript, provide photos, draw illustrations, proofread copy, prepare indexes, and do many of the other tasks that are part of the process of producing books. The completed manuscript then goes to independent printers and bookbinders who manufacture the finished product, whereas, until recent decades, publishers ran their own printing plants, binderies, and even bookstores.

Today, few book publishers are likely to express interest in noteworthy but unprofitable manuscripts. University presses and nonprofit think tanks are an exception, but even they have a threshold for the bottom line. Most book publishers are more likely to consider themselves simply as entrepreneurs, little different in principle from producers of beer, soap, or soup. Their aim is to manufacture a product that they can persuade consumers to buy, regardless of its other qualities. Thus, publishing today looks less like a craft or an intellectual enterprise and more like any other modern industry. Critics fear that neither the meticulous craftsmanship of the traditional publishing industry nor intellectual standards will survive and that in their place we will soon find only "conformity to the median of popular tastes."[19] In the words of one critic:

> Of late, books and book publishing have come under fire not only as a doomed medium, but as a once-great institution fallen to schlock and profit mongering. Publishing houses have turned into houses of ill repute, the critics sniff, charging that the bottom line and market-oriented decision making has resulted in such a lowering of quality that book publishers, if not doomed by illiteracy and competition, should be nonetheless put out of their low-brow misery.[20]

Not everyone feels so gloomy, however. Just as consolidation in other industries, such as cosmetics or beer, created opportunities for small new companies to flourish with high-quality, "niche" products, many small publishing houses flourish across the country, producing specialized books. A publishing company can begin with only one or two people and little equipment, hiring outside suppliers on a book-by-book basis. Unlike the small radio or TV station, the small book publisher needs no federal license, and unlike a small

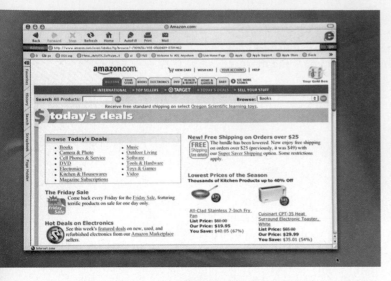

Amazon.com and other online booksellers have revolutionized the marketing and selling of books.

newspaper, the enterprise is not limited to a local audience. Through selective promotion, direct-mail, and on-line marketing, a new firm can command national attention and sales. Book publishers can thus begin with limited capital, publishing only a few titles until they begin to show a profit.

MARKETING AND SELLING BOOKS.   As we've noted, consolidation brought corporate marketing expertise to publishing. Buying a traditional book today, for example, is not as difficult as it was twenty years ago. We've already discussed online bookselllng. Corporate influence has wrought great change to the places where books can be bought in person. "Mom and pop" bookstores and small ones in shopping malls, both with limited inventories, are rapidly being replaced by huge stores operated by national chains. These **superstores**, or megastores, have hundreds of thousands of titles—a book for every reading level, interest, and taste. Even though some critics mourn the loss of the personal attention they claim to have received in the smaller stores, the "mom and pop" enterprise is not likely to make a comeback.

The contemporary book industry also uses a variety of marketing techniques. Included are direct mail, telephone marketing, websites, professional meeting displays, book clubs, and magazine ads. Publishers sometimes offer a reduced rate for buying the book in advance of the publication date. Virtually every promotional device used to market other products has been tried. However, traditionally, publishers have tiny advertising budgets compared with other consumer product industries.

Because of their small budgets, perhaps more than other forms of print, books depend on other media. For example:

- Books depend on reviews in magazines and newspapers to promote books, as a way to supplement paid advertising.
- Authors, especially those producing nonfiction, frequently appear as guests on television and radio talk shows, where they promote their books. Such programs as *The View*, hosted by Barbara Walters, or *Oprah!* are important venues for authors, as are various cable shows, late-night talk shows, and others. Indeed, the venerable Ms. Walters produced a massive, best-selling autobiography titled *Audition* in 2008, and she appeared on scores of talk shows promoting it. Without current books, many of them controversial, some of these programs would be hard pressed to fill their time.
- Book publishers typically have modest-budget **book tours**, in which authors travel from place to place to promote their books, but increasingly books are promoted online, through online chats, podcasts, and other means. Still authors covet the book tours, in part because they generate important coverage from local media in the locations the authors visit, especially in America's most literate cities, as indicated in Figure 3.3.

The New York Times Book Review "Best Sellers" list plays an influential role with readers.

Perhaps as a result of these efforts, Americans are currently buying books in numbers never thought possible in earlier years. Since the middle of the recently concluded twentieth century, the number of titles being published in the United States has soared by more than 500%, as we saw in Figure 3.1 (on page 50). In 1999 alone, 70,000 titles of all kinds were sold to people of all ages and backgrounds. By 2006 that number was over 290,000. And sales of e-books, which we described earlier, add to these totals.

Overall, the outlook for books remains positive, though not perhaps in the romantic way that some writers, editors, and critics think. Some fear that the consolidation of the book publishing industry will crowd out some important books with limited appeal—and even university presses, once the subsidized pride of institutions of higher education, are scrambling to survive. At the same time, as Jonathan Karp has pointed out in a *Washington Post* article, "Turning the Page on the Disposable Book" (June 29, 2008, B01), "the barriers to entry in the book publishing business get lower each year," with thousands of independent publishers and self publishers. With on-demand technology, a person can write and publish only a few copies, for example. One loss the book publishing industry can probably count on, though, is the decline of reference books such as encyclopedias, medical books, and practical nonfiction (how-to books), which are ideal for online distribution, as readers may not want the whole book but only a part of it. There are, of course, expanding markets for books, new retailing systems, vigorous publishers, and increasingly user-friendly technology for downloading and reading books. The business of books, both fragile and robust at the same time, is the factory for the transmission of knowledge, creative thought, and the general culture. Books are more than a business; they are a part of culture itself and thus likely to be on the scene for a long time.

TV star Oprah Winfrey is a major force in book sales as this interview with author Toni Morrison suggests.

The Top Ten	
Minneapolis, MN	1
Seattle, WA	2
St. Paul, MN	3
Denver, CO	4
Washington, DC	5
St. Louis, MO	6
San Francisco, CA	7
Atlanta, GA	8
Pittsburgh, PA	9
Boston, MA	10

FIGURE 3.3
America's Most Literate Cities, 2007

Source: Dr. John Miller, President, Central Connecticut State University, is the author of this study. Research was conducted in collaboration with the Center for Public Policy and Social Research at CCSU.

CHAPTER REVIEW

- Books began after writing and portable media were developed. They have undergone at least three significant transformations over the last six centuries.
- Cave paintings were human beings' first attempts to represent ideas graphically. Such efforts represent a transition from purely oral description to the graphic depiction of ideas.
- Ideographic systems based on pictographs began about 4,000 B.C. Improvements came slowly over about 2,000 years until phonograms came into use. Eventually writing was greatly simplified when alphabets were invented.
- When portable media replaced stone, longer documents and even libraries of scrolls became possible. The Romans made the first books with letters on both sides of cut and bound pages and end boards or covers. They also developed many of the written language formats that we still use in books and other printed material.
- The skills of writing and manuscript preparation were kept alive during the Dark Ages by the Christian monasteries, but after the twelfth and thirteenth centuries they passed into lay hands as well. Meanwhile, paper had come into use, and the stage was set for print.
- A great technological advance came when Johannes Gutenberg developed both a workable press and cast metal type. His invention was enormously important and quickly spread throughout the Western world.
- Books printed on paper are likely to survive in the near future due to their portability, permanence, and cost-effectiveness. However, as technology continues to develop, major changes lie ahead in the way in which books are produced, stored, distributed, purchased, and read. Digital systems may bring about a fourth transition in the form of this venerable medium. Nevertheless, books, whatever their physical form will remain our most respected medium and essential to our civilization.

STRATEGIC QUESTIONS

1. How did books evolve in the context of society and culture?
2. What value does the history of book publishing have in understanding books today?
3. What functions of communication does a book carry out?
4. How have books used new technologies in their development?
5. What barriers has the book faced in the digital age?
6. How would you characterize the future of book publishing—and what factors will affect it?

KEY CONCEPTS & TERMS

Book publisher   47
Copyright   54
Electronic publishing   45
Best seller   54

Literary agent   51
Returns   45
Amazon.com   46

Kindle or Sony Reader   46
Demand publishing   45
Digital publishing   43

ENDNOTES

1. Steven Levy, "It's Time to Turn the Last Page," *Newsweek,* Jan. 1, 2000, p. 96.
2. Dermot McEvoy, "Want Political Truth? Buy a Book," *Publishers Weekly,* June 16, 2008, pp. 22–23.
3. Frederick Seibert, *Freedom of the Press in England, 1476–1622* (Urbana, IL: University of Illinois Press, 1952), Chapters 1–3.
4. The sections on writing, the alphabet, early books, and the invention of printing are based on the following sources: Albertine Gar, *A History of Writing* (London: Scribner's, 1984); Joseph Naveh, *Early History of the Alphabet* (Jerusalem: Magnes, 1982); Donald Jackson, *The Story of Writing* (New York: Taplinger, 1981); and Douglas McMurtrie, *The Book: A History of Printing and Book-Making* (New York: Oxford University Press, 1943).
5. McMurtie, *The Book,* pp. 76–77.
6. Francis Falconer Madan, *Books in Manuscript: A Short Introduction to Their Study and Use,* 2nd ed. (Oxford: Oxford University Press, 1920).

7. Robert Hamilton Clapper, *Paper, An Historical Account of Its Making by Hand from the Earliest Times Down to the Present Day* (Oxford: Oxford University Press, 1934).

8. James Moran, *Printing Presses: History and Development from the Fifteenth Century to Modern Times* (Berkely: University of California Press, 1978), p. 18.

9. The actual number will forever remain elusive. But it was clearly a great communication revolution, rivaling that which has occurred in the twentieth century. For a detailed analysis of the implications of that revolution, see Elizabeth Eisentstein, *The Printing Press as an Agent of Change,* vols. 1 and 2 (Cambridge: Cambridge University Press, 1979).

10. Brad Stone, "Envisioning the Next Chapter for Electronic Books," *New York Times,* Sept. 6, 2007.

11. Steven Levy, "The Future of Reading," *Newsweek,* November 17, 2007, at www.newsweek.com/id/70983; also see "Amazon Kindle Sells Out on Debut," BBC News, Nov. 22, 2007.

12. For a summary of the state of electronic publishing as of the end of 1999, see Steven Zeitchek, "Pixel Power," *Publishers Weekly,* Dec. 20, 1999, pp. 38–44.

13. See John E. Pomfret, *Founding the American Colonies: 1583-1660* (New York: Harper & Row, 1970).

14. John Tebbel, *The Media in America* (New York: Crowell, 1974).

15. There is considerable lag in the process of gathering and reporting such figures because publishers are often reluctant to disclose current sales trends. Therefore, completely current unit and dollar sales are not always available. The figures of trade and college textbook publishing in this chapter were obtained from the 2006 Veronis Suhler Stevenson's *Communication Industry Forecast 2006–2010,* an annual industry information publication.

16. Dan Lacy, "The Economics of Publishing, or Adam Smith and Literature," *The American Reading Public* (New York: Bowker, 1965), based on an issue of *Daedalus.*

17. Lacy, "Economics of Publishing."

18. See *Books in Print* (New York: R.R. Bowker Inc., 1991).

19. Charles A. Madison, *Book Publishing in America* (New York: MGraw-Hill, 1966), p. 402. See also Albert N. Greco, *The Book Publishing Industry* (Mahwah, NJ: Lawrence Erlbaum Associates, 2004). Benjamin M. Compaine, *The Book Industry in Transition* (White Plains, NY: Knowledge Industry, 1978).

20. Everette E. Dennis, Craig Lamay, and Edward C. Pease, eds., *Publishing Books* (New Brunswick, NJ: Transaction, 1997), p. xiv. Two excellent books on publishing are Jason Epstein, *Book Business: Past, Present, and Future* (New York: Random House, 2001) and Andre Schiffrin, *The Business of Books: How the International Conglomerates Took Over Publishing and Changed the Way We Read* (New York: Verso Books, 2000).

Newspapers and News Media: Delivering Information to Society

A group of strategic planners is gathered around a large conference table at a major media company, speculating about plans for the "newspaper of the future." The newspaper, in these first decades of the twenty-first century, is "a dinosaur, part of a dying breed and a dying industry," says one young executive. Why? "It is expensive to produce, reaches a limited audience, doesn't last very long and is unpopular with young people," says another. The solution to these problems, one participant says, "is to create an all-purpose electronic newspaper, one that is interactive, offers as much information as anyone wants to click on, instantly and at little or no cost."

Several decades earlier, in the 1960s, the notable Canadian media guru Marshall McLuhan, a brilliant analyst who foresaw the "global village" of the Internet, predicted the "death of print." So far, however, the print media in general, and the newspaper in particular, have survived and succeeded through the decades, even as their shortcomings were being trumpeted by many, like these strategic planners.

Back in that boardroom, the speakers have begun to size up the reasons for the newspaper's success. They have agreed that today newspapers have the following advantages:

Portable. They go anywhere a person goes, without equipment, software, or plug-ins.
Predictable. Users know what to expect; they know how the newspaper is organized and what's where.
Accessible. There is no mystery about where you get a newspaper and how.
Cost Effective. Newspapers are quite cheap to purchase, and you get a lot for your money.

On the negative side of the ledger, ink on paper newspapers are:

- Perishable products that lack permanence.
- Difficult to store.
- Impossible to update.
- Appealing mostly to middle-aged and older readers.
- Likely to cause ink smudges on your hands.

The newspaper has sometimes been called the gold standard for news and information. Newspapers offer comprehensive, detailed coverage of almost everything. The respected *New York Times*, for example, with its motto, "All the news that's fit to print," built its reputation as "the newspaper of record."

Today, however, newspapers are in the fight of their lives. Some critics have suggested that the newspaper is a dying medium, one that will be surpassed by the forces of technology and new competitors, at a time when young people prefer hipper and cooler media. Indeed, the print editions of some newspapers have died in recent years including the once venerable *Rocky Mountain News* of Denver and the *Seattle Post Intelligencer*, both in 2009. They also point out that newspapers are being bought and sold by private investors who know nothing about the news business. The newspaper, with its 200-year history, has long survived the challenges of other media—radio, television, cable, and now digital delivery and distribution—but never before has it had so much competition. There are now tens of thousands of Internet "newspapers" and news services that also court advertisers and readers. Readers can pick up on street corners free ink-on-paper newspapers that not only offer well-edited-and-packaged news but advertising content as well. Newspapers' two major sources of revenue, sales of copies through home subscriptions and street newsstand sales and display advertising, are greatly challenged. Classified advertising, once a mainstream source of revenue, has nearly been wiped out by interactive ads on the Internet.

Newspapers have always been sensitive to economic trends and have suffered during hard times. During the global economic crisis of 2008 and beyond, newspapers saw massive losses of advertising and circulation while profits dropped accordingly. These problems began before the crisis, but deepened during that period as thousands of employees were laid off and newspapers desperately sought new economic models, ranging from non-profit news services to suggestions that involved micro-payments for information and news. While also embracing Internet trends and using social networking media, newspapers nonetheless also lost ground to new, online media. Some financial analysts openly predict the death of newspapers, once again, while others say that there will be fewer papers and less competition than there is today.

Just how this venerable medium evolved, developed, and survives in the media marketplace today is the subject of this chapter. Of course, newspapers as organizations, products for sale, and vehicles for information must be understood in the context of the nature, purpose, and extensions of *news—the surveillance function of the mass media*. We explore news in greater detail in Chapter 9. Whether the newspaper of the future is still printed on paper or sent electronically or in some yet-to-be-discovered way is not as important as understanding the architecture of news; the role played by the newspaper, historically and at present; and its place in the current news media, themselves now part of the larger landscape of information, entertainment, and communication industries.

THE IMPORTANCE OF NEWSPAPERS AS A NEWS MEDIUM

Of course, almost everyone understands that a **newspaper** is a printed product containing news and printed daily or weekly. This chapter recognizes that newspapers can no longer be seen as singular media, separated from the rest of the media family, but must be viewed as an integral part of a larger system. Newspapers, among the oldest mass media, are still highly visible and profoundly important, even in an era of interactive media. Just what they are, what they do, and how they do it, once considered settled issues, are now in dispute at the dawn of a digital age. Some industry leaders, for example, say that newspapers are simply "platforms," or the technical means of packaging information in an ink-on-paper form that contains news articles, opinion, advertising, and other material, some of it entertainment. Some "newspapers" do not use paper or ink at all and are instead delivered online in electronic form.

The premier place of newspapers among the media is reflected in these papers laid out for customers at a newsstand near the New York Stock Exchange.

The Premier Place of Newspapers in the News Media

News, the main commodity delivered by newspapers and other news media, is current or fresh information about an event or subject that is gathered, processed, and disseminated via a medium to a significant number of people. Once lone sentinels delivering news of public affairs and the private sector, newspapers are now part of a multimedia mix of newsmagazines, radio, television, cable, digital, and other means of storing, packaging, and delivering information. Newspapers are thus part of the **news media.**

News is still the principal concern of the newspaper, no matter what form it takes—print or electronic. The same cannot really be said for most other news media, even if they do offer news to their readers, viewers, listeners, and users. News is the primary business of the newspaper, and it is offered in more depth and detail there than anywhere else.

Now on the scene in America and the world for more than two centuries, newspapers are said to have *gravitas,* or intellectual and cultural weight in the work they do. They are still the most prestigious and serious enclaves of high-caliber people devoted to the gathering, processing, and dissemination of news.

The newspaper shapes our current expectations for formatting of news. In the pages that follow, as we consider the history and development of the newspaper and the modern articulation of the concept of news, it is important to remember that the newspaper was the first medium to organize and package the news in a coherent, systematic, and predictable manner. From the earliest times to the present, newspapers had visual rules and a "grammar" of presentation. World affairs were in one place, financial news was in another, and national and local affairs in still another. From editorial pages to sports pages and special sections, newspapers created an "architecture" for the presentation of news, a framework for organizing news and information in a manner that would appeal to readers and bring them back for more.

Newspapers also play a leading role in the creation of news content. Some of the news seen or heard elsewhere is actually drawn from newspapers, because of their large and sometimes superior capacity for assembling information. Because of this influence, newspapers play an extremely important role in shaping the news and, in turn, portraying society.

Newspapers and News in a Digital Era

Commentators speak of the "decline" of the American newspaper and argue that newspapers are in deep trouble. As we saw at the beginning of the chapter, newspapers are losing readers and reader loyalty, ignored by younger readers who get their news from electronic and digital sources. During the worldwide financial crisis of 2008 and 2009, several leading newspapers were shattered and others converted into online editions only.

The digital revolution is radically different and has been troubling for this industry, which deals with cutting-edge news, but at the same time has been painfully slow in adapting to technological change.[1] As columnist Michael Kinsley (the first editor of *Slate*) wrote in the *Washington Post,* "As we live through the second industrial revolution, your daily newspaper remains a tribune to the wonders of the first one." Kinsley explains that producing newspapers is essentially a manufacturing, or industrial, process that begins with cutting down trees.

Habits die hard, however, and many readers still prefer the traditional newspaper. Although its death has long been predicted, the newspaper still lives on. Furthermore, even leaders of the new media admit they depend on traditional newspapers and their large staffs for content, which they happily "repurpose" for their own audiences.

At one time, newspapers fought the onset of new technology, decrying the plans of telecommunications companies to "deliver information" and create electronic classified ads. In time, however, the newspaper industry adapted to technological change. Newspaper organizations either embraced digital newsgathering, processing, and delivery throughout their enterprises or they set up separate online divisions.

Today, many venerable ink-on-paper newspapers live alongside their own online, digital offspring. Some have parallel websites that simply replicate the printed publication, whereas others offer sites that look different and offer information services along with menus for finding them. The Gannett Company, for example, sought a new lease on news by promoting interactive, digital journalism in an initiative where ordinary citizens (amateurs) work alongside journalists (professionals) in a "pro-am" arrangement that "harnesses the power of citizen journalism."[2]

MEDIA LEADERS INSIGHTS: NEWSPAPERS

JENNIFER CARROLL

VP/Digital Content

Gannett Co., Inc.

Connecting content to new technological platforms is central to Jennifer Carroll's assignment at the 90-newspaper Gannett Company, one of the world's largest newspaper groups. A graduate of Michigan State University, she began as a reporter for the small *Times-Herald* of Port Huron, Michigan, then moved to the *Lansing* (MI) *State Journal*, where she rose from reporter to managing editor before joining Gannett's corporate staff. At Gannett, she has been cited for her "extraordinary and creative work" in extending the reach and scope of news content to new platforms, demonstrating a real mastery of the digital age. She's been especially adroit in understanding the demographics of the news audience and building loyalty with groups, such as moms, who were previously neglected. Ms. Carroll is a national leader in the newspaper industry.

1. When and under what circumstances did you first realize the import of new media or the digital age?

   Ever since I was a reporter, I've been interested in expanding the way journalists think of themselves in every respect, including both where stories appear and what tools are available to do our work. Like many, I got into journalism because I am very passionate about different aspects of the business. Some care deeply about public service, about being a government watchdog and ensuring a continuing freedom of the press. Others thrive on immediacy and breaking news and being part of the buzz, while still others love being part of the community conversation.

   It has struck me all along that, while all those reasons to be passionate about the business are still there, we have an obligation to use a broader palette of tools to expand our reach, to engage our communities more deeply and with more relevance than ever before. So I have been an early adopter, experimenting with new technology and platforms for years. I can't isolate a single moment; it has been a constant, growing interest and area of focus for me.

2. What impact did that experience have on you personally or professionally?

   I believe it has led me to the position I have now: to help lead and innovate and reinforce ways we can survive and thrive. I truly enjoy testing and expanding our potential with colleagues in all corners of the business.

3. What is the greatest challenge or benefit of the digital revolution for newspaper publishing? Your work at Gannett has been cited as an example of engaging the communities as true contributors to your content.

   We are expanding news and information in myriad ways on our websites, mobile and beyond. Our deep community sites are rich with photo galleries, reader forums, calendars and beyond. We welcome contributions from readers and actively seek their thoughts, photos, videos. We offer ways to help them connect with others in specific areas of their communities.

   Also, our searchable databases on areas ranging from property taxes to crime reports have expansive potential in local information and elevated public-service coverage. We're providing deeper, richer local data than ever before. And we have the tools not only to break stories based on data analysis but also to give readers the ability to search and analyze in powerful ways. Our First Amendment work is being strengthened as we layer tools, including forums and original documents, with databases that significantly inform our readers and enhance relevance to their lives.

4. Are you optimistic about newspapers' future? How so?

I am optimistic when considering the total reach of print newspapers, magazines, weeklies, websites and mobile, all of which we now produce for different geographic and demographic audiences. We are dramatically growing our readership on our websites, including the time spent on the sites overall and frequency of return visits. We are designing specific websites that better reflect the lifestyle and needs of readers and are more attractive to advertisers. The idea is to expand by being a lot smarter about the gender, age, and preferences of whom we are trying to reach, whether it is gaming and video for young men or social media tools for engaged community groups.

A great example of this is our growing network of mom's sites across the company. They have extensive forums, photo sharing and galleries, and calendar events targeted at families. They are places where moms can network with each other, identify mutual concerns, and organize everything from carpools to daycare. Many moms return to the sites frequently throughout the day. And we have new revenue streams from advertisers ranging from children's hospitals to daycare services.

5. What, if any, advice do you have for a person who aspires to a career in the newspaper industry?

Be multi-platform and multifaceted. Traditional print newspaper companies now produce content across a range of devices, and book publishers must do the same. There is a strong place for quality research and narrative prose. That can be augmented with a range of electronic devices and new tools, including blogs that allow readers to access the content in whatever form they choose.

Visionary leaders of the newspaper industry have long declared that they are "information companies" and "information providers," more than old-school publishers and manufacturers of paper products. Arthur S. Sulzberger, Jr., publisher of *The New York Times*, has famously declared, "We are platform-neutral," meaning that newspapers can adapt to any delivery mode—online, wireless, and others yet unimagined. As another industry executive said, "It is what we do (in gathering news and information) to not how we do (the way it reaches people) it that counts."

NEWSPAPERS: THE FIRST MEDIUM FOR THE MASS SOCIETY

Essentially, the story of newspapers begins with Gutenberg's press. Soon after it was invented, printed descriptions of important events began to appear. These brief documents were the forerunners of newspapers, and they were sent relatively quickly to distant places. For example, the story of the voyage and discoveries of Christopher Columbus spread through Spain within a few months of his return, in the form of printed copies of his own accounts.

The First Newspapers

The printing press was used in a variety of ways to provide news, even during its earliest years. In the mid-1500s, leaders in Venice regularly made available to the public printed newssheets about the war in Dalmatia. To receive a copy, Venetians had to pay a *gazetta*, a small coin. (The term "gazette," so frequently used in newspaper titles, comes from that source.) During the early 1600s, brief printed newssheets called *corantos* originated

Newspapers of the U.S. colonial period often emphasized news of commerce and government, as with this 1770 issue of *The Boston Gazette & Country Journal.*

in Holland and were soon being published periodically for commercial communities in several countries. The oldest surviving example was printed in 1602. The coranto could be regarded as the first newspaper in English, although it lacks certain features of a true newspaper as we define them today. Newspapers of more modern times have several characteristics not found in these earlier publications. One view is that a true newspaper:

- Is published (at least) weekly.
- Is produced by a mechanical printing process.
- Is available (for a price) to people of all walks of life.
- Prints news of general interest rather than items on specialized topics such as religion or business.
- Is readable by people of ordinary literacy.
- Is timely.
- Is stable over time.[3]

By this definition, the first true newspaper was the *Oxford Gazette* (later called the *London Gazette*). First published in Latin in 1665 under the authority of King Charles II, the *Gazette* appeared twice a week and continued publication well into the twentieth century. This was an "authorized" newspaper, which means that its content was controlled and screened by the royal government.

The first daily newspaper in English, the *Daily Courant* (from *coranto*), began publication in London on March 11, 1702. A newspaper of high quality and considerable integrity, the *Courant* was not really a "mass" medium, because it maintained a sophisticated literary style and appealed primarily to an affluent and educated elite. However, like the more popular newspapers that would come in the nineteenth century, it recovered some of its costs from advertising.[4]

After the late 1600s, censorship was rarely enforced in England. It was a different story in the American colonies. The press was tightly controlled by British governors in each of the colonies, because insurrection was always regarded as a possibility in such remote colonies. Soon, however, colonial governments faced lively and independent newspapers.

The Press in the American Colonies

The growth of newspapers in the American colonies was tied closely to cultural, economic, and political circumstances that existed at the time. Both the population and commerce grew steadily, creating a market for news of shipping and trading as well as a need for a limited amount of advertising. As political tensions over such issues as taxes and control of trade grew, the colonial newspapers often published criticisms of the Crown's policies. One of the more significant criticisms appeared in Boston on September 25, 1690—the first (and last) issue of a paper titled *Publick Occurrences Both Foreign and Domestick.*

This four-page paper was the work of Benjamin Harris, a printer who had come to Boston fleeing punishment for publishing a controversial paper in London. The governor of Massachusetts banned Harris's paper on the grounds that it was published "without authority," meaning prior approval by the government, and that it contained material disapproved by the government.

Although it survived only a single issue, *Publick Occurrences* was important, not only because it was the earliest paper published but also because it spoke out against the government.

Because it was not published continually, however, *Publick Occurrences* does not really fit our definition of a newspaper. The honor of being the first American paper in that sense should go instead to a dull publication called the *Boston News-Letter*, which first appeared "published by authority" in April 1704. John Campbell, the publisher, was also the postmaster of Boston. As postmaster he was able to mail the paper without postal charges. For early colonial papers, a connection with a post office was almost indispensable, because there really was no other way to distribute the paper.

The *Boston News-Letter*'s content consisted mainly of dull treatises on European politics, shipping reports, and some advertising. The result, according to Edwin Emery, was a paper that was "libel-proof, censor-proof, and well-nigh reader-proof."

Establishing Traditions in American Journalism

The manner in which the American press operates today is very different from conditions faced by colonial papers. Newspapers today are protected by the **First Amendment** to the Constitution, which explicitly provides for freedom of the press, and by a body of law developed over more than two centuries. Those protections are an end of a long chain of events that started during the colonial period. As the eighteenth century progressed, colonial governors continued to suppress articles that criticized the government. However, their control was gradually subverted by rather bold printers and publishers in a long struggle marked by numerous conflicts and harsh repressions.[5]

THE PRESS AS WATCHDOG OF THE PUBLIC INTEREST   In 1721, James Franklin, an older brother of Benjamin Franklin, started his own paper, the *New England Courant*. It was something of a departure from the restrictive colonial tradition because it was not "published by authority" and had no connection with a post office. It was aimed at a well-educated and prosperous elite. Although it also contained the shipping reports and information from nearby towns, it appealed mainly to those who liked literary essays and controversial political opinions.

The *Courant* was the first newspaper in the colonies to crusade on a public issue. During an outbreak of smallpox in Boston, it argued strongly against the newly invented medical procedure of smallpox inoculation. From a medical standpoint, its position turned out to be wrong, but using the newspaper to speak out against a situation seen as harmful to the public began an important tradition that would come to characterize American newspapers. Increasingly newspapers would become "**watchdogs** of the public interest," a role that they continue vigorously today.

Benjamin Franklin (1706–1790), an American statesman, was also the most prominent newspaper publisher of his day.

Successful and humorous, the *Courant* criticized one person, poked fun at another, and finally attacked the governor himself. As a result, the governor cracked down. James Franklin was thrown in jail for a month and ultimately forbidden to publish *Courant* or any paper "of like nature." Franklin was clever, though, and he got around the restriction by making his brother Benjamin the publisher.

Young Ben Franklin had been apprenticed to his brother at age thirteen and began to gain firsthand experience with printing. When his brother was in jail, young Ben operated the print shop and paper. By 1729 he had moved on to take over the *Pennsylvania Gazette* in Philadelphia. Franklin not only made that paper a success, but he also anticipated another tradition, a small chain of newspapers.

ESTABLISHING THE PRINCIPLE OF FREEDOM OF THE PRESS   A court trial that pitted newspaper publisher John Peter Zenger against William Cosby, governor of New York, helped to establish the principle of freedom of the press in the colonies.

Zenger was persuaded (and funded) by a group of businessmen in New York to establish a newspaper, the *New York Weekly Journal,* because they wanted to have a paper in opposition to the officially authorized *New York Gazette.* Zenger began publication in 1733, and his paper ran articles openly critical of the governor and his policies. In response, Governor Crosby had Zenger clapped in jail, on a charge of "seditious libel." **Sedition** means promoting disaffection with government or inciting people to revolt against constituted authority. **Libel** means publicizing untruths. However, under British law at the time, it really did not matter whether what the defendant published was true; it was the seditious intent that was considered the major offense and the central issue of the case.

Zenger was brought to trial before a jury of fellow colonials in 1735. The governor's case seemed airtight. Zenger had, in fact, broken the existing law. However, Andrew Hamilton, a distinguished lawyer, undertook his defense. Hamilton freely admitted that Zenger had published articles criticizing the government. However, he argued with great conviction that the articles were true and that, in spite of what the law said, no one should be punished for printing the truth. Hamilton's argument convinced the jury that they should ignore the judge's instructions and declare Zenger not guilty. They did so, in a stunning upset. The governor was furious. The significance of Zenger's trial was that it established an important principle: the press should be allowed to criticize government. That idea would eventually find its way into the First Amendment to the Constitution, which would be formulated a half-century later.

Characteristics of Colonial Press

By 1750, most Americans who could read had access to some kind of newspaper. However, although many newspapers were started during the period, few were successful. The majority failed after only a few issues. Newspapers were difficult to support financially, because the two main sources of income for newspapers, sales of copies and advertising, were both limited. Literacy rates were low by comparison with later centuries, so few people actually read newspapers. All the papers were aimed at comparatively well-educated and relatively affluent subscribers, who made up only a small part of society. They were also very expensive, which made them unavailable to the common people. Around the time of the American Revolution, a newspaper might cost $6 to $10 a year, about as much as a worker's salary for one or two weeks. In today's terms, that would be like paying several hundred dollars for a year's subscription. Few people would be willing to pay that much.

We noted earlier that advertising is an important source of financial support for newspapers. However, there really was a limited need for advertising in colonial times. The great rise in consumerism that we know today had not yet arrived. It was a product of the industrial revolution, the advent of easy distribution by improving transportation, and the development of well-coordinated retail systems. Thus, there were not many products to be advertised, and few markets could provide a solid financial base for the support of newspapers.

The colonial papers were limited in many other ways as well:

- *Their news was seldom up to date.*
- *They were published infrequently.* Until 1783, when the *Pennsylvania Evening Post and Advertiser* was started, the colonies had no daily newspaper.
- *They were slow to reach subscribers.* The papers were usually delivered by mail, traveling to subscribers by horse and carriage, pack trains, or sailing vessels.

The colonial papers were also limited by existing technology. The hand press used by Benjamin Franklin and others in the late 1700s was little different from the one used by Gutenberg in the mid-1400s. Paper was still made from rags, not wood, and was both expensive and always in short supply. As a result, colonial papers were small, usually about four pages of a mere ten by fifteen inches each.

Another factor limiting colonial papers was that they restricted their own audiences. Many were **partisan** papers. They consistently argued for only one point of view. When political parties developed at the end of the eighteenth century, each had certain newspapers under its control. Some even subsidized their papers.

In spite of these many limitations, the colonial press established valuable traditions of journalism that were to become an important part of the emerging American press.

Newspapers for Ordinary Citizens

At the dawn of the industrial revolution, innovators were beginning to solve the technological and other problems needed to provide widely circulated newspapers for the public. By 1830, steam-powered rotary presses were introduced. They were an astonishing improvement in technology. With the old screw-type press, a well-trained team of two printers working full speed could put out only a few hundred sheets per day at best. By contrast, even the earliest steam-powered press could produce four thousand sheets per hour, printed on both sides.[6]

THE EMERGENCE OF THE PENNY PRESS   On September 3, 1833, a strange little newspaper appeared on the streets of New York. Published by Benjamin Day and called *The (New York) Sun,* its masthead carried the slogan "It Shines for All." That slogan was somewhat misleading. The *Sun* was not designed to appeal to everyone but specifically to the less sophisticated. The *Sun* was filled with human-interest items about common people.

Day began an important newspaper tradition when he hired the first salaried **reporter**, who went to the local courts each morning and wrote lively stories about local happenings, with an emphasis on crime, human interest, accidents, and humorous anecdotes. (The term "reporter" is derived from those recorded court proceedings.) Another feature of this newspaper was that it was sold on the streets by **newsboys** for only a penny. This system of distribution worked well. The newsboys (some of whom apparently were girls dressed as boys) bought the papers in lots of a hundred for sixty-seven cents. If they sold the entire hundred, they earned thirty-three cents, which was quite a profit for a youngster at the time.

One of the most important features of the *Sun* was that advertising played the central financial role in Day's system. In its first issue, on page one, Day declared: "The object of the paper is to lay before the public, at a price within the means of everyone, all the news of the day, and at the same time afford an advantageous medium for advertising." The penny that buyers paid for their copy did not recover the costs of production. The *Sun* made its profit by selling advertising space for a great variety of products and services. This was possible at the time because the new factories were producing a greater variety of goods, and new retail establishments were selling to larger and larger markets.

The paper was an instant success. Soon it was selling more than eight thousand copies per day. From there, its sales doubled, and within three years it was selling an astonishing thirty thousand copies daily. Other journalists were astounded, and they scrambled to imitate Day's model.

Within a few months the *Sun* had competitors, and the mass press became reality. Together, all the competing newspapers that adopted Day's basic

Enterprising "newsboys"—some of whom were girls—began to sell papers on the streets in the 1830s as part of the penny press proprietors' efforts to reach large audiences faster than conventional mail service would allow. Street selling of newspapers by children, still common in some countries, has virtually disappeared in the United States, though house-to-house distribution continues.

The first copy of *The* (New York) *Sun*—a penny newspaper—circa 1833.

formula were known as the **penny press**. Particularly noteworthy was the *New York Herald,* founded in 1835 by the colorful James Gordon Bennett. Bennett imitated Day, but he also added many features that became part of modern newspapers, including a financial page; editorial comment; and more serious local, foreign, and national news. Horace Greeley's *Tribune* and Henry Jarvis Raymond's now famous *The New York Times* were also started during this period.

The penny papers had very distinctive characteristics that made them completely different from the colonial press. They were vulgar, sensational, and trivial in many respects. Publishers after Bennett, however, began to give increasing amounts of basic economic and political news, as well as editorial viewpoints regarding public matters. As they developed, then, the penny newspapers brought at least some significant first-hand information and ideas to large numbers of people who had not been readers of newspapers up to that time.

The Impact of Society on the Growth of Newspapers

During the nineteenth century, three great changes took place in American society that had significant influences on the growth of the nation's newspaper industry:

1. Rapid expansion of the population, leading to larger numbers of newspaper readers
2. Remarkable developments in technology, which increased enormously the ability of journalists to gather, transmit, print, and distribute news
3. The Civil War, which stimulated a great demand for news and the development of increasingly efficient systems for getting it to newspapers and from there to subscribers

RAPID POPULATION GROWTH   The rate of population growth in the United States during the nineteenth century was unprecedented in history. During the two decades preceding the Civil War (1840–1860), millions of new people arrived, especially from northern Europe. Even higher levels of immigration, especially from southern and eastern Europe, came during the last half of the century. Most newcomers settled in the eastern states and the Great Lakes region. At the same time, steady streams of internal migrants moved westward, settling along a continuously expanding frontier, establishing new towns and cities where newspapers were needed. People were needed to occupy the vast lands that had been acquired from France and Mexico. As these new residents acquired English, they subscribed in ever-increasing numbers to daily newspapers.

THE REVOLUTION IN TECHNOLOGY   As the nineteenth century progressed, the industrial and mechanical arts flourished at a remarkable pace. Beginning about 1839, ever larger and more elaborate steam-powered rotary presses could print, cut, and fold, increasing thousands of finished newspapers per hour. Cheap paper to feed these presses was being made from wood as early as 1867.

In another great advance in technology, telegraph wires along the rail lines linked major cities and made possible the rapid transmission of news stories to editors' desks. As we will see later in the chapter, the telegraph opened a new era in the history of newspapers, as associations were formed to transmit news along the new network of wires.

The telegraph was the beginning of a fourth great revolution in human communications (following speech, writing, and printing). It ushered in an era of instantaneous communication across great distances. From the dawn of human's awareness until the invention of the steam train, communication between two people over a distance had been limited to the speed of a swift runner (about 15 miles per hour), or a galloping horse (about 25 miles per hour), or at most a flying pigeon (about 35 miles per hour over distance). But by the early 1840s, trains had achieved the awesome speed of 45 miles per hour. Many people regarded this as a final limit and thought that any further increase would be a violation of God's plan for humankind. They warned that people might fly apart if such dangerous speeds were exceeded.

It is difficult today to imagine what people thought when it was announced that a means had been devised to send a message at the mind boggling speed of *186,000 miles per second*—more than fifteen times around the world in a mere wink of the eye. It was, in words of moon astronaut Neil Armstrong more than a century later, "a giant leap for mankind."

The rapid expansion of the railroads and steamboat lines also promoted the growth of newspapers. Now daily papers printed in the city could be delivered across substantial distances, so that people in surrounding communities could receive the news in a timely manner. The ancient dream of conquering both time and distance with an effective medium of communication was becoming a reality.

THE CIVIL WAR The great conflict between the North and the South enormously stimulated the development of newspapers. Its battles resulted in terrible slaughter, the worst loss of life our country has ever known. People on both sides of the conflict were desperate for reports of the battles and news about the fates of their loved ones. Faster and faster steam presses across the nation churned out millions of copies daily.

By 1839, photography had developed. It would be more than three decades before photographs could be printed in newspapers, but the existence of the technology stimulated the beginnings of pictorial journalism, as photographers captured the nation's history on their plates. During the Civil War, one of the country's leading photographers, Matthew Brady, persuaded President Lincoln to let him make a photographic record of the battlefields. Brady was given unrestricted access to military operations, together with protection by the Secret Service. He and his team took some 3,500 photographs—one of the most remarkable photographic achievements of all time.[7] More recently, historians have asserted that Brady posted many of his photos, something modern photojournalists would deplore.

During the Civil War, newspapers sent hundreds of reporters to the fields of action, where they lived and traveled with military forces. Above left: Reporters gather at the *New York Herald's* field headquarters. Above right: A few photographers, notably Matthew Brady, captured the grimmer side of the war in their vivid photographs, but newspapers lacked the mechanical processes to reproduce photos. It was not until decades later that photos were commonly used in newspapers, thanks to the zinc engraving. Nonetheless, Brady and others provided a gripping documentary record for the archives and later use.

By the end of the nineteenth century, the newspaper was a technologically sophisticated and complex mass medium. Newspaper publishers had at their disposal a rapid telegraphic news-gathering system, cheap paper, linotype (which set type with the aid of electricity), color printing, cartoons, electric presses, and, above all, a corps of skillful journalists. The newspaper had settled into more or less standard format, much like what we have today. Its features included not only domestic and foreign news but also a financial page, letters to the editor, sports news, society reports, "women's pages," classified sections, and advice to the lovelorn. Newspapers were complex, extremely competitive, and very popular. Furthermore, they had no competition from other media.

The Era of Yellow Journalism

Because newspapers in the United States were profit-oriented, privately owned businesses, they were very competitive. The key to financial success in a newspaper, then as now, was to attract as many readers as possible. By showing advertisers that more people would see their messages than in a competing paper, a publisher could sell more ad space, at higher prices, and enjoy greater revenues. During the last decade of the 1800s, fierce competition for readers among the large metropolitan papers led to a remarkable period of sensational journalism.

The penny papers had already taken the first steps, with their emphasis on crime, human interest, and humor. Then, by the early 1890s, Joseph Pulitzer succeeded in building the circulation of the New York Sunday *World* to more than 300,000. Pulitzer intensified reader interest by combining good reporting with "crusades," an emphasis on disasters and melodramatics, sensational photographs, and comic strips. Pulitzer crusaded against corrupt officials, for civil service reform, and for populist causes, such as taxes on luxuries, large incomes, and inheritances. He pioneered the use of color printing of comics in newspapers, which did much to spur the circulation of his Sunday editions.

One popular cartoon in the *World* made history. It features a bald-headed toothless, grinning kid, clad in a yellow sack-like garment. The "Yellow Kid," as the character came to be called, appeared in settings that depicted life in the slums of New York. The comic was soon at the center of controversy, when William Randolph Hearst, who founded the *San Francisco Examiner,* set out to master the art of attracting readers. Hearst expanded to the east and purchased the *New York Journal* in 1895. Determined to build the *Journal's* flagging circulation to surpass Pulitzer's *World,* Hearst simply bought the Yellow Kid cartoonist from his rival with a large salary and added other writing and editorial talent. Then he published more comics, more sensational reports, and more human-interest material, all of which led to greater circulation.

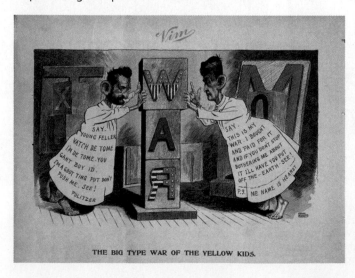

Newspaper publishers Joseph Pulitzer and William Randolph Hearst dressed in the manner of the 1890's comic strip character, "The Yellow Kid," as they practice yellow journalism, promoting the Spanish-American War.

THE BIG TYPE WAR OF THE YELLOW KIDS.

As each issue of Hearst's *Journal* began to rival that of Pulitzer's *World,* the two newspaper barons led their papers further into practices that would significantly influence the style of American journalism. Many smaller papers resisted the trend, but for more than a decade, many large metropolitan newspapers came to be preoccupied with crime, sex, sob stories, exposés of sin, disclosures of corruption in high places (many of which were gross exaggerations), sports, dramatic photographs, and misrepresentations of scientific facts—indeed, anything that would attract additional readers.

It was also said that each issue of Hearst's papers was designed to provoke one reaction from its readers: when they saw the headlines, Hearst wanted them to say, "Gee whiz!" Responsibility to the public seemed to have been abandoned. The new, sensationalist style came to be called **yellow journalism.**

Many historians believe the label derived from the Yellow Kid cartoon character, because it symbolized the newspaper's mindless intellectual level.

As the nineteenth century came to a close, yellow journalism in the Pulitzer/Hearst tradition died with it. Newspapers were nearing a saturation penetration of American homes, and it was no longer possible to gain large increases in circulation by such tactics. In addition, people were tired of that type of newspaper and wanted a more responsible press. As we will see, however, sensational journalism is alive and well in some metropolitan newspapers, especially in the curious tabloids commonly sold in the supermarkets.

TRENDS THAT SHAPED TODAY'S NEWSPAPERS

Several trends that developed over the course of the twentieth century continue to affect the way newspapers are produced and used today:

1. We'll see that the U.S. pattern of purchasing newspaper subscriptions followed a *curve of adoption* similar to that of many new innovations and that subscription rates reflect the ever-changing number of households in the country during each decade.
2. Development of two major *auxiliary services* that supply newspapers with content actually began even earlier, in the nineteenth century.
3. *Changing patterns of ownership* also characterized American newspapers in the twentieth century.

Newspapers as Cultural Innovation

As daily newspapers became available to the public, they were not immediately subscribed to by every family in the nation. Instead, over time, the pattern of use of daily newspapers in the United States forms a typical curve of adoption, commonly seen as people start to use new technological or other innovations: an S-shaped pattern that starts slowly, rises swiftly, and then levels off. As Figure 4.1 shows, after a slow start during the nineteenth century, subscriptions to daily newspapers per household did grow sharply during the last decades of the 1800s, reaching a peak early in the nineteenth century and lasting until about the time of World War I.

These major features of the pattern can best be understood in terms of the relationship between newspapers and other mass media in America. During the early decades of the twentieth century, between 1910 and 1930, newspapers enjoyed a kind of "golden age," when subscriptions per household were twice what they are today. By the time of World War I, for example, circulations had grown to a point where many households in the United States were subscribing to both a morning and an afternoon paper. But, as the curve of adoption indicates, it would not last.

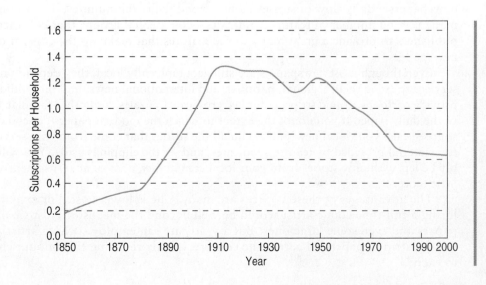

FIGURE 4.1

The Curve of Adoption of Daily Newspapers in the United States, 1850–2000

Subscriptions to daily newspapers rose at an increasing pace during the last half of the nineteenth century. Newspaper usage peaked around the time of World War I. It was the medium's golden age. Later, radio, magazines, and television offered competition and subscriptions declined steadily.

FIGURE 4.2

Number of Daily U.S. Newspapers 1950–2006

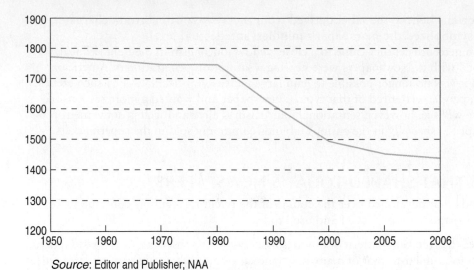

Source: Editor and Publisher; NAA

Once newer media arrived, newspapers entered a decline in subscriptions per household that continues to this day. Competition for both audiences and advertising dollars came first from radio and eventually from television, and it continued to rise relentlessly.

In addition, although newspapers had, by that time, both impressive technologies and elaborate news-gathering systems, the costs of news-gathering and all other aspects of publishing began increasing after 1930. Consequently, papers began to fail financially or were purchased by their rivals to consolidate production and other facilities. These trends have continued up to the present time and are likely to continue. In 1910, the country had more than 2,200 English-language and nearly 400 foreign-language dailies. As Figure 4.2 shows, however, the number of papers grew smaller and smaller after this time. Some papers merged, some dailies became weeklies, and others suspended publication completely. The U.S. Census reports that the number of daily newspapers declined from 2,042 in 1920 to just over 1,500 in 2000 and dwindled to 1,452 by 2006.[8]

The Growth of Wire Services and Feature Syndicates

The second trend influencing newspapers is the growth of two kinds of national organizations that supply them with much of their daily content. One such auxiliary is **wire services**, national and worldwide news-gathering associations that bring to local newspapers a daily flow of stories from beyond their communities. The second is made up of a number of **feature syndicates**—commercial groups that contract with publishers to provide a great many of the features that make up the content of today's newspapers.

Even though most newspapers are still geographically local, they depend on the wire services to bring them regional, national, and international news, and on syndicates to provide cartoons, comic strips, columns, crossword puzzles, and other familiar features of the daily paper. If you doubt the extent to which the modern papers depend on these sources, take your local newspaper, clip all the stories that come from wire services and the material provided by feature syndicates, and set the clippings aside. You will probably be left with only stories from your local community, a lot of advertisements, and little more.

The advantages of these services are many. One is lower cost. For example, hiring a full-time comic artist would be well beyond the means of most small newspapers and even some large ones. But a syndicate can employ such an artist and sell the strip to papers all across the country, greatly reducing the amount charged to each.

WIRE SERVICES   Today's wire services grew out of an agreement in the early 1840s between several newspapers in New York, Baltimore, and Philadelphia, who pooled their resources to provide faster, cheaper, and more comprehensive news of the Mexican War. This temporary but innovative agreement set a precedent, in that the newspapers were cooperating rather than competing in covering the news. Then, in 1848, several small papers in upstate New York agreed to share the cost of having a reporter telegraph news stories to them all from the state capital at Albany.

The idea of a wire service worked well, and others decided to try it on a larger scale. A few months later, six New York newspapers signed an agreement to share the costs of telegraphing foreign news from Boston, where ships first arrived with the latest dispatches from Europe. This agreement was the forerunner of the modern **Associated Press (AP)**. During its earliest years, the AP was mainly an organization linking eastern newspapers. Then, as Americans moved westward and railroads grew, the news service began to cover the nation rather than just the East. During the Civil War, AP newspapers covered the great battles and troop movements, providing subscribing papers with detailed accounts.[9]

After the Civil War, newspapers that lacked the advantages of AP membership and its extensive news coverage began to have trouble keeping their readers. These papers provided a market for competing wire services. Shortly after the turn of the century, Edward Wyllis Scripps, the owner of the Scripps chain of newspapers, founded the United Press Association (UP), which began operation in 1907. William Randolph Hearst formed his own press association, the International News Service (INS), in 1909. From that time until 1958, the United States was served by the three rival services (although AP always outdistanced the other two). In 1958 UP and INS merged into United Press International (UPI), to promote more vigorous competition with AP. This, however, never happened, and UPI's demise has been predicted for years. Its present role is much diminished, and it is no longer seen as a serious competitor to the AP. A more significant role is played by North American Reuters, the British service, owned by Thompson Media, which has a large client base in the United States. Added to the mix are a number of vigorous supplemental wire services organized to provide a variety of news and feature material. Examples are The New York Times Service, the Washington Post/Los Angeles Times Service, the Bloomberg News Service, and Gannett News Service.

Thus, almost from the beginning, the wire services broadened the content of news, allowing more newspapers to have a wide range of coverage from distant points, codifying and defining journalistic style and increasing the level of objectivity in news coverage. Today, stories are not sent by telegraphic wire but are transmitted to subscribing newspapers via computers linked in various ways, by telephone line, optical cable, or satellite.

FEATURE SYNDICATES   The feature syndicates, like the wire services, trace their origins to the mid- and late nineteenth century. Early on, journalists recognized the importance of entertaining readers as well as informing them. Entrepreneurs among them surmised rightly that they could profit by offering newspapers a package of ready-to-print "features," including opinion columns, poetry, cartoons, short stories, and many other kinds of non-news content. They formed companies to provide such material. The earliest syndicates directed their appeals to small papers that could not afford to produce their own material. Eventually, they also sold to larger papers. Today there are more than three hundred syndicates, ranging from those with billings of more than $100 million per year to small firms that represent one or two writers.

The role of the syndicates is not without its critics. Some are concerned that they exert too great an influence on newspapers. Certainly, the syndicates provide a remarkable variety of entertainment and opinion material for newspapers, including editorial cartoons, serializations of popular books, columns by noted political commentators, comic strips, puzzles and games, movie critics, plus columnists who write about astrology, automobiles, books, bridge, politics, gossip, consumer advice, human relations, music, religion, and television. In addition, some syndicates sell design services, graphics, and even newsstand racks. They promise that their material will bring circulation gains, and readership studies indicate that they are sometimes right. Advice columns, such as Dear Abby, often head the list of the most-read items in a newspaper, and the comics have always had strong appeal. Newspapers have occasionally fought vicious court battles to retain a particular columnist or cartoonist.

Because relatively little is written about syndicates and all are privately held companies, even their size and scope remains something of a mystery. One way to measure the reach of a syndicate is by the number of newspapers or magazines it serves. The top five by this criterion are King Features Syndicate (started in 1914 by William Randolph Hearst), United Media (owned by Scripps Howard), North American Syndicate (founded by Rupert Murdoch), Tribune Media Services (owned by the Tribune Co.), and Universal Press Syndicate.

Changing Patterns of Ownership

A third major trend that has shaped today's newspapers is the *consolidation of their ownership,* the concentration of newspapers under the control of fewer owners. Only a small proportion of our nation's papers remain in the hands of the families who started them. Increasingly, newspapers are owned by **chains** or groups, in which the same company owns several papers. Some of the chains are, in their turn, owned by even larger groups, conglomerates that also own other kinds of businesses and industries. This concentration of ownership has contributed to the significant decline in the number of daily newspapers published in the United States and generated a great deal of debate as to whether the nation is being well served by its contemporary press.

THE GROWTH OF CHAINS   Like the mom-and-pop hamburger stand, the independently owned newspaper is very close to extinction. Economic forces—including soaring costs in labor, material, and services—have made it difficult for individual newspapers to survive. Groups of newspapers are able to split many costs, reducing the expense of publishing each individual paper in the chain. In fact, newspapers are good sources of profit for chain owners. In spite of the fact that newspapers have lost the enviable position they held early in the twentieth century as the *only* source of news and that they compete now for advertising dollars with other media, they continue to earn a great deal of money. Newspapers, on average, return almost *twice* the earnings per dollar of investment as do stocks in the nation's five hundred leading corporations!

By 2008 the Gannett Corporation owned 90 daily newspapers in the United States as well as television stations and radio stations in the United States, Guam, and the Virgin Islands. Gannett, which owns *USA Today,* one of the nation's largest newspapers, also owns *Sports Weekly, Sunday Magazine,* a printing company, new media, offset printing firms, and other holdings including some 1,000 non-daily publications. Such media empires also own other kinds of businesses.

Determining the relative size and scope of a newspaper chain or group is more difficult than it may seem. Some critics are fond of counting the number of newspapers owned, whereas others look more to circulation figures. What is easier to assess is the pattern of change over time. Going back to 1920, during the period when newspapers were enjoying a virtual monopoly on the news industry, there were only 31 chains or newspaper groups in the United States, and each owned on the average fewer than five newspapers. By 1960, there were 109 chains, and they controlled an average of five newspapers each. By 1986, the number of chains had risen to 127 with an average of nine dailies per chain. Looked at another way, the number of actual papers owned by chains rose from 153 in 1920 to just over 1,200 by 1990. Today, chains own about 75% of all the daily newspapers published in the United States.[10]

The trend will slow in the years ahead because there are fewer independently owned newspapers left to be absorbed. Chains are not likely to establish additional papers, because they would then be competing either with themselves or with well-established papers that already dominate local markets. In the decades ahead, however, big chains most likely will continue gobbling up smaller ones. A pattern will probably emerge that looks very much like what happened to American automobile manufacturers. In 1920, there were more than a hundred kinds of car manufactured in the United States. By 2009, only three somewhat shaky U.S. companies, Ford, Chrysler, and General Motors, remained. In like manner we may soon see a "Big Three" of chains controlling our nation's newspapers or a few so-called big name brands.

THE IMPLICATIONS OF CONCENTRATED OWNERSHIP   For many critics, the change in newspaper ownership has ominous implications. As author Richard McCord points out, those who established the chains often used dubious financial practices and were ruthless competitors.[11] Moreover, chain ownership implies an ability on the part of the ownership group to control the news and thereby potentially to shape how readers think about events. (We discuss this agenda-setting function of the news in Chapter 9.) As First Amendment scholar C. Edwin Baker flatly states, "Ownership matters." Baker believes that concentration of media ownership put democracy at a crossroads. He gives three main reasons for opposing media concentration, including "a more democratic distribution of communicative power, democratic safeguards, as well as quality and the bottom line."[12] He believes that too few owners control the media and that there needs to be more regulation in the public interest and less concern for profit.

Media critics warn that in a few years a handful of corporate conglomerates might have a stranglehold on the nation's newspapers. Even more worry that there will be so few newspapers left at all that complaining about who owns them may be a moot point.

Another troublesome factor is that, although in the past most communications enterprises were owned by companies that specialized in communications, now other corporations have moved into the field. In recent years there has been much turmoil in the ownership of newspapers including the purchase by Rupert Murdoch's News Corp. of the venerable *Wall Street Journal,* owned for more than a century by Dow Jones.[13] Earlier, the Tribune group sold its famed stable of papers, including the *Chicago Tribune* and *Los Angeles Times,* to entrepreneur/investor Sam Zell. And the much praised Knight Ridder newspapers were sold to McClatchy Corp., another respected newspaper company that quickly resold some of the papers, including the *Philadelphia Inquirer,* to local business leaders. Some of these sales involved heretofore non-media owners, and critics worried about the future of these enterprises.

There are three reasons why control by such "absentee owners" is more alarming than dominance by large communication industries:

1. Absentee owners, with far-flung and diverse economic interests, are likely to have little commitment to local communities.
2. Corporations without a strong communications tradition are not likely to be committed to expensive but critical journalistic watchdog traditions.
3. A conglomerate is designed primarily to make profits on "products," and news may come to be defined as only one of many products in a conglomerate's portfolio.

As we mentioned earlier, some of today's "local owners" are investors with only recent interest in the news or information business. Still, there are examples of entrepreneurs saving newspapers that might otherwise have died. Boston real estate magnate Mortimer Zuckerman bought the *New York Daily News* in the 1980s and also owns the magazine *U.S. News & World Report*, both of which have thrived under his stewardship, and he himself has become a television commentator.

When all is said and done, however, the big question is whether the trend toward consolidation of newspaper ownership will actually restrict debate and robust discussion of issues in such a way that it will change the missions and quality of the American press. In the days of William Randolph Hearst, the corporate offices in New York dominated his chain's papers. As our account of yellow journalism showed, that *did* change their mission and quality. Today, however, only a few newspaper groups issue direct orders to local editors about editorial policies, although they do firmly control finances and have generally high expectations about local newspaper profits.

Overall, the implications of ownership remain an open question. At some point in the future, Americans may find that the papers they read have about as much local autonomy in what they print as a KFC franchise has in what it cooks. On the other hand, as we have seen, the search in the past decades has not been for ways to dominate readers' opinions regarding political or moral positions. Newspapers' search instead has focused on ways to maximize profits by giving readers more of what *they* want and think they need. In other words, newspaper content in a profit-oriented economic system is audience-driven. Although that may limit corporate control of news, it may also mean that, in the search for greater returns on investment, the focus on entertainment will increase at the expense of providing information to the public.

Serious journalism may move into the nonprofit arena. Not-for-profit news operations, including public radio and television, rely on public pledge drives and grants from foundations and corporations to fund their operations, rather than on subscriptions or advertising. Efforts to promote nonprofit media to produce better journalism and more investigative reporting have captured the imagination of various media foundations, which have underwritten experimental programs and news services. *Pro Publica*, a highly touted service headed by Paul Steiger, longtime managing editor of the *Wall Street Journal*, was launched in 2007 to encourage long-form journalism and investigative reporting, which cost-conscious, profit-making media have downgraded in recent years.

THE NEWSPAPER AS A CONTEMPORARY MEDIUM

The difference is great between the simple colonial newspaper run by a single printer in a tiny shop and the complicated computerized operations of today's major dailies. As we have noted, some 1,422 newspapers now sell some 51 million printed copies every day while some 69 million visit their websites. To examine this huge medium within a contemporary perspective, this section begins by examining various *types* of newspapers currently published. We then identify the *functions* that these newspapers serve for their readers. Our focus then turns to the *dual identity* that is shaped by both the political and economic environment of newspapers. And finally, we summarize briefly the way newspaper work is *organized*. Increasingly the role of newspapers is that of content provider for other media since they are still vitally important content producers, as they gather and publish news and information across many fields and interests.

Types of Newspapers

Contemporary American newspapers come in all types and sizes, but most, past and present, have shared at least one characteristic: they are very *local* in their orientation and coverage. Although most American dailies cover national and international news, community and regional sections emphasize local news and concerns. The United States does have a few national newspapers—for example, *USA Today,* the *Christian Science Monitor,* and the *Wall Street Journal.* In addition, *The New York Times* and to some extent the *Washington Post* are read nationwide, although both depend on their respective cities for most of their readers and each gives special attention to its area. Each carries at least some news of its city on the front page and devotes a section to its region. Other large American papers, such as the *Boston Globe* and the *Seattle Times,* are regional papers with a distinctive local stamp.

We can divide almost all of America's newspapers into two very broad categories. **General news papers** are intended for readers within their area, while **specialized papers** aim at a particular kind of reader, such as a specific minority group, those of a particular religious faith, or people with a well-focused interest. Both can be further classified in terms of how *often* they publish (daily, weekly, etc.)

Until recently newspapers were mostly confined to readers in particular geographic areas as with this man reading a newspaper during a lunch break in Rome.

and their **circulations**—that is, how many people they reach. Using these criteria, most of America's newspapers fall into one of the following categories: metropolitan dailies, medium-sized and small dailies, non-daily newspapers, free dailies, the ethnic press, and specialized newspapers.

METROPOLITAN DAILIES   Newspapers in the nation's largest cities have circulations (copies sold) that usually exceed 250,000 and a potential readership several times larger. Examples are the *Chicago Tribune* and the *Los Angeles Times.* Many such papers reach readers not only within their metropolitan areas but also across large, multistate areas. Others, such as the *Star Tribune* of Minneapolis, serve more limited regions around their cities. Still others, like the *Emporia* (Kansas) *Gazette,* have a primarily local readership. All, however, are distributed house-to-house by carriers, on the street in coin boxes or newsstands, and occasionally by mail.

Metropolitan dailies usually publish seven days a week. The major dailies include news, features, entertainment, sports, and opinion. Their Sunday editions typically devote considerable space to books, travel, the arts, personalities, and similar topics. They rely on the wire services for much of their content, but some of them have national staffs (usually based in Washington), and a few have foreign correspondents in important cities around the world, although this once proud tradition has declined greatly. Several have set up special investigative teams, which put together detailed analyses of local or even national issues, problems, or scandals.

Most metropolitan newspapers are printed full size—usually fourteen by twenty-two inches with six or seven columns. Some metropolitan dailies are **tabloids**. Today, the term refers mainly to a special size, twelve by sixteen inches, with five columns. At one time, however, a tabloid newspaper was one of low quality and sensational content. The big-city tabloids were usually splashy, designed to capture attention and high street sales with large bold headlines. Today, the distinctions are less clear because tabloids (in the sense of size and format) include papers that mix sensationalism and professionalism (*New York Post* and *Boston Herald*), as well as the more sedate *Christian Science Monitor.*

Quite another category of tabloids are those displayed and sold at checkout counters in supermarkets and that feature unusual and bizarre stories often defying the imagination. Examples are the *National Enquirer,* the *Star,* and *The Globe.* Despite their content (or maybe because of it), these tabloids sell briskly and generate impressive revenues.

MEDIUM-SIZED AND SMALL DAILIES   Middle-sized newspapers in this category have a more modest circulation (50,000–100,000) but are often physically hefty. They may have fewer of their own editorial resources than the major dailies, but they use wire service news and subscribe to syndicates that provide much of their feature material.

Small dailies have a circulation under 50,000. They are even more locally focused than medium-sized dailies and sometimes are meant to be read along with a larger nearby regional paper. Their size is usually small relative to other dailies, and they use less material from external sources.

NON-DAILY NEWSPAPERS   Sometimes called **community** or *grassroots* press, weekly papers were once exclusively rural or suburban publications. They ranged from suburban papers that featured lifestyle stories (for example, on apartment living or how to fund day-care centers) to small country papers dominated by local events and country correspondence. During the 1980s, an increasing number of new urban weeklies were founded. Some concentrate on their neighborhoods. Others are sophisticated, cosmopolitan publications that review such topics as politics and the arts. Urban weeklies like New York's *Village Voice,* Chicago's *Reader,* or San Francisco's *Bay Guardian* are mainly supplementary reading for people who are already informed about news and public affairs from other media.

FREE DAILIES   Free-distribution daily newspapers with extensive news coverage and ad service inserts are relatively new on the American scene, although they have long been a factor in Europe. Indeed, in Europe, free dailies account for 50% of the newspaper market. In contrast, the figure in the United States is just 6%.

One report indicated that there are some thirty-five free dailies in the United States, including several called *Metro,* which were first introduced in Sweden. This paper and others like it, such as *AM New York,* are distributed around public transportation hubs where people wait for buses, subways, and rapid transit. In New York City, *Metro* and *AM New York* each have circulations of 300,000-plus and vie with traditional papers for advertising. In Philadelphia and other cities, local media companies have tried, without success, to block the free papers, which aim at a younger audience than their larger and better-established counterparts.

THE ETHNIC PRESS   This category includes both foreign-language papers and papers written in English but aimed at a particular ethnic group. During those periods of our history when massive numbers of immigrants were pouring into the United States, the foreign-language press was substantial. In colonial times, French papers were common. During the late nineteenth century, German and Scandinavian papers prospered. Today, because of continuing immigration from Mexico and Latin American countries, the number of Spanish papers is increasing, as witnessed by *El Diario* and *El Mundo.*

Many papers serve racial and cultural minorities. The African-American press began in the nineteenth century. Today the United States has several black-oriented newspapers, including the *Baltimore Afro-American,* New York City's *Amsterdam News,* and the *Chicago Defender.* Most of these newspapers emerged because of segregation in the white press, which virtually ignored African-American people and their concerns. For many years it was difficult for blacks to get jobs within the mainstream media. By and large, the press itself took steps to reverse this situation. Many industry and professional newspaper organizations have developed special programs for recruiting and training minorities, although many fall short of their goals. There has also been greater emphasis on reporting on the minority community, although many media critics consider this coverage inconsistent.

OTHER SPECIALIZED PAPERS   The list of specialized papers can go on and on, including industrial and commercial newspapers, labor newspapers, religious newspapers, and those serving environmental interests, people pursuing unconventional lifestyles, special hobbyists, members of voluntary associations, and, of course, college students. There are even prison newspapers. Some of these papers are supported by membership fees or an organization's profits, rather than by advertising.

Changing Functions and Content

Whatever the size of a newspaper, running it as a business means knowing how to make a profit, which means knowing how to sell the paper to the largest possible audience. A newspaper must derive income to survive. The struggle for existence, in the case of the newspaper, has been a struggle for circulation. In recent years this has meant, for the most part, a struggle to appeal to young readers. A 2007 Harvard study showed that only 16% of young adults read a newspaper every day, and only 9% of teenagers said they did. Most young adults, said study director Thomas Patterson, "don't have an engrained news habit." He noted that the most common news sources for these groups are television, followed by the Internet.[14] Further, Patterson doubts that newspapers will ever recapture this audience.

To win the readership struggle and to maintain a flow of income from advertisers, newspaper publishers have had to adjust to the changing demands of their audiences. They have done this by fulfilling a variety of needs among their readers and offering them many kinds of content that provide gratifications. The ways in which they do this can be called the *functions* of the newspaper. Even though they change from time to time, at least six major functions can be identified: persuading, informing, entertaining, providing in-depth coverage and analysis, serving as the official communicator, and appealing to specialized interests.

PERSUADING   Around the time of the American Revolution, the number of functions served by newspapers was limited. As we have indicated, one major category at the time was political papers, whose main function was persuading readers (or at least reinforcing the views of those already committed to the paper's point of view). To some extent today's newspapers continue to serve this *persuasion* function by supporting particular political candidates, promoting public policies, endorsing programs, and taking positions in their editorial pages. Some provide favorable or unfavorable news coverage of institutions, candidates, and issues. However, contemporary papers are more restrained and balanced in this function than their counterparts were a century ago.

INFORMING   In modern times the *information* function of the newspaper is especially alive and well, served in part by that portion of the paper actually devoted to news. This can be surprisingly small. After all the regular material—such as feature stories, comics, syndicated columns, and advertising—is given space, room remains for important and unimportant news stories. This space, referred to as the **news hole**, makes up only about one-fifth of the paper. Other parts of the paper, such as weather forecasts and stock market reports, also serve this function.

ENTERTAINING   To stay alive financially, contemporary newspapers must also serve an *entertainment* function. For this reason, a large amount of their content has little to do with news. It is designed to amuse and gratify readers. Newspapers offer human-interest stories, crosswords puzzles, recipes, gardening hints, sports, and advice on everything from medical problems and fashion to how to rear your child.

PROVIDING IN-DEPTH COVERAGE AND ANALYSIS   The *in-depth* or *analytic* function is closely related to informing. It goes beyond merely transmitting information, however, by providing background details relevant to the news, explanations of related events, and analyses of their importance and implications. Newspapers are able to do this better than most other media. An increasing emphasis on this function in newspapers occurred when radio began to broadcast news reports. Radio posed a real threat, because newspapers lost their edge in timeliness. Radio (and later television and the Internet) could always get the news out faster. Indeed, blogs and citizen journalism posts often break stories long before traditional newspaper reporters get them. However, broadcast and even online formats provide for little more than a summary of the day's events. Consequently, newspapers today place less emphasis on the news "scoop" and more on the details, along with discussions of the meaning and significance of events.

SERVING AS THE "OFFICIAL" COMMUNICATOR   Increasingly over the years newspapers have worked out a special function as their local government's *medium of public record*. According to *Black's Law Dictionary*, an "official" newspaper is one "designated by a state or municipal legislative body, or agents empowered by them, in which the public acts, resolves, advertisements, and notices are required to be published." The laws of a city or state may require that the government publish (in the sense of making public) notices of candidates filing for elections, auctions of property seized for failure to pay taxes, or building contracts open for bids. When a local government designates a newspaper as its official news outlet, it pays the paper to print these notices and advertisements as a means of placing them in the public record.

Local governments often subsidize selected newspapers to serve as their official means of communication. In large cities, there is often a specialized legal or commercial publication. Sometimes, however, the subsidy has made the difference between survival or not for a smaller community's main daily or weekly.

APPEALING TO SPECIALIZED INTERESTS   During the second half of the twentieth century, newspapers took on the function of appealing to specific reader interests with whole sections of the paper devoted to particular kinds of content. For example, even *The New York Times,* known for its coverage of hard news in a staid, serious, and reliable style, now includes special sections each week called "Home" and "Living." Other papers appeal to readers' specialized interests with sections on food, personal ads, automobiles, and travel. Today, a typical newspaper might allot 20% of its space—about the same as for news—to various kinds of such interest-related sections.

Newspapers' Dual Identity and Built-in Conflict of Interest

Earlier in this chapter, we defined newspapers with a simple list of characteristics. However, not everyone sees newspapers in those terms. In fact, they can be different things to different people, because contemporary newspapers have a *dual identity*. On one hand, the newspaper is a quasi-public institution charged with being the watchdog of the public interest, often making it an antagonist of government and other forces in power. This identity is a product of many honored traditions of journalism established over more than two hundred years. On the other hand, as a business, the newspaper seeks to make a profit and function as a member of the business community, a major employer, and a member of the chamber of commerce.

This dual identity often brings with it an inherent conflict, as business values and those of serious journalists clash. A few years ago, for example, the *Los Angeles Times* nearly exploded when the publisher agreed to share revenues for a special magazine section with a sports section. This breach of editorial and advertising functions was said to damage the paper's credibility and led to the departure of both the editor and publisher.

How Newspaper Work Is Organized

Although newspapers range in size from *The New York Times,* with a staff of about six thousand employees, to the country weekly with a staff of three or four, all papers have two basic operations: the business and the editorial. Generally, the business side manages the paper's financial affairs and its advertising, which generates the income that keeps the paper alive. The editorial side includes reporters, editors, and all the others who acquire and process the information that goes into the paper's news stories and other editorial (non-advertising) content.

OVERVIEW OF DEPARTMENTS   The larger the paper, the more complex the organization. On the business side, several essential activities are often organized as separate departments.

- The *advertising* department handles both display or non-classified advertisements from merchants and businesses and the classified announcements, such as apartments for rent, used autos for sale, and help wanted.
- The *production* department is responsible for typesetting (which today is done largely by complex computerized systems) and printing.
- The *circulation* department is responsible for arranging for home or mail delivery or sale by street vendors.
- A general *business* department handles such things as accounting, personnel, and building maintenance.

THE EDITORIAL STAFF   The people who produce the news content of the paper are those who gather, write, and edit stories; handle photographs; select what to publish from the wire services and syndicates; and prepare final selections for printing. They are organized into a ranked system of power and prestige.

Editors.   A number of supervisory people have titles that include the term "editor," and this can be confusing. However, each has a different level of authority and is responsible for different forms of content. Supervisory newspaper staff include the following people:

- The *publisher* is either the owner or the principal owner's representative.
- The *editor-in-chief*—sometimes simply called the *editor* or, with the advent of chain ownership, the *executive editor*—heads the entire editorial department. The editor is responsible for all the paper's content, with the exception of advertising.

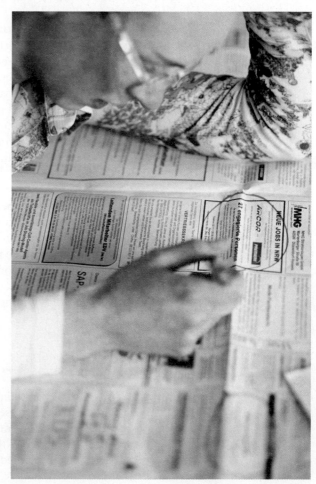

Historically classified advertising play a key role in newspaper advertising revenues.

- Reporting to the editor-in-chief is the editorial page editor (sometimes called the *associate editor*), who is responsible for the editorial page and the "op ed" page (opposite the editorial page). The editorial page editor reports directly to the editor because newspapers try to separate "opinion" from "news" to the greatest extent possible.
- Also reporting to the editor is the *managing editor,* who is responsible for the day-to-day operation of the newsroom. The managing editor is a relatively powerful figure, who hires and fires staff members and supervises various specialized editors.
- Specialized editors include the city editor (or *metropolitan editor* in large papers), who is responsible for local news coverage, including assignments for local reporters. Depending on the size of the paper, other news-gathering sections such as sports, business, entertainment, and features will also have editors supervising them. The number of separate sections working within a newsroom is determined by the size of the paper more than any other factor.
- Also working for the managing editor is the *news editor,* who is responsible for preparing copy for insertion into the pages. The news editor supervises *copy editors* (who really do "edit" stories and write headlines). The news editor also oversees the design of the pages and decides where stories will be placed. On major stories, the news editor will often consult with the managing editor and other lower-level editors before a decision is made.
- Finally, the *wire* or *news service editor* selects, edits, and coordinates the national and international news from the news services, such as the Associated Press (AP).

Editors gather to discuss news priorities in the newsroom of the Orange County Register in Southern California.

Although smaller papers may not have personnel with all of these specific titles, someone on the newspaper staff must perform each of the activities in order to see that a paper gets produced.

Reporters.   A familiar part of the editorial staff are the **reporters**, journalists who seek out news information and initially write stories. There are basically three kinds of reporters:

- *General assignment reporters* cover a wide range of news as it happens, regardless of the topic. They also rewrite stories.
- *Beat reporters* are assigned to particular areas of government, such as the courts, police, and state government.
- *Specialist reporters* cover fields such as business, science, and urban issues.

In a special category, about which we have much to say in our discussion of news in Chapter 9 ("The News Process"), are the *investigative reporters,* whose probes help the press carry out its vital "watchdog" activities. Larger and more complex newspapers obviously have more specialized categories of business reporters, columnists, and editors, who monitor various areas of commercial and industrial interest. Some papers have local **columnists** who write about colorful people or events and reflect the general character of the city. Other columnists might specialize in politics or race relations.

Other Specialists.   **Photojournalists** have played a major role in the American press since before the turn of the century. Today, their major work is indispensable, as stylized, illustrative photography has become more vital to overall newspaper design. Photography came into its own when newspapers began to use more and more color. Until a few years ago, for example, most newspapers (except Sunday editions) were produced exclusively in black and white. Spurred by *USA Today's* eye-catching color photography and elaborate graphics, many other papers followed suit during the 1990s, in an effort to be more attractive to readers. Many papers now employ art and design directors who work with editors to design the paper and its special sections.

Online Staff.   Some papers have a parallel website that simply mirrors the printed edition, while others have completely different sites, even with different names. At the beginning of digital or online publishing, most newspapers separated their online product from the more tactile paper edition. There were often different traditions of the two staffs, and often they produced very different newspapers. That began to change a few years ago, as more and more newspapers integrated their online staffs into the more traditional staff, including the requirement at some papers that all reporters and columnists have blogs.

THE FUTURE OF THE NEWSPAPER

As we saw at the beginning of this chapter, some observers and pundits proclaim that the printed newspaper represents the past and that it is doomed to extinction as the technology of the Internet continues to advance. A 2006 headline in the *The Economist,* for example, asked, "Who Killed the Newspaper?" The article went on to state that "the most useful bit of the media is disappearing."[15] Investor and newspaper booster Warren Buffet also joined doomsayers in predicting the death of the medium.

Indeed, for at least two decades, newspapers have had a precarious existence. As we noted, newspapers are slowly declining in terms of the percentage of the population who subscribe to them. They are also declining in terms of the share of the total amount of money spent by the nation's advertisers. A few have historically made huge profits, while others worry about all the barriers to their survival and success.

Several financial factors will probably continue to reduce both the proportions of Americans who read newspapers and their revenues in the future.

- Many newspapers are owned by corporations that also own radio and television stations that could reduce competitive efforts.
- There are a finite number of advertising dollars available in our economy. Media consultants maintain that consumers will spend only a certain constant percentage of their income on information and entertainment, no matter how many outlets and services are available. Those dollars are being chased by an increasing number of competitors, including newspapers, radio, television, cable, magazines, direct mail, as well as phone companies and Internet companies. As the number of media competitors increases, they will have to cut the same-sized "revenue pie" into smaller and smaller pieces, and newspapers will get a shrinking slice.
- Newspapers suffer from rising labor and newsprint prices.[16]

Many people, however, believe that it is too soon to declare the death of newspapers. They predict that the newspaper will survive in its present form, at least for the foreseeable future. Even the *Economist* article suggesting the death of the newspaper concluded that current challenges are "a cause for concern, but not for panic."[17]

These observers point out that newspapers remain quite profitable for their owners. This is because newspapers command the largest share of American advertising dollars—spent by local businesses that must advertise their goods and services to local customers. Moreover, newspapers remain a personal and local medium, where people find information about events, people, and illustrations in their own communities. At this time, newspapers thus continue to serve needs that are difficult for any other medium to fulfill. Their long-range prospects, however, are less clear. As we saw at the beginning of the chapter, many believe that the future of newspapers definitely includes embracing digital technology.

Like other online newspaper editions, *The Philadelphia Inquirer* website lists top news stories in several different categories.

Interactive Media and Online Newspapers

Newspapers flirted with new technologies as early as the 1950s when they introduced electronic typesetting. Eventually the computer played a role in newsgathering, as reporters used it as a tool in their work. Starting back in the 1930s, various news organizations experimented with "electronic newspapers." Although a variety of methods proved unsuccessful, these early efforts were still instructive for newspaper executives and their competitors when online, interactive newspapers were developed in the 1990s using the Internet.

By 2009, virtually all large U.S. and international newspapers had an interactive or digital edition, and some online newspapers existed only on the web. The potential impact of Internet newspapers was noted by researcher Enrique Dans, of the Institute of the Press in Madrid, Spain, who wrote:

In 450 years of existence, the written press has never faced a change with the intensity and consequences as those of the Internet. The decision of going online represents a set of opportunities and threats that publishers must carefully weigh. Once they have made the step, newspapers find themselves in a completely different competitive environment. They deal with different competitors, business models, customers and patterns of consumption.[18]

A more recent article reported that newspapers are making progress with the Internet, but most are still too timid, defensive, or high minded. A look at the operations of many Internet newspaper services is also somewhat disappointing. Most have only small staffs, and only a little more than one-third update their material more than once a day, thus missing one of the major advantages of the Internet: the ability for constant updating.

It is also difficult for online news resources to make money. Efforts by newspapers to leverage their Internet assets to increase their value on the market and profits have fallen short. One reason is that they must coordinate and balance old physical assets like buildings and presses to embrace the less capital intensive new economy of the Internet. They still have the same industrial problems that slowed newspapers for years—"shrinking circulation, rising newsprint prices and the slow growth nature of their core businesses."[19] A study by market researchers Insight Express had more bad news when it reported that some 55% of online users are not willing to pay for news.[20]

However, scholars are not counting out the Internet newspapers. They have a following among younger people. Internet sites also take the newspaper into the world of e-commerce. For example, a paper with an online presence can have an enormous capacity to handle classified advertising and other quick-turnaround commercial transactions. Indeed, some newspapers like the *Christian Science Monitor* dropped its printed edition in 2008 and now only publish online. This could reflect a growing trend in a world where newspaper advertising revenues are declining.

CHAPTER REVIEW

- Newspapers, once ink-on-paper products, are now part of the digital world, quite dependent on computer hardware and software for all aspects of their operations.
- Newspapers are distinguishable from other media because they are portable, predictable, accessible, and cost-effective.
- News, the main commodity delivered by newspapers and other news media, is current or fresh information about an event or subject that is gathered, processed, and disseminated via a medium to a significant number of people.
- Newspapers were slow in coming to the American colonies. The first to publish more than a single issue was the *Boston News-Letter* of 1704. A succession of small colonial newspapers followed, and a tradition of free expression was slowly established. The dramatic trial of Peter Zenger in 1734 was an important landmark in establishing the concept of a free press.
- The colonial papers were small, slow, aimed at affluent readers, and limited in coverage. Some were partisan papers published to express and support a particular political position; others were commercial papers of interest mainly to merchants and traders. Nevertheless, they established important traditions as guardians of the public interest and played a key role in spreading ideas that became important to the founding of the new nation.
- Newspapers for common people became increasingly possible as the industrial revolution brought new technologies and as immigration, the growth of cities, and the increased literacy led to larger potential audiences. In *The New York Sun*, Benjamin Day put together the necessary components of printing technology, advertising support, new content with wide popular appeal, and an effective distribution system. Quickly, the penny papers spread to America's other cities.

- A number of changes in American society spurred the growth of newspapers: among these were rapid population growth through immigration, increasing literacy, and technological changes brought about by the steam press, telegraph, trains, and steamboats. Intense competition for readers among competing urban newspapers fostered an era of yellow journalism.
- Early in the twentieth century, the newspaper was the nation's only mass medium and was adopted by most American households. However, as other media arrived, its number of subscriptions per household declined. That downward trend continues today.
- The functions of newspapers began to change with increased emphasis on corporate profits. The older function of informing readers is still there, but entertaining them has assumed growing importance. Newspapers increasingly emphasize their tradition of in-depth coverage and interpretation because of competition from radio and television, which get the news out much faster.
- As a contemporary medium, newspapers have altered their functions to respond to competing media (such as television and the Internet) with less focus on immediacy and more detailed coverage.
- There are several types of newspapers from large metropolitan dailies to small free papers given away on or near public transportation.
- The digital revolution has led some struggling papers to do away with their paper editions and go exclusively to an online edition.

STRATEGIC QUESTIONS

1. What is the principal role of the newspaper in contemporary society?
2. What has been the historical role of the newspaper in American society—how has that role changed?
3. Why do newspapers command so much advertising even as their importance in society—and the economy—has diminished?
4. What have been the major drivers or trends that have shaped today's newspapers?
5. How is the newspaper adapting to the digital revolution? Is it a leader or follower?
6. What have been the newspaper's most important characteristics—and are they likely to survive?

KEY CONCEPTS & TERMS

News 60	Electronic or digital	Wire services 72
Penny press 68	newspaper 83	Feature syndicates 72
Yellow journalism 70	Watchdog role 65	
First Amendment 65	Dual identity 76	

ENDNOTES

1. "The Decline of the American Newspaper," *The Week*, Jan. 19, 2007, p. 11.
2. Jon Fine, "Gannett's New Lease on News," *BusinessWeek*, Feb. 26, 2007, p. 28.
3. Edwin Emery, *The Press in America*, 5th ed. (Englewood Cliffs, NJ: Prentice-Hall, 1972), p. 3.
4. Marvin Rosenberg, "The Rise of England's First Daily Newspaper," *Journalism Quarterly* 30 (Winter 1953), pp. 3–14.
5. Emery, *The Press in America*, p. 31.
6. For an especially insightful view of the newspaper and other media, see Hiley H. Ward, *Mainstreams of American Media History* (Boston: Allyn & Bacon, 1997); for an excellent discussion of early press technology, see John W. Moore, *Historical Notes on Printers and Printing*, 1420–1886 (1186; reprint, New York: Burt Franklin, 1968).
7. An excellent selection of Brady's photographs is reproduced in Phillip B. Kunhart, Jr., *Matthew Brady and His World* (New York: Time-Life, 1977).
8. See U.S. Bureau of Census, *Statistical Abstract of the United States* (Washington, DC: U.S. Government Printing Office).
9. A thorough history of the development of auxiliaries can be found in Richard A. Schwartzlose, *The Nation's Newsbrokers*, 2 vols. (Chicago: Northwestern University Press, 1989).

10. The sources for these various figures on trends in ownership are Lynch, Jones and Ryan, Inc. and John Morton Research, Inc.

11. Richard McCord, *The Chain Gang: One Newspaper Versus the Gannet Empire* (Columbia, MO: University of Missouri Press, 1996).

12. C. Edwin Baker, *Media Concentration and Democracy, Why Ownership Matters* (New York: Cambridge University Press, 2008), pp. 6–28.

13. Richard Siklos, "Reinventing Newspapers Is Murdoch's Long-Range Goal," *International Herald Tribune,* http://www.uht/com/articles/2007/05/13/business/murdoch.

14. Robert E. Park, "The Natural History of the Newspaper," *American Sociological Review* 29 (1923), pp. 273–289.

15. "Who Killed the Newspaper?" http://economist.com/research.articles/cfm?story_ID=7830218.

16. Felicity Barringer, "Newspapers Bring Threat of Web into Perspective," *New York Times,* May 15, 2000, p. C21.

17. "Who Killed the Newspaper?" http://economist.com/research.articles/cfm?story_ID=7830218.

18. Enrique Dans, "Internet Newspapers: Are Some More Equal than Others?" *International Journal on Media Management,* Spring 2000, p. 11.

19. Susan McGee and Matthew Rose, "Newspapers' Internet Stories Haven't Clicked with Investors," *Wall Street Journal,* July 11, 2000, C1, C4.

20. "Newspapers' Internet Stories Haven't Clicked with Investors."

Magazines: Voices for Many Interests

In many ways, observing the magazine landscape in the digital age is like witnessing diverse individuals in a teeming crowd. Thousands vie for attention and advertising support. Some gain attention and survive; others wither and die as new entries, called **start-ups**, join the crowd announcing their presence as the newest or latest answer to readers' needs and wants. Magazines represent a complex and challenging segment of the media industry as they compete with other members of the print or publishing family in a ruthless and often unforgiving economic and social marketplace.

In their beginnings, magazines depended on the same technological developments in movable types, presses, printing, and paper as did books and newspapers. However, magazines are not like other print media. Although they have some of the features of books and are published on some regular schedule like newspapers, they are a unique medium in their own right. We'll see in this chapter that magazines have always served specific functions in society that differ from those of either newspapers or books. Furthermore, those who read and subscribe to magazines constitute a distinct segment of U.S. society.

We'll also see that magazines are not just a print phenomenon anymore. The magazine format, with information organized by topic and theme, was long ago borrowed by television and cable, for example. This makes the magazine a media product, a medium of communication (or platform) and a communication format.[1]

Magazines entered the twenty-first century in a state of confusion, as part of old media, but with an early interest in using the Internet as a platform. Magazines soon were seamlessly identified with blogs and podcasts, offering their readers full-motion video and almost endless interactivity, as well as search capacity. They went from seeing the Internet as just another mode of delivery to one of melding into social networking and search sites. Today, many magazines, like newspapers, operate both in the traditional ink-on-paper forms and online.

Understanding magazines in an integrated, converging media world requires awareness of what they are, how they operate, and their likely future course in the context of how they actually evolved.

DISTINGUISHING MAGAZINES FROM OTHER MEDIA

You may feel that you already know a lot about what a magazine is and how it differs from a newspaper, but in contemporary publishing it is sometimes difficult to distinguish between the two. Magazines today are becoming more difficult to differentiate from other media as well. Yet magazines still maintain their identity as a distinct media industry and platform. To understand how, we must examine the form, audiences, and functions of contemporary magazines.

There are usually some fairly noticeable differences in form that satisfactorily distinguish magazines from newspapers. Generally, a magazine is published less frequently than a newspaper. It is also manufactured in a different format, usually on better quality paper, bound rather than merely folded, and has some kind of cover.

The long-held distinction among newspapers, published magazines, and electronic magazines is becoming increasingly blurred, however. Indeed, when newspapers have made major changes in packaging and presentation,

"It's on-line, subscribers pay only for the articles they want, it's updated everyday—are you sure we can call it a magazine?"

it is often said that they are adopting a "magazine format." Even television has been influenced: CBS's *60 Minutes* and its current imitators call themselves "television magazine" shows.

What complicates the matter further in the digital age is the fact that both newspapers and magazines have websites, as well as print delivery. Online versions of magazines may run differently from their print counterparts. While printed magazines are only updated on a weekly or monthly basis, the dot-com magazine today is often edited and infused with new material hourly.

The content of magazines has historically distinguished them from other media. Historically, magazines have appealed to a regional or national audience and have been free from the fierce localism of newspapers. Unburdened by daily deadlines, magazines have also usually probed issues and situations more carefully than newspapers, for example. However, with an increasing interest in investigative reporting on the part of today's larger newspapers, that is not always the case. What we do find in magazine content is less concern for the details of daily events and more concern for interpreting topics in a broad context.

Recall that, in Chapter 1, we discussed Harold Lasswell's list of the functions of all media. That list included:

- Surveillance of the environment.
- Correlation of the parts of society responding to the environment.
- Transmission of the social heritage from one generation to another.

We also added entertainment to this list. Magazines today perform all of these traditional functions. They are a major medium of surveillance, often delivering information ahead of the rest of the media. Some magazines, like *Newsweek,* are intended mainly to fill the surveillance function by informing readers. Others, like *Playboy,* aim primarily to entertain. Other print media also inform and entertain, but it is in performance of the *correlation* function that magazines stand out. Among the various functions served by magazines, they are most successful in providing in-depth analysis that helps readers to understand contemporary society and its parts. Magazines excel in projecting trends and explaining the meaning of the news by bringing together fragmented facts. Magazines, in other words, are the great interpreters. Magazine scholar Theodore Peterson offered this succinct description of the modern magazine:

> Although the magazine lacked the immediacy of the broadcast media and the newspaper, it nevertheless was timely enough to deal with the flow of events. Its timeliness and continuity set it apart from the book. As a continuing publication, it could provide a form of discussion by carrying responses from its audience, could sustain campaigns for indefinite periods, and could work for cumulative rather than single impact. Yet its available space and the reading habits of its audience enabled it to give fairly lengthy treatment to the subjects it covered. Like the other print media it appealed more to the intellect than to the senses and emotions of its audience. It was not as transient as the broadcast media, nor did it require attention at a given time; it was not as soon discarded as the newspaper; its issues remained in readers' homes for weeks, for months, sometimes even for years. In short, the magazine by its nature met well the requirements for a medium of instruction and interpretation for the leisurely, critical reader.[2]

THE HISTORY OF MAGAZINES

The word "magazine" entered the English language in the late 1500s, but it did not refer then to a printed medium. The term comes originally from the Arabic *makhasin,* which means "storehouse." In ancient times the term magazine referred to a place containing a collection of items, usually military stores. We still use the word to describe many kinds of military enclosures where explosives are kept. In the 1700s, when the earliest printed periodicals began to appear, they eventually came to be called magazines because they were, in a sense, storehouses of writings about various topics.

The formats, functions, and audiences of magazines have a long and colorful history, and although all have changed greatly over time, at least some remain remarkably similar to what they were from their beginnings. In our review of the history of magazines, we'll see that:

■ The first magazines were originally established in London, where they prospered in a great city inhabited by many urbane and educated residents.

■ Rougher societal conditions prevailing in America during the eighteenth century held back the development of periodicals on this side of the Atlantic. As the nation expanded, became urban, and developed improved transportation, magazines began to prosper in the United States.

■ By the end of the nineteenth century, magazines were a serious and respected medium serving millions of readers.

■ During the early twentieth century, magazines played an important role in exposing unacceptable social conditions and stimulating social reform.

■ Between the two world wars, before television became a household medium, magazines were one of the major mass media, advertising nationally distributed products.

■ After World War II, the growth of television had a significant impact on the magazine industry. Large-circulation general magazines were severely hurt financially, but new kinds of magazines were founded to meet new demands, and the industry thrives today.

The First Magazines

The history of the magazine began in London in 1704 with the first issue of a small periodical called *The Review*. In some ways, this little publication resembled a newspaper of the time: it was printed on about four small pages and (at first) was published weekly. Yet it was different from the early newspapers in being much less concerned with news; it focused mainly on articles about domestic affairs and national policy.[3] It was still a time in England when people could be thrown in jail for writing and publishing material contrary to the Crown, and, as it happened, the founder of *The Review* had been doing precisely that just before his new publication began to appear. The founder was the outspoken Daniel Defoe (who later wrote *Robinson Crusoe*). He wrote the first issue while in Newgate Prison, where he was being held because of his critical writings denouncing certain policies of the Church of England.

The Review, like many magazines that would follow it, was a vehicle for political commentary, and it was intended to influence its readers' beliefs and opinions. At the same time, it was an instrument of entertainment—at least for sophisticated readers—in that it also contained essays on literature, manners, and morals. Both of these functions were central to the medium from the beginning and, for many magazines that followed, remain so today.

After his release from prison, Defoe continued to produce *The Review* on a frequent schedule, about three times

The first issue of *The Pennsylvania Magazine or American Monthly Museum* was published in Philadelphia in 1775 by Thomas Paine.

a week, until 1712. Defoe's little publication was almost immediately imitated, and the idea of magazines as a separate kind of print medium began to catch on. Although seen as the first magazines, these early publications were not called that at the time. The term was not applied to printed works until 1731, when Edward Cave, a London printer, first published his monthly *Gentlemen's Magazine,* which was so successful that it eventually reached some 15,000 subscribers, truly a remarkable circulation for that time.

Early magazines differed from newspapers of the period not only in their content but also in their authors. From the beginning, the magazines became a medium for some of the ablest writers of the time. Their pages contained essays, stories, and entertaining commentaries by such figures as Samuel Johnson, Alexander Pope, and, as noted, Daniel Defoe, Joseph Addison, and Richard Steele—among the most respected English writers of the eighteenth century.

As the form and substance of the new medium came together by the middle of the 1700s, the functions it was serving in society remained unique. The magazine was clearly designed to make a profit. It depended on subscription payments by its readers and, to a limited extent, on advertising revenues. It sought to attract readers with a mixture that was heavy on political commentary but also included discussions of controversial topics and issues and opinion-shaping essays. Its literary quality was high and its typical reader was a member of the affluent, well-educated elite. It was not a medium for the masses. Magazines, then and now, were different from pamphlets or promotional and marketing materials whether printed or stored electronically.

By the middle of the century, a number of rival magazines were being published successfully in England, and the concept was spreading to other parts of the world. Thus, by the time of the American Revolution, hundreds of publications that we would recognize as magazines today were being produced in the major cities of Europe. What was happening across the Atlantic, in the American colonies?

American Magazines in the 1700s: Barriers to Development

The magazines that had been established in England were impressive models. To some intellectuals it seemed like a great idea to begin publication of such a periodical in the colonies. In fact, Benjamin Franklin, ever the innovator, tried to get one started in 1741. It had the awesome title of *The General Magazine, and Historical Chronicle, for All the British Plantations in America.* It even had a competitor with an equally awesome title, Andrew Bradford's *The American Magazine, or A Monthly View of the Political State of the British Colonies.* Franklin's effort lasted only six issues; Bradford's failed after three.[4] For the next decade after that, attempts to produce magazines were sporadic.[5]

If Franklin, Bradford, and others had been able to hire a modern market researcher to try to determine if there was a realistic magazine market, it would not have taken much research to reveal why such projects were doomed before they started. There were four major conditions that created barriers to the successful establishment of magazines in America and caused their development to lag considerably behind that of their European counterparts: (1) the nature and dispersion of the population, (2) the economics of publishing at that time, (3) the state of transportation and the postal system needed for delivery, and (4) the costs of subscribing.

COLONIAL POPULATIONS   At the time Franklin and Bradford brought out their rival magazines, the population of the entire thirteen colonies was only about one million people, who were spread over a huge land area, about twelve hundred miles along the seacoast and just a few hundred miles inland. In addition, the majority of these colonists lived on farms, often in isolated locations. Even fifty years later in 1790, when the first official U.S. census was taken, only 3.9 million white and black people lived throughout the entire original thirteen states, and the only cities with populations over twenty-five thousand were Philadelphia and Boston. Altogether, city dwellers made up only 3.5% of the entire American population.[6]

As a consequence of these population conditions, no accessible market existed for a magazine in eighteenth-century America. If Franklin and Bradford and those who tried later

This fanciful rendering contrasts the obstacles in transporting magazines and other products in colonial days as opposed to the modern era.

to start magazines had understood how these factors were related to the success of their medium, they probably would not have even taken the trouble.

MAGAZINE ECONOMICS   The economics of magazine publishing in this period were fragile indeed. An individual entrepreneur or publisher had to do everything—conceive and produce the publication, print it on their own printing press, distribute it, and so on. The business model for magazines was sometimes paid entirely by the subscriber, sometimes a mix of subscriptions and advertising. There were no national or even regional markets, so most magazines were strictly local, driven by the intuition and interests of their owners, who were, as we said, publishers, editors, writers, printers, and distributors. The age of specialization and distribution of labor was still a long way off.

OBSTACLES TO TRANSPORTATION AND DELIVERY   Today we receive magazines in the mail routinely and reliably. In the 1700s, however, transportation conditions made mail delivery to the country's sparse and dispersed population extremely difficult and expensive. Traveling from New York to Boston today, for example, requires only minutes by air and just over four hours by car on the interstate highway. In the middle of the eighteenth century, it was a rough eight- to ten-day trip by stagecoach, and just getting there was an accomplishment. Hauling goods (such as bundles of magazines) by wagon or pack animal was much slower. In the less-settled areas there were few roads of any kind, and most travelers went by horseback, sailing vessels, or even canoes.

Today's magazine subscribers seldom think about postage, because it is paid by the publisher (and is really quite inexpensive). Getting magazines to subscribers in the eighteenth century was a different matter. Magazines were not even allowed to be carried by mail until the 1790s. The fees were not practical at first, because they were based on weight, which made mailing heavy magazines prohibitively expensive. A few years later the Congress changed to a system based on the number of pages plus the distance required for delivery. This did not work well either, because of the expense to people in remote areas. Postage, which had to be paid in advance by the subscriber, added 20 to 40% to the cost of the periodical.

It was not until 1852 that postal rates for magazines could be paid at the point of mailing by the publisher. By that time, roads had been greatly improved, and both steamship lines and railroads were operating on regular schedules to carry mail quickly, cheaply, and efficiently. The lower costs led most publishers to absorb the postage as part of the subscription price.

THE COST OF SUBSCRIBING   A magazine in the early days was a real luxury. The first magazines produced by Franklin and Bradford, for instance, sold for a shilling per issue, which in the currency of the time, was about half a day's wages for a farm laborer. A year's subscription would equal what a laborer could earn in about four or five days. Added was the cost of delivery, about another day's wages. Payment for comparable amount of labor, at today's minimum wage, would be around $315. Few among us would be willing to pay that much for a magazine subscription.

Magazines were then, and would remain for a substantial period, a medium for the well-to-do. The elite of European cities like London and Paris made up a pool of potential subscribers, but the farmers and laborers of America, thinly scattered over a vast area, were not a potential market.

American Magazines in the 1800s

Although virtually every imaginable factor conspired against the development of magazines in America during the 1700s, the situation started to change significantly after the next century began. The 1800s brought just the conditions needed for a great flowering of magazines.

CATALYSTS FOR DEVELOPMENT IN THE NINETEENTH CENTURY   A number of factors contributed to the growth of magazines in the 1800s:

- The population of the United States exploded.
- Many of those people moved into cities.
- Transportation improved quickly.
- People became better educated.
- There were great issues about which the population urgently needed detailed information.

Rapid Population Growth.   In 1800, ten years after America's first census, the population had increased to 5.3 million. Then, during only five decades, the population soared to 23.2 million, an increase of more than 400%. By the end of the nineteenth century, due in large part to massive immigration, it had skyrocketed to 75.9 million. Few nations in history have ever recorded such an astonishing rate of population growth. The golden age of magazine growth during the nineteenth century would never have occurred without these long-term population trends. As we will see, that population growth also characterized the first half of the twentieth century.

Urbanization.   Not only did the population grow numerically, it also became more urban, as Table 5.1 demonstrated. Increasing proportions lived in towns and cities and earned salaries and wages. During the same period, smaller and smaller proportions were living on farms. The growth of towns and cities meant more concentrated populations with larger cash incomes and higher levels of education. These were precisely the conditions required for an expanding market for magazines. To give some idea of the shift, in 1790 more than 95% of American families lived on farms. By 1820, this figure had dropped to 80%. At the time of the Civil War, it was about 70%. The flow of people from farm to city continued and even accelerated in the present century. By 1920, only half of the nation's families lived on farms. Today it is less than 2%. We truly are an urban nation. More than half of us live on only 1% of the landmass.

Transportation.   In part, this trend toward urban living arose from the spread of transportation networks that made it possible to move farm goods to domestic and foreign market centers. Completion of the great Erie Canal created a network linking lakes and rivers so travelers and goods could journey cheaply from New York City to the new city of Chicago. As farm products and consumer goods moved over this great transportation system, hundreds of communities sprang up in the Midwest and in northern parts of

TABLE 5.1

U.S. POPULATION MOVES TO CITIES

Year	Percent of Americans Living on Farms
1790	more than 95%
1820	72%
1850	64%
1861 (start of Civil War)	58%
1920	30.2%
Today	less than 2%

Source: AP, "Farm Population Lowest Since 1850s," *New York Times*, July 20, 1988, and USDA.

Pennsylvania, New York, Indiana, and Ohio. Southward links allowed barge traffic to travel all the way to New Orleans. New York City itself, at the eastern end of the system, grew into a great port for exports and imports. It became the largest and most important city of the nation's mass communication industries. Between about 1840 and 1900, the railroads, too, had spread to most parts of the country, fostering their own share of towns and cities.

Increasing Education. Although sheer numbers and their concentrations are important, the quality of the population is also a factor shaping the market for a product like a magazine. In its early years, the United States was a nation whose citizens for the most part had received little or no formal instruction in reading. Even at the beginning of the nineteenth century, education beyond the rudiments was largely a matter of training the elite. Few ordinary people went to secondary school, and only the wealthy attended college.

By 1834, however, Horace Mann of Massachusetts persuaded his state's legislature to adopt a system of free public education and to make it mandatory for all children. The Massachusetts system for educating all citizens quickly spread to other states. In the 1860s the Civil War greatly disrupted society, including educational development, but following that conflict the proportion of the nation's children enrolled in schools increased for more than a century. This great social change had profound implications for the development of magazine markets, as new generations of literate citizens sought out reading material for information and entertainment.

The Great Issues. As population changes occurred during the 1800s, growing demands for specialized types of information played a part in the spread of the modern magazine. The entire century was marked by extraordinary events, sweeping changes, and truly significant movements in thought, politics, and religion. Magazines were an instrument uniquely qualified to present positions, details, opinions, and analyses in ways quite different from the newspaper and in much greater depth. It was from the perspective of magazines that Americans began to learn about important trends, controversies, and significant issues affecting their society, including the following:

Great social issues such as women's rights have been important content for muckraking advocacy and opinion magazines.

- *The Civil War* and its accompanying debates over slavery. Works like Harriet Beecher Stowe's antislavery novel, *Uncle Tom's Cabin,* were serialized in magazines and reached a reading public far exceeding the number who had access to the book.
- *Intellectual debates.* An example was the explosive issue of Darwin's explanation of the origin of species. Magazines were an important forum in the debate over evolution versus creation. Magazines also delved into topics like financial panics and depressions, controversial discoveries in medicine, great religious revivals, and the continuously expanding frontier.
- *Women's issues.* Many magazines were aimed directly at women and provided stories and commentary on changes advocated by leaders of the growing women's movement. There was an emotionally charged debate between those who advocated and those who wanted to prevent women's suffrage, or voting. Others believed that women should have the right to obtain credit, to get a mortgage, to initiate divorce, to wear more comfortable clothing, and even to work outside the home in jobs traditionally reserved for men. Magazines presented views on all aspects of these issues.

AMERICAN MAGAZINE CHARACTERISTICS IN THE NINETEENTH CENTURY   With the catalysts noted above, the U.S. magazine industry flowered during the nineteenth century. It was a dynamic industry, constantly seeking new formats, new audiences, new appeals, and new ways to increase profits. Although thousands of magazines were started only to die within a short time, some lasted for generations.

Numbers and Circulations of Magazines.   The number of magazines published in the United States showed a remarkable pattern of growth over a seventy-five-year period. In 1825 there were fewer than 100 magazines in circulation.[7]

Paralleling this rapid expansion in the number of magazines published was growth in circulation rates. Actual circulation amounts were not systematically recorded during the century, but various figures are available that show a sharply increasing trend. For example, during the late 1700s a magazine would have been lucky to have 1,500 subscribers. Most had fewer. In contrast, the *Country Gentleman* in 1858 had 25,000 subscribers. Other magazines that year were within the same range. *Godey's Lady Book,* a very popular magazine for women, had 15,000 subscribers. Within fifteen years the circulation had skyrocketed even higher. In 1885, the *Youth's Companion* was the leader with 300,000 subscribers, and the more literate *Scribner's Monthly* had a respectable 200,000.

A Magazine for Every Taste and Interest.   During the last years of the nineteenth century, magazine publishers came to understand their markets very well. "Every interest had its own journal or journals—all the ideologies and movements, all the arts, all the schools of philosophy and education, all the sciences, all the trades and industries, all the professions and callings, all organizations of importance, all hobbies and recreations."[8] Whereas newspapers provided their readers with a daily cafeteria of many different types of content, magazines zeroed in on specific categories—on people who shared an interest in a particular subject.

As the century came to a close, the world of magazines was varied indeed. In particular, the religious periodicals were thriving. By 1885 there were some 650 publications aimed at different denominations. Scores of magazines were also devoted to the arts,

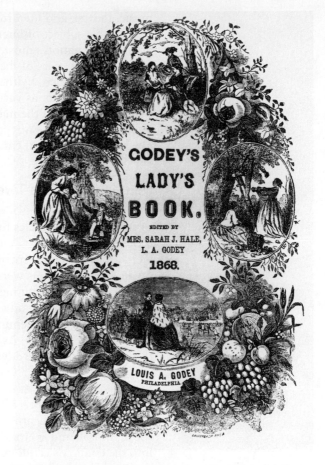

Magazines aimed at women such as *Godey's Lady's Book* were important in increasing the circulation, reach and popularity of magazines.

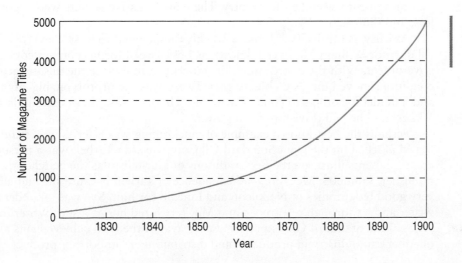

FIGURE 5.1
Increase in Magazine Titles in the 19th Century

music, theater, and literature. Short stories, travel accounts, and virtually every other conceivable subject of interest were all served by some form of periodical. Many of what are now the nation's most prestigious professional and technical journals were started during the last years of the nineteenth century.

Generally, then, by the end of the 1800s, the magazine had become a mature and important medium, as varied as the country's interests and concerns. For many citizens, magazines supplied the major source of opinions and analyses concerning complex issues and topics that were not covered in depth by newspapers. For other people, they offered amusement and trivial entertainment.

Magazines in the Twentieth Century

Magazines gained additional respect early in the twentieth century, when a number of them became vehicles for exposing political corruption, social problems, and economic exploitation. Yet ultimately magazines, like all other American mass media, were produced and distributed for the most part because they made a profit for their owners. Subscriptions were important, paying a considerable portion toward the costs of producing and distributing the publications. But the real profit, as in newspapers, was to be found in attracting advertisers. This advertising function led to success during the first half of the twentieth century for several large-circulation general magazines aimed at a nationwide readership. As we'll see, however, by mid-century television had taken away the role of nationwide advertiser. Magazines had to find a new way to survive.

MAGAZINES AS REFORMERS   One of the most important periods in the history of magazines began just before 1900 and lasted until the end of World War I. During the first decade of the new century, prestigious magazines took the lead in pricking the nation's social, moral, and political conscience as their writers, editors, and publishers probed into the country's economic and political life. As we will see, the conditions revealed during this period resulted in many needed reforms and corrective legislation.

These magazines were the leaders in what we would now call **investigative reporting**. At the time it was called **muckraking**, a term coined by President Theodore Roosevelt to characterize journalists who, instead of extolling the virtues of America, were determined to expose its dark and seamy side. Roosevelt compared such journalists to the "man with the muckrake" in John Bunyan's classic book, *Pilgrim's Progress*. This character would not look up from the filth on the floor even when offered a glittering crown.

Particularly forceful in the muckraking movement were *McClure's, The North American Review, Forum,* the *Atlantic Monthly,* and even the *Saturday Evening Post.* These were national publications with a huge combined circulation. A number of their writer-investigators probed political, social, and economic conditions as part of the popular movement sweeping the country. These investigative writers were vigorous, relentless, and thorough.

As early as the 1870s, *Harper's Weekly* campaigned to oust New York City's political dictator William M. Tweed, known as Boss Tweed for his corrupt control of city government. With the new century, the movement to expose the unsatisfactory social conditions moved into even higher gear. Tweed was the prototypic big city political boss and a model for others to come. Cartoonist Thomas Nast skewered him in *Harper's Weekly* and helped drive him from power.

Perhaps the best-known example of muckraking was a series in *McClure's* by Ida M. Tarbell on the giant Standard Oil Company. Ida Tarbell was a person whose accomplishments illustrate the best traditions of journalism as the watchdog of society. The publisher, Samuel S. McClure, had confidence in Tarbell because she had already written very good biographies of Napoleon and Lincoln for him. She was an understanding writer and a thorough researcher, and McClure hired her as a staff writer to produce the series about Standard Oil, expecting a portrayal of the high achievements and efficiency of American industry in producing and distributing an important product.

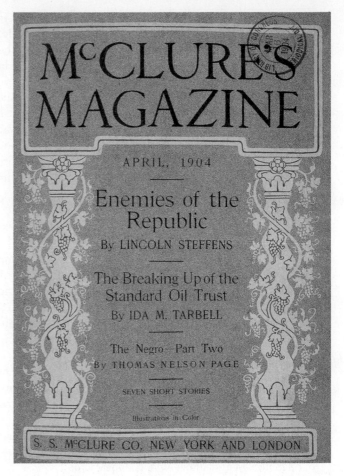

MᶜCLURE'S
MAGAZINE

APRIL, 1904

Enemies of the
Republic
By LINCOLN STEFFENS

The Breaking Up of the
Standard Oil Trust
By IDA M. TARBELL

The Negro—Part Two
By THOMAS NELSON PAGE

SEVEN SHORT STORIES

Illustrations in Color

S. S. MᶜCLURE CO., NEW YORK AND LONDON

Ida Tarbell was a great muckraking journalist and author best known for her "history of the standard oil company." She and other investigative journalists such as Lincoln Steffens published their work in *McClure's Magazine*.

What he got turned out to be something very different. Tarbell spent five years preparing and writing seventeen articles about the giant trust. She dug into every public record she could find; interviewed people; and examined letters, court transcripts, and thousands of other documents. She did report that Standard Oil was superbly organized and that it achieved its objectives with great efficiency. But she also revealed, in merciless detail, how John D. Rockefeller and his corporation had used "bribery, fraud, violence, corruption of public officials and railroads, and the wrecking of competitors by fair means and foul."[9] The public was outraged, and McClure's circulation soared. Tarbell's series gained worldwide recognition as an example of thorough investigative reporting.

The names of other reform-minded writers, like Lincoln Steffens and Ray Stannard Baker, also became household words. Steffens produced the widely praised "Shame of the Cities" series, showing how corrupt governments worked in a number of American communities. Baker's "The Right To Work" was a series on the problems of workers and corruption in labor unions. These writers and dozens of others of the muckraking period made a tremendous impression on the public and became the conscience of the nation. Powerful political figures took up their cry for reform, and both federal and state governments acted to correct the political and economic abuses that were exposed. Eventually, a great many magazines turned to this kind of material. Some did well, but many churned out poorly researched criticisms of virtually everything about which stories could be written. Eventually, the public got tired of this tidal wave of criticism, and magazines had to change. The muckraking period ended with World War I, but it may have been the high point in the social and political importance of magazines.

Time's cover has set news agendas and heralded the rise of celebrities. Martin Luther King, Jr. appeared on the magazine's cover as early as 1957, in the heat of the Civil Rights Movement.

THE CHALLENGE OF TELEVISION   After interest in muckraking declined, new classes of magazines began to appear. One was the **newsmagazine**, a term coined by Henry Luce and Briton Hadden in 1923 when they founded *Time*. New concepts arose, too (or, more accurately, old concepts were revived), such as the **digest**—a collection of excerpts from other publications. Even today, *Reader's Digest* remains one of the most successful magazines of all time. The *New Yorker* was also founded in the 1920s. In 1936 the picture magazine *Life* was first published and met instant success. In 1945 the black picture magazine *Ebony* was founded.

As an advertising medium, the magazines of the nineteenth and early twentieth century were formidable. There were no other widely distributed media for touting wares to the national market; radio would not arrive as a household medium until the 1920s, and television would not be a reality for decades. Newspapers were local, and neither books nor movies were nationally advertising in the same way. For the cost of the space, a magazine circulated nationwide could guarantee that potential customers all over the country would be exposed to the same message.

This advertising function led to the large-circulation general magazines of the first half of the twentieth century. Aimed at a nationwide readership drawn from all walks of life, they truly were magazines in the original, storehouse meaning of the term. For almost thirty years, from the 1920s into the 1950s, large general circulation magazines such as *Life, Look, Collier's,* and the *Saturday Evening Post* dominated the market. National circulations reached into the tens of millions. They had something for everyone in every issue—fiction, biography, travel, humor, advice for the homemaker, a sprinkling of political commentary (but not too much), and sports. Magazines were far ahead of newspapers and books in the effective, sophisticated use of photographs and graphic design. They were beautifully printed, efficiently distributed, rewarding to read, great as an advertising medium, and enormously profitable for their owners. People loved them, and they seemed to be a part of society that would last forever.

Then came television. As this new medium's popularity grew, the general large-circulation magazine found its subscriber pool shrinking and its advertising revenues dwindling. Television was its own kind of "magazine," and it was much easier to use. Furthermore, it was free to the user. Advertisers who were marketing products nationally began turning in droves to the networks and TV commercials.

Within a few years, the magazine industry had to make major adjustments. As it turned out, most of the big general magazines with the "something for everyone" approach died. *Collier's* and *American* were early casualties, succumbing to economic pressures in the 1950s. In the 1960s many others failed, including the large picture magazines *Life* and *Look*. Some, like *Life,* returned in the 1970s and 1980s, but in their new form they have smaller, more carefully targeted circulations.

There are still a few immensely popular magazines appealing to the general population, including *Reader's Digest* (guaranteed circulation 8 million), *TV Guide* (3.2 million), and *National Geographic* (600,000). But most magazines today are not directed to a broad heterogeneous audience preferring a "storehouse" of mixed content. Instead, they aim toward a more defined group with distinct interests. As we'll see next, in place of general, large-circulation magazines there are now thousands of more narrowly focused, special-interest publications.

Meanwhile, the venerable newsmagazines like *Time, Newsweek, U.S. News & World Report,* and *The Economist* have experienced difficulties fighting off the immediacy of the web and electronic media. Although their circulations have either held even or decreased slightly, the demographic category at which they aim—college-educated readers between the ages of twenty-five and forty-four—has nearly tripled during the same period. Thus, they have lost a large share of their target group during a time when their circulations should have boomed. In efforts to regain readers, they have grown slimmer and developed sleek online editions. Whether this type of magazine can survive in today's competitive news and advertising environment, however, remains to be seen.[10]

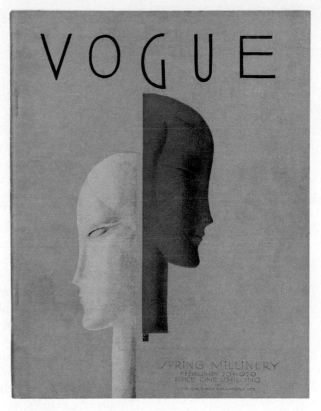

Vogue's cover from February 20, 1929 demonstrates the magazine's commitment to high design.

THE MAGAZINE INDUSTRY TODAY

Types of Magazines

Currently, there are nearly 20,000 periodicals of all kinds in circulation in the United States, and, as previously noted, most of them focus on special interests. There is a specialty magazine (in fact, there are often several) for every conceivable interest, hobby, and taste, from tennis, fly-fishing, and model trains to wine collecting and equestrian pursuits. There is even one called *SUV Power Magazine* for devotees of these vehicles.[11] Some enjoy huge circulations, such as *AARP, The Magazine,* which is the publication of the American Association of Retired Persons (with a guaranteed circulation of 23.5 million). *Consumer Reports,* published by Consumer Union, claims a circulation of 4.5 million.

Although there are various ways to categorize all of these magazines, the industry typically speaks of two broad categories: consumer magazines and business magazines. **Consumer magazines** are those readily available to the public by subscription—to be received through the mail—or by direct purchase at newsstands. **Business magazines,** on the other hand, cover particular industries, trades, and professions and go mainly to persons in those fields. Table 5.2 describes the main types of consumer magazines.

Writer's Digest, a publication with a considerable focus on magazines, provides another classification scheme, this one with four major types:

- **Consumer magazines**—periodicals purchased on newsstands or subscribed to by the general public for home delivery, such as *Reader's Digest, Life, Ebony, TV Guide, Sports Illustrated*
- **Trade journals**—Magazines aimed at a particular trade or industry, such as *Nightclub & Bar* magazine or *International Boat Industry*
- **Sponsored publications**—Internal publications of particular organizations, unions, and other groups, including college and university magazines, customers' publications, and employee magazines, such as *American Legion, Elks Magazine, Consumer Report,* or *Harvard Magazine*
- **Farm publications**—These magazines, like *Farm Journal* and *American Small Farm,* that cover agriculture and agribusiness are given a category of their own because of their large number and the degree of specialization within farm periodicals.

Magazines, however, are more complex than this list suggests. Our own view is indicated below.

- **Newsmagazines:** Serving as national newspapers in America, newsmagazines include *Time,* which was once known for its strong Republican bias but is now more moderately political; *Newsweek,* a less doctrinaire publication, with a generally liberal bias; and *U.S. News & World Report,* with a strong business orientation.

■ **City magazines:** Publications such as *New York, San Diego, The Washingtonian,* and *Boston* exemplify city magazines, which tend to concentrate on the activities of a particular city or region. Most major cities (such as Columbus) and many smaller ones (for example Albuquerque) now have city magazines that investigate public affairs and try to critique the local scene (especially entertainment and restaurants).

■ **Adult interest magazines:** These publications have substantial circulations and generate considerable revenues. They take pride in their fiction and nonfiction articles and interviews as well as their suggestive photographs. This group includes such general-interest adult magazines as *Playboy, Playgirl,* and *Penthouse.* Publications such as *Hustler* and *Screw* cater to people with explicit sexual appetites.

■ **Gay and lesbian magazines:** These are largely style publications aimed at gays and lesbians and include titles such as *The Advocate* and *Out* and feature gender and identity issues and concerns. They cater to a large and growing gay and lesbian demographic and also have specialized titles for transgender and bisexual individuals as well. They have an air of advocacy for gay causes and interests—and feature ads for gay-interest and -oriented products and services, such as travel. They are distinctly different from traditional men's and women's magazines.

■ **Sports magazines:** Americans are preoccupied with sports of all kinds, and there are scores of magazines to satisfy their interests, ranging from *Sports Illustrated* and *ESPN,* which cover a variety of sports, to specialized magazines covering just one sport, such as *Golf, Racquetball,* and *Skiing.* A new sports fashion will quickly generate magazines. When racquetball gained enthusiasts in the 1980s, several racquetball magazines appeared. Sports magazines, like sex magazines, once seemed to be intended for men only, but women now make up more of the audience for general sports magazines, and some sports magazines are designed especially for women.

■ **Opinion magazines:** These include some of the oldest and most respected journals in the United States. They range from the left-leaning *The Nation,* which has been published since the Civil War, to the *National Review,* a conservative magazine founded in the 1950s by columnist William F. Buckley, and the *Weekly Standard,* an entry from the 1990s. Some others are the liberal *American, Prospect, New Republic,* and *The Progressive.*

■ **Intellectual magazines:** These small-circulation publications are very similar to opinion magazines, but they usually have denser copy and are aimed at a more

---

TABLE 5.2

TYPES OF CONSUMER MAGAZINES

Type	Description	Examples
Newsmagazines	Serve as national newspapers in the United States	• *Time* • *Newsweek* • *U.S. News & World Report*
City Magazines	Investigate public affairs of a particular city or region and critique the local scene (especially entertainment and restaurants)	• *New York* • *San Diego* • *The Washingtonian* • *Boston* • *Los Angeles*
Adult Interest Magazines	Generate considerable revenues and substantial subscriptions with fiction and nonfiction articles and interviews, as well as suggestive photographs	General-interest adult magazines: • *Playboy* • *Playgirl* • *Penthouse* Publications for people with explicit sexual appetites: • *Hustler* • *Screw*

Type	Description	Examples
Gay and Lesbian Magazines	Largely style publications for gays and lesbians, with specialized titles for transgender and bisexual individuals. Feature gender and identity issues and concerns, advocacy for gay causes and interests, ads for gay-interest and -oriented products and services, such as travel	• *The Advocate* • *Out* • *Curve* • *Unzipped*
Sports Magazines	For readers interested in sports of all kinds. A new sports fashion will quickly generate magazines. Sports magazines, like sex magazines, once seemed to be intended for men only, but women now make up more of the audience for general sports magazines, and some sports magazines are designed especially for women.	General, covering a variety of sports: • *Sports Illustrated* • *ESPN* Specialized, covering just one sport: • *Golf* • *Racquetball* • *Skiing*
Opinion Magazines	These include some of the oldest and most respected journals in the United States.	• *The Nation* • *National Review* • *Weekly Standard* • *Prospect* • *New Republic* • *The Progressive*
Intellectual Magazines	Small-circulation publications very similar to opinion magazines but usually have denser copy and are aimed at a more intellectual audience. Both opinion magazines and intellectual magazines pride themselves on "influencing the influential."	• *Commentary* • *American Scholar* • *Tikkun*
Quality Magazines	Similar to opinion and intellectual magazines but usually have larger circulations (perhaps as high as 500,000) and reach a more general audience.	• *Atlantic Monthly* • *Harper's* • *The Smithsonian* • *The New Yorker*
Men's Interest Magazines	Sometimes overlap with health magazines and sports magazines; other similar magazines represent men's preoccupation with fashion and grooming. And there are the so-called "laddie" magazines for hip young men.	Men's Fashion and Health: • *Men's Health* • *GQ* Laddie magazines: • *FHM* • *Razor* • *Maxim*
Women's Interest Magazines	Some of the most successful magazines in the country, with the highest circulations, are aimed at women.	Homemaking emphasis: • *Ladies' Home Journal* • *Better Homes and Gardens* • *Good Housekeeping* Fashion/Lifestyle: • *O, The Oprah Magazine* • *Vogue* Feminist: • *More*

continued

TABLE 5.2 *continued*		
Type	**Description**	**Examples**
Humor Magazines	Taking hold in the 1870s with *Puck, The Comic Weekly*, humor magazines have been with us ever since.	• *Harvard Lampoon* • *Mad*
Business Magazines	Some business magazines offer broad-based news coverage; others are designed to advise their readers on the machinations of the stock market. There are also magazines covering high technology and electronics.	Leading business magazines: • *Business Week* • *The Economist* • *Fortune* • *Smart Money* • *Forbes* • *Barron's* Technology: • *Wired* • *Computerworld*

intellectual audience. Examples include *Commentary, American Scholar,* and *Tikkun.* Both opinion magazines and intellectual magazines pride themselves on "influencing the influential."

■ **Quality magazines:** Although these magazines are similar to opinion and intellectual magazines, they usually have larger circulations (perhaps as high as 500,000) and reach a more general audience. Some examples are *Atlantic Monthly, Harper's, The Smithsonian,* and *The New Yorker.*

■ **Men's interest magazines:** These publications, such as *Men's Health,* sometimes overlap with health magazines and sports magazines. *GQ* and other similar magazines represent men's preoccupation with fashion and grooming. And there are the so-called "laddie" magazines like *FHM, Razor,* and *Maxim* for hip young men.

■ **Women's interest magazines:** Some of the most successful magazines in the country with the highest circulations are aimed at women. The first American magazine in the nineteenth century to have a circulation of more than 1 million was *Ladies' Home Journal,* which continues today. Other magazines in this class are *O, The Oprah Magazine; Vogue; Better Homes and Gardens; and Good Housekeeping.* A women's interest magazine that departs from the traditional mold of women's periodicals is *Ms.,* which reflects a moderate feminist viewpoint (*Ms.* led the way

Two conservative opinion magazines, *National Review* and *Weekly Standard,* were established by different generations of ideologically oriented editors who offer thoughtful analysis of public affairs from a right of center perspective.

for feminist magazines, and today there are several available with varying editorial formulas and viewpoints). There are many magazines for teenaged girls and young women, one of the best known being *Seventeen*.

■ **Humor magazines:** Taking hold in the 1870s with *Puck, The Comic Weekly,* humor magazines have been with us ever since and include *Harvard Lampoon* and *Mad*. Related to humor magazines are comic books, forming an industry in themselves. Many of these publications are not humorous at all but use cartoon-style artwork to present complex plots and characters and diverse views and social commentary. Comics, of course, fit into this category though they are quite numerous and have wide appeal.

■ **Business magazines:** Few subjects are more compelling to the American audience than business. Among leading business magazines are *Business Week,* published by McGraw-Hill; *Fortune,* a Time-Warner publication; *Smart Money,* a personal business magazine published by Hearst; and *Forbes,* which once used the whimsical slogan "A Capitalist Tool." *Barron's* is published by Dow Jones, which also produces the *Wall Street Journal*. Some business magazines offer broad-based news coverage; others are designed to advise their readers on the machinations of the stock market. There are also magazines covering high technology and electronics such as *Wired* and *Computerworld* (in fact, the publishing industry has benefited a great deal from changes in technology; there are many new publications just on computers).

Consumer magazines, like *Wine Enthusiast* and *Ebony,* are also called "slicks," because of their coated paper. Many in this category are mass-circulation magazines, but a subcategory, the secondary consumer magazine, includes broadly circulated magazines that concentrate on a specialized topic or a specific interest—examples are *Private Pilot, Yachting,* and *Gourmet*.

The Life Cycle of Magazines

American magazines seem to be in a continual process of birth, adaptation, and death. Jay McGill, a senior vice president at Hearst Magazines (profiled in this chapter's Media Leaders Insights feature) says the life cycle of magazines is quite predictable, and it includes the following stages:

LAUNCH.   A publisher usually starts a new magazine in response to a social or economic phenomenon that points out an information need not being met for a given target audience. For example, if more individuals began to make investments, and traditional businesses were not providing pertinent information, there might be a need for a new personal finance magazine.

GROWTH.   A demand for the publication is established, and the publisher makes a strategic investment in circulation with an aggressive search for primary and secondary audiences, that is, those for whom the magazine is specifically directed plus others who will need it occasionally. Content is seen as fresh and relevant, and advertising revenues grow.

MATURITY.   After relative stability, growth slows as competitors enter the market, and levels of circulation and advertising growth slow down. Content may seem "old school," and there is a struggle to manage costs.

DECLINE.   Social or economic shifts cause reader interest to decrease. Advertising rates decline, leading to less revenue. The downturn is marked by fewer pages, staff cuts, and

MEDIA LEADERS INSIGHTS: MAGAZINES

JAY MCGILL

Senior Vice President

Hearst Magazines International

Jay McGill has extensive experience as the publisher of well-known, large circulation magazines, including *Popular Mechanics* and *Smart Money.* He began his career in advertising sales for community newspapers outside Chicago after graduating from Marquette University. His sales work led him to his first job in magazines, as an ad representative for *Popular Mechanics,* one of the magazines owned by the Hearst Group. He worked his way up in the company to vice president and publisher. He currently serves as a senior vice president of the company, a position he held while leading *Smart Money* as its publisher. In the course of his successful tenure in magazines, he has been publisher of several other titles, including *Country Living*, *Sports Afield*, and *Motor Boating and Sailing.* Magazines he has led have won National Magazine Awards, and one was named "Magazine of the Year" by *Advertising Age.* McGill's keen understanding of the life cycle of magazines is much appreciated by anyone tracking their development.

1. **When and under what circumstances did you first realize the import of new media or the digital age?**

   I was the publisher of *Country Living* in 1995 when Cathie Black came in as the new president of the Magazine Division. Her first edict was "no more memos." All written correspondence was to be conducted via email. I did not even have an email address at the time and my typing skills were lousy (still are). I learned quickly that communicating digitally was both efficient and dangerous. One had to be diligent not to hit "reply all" or respond to messages sent as bcc's. It was also much easier for others to misinterpret one's "tone." I realized the shorter, the better.

2. **What impact did that experience have on you personally or professionally?**

   I believe it greatly increased my overall communication skills and demystified the computer. Until that time, I was what I would call "compu-phobic." Soon after mastering the skills of email and word processing, I was surfing the "information superhighway" in search of anything that was in any way useful. Back in the mid-nineties, the content offerings online were not very focused, but even then I realized that the web was going to have a profound impact on consumers' information, entertainment, and communication needs. The big question then was how websites would sustain themselves after they had burned through their venture capital?

3. **How have digital technologies and/or thinking influenced your work at Hearst Magazines or in the magazine industry generally? What is being done to harness these new possibilities?**

   Digital technologies have created just-in-time and on-demand information and entertainment options for consumers. It has changed the demands and expectations users have of all media. We, as publishers, must embrace the web and use it to keep information flowing to our customers. It's not enough for magazine brands to interact with readers once a week or month. Web and mobile platforms now allow for an ongoing dialog with users/readers. We learn what is of most interest to them, allowing us to refine and focus our content.

4. **What is the greatest challenge or benefit of the digital revolution for magazines from your perspective as a publisher and global executive?**

   Digital technology offers publishers the opportunity to deliver their content across multiple channels more efficiently. The challenge lies in how to package the content so it will meet reader's needs and expectations. So far, offering exact replicas of magazine pages via the web has not been successful. Getting customers to pay for content delivered digitally has been a challenge as well.

5. Are you optimistic about the digital future?

Absolutely! I read the *NY Times* every morning on my Kindle reader. I believe that eventually all print media will be transmitted digitally to some sort of "reader," eliminating the need for paper, printing plants, and postage. I also believe readers will become editors, able to tailor-make the content delivered to them.

6. What, if any, advice do you have for a person who aspires to a career in magazines?

I would advise anyone to forget whatever they know about magazines as they are today. Magazine publishing in the future will require an open mind and a willingness to experiment with content and the multiple delivery platforms technology provides.

a sense of drift—sometimes accompanied by frequent remakes and efforts to revive a once-healthy publication.

DEATH.   The magazine stops publishing, a move generally caused by an inability to adapt the publication to social or economic shifts, allowing readers and advertisers to lose interest.

The length of the life span during which these stages happen varies considerably. McGill provides the example of magazines associated with celebrities: "Some, like *O, The Oprah Magazine,* with 2.5 million readers are highly successful and last for years. Others like *Rosie* (the former *McCall*'s, which was renamed for comedienne Rosie O'Donnell) or *Sly,* a magazine that presumed that young men would be inspired by Sylvester Stallone, do not."[12] In the case of *Sly,* now largely forgotten, the period from launch to death took only two issues!

A lot of magazines go through this life cycle. The number of new magazines that appear each year has grown sharply in recent times and is now nothing short of phenomenal. Industry sources indicate that literally hundreds of new consumer magazines are introduced every year. During the 1990s, for example, about 5,000 new consumer magazines were established; reportedly, the number of titles grew by 68%. In 2007, the number of consumer magazines rose to 6,800 titles.

The Magazine Publishers Association, a trade group, charts magazine launches each year, using convenient topical categories (which denote content somewhat narrowly), rather than the type of magazine, although there is some overlap. See Table 5.3. Some of the newcomers on the list were established by large publishing companies; others were low-budget projects begun by individuals.

In recent years, magazine starts and failures have paralleled changes in the general economy. As America has moved from an economy based on heavy manufacturing and extractive industries (such as coal, iron, and oil) to one based on information, communication, and services, a corresponding decline has occurred in business publications serving the older industries, with an increase in magazines aimed at covering the computer, electronic, and financial services.

Magazines like newspapers have a value chain, which organizes both editorial and advertising content. Moreover, there are six distinct stages or activities in magazine publishing, namely:

- Content creation and acquisition
- Editing and content processing
- Production for publication
- Printing and binding
- Advertising sales, marketing, and circulation
- Distribution

TABLE 5.3

NEW U.S. MAGAZINE LAUNCHES BY INTEREST CATEGORY 2007

38	Metropolitan/Regional/State	4	Pop Culture
27	Crafts/Games/Hobbies/Models	3	Sex
15	Automotive	3	Fishing/Hunting
13	Fashion/Beauty/Grooming	3	Dogs/Pets
13	Special Interest	2	Science/Technology
12	Entertainment/Performing Arts	2	Military/Naval
11	Black/Ethnic	2	Comic Technique
10	Home/Home Service	2	Gay/Lesbian
8	Health	2	Nature/Ecology
8	Sports	2	Teen
7	Children's	2	Literary/Reviews/Writing
7	Women's	2	Political/Social Topics
6	Arts/Antiques	2	Fitness
5	Camping/Outdoor Recreation	2	Travel
5	Computers	1	Gardening
5	Business/Finance	1	Gaming
4	Epicurean	1	TV/Radio/Communications/Electronics
4	Motorcycles	1	Media Personalities
4	Bridal	1	Horses/Riding/Breeding
4	Music		
4	Men's	**248**	**Total New U.S. Magazine Launches**

Note: This list represents weekly, bimonthly, monthly, and quarterly titles only.

Source: *Samir Husni's Guide to New Consumer Magazines*, 2008.

While these functions have been pretty constant for decades, in each area there is an active connection to the digital world. For example, content comes online as writers increasingly are outsourced—and some content is aggregated from other sources, often thanks to digital sources. Similarly, editing and content processing benefits from computer systems, graphics, and outsourced staffing. Production can also be done on- or offsite and is guided now by software systems. Printing and binding is usually farmed out to vendors. Ad sales, marketing, and circulation are strongly supported by Internet

TABLE 5.4

NUMBER OF MAGAZINES 1997–2007

Year	Total	Consumer Only
1997	18,047	7,712
1998	18,606	7,864
1999	17,970	9,311
2000	17,815	8,138
2001	17,694	6,336
2002	17,321	5,340
2003	17,254	6,234
2004	18,821	7,188
2005	18,267	6,325
2006	19,419	6,734
2007	**19,532**	**6,809**

Note: Includes, but is not limited to, magazines in North America regardless of publishing frequency

Source: MRI Fall, 2007, *National Directory of Magazines*, 2008, Oxbridge Communications.

links and strategies. Distribution can be done much more precisely, connecting potential sales sites, newsstands, and stores with direct orders, rather than engaging in a speculative guessing game.

Typically, entrepreneurs who want to start a new magazine develop a business plan charting a course for the magazine and "proving" with statistics (on potential readership and related marketing questions) that there is a niche (market) for the new publication. Then a staff is hired and offices are established. Typically, printing is contracted out, as are arrangements for distribution and circulation. Advertising space can be sold either by the magazine staff or by national advertising media representatives.

Because, as we have noted, magazine publishers rarely own their own printing presses, the initial investment needed to found a magazine is rather modest, and so starting a magazine is relatively easy. Maintaining it is much more difficult. On average, only two in ten of the newcomers are expected to survive for more than ten years. Many new magazines start with high hopes, only to find that no significant niche exists to make the new publication profitable. Most leading observers agree that many magazines die because the publisher failed to strike a balance between revenue from circulation and revenue from advertising. Some magazines die because the publisher failed to fine-tune the product to meet changing fashions and interest.

The Magazine Staff

The magazine staff is organized to carry out the functions indicated above and includes the editorial staff and the business staff.

The **editorial staff**, which establishes an "editorial formula" and determines what the content will be, will produce the magazine and prepare it for publication. The staff includes the:

- **Editor-in-chief** or **editor**—has overall responsibility for planning and organizing the magazine and often consults with the publisher and advertising director, among others.
- **Managing editor**—typically hires and supervises the staff and also arranges for freelancers and other content sources.
- **Associate editor**—responsible for specific departments or coverage areas of the magazine.
- **Senior, assistant, and departmental editors**—usually report to the associate editor and handle specialized areas (national affairs, science, etc.) or types of content (articles, special sections, letters, and commentary).
- **Writers, reporters, columnists, and bloggers**—cover specific assignments and report to supervising editors, above.
- **Editorial assistants**—junior staff who assist others; some magazines also have fact checkers, copy editors, and others.
- **Art or design director**—designs the graphic presentation of the magazine and may have various assistants for photography, art direction, and other areas.
- **Webmaster or digital content director**—produces the online version of the magazine, either drawing on overall content or sometimes special material only available online.

The **business staff** of the magazine handles all general organizational, finance, advertising, circulation, and other activities and can include the:

- **Publisher**—has operational and fiscal responsibility for the magazine. This person may be the overall boss or report to the editor-in-chief or to a president or chief executive.
- **Advertising manager or director**—responsible for acquiring all advertising and supervising the sales force and other specialists, such as designers.

- **Associate and assistant advertising managers**—do work delegated by the advertising manager.
- **Advertising sales person**—sells advertising to advertisers or to ad buyers at ad agencies or with digital advertising networks.
- **Circulation or distribution manager**—connects published magazines to distribution agents and services, including persuading them to stock the magazine at their newsstands or other points of sale.
- **Production manager**—responsible for transforming the raw content into a finished product ready for distribution and sale.

Some other positions in magazines include business development specialists and audience development managers, both responsible for finding new business and sources of revenue for the magazine as well as thinking creatively about the audience—and potential audiences that will drive ad sales.

There are many other specialists and assistants in the magazine business, and the number of these at a given magazine depends on the size of the publication and its rate of growth. Magazines range from small operations with only a few staff members to those with hundreds of staffers. A careful look at the masthead will provide a portrait of the staffing of any given magazine.

Making a Profit

Consumer magazines are the industry's major moneymakers. According to Magazine Publishers of America (MPA), revenues from consumer magazine advertising and circulation totaled $35 billion in 2007, and of that amount circulation generated $10 billion, composed of subscriptions at $6.8 billion and single-copy sales at $3.2 billion, whereas advertising accounted for $25 billion. As we have noted, magazines earn money in two ways: through **circulation**, or selling copies of the magazine, and through advertising. *Circulation* is the number of copies of magazines published and sold. Unsold magazines are called *returns*.

CIRCULATION   About half of the total earnings of consumer magazines comes from circulation, and the other half comes from advertising. The vast majority of sales are through mailed subscriptions. Approximately 75 to 80% are accounted for by subscription while about 15 to 20% are sold on newsstands. The term *newsstand* actually refers to a variety of places magazines are sold, as listed in Table 5.5.

TABLE 5.5

WHERE MAGAZINES WERE SOLD 1998–2007

	1998	2007
Supermarkets* (Safeway, A&P, Shoprite, Walmart, Target)	45%	44%
Discount Stores/Mass Merchandisers* (Walmart, Target, K-mart)	15	9
Bookstores (Borders, Barnes & Noble)	8	11
Drugstores (CVS, Rite Aid, Walgreens)	10	10
Terminals (Bus Terminals, Airports, Train Stations)	4	7
Convenience (7-Eleven)	6	5
Newsstands (Hudson News, city street newsstands)	3	2
Club Bargain (Costco, Sams Club)	–	1
Others	9	11
Total	**100%**	**100%**

*As of 2005, magazine sales in supercencer stores (huge retail formats that combine grocery and discount store formats) are reported in the supermarket category.

Source: Harrington Associates, 1999, 2008.

For the U.S. B-to-B (business-to-business) magazines, the revenue picture is radically different. In 2008, forecasters say, revenues will reach $11.9 billion, of which a bulk will come from advertising. Thus, subscriptions are not a significant part of the profit picture in the business magazine.

In fact, many business and trade magazines are actually given away free; that is, they have what are called **controlled nonpaying distributions**. The magazines using this pattern of distribution can afford to do so because they literally blanket the relevant field or industry, which makes them especially attractive to advertisers. Magazines aimed directly at a given industry tend to be read by a large percentage of people in that field—exactly the people who the advertisers want to reach.

ADVERTISING   Like all other media that are supported by advertising, a magazine must pay keen attention to its audience in order to survive. For magazines, as for other media, audience ratings and audience surveys are important in determining advertising rates. But as Philip Dougherty has pointed out, there is an interesting twist for magazines:

> If an editor creates a magazine that is so on target that subscribers refuse to part with it, that's bad. If, however, the editor puts out a magazine that means so little to each individual that it gets passed from hand to hand, that's good. Reason: the more the magazine is passed along, the higher the total audience figure will be. In that way, the ad agency rates will look more efficient to agency people, who will be more likely to put the magazine on their schedule [for advertising].[13]

Of course today much magazine content is forwarded online by web visitors. The old methods of simply counting circulation figures and estimating **pass-along rates** (whereby a magazine is read by several people who are not its primary subscribers) are no longer adequate. In the Internet age, magazines have not only vigorously sought advertising revenues via the Internet but have also worked diligently to create new **metrics**, or measurement methods, for the web.[14] Web metrics include unique visitors to a site as well as usage patterns, transactions, site performance, and usability.

Advertisers love specialized magazines because they are so effective in reaching precisely the categories of consumers who buy their kind of product. For example, no maker of expensive handcrafted bamboo fly-fishing rods would advertise those wares on national television, in a newspaper, or on local radio, because most people using those media would not be interested. To reach the attention of relatively affluent buyers with a potential interest in such equipment, scattered all over the nation, and perhaps even in foreign countries, the maker has a better chance with a single ad placed in one or more magazines devoted to fly-fishing. Subscribers will see the ad, and the magazine will likely be passed on to other fly-fishing enthusiasts. Furthermore, such advertising is cheap by comparison with other media. It is because of these factors that so many narrowly focused magazines can make a profit today. By this pattern of targeting its markets, the magazine industry has adapted to and survived the challenge posed by television.

Magazines are very much a creature of the economy and especially sensitive to individual wealth, because they deal largely with specialized topics that often require affluent readers. An executive at *Esquire* explained that magazines are after "the new affluent reader," who is more *psychographic* than *demographic*, meaning that people with midrange incomes are also buying products like Gucci shoes and clothes by Ralph Lauren. Luxury advertisers marketing expensive cars, home furnishings, clothing, watches, and electronic toys often choose magazines for their media buys. Indeed, many new media and e-commerce companies also pick magazines aimed at the luxury market, which increasingly crosses income lines, once thought to be barriers.

Like other media, magazines are creatures of the marketplace. Although they can be a powerful medium for precise, demographically defined advertising, they are also susceptible to fickle consumer demands. As Chapter 11 explains, media advertising is a complex and dynamic process that links together specific forms of advertising content, specific media, and consumer demands for particular products. Thus, when consumer demands change, advertising content in magazines moves up and down in volume, causing the magazine industry to prosper or decline accordingly.

To some the way magazines court business may sound a bit crass. For example, an article in *Folio,* which serves the magazine industry, began as follows:

> That din you hear is the sound of media players fighting to be the publication, or the network, or the Web site to deliver any given advertiser's message to a potential customer.... Any magazine publisher who wants to stand out from the crowd has to understand how media buyers interact with the marketers they serve, and show how his or her magazine can help.[15]

And here is what advertising agency executives recommend to magazines that want to survive in an increasingly competitive market:

- Spend a lot of time creating your pitch.
- Customize your offerings to match clients' objectives.
- Impact the bottom line.
- Research reach, circ, and buzz.[16]

This "insider's lingo" needs some explanation. The "pitch" is a term used in media and business for the approach or persuasive messaged aimed at persuading the client or advertiser to accept the proposal being made. "Customizing" or addressability means tailoring the message to the needs and interests of the clients. The "bottom line" is the financial benefit that will come from the transaction in terms of a net gain of revenue or profit. "Reach" is the geographic or demographic scope the message will cover. Some ad people speak of the "penetration" or "footprint," which can mean the same thing. Finally "circ" is circulation, or just where the magazines go and to whom, and "buzz" is the talk about the product or service—whether anyone cares and thinks it is cool or interesting.

Ownership Trends

Much that was said in earlier chapters about trends in media ownership also applies to magazines. Today, many are owned by chains. The competitive environment of specialized publishing makes chain ownership especially suitable for magazines. The most successful magazine publishers produce more than one magazine, because if one magazine fails (and, as we have seen, failure is common), the company still has others to keep their company alive. In fact, new magazines that succeed are often quickly sold to large magazine and media companies, whose economies of scale make it profitable to publish many different magazines under the same corporate roof. The resulting concentration of magazine ownership, whether by multinational firms from abroad or by large media corporations in the United States, appears to be continuing unabated.

The Influence and Importance of Magazines

As we have shown, magazines differ greatly in their circulations. But the largest magazines are not necessarily the most powerful or important, nor can total revenues be equated with power and influence. Under such an evaluation *TV Guide,* once the nation's most financially successful publication, boasting a large circulation, would seem more important than a magazine like *Foreign Affairs,* an influential quarterly with a very modest circulation. But whereas millions may read the former and only a few thousand the latter, the smaller magazine may influence a much more powerful audience.

The journals of opinion like *The Nation* and *Weekly Standard* exert influence far beyond their numbers, as their articles are frequently picked up by blogs and cable news shows. They are read by government officials, business leaders, educators, intellectuals, and others who affect public affairs more than does the average person. The opinion magazines set agendas, shape ideas, start trends, and offer labels for virtually everything (including people, such as "millenials" and the "Gen X'ers"). Perhaps more importantly, they speak to what it is that magazines do better than almost any other medium.

Clearly, magazines inform, but compared with the reach of television news or the immediacy and impact of daily newspapers, this function is modest in any overall assessment.

The same is true for entertainment, where television and movies are champions. Even fiction, where magazines were once very important, accounts for little of their content today. In none of these is the magazine a strong contender.

It is in the realm of *opinion* that magazines triumph. They have the luxury of expressing their biases, being openly liberal or conservative and as grumpy or savage as they choose. Other media, trying to court larger audiences, could never accomplish this.

Magazines also can make longer investigations and present their findings in equally lengthy form. For example, the *New Yorker,* a widely respected opinion magazine, can have lengthy articles that take up topics such as law and justice in a cerebral and philosophical sense, or it can present articles about the United Nations that severely challenge the moral authority of that institution. The *New Yorker* does this kind of thing in the context of a ninety-year history during which it has earned a high reputation for such analyses. As with other respected opinion magazines, when the *New Yorker* speaks on an issue, people listen, and the ideas it presents are picked up and diffused to more popular magazines and newspapers and even to television audiences, which is far beyond its readership. Thus, a respected opinion magazine can have an influence well over what the number of its subscribers would suggest.

THE FUTURE OF MAGAZINES

Many of the same challenges faced by newspapers, because of the development of multimedia computers and the World Wide Web, also confront magazines. Changes are taking place very rapidly in this technological world, and it is impossible to predict over the long run how they will influence any of the print media. Increasingly, some magazines are mostly online, and some are actually dispensing their print editions. With, search engines and portals like Google or Yahoo! and social networking sites like Facebook, MySpace, or YouTube, people create their own specialized "magazines" without benefit of paper or traditional magazine editors.

The demise of magazines has been predicted many times past. However, for the foreseeable future, most analysts think the magazine will continue to exist in its present form, because of its portability and its permanence, whether online[17] or on paper. As magazine expert Charles P. Daly and his colleagues note:

> On more than one occasion in the past 250 years or so, someone has sounded the death knell for the American magazine. Improvements in the printing press and mail distribution in the late 1880s enabled some magazines to increase their circulations dramatically. That was bad news for one editor who gloomily predicted that magazines wouldn't be worth reading anymore because large circulations could only mean mediocrity and conservatism.[18]

Of particular importance for the future are magazines that are on the Internet. New terms have been developed to label magazines that are available online. For example, the term **e-zines** has come into use to identify magazines available in this form. These range from highly specialized and crude tracts to truly sophisticated electronic magazines. Web pages are easily found for subscribing to magazines, often at significant discounts. A number of pay-per-read sites provide full-text articles. A good source for finding information about magazines on the World Wide Web is www.newslink.org or www.foliomag.com.

MAGAZINES AND THE DIGITAL REVOLUTION

Given the capacity for digital communication to target specific magazine subscribers for advertisers and to more effectively create magazine content that speaks directly to readers, some analysts say that the impact of the Internet on magazines has been disappointing, at least up to 2008 or so. As media economist Lucy Küng has written, "to date many predictions concerning the impact of the Internet on the magazine sector have not held true. Magazines have not shifted wholesale from paper to online versions, and the spate of online only magazines has [been] largely subsidized"[19] with only a few notable exceptions such as *Salon* and *Slate*. This will no doubt change as the cost benefits of online publishing are clearer.

From the earliest days of the digital revolution, magazines used computer power and digitization for such mechanical operations as typesetting and production and were among the first to pioneer so-called digital ink, transmitting their products on a flat screen. Various digital reader devices, such as the Amazon Kindle and Sony Reader, for example, offer magazine subscriptions without benefit of ink on paper. Most magazines, as noted earlier, have a web presence. In some instances the entire content of an issue is available free online. In other instances the web content is only a teaser to get readers to buy the paper magazine. Still, the websites of magazines include large numbers of blogs on specific topics and some that are maintained by specific writers and columnists, among others. Podcasts, which offer audio transmissions of magazine articles, are also available, and increasingly handheld devices and smart phones have evolved; magazine content is directed to that platform as well. Several magazines also offer readers' blogs and other social networking features. And, of course, magazine content is often linked and forwarded by readers to their friends and contacts.

The Magazine Publishers Association has an annual digital conference—its fifth was in 2009—to bring together so-called digital thought leaders with digital pioneers, mobile and Internet executives, and even digital journalists. Topics included "digital drivers," with magazine publishers explaining how they use video, social networking, and mobile platforms in their businesses. Increasingly magazines are getting their "readers" to tune into online video. Especially hard for magazines has been allowing digital media to "slice, dice, and aggregate" their content with only small segments being used by other media sources. However, this may be a great benefit to magazines. After all, word of mouth and old-fashioned legacy advertising was the traditional way for magazines to attract readers. Now people who use a search site might learn about a magazine through that publication's web advertising. Similarly, social networking sites like MySpace or Facebook—or micro sites like Twitter—can be a source of information about a magazine and drive potential readers in that way. Magazines that have historically sold their content find it difficult to give it away.

Individual magazines and magazine groups have experimented in various ways to harness the digital future on their behalf, including having ad-supported titles online, selling selected content in digital form, getting companies to sell their products on a magazine website, using digital promotion to spur print sales, and using social networking and an online presence to build relationships with subscribers.[20]

Whatever the relationship between their print and electronic form in the future, the magazine is not only likely to survive as a medium, it may also thrive in the decades ahead. Over their long history, magazines have faced many challenges. They survived by adapting to an ever-changing system of mass communication. The great diversity to be

TABLE 5.6

NUMBER OF MAGAZINES WITH WEBSITES 2004–2008

Year	Total	Consumer Only
2004	9,355	4,210
2005	10,131	4,712
2006	10,818	5,395
2007	11,623	5,950
2008	**13,247**	**6,453**

Note: Data as of March 2008

Source: *Oxbridge Communications*, 2008.

found in the magazine industry provides something for everyone and in a form that is current, portable, permanent, and presented at a level within the readers' capability. That is a formidable formula. So although the medium may have to adapt to a new mix in the media system over time, it seems at this point that Americans will continue to support this voice for their many interests.

CHAPTER REVIEW

- The magazine as a contemporary medium serves the traditional media functions of surveillance, monitoring what is going on, transmitting the culture, and entertaining the population. Its most notable function, however, is correlation, interpreting the society by bringing together diverse facts, trends, and sequences of events.

- Magazines as we know them today started in London, where there was a concentration of urbane, affluent, and literate people. The earliest magazines were mainly instruments of politics, both in England and in the United States.

- It was difficult to establish magazines in the American colonies because people were spread out, literacy was not widespread, and the population was not affluent. In addition, such factors as transportation and mail service were uncertain at best.

- During the 1800s societal changes encouraged the growth of magazines in the United States. The population grew, cities became larger, more citizens were educated, the mail became more reliable and less costly, and all forms of transportation improved. In addition, it was a century of great issues.

- The magazine flourished early in this century during the era of the "muckrakers." Prestigious magazines took the lead in exposing corruption in business and government and unacceptable social conditions. Magazines played a significant role in the reform movement that characterized the first decade of the 1900s.

- New kinds of magazines appeared in the 1920s. One category was the newsmagazine. Another was the large-circulation magazine containing something for everyone. Such magazines had huge circulations, making them important vehicles for national advertising. They were very successful, and it seemed that they would be a permanent feature of society.

- When television arrived it absorbed much of the advertising that had previously gone to the large general magazines, many of which failed in consequence. However, the industry adapted remarkably well by developing a host of specialty magazines aimed at markets with well-defined interests and characteristics.

- The magazine business today is fiercely competitive and very dynamic. An impressive variety of magazines are published. Every year, many are started, although the majority fail. The two basic types are consumer and business magazines; of the two, the consumer predominates.

- Trends in American magazine ownership parallel other media; that is, most are owned by chains. Large conglomerates, with many kinds of businesses, buy magazines and add them to their diverse holdings.

- The sheer number of people who subscribe to or even read a magazine is no indicator of either its ability to make a profit or its influence. The most influential periodicals are the opinion magazines. Their circulations are small compared with more popular magazines, but the people who read such magazines tend more than others to occupy positions of power and leadership, where their decisions can markedly influence public affairs.

- Although the new computer technologies challenge magazines as well as newspapers generally, the magazine is likely to survive in its present form. It is a medium that presents material tailored for the interests of specific kinds of people in a manner that they prefer. It is likely that Americans will be reading magazines for a long time to come.

- Magazines increasingly have digital strategies—online editions and connections to search engines, social networking, and mobile media.

STRATEGIC QUESTIONS

1. What communications functions do magazines serve—and which, if any, are most important?
2. Why are magazines called "specialized" media?
3. How does the history of magazines inform magazine publishing today?
4. How have magazines adapted to the digital revolution?
5. What has been the social role of magazines?
6. How does the life cycle of the magazine inform magazine publishers about the likelihood of success of a new magazine?

KEY CONCEPTS & TERMS

Muckrakers 96
Newsmagazine 98
Consumer magazine 99

Opinion magazine 102
Business magazine 99
E-zines 111

Start-up 88
Web magazines 111

ENDNOTES

1. For a comprehensive look at the magazine industry, see *Magazines, A Comprehensive Guide and Handbook,* 2008–09 (New York: Magazine Publishers Association, 2008); also see www.magazine.org.
2. Theodore Peterson, *Magazines in the Twentieth Century,* 2nd ed. (Urbana, IL: University of Illinois Press, 1964), p. 442.
3. Many of the details in this section concerning the first magazines were drawn from James P. Wood, *Magazines in the United States* (New York: Ronald, 1949), pp. 3–9.
4. Wood, *Magazines in the United States,* p. 10.
5. The details of these early American attempts to produce magazines are drawn from Frank Luther Mott, *A History of American Magazines, 1741–1850* (Cambridge, MA: Harvard University Press, 1930), vol. 1, pp. 13–72.
6. Melvin L. DeFleur, William V. D'Antonio, and Lois DeFleur, *Sociology* (Glenview, IL: Scott, Foresman, 1972), p. 279.
7. These various figures were painstakingly assembled from historical accounts and various early government documents by Mott in his five-volume *History of American Magazines.* As he notes, many are approximations. The present section is a compilation of figures from several of his volumes. A useful contemporary scorecard on magazines is Samir Husni's *New Guide to Consumer Magazines* (New York: Oxbridge Communications, 1997).
8. Mott, *History of American Magazines,* vol. 4, p. 10.
9. Wood, *Magazines in the United States,* p. 131.
10. Fleming Meeks, "God Is Not Providing," *Forbes,* Oct. 30, 1989, pp. 151–158. See also Magazine Publishers Association (MPA) Fact Sheet on "Average Circulation for Top ABC Magazines, 2007." See also www.magazine.org.
11. See MPA Fact Sheet on "New and Noted Magazines, 2007."
12. Lecture by Jay McGill, Hearst Magazine International, Fordham Graduate School of Business, Nov. 7, 2007.
13. Philip Dougherty, "Saturday Review's New Drive," *The New York Times,* April 2, 1979.
14. Maria Aspan, "The Web Way to Magazine Ad Sales," *The New York Times,* Aug. 21, 2007, and Louise Story, "How Many Hits? Depending on Who's Counting," *The New York Times,* Oct. 22, 2007.
15. Susan Thea Posnock, "Inside Media Minds," *Folio,* May 2000, p. 14.
16. Posnock, "Inside Media Minds," p. 2.
17. Jon Fine, "A Dogged Web Mag Pioneer," *BusinessWeek,* June 18, 2007, p. 22; see also www.nerve.com for updated information.
18. Charles P. Daly, Patrick Henry, and Ellen Ryder, *The Magazine Publishing Industry* (Boston, MA: Allyn and Bacon, 1997), p. xii.
19. Kung, Lucy, *Strategic Management in Media* (Los Angeles, CA: Sage Publications), 2008, pp. 48–49.
20. Laura Petrecca, "Magazines Experiment with Digital Platforms," *USA Today,* http://www.usatoday.com/tech/news/techinnovations/2006-06-22-digital-magazine_x.htm.

Motion Pictures: The Great Entertainer

Movies, the great entertainer that had their origins on the stage, have moved with dispatch to capitalize on the digital age. First there is digital cinema, explained later in this chapter, which is responsible for vast improvements in pictures and sound. Second, movies have adapted to virtually every new technical platform of the digital age from iPods and other smart phones to websites, video-on-demand, and others. If the digital age is largely about distribution and interactive messages, the movies have stepped up to provide full motion visual content on social networking and search websites among others. There are websites for motion picture companies, individual movies, actors, and other players in this most imaginative of industries. Far from being left behind as old-school media, movies are using the fruits of the digital age to their advantage—and with gusto. They are not only using the three-screen universe (TV, computers and smart phones) to expand beyond the "big screen" of movie houses for distribution, but also producing movies especially for them. More on this as the chapter unfolds, but first to the industry's origins, purposes, and current status.

Perhaps more than any other medium, the motion picture industry has attracted the popular imagination. Screaming supermarket tabloids, gushing movie magazines, and caustic television and cable commentators pass on the latest Hollywood gossip and speculation to a fascinated public. The pictures themselves, from 1915's *The Birth of a Nation* to the latest "blockbuster," can be seen by tens of millions. Movie stars, from the earliest times, have had outsized reputations and an iconic place in our culture, with fans fascinated by the smallest details of their lives. Movies continue to be the great entertainer, more concerned with pure entertainment than are any other media.

But the movies are more than entertainment. Above all, the movies have left, and continue to leave, an indelible stamp on our nation and its culture. Our standards of female beauty and sexual attractiveness have for generations been derived in some part from movies. It started early in the century when Lillian Gish began to set the norms. It continued with the "vamps" of the 1920s and great beauties like Greta Garbo in the 1930s and Ingrid Bergman in the 1940s. By mid-century "sex goddesses" such as Marilyn Monroe and Elizabeth Taylor served as models. Today the definition of female sexual attractiveness is set by actresses such as Angelina Jolie and Eva Mendes. Similarly, our conceptions of handsome manliness have been influenced by such figures as John Wayne, Clark Gable, and more recently Tom Cruise, Brad Pitt, and Will Smith. These standards can have a profound influence on the behavior of millions, in everything from using cosmetics to criteria for selecting a mate.

Behind the gossip and the glamour lie the complex realities of movies as a mass medium, different from the others. In superficial ways, for example, movies and television are alike. They both have moving images in color and sound. As mass media, however, the similarities end there. We have long had a dynamic, separate industry that makes films, although the industry lines have blurred and distribution now includes the Internet, which means that TV and movies sometimes share the same technological platform. We'll also see in this chapter that movies also existed long before television was even a dream in the heads of electronic engineers. Today, although the motion-picture medium has had to change in many ways to adjust to the impact of television, it remains a vital industry.

In addition to being a medium of communication and a form of popular culture, motion pictures are also a social force, a huge and diversified industry, and an intricate art form. As a social force, film raises issues concerning the medium and industry's presumed influences on morals, manners, beliefs, and behavior that we consider in this and later chapters. Evaluating the artistic merit of films is beyond the scope of this book, but we can say that, as art, film takes in the whole spectrum of forms that the term implies. It is a performing art, like the theater and dance; it is representational, like a painting; and, like music, it is a recording art.

Movies are also, of course, big business. To a large degree for most of their history they have been essentially a manufacturing industry, making actual films, then producing and distributing them as cultural products. However, the motion picture industry, unlike other media industries, lives and functions amid new technologies, and it and always has. So the digital age is just the latest challenge.

In the digital age, movies live within the same media economy affecting their sister industries. Many movie-making companies saw themselves acquired by giant conglomerates, which themselves are the products of technology and media. Inside the movie industry, digital technologies have nearly revolutionized production and changed content. And even in the world of distribution, from theaters to DVDs, the digital age was being seen and felt. Critics ask, "In the digital age, is film dead? As audiences gravitate to DVDs [and Blu-ray players], Hollywood wonders if the movie theater can survive."[1]

THE DEVELOPMENT OF MOVIE TECHNOLOGY

Because movies focus so strongly on popular entertainment, it is easy to think of them in less-than-serious terms and to overlook the fact that they depend on a highly sophisticated base of scientific knowledge. The technological components in the motion picture are far more complex than those of print, and they were a very long time coming. A motion picture, after all, is a series of still pictures rapidly projected on a screen in such a way that the viewer perceives smooth motion. To achieve this illusion of motion, problems in optics, chemistry, and even human physiology had to be overcome. Lenses, projectors, cameras, and roll film had to be invented. Only a little over a century ago did all the technology come together so that "the movies" were born.

Magic Shadows on the Wall

The first problem to be solved was how to focus and project an image. Convex quartz lenses for magnifying and focusing the sun's rays were used as early as 600 B.C. In 212 B.C., Archimedes earned fame by frightening the Romans with a lens during the defense of Syracuse. He is said to have mounted on the wall of the city a large "burning glass" that could concentrate the sun's rays enough to set fire to the Roman ships. The story may or may not be true, but it indicates the ancients had begun to grapple with one of the main problems that would later be associated with cameras and projectors—how to use lenses to focus light.

The next major advance came nearly two thousand years later. A German priest, Athanasius Kirscher, conducted experiments on projecting a visual image by passing light through a transparency. In 1645, he put on a "magic lantern show" for his fellow scholars at the Collegio Romano, using slides he had painted himself. His projected images of religious figures could barely be seen, but his show was a sensation. No one had ever seen anything like it. The images on the wall looked like ghosts. In fact, there were dark rumors that he was in league with the devil and was conjuring up spirits through the practice of "black arts."[2]

In the eighteenth century, the public became increasingly aware of the idea of the projected image. Traveling magicians and showfolk entertained audiences with shadow plays and projected images of ghostlike figures. By the mid-1800s, improved lanterns with reflecting mirrors, and condensing lenses provided fairly reliable sources of light. By the 1870s, the simple oil-burning lantern had been replaced by a powerful light produced by burning hydrogen gas and oxygen through a cylinder of hard lime. That form of illumination was widely used in the theater to spotlight acts and events (hence, the expression *limelight*). Ultimately, of course, electric lights provided the necessary illumination.

Photography

The science of lenses and projection advanced earlier than that of photography. Until the nineteenth century, people could project images, but no one had been able to capture images to form a still picture. Several experimenters in the late 1700s and early 1800s worked to perfect a photographic process. However, it was a French artist and inventor, Louis Daguerre, and a chemist, Joseph Niepce, who arrived at the best method after years of work. Niepce died shortly before success was achieved, but his partner, Daguerre, carried on.

In 1839, Daguerre announced the success of his work and showed examples of his sharp, clear photographs to the public. He called his process, in which the photos were made on very thin polished copper plates, the **daguerreotype**. Because Daguerre's pictures were much clearer and sharper than those of others (who tried to use paper), his process was rapidly adopted all over the world.[3]

Photography was received enthusiastically in the United States. By the time of the Civil War, there were daguerreotype studios in every city. All of society wanted their picture taken and photos of their loved ones. It was even common to photograph the recently deceased in their coffins so that the family could retain a final image. Photographers traveled the backcountry in wagons to meet the surging demand.

By the 1880s, as chemistry and technology improved, such pioneers as George Eastman transformed photography from an art practiced by trained technicians to a popular hobby. More than anything else, it was Eastman's development and marketing of flexible celluloid roll film and a simple box camera that made popular photography a success.[4] The availability of flexible film also made motion pictures technically feasible. Before they could become a reality, however, the development of photography had to be matched by progress in understanding visual processes and the perception of motion.

Phenakistoscope or wheel of life as it was popularly known was a rotating disc that gave a sense of movement as with this seated man in turban.

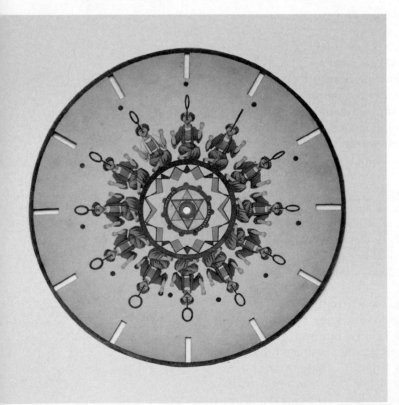

The Illusion of Motion

Motion pictures, of course, do not "move." They consist of a series of still pictures that capture the moving object in progressively different positions. When the stills are run through a projector at the correct speed, the viewer perceives an illusion of smooth motion. At the heart of this illusion is a process called visual lag or **visual persistence**: "The brain will persist in seeing an object when it is no longer before the eye itself."[5] We "see" an image for a fraction of a second after the thing itself has changed or disappeared. If we are rapidly presented with one image after the other, the visual persistence of the first image fills in the time lag between the two images, so they seem to be continuous.

The discovery of visual persistence by Dr. Peter Mark Roget in 1824 and its study by eminent scientists of the time led to widespread interest in the phenomenon. Toys and gadgets were produced that were based on visual lag. For example, a simple card with a string attached to each end can be twirled with the fingers. If a figure, say a bird, is drawn on one side of the card and a cage on the other, the bird will seem to be inside the cage when the device is spun. The reason for this is that both the bird and the cage are retained by the human retina for a brief period during the rotation. Today, for the same reason, children who rapidly twirl a

Fourth of July "sparkler" see the entire circular pattern made by the moving point of light.

By the middle of the century, the wheel of life (or *phenakistoscope*, as it came to be called) was highly developed. It generally consisted of a large disk on which was mounted a series of drawings showing a person or animal in progressively different positions. By rotating the disk and viewing the drawings through an aperture, or opening, as the wheel turned, a person could "see" smooth motion. When elaborated and combined with the photography of things in motion, the same principles provided the basis for movies.

Capturing and Projecting Motion with Film

During the closing decades of the nineteenth century, a number of people tried to photograph motion using a series of still cameras. One major advance was the result of a bet. Governor Leland Stanford of California and some of his friends made a large wager over whether a running horse ever had all its feet off the ground at once. To settle the bet, they hired an obscure photographer with an odd name, Eadweard Muybridge. Muybridge photographed moving horses by setting up a bank of twenty-four still cameras, each of which was tripped by a thread as the horse galloped by. His photographs showed that a horse did indeed have all four feet off the ground at once. Interest in the photography of motion became intense, but no one had yet taken motion pictures as we do today. Further advances in both cameras and projectors were needed.

During the late 1880s and early 1890s, various crude motion picture cameras were under development, and a number of showmen were entertaining people with moving pictures based on serially projected drawings. Then, during the 1890s, applications of film and viewing procedures virtually exploded. By 1895, greatly impressed French audiences were seeing brief motion pictures projected on a screen by August and Luis Lumiere. Other applications of the new technology soon followed, and several individuals clamored for the title of inventor of the motion picture. But it was William Dickson, assistant to Thomas Alva Edison, who developed the first practical motion picture camera.

Meanwhile, Edison and another assistant, Thomas Armat, developed a reliable projection system. Edison and Armat obtained U.S. patents and began to manufacture their projector, which they called the **Vitascope**. Edison also set up a studio to produce short films—mostly of vaudeville acts. Although it had many shortcomings, the Vitascope worked quite well. Its major flaw was that it projected at a wasteful forty-eight frames per second, whereas sixteen frames easily provide the illusion of smooth motion.

Because Edison, ever the penny pincher, declined to spend $150 to obtain foreign patents, his machines were quickly duplicated and patented in Europe. In fact, numerous improvements soon made Edison's original machines obsolete. Furious patent fights in the courts later threatened to kill the new medium.

Then Edison decided to exhibit his moving pictures in a peep-show device that he called the **Kinetescope**. For a nickel, a single viewer could turn a crank, look inside the machine, and see a brief film on a small screen. This one-viewer-at-a-time approach, Edison thought, would bring a larger return on investment than projecting to many people at once. Edison's

An illustration from the New York Herald newspaper of April 24, 1896 depicts the Edison Vitascope projecting an image on a large screen overlooking a man conducting an orchestra in front of a large audience in a theater.

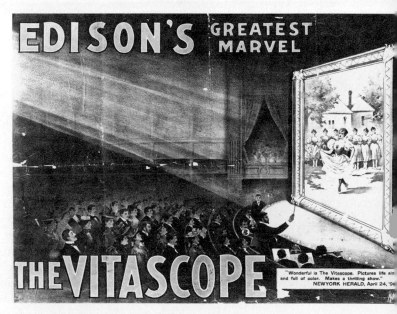

Iconic inventor Thomas Edison and his associates played a vital role in motion picture technology as seen in this view of him examining a home projecting kinetoscope in West Orange, New Jersey.

approach did not catch on; instead, in the end the industry developed along the lines of the traditional theater model. The Lumiere brothers and others in Europe had seen clearly that this was the way to exhibit films. By 1896, however, Edison was projecting motion pictures to the public in New York for the first time in America.

By 1900, all the scientific and technological underpinnings of the motion picture were in place, and the new device was now ready for mass use. Millions of people were eager to pay to be entertained. It was now a matter of developing the medium to present content that people wanted to see and to identify ways to maximize profits to be obtained from the movies.

THE MOVIES BECOME A MEDIUM

The first few years of the fledgling medium in the new century were marked by experimentation. Many of the early films ran for only a minute or two. Just the sight of something moving on the screen could thrill an audience. Inevitably, however, the novelty wore off, and patrons wanted something different. In response, the motion-picture makers began to try longer films offering more interesting content. The fledgling medium developed at a rapid pace.

By 1903, both American and European producers were making "one-reelers" that lasted ten to twelve minutes and told a story. One-reel films were produced on every conceivable topic, from prizefights to religious plays, for houses. Some have become classics, such as *A Trip to the Moon* (1902), *Life of an American Fireman* (1903), and *The Great Train Robbery* (1903). Many others have been lost or perhaps were not worth preserving.

By 1905, two-reelers were becoming increasingly common, lasting up to twenty-five minutes. These were more interesting for audiences. As the popularity of the new movies increased, production and distribution of films expanded at an extraordinary pace.

The Nickelodeons

The idea of renting films may seem to be of little significance, but it made possible the local motion picture theater as a small business venture. For a fairly modest investment, a theater manager could make high profits. One could rent a film and a vacant store, add some cheap decorations, install folding chairs, buy a projector, a piano, and a screen, and open the doors for business. In 1905, two entrepreneurs from Pittsburgh, Harry P. Davis and John P. Harris, did just that. They charged five cents for admission and called their theater "The Nickelodeon." In a week they made $1,000, playing to near-capacity houses. At the time, this was the next best thing to owning an Alaska gold mine.

The success of the first **nickelodeon** greatly impressed the entertainment world, and there was a stampede to set up others in cities across the nation. Within a year, one thousand were in operation, and by 1910, ten thousand were showing films. National gross receipts for 1910 have been estimated at $91 million.[6] The motion picture medium was skyrocketing to success.

Most of the early theaters were located in the hearts of industrial cities of the Northeast. Movies were made to order for that time and place. America was a nation of immigrants, most of whom were newly arrived and many of whom lived in the larger urban centers. Many of these people spoke either no English or very little.

Because of their near-universal appeal and modest price, the nickelodeons have been called "democracy's theaters." Early movies were silent, so language posed no barrier for an immigrant audience. Going to the movies was cheap, so they provided entertainment for people in the bottom rungs of the economic ladder. They showed stereotyped plots, overdramatized acting, and slapstick humor—all needed for their audiences at that time. Even the least educated could understand a pie in the face, a lover crawling out of a window as the husband came in the front door, or a mean boss.

The early movies prove to be popular beyond the wildest dreams of their pioneers. In New York City alone, more than a million patrons attended the nickelodeons each week in the early 1900s. Although the nickelodeons were associated with slums and ghettos, movies had become big business, and corporations were quickly formed to produce, distribute, and exhibit films.

Ornate movie theaters of the 1920s and 1930s, like Warner's Western Theater in Los Angeles, here ablaze with lights for a premiere, have given way to smaller-screened multiplex and individual theaters.

Movies for the Middle Class

The nickelodeons brought the motion picture to the urban poor, but the industry was anxious to lure other kinds of customers into the theaters, especially the huge mass of middle-class families. At first, such people viewed movies as vulgar and trivial. The young medium not only bore the stigma of low taste but also was associated with the least prestigious elements of society. Even poor immigrant women were afraid to sit in the dark surrounded by strange men.

To shake this image and bring middle-class patrons to the box office, attractive theaters were built in better neighborhoods, and movie "palaces" opened in the business districts. Moviemakers produced longer, more sophisticated films to exhibit in such improved surroundings.

While striving for a better product, producers discovered that they could increase attendance by giving prominent roles and media attention to particular actors and actresses. They hired "press agents" to publicize them as artists and important personalities. These early public-relations specialists created masculine idols and love goddesses of the "silver screen" that could be adored from afar by unsophisticated fans. Thus the "star" system was born—and gave a tremendous boost to the popularity of motion pictures.

By 1914, an estimated 40 million patrons attended movies every week, including an increasing number of women and children. The movies were being accepted by the middle class. Movie theaters were respectable, and the era of the tacky nickelodeon was over.

Meanwhile, as Europe entered World War I, Hollywood had been established as the center of American movie making. The film industries in Europe had to close because of the war, leaving production and the world market to American filmmakers. They took swift advantage of the opportunity, and a huge growth in film attendance occurred all over the globe. American films have been popular in the world market ever since.

The Talkies

Since the 1890s, inventors had tried to combine the phonograph and the motion picture to produce movies with synchronized sound. Few of their contraptions worked well. The sound was either weak and scratchy or poorly coordinated with the action in the film. The public soon tired of such experiments, and the moviemakers thought that talking pictures posed insurmountable technical problems.

However, the difficulties were overcome by the mid-1920s. American Telephone & Telegraph (AT&T) used enormous capital resources to produce a reliable sound system based on optical recording of sound incorporated directly into the actual film. It eliminated the problem of people being seen speaking with the sound coming earlier or later. By 1926 Warner Brothers had signed an agreement with AT&T, and the transition to sound was under way. Warner produced a new feature including sound for the 1927–1928 season. Starring Al Jolson, *The Jazz Singer* actually did not have a full soundtrack. It included a few songs and a few minutes of dialogue; the rest of the film was silent. It was an enormous success, however, and the other **talkies** followed quickly.

Almost overnight the silent movie was obsolete; the motion picture with a full soundtrack became the norm. As technical quality, theaters, acting, and other aspects of the medium improved, motion pictures entered their maturity. Within little more than a decade, color would be possible, and the movies as we know them would be a reality.

Portrayals of the Fast Life

The 1920s were a time of great transition. The old Victorian codes of morality simply crumbled following World War I. As the 1920s progressed, there was a great emancipation from—some said deterioration of—the old rules. In 1920, U.S. women gained the right to vote. They also gained a number of social freedoms. Women had been confined to lengthy dresses stretching from wrist and chin to the ground, tight corsets, and long hair. Prim codes of conduct made demure behavior and even chaperones mandatory for generations. By the mid-1920s, women could smoke, wear short dresses and cosmetics, cut their hair short, and even drink alcohol without being branded as harlots for life. It was a time of fast music, fast cars, "fast bucks," and, many thought, "fast women." These changes shocked an older generation but delighted the "flaming youth" of the 1920s.

It is hard to say whether the movies of the time contributed to these changes in social norms or merely portrayed them as they developed. In any case, in its struggle for increased profits, the movie industry began to introduce subject matters that, for the times, were sexually frank and portrayed modes of behavior that were very clearly unacceptable by the standard of the older generation. Within a short time, major religious groups actively opposed portrayals in the movies of easy money, gangsterism, alcohol use, and sexual themes. These were powerful critics, and the industry was forced to take steps to police itself. As we will see in more detail later, in 1930 the industry adopted its first voluntary code for censoring films before exhibition.

The "Golden Age"

During the 1930s the movies increasingly tried to appeal to entire families and become families' major form of entertainment. In the process, the standards in the motion picture code made the conduct of movie characters about as sinful as a Norman Rockwell painting. By the mid-1930s, for example, the code banned words such as *broad, hot,* (when used about a woman), *fairy, pansy, tart,* and *whore.* Bedroom scenes always featured fully clad actors in rooms furnished with twin beds with a table and a lamp between them. The code was rigidly enforced, and by the 1940s the movies had become a wholesome, if bland, form of family entertainment.

Throughout most of the 1930s and 1940s, movies were the most popular form of mass entertainment in America. In the Depression decade of the 1930s, there really was not much else one could enjoy in the way of popular entertainment for so little money. The price of admission for adults was usually less than fifty cents. Children could get in for half price or less. A whole family could go to the movies together, have a snack afterward, and generally have what was regarded as a "swell time" while barely denting the hard-earned family resources. The golden age of movies had arrived, and people loved them. On average, between two and three tickets to the movies were sold each week for every household in America.

The Decline

Box office receipts held steady until the late 1940s. Movies were especially popular during the World War II years of 1941 to 1945. By 1946, some 90 million tickets were being sold weekly.

Then, with extraordinary speed, a new medium arrived. Television's massive adoption by the public had a devastating impact on motion picture theaters. By 1960, when television had been widely adopted, sales of movie tickets to families were only one-fourth what they had been in 1948 (just before TV arrived). The box in the living room was displacing the silver screen downtown, in the neighborhood, and at the drive-in theaters (which declined from 3,720 in 1971 to a mere 730 by 2007). Even before DVDs and cable, people increasingly preferred to watch free entertainment on their TV receiver than travel to a theater and pay to get in.

To try to draw patrons back to the theaters, moviemakers turned to a variety of gimmicks and innovations. They tried increasing the use of color, escalating levels of violence, increasingly explicit portrayals, horror themes, spectacular special effects, space fantasies, and even an occasional three-dimensional (3D) production. None of those efforts really helped. Attendance at motion picture theaters has shown a downward trend ever since the arrival of television.

The Digital Age

It is clear that, on a per capita basis, movie attendance will never again be what it was before television. **Movie exhibitors**, those who own theaters and show films, continue to be plagued by a number of negative trends. Audiences today do not consist of entire families, as in earlier decades, but mainly of young people for whom going to the movies can be a cheap date or a peer activity. The older neighborhood theaters and drive-ins closed long ago, when TV became popular. Today **multiplexes**, multi-theater cinemas, often located in or near malls, offer young viewers a range of films from which to choose.

DVDs available in a rental store have been a major distributor for movies in the digital age.

What is especially important today—and a likely indicator of the future of movies—is digital cinema, or the use of digital technologies to distribute and display movies. Worldwide there are 6,455 digital cinema screens, 72% of those in the United States. This allows for high-quality sound and visual images. As noted by Tim Stevens in this chapter's Media Leaders Insight feature, digital cinema can also draw moviegoers who come to see specially produced events. In the 2008–2009 season, for example, the Metropolitan Opera distributed live events from Lincoln Center to screens worldwide to great success. Major sports events also use this technology as do some Broadway productions. Digital cinema usually involves replacing conventional projectors with digital projection that uses hard drives, DVDs, and satellite technology to produce high-quality images and sounds.

In spite of downward theater-going trends, the movie as a medium is here to stay. Fewer people may pay at the box office, but they see movies in other ways. The original social and cultural forces that drove the motion picture to heights of popularity are still in place. The United States is still an urban-industrial society in which people who work all day

MEDIA LEADERS INSIGHTS: MOTION PICTURES

TIM STEVENS

Senior Vice President, Administration

New Line Cinema

Tim Stevens is said to be "intuitive, solution driven, and visionary," a person capable of connecting the complex organizational needs that characterize the movie industry, who can formulate a strategy and execute it too.

As a senior vice president at New Line Cinema, a Time Warner Company, Stevens oversees all administrative functions. After completing a BA in English and communications at New Jersey's Kean University, Stevens worked as a customer service manager for an airline, head of telecom for *Newsweek*, and, subsequently, corporate vice president at Viacom International and senior vice president for network operations at MTV Networks. He sees the digital age from a technological and people-management perspective.

1. When and under what circumstances did you first realize the import of new media or the digital age?

   That happened even before I got to New Line, while I was at MTV Networks. However, it was clear to me when I began working at New Line that, like many companies, it had not yet taken full advantage of the technological opportunities available for either its production or distribution needs. Unlike other media industries, motion pictures had not been forced to modify their operations for decades. The same basic operating principles that guided the industry at its inception were still pretty much in place, with minor exceptions. Still, I thought New Line was poised for an evolution and was the perfect candidate to be an early adoption of digital technologies.

2. What impact did that experience have on you personally or professionally?

   Personally, I struggled between trying to position myself for the future while continuing to provide support to the legacy systems and operations in place. As a manager, you are acutely aware that some projects have no long-term value, yet you must continue them in order to support the current operation.

   Professionally, because the industry lacked a clear direction, in part because of its resistance to change, I frequently found myself struggling to make the appropriate decisions for the organization. This conflict often put me at odds with the senior management team, as their goals appeared to be more short term.

3. How have digital technologies and/or thinking influenced your work at New Line Cinema and in the motion picture industries generally? What is being done to harness these new possibilities?

   I was a huge proponent of creating a digital strategy at New Line and worked very closely with the senior vice president of IT [Information Technology] to move an agenda forward—specifically focused on digital distribution. Our small size would have made us the ideal lab environment for the industry, by organizing a limited roll-out to test the economic impact of a new, digital distribution model. I saw digital distribution as the foundation for a new economic model for the industry, but unfortunately adoption has been extremely slow. When I pressed the chief financial officer at the time, he had little interest in leading, instead preferring to follow whatever direction Warner Bros [another division of the Time Warner conglomerate] was heading.

4. What is the greatest challenge or benefit of the digital revolution for the movies and other video production? To what extent does New Line (in the context of Time Warner) have a digital strategy?

Video production will continue to benefit from the advances in digital media by allowing long-distance collaboration in content creation. Teams of professionals can realize a product that, prior to the availability of these tool sets, would have been enormously expensive and time consuming.

The greatest benefit to the industry, as a whole, is also its greatest challenge. The adoption of digital distribution to theatrical exhibitors will completely change the economics of the industry. The opportunity for the theater owner is the ability to quickly add screens for blockbusters, while shrinking screens for less desirable products. And they can offer new digital content not seen before in theaters: pay-per-view, local events, sports, Broadway shows, and so on. Still, none of these products has been fully tested, so this promise remains theoretical. I believe that the greatest immediate benefit to the industry will be to the distributors, in terms of cost reductions, but only if the theater owners decide to expend the capital for the digital systems.

5. Are you optimistic about the digital future?

Extremely. We are seeing an enormous amount of pressure on many industries given today's economic issues, and, as such, the time is ripe for change. The most obvious change will be the implementation of digital cinema throughout the U.S. and global markets. This will change the distribution model completely, allowing product availability to shrink or expand based on its demand. And it will provide unprecedented opportunity for new filmmakers to easily and quickly deliver their products.

The only caveat to this digital future is the realization that with the overwhelming amount of content comes the need for careful and creative programming. Studio heads and network programmers need to connect more effectively with consumers to understand how they want to spend their time. I see an important role for YouTube or Facebook to monitor our preferences and guide our consumption habits.

6. What, if any, advice do you have for a person who aspires to a career in filmed entertainment/motion pictures?

Remember first that it is a business. It has all of the functional responsibilities and opportunities of any business. Even more importantly, it is a manufacturing and distribution business, with a long product cycle and a fickle consumer. Like any media business, there is often a clear separation between the creative aspects of the product and the business side, responsible for the manufacturing and distribution of that product. Unlike television, which is essentially an advertising business, the movie industry is filled with creative people in every area of its operations. For anyone who wants to work in this industry, patience, a thick skin, and an appreciation for talent and the personality challenges that come with talent are essential. It's an industry that will test your patience and your lifestyle, but it rewards loyalty, and it provides many benefits—including access to a glamorous and exciting field—that can balance the lower pay and the emotional compromises required at the outset.

want to enjoy popular culture during evenings and weekends. In such a society there is an almost insatiable demand for popular entertainment that costs very little and makes few intellectual demands. Movies fill that need very well indeed.

When there was no other way to see a movie, people left home, traveled to a theater, and paid at the box office. They had no options. Today, huge numbers of people want to sit back and have movies come to them. Thus, the industry has survived and prospered by adapting to new technologies in movie delivery. Moviemakers today produce movies for broadcast and cable television. They have also reaped revenue from rapid growth in movie rentals for home showings and benefited from such mail distribution systems as Netflix, as well as from services that allow viewers to download movies. International distribution of this early player in the global marketplace adds still another dimension to the profit picture.

There is something ironic about this. The motion picture has often faced the challenges of new technology but not always with great vision. In 1982, Jack Valenti, then president of the Motion Picture Association of America, appeared before a Congressional Committee and declared, "The growing and dangerous intrusion of this new technology threatens an entire industry's economic vitality and future security."[7] He was talking about the VCR, and he was worried that home taping of movies would ruin the movie industry. Of course, that didn't happen. Instead VCR rental became a whole new revenue stream for the movies.

The industry's initial reluctance about new technologies can be seen in other instances as well. In 2008, the motion picture industry was engaged in a battle between delivering movies on high-definition (HD), large-storage-capacity Blu-ray discs and standard DVDs. Blu-ray (Blu-ray disc or BD, an optical storage medium) was at the center of a format war, which ended in February 2008 when the Japanese firm Toshiba threw in the towel and decided to stop manufacturing HD DVD players and recorders. Blu-ray, the brainchild of the Blu-ray Disc Association, a consortium of the world's leading electronics and computer firms, won the format war. And, as mentioned earlier, downloading movies on one's personal computer, laptop, Blackberry, or cell phone is another way for consumers to get movies.

Downloading began with Internet users sharing ways to break encryption codes, a digital signature that locks out those who cannot decipher it, which companies used to protect media delivered on digital discs, such as audio CDs and DVDs. The downloaders could then pass along the contents of these discs from one user to another for free. Such downloading was obviously initially very unpopular with media companies, as it cut into profits. In 2000, for example, the Recording Industry Association of America prevailed in court to stop the Internet music service Napster from freely distributing music that people could download without paying for CDs. Movie studios are also pursuing strategies to prevent such "piracy." In the case of movies, it is infinitely easier to copy movies on DVDs this way than it was in making tapes from VCRs because that required two recorders. The VCR case went to the U.S. Supreme Court before it was eventually settled, and perhaps this will happen again. Once again First Amendment arguments about the free flow of information run head on into the intellectual property rights of movie studios. Some of this seems unstoppable as film clips from movie trailers end up on YouTube with great regularity. Some argue this actually helps promote the movie and thus has economic benefit.

FILM AS A CONTEMPORARY MEDIUM

In this section, we are most concerned with film as a contemporary medium of communication with different kinds of content that serve distinctive functions. Both the content and the functions are determined by professional communicators—the industry that produces the pictures—and their large and diverse audience.

The Functions of Films

A movie may be frivolous and diverting, it may provide information or training, it may make a social or political statement, or it may have important aesthetic qualities. In terms of the media functions we have discussed throughout this book, a particular movie may seek to:

- *Entertain* or amuse, by providing diversion and enjoyment.
- *Educate,* as many documentaries do.
- *Persuade* or influence, as in the case of wartime propaganda films.
- *Enrich* our cultural experiences.

Most often, a film will have combined functions: For the audience, a film may be informative, an escape, or an engaging lesson in history, morality, or human relationships. For its producers, the same film is a source of profit. For directors and actors, it can be a means of supporting artistic values, whereas for writers, the film may be a way of raising consciousness about social causes.

Even within these groups, people may perceive different functions. For example, many people consider vintage Walt Disney films to be wholesome family entertainment. Others interpret them as rigid ideological statements that praise an unrealistic image of America, showing artificial, antiseptic WASP communities devoid of social problems.

It is safe to say, however, that the main function of American films has been, throughout their history, to *entertain*. In this very important respect, movies differ from the print and broadcast media. The origins of magazines and newspapers were related to the functions of providing information and influencing opinion, but films grew from the traditions of both theater and popular amusements. Their central focus was always on entertainment.

Today, films continue those traditions, and their principal function has always been to take their viewers away from the pressing issues and mundane details of everyday life, rather than to focus their attention on them.

The Development of Themes and Styles

The early movies looked to the established forms of drama (comedy, tragedy, musical) for their themes. Then, as now, they often turned to books for ideas and screenplays. Due to the lack of sound and the nature of their audiences, the early films also relied on the art of mime. Soon, however, American films developed their own forms and traditions. They were influenced less by the approaches of plays or books and more by film's own emerging traditions.

The 1930s research of Edgar Dale provides a glimpse of those traditions. Dale analyzed the content of fifteen hundred films that had been released from the early 1900s until 1930. He found that just three major themes—crime, sex, and love—accounted for approximately three-fourths of the movies produced during the period.[8] In many ways, these three are still the major themes of the industry.

Different members of the filmmaking teams may dominate at any time and in any film. In general, directors were the dominating force shaping films until the 1930s. In the early period, the pioneering D. W. Griffith had a profound influence on the film medium as movies moved from side-show curiosity to dream machine. Some say he, more than anyone else, was responsible for developing the grammar and syntax of the movies. In the silent film era, Mack Sennett, Charlie Chaplin, Buster Keaton, Harold Lloyd, and others created their own forms of acting and storytelling. Later, directors such as Eric von Stroheim and Cecil B. DeMille added their mark. These and filmmakers of today such as Gus Van Sant and the Coen Brothers, who create films with a distinctive style, are known as **auteurs**. Auteurs are filmmakers with a personal style and keep creative control over their pictures.

In the 1930s and 1940s, the **studios**, or major movie-making companies, became dominant in shaping the style and themes of motion pictures. Several studios came to have recognizable styles. MGM was long known for

Film director Alfred Hitchcock is a master of the action thriller including the classic film *Psycho*.

its richly produced, glossy epics aimed at tastes that appeal to the mainstream of Americans. Paramount was said to give its films a European sensibility. Warner Brothers developed a reputation for realism because the studio often shot movies on location to avoid the expense of building sets.[9] Today these differences in production styles have disappeared as the influence of the major studios has declined. However, even in the heyday of the studios, some individual directors, actors, or cinematographers were able to mark their films with their own distinct stamp.

Beginning in the last decades of the twentieth century, the director once again became the main force in determining a picture's style. Today, on the whole, there is a heightened awareness of the individual movie-making styles of different directors, although movie stars still have an enormous influence on film because of their economic clout.

Ultimately, though, the people who pay for movies to be made still hold a good deal of power over how they turn out. "Studio chiefs are focused on the particular elements in films that will keep money flowing into their clearinghouses," says author and critic Edward J. Epstein.

Epstein also notes, however, that "studios require more than commercially successful projects."[10] As we'll see next, content and production styles of films are driven, on the one hand, by a need to appeal to those who finance films—industry executives and merchandisers—and, on the other hand, by creative input of their stars, directors, and producers.

The Content of American Films

A film's content is almost always shaped by conflicting forces. The audience, technology, economics, and filmmakers themselves play a part. Producers look carefully at the balance sheet, continually worrying about audience interests. They ask two key questions: 1) What is technically and economically possible and efficient? 2) What does the audience want? Studios' constant searches for efficiency and audiences have led to a number of the characteristics common in today's movies, including the following:

- *Standardized lengths* for films, although those lengths have changed through the decades.
- *Realistic locations* or settings for films, whether in jungles, cities, or submarines.
- *Special effects* that seem realistic.
- *Coherent plot structures.* Old Westerns, for example, were usually melodramas with a hero, a villain, a beautiful girl, a sidekick, a handsome horse, and perhaps inaccurately portrayed Native Americans. The audience had particular expectations of what they would see, and plots usually conformed to those expectations. That principle still prevails.

However, old formulas can become trite. Over time, audiences change, in terms of both their characteristics and what they want to see. Anxious to keep track of audience composition and tastes, the Motion Picture Association of America (MPAA) conducts annual surveys that yield a profile of moviegoers. In fiscal year 2007, for example, 38% of all ticket purchases were in the twelve to twenty-four age group, 29% were twenty-five to thirty-nine, 24% were forty to fifty-nine, and only 9% were sixty or older.[11] Clearly, making movies for the young is a more certain way to make money than making them for mature audiences (and has been for a long time).

Still, the balance sheet is not the only factor that determines the shape of films. Directors, actors, and even producers may also want to put the mark of their own imagination on a film. Studios strive to balance the filmmaker's desire for individuality against the need to give the audience a message it will understand and accept—the need for successful dream building. According to one film historian, this conflict is what "drove the Hollywood cinema: the clash between the artist's sensibility and the classic mythic structure of the story types that were identified and popular."[12] Out of this clash came a broad range of films and film genres.

GENRES   **Genres,** or story types, are more or less standardized plots, recognizable categories of films with the same basic kinds of characters, settings, and general sequence of events. The gangster film is an example. Another is the war film. Still another is the slapstick comedy. Probably the most popular film genre of all time has been the Western. It was a completely American invention, with brave men and women living the rugged life of the range or moving across the frontier where they met hardship in battle with the elements, the Native Americans, and the law. Films starring cowboy hcrocs—Tom Mix, Roy Rogers, and John Wayne—and later epic Western themes dominated this genre.

Musicals were once immensely popular, and some studios, such as Warner Brothers, virtually specialized in this genre. It was Warner Brothers that produced Busby Berkeley's elaborate, geometrically choreographed dance films of the 1930s, featuring group dancing with performers forming intricate patterns when photographed from overhead. Many of Berkeley's "dancers" knew nothing (and did not need to know anything) about genuine dance. All they had to do was to move precisely together in a few scenes. He used unusual camera angles and fast-paced editing to create spectacular effects.

Comedies have always attracted wide audiences. They have ranged from dry-witted, British-inspired parlor comedies to screwball films by the Marx Brothers, the Three Stooges, and Laurel and Hardy and to those of contemporary comics like Jim Carrey, Chris Rock, or Ben Stiller. Other genres include horror films, historical romances, and detective thrillers.

Occasionally public taste dictates development of a new genre. The 1950s, for example, saw the development of science-fiction thrillers, which were followed by teen-horror movies of the 1960s, and action-thrillers in the 1990s. More recently, with the use of computer technology, a new cyborg genre, as in "The Terminator," was developed as were blockbuster animated films.

Public attitudes and social conditions have often influenced (some would say dictated) the treatment of racial and ethnic minorities in film. For many years it was difficult for African-American and Latino actors to get good film roles. They were often depicted in a subservient position that reinforced racial stereotypes. In more recent years, however, there have been new images for minorities in screen roles. Additionally, more people of color have gotten key industry roles, although many critics say that the diversity of the industry is still woefully lacking and thus accounts for a lag between changing cultural values and what one sees on the screen.

Films depicting women and women's issues have also gone through a number of phases. In the early films, women were usually melodramatic heroines: pretty girls threatened by evil villains and saved by virile heroes. However, by the 1930s and 1940s, actresses such as Bette Davis, Joan Crawford, and Barbara Stanwyck portrayed very strong women. In the 1950s, the "sexy blond" role, most prominently associated with Marilyn Monroe, brought a different and much weaker image of women. Subsequently, with the rise of the women's movement and the general acceptance of feminism, women returned as strong lead actors and in fewer demeaning film roles. Indeed, a number of popular films took on clear feminist themes, with actors playing important roles dealing with issues and problems of special interest to women. That said, even today, few female stars are typically as "bankable" as top male stars, who continue to get higher salaries and mega-buck, multimillion-dollar deals.

DOCUMENTARIES   Although the public overwhelmingly identifies "the movies" (both as an industry and as a product for consumption) with the entertainment function, an important category of nonfiction films providing an education function are **documentaries.** The term was first introduced by British filmmaker John Grierson, although his film was not the first of the category. His notification film *The Drifters* (1929) depicted the lives of herring fishermen in the North Sea. In the documentary's purest form, the filmmaker intrudes as little as possible; the director, for example, does not direct actors or set up scenes.

From an intellectual perspective, documentaries can have a lasting importance, far exceeding entertainment films, as records of human culture in particular periods. Imagine

Filmmaker Michael Moore has helped usher in a new era for documentaries such as his movie *Fahrenheit 9/11*.

what we might see if someone at the time could have made documentaries of the ancient Egyptians building pyramids, of Gutenberg developing printing, or of the first encounters of Columbus with the people of the New World. At some point in the future, some of the documentaries produced in this century will have precisely that value. An example is the World War II documentary series, *Victory at Sea,* which recorded that global conflict for future generations. The film and video recordings of the first human beings on the moon provide another example. These are priceless records of human struggle and achievement that will have immense value to future generations far beyond the latest film produced for entertainment.

Through the years, documentaries have dealt with people at work, the efforts of nations at war, social problems, and other issues. Some are timeless and artful classics that are now intellectual treasures, like Robert Flaherty's *Nanook of the North* (1922), which depicted Inuit life just before the native culture was transformed into a more contemporary form. Some documentaries take bits and pieces of a process and weld them into a film. For example, directors Emile de Antonio and Daniel Talbots creatively put together the work of other filmmakers and of camera operators not under their direction to produce the award-winning *Point of Order!* (1963) of the anticommunist hearings chaired by Senator Joseph McCarthy during the 1950s. Documentaries often carry a powerful message, like Peter Davis's *Heart of Minds* (1975), which traced the painful relationship between the United States and Vietnam.

By the 1990s, after years of slow growth in the documentary filmmaking sector, documentaries began to reach large audiences. Some were shown in movie theaters; others came via television. For example, the four-part documentary directed by Ken Burns, *The Civil War,* electrified Americans when it was presented on public television in 1990, even though it was based mainly on still pictures from the period. In theaters, documentaries and docudramas, depicting real events, have triumphed in recent years ranging from Michael Moore's pointed critiques of American society to films like *The Fog of War* and *Grey Gardens*. There is even a website featuring the top 50 most popular documentaries. See www.imdb.com.

PUBLIC PREFERENCES   As we've noted, studios are very sensitive to public preference in movie content. Many factors influence preferences: trends in morality and standards, current fads and styles, and recent events. Over the decades, content has reflected these changing factors:

- The 1930s fostered stark realism and grim themes of the Great Depression, as well as cheerful musicals that helped the public escape from its troubles.
- Historical and patriotic themes as well as films were popular during World War II and after, but so were light comedies.
- In the 1950s, films seemed to reflect the lighthearted mood of the country. Comedies and Westerns were increasingly popular, and sexual themes were becoming more explicit.
- In the late 1960s, during a period of dissatisfaction with prevailing standards and styles, some films successfully celebrated the antihero and began to take on controversial social topics.

Films from the late 1960s into the first decade of the twenty-first century have explored such themes as racism, drug use, feminism as well as gay and lesbian issues. However, there was still time for the nonsense comedy and the lighthearted musical. Recent films have also explored international espionage and organized crime, as well as labor strikes, sports, and the supernatural.

THE MOVIE INDUSTRY

Art has never really been a prime mover of the motion picture industry. Charlie Chaplin, whose *Little Tramp* films are now regarded as art, put it pointedly at the Oscars in 1972: "I went into the business for money, and the art grew out of it. If people are disillusioned by that remark, I can't help it. It's the truth."[13] Above all, makers of motion pictures want profit.

To sketch a profile of this industry, we will first look briefly at the process of how a movie gets made. Then, we'll examine the organization of the industry—its ownership patterns, studios, and employees. Finally, we'll examine the complex economics of the movie business.

Making a Movie

Making movies is a communal process. They are the product not of one person but of many. As film historian John L. Fell remarked in a classic formulation:

> The substance of any particular production is likely to change appreciably between its early idea stages and the final release print. These changes may be dominated by some individual's vision, ordered by his own evolving understanding of what the movie is, but such a happy circumstance is never altogether the case . . . even if most of the time someone pretends to be in charge.[14]

In other words, films are put together under chaotic conditions with a variety of artistic, technical, and organizational people. Every film requires the solution of both mechanical and aesthetic problems. The people who are part of the team making the film must have, among them, many different skills. Just consider the various unions, or worker's organizations, involved in filmmaking: the Writers Guild of America, the American Cinema Editors, the Directors Guild of America, the Screen Actors Guild, and the International Association of Theatrical and Stage Employees.

Fell has identified seven stages or elements in the process of filmmaking:

1. *Conceptualization.* The idea for a film may come from any one of a variety of people. Early directors often wrote their own scripts.
2. *Production.* To produce a film means to get the money together, organize all the people involved in the schedule, and continue supervising the process until the film is ready for distribution.
3. *Direction.* Once financial backing is secured and the script is acquired, then the director is chosen.
4. *Performance.* Actors must be chosen and their performances calibrated to the script and to other personnel involved in the film.
5. *Visualization.* The planning and execution of the actual filming involves cinematographers, lighting technicians, and others.
6. *Special effects.* Everything from camera trickery to monsters to stuntmen and stuntwomen comes under this heading.
7. *Editing.* This process involves choosing takes from all the film that has been shot and processing a finished film.

The **producer** is a key figure in putting all these elements together. In most cases he or she is part of a film studio that has the space, facilities, and personnel to complete the film. It is the producer who carries the responsibility for most of the central decisions, other than technical ones, about acting, editing, and so on. The producer initiates the development of a film by acquiring a story or a script, or the producer may merely take an **option** on a story (that is, an agreement giving one the right to purchase at a later date) until he or she sees if the talent and the money are available to produce the film. If financial backing is available and suitable acting talent can be placed under contract, then the producer finds a director, who will be in charge of actually shooting the movie, and assembles the rest of the filmmaking team.

The Filmmakers

By the late 1920s, the movies were a billion-dollar-a-year industry employing thousands and claiming a lion's share of America's entertainment dollar. Because of its benign weather and abundant sunshine for filming, the early studios of the 1920s chose southern California—specifically Hollywood—as the home for their huge dream factories. They established their studios on back "lots" that could be made into a Western town or a jungle paradise.

As the industry matured, Hollywood became in some ways more of an administrative than a production capital. Nevertheless, it remained a symbol of glamour. The glamour myth of Hollywood overstated the geographic concentration of the film industry. From its beginnings, the industry forged financial links with Wall Street as well as artistic and production ties with European countries, and movies were often filmed on remote locations. As editor Peter Buckley wrote, "Hollywood was synonymous with everything that came out of the U.S. film industry, yet few films were actually made there.... Hollywood was a wonderful, fanciful state of mind: the film capital that never really was."[15]

OWNERS AND STUDIOS   Concentration of control and ownership was always part of the equation in American film. Major studios have been the dominant force in Hollywood since its early days.

Founded by legendary motion picture moguls, such as Samuel Goldwyn and Louis B. Mayer, the early studios ran their huge production plants in high gear. If you wanted to work in the movies in the heyday of the 1930s and 1940s, you worked for a studio. Each major studio had its own writers, directors, actors, and actresses under contract, as well as its own technicians, equipment, and lots.

The studios had tight control not only over the whole production process but also over **distribution**, scheduling and promoting the showings of their movies. Through a practice know as **block booking**, each studio forced theater owners to show its bad films if they wanted a chance to show the good ones. The studios even owned their own chains of theaters, controlling exhibition of movies, too. Thus, major studios had an assured outlet for their films—good or bad—whereas other smaller producers found it difficult to have their movies exhibited. In short, the studios had control from idea to camera to box office. It was little wonder that smaller companies had difficulty breaking into the business.

Then in 1948 with the Paramount decision, the federal government stepped in. The courts ruled that major studios must stop block booking and give up their theaters. Because of this decision, filmmaking became a riskier business, and the major studios became less powerful.

In the 1960s various corporations bought up theaters, integrating these holdings with other kinds of investments. Large corporations also bought up the old major studios. In 1966, Gulf & Western bought Paramount. Warner Brothers was bought by Kinney National, which also owned funeral parlors, parking lots, and magazines, among other things. In the 1970s, the trend toward conglomerate ownership of studios abated in favor of emphasis on independent production companies, which continued into the 2000s. The two decades saw a number of new purchases. The whole Kinney conglomerate became Time Warner, which was, in turn, acquired by AOL in 2000. In the early 1990s, Columbia Pictures was purchased by Sony, the

Japanese conglomerate. Some studios themselves became conglomerates. Disney, for example, bought ABC Television.

Although the names of the major studios have survived for many decades, they are no longer what they once were: the private empires of single movie moguls. They are now publicly held by numerous stockholders.[16] What's more, writers like Edward J. Epstein, an expert on motion pictures, and others note that movie studios are a relatively unimportant part of the revenues of the conglomerates that own them. Studios account for anywhere from 7 to 21% of total revenues, and that includes TV licensing, DVD sales, and other sources of income not directly related to showing movies in theaters.[17]

The movie industry is more diverse and scattered today than it was in the first half of the century, with many more independent producers making films. The major studios continue to lead the industry, however, in financing and distributing movies. The top motion picture studios today, such as Sony (Columbia-Tri Star), Buena Vista (owned by Disney), MGM, Universal, and 20th Century Fox, dominate theatrical film distribution, because these studios distribute most films produced by independents, as well as producing their own. They collect more than 90% of the total income of movie distributors, although they share this income with the independent producers and directors whom they hire for particular services or assignments.

CAREERS IN THE FILM INDUSTRY   A host of specialists work for movie studios: electricians, makeup artists, property workers, grips (people who move cables), projectionists, studio teamsters (or drivers), costumers, craft workers, ornamental plasterers, script supervisors, extras, film editors, writers, composers, musicians, camera operators, sound technicians, directors, art directors, and set directors, not to mention the stars. Almost all the technical workers are unionized.

Recently, the number of those employed in the motion picture industry has slightly increased, as Table 6.1 indicates. Some of this is due to digitization. For example, the studios also had teams of animators who did their painstaking work by hand. Today, computer graphics has taken over and traditional animators have been phased out.

Most of those who work in the industry are engaged in making films or advertising and distributing them to exhibitors. While film schools supply much of the talent for the industry, business schools are also sources for recruiters. Some business schools, like those at UCLA and the University of Southern California, have specialized courses and tracks for entertainment and media industries, with a special emphasis on motion pictures.

TABLE 6.1

NUMBER OF EMPLOYEES IN THE NOTION PICTURE INDUSTRY

U.S. Motion Picture Industry Employment Areas: Bureau of Labor Statistics

	Production & Services (000s)	Video Exhibition (000s)	Other (000s)	Total (000s)	Total % Change vs. Previous Period	2007
2007	192.8	136.2	28.3	357.3	0.8%	—
2006	192.2	133.7	28.5	354.4	−0.8%	0.8%
2005	195.6	133.2	28.4	357.2	−1.7%	0.0%
2004	196.5	137.4	29.3	363.2	3.3%	−1.6%
2003	183.1	139.2	29.4	351.7	−2.5%	1.6%
2002	191.7	138.4	30.6	360.7	4.0%	−0.9%
2001	180.9	133.2	32.6	346.7	−1.4%	3.1%
2000	182.1	136.9	32.6	351.6	−0.7%	1.6%
1999	182.5	138.6	32.9	354.0	4.5%	0.9%
1998	172.0	135.0	31.7	338.7	—	5.5%

Movies and Money: The Economics of the Business

Like books, where most of what is published loses money and only a few best sellers make profits, most movies also lose money. Of the six hundred films made each year in the United States, fewer than two hundred get the kind of favorable release that permits any financial return at all, let alone a profit. Nevertheless, the motion picture industry is a lively and important part of the media industries, generating considerable profits. As film industry attorney Schuyler Moore has written, "The saving grace in the film industry is that, when the rare blockbuster occurs, it can make up for the losses of a lot of other films."[18]

Moore compares movies to wildcat oil drilling: a lot of capital is required to make enough films to produce a rare blockbuster. This system naturally favors the big studios that take care of their own distribution and have continuing relationships with theaters. Independent filmmakers farm their distribution out to major studios or to other third-party distributors, a costly but necessary operation. Not surprisingly, over the years in this fiscally fragile field, many independent filmmakers have gone out of business, while distribution companies have a longer life cycle. As Peter Bart of the premier movie magazine *Variety* has written:

> A mere twenty years ago, it was common practice to open a movie in a few theaters across the country, build on word of mouth, adjust advertising strategies to audience response and then slowly expand to an ever broader audience. Today a movie is un-veiled, not with a quietly orchestrated build, but with a cosmic paroxysm, a global spasm of hype involving giant marketing partners like McDonalds and profligate network ad buys on the Super Bowl or the Olympics. A new film is thus machine-tooled to become either an instant blockbuster or an overnight flop. There is no room for adjustment or strategic change.[19]

Much has been written about the shady nature of the motion picture industry, where billions of dollars swirl around films that are often said to be unprofitable. (Domestic box office figures for 2007 alone were $9.63 billion.) As one recent book declares, "motion picture can elicit deep passion" and like oil gushers motion pictures "can create a flood of cash."[20]

How is it that a movie can generate millions of dollars more in ticket sales than it cost to make but still not make a profit? The seemingly endless credits at the end of a motion picture are a cue to what a complex industry this really is. Understanding the movie business requires a look at the industry's creative and even arcane accounting practices.

Unlike other media companies and firms where there are owners and employees, the motion picture industry has many players who bring talent and financing to the table. Many of these contributors to a movie also participate in the profits. For example, a star might receive not only a salary for making a picture but also a percentage of the money it makes. After various percentages are paid to different participants, the movie may end up not only unprofitable but actually losing money. Some critics say that this *participation system* of the industry "amounts to nothing more than a price-fixing conspiracy by the major powers in a company town,"[21] while others "defend the fairness of the system with vigor."[22]

Of course, some movies simply never earn more money than it cost to make them. As we have noted, many people are involved in making movies, and paying them can take a lot of money. A film's overall costs can soar because of superstar salaries and other demands that tend to drive up all other costs. In movie budgeting there is a well-known division: *above the line* and *below the line*. There is actually a line in the budgets that separate the above-the-line costs that must be spent before filming even begins—literary material, writers, producers, directors, and leading actors—from all the other actual production costs below the line. As Table 6.2 shows, many of these costs are for personnel.

Wages, of course, are only part of the cost of movies. By one estimate, the stars and other members of the acting cast account for only 20% of the costs, whereas sets and

TABLE 6.2

ABOVE-AND BELOW-THE-LINE POSITIONS IN FILMMAKING

People Above the Line

- Producers
- Directors
- Actors
- Writers

People Below the Line

- Casting directors
- Production assistants
- Assistant directors
- Camera operators
- Gaffers and best boys
- Wardrobe coordinators
- Stunt coordinators
- Film editors
- Post-production staff
- Composers and musicians
- Technical advisers (and many others)

physical properties ("props," the cars, furniture, and other items used by actors in movies) account for 35%.[23] The average cost of making a film in 2007 was $106.6 million. Many cost far more. Advertising and other costs were an additional $35.9 million per film on average. The money that the studios take in to balance such costs obviously depends on the number of films they distribute, the size of their audience, and the cost of admission.

THE MOVIE AUDIENCE

After the film is made, the next step is to distribute it in such a way that a maximum number of people will pay to see it. Although, as we have mentioned, increasing numbers of people prefer to watch movies at home (or on their mobile devices), moviemakers still place major emphasis on box-office performance, the money people spend to see a picture in the theater. Key factors that affect the size and makeup of theater audiences include:

Teenagers talking as they wait in line at a theater box office. They are a mainstay of the movie audience.

- The availability and cost of theater seats.
- Film ratings that indicate levels of objectionable content such as sex and violence.
- Influence and information provided by critics and movie awards.

Theaters and Cost of Admission

Movie distributors—generally the major movie studios—rent movies to exhibitors who operate theaters. Some exhibitors are independent, but, like newspapers, more and more are owned by chains. Deregulating media industries generally has benefited the motion picture industry. For example, motion pictures were once reluctant to work with cable and television, but they no longer are. As a result, at least four of the major studios now own theaters or shares in companies that do.[24]

HOW MANY PEOPLE GO TO THE MOVIES? The average weekly attendance at movies reached a peak of more than 90 million in the late 1940s; it was down to just over 18.5 million by 1992. The rate of decline leveled off during the 1990s, but as we noted earlier in the chapter, there is little prospect that it will rise significantly again.

Fewer people have, in turn, led to fewer theater seats. In the late 1940s there were just over 20,000 (single-screen) theaters in the United States. By 2007, there were 40,077 total screens, but only 6,356 theaters. That is, there are more screens available today, but they are in fewer theaters. In 2007 multiplexes with 16 or more screens grew by 4%. At the same time, the number of seats per theater has declined. Whereas in 1950 the average indoor movie theater had about 750 seats, by the late 1990s the average theater had just under 500.

It should also be noted that the number of people employed in movie theaters has declined steadily over the years, as movie attendance has decreased. Multiscreen establishments with more automated equipment require fewer people to run them than the old single-screen theaters.

Clearly, television and movie rentals have been the major factors in this precipitous decline, but the increasing price of admission may also have discouraged moviegoing. The price of a single adult ticket to a first-run picture (or new major release) rose from an average of only 23 cents in 1933 to more than $10 in most mid-sized and larger U.S. cities at a typical mall theater. In many metropolitan areas, admissions are even higher.

Overall, Americans are now spending more money on movies than ever before. However, in real terms, the industry is attracting a much smaller part of the family entertainment dollar than before. For example, in 1943 Americans spent more than 25% of their recreational expenditures on movies. By 2007, this figure had dropped to less than 5%.

WHO PAYS AT THE BOX OFFICE? As indicated earlier, movie theaters draw a youthful audience and appeal less to those who are older (see Figure 6.1). Most mass communication industries see young audiences as very desirable, because it is that portion of the population that will, in the future, buy goods and services and participate in the political process. The youthful vitality of the theater audience and its relative stability in makeup are an important force in keeping the industry alive and well. For about twenty years, starting in about 1970, due to a declining number of births earlier, the young movie audience was slowly shrinking. By the mid 1990s, however, the number of teenagers in the population started an upward trend. Today, with the nation's schools crammed

I FIGURE 6.1

Percent of Admissions by Age Group

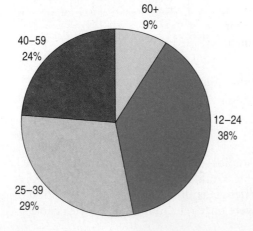

with rising numbers of students, the young movie audience will increase steadily in the years ahead.

How often do people pay to see a movie in a theater? For most people, not very often, according to national studies. Those who do go, however, attend and pay quite often. These so-called *frequent moviegoers* made up only about a fifth of the public (22%) in 2007, which represented a five-year low. In the twelve to twenty-four age group, however, 41% are frequent moviegoers. Although detailed data on the social characteristics of moviegoers are not easily obtained, research that is available indicates the following:

Objectionable content includes movie violence as in Quentin Tarantino's film *Reservoir Dogs*.

- Single people continue to be more frequent moviegoers than those who are married. In fact, about twice as many single people, compared with those who are married, go frequently to the movies. At the other end of the attendance scale, at least a third of married people say they *never* go to the movies, somewhat more than the number of single people who never go.
- More males than females describe themselves as frequent moviegoers.
- Movie attendance tends to increase with higher educational levels among adults, suggesting that the moviegoing audience tends to be better educated than those who do not go.

Ratings and Objectionable Content

As the movie industry grew massively earlier in the twentieth century, much of the public feared that films were having both powerful and harmful effects. (We discuss research on whether or not movies do indeed have a powerful effect in this chapter's Big Ideas feature.) A number of people believed the new medium was negatively influencing children and teaching them unwholesome ideas. Many civic and religious leaders concluded that the movies would bring a general deterioration of moral norms and harmful political changes to American life. These concerns pressured the industry to "clean up" its product, and efforts to suppress certain kinds of content in the movies, as well as to alert viewers to potentially objectionable themes, have continued. Most of the criticism now centers on films with "mature" themes—by which people usually mean those that deal with sex.

THE EVOLUTION OF MOVIE RATINGS As we noted earlier, the first strong pressures to censor films arose during the 1920s. The industry responded by cleaning up its own house. The Motion Picture Producers and Distributors Association appointed a former postmaster general, Will H. Hays, to head their organization. Hays developed a tough self-censorship code, which all producers in the association had to follow. A film that did not meet the standards of the "Hays Code" could not be shown in American theaters. Film producers who tried to defy this dictum were subjected to costly legal battles. The code restricted depictions of sex in particular. From the mid-1930s until the rise of television threatened the industry, movies avoided direct treatment of sexual themes and sexual behavior.

Meanwhile, a number of local governments screened and censored films. Even through the 1960s, Chicago gave this assignment to its police department, which called on a group of citizens to screen controversial films. Among the private groups most active in efforts to censor films was the Catholic Legion of Decency, which was established in 1934. It developed a list of recommended and non-recommended films, and it promoted the list to both Catholics and the general public.

BIG IDEAS: MEDIA THEORIES EXPLAINED

Selective and Limited Influences Theory

Research on the effects of mass communication began during the late 1920s with the Payne fund studies of the influence of movies on children. The results seemed to support the "magic bullet" theory (described in Chapter 1), indicating that motion pictures had widespread and powerful effects on their audiences. But newer research offered a different interpretation.

In 1940, a major study of a presidential election was conducted in Eric County, Ohio. The results showed that media had only three kinds of *limited* influences: 1) The media *activated* some people to vote who might have stayed home. 2) They *reinforced* the already firm views of others. 3) Only a few people, weakly tied to their initial choice, were persuaded to *change* their vote from one party's candidate to the other.

These results revealed that two kinds of factors were important as influences on what people *selected* from the media to read and hear. These were their social category memberships (such as income, religion, age, and gender) and their social relationships with friends and family. Thus, the results of the mass communicated campaign were selective and limited.

Research done for the army during World War II also led to a conclusion of selective and limited effects. Soldiers who were shown training films about the reasons for the war and the nature of the enemy learned a number of facts from their exposure. However, they underwent only minor changes in their opinions and no changes in their more general attitudes about the war or their motivation to fight. What changes did occur among these soldiers were linked to their individual differences in such matters as intelligence and their level of formal schooling.

Following the war, a number of additional experiments confirmed that exposure to, interpretation of, and response to a persuasive message was influenced by a host of factors. Specifically, the degree to which a person was influenced was related to both the characteristics of the message and the receiver.

This accumulation of research made it necessary to abandon the earlier "magic bullet" theory that forecast powerful, uniform, and immediate effects. It was necessary to develop explanations that took into account the fact that different kinds of people selected different kinds of content from the media and interpreted it in many different ways. Thus, the new theory emphasized both selective and limited influences. It is summarized in the following propositions:

1. People in contemporary society are characterized by great psychological diversity, due to *individual differences* in their psychological makeup.
2. People are also members of a variety of *social categories* (income, religion, age, gender, and many more). Such categories are characterized by subcultures of shared beliefs, attitudes, and values.
3. People in contemporary society are not isolated but are bound together in webs *of social relationships* based on family, neighborhood ties, and work relationships.
4. People's individual differences, social category subcultures, and patterns of social relationships lead them to be interested in, attend to, and interpret the content of mass communication in very *selective* ways.
5. **Therefore**, because exposure to media messages is highly selective and interpretation of content varies greatly from person to person, a mass communicated message will have only *limited* effects on the public as a whole.

Source: Brian Martin, "The Selective Usefulness of Game Theory," *Social Studies of Science*, Vol. 8, 1978, pp. 85-110.

Efforts like those of the Legion of Decency and other critical groups influenced the specifics of the Motion Picture Production Code developed by Hays. Although the code was not tough enough for groups such as the Legion of Decency, others regarded it as harsh, repressive, and too legalistic. Some film historians think the code hindered the development of American motion pictures.

By the late 1960s, the production code had been modified greatly. Numerous legal actions had broken efforts to apply rigid censorship. The industry entered a new era of self-regulation by establishing a movie classification, or **ratings**, system. Instead of barring certain films from theaters, the new system required that the public be warned of what to expect in a film. The result, which has been modified four times since it was adopted in 1968, is the following system of ratings:

G: All ages admitted, general audiences
PG: Parental guidance suggested, for mature audiences
PG-13: Parents are strongly cautioned to give special guidance to children under thirteen
R: Restricted, children under seventeen must be accompanied by a parent or other adult
NC-17: No one under seventeen admitted

The classification does not indicate quality; it is only a guide for parents considering what motion pictures their children should see. In recent years, a number of parents' groups and various magazines, newspapers, and websites offer movie recommendations for children calling attention to prevalence of violence and sex.

This system won public support and stilled some criticism, but some film producers feel that the system is too restrictive. The industry, through the Motion Picture Association of America, in effect puts its seal of approval on the first four categories of films and denies it to the fifth. There has been no active move to overturn it, however.

Interestingly, there are less than half as many G- and PG-rated films as there are films with PG-13, R, or NC-17 ratings. In fact, R ratings accounted for 59% of all films rated in 2007.

From time to time other films arouse public ire or that of particular groups who feel they are poorly or inaccurately portrayed. Sometimes there are boycotts of films and other efforts to urge the public to stay away. Efforts to suppress a particular motion picture can backfire, however. Perhaps no film in recent times has aroused such an outcry as *The Last Temptation of Christ* (1988), a low-budget movie that became something of a financial success at the box office—largely as a result of the furor. Various church groups and other critical people threatened and carried out boycotts and protest demonstrations. These efforts were thoroughly covered by both national and local news. The publicity brought crowds of curious viewers to the theaters to see what all the fuss was about. Some observers have speculated that if the film had been ignored, it would quickly have died as a dud.

CREEPING DESENSITIZATION   As television became a highly competitive medium for motion pictures, the industry turned away from the earlier production and review code developed by Will Hays. To meet the competition from network television, the movies began to alter their content. Once again, as they had done during the 1920s, they turned to depictions that went beyond the more conservative norms of the traditional segment of the public. Aside from the sexual portrayals previously discussed, which were always the most controversial, the producers also began to incorporate an increasing level of violence and vulgarity into their films.

Fast-action drama, packed with violence and with the actors using vulgar language, was a clear change from the older, sanitized movies that had been governed by the Hays code. Increasingly, the industry began producing fast-paced films in which macho heroes shot it out, had brutal fistfights, and raced through the streets in spectacular crash-filled car chases. New genres, such as horror, surf and beach epics, and more sophisticated special-effects monsters also proved to be popular.

In some ways this shift was successful, and in some ways it was not. There was limited success in that, after about the mid-1960s, the rate of decline in box office ticket sales slowed down. However, with these changes in content, a transformation of the audience was under way in which the movies changed from a form of family entertainment that mom, pop, and the kids all attended together into one made up of younger, single people. In particular, themes of violence and vulgarity were just right for younger audiences, but they were not appealing to older married people and were unsuitable for their children. Thus, while the loss of ticket sales slowed, the movies effectively shut out the more conservative majority of older, married people.

A very interesting pattern can be seen when looking back at the history of the relationship between audiences, their moral norms and the content of the movies. During the period just before and after World War I, the content of the films did not transgress general norms concerning sexual depictions, violence, or vulgarity. As the country entered the changing period of the 1920s, as noted earlier, movies increasingly challenged those norms. The Hays code temporarily halted that and reversed the trend. Challenged by television, however, movies once began to cross the line in terms of what many people wanted to see on the screen. In most recent years, further competition came to the industry from cable TV and from DVDs. Again, seeking increased audiences and profits, movies seemed to many to transgress traditional norms regarding sex, violence, and vulgarity.

The result has been a pattern of pressing forward to the limits of such norms, then drawing back when public outcries become too shrill, to wait until people adapted to the new standards being set. When outcries become fewer, the industry presses on once more until it again encounters resistance. Because of this cycle, the public gradually becames *desensitized* to content of the movies that at one time would have caused a serious problem for the industry. This "creeping cycle of desensitization" is not unique to motion pictures. It can apply to other media as well.

This cycle suggests that, when movies get sexier, more vulgar, and increasingly violent, these changes are not simply due to immoral decisions made by bad and greedy people who are in charge of the movie industry. Such people may not be saints or leaders in a movement to purify the popular culture of America, but their decisions are largely products of the economic system in which our media are embedded. Their choices can be stark: make money for their investors (highly approved) or go bankrupt (highly disapproved). With no political system of censorship to retain them, they supply the public with what it appears to want and back off only temporarily when critics stand their ground.

Censorship and Politics

Sex, violence, and vulgarity have not been the only categories of content at the center of outcries against movies over the years. Politics, too, has been the basis for censorship efforts.

Many films with political themes were widely criticized during the 1930s. Some large corporations of the time were fighting against unionization of their workforces, and some charged that unions were tools of Communists. Resulting accusations that some films were Communist propaganda split Hollywood in the years before World War II. During World War II, political differences were submerged as the industry united behind the war effort. However, when fear of communism ignited again in the late 1940s and 1950s, political censorship came to Hollywood as never before. The House Un-American Activities Committee, an official group of the U.S. Congress that had been active since the 1930s, held hearings under the leadership of Senator Joseph McCarthy. The Committee charged scores of people, including many in the film industry, with Communist activity. The hearings resulted in prison sentences for some people in the film, broadcast, and print industries.

Many others were blacklisted. **Blacklisting** was the work not of government but of private groups, and it was decidedly not a democratic activity. Various lobbying groups put together lists of people they suspected of being Communists. They circulated the lists privately and threatened to boycott advertisers who sponsored shows, newspapers, or magazines that hired anyone on the list, as well as producers who gave listed people work. Most of those blacklisted were not publicly accused, so they had no chance to defend themselves. Some actors, producers, writers, and others did not even know they were on such a list until no one wanted to hire them and their careers crashed. For a time performers had to be "cleared" by one of the anti-Communist groups before they would be hired. This period, when unsupported charges were frequent, is one of the darkest in media history. Postwar fear of communism was the culprit, and the film industry was hard hit by the informal censorship that resulted.

In the 1950s, the House Committee on Un-American Activities often created a media circus as they took on alleged subversive influences in the United States. They often targeted the movie industry.

The end of the Cold War late in the last century did not end political charges against movies and their producers. Many groups outside the movie industry have exerted influence on the content of films. Congress has summoned actors and directors to public hearings. The Supreme Court has tried to define what is and is not obscene in order to control objectionable depictions. Church groups and officials of local governments have also tried various strategies to shape, suppress, or ban American movies.

Censorship efforts often constrain the artistic freedom of filmmakers while providing little, if any, useful feedback for them. The groups pressuring the filmmakers are often too small, and their interests too narrow, for their efforts to constitute effective feedback for a medium intended for a mass audience. Nevertheless, their efforts can seriously distort communication between filmmaker and audience. Still, consumers of films have the same First Amendment rights that filmmakers do, and this includes the right to protest against content they do not like.

Many people in Hollywood, in their turn, exercise the right to attempt to influence the government. Conservative talk show hosts and other critics decry Hollywood's "liberal bias" and delight in denouncing actors who engage in political activity. Such politically active actors as Susan Sarandon and Sean Penn, for example, have taken considerable heat. Much of the Hollywood establishment weighs in during presidential campaigns and in recent years has raised notable amounts of money for Democratic candidates (although Republicans are certainly not without their own Hollywood supporters). Over the years a number of entertainment industry figures have even been elected to public office, most famously Arnold Schwarzenegger, who became governor of California.

The Influence of Evaluation: Criticism and Awards

Film ratings or public protests are only part of the many assessments that audiences use to help them choose movies. The writings of critics, the selections made for film festivals and awards, and surveys of public opinions of films provide other evaluations. These assessments might suggest that there are uniform standards of excellence in films, but that is not the case. Although occasionally there may be widespread agreement on which film was the best of a year or decade, there are about as many standards for criticism as there are critics and awards.

THE CRITICS   Although some people distinguish between **reviewers**—who make assessments about the appeal of films for a general audience—and **critics**—who judge a film

Awards like the Oscar given by the Academy of Motion Picture Arts and Sciences confer status on movies and help with marketing.

by more artistic and theoretical criteria and try to ascertain its social importance, the terms are used interchangeably by most people.

Film criticism appears in many places. Specialized industry magazines speak mainly to the movie community and to film scholars. Many magazines and newspapers have movie reviews and criticisms. *Time* and *New York Times,* as well as others, publish annual "ten best movies" lists. NBC's popular *Today* show offers regular movie reviews. PBS has a half-hour show devoted to movie reviews called "At the Movies," which is a sort of "consumers' guide" for what is worth seeing. Local television and radio stations review films on the air. Various Internet services also list, critique, and rate films. In fact, the Internet plays a significant role in driving people to movies. A survey conducted by the MPAA and Yahoo indicated in 2008 that some 73% of respondents reported that they first heard of a movie on the Internet before actually seeing it in a theater. Sometimes it seems like more energy is devoted to reviewing and criticizing films than to making them. There are even annual awards for the best film criticism.

THE AWARDS   The granddaddy of all the movie awards is the **Oscar,** a gold-plated statue about a foot high awarded each year in a nationally televised spectacle by the Academy of Motion Picture Arts and Sciences. The Oscars are prizes from the industry itself to its honored few, and even though the little statues themselves are rather tacky and cheaply produced, they are the most coveted of all the movie awards. Winning an Oscar has real economic value, because films that win them are usually re-released with a lot of publicity. Audience members use the Oscars as a source of information about whether a movie is worth seeing, so the re-released winners draw thousands more viewers and box-office receipts. Once a film gets nominated for an Oscar—or actually receives one— it gains prestige and often an additional audience that didn't see it the first time around.

The Academy makes awards in an almost-endless list of categories: It includes best picture, best director, best actor, best actress, best supporting actor, best supporting actress, best screenplay adaptation, best original screenplay, best cinematography, and best foreign-language film. There are also awards for art direction, sound, short subjects, music, film editing, and costume design, as well as honorary awards, scientific and technical awards, and various awards for service to the industry.

The Academy Awards have not been without their critics. Some charge that those giving the awards concentrate on the most popular films, rather than on the best or most socially significant. There is some truth to this argument. For example, one of the best films of all time, Orson Welles' brilliant *Citizen Kane* (1941), received only one award, for best screenplay. Still, the list of Oscar winners is a kind of "Who's Who" of well-known films and filmmakers.

Other honors and prizes are less well known. Both the Writers Guild and the Directors Guild give awards, and there are a number of awards by groups independent of the industry. The National Board of Review Awards are given for films that are recommended for children. Both the National Society of Film Critics and the New York Film Critics give annual awards for exemplary films, and the foreign press corps covering Hollywood gives annual Golden Globe Awards.

Of course, another source of recognition is the inclusion of films at major film festivals, from Cannes to Los Angeles, New York and Sundance. These festivals are major marketing tools for the industry and provide a stamp of recognition and approval.

CHAPTER REVIEW

- Motion pictures have a technological history that includes inventions in optics, photography, and electronics and discoveries in the psychology of the perception of motion.

- The movie theaters as we know them began after the turn of the century with the nickelodeons. Within a few years, movies were being made for the middle class, and the industry expanded to become a popular mode of family entertainment.

- As society changed rapidly after World War I, movies mirrored the new ways of life. Conservative people were alarmed at portrayals of alcohol use, easy money, fast cars, and loose morals. Extensive efforts to control movies arose.

- Between 1930 and 1960, the great Golden Age of movies dawned and then declined. The American film industry has gone through many changes in its short history. For the most part, it has been a medium for entertainment.

- Motion pictures are much affected by digital technologies that have revolutionized production and changed content and distribution patterns.

- Every film is a product of technology, artistry, managerial skill and showmanship. Making a film involves a wide range of professionals and craft workers. At various times different members of the filmmaking team have tended to dominate in shaping films.

- The content of a film is influenced by conflicting forces: the desire for efficiency, a view of what the audience wants, and an individual's desire to shape the film. The result of this conflict has been a wide range of genres and styles in American films.

- Audiences are influenced by ticket prices and availability, ratings, and the evaluations of movies conveyed by reviews and awards.

- Traditional film (shown in theaters) was once a more important medium of entertainment than it is today, but the industry has responded to the demands of new competition, changing technology, and changing audiences. Because it has adapted with digital screens and other digital applications, it will likely remain a large, lively, and significant medium.

STRATEGIC QUESTIONS

1. How did the motion picture become a successful medium of entertainment? Does the history of the medium explain this?
2. What has been the role and function of motion pictures in society? Has that changed?
3. Why does the popularity of film genres change over time? How do today's most popular film forms compare with those of the Golden Age of Hollywood?
4. What is the economic or business model for the movies? Has that changed over time?
5. How is the motion picture industry adapting to and making use of the digital revolution?
6. How do movies compete with or collaborate with other entertainment media such as cable, video-on-demand, and other forms?

KEY CONCEPTS & TERMS

Nickelodeons 120	Home Video 126	Censorship 140
Talkies 121	Producer 131	Piracy 126
Golden Age 122	Above the line 134	Movie audience 135
Moguls 132	Blockbuster 116	Multiplex 123

ENDNOTES

1. Richard Corliss, "Can This Man Save the Movies? (Again?)," *Time*, March 20, 2006, p. 67. See also "Everything's Gone Blu," *The Economist*, Jan. 10, 2008.

2. Martin Quigley, Jr., *Magic Shadows: The Story of the Origin of Motion Pictures* (Washington, DC: Georgetown University Press, 1948), pp. 9–10.

3. Josef M. Eder, *History of Photography* (New York: Columbia Press, 1948), pp. 209–245, 263–264, 316–321. For a contemporary look at a motion picture technology, see Steve Barclay, *The Motion Picture Image— From Film to Digital* (New York: Focal Press, 1999).

4. There were several claimants to the invention of celluloid roll film in the late 1880s. Eventually the courts decided a case on the matter in favor of the Reverend Hannibal Goodwin. However, George Eastman produced the film in his factory and marketed it to the public. See Frederick A. Talbot, *Moving Pictures: How They Are Made and Work* (London: Heinemann, 1923).

5. Talbot, *Moving Pictures*, p. 2. Also see Gail Resnik and Scott Trost, *All You Need To Know About the Movie and TV Business* (New York: Fireside, 1996).

6. Tino Balio, ed., *The American Film Industry* (Madison: University of Wisconsin Press, 1976), p. 63.

7. Adam Liptak, "Is Litigation the Best Way to Tame New Technology," *New York Times*, Sept. 2, 2000, p. B9.

8. Edgar Dale, *The Content of Motion Pictures* (New York: Macmillan, 1935).

9. Dale, *The Contents of Motion Picture*, p. 208. See also an excellent summary history of the major studios in Cobbett Feinberg, *Reel Facts: The Movie Book of Records* (New York: Vintage, 1978), pp. 376–389.

10. Edward J. Epstein, *The Big Picture, Money and Power in Hollywood* (New York: Random House, 2005), pp. 130–131. Also see Epstein, "The Next Big Thing, Sony's Blu-Ray DVD," *Slate*, Aug. 22, 2005.

11. Motion Picture Association of America, 2007. The MPAA maintains a website with detailed industry statistics, including its annual *Movie Attendance Study* and *Theatrical Market Statistics*, both for fiscal year 2007; see www.mpa.org.

12. James Monaco, *How to Read a Film*, rev. ed. (New York: Oxford University Press, 1977), p. 246.

13. Feinberg, *Reel Facts*, p. xiii.

14. John L. Fell, *An Introduction to Film* (New York: Praeger, 1975), p. 127.

15. For an excellent abbreviated analysis of the movies, see Garth Jowett and James M. Linton, *Movies as Mass Communication* (Beverly Hills, CA: Sage, 1990).

16. Douglas Gomery, "The Hollywood Film Industry: Theatrical Exhibition, Pay TV and Home Video," in Benjamin Compaine and Douglas Gomery, *Who Owns the Media*, 3rd ed. (Mahwah, NJ: Lawrence Erlbaum, 2000). Also see Jason Squire, *The Movie Business Book*, 3rd ed. (New York: Fireside, 2005).

17. Epstein, *The Big Picture*. Also see Epstein, "The Next Big Thing."

18. Schuyler M. Moore, *The Biz—The Basics: Legal and Financial Aspects of the Film Industry* (Los Angeles: Silman James Press, 2000), p.12.

19. Peter Bart, *The Gross: The Hits, The Flops, The Summer That Ate Hollywood* (New York: St. Martin's Griffin, 1999), p. 3.

20. Bill Daniels, David Leedy, and Steven D. Sills, *Movie Money—Understanding Hollywood's (Creative) Accounting Practices* (Los Angeles: Silman James, 1998), xxi. See also Kelly Charles Crabb, *The Movie Business: The Definitive Guide to the Legal and Financial Aspects of Getting Your Movie Made* (New York: Simon & Schuster, 2005) and Charles C. Moul, *A Concise Handbook of Movie Industry Economics* (New York: Cambridge University Press, 2005).

21. Gail Resnik and Scott Trost, *All You Need to Know About the Movie and TV Business* (New York: Fireside, 1996) pp. 33, 35–36, and 57–78 for an excellent discussion of "above-the-line" and "below-the-line" people in the motion picture industry.

22. Daniels, Leedy, and Sills, *Movie Money*, xxi–xxii.

23. These estimates were obtained by one of the authors in an interview with the National Association of Theater Owners.

24. Motion Picture Association of America, Inc., op. cit, 2007 studies.

Radio: The Resilient Medium

Radio—the oldest broadcast medium—is also one of the most modern, taking full advantage of the digital revolution. Once the radio industry, whose history we will detail later in this chapter, was a fairly simple proposition: First, there was the *tower* (or transmission station and means of production and distribution). Second, there was the *talent*, the people who operate radio stations from station managers and news directors to disc jockeys and talk show hosts, among others. Next came the *audience* for radio, people attracted to particular programs or radio content and formats from news to rock music, for example. Finally, there was the *advertising*, the fuel for financing radio operations.

In the digital age, radio has changed the listening experience with better quality sound, distribution on the Internet, and such audio innovations as podcasts as well as digital satellite radio with scores of channels available to the listener. Radio is somewhat a paradoxical medium—at once, a highly concentrated industry with a single company owning over 1,000 stations and at the same time a medium where a single individual can use the Internet to become a web broadcaster. While it is a vigorous business in the United States and most of the world, radio also has a long relationship with the government, both as a regulated medium and as one sometimes owned (or supported) by governments, from government-run radio stations and networks in some countries to our own public radio, which gets some taxpayer support to operate. Now to radio's colorful and continuing history.

Until a little over a century ago, the lack of rapid, long-distance communication was a severe handicap in coordinating complex human activities. In fact, the inability to communicate quickly over distance has more than once altered the fate of the entire world.

For example, in 1588, King Philip II of Spain sent the Armada, a great fleet of 130 warships under the command of the Duke of Medina-Sidonia, to crush the English. The plan was for the Spanish ships to pick up the army of Alessandro Farnese, the Duke of Palma, on the shores of Flanders and take them across the channel to invade and conquer England.

This was the largest military venture ever planned up until that time. It should have succeeded, since the English had no effective standing army. Instead, the venture was a miserable failure, largely due to a lack of adequate communication.

The Armada and Palma's army never found each other. English ships sailed out to harry the Armada in the channel, doing only minor damage but forcing Spanish ships northward. Problems of coordination quickly mounted. Unable to contact the nearby army that he was supposed to meet and, indeed, uncertain that it was even there, Medina-Sidonia had to abandon the invasion plan. Bad storms arose as the ships tried to return to Spain. Dozens of vessels foundered, with great loss of life, and the whole effort ended in disaster.

If the commanders of the Armada and the shore-bound army had possessed just one little CB radio each, they could have coordinated their efforts effectively. The entire history of the world would have changed, and in the United States, we would probably all be speaking, reading, and writing Spanish today!

It wasn't until about 350 years after the Armada sailed that the technologies were all in place and radio took off as a mass medium becoming, as we'll see, almost an instant success. Although it faced significant competition from television, radio has adapted and found a viable niche among our current media. It is now a source for music entertainment, a means by which many people receive the latest news, and a forum where ideas—both important and unimportant—are debated on talk shows.

With so much competitive activity and clutter transforming media in a digital age, it would be easy to assume that radio—our oldest broadcast medium—might be overlooked and even left behind as exciting new devices and platforms vie for attention. But this is not the case. Instead of shutting off radio, the Internet opened new channels for radio. It is now possible to listen to radio stations from all over the world, not just those within a limited local or geographic range. Radio has also taken advantage of the cell phone and other handheld devices, like the Blackberry and its various competitors. There is hardly anywhere in the media world where radio is not available. A completely new development is satellite radio. Its multi-channel offerings, mostly received in cars, are actually paid for by listeners, a new development in radio industry. Similarly, the digital age has expanded the capacity of radio stations broadcasting the "old-fashioned" way, over the airwaves. Those stations now have websites, offering their listeners podcasts and full-motion video reports, as well as other services.[1] The web allows broadcast radio, an early interactive medium, to be even more interactive now, with online chats accompanying on-the-air programming.

Radio was, is, and remains our most attended-to medium, making it attractive to advertisers. Radio stations are, therefore, profitable—so much so that radio is an attractive investment for media companies. We'll see in this chapter that radio has become one of the most concentrated of the media industries, with a few firms literally owning hundreds of stations.[2] Radio, in short, has found a successful place among our current media, and it seems likely to remain viable.

THE DEVELOPMENT OF RADIO TECHNOLOGY

Communication devices that could conquer distance at high speed were a dream for many centuries before they actually existed. Giovanni della Porta, a scientist in the 1500s, described in his book, *Natural Magik,* a "sympathetic telegraph" that would be able to "write at a distance."[3] (In Greek, *tele* means far off and *graphos,* to write.) The instrument would be prepared with a special lodestone, a natural magnet that would sensitize two needles so they would act "in sympathy." The needles would be mounted on separate dials, something like compasses, but with the letters of the alphabet around the edge. If one needle were to be moved to a given position on its dial, such as to point to the letter *A,* the other would move to a similar position immediately, even though the devices were far from each other and not connected with wires.

It was a great idea. Unfortunately the special lodestone was never found. During the next three centuries, however, there was a slow accumulation of science that eventually made such long-distance and instantaneous communication possible. Indeed, devices were developed during the 1900s that would have astounded della Porta.

Starting in the 1840s, swift, long-distance communication technologies came quickly, one after the other, within a span of about fifty years. The first was the electric dot-and-dash telegraph (1844). It was followed by the telephone (1876), the wireless telegraph (1896), and finally the radiotelephone (1906). Then, with adaptations of radiotelephone technology in the early 1920s, radio became a mass medium for household use. We saw earlier that the movies also came into existence during the last decade of the nineteenth century. By the mid-1920s, even the principles needed for television were understood, and the first scheduled broadcasts took place in the 1930s.

This chapter focuses on only part of that set of swift changes—the development of radio. As will be clear, radio and television share a common background of technological development. They also share a common economic base and a system of societal control. For that reason, the events of history common to both media will be reviewed in the present chapter, but what is unique to TV will be presented in Chapter 8.

The original telegraph receiver printed Morse codes onto a ticker tape.

The Social Conditions that Spawned Radio

To understand the ways in which the development of broadcasting was a part of more general trends taking place, we need to review very briefly what was happening more broadly in Western society at different times during the nineteenth century. Few citizens at the beginning of the period could have imagined the changes in lifestyle that would soon take place in the United States. During the first decade of that century, people still traveled between towns on foot, on horseback, or on vehicles pulled by animals. Trips to distant places often took months. Goods to be purchased were handcrafted rather than factory-made. Food was either grown at home or produced on nearby farms. Only a limited selection of items came to a community from distant places. Long-distance communication was by sailing ship or by postal and courier services that used horses. The pace of society was slow indeed, and most people lived a simple rural or small-town existence.

The century was not even half over before travel time had been drastically reduced. Awesome machines, belching smoke and steam and pulling long strings of wagons, were rolling across the countryside on iron rails at what were then considered incredible speeds. Powerful boats, thrust forward by steam-driven paddle wheels, were plying the nation's waterways. Power-driven factories spewed forth standardized goods. The scope and pace of commercial activities had increased greatly. Thus, even before the Civil War, the industrial revolution had transformed much of the nation.

After the war ended, the process continued. Railroads soon offered scheduled service connecting most major American cities, and steam-driven ships regularly crossed the great oceans. Hundreds of factories were producing shoes, farm implements, clocks, guns, cooking pots, woven cloth, tools, and a great variety of other manufactured goods. Small towns had become cities, and large metropolitan centers thrived. Food came not just from local farms but also by rail and ship from more distant sources. The process of industrialization had generated a parallel revolution in the production, distribution, and consumption of goods and services of many kinds.

The development of radio was a part of these great changes. As we have already suggested, it was by applying principles discovered in the basic sciences that practical devices were developed to communicate rapidly over long distances.

Unraveling the mysteries of electricity was a first step toward broadcasting. The Greeks marveled at static electricity but did not understand its nature. By the 1700s, Europeans were generating gigantic static charges, but they still did not understand the nature of electricity. Within one hundred years, however, researchers succeeded in revealing how electricity works, how it could be stored in batteries, and how it could be used in practical applications. The great dream of the sympathetic telegraph seemed increasingly achievable as the nature of electricity and ways to control it began to be understood. Discoveries made by scientists such as Alessandro Volta, Andre Ampere, Michael Faraday, and James Clerk Maxwell laid the scientific foundations for applications such as the telegraph, the electric motor, and, later, radio and television.

Communicating over a Wire

At the end of the 1700s, devices were developed by which electrical impulses could be used to send a message over wires. They were very cumbersome and limited to short distances (such as between two rooms). The system relied on static electricity and a number of separate wires, each connected to a hinged card—one for each letter of the alphabet. On a special desk-like console, a charge applied at one end of a specific wire caused a spark at the other end. This, in turn, caused its hinged letter card to flop down. With great patience and constant resetting of the letters, a message could be sent. Actually, it was a lot faster and easier just to shout from one room to the other. Nevertheless, this fascinating toy demonstrated two problems needed to be solved in order to develop an electric telegraph: controlling the electricity traveling along wires and developing some means to identify individual letters at the receiving end.

The first important discovery came in 1819 in England when Hans Oerstead found that a pulse of electrical current traveling a considerable distance could deflect a magnetic needle in a sort of dial at the end of the wire. He also noted that reversing the direction of the current in the circuit would reverse the deflection of the needle, allowing the device to serve as a crude telegraph. This led a number of scientists, including Andre Ampere and Karl Gauss, to study and improve the process. By 1837, Wilhelm Cooke and Charles Wheatstone developed a working telegraph system based on this needle-deflection principle. It was actually used by railroads in England.

The Contribution of Samuel B. Morse

A much more efficient system, based on the electromagnet, was developed by Samuel B. Morse in 1844. The electromagnet itself had been discovered by William Sturgeon in 1825 and then refined by Michael Faraday and Joseph Henry. It was a rather simple device: A bar of soft iron, about the size of a highlighter or whiteboard marker, is tightly wrapped in copper wire. When a steady flow of electricity from a battery is passed through the wire, the bar becomes a fairly

PROFESSOR MORSE EXHIBITING HIS ELECTRIC TELEGRAPH.

The first communication over a wire came with the invention of the electric telegraph by Samuel Morse (1791–1872) here exhibiting his invention in this 19th century wood engraving.

strong magnet. Stop the electricity and the bar loses most of its magnetic property. By starting and stopping the flow of electricity, an operator can make the electromagnet attract and release another piece of iron. Using this principle, Morse constructed a telegraph machine. He attached a pencil to the piece of metal that his electromagnet attracted, so as to leave a record of the transmission on a moving strip of paper. Morse also devised a code for each letter by using long and short pulses of electricity. His alphabetic system of "dots" and "dashes" became known as Morse code.

By today's standards, Morse's was a crude system. But in comparison to what was available at the time, it was a fantastic practical advance in communication technology. After the device proved reliable, Morse was able to obtain a grant from the U.S. government to field-test the system. He had a copper wire strung on poles between Baltimore, Maryland, and Washington, D.C., a distance of about forty miles. From Baltimore, on the morning of May 25, 1844, he sent the dramatic message, "What hath God wrought?" It was received in Washington with wild cheering and awe. The speed of communication was no longer limited to the speed people could travel. Information could now be flashed to a distant location at the speed of lightning. It did indeed seem to many observers like something that God had personally wrought.

Within a few years, with wires on poles along the railroad lines, most of the major cities of the United States were connected by telegraph. Business, the military, and, as we saw in Chapter 4, newspapers began to depend on the system for rapid communication. Undersea cables were laid even before the Civil War. Regular telegraph service between the United States and Europe was available by 1866. Yet the telegraph obviously was not a medium for the general public to use at home. It would be more than half a century before ordinary people would have a device in their homes for instantaneous mass communication without wires.

The telegraph not only initiated the era of instantaneous communication; it also set the model for the *structure of ownership* that would eventually characterize the electronic media in the United States. Even though the federal government had paid for Morse's experimental line between Baltimore and Washington, it declined to exercise control over the telegraph. The medium became the property of a private corporation to be operated for profit. This was a critical decision because it set the pattern for telephone, radio, and television as they developed.

Guglielmo Marconi (1874–1937), the Italian electrical engineer and inventor, sent coded messages without wires in 1895 and played a major role in the development of radio.

Communicating with Radio Waves

Meanwhile, a German scientist, Heinrich Hertz, had been experimenting with some curious electromagnetic phenomena that he had produced in the laboratory. By 1887 he had constructed a simple transmitter and receiver and had demonstrated the existence of what we know today as **radio waves**, the longest waves in the electromagnetic spectrum, which also includes light waves. Although our eyes cannot perceive radio waves, they can be received by devices such as radios, televisions, and cellular phones. The accomplishment amazed the scientific world, and experimentation with these mysterious new waves that traveled at the speed of light began in laboratories in many countries. This basic scientific discovery was to become the foundation of radio broadcasting.

MARCONI'S WIRELESS TELEGRAPH   A few years later, Guglielmo Marconi, a twenty-year-old youth from a wealthy Italian family, had read everything he could find about the Hertzian waves, bought the necessary parts, and built his own devices to produce and detect them. He experimented with different wavelengths, types of antennae, and other features of the system. His idea was that by systematically interrupting the wave as it was being generated, he could send and receive messages in Morse code— without wires.

By 1895, Marconi had succeeded in sending coded messages over a modest distance across his father's estate. Thinking that his invention probably could have important uses, he offered it to the Italian government and tried to persuade them to help finance his work. But his government, deciding the device was only a novelty without practical importance, was not interested. Undaunted, and at the urging of his English mother, Marconi took his ideas to London, where in 1897 he was able to obtain a patent as well as financial backing to develop further his "wireless telegraph." Soon after, by 1901, he had built a much more powerful transmitter and succeeded in sending a message (a sequence of eighteen repetitions of the coded letter S) across the Atlantic. It was a startling achievement.

Radio, in this dot-and-dash form, had enormous practical advantages over the land-based telegraph that required wires. Ships at sea could communicate with each other and with stations on land. A number of remote stations could hear and reply to the broadcast of a central station. For England, with numerous colonies, a large navy, a huge merchant marine, and far-flung commercial enterprises, the wireless telegraph was a godsend.

The principal drawback of the earliest sets was that they required large, heavy equipment to achieve long-range transmission. Such a set could barely fit into a room. Not being a scientist, Marconi had chosen the wrong end of the frequency band. He reasoned that long radio waves would go farther than short ones. But it took great electrical energy to transmit them over long distances. Thus, his system required powerful electric currents, heavy wiring and switches, and massive antennae. If he had used the very short waves, he could have developed a much smaller, more portable machine. However, within a few years that became evident.

Marconi was not only an inventor but also a shrewd businessman. He successfully fought patent challenges to protect his ownership, and he established profit-oriented corporations to exploit wireless communication. He founded the American Marconi Company in 1899, and by 1913 it had a virtual monopoly on the use of the wireless telegraph in the United States. By that time dot-and-dash radio had come into worldwide use, and Marconi became a rich man indeed. As earlier, with telegraph by wire, the principle of private ownership and profit in broadcasting was established from the outset.

Marconi also invented a device for generating and detecting a particular wavelength, for the more precise transmission of signals. He patented it in 1904. This was important because it allowed the transmitter to broadcast on a specific wavelength, or **frequency**. With the receiving instrument "tuned" to a similar wavelength, signals on other frequencies could not interfere. We still tune radios to specific frequencies in this manner for transmission and reception.

THE RADIOTELEPHONE   During the first decade of the twentieth century, radio quickly became more than a wireless telegraph. On Christmas Eve in 1906, radio operators along the lonely Atlantic sea lanes could not believe their ears when suddenly they heard a human voice over their sets. A man read from the Bible, then played a phonograph record and a violin. Up to that time, only dots and dashes had ever come out of their earphones. It was Reginald A. Fessenden broadcasting from an experimental station near Boston. He used a telephone mouthpiece as a "microphone" and a special alternator to generate his radio waves. The dot-and-dash receivers were able to detect his complex signals.

It was Lee De Forest who in 1906 brought the radio into its own by inventing what he called the *audion,* a three-element vacuum tube, which allowed much more sophisticated circuits and applications. De Forest's tube made amplification of radio signals possible. This, in turn, permitted the development of small, reliable receivers. As a result, portable radio transmitters and receivers about the size of a large shoebox played important roles in World War I. By 1918, radio communication had advanced sufficiently for a pilot to receive and transmit signals from an airplane to people on the ground. Even at this time, however, radio was still either the older dot-and-dash wireless system introduced by Marconi or essentially an experimental device. It was by no means something that people used at home to listen to scheduled broadcasts. In other words, it was a private, rather than a public, medium.

Nevertheless, radio captured the imagination of the public in the early days. It seemed like a scientific marvel at the cutting edge of new technology. People had the same fascination with it that later generations would have with early space vehicles and the Internet. For example, when ships got into trouble, it was possible to summon aid by radio. One of the first examples occurred in 1898, when radio signals were used to bring aid to a vessel in difficulty. But a really dramatic rescue at sea took place in 1909. When the *SS Republic* began to sink off the coast of New York after being struck by another ship, Jack Binns, the ship's wireless operator, stayed at his post in the freezing weather for hours, sending out a distress signal. Other ships detected it and came as quickly as possible to the position indicated. All fifteen hundred passengers were rescued. It made great newspaper headlines, and the public was enthralled. Binns was regarded as a hero and was given a ticker-tape parade in New York City. Chorus girls, it was said, threw themselves at him. His employers were so pleased with him that they were going to promote him to a better post—as wireless operator on their new superliner, the *SS Titanic,* when it went into service. Binns, however, could not accept that honor, as he was to be married the same day the *Titanic* set sail.

On its maiden voyage, in 1912 (without Binns), the "unsinkable" *Titanic* struck an iceberg in the North Atlantic. The wireless operator tried to alert nearby ships, but their radio crews had gone to bed for the night. However, contact was made with a shore station (in Wanamaker's department store in New York), whose stronger signal could reach more distant points. The young operator, David Sarnoff, stayed at his post for many hours, making contact with other vessels. Unfortunately, by the time those ships arrived the next morning, the great passenger liner had gone to the bottom of the ocean. Some fifteen hundred people drowned, including the *Titanic's* heroic wireless operator, who tried all night to summon aid until he went down with the ship.

RADIO BECOMES A MASS MEDIUM

In increasing numbers, amateur radio fans were attracted to the medium after World War I. Although assembled sets could be purchased, they were expensive, so thousands bought parts and put together their own receivers. Plans for "crystal set" radio receivers appeared in popular magazines aimed at the home mechanic and tinkerer. Companies marketed kits through the mail for crystal sets that even a bright child could put together. With a length of copper wire wrapped around a Quaker Oats box, a device to slide along the resulting coil to "tune" the device, and the right kinds of crystal, battery, earphones, and aerial, the home listener could pick up audible signals. Radio was the scientific wonder of the age, and the public expressed a broad interest in the medium even before regular broadcasting began.

The Period of Transition

Before radio broadcasting could be a mass medium, it had to be transformed from a long-range, rather cumbersome device for maritime, commercial, governmental, and hobby communication to an easy-to-use system that would bring program content to people in their homes.[4] That meant that radio needed to develop several characteristics:

1. *Small size.* Radio sets had to be small enough for use in the home. In part, the home-built set helped to fulfill that need, but those who were not tinkerers wanted to purchase their sets ready-made.
2. *Low price.* The cost of radios had to be brought within the means of large numbers of families.

NBC's founding mogul David Sarnoff at a demonstration of the RCA Electronic Light Amplifier, which had important applications in television, radar, x-ray and other fields.

3. *Regularly scheduled programs,* to which people would want to listen. This was a real barrier because there simply were no stations providing content that would interest most potential listeners.
4. *Clear reception*—that is, without annoying static and overlap between stations. This meant that there had to be a means of regulating the use of the airwaves, either by voluntary agreements or through some government licensing scheme. Not everyone who wanted to broadcast would be able to do so without interfering with others on the same wavelength.
5. *Money-making capability.* Perhaps most important of all, there had to be a means of paying for the broadcasts. While by today's standards, the transmission equipment itself was not all that expensive, there were other costs involved. Broadcasters had to provide space to house the station, with its attendant costs of heat, light, rent, and so forth. They also had to pay the staff: engineers, people who said things over the air, and even janitors who cleaned up.

Within a few years all of these barriers would be overcome, and the transition to a true mass medium would take place very quickly.

THE "RADIO MUSIC BOX"   In 1916, David Sarnoff (who played a part in trying to summon aid for the Titanic), had gone to work for the American Marconi Company. He wrote a now-famous memorandum to his boss that outlined the way that radio could become a medium for home use:

> I have in mind a plan of development which would make radio a "household utility" in the same sense as a piano or phonograph. The idea is to bring music into the house by wireless.... The receiver can be designed in the form of a simple "Radio Music Box" and arranged for several different wave lengths, which should be changeable with the throwing of a single switch or pressing of a single button. The "Radio Music Box" can be supplied with amplifying tubes and a loudspeaking telephone, all of which can be neatly mounted in one box. The box can be placed on a table in the parlor or living room, the switch set accordingly and the transmitted music received.[5]

Sarnoff went on in his memo to suggest that people listening at home could receive news, sports scores, lectures, weather reports, and concerts. He also suggested that such machines could be manufactured and sold by the thousands. All his scheme needed was the addition of advertising as a source of financial support for regularly scheduled broadcasts, plus government control over frequency allocation, and it would have been a very accurate description of the future of radio as a mass medium. Sarnoff's proposal was rejected by his superiors as impractical and too visionary. However, by 1919 he had become the manager of a new company called the Radio Corporation of America (RCA), and he played a major role in bringing radio to the public as a mass medium.

Pittsburgh's station KDKA, where this engineer is at work, is the oldest continuously operated radio station in the U.S.

SCHEDULED PROGRAMS BEGIN The broadcasting of regularly scheduled programs over the airwaves did not begin in all parts of the country at once. A sort of amateur version of such broadcasts started in Pittsburgh in April 1920. An engineer, Dr. Frank Conrad, was developing transmitting systems for the Westinghouse Corporation. He needed to test equipment after hours, so he built a transmitter over his garage at home. It was licensed as station 8XK. With the help of his family, Conrad began making regular broadcasts two evenings a week. He invited people to send him postcards. Many did so or called on the telephone requesting particular Victrola records. This feedback from the audience enabled Conrad to understand the reach of his station's signal.

The directors of Westinghouse, seeing the growing public interest in home radio in 1920 and intrigued by Conrad's example, decided to establish a radio station to produce regularly scheduled broadcasts in the Pittsburgh area. The idea was to provide programming for people who bought the home receivers that Westinghouse was manufacturing and selling. The firm built a transmitter in a tin "radio shack" on top of its building in Pittsburgh and licensed it as radio station KDKA. To dramatize the establishment of the station, it announced that for its first broadcast it would transmit the returns of the 1920 presidential election (Warren G. Harding versus James M. Cox).

Actually, the station received its election information from a local newspaper by phone. Nevertheless, several hundred people with sets in the Pittsburgh area learned from signals sent over the evening sky that Harding had won. The event was a dramatic success, greatly stimulating the sale of receivers. The station continued to broadcast regularly, presenting music, religious services, sports information, political talks, and even market reports. Its signal carried over a long distance, and people in many parts of the country tuned in. Radio station KDKA is still on the air and is recognized as the oldest station in continuous operation in the nation.

CHAOS ON THE AIRWAVES Within months, dozens of other stations went on the air in various cities. Soon there were hundreds, and the infant mass medium became a chaotic mess. Transmitters were paid for and operated by just about anyone who wanted to transmit messages. This included department stores, wealthy individuals, automobile dealers, corporations, churches, schools, and, of course, manufacturers of radio equipment. By the end of 1922, some 254 federal licenses had been issued for transmitters that complied with the provisions of the Radio Act of 1912. The very next year, in 1923, dozens of stations came onto the air every month, and about 600 were broadcasting by the end of the year.

There simply were not enough locations in the frequency spectrum to accommodate everyone. Each position had at least one and sometimes several stations. Furthermore, the amplitude modulation (AM) broadcasting system in use could carry over very long distances, especially at night. People trying to listen to a local station would, at the same time, hear a jumble of broadcasts from other parts of the country.

NETWORKS EMERGE   In 1926 the National Broadcasting Corporation (NBC, led by David Sarnoff) initiated **network broadcasting**. The Columbia Broadcasting System (CBS) and others soon followed, and near the end of the decade, people all over the country could simultaneously hear a broadcast of the same radio program. Radio networks were a group of radio stations, either affiliates of a given company or owned by them, which broadcast the same content at the same time across a wide geographic territory. The idea was that each station would broadcast to a particular area until its signal ran out and was then joined by the next station, and so on. First proposed by AT&T in 1921 as a broadcast system supported by advertising, General Electric, Westinghouse, and RCA formed their own networks and eventually in 1926 bought out AT&T. These became the basis for such radio networks as ABC, CBS, and NBC, which eventually morphed into television networks. There are radio networks across the world such as the BBC (UK), CBC (Canada), NHK (Japan), China National Radio (People's Republic of China), and many others. The expanded audience for programming, thanks to networks, became the basis for a radio industry in which programs were sold to local stations—and audiences were sold to advertisers.

REGULATING BROADCASTING   Because radio transmissions respect no national boundaries, it was clear from the beginning that international agreements of some sort were needed to maintain order on the airwaves. An international structure designed to regulate telecommunications already existed, long before radio was even developed. It was quite successful, and it provided a model that could be used to forge agreements on radio broadcasting. Similar radio agreements, made in 1903 and 1906, regulated international and maritime broadcasting, giving priority to humanitarian and emergency uses of radio.[6] These agreements, however, had nothing to do with home radio.

With the Radio Act of 1912, the U.S. Congress tried to create a system for licensing of transmitters. The law required citizens to obtain a license to operate a transmitter, but it did not work because it provided no real way that the government could turn anyone down. Furthermore, it established no criteria for approving the operations of a new transmitter, such as a broadcasting frequency, its power, or time on the air.

Because the 1912 legislation did not prescribe a frequency for a new station, its owner could choose the one that he or she preferred. If several operators decided to use the same frequency, as often happened, interference and overlap increased. Some stations solved the problem by agreeing informally to broadcast only on certain days or hours. Others, less cooperative, simply increased their power sharply to blast competing stations off the air. There was some experimentation with networks, with several stations sending signals on the same frequency. However, none of these solutions were effective.

As more and more stations began transmitting, the overlapping of frequencies and broadcast hours finally made it virtually impossible to tune in to any clear signal. The chaos first brought the establishment of new stations to a halt, then sharply reversed the growth trend. Hundreds of stations simply went off the air and never returned.[7] They had no way of recovering their costs, and their signals were lost in a chaos of noise.

Obviously, some sort of tight government control was needed to make the system work. However, the federal government was very reluctant to try to control the new medium. It was still a time when Americans looked on government regulation of anything as unwanted interference. Decades earlier, Congress had shied away from taking over the telegraph, and it was not about to step in and be charged with trying to limit free speech through control of the airwaves.

The Secretary of Commerce at the time was Herbert Hoover, later President of the United States. He tried to assign frequencies to new stations on an informal basis as licenses were granted, and it did seem to help for a while. However, the courts decided in 1926 that his agency lacked the legal power to do even that. The chaos that had prevailed earlier started to return and again threatened to ruin the fledgling industry.

Finally, Congress stepped in, held lengthy conferences and hearings, and provided new legislation—the Radio Act of 1927. This legislation established a very important principle: the *airwaves belonged to the people,* and this gave the government the right to regulate their use in the public interest. Thus, the Act of 1927 temporarily gave the government new authority to regulate virtually all technical aspects of broadcasting. The act provided for a Federal Radio Commission (FRC) with broad new powers. In particular, the rules for licensing became very demanding, and those who wanted to transmit had to agree to do so only on assigned frequencies, at specified power levels, and at scheduled times. Even though the 1927 act brought strong and effective controls to the medium, it was applauded by the industry, which had been totally unable to regulate itself.

This interim Radio Act of 1927 prevailed during the new mass medium's early years of growth and development. Within a few years, it was replaced by the Federal Communications Act of 1934, with complex legislation administered by a permanent **Federal Communication Commission (FCC)**, the government agency that continues, to this day, to oversee licensing and issue rules as needed. The 1934 act, with numerous revisions, remains the legislative foundation governing the broadcast industries, as well as all other forms of radio transmission in the United States.

Establishing the Economic Base of the New Medium

Radio was so new that no one was sure how to pay for the costs of transmitting or, in particular, how to make a profit from the broadcasts. At first, there seemed to be a number of alternatives:

- *Operation by the government* was one possible answer. That was the solution settled on by many societies in different parts of the world. In such a system, radio and television are operated by government bureaucrats, and the content of the media is rigidly controlled. In the United States, however, few citizens wanted that kind of arrangement. The basic values of democracy conflict with government intervention in the flow of information. Therefore such a government-operated and -controlled system was never seriously considered.
- *Subscription systems* were considered by some visionaries. Each owner of a radio receiver would have to get an annual license to operate it and pay a fee that would support the programming. Although that system was adopted in Great Britain, it was never seriously tried in the United States.
- *A common carrier approach* was actually tried by AT&T. The idea was that AT&T would lease its transmitter to whoever wanted to go on the air to broadcast whatever content they prepared. There were not enough takers, however, and the idea was abandoned.
- *An endowment* was another option. Rich philanthropists would be invited to endow radio stations with large money gifts, and then the station could use the earnings on investments to pay the costs of broadcasting. That system had worked well in funding universities, museums, and libraries. However, no rich philanthropists stepped forward.

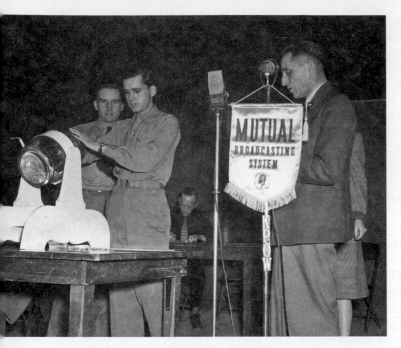

Two U.S. soldiers draw numbers from a tumbler, as a radio announcer reads the results into a microphone, for a lottery drawing for the U.S. draft in World War II. The microphone is draped with a sign advertising the Mutual Broadcasting System, and station KPOW.

ADVERTISING AS THE SOURCE OF PROFIT   The challenge, then, was how to make a profit by broadcasting programs to a general public who could tune in and listen for free. About the only obvious possibility was to transmit advertising messages over the air and charge the advertiser for the time, just as newspapers made a profit by presenting such messages in print. However, there was great resistance to the use of the airwaves for advertising, at least at first.

Radio seemed to most people to be a wonderful new medium at the forefront of human accomplishment and destined for nobler purposes. To use it crassly for advertising seemed a disgusting idea. Herbert Hoover strongly opposed it, saying, "It is inconceivable that we should allow so great a possibility for service, for news, for entertainment, and for vital commercial purposes to be drowned in advertising chatter."[8]

In spite of these early airwave "environmentalists," advertising once again won over good taste. There simply did not seem to be any alternative solution that could make the medium financially viable. Although scattered uses of advertising over the airwaves had been tried earlier, the system as we know it was initiated by station WEAF in New York, which made the decision to lease time to present advertising promotions. There was no particular limit on the amount of time (the idea of brief "commercials" sandwiched in between segments of a program would come later). In the summer of 1922, a real-estate firm leased a ten-minute segment to extol the virtues of some apartments in New York. It cost the firm $50.

After the idea caught on, advertisers warmed to the idea of becoming regular **sponsors**, who paid the costs of producing weekly programs in exchange for the privilege of being the sole advertiser on the show. The show might feature dance music, readings of the news, ball-game scores, and so on. With the number of home-owned receivers growing astronomically (see Figure 7.1), it soon became clear that radio was a very important medium by which advertising messages could reach consumers.

Early radio advertising was very polite and restrained. The initial model was **institutional advertising**; that is, the corporation sponsoring a particular presentation or program would be identified by name, but no information was provided about a specific product that it produced. To illustrate, advertising in the early days of radio would have consisted of a dignified voice saying, "This program is sponsored by the XYZ Pharmaceutical Corporation, and we are pleased to present the following program." That was it!

Today, advertising messages openly identify a specific product. Some become truly tacky, such as certain brands of laxative that go into grim details about such matters as "constipation," the "softening effects" of the product, the time it takes to "gain relief," and feelings of comfort and joy that result from elimination. Other current ads openly address such indelicate issues as diapers for incontinence among the elderly, preparations for itchy anal hemorrhoids, and products to combat erectile dysfunction. The public in radio's early days would have been truly horrified by the mention of such matters over the air, and the resulting outcry would have caused the station's license to be instantly withdrawn. Obviously, times and standards of taste have changed.

Selling Receivers for Home Use

Throughout the early 1920s, manufacturers marketed various kinds of radio sets, and the public eagerly bought as many as could be produced. For several years, demand

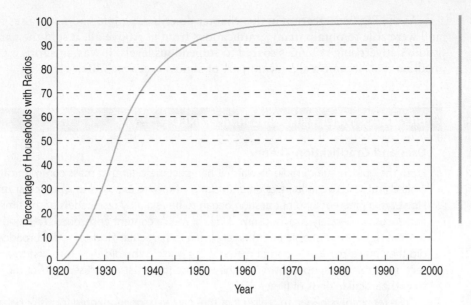

FIGURE 7.1

The Curve of Adoption of Household Radio, 1920–2000

The acquisition of radio sets by American families followed a classic adoption curve after the beginning of regular broadcasts in the 1920s. Virtual saturation of households was reached after about mid-twentieth century.

often outstripped supply. Figure 7.1 shows the spread of radios. By 1922 an estimated half million sets were in use. In 1925 that number escalated to about 5 million. By the end of the decade, some 14 million radio receivers were in American homes. (They no longer required batteries and were operated on house current.)

Thus, in the brief span of a single decade during the 1920s, radio was transformed from a long-distance signaling device serving limited interests into a medium that served an entire nation with broadcasts to home receivers. A great industry had come into existence. It was privately owned, dedicated to making a profit, and linked firmly to the world of commercial advertising. Unlike other media of the time, however, it was regulated to a considerable degree by government, especially in terms of the mechanics of broadcasting. It retains all of these features today.

Listening to the radio was rapidly becoming one of everyone's most important leisure-time activities. Marconi's device had truly become a mass medium.

THE GOLDEN AGE OF RADIO

During the years between 1930 and America's entry into World War II in December 1941, radio continued to develop into a medium of increasing national and worldwide importance. Following the war, radio would enjoy only five additional years of unchallenged dominance as the major broadcast medium in the United States, from 1945 to about 1950. It would then have to meet the challenge of television. Thus, we can identify the fifteen-year period between the mid-1930s and about 1950 as the *golden age of radio*.

The programs and diversity that we see on television today are contemporary versions of much of what was on radio during its golden age. It offered an enormous variety of content:

- *Comedians* became household names and made the entire nation laugh.
- *Popular dance bands and singers* gained national followings. Broadcasts promoted ever-changing dance styles and new forms of popular music.
- *Sports events* drew millions of fans.
- *Politicians* used the medium to get elected and to persuade the public to support new programs.
- *News broadcasts* were an immediate source of important information for huge audiences. Radio brought a constant flow of fads.
- *Daytime "soap opera"* developments were eagerly awaited by housewives and many others across the country.

As the Big Ideas feature in this chapter describes, people had many uses for radio and were able to obtain many gratifications from it. Above all, it sold the nation's goods. Radio's advertising revenues soared to stupendous levels. It was, in short, a great medium that became a significant part of almost everyone's life.

BIG IDEAS: MEDIA THEORIES EXPLAINED

Uses and Gratification Theory

From the golden age of radio forward, it had become clear that mass communications had limited and selective influences on individuals who were exposed to a particular message. However, a different kind of question began to be asked by researchers of the time. Why did audiences deliberately seek out some kinds of media content and completely ignore others?

That is, why did people intentionally listen to particular kinds of radio broadcasts? Why did they buy a particular kind of magazine or book? Why did they turn first to a particular section of the newspaper? Why did they peruse the latest advertisements of movies so as to find particular kinds of films?

The researchers began to realize that these are very goal-oriented forms of behavior. They indicated clearly that audiences did not simply wait placidly to receive whatever content happened to come their way. Audiences were seeking content from the media that they anticipated would provide them with certain kinds of satisfactions. In other words, receivers wanted to *use* the information in some way to obtain *gratifications* for their needs.

After several massive studies of the audiences for the daytime radio serials of the late 1930s and early 1940s, media researchers formulated the *uses for gratification theory* to try to explain why audiences do not passively wait for media messages to arrive. Instead, the theory sought to explain why audiences are active, deliberately seeking out forms of content that provide them with information that fulfills their needs.

This theory focuses on psychological factors. Each member of the audience has a structure of interests, needs, attitudes, and values that plays a part in shaping his or her selections from the media. Thus, one person with a particular set of needs and interests might seek satisfactions through exposure to sports, popular music, wrestling, and detective dramas. Another, with a different psychological makeup, might prefer wildlife programs, political analyses, symphonic music, and literary classics.

The central propositions of the uses for gratification theory emerged from a long list of investigations that have been completed over a number of decades. It has remained as an important explanation of why people select the media content that they do. While it has not previously been stated in formal propositions, in summary, its basic ideas can be expressed in the following statements:

1. Consumers of mass communications do not passively wait for messages to be presented to them by the media.
2. Members of audiences are, instead, active. They make their own decisions in selecting and attending to specific forms of content from the available media.
3. Those choices are made on the basis of individual differences in interests, needs, values, and motives that have been shaped by the individual's learning and socialization within a web of social relationships and social category memberships.
4. Those psychological factors predispose the person to have an interest in particular categories of media content, from which they can obtain diversion, entertainment, and respite.
5. **Therefore**, members of the audience will actively select and attend to specific forms of media content, while ignoring or rejecting others, in order to *fulfill their needs* and to *provide gratifications* of their interests and motives.

Source: J. Raacke and Jennifer Bonds-Raacke, "MySpace and Facebook: Applying the Uses and Gratifications Theory to Exploring Friend-Networking Sites," *Cyberpsychology & Behavior*, Vol. 11, Number 2, 2008 (New Rochelle, NY: Mary Ann Liebert, Inc).

Radio During the Great Depression

If ever there was a population in need of free entertainment, it was the people of the United States during the 1930s. At the depths of the Great Depression, 15 million workers were unemployed in a population less than half of what we have today. That calculates to about 5% of the labor force. The unemployment rate is always one of the key indicators of the economy, especially in hard times as was the case in the recession of 2008–09.

As the Great Depression began, there was no national system of public welfare, no unemployment compensation, no Social Security or Medicare for older people, and no Medicaid for the poor. There were also no government programs of public works to absorb the unemployed. All those would come later in the 1930s. Farmers could not sell their crops; factories could not sell their goods. Many businesses simply shut down and locked out their employees. Mortgages went unpaid, and families were evicted from homes and farms. People went without meals, without medical treatment, and even without shoes. Hundreds of thousands of children wandered without adult supervision. Hungry people foraged in the streets. Anyone who had a steady job was among society's fortunate, no matter how mean the work.

President Franklin Delano Roosevelt, the first mass communication President, during a radio broadcast.

But people did have radio. It was free, in the sense that all one needed to do was plug a receiver into a socket. During the Depression, radio stars emerged in all the program types list above. Comedy broadcasts made national names of such former vaudeville stars as Fred Allen, Jack Benny, Eddie Cantor, and Ed Wynn. Listeners laughed at the antics of "Amos and Andy" (a show with two white actors working in blackface in the old minstrel tradition). They thrilled to the heroism of the Lone Ranger, who brought simple justice to the old West. They were kept in suspense by The Shadow, a mysterious figure who vanquished the forces of evil. Children were excited by the airborne adventures of Sky King and the incredible space exploits of Buck Rogers. For those with more rural tastes, there were regular programs of country music. Urbanites probably preferred the dance music of the "big bands," which transmitted live "swing" music from various hotels and ballrooms. News programs reported the latest policies of the Roosevelt administration and called attention to events overseas, such as the military buildups of Adolf Hitler in Germany, Benito Mussolini in Italy, and the Japanese conquest of Manchuria. All of that did not seem very important to most listeners; few Americans were interested in the political problems of places like Europe or China.

Although one might think that the Great Depression should have held back the development of the radio, that was not the case. An increasing number of stations came on the air, and an ever-growing number of homes purchased radio sets. Advertising revenues grew sharply, from about $40 million per year at the start of the Depression in 1930, to more than $112 million during the worst of the Depression in 1935. Programming became more and more diversified and sophisticated, attracting a growing number of listeners. The networks continued to expand and dominate broadcasting.

In the mid-1930s two things happened that were very important to the future of broadcasting. One was the establishment of the federal legislation we noted earlier (the Federal Communications Act of 1934), with a new government agency (the FCC) to supervise broadcasting in the United States. The other was the development of an entirely different technology for broadcasting.

FREQUENCY MODULATION (FM) BROADCASTING   In 1933, a relatively obscure inventor, Edwin Armstrong, developed and patented a new kind of radio signal based on **frequency modulation (FM)** rather than amplitude modulation (AM). The world took little note, because Mr. Armstrong did nothing to publicize his innovation. The advantages of the new system were that it was static free and that it could carry much higher and lower audio frequencies than AM, making it an ideal carrier for music.

At first, it seemed to be a disadvantage that, at most parts of the frequency spectrum, FM reaches only to the horizon. AM can carry signals over very long distances (such as across the Atlantic), but the FM signal is different. At very high and ultrahigh frequencies (VHF and UHF), it simply travels in a straight line in all directions and does not bounce up and down. Because the earth is not flat, such broadcasts cannot be effectively detected beyond the horizon. Furthermore, a big building or mountain that gets in the way of FM signals can garble or even stop them.

These might sound like serious limitations, and for some purposes they were. However, FM turned out to be exactly what was needed as a basic carrier of the audio signals for the new system of *television*, with which RCA and other corporations were experimenting. The FM audio carrier was ideal for television because it could confine a signal to a local area and not interfere with other transmitters some distance away, meaning that TV channels could be kept from interfering with each other. The same was true for radio stations that wanted to confine their broadcasts to a local area.

Unfortunately, Armstrong had to fight RCA in the courts when it started using his system for TV broadcasts. Although his case was ultimately won, his bitterness and frustration led him to commit suicide some years before the settlement.

RADIO AND THE NEWS   Another great battle fought during the period was over who had proprietary rights to the news. In 1930, Lowell Thomas, who was to become a well-known radio news personality, began a trend by reading the news over the air. Frightened by the competition radio was giving them, newspapers tried to stop local stations from using the early editions of papers as the source for their news, claiming that the radio stations were violating copyright laws. But the courts ruled that, although the particular expression of a writer can be copyrighted, the factual content of news is in the **public domain**—thus, no one "owns" the news. The radio stations could broadcast news shows even if they could not afford to hire their own reporters.

Edward R. Murrow, CBS London war correspondent during World War II, became an iconic figure in broadcast news.

As it turned out, radio coverage actually stimulated rather than deterred interest in newspaper reading. The brief news broadcasts and bulletins provided by radio caused people to follow up to get more detailed accounts in print. Before long, the major networks had developed their own separate news-gathering operations—a system that still brings us the broadcast news today.

Radio During World War II

Even before the U.S. entry into World War II, radio reporters around the world were able to transmit live, eyewitness reports on major events by short wave to New York. From there, the stories were picked up by the major networks and relayed over standard frequencies to listeners at home. Americans heard dramatic firsthand accounts from Edward R. Murrow, reporting from London in 1940 during the bombardment by the German Luftwaffe. Later, such news personalities as Robert Trout, H. V. Kaltenborn, and Elmer Davis used the medium to bring reports and interpretations of the war in Europe.

On Sunday, December 7, 1941, American families could scarcely believe their ears when they learned by home radio that the Japanese had attacked the U.S. Pacific fleet in Pearl Harbor. As the war progressed, firsthand news reports came from battlefields in strange places people had never heard of—Guadalcanal, Attu, Anzio, Iwo Jima. Throughout, President Roosevelt calmed the American public with frequent radio talks, reassuring the nation of ultimate victory. By the time the dreadful conflict came to an end, radio was the unchallenged news medium of America.

Radio's expansion to worldwide news coverage built a foundation of audience expectations that contemporary broadcasters still address by providing news from around the globe. For example, when CNN Headline News presents summaries of what is happening "Around the World in Thirty Minutes" on a 24-hour basis, it is following a tradition that was pioneered by radio broadcasters during the late 1930s and the dark days of World War II.

THE CHALLENGE OF TELEVISION

After World War II, radio lived on in its glory for roughly five years. But, starting in 1948, television stations began to go on the air with regular broadcasts. Early in that first year, only seventeen were in operation. Before the end of the year, however, the number more than doubled, to forty-eight. Sales of television sets increased 500%, and the audience for TV broadcasts grew at an astounding 4,000% in only two years! Coaxial cables began to connect communities, and the same networks that had fostered radio enthusiastically developed the new medium.

No one in radio knew quite what to do. Many radio executives announced that TV was only a fad and that audiences would remain loyal to the original broadcast medium that had served them so well.

As television continued to take over audiences, however, it became clear that radio was in deep trouble. In fact, it was in danger of disappearing altogether as a mass medium. Profits plummeted and radio audiences melted away as both talent and audience interest switched to television.

Radio Adapts

Radio might have died completely had it not been for its resourceful response to the challenge of television. At first, the medium tightened its belt and took on advertising accounts that could not afford costly television commercials. Then it made two sweeping changes that permitted it to survive on a more permanent basis:

- *New Content.* Out went the well-developed radio drama, the soap opera, the quiz show, and other amusement fare that had been the mainstay of radio entertainment. All of that type of programming could now be found on television. In came the disc jockey, continuous music, frequent spot news, weather reports, and call-in talk shows.
- *Localization.* For the most part, radio ceased to be a national medium. Network-type programming decreased, and radio became a medium providing services to local rather than national audiences.

In effect, then, radio drastically changed its functions. It gave more emphasis to music, news summaries, and call-in talk shows and less attention to its earlier forms of drama and similar entertainment. In this way radio survived as an intimate and community-oriented medium.

PUBLIC BROADCASTING   One additional set of changes that influenced radio (as well as television) was the development of **public broadcasting**, government-supported, noncommercial radio and TV. As early as 1941, the FCC had reserved a number of FM channels for noncommercial use. In effect, this meant educational broadcasting. However, Congress provided no funding for such programming. A number of small radio stations eked out an existence with support from churches, colleges, and universities. Some lived on public funds, some from donations or from foundation support.

In 1967, however, Congress passed the Public Broadcasting Act, creating the **Corporation for Public Broadcasting(CPB)**, serving both radio and television. It was not actually a corporation, in the sense of a profit-oriented business, and it was not exactly an arm of government. It was set up as an independent, nonprofit organization that receives federal funds and allocates them to local stations within networks.

The radio part of the CPB package was **National Public Radio (NPR).** This division not only links radio stations into a network, but it also produces various kinds of non-commercial programming for broadcasts. Today, there are about two hundred FM radio stations in the NPR system. They all produce some programs and make at least some use of the nationally produced material. Such stations also solicit local donations and sponsors. For the many people who tire of regular AM or FM stations, with their continuous broadcasts of rock 'n' roll, country-western, or classical music and frequent commercial advertising, NPR is a pleasant relief. The nationally produced content is heavy on news, public affairs analyses, interactive talk shows, and information about music, theater, and the arts. There is even some attention to sports.

MEDIA LEADERS INSIGHTS: RADIO

DICK MEYER

Executive Director

National Public Radio

A much honored reporter and producer both in television and radio, Dick Meyer is in charge of all news, entertainment, and music content on NPR.org and NPR's other digital platforms. He has taken lessons from the best of legacy media to the new media. A graduate of Columbia College, he later studied at Oxford, where he received a master's degree in the history of political philosophy.

Meyer's first media job was as a researcher for CBS's election unit. Before joining NPR, arguably the most respected news outlet in radio, and perhaps other media, he was editorial director of CBSNEWS.com and, for several years, produced the CBS Evening News.

Programs that Meyer produced have garnered such coveted honors as the Columbia-DuPont award and others from the Society of Professional Journalists and the Investigative Reporters and Editors and the Online News Association. His many articles and books include *Why We Hate Us* (Crown/Random House, 2008).

1. When and under what circumstances did you first realize the import of new media or the digital age?

   It wasn't until I first began using eBay around 1998 that I deeply and intuitively understood how profoundly new technology was going to affect society and journalism. I was a relatively late adoptor. But using eBay for ten minutes, I found a bit of memorabilia that I had been searching for over five years. It was a stunning revelation about the power of the web.

2. What impact did that experience have on you personally or professionally?

   At the time I was working as a producer on *The CBS Evening News*. I quickly realized the extinction of that genre was a certainty, not a possibility. I also realized that CBS News itself was in peril if it didn't understand it needed to deliver news on-demand and well. By the end of 1999, I was the editorial director of CBSNews.com.

3. How have digital technologies and/or thinking influenced NPR specifically and radio more generally? That is, what is being done to harness these new possibilities?

   I think new media have pretty much killed commercial radio. Maybe it will survive on satellite, I don't know. But digital technology can now provide music, entertainment, and news more efficiently, cheaply, and satisfyingly than radio. NPR is in a different position for the simplest of reasons: No one also produces comparable content. There is a demand for what NPR produces, and roughly 30 million people a month are still willing to endure using that old-fashioned thing called a radio to consume NPR content.

Before new media became regular media, I don't think NPR thought about sharing its news and reporting with the public except through radios. That has changed. The mission of NPR is now not to produce radio; it is to produce content with NPRnews and to share it with the greatest possible audience on the platforms the audience chooses. That is a sea change. So NPR is redesigning its site and online production process, investing in digital assets, and training broadcast people to produce NPR-quality web content.

4. What is the greatest challenge or benefit of the digital revolution for public radio? To what extent does NPR have a digital strategy in an environment where satellite radio and digital transmission seems to be changing everything and increasing competition?

The greatest challenge is simply overload. The competition for the bandwidth of smart American brains is intense and flooded. NPR's only hope—and thus its best strategy—is to produce programming that stands out, that is different, that isn't a commodity, that meets a real need, and that provides a true pleasure. That can't be done with automated aggregation, editorial algorithms, narcisstic blogs, and Twitters.

So NPR has to use its unique nonprofit model to produce material commercial operations simply won't. The demand for that—for news that is not obnoxious, for entertainment with dignity, for cultural news instead of celebrity sleaze—is enormous. Meeting that demand will not create billionaires, and hedge funds won't back it. But an important part of society will be served, and the so-called information economy will have an important, very different source of information.

5. Are you optimistic about the digital future?

I can't make a distinction between the digital and non-digital future. The future will be filled with many things we think of now as digital, but soon they will just be things. Am I optimistic that the flow of news and cultural, political, and social information will serve our democracy, our economy, and our individual pursuits of happiness? No.

I think the "wisdom of crowds" will be harnessed in unknown ways that will do great things and facilitate great achievements. My concern more is that individuals will not get enough "soul food" from the overladen buffet tables of information age.

6. What, if any, advice do you have for a person who aspires to a career in radio, whether public or commercial? Or is there any difference?

Commercial radio is in deep trouble, and what it is producing right now is rarely something I can imagine giving a career to. I think public radio has the possibility of becoming bigger and more influential than it ever has been in America—but online. Thinking about a radio career wholly separate from an online career is a recipe for frustration.

THE GROWTH OF FM BROADCASTING   In its various formats, radio is surviving the challenge of television. A significant trend has been the decline in listening to AM stations and the steady increase in those tuning into FM stations. Before about 1977, more people listened to AM stations. After that year, the pattern switched and FM listenership grew increasingly dominant. FM broadcasting has now become the dominant system (see Figure 7.2).[9] Today, nearly 70% of radio listeners are tuned into an FM station.

FIGURE 7.2
AM vs. FM
Commercial Radio
Stations in the
United States,
1970–2007

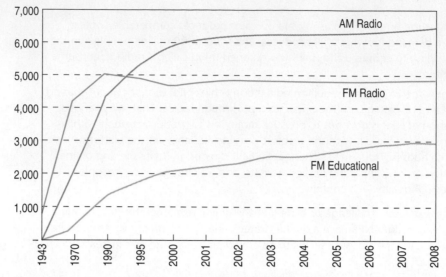

Source: Federal Communications Commission, http://www.fcc.gov/mb/audio/totals/

That switch is unlikely to be reversed. The future of the older, more static-prone AM band is less and less clear. Today, AM stations tend to present news, talk radio and analyses, more "oldies," and low-key background-type music. In contrast, FM radio tends to be more focused on musical formats. NPR survives on FM with a small, but dedicated, following.

RADIO AS A CONTEMPORARY MEDIUM

Today, radio is a mature medium with a clear niche in the media spectrum. Radio still commands larger cumulative audiences than any other medium in America. Local advertisers remain convinced of the worth of radio advertising, and their advertising success keeps radio stations profitable for owners. Much of the content of radio today is carefully planned in several predictable formats, although talk radio still creates surprises. As we'll see, such surprises can be controversial because they cross the boundaries of good taste. Although radio is still prospering in its present form, there are several new radio options and alternatives in the digital age.

The radio continues as a force in the media industries as this billboard for Radio Disney in Southern California indicates.

Radio's Role in Today's Media Mix

A total of more than thirteen thousand radio stations stretch across the country, with numerous signals reaching every community and neighborhood.[10] Studies show that 96% of the population over age twelve listens to the radio during an average week. Radio actually wins out over weekly television viewing (90%) and newspaper reading (76%). One reason so many people listen is because radio is the most portable of the broadcast media. It's accessible at home, in the office, in the car, on the street or beach, or virtually everywhere at any time.

Because radio listening is so widespread, it has prospered as an advertising medium. Between 16 and 17% of all money spent on media advertising in the

United States goes to radio. This compares with 26% for daily newspapers and 22% for television stations, not including cable systems, according the investment firm Veronis Suhler Stevenson.

Total spending on radio was about $21 billion in 2008 according to industry forecasts. Statistics on the radio industry usually exclude satellite radio, Internet radio, podcasting, and mobile phone broadcasts. They do, however, count advertising revenues associated with radio websites, a major growth area since the turn of the century.

What is accounting for radio's continuing economic viability? Experts say it is the high cost of commercial television time, which is still prohibitive for many local advertisers who can afford radio's more reasonable ad rates. Radio stations reach local rather than national audiences and are thus very useful for merchants who want to advertise their wares and services to people in their own communities. In addition, the advertising sales forces for radio stations offer a good deal of assistance to local advertisers in preparing their spots for broadcasting.

Surveys show that radio gets more than 75% of its revenues from local advertising, about 22% from national advertising, and a tiny sliver (around 1%) from network compensation. It is thought that radio's ability to attract local advertisers hurts mainly newspapers, since television is less attractive to the small, local advertiser.

Furthermore, radio serves small, highly targeted audiences, which makes it an excellent advertising medium for many kinds of specialized products and services. As we explained in the case of magazines, this feature appeals to advertisers, who realize it would be inefficient and prohibitively expensive to tout a special-interest product to heterogeneous audiences drawn to nationally popular entertainment programs.

Another key factor may be the popularity of remote controls, as well as TiVo, DVDs, and various other recording devices that allow viewers to avoid watching TV commercials. Many suggest that these tools cut the effectiveness of television advertising. The radio audience, on the other hand, is more captive, not able to tune out commercials quite so easily without changing stations.

Radio's advantage in offering less-escapable ads may be nearing an end, however. Satellite radio, which we discuss in more detail later in this chapter, is largely commercial-free, with dedicated music format channels, news programs, and specialized fare that remove its listeners from the broadcast radio audience. Podcasts offer another way to avoid ads. Indeed, terrestrial radio has declined in advertising rankings since 2000, due to competition from the Internet and other sources.

As mentioned earlier, the radio industry is dominated by giants like Clear Channel Communications, which owned and operated more than 1,200 radio stations in the United States, hundreds of stations ahead of its nearest competitors in the 1990s. This number declined to 900 or so. These stations dominate local markets, as Table 7.1

TABLE 7.1

NUMBER OF STATIONS OWNED BY TOP BROADCASTING COMPANIES, 2006 VS. 2007

Owner	Number of Stations Owned, Year End 2006	Number of Stations Owned, December 2007
Clear Channel	1134	636
Cumulus*	305	286
Citadel Communications	212	204
CBS Radio	140	140
Entercom	120	114
Salem Communications Corporation	98	97
Saga Communications Inc.	89	91
Cox Radio Inc.	79	79

continued

TABLE 7.1   *continued*

Owner	Number of Stations Owned, Year End 2006	Number of Stations Owned, December 2007
Univision	74	74
Radio One Inc.	69	53
Regent Communications Inc.	68	68
ABC/Disney	47	47
Entravision	47	47
Cumulus Media Partners LLC	37	37
Journal Broadcast Group Inc.	36	35
Citadel/ABC	24	24
Emmis Communications	23	23

Source: BIAfn Media Access Pro, PEJ Research, December 2007

Note: Clear Channel numbers include pending sales. Year-end numbers not offered for Cumulus for 2006: year-end 2005 numbers offered instead.

indicates. Radio industry concentration stems from the loosening of regulatory rules on ownership beginning in the 1990s, which brought a flurry of activity leading to the dominance of Clear Channel, as Figure 7.3 shows. However, in 2006, in the face of declining revenues, the company agreed to sell off some 450 small-market stations. Other leading companies are Cumulus, Citadel, Infinity, and Educational Media Foundation. It is argued that concentration of ownership leads to homogenized content, smaller local staffs and news coverage and other negative effects. Other critics say media concentration in radio is a myth since there are so many digital channels and other means of producing and distributing radio programming.

Media economists say that broadcast radio—not including the Internet and other new forms—is evolving from what was once a growth medium to a mature one, more stable and fighting for its place in the media family amid great fragmentation. So far,

FIGURE 7.3

Number of Markets Reached by Top Companies in 2007

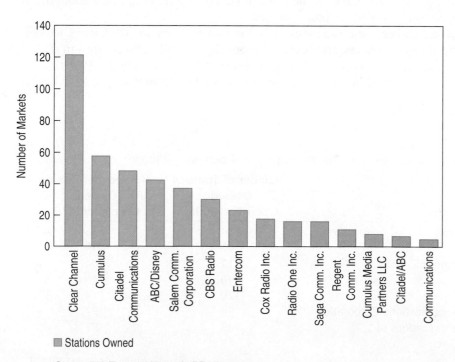

■ Stations Owned

Source: BIA Financial Network, PEJ Research

however, according to the Veronis, Suhler & Associates' *Industry Forecast,* radio's growth has still exceeded that of the overall economy, reflecting the radio industry's robust progress.[11]

Radio Ownership Today

Like all media today, radio is sometimes owned by medium-specific companies that have mostly radio properties. Increasingly, however, stations are being purchased by large media companies that are likely to own newspapers, magazines, television stations, databases, and other communication enterprises. A new development, however, allows smaller groups, even individuals, to own very small radio stations.

College radio an important cultural and social force often uses low-power FM radio to reach its audiences in a limited geographical area but now can achieve greater distribution on the Internet.

YOU, TOO, COULD OWN A RADIO STATION: LOW-POWER FM RADIO   In an effort to give private citizens and nonprofit groups a chance to have their own radio outlets, the Federal Communications Commission, in 2000, created a special class of licenses called **low-power FM radio (LPFM)**. Full-power FM radio stations usually operate between 6,000 and 100,000 watts. In contrast, according to the FCC, LPFM service consists of two types of radio stations:

- *100-watt stations,* which reach an area with a radius of approximately three and a half miles
- *10-watt stations,* which generally reach a radius between one and two miles.

LPFM potentially opens the airwaves to thousands of individuals and groups. The social value of such radio stations, many of which operate successfully, was underscored at the 2008 National Conference on Media Reform, which pointed out that "the future of the media doesn't belong to [media baron Rupert] Murdoch." [12] It is the fear and resentment of Big Radio as represented by the giant entity Clear Channel that gives heart to those who see some salvation in LPFM and other radio outlets where there are few barriers to entry into the market. Internet radio and several others are also seen as one way to counter this highly concentrated industry.

Today's Radio Content

The arguments involving concentration of ownership in radio are usually centered on diversity of voices (and content) in the marketplace. This goes hand in hand with diversity of ownership wherein minority groups, especially African Americans, have been identified as not having much opportunity to own radio stations, an issue noted elsewhere in this chapter. Over the years, the Federal Communications Commission (FCC) has championed diversity of ownership but has had a "hands-off policy" with regard to content formats, which are left up to local stations, networks, and station groups. In radio, as in other media, a format is a programming genre that refers to the content featured on the radio station. Once there were relatively few formats—for example, news and public affairs, music, sports, and drama. At one time a station or network would feature a variety of formats, but, in recent years, stations have most often had a single format (such talk radio, country and western music, or rock music), and generally the format tries to court a particular audience—or demographic. Stations sometimes switch or modify their formats depending on their fortune in the audience ratings that are collected by the research firm Arbitron. Of course, advertisers look to particular formats to draw the audiences they are courting. Arbitron lists some fifty-four radio station formats, as Table 7.2 indicates.

TABLE 7.2

RADIO STATION FORMATS

The list below includes all of the radio formats measured in Arbitron listening surveys.

'80s Hits	News/Talk/Information
Active Rock	Nostalgia
Adult Contemporary (AC)	Oldies
Adult Hits	Other
Adult Standards/MOR	Pop Contemporary Hit Radio
Album Adult Alternative (AAA)	Religious
Album-Oriented Rock (AOR)	Rhythmic AC
All News	Rhythmic Contemporary Hit Radio
All Sports	Rhythmic Oldies
Alternative	Smooth AC
Children's Radio	Soft AC
Classical	Southern Gospel
Classic Country	Spanish Adult Hits
Classic Hits	Spanish Contemporary
Classic Rock	Spanish Contemporary Christian
Contemporary Christian	Spanish News/Talk
Contemporary Inspirational	Spanish Oldies
Country	Spanish Religious
Easy Listening	Spanish Sports
Educational	Spanish Tropical
Family Hits	Spanish Variety
Gospel	Talk/Personality
Hot AC	Tejano
Jazz	Urban AC
Latino Urban	Urban Contemporary
Mexican Regional	Urban Oldies
Modern AC	Variety
New AC (NAC)/Smooth Jazz	World Ethnic
New Country	

Source: 2008 Arbitron, Inc.

Radio Station World, which covers streaming radio drawn from traditional stations for the Internet, mentions these formats:

- News, talk, sports
- Country music formats
- Contemporary hit music
- Adult contemporary music
- Rock and alternative music
- Urban music
- Jazz and classical music
- Oldies, adult hits, and nostalgia
- Spanish and Latin music
- World music
- Religious programming
- Government, public, community radio
- College, student radio
- Other (children's, ethnic, brokered)

Radio stations make creative use of formats to draw audiences and sell them to advertisers. Along the way, they have created various radio clock wheels to coordinate

FIGURE 7.4
Current Hit Radio
Clock Wheel

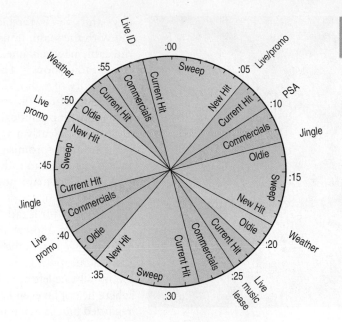

Source: Tobasco's Amazing Clock Wheel

the nuances of formats with commercials. One such clock wheel that is used for current hits is shown in Figure 7.4.

PREDICTABLE FORMATS   The most predictable formats, as noted previously, are the news/talk/sports stations and the most popular music form—country and western. As noted earlier, radio provides much for ethnic communities. There are Spanish-language, Native American, and African American radio stations (and even a national African American network) as well as stations that feature programming in Greek, Irish, Scandinavian, Chinese, Japanese, and other languages.

Public radio, especially NPR, mentioned earlier, and other forms of noncommercial broadcasting, provide important services and typically reach a large, upscale market, especially in university communities. Many noncommercial stations are owned by educational institutions, religious organizations, cities and towns, and other groups. However, most U.S. radio, like U.S. television, consists of commercial stations that rely on advertising sales to stay on the air.

CONTENT CONTROVERSIES   As noted earlier, radio exists in a very competitive economic environment. Stations in every community compete vigorously for audience share. This can lead them to present content that may cross the lines of good taste or acceptable topics that might offend more conservative members of the community. Like movies and television, radio can at times be quite controversial. Some radio hosts and shows have been criticized because of coarse content and explosively insensitive remarks, others because of highly charged political content.

In recent decades, the term "shock jock" has come into popular use to refer to radio hosts who make it a regular practice to cross common boundaries of good taste. Some famous shock jocks have suffered severe penalties when they crossed one line too many. For example, the craggy and cranky "shock jock" Don Imus made "crude, tasteless and racially charged" remarks about African American members of the Rutgers women's basketball team. Although he had made objectionable comments before, invoking racial and ethnic slurs as a type of shock-jock humor, this time his comments—made early in the morning and picked up by an Internet blogger who was monitoring radio programs—stirred a storm. Imus was under fire from the public; employees at CBS, where his show was broadcast nationally; civil rights leaders; and even advertisers. After a few

Radio personality Howard Stern responds to a question at an on-air news conference during his much ballyhooed debut on Sirius Satellite Radio in 2006.

days and even in the face of public apology and a meeting with the team, Imus was fired by CBS and MSNBC, the cable news channel, which also dropped the telecast of his radio show.[13] The controversy illustrated the complexity of radio, since the Imus show was also a venue for serious political and social talk and had long hosted leading political candidates, media celebrities, and others. Nearly a year later, Imus, with an apologetic air and a promise to be more sensitive in the future, returned to radio, though not on CBS, where he had been a major money maker. The Imus case was the cause for much media hand-wringing about how far is too far for a radio talk show.

Similarly, another vulgar shock jock, the popular Howard Stern, was the subject of fines from the Federal Communications Commission and a public scolding. Eventually, he left broadcast radio for satellite radio, where he got an even larger salary since the new network regarded him as a magnet for audience. Other controversial programming includes such talk shows as *The Savage Nation,* with Michael Savage, who screams invectives at those he opposes in a bracing interactive talk show.

Several of the most listened-to radio commentators are the political talk show hosts. Conservative hosts are particularly popular, including Rush Limbaugh, who has a massive audience, and Sean Hannity. Both decry the liberal media and liberal politicians in their highly charged shows. Less successful is the unabashed liberal network, Air America, whose hosts and programs push their own ideology as well. Although a major target of their criticism was the unpopular Bush administration, this network struggled to get financial support, unable to emulate the successful business model of the conservative talkmeisters.

As we noted earlier, the content of radio today would appall listeners of the 1920s and 1930s, if they could hear it. Yet only exceptionally coarse or political talk raises comment these days. The explanation of such changes lies in the same factors that influence content in other media, such as film and television. In some cases, at least, a "creeping cycle of desensitization," as we discussed in Chapter 6 on movies, can be observed, as stations driven by competition for survival press the boundaries of good taste and moral norms. On the other hand, audiences and programmers are not entirely desensitized. Radio stations have universally banned pornography star Robin Byrd's song, "Bang Your Box." She says that it is about the piano, but many DJs doubt that.

College radio, an important cultural and social force, often uses low-power FM radio to reach its audiences in a limited geographical area but now can achieve greater distribution on the Internet.

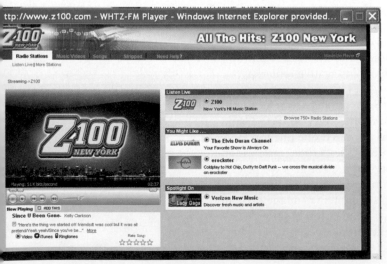

Radio in the Digital Age

The digital age has spawned a number of new options for radio listeners, including satellite radio, high-definition (HD) radio, and radio programming available on mobile "phone" devices. In addition, digital developments are changing the business of traditional radio broadcasting. "Listeners" can now be "users," whose interactions with their favorite radio stations include downloading podcasts or posting to the blogs of their favorite DJs at the station's website. And stations can use digital technology to track listeners more closely and to squeeze more ads into their on-air broadcasts.

SATELLITE BROADCASTING   Satellite radio emerged in 2000, offering great promise for a new diversity in radio programming and quality reception, mostly in cars. Unlike broadcast radio, free to anyone with a receiver, satellite radio is paid radio. The consumer pays an initial fee of around $200 for the reception device, which includes a tiny (two-inch) satellite dish. The dish, which receives the radio signals, is mounted on the vehicle and wired to a dashboard device that allows the user to choose channels, set volume, and perform other traditional functions.

Users also pay a monthly subscription fee of $10 to $12 per month for access to approximately 130 channels, most without advertising. The idea, according to those promoting it, is to give customers many choices twenty-four hours a day, beyond what they can get from the standard commercial stations. Satellite radio, for example, has hired hosts such as shock jock Howard Stern away from broadcast radio.

Two companies originally entered the satellite radio market: Sirius and XM. In 2008, financially struggling in the midst of a difficult economy, the first two players merged into a single company as they sought to establish a foothold among consumers used to getting their radio service free.[14]

The jury is still out as to whether the public will respond in large enough numbers to support this new and high-caliber medium. The main audience presently consists of people who drive their cars to work and elsewhere. Luxury car companies, in particular, have been big promoters of satellite radio, which they sometimes provide as an incentive. Approximately 17 million Americans had Satellite radio at home or in the car by 2008. With millions sitting in rush-hour traffic and others listening at home, in the office, or on the beach, the promise of consistent high-quality sound and a vast array of programming might have the seeds of success for this new product of the digital revolution.

If this system is successful, it may eventually have an influence on commercial broadcast stations—just as cable TV and the VCR caused many problems for over-the-air network television broadcasting. Standard stations may find their share of the radio audience declining, which would hurt their profits from advertising. However, all of that remains to be seen. It may well be that commercial stations will alter what they do to meet such a challenge. Radio has adapted effectively before. A number of evolving technologies and applications have enriched radio in the digital age. They include:

- **Internet Radio**—This is a streaming audio service in which radio stations are transmitted over the Internet. This is also called net radio, e-radio, and streaming radio and is simply a distribution service whereby stations from all over the country and world are available online—in real time—over which the listener has no control. If you are in Ohio and want to listen to a San Francisco station, this is the way to do it. Individual stations are tied into this network—and sometimes offer podcasts (recorded programs), which can be downloaded. Internet radio, which uses streaming, is not the same as podcasts, though, which can be retrieved on demand. Virtually all radio stations have their own websites to promote their services.

- **HD Radio**—Both AM and FM stations use HD (high definition) radio to connect their analog signals with digital signals, thus improving their reach and sound quality. Conventional radio stations speak of simulcasting in both analog and digital radio signals as well as a third signal for text data. HD radio is free to the consumer, unlike satellite radio, which charges a subscription fee. HD radio is mostly used to broadcast local stations and can be received on ordinary radios, though eventually all AM and FM radios will be equipped with digital technology. As the website Crutchfield.com has noted, some stereo brands like Kenwood offer an add-on HKD radio module that can be connected to existing car stereo systems without subscribing to satellite radio. By October 2008, some 1,800 radio stations, which reached 85% of the United States, were offering HD Radio.

- **Digital Radio**—Another popular form of broadcasting is digital radio, which is the transmission and reception of sound with technology like that used in CD players. Digital radio processes sounds into patterns or numbers or digits. By contrast, according to the FCC, traditional analog radios process sounds into patterns of electrical signals much like sound waves.

This is digital, wireless communication and can be either one-way or two-way communication, but it has been hampered by the lack of a global agreement on standards. Both AM and FM digital radio bring better sound to their listeners and are resistant to interference as one gets farther from the originating radio station. Much of the poor radio reception in cars can be eliminated by this technology.

■ **Mobile Radio**—This is a hand-held, two-way radio system most often used by police and fire departments or taxi companies. This is especially useful for internal communications for a given firm or organization. It allows both point-to-point and multi-point, an advantage over cell phones, which are point-to-point only. This is for closed user groups and can cover a large area. Again, this form of radio is a niche communication system, not open to the general public but useful to members of the public who are served by the organizations that employ it.

MONITORING YOUR LISTENING   A shoebox-sized device called MOBILTRAK has been developed to detect the radio station that your receiver in your car is tuned to as you arrive at a shopping center, concert parking lot, or mall. Critics such as John Roberts, director of the American Civil Liberties Union in Massachusetts, have denounced the technology as an invasion of privacy.[15] It does not record your conversations or any other automobile or personal information, however, just the station to which you have tuned in. Such monitoring systems are already in use in a number of major cities. The information provided is a kind of "ratings" system by which stations in the area can tell which has the largest audience at a particular time and what kinds of music or programs people are listening to at any particular moment. Such information is valuable to broadcasters who want to convince advertisers that they have a large market share and are providing the content that people desire.

SQUEEZING IN MORE ADS   Another interesting new technology, used in both radio and television, reviews taped material moment by moment. The purpose is to find small places on the tape that can be deleted, without altering the content of what people are saying. This reduces the time devoted to on-air program content by squeezing out a second here and a second there. These seconds can add up to minutes over the length of an entire program. The time saved is then devoted to more commercials. Radio stations and advertisers love it. The public may not appreciate it, but chances are they will never detect it.

Conclusions About Radio Today

Overall, radio has proved itself a versatile and adaptive medium, one that supplies a good deal of information and entertainment, some opinion, and relatively inexpensive local advertising. It has effectively met challenges to its place in the media mix. Radio will continue to readjust and recalibrate itself as audience tastes and interests change, and as technology advances.

CHAPTER REVIEW

■ Radio developed as a logical extension of the electric telegraph, which became a reality in the 1840s. Reliable electric telegraphy was not possible until after the invention of the electromagnet, which was at the heart of the system developed by Samuel F. B. Morse.

■ When Morse sent his famous message, "What hath God wrought?" over 40 miles of wire between Baltimore and Washington, D.C., the speed with which information could move changed from that of a train or a flying pigeon to that of lightning. It was a truly startling advance.

■ Radio shares its early history with the telegraph. The wireless represented the achievement of an ancient dream of conquering both time and long distance to communicate quickly without wires. The first wireless patent went to Guglielmo Marconi, who spanned the English Channel in 1897–and then the Atlantic in 1901–with a wireless telegraph message.

- The new form of telegraphy was an enormously useful device for communicating with ships at sea and with far-flung business, military, and diplomatic enterprises around the globe.

- Radio took on an aura of glamour very early when it played a critical role in rescue efforts at sea. While it would be many years before it would even start to become a household communications medium, it quickly gained a large and enthusiastic following in the population.

- During the early 1920s, under existing legislation, virtually anyone could obtain a license, build a relatively inexpensive transmitter, and go on the air. Hundreds did just that. Soon, the airwaves were cluttered with conflicting signals. With considerable reluctance, Congress first passed the Radio Act of 1927 and finally the Federal Communications Act of 1934, which brought radio broadcasting under the technical control of the federal government.

- An important problem that had to be solved before radio could become a household medium was how to pay for the broadcasts. After several alternatives were considered, the answer came in the form of selling airtime to advertisers, a close parallel to selling space to advertisers in the print media. This permitted the development of sponsored shows, regularly scheduled broadcasts, and a star system.

- The golden age of radio was between the 1930s, after the medium had matured, up until it was almost displaced by television during the early 1950s. Many important features developed during the period, including worldwide radio news, FM broadcasting, and the ultimate adjustment of radio to its current format and style.

- As a contemporary medium, radio is surviving well, largely as a local medium. It has successfully become a player in the digital age, drawing on the benefits of the Internet while continuing its cost-efficient over-the-air transmission. Listening is widespread, and radio captures about 7.4% of the nation's expenditures for media advertising. Its formats and content range from various kinds of music to talk shows, news, and sports. The majority of listeners today tune in to FM stations.

- Radio has many predictable formats, which are linked to specialized content and are aimed at particular demographic groups.

- New technologies based on satellite transmission were introduced in 2000, and the two major satellite firms merged in 2008. Satellite radio is a subscription service with multi-channel offerings free of commercials and high quality sound. Internet radio and podcasting are also expanding the reach of radio.

- Other new technologies have enriched radio, and they include HD radio, Internet radio, and mobile radio.

- Radio's future seems secure. It has worked out its own niche in our system of mass communications. It is a flexible medium, capable of responding to changes that may come in the future. At present, in financial terms, radio is enjoying a period of relative prosperity.

STRATEGIC QUESTIONS

1. How has radio evolved as a medium of mass communications in terms of the functions of communication it has embraced and contributed to in the process?
2. What appeals did each of radio's major technological innovations have for the public?
3. How did radio cope with the development and subsequent competition of television?
4. How do radio formats appeal to the public?
5. What impact is the digital revolution having on the radio industry?
6. Why is radio sometimes a controversial medium? Can you think of a recent radio controversy?

KEY CONCEPTS & TERMS

Marconi's wireless   150
Radio networks   154
Broadcast regulation   154
Commercial
   broadcasting   156

Public (or public service)
   broadcasting   161
Radio formats   168
Internet radio   171

Radio ownership
   concentration   167
Satellite radio   171

ENDNOTES

1. *Communications Industry Forecast 2006–2010* (New York: Veronis Suhler Stevenson, 2006). See p. 67 and Chapter 8, "Broadcast and Satellite Radio," pp. 326–351; also see Chelsi Spooner, "The State of the Music Industry and Radio Stations" (Associated Content, 2007), www.Associatedcontent.com/pop_print

2. Richard Siklos, "Changing Its Tune," *New York Times,* Sept. 15, 2006, www.nytimes.com/2006/09/15/business/media/15radio.html. Most of the data mentioned here is found in *Advertising Age's 2006 Fact Pack, 4th Annual Guide to Advertising Media* (New York: Crain Communication, 2006).

3. John Baptista Porta (or Giovanni Battista della Porta), *Natural Magik* (New York: Smithsonian Institute for Basic Books, 1957). This is a modern reprint of a book first printed in the late 1500s, just after the invention of the press.

4. The details of the history of radio presented in these sections are a summary of a more extended treatment of the subject in Melvin L. DeFleur, *Theories of Mass Communication,* 1st ed. (New York: McKay, 1966), pp. 44–69.

5. Gleason L. Archer, *History of Radio to 1926* (New York: American Historical Society, 1938), pp. 112–113.

6. For an excellent discussion of these early developments (from which the authors have drawn many insights), see Sydney W. Head and Christopher H. Sterling, *Broadcasting in America,* 5th ed. (Boston: Houghton Mifflin, 1987) pp. 62–65, 435–99; also see Head, et al, 9th ed. (Boston: Houghton Mifflin, 2000).

7. For the most thorough and more contemporary discussion on the rise of the broadcasting industry and the details of its development, see Sydney W. Head

et al, *Broadcasting in America,* 9th ed. (Boston: Houghton Mifflin, 2000); see also Alfred Balk, *The Rise of Radio: From Marconi Through the Golden Age* (Jefferson, NC: McFarland & Co., 2005).

8. Alfred G. Goldsmith and Austin C. Lescarboura, *This Thing Called Broadcasting* (New York: Holt, 1930), p. 279.

9. Radio Advertising Bureau (www.rab.com) and Veronis Suhler Stevenson, Communications Industry Forecast, 2006–2010.

10. Provided by the Federal Communications Commission, Washington, D.C., this number is for December 31, 1992.

11. *Communications Industry Forecast 2006–2010* (New York: Veronis Suhler Stevenson, 2006).

12. Federal Communications Commission, Consumer and Governmental Affairs Bureau, http://ftp.fcc.gov/cgb/lpfm.html

13. Don Jeffrey, "CBS Settles with Radio Host Don Imus Over his Firing," Bloomberg.com/app/news?pid=20670001&refer=home&side=a4g17kdNoH2Y; and Weston Kosova, "Imus: Race, Power and the Media," *Newsweek* cover story; www.msnbc.com/id/18110453/site/newsweek

14. Eric A. Taub, "The Future for XM, With or Without a Sirius Merger," *New York Times,* Sept. 15, 2007, p. C2; Richard Martin, "Satellite Radio Stumbles, Still Shines," Off the Air/Information Week at www.informationweek.com, June 20, 2008; and Jeffrey McCall, "Agency Likely to Pull Plug on Planned Satellite Radio Merger," www.indystar.com/apps/pbcs.dll/article?AID+/20080621/OPINION12/806210384/1

15. Erica Noonan, "Stadiums Listen in on Concert-Goers' Radio Choices," *The Associated Press State and Local Wire,* January 11, 2000.

Television: The Most Influential Medium

If most media have moved into the digital age on their own timetable, television has had a more precise deadline: February 17, 2009. This date was established by Congress years earlier to accomplish the nationwide switch from old analog to digital broadcast television signals. However, after much controversy and warnings that this was not workable, the date was changed to June 12, 2009. After more than sixty years, conventional over-the-air television came to an end that day, and "with that ending will come this new digital world, this much greater world,"[1] declared Richard E. Wiley, a former chairman of the Federal Communications Commission, who had long advocated what he called "advanced television." Of course, most consumers had long ago put away rooftop antennas and rabbit ears on their sets, opting for cable or satellite transmission, so the **DTV** transition was somewhat anticlimactic except for those viewers who needed an adapter box on their old-style TV set.

But TV's confluence with the digital world is more than this. Beginning at the turn of the new century, TiVo and other digital recording devices allowed viewers to create their own programming schedules. Programs became linked with Net-TV or Web TV, using high-speed Internet services to extend the reach of viewers' favorite shows, establish interactive online communities, and get more advertising and wider viewership.[2] Mobile technologies allowed viewers to carry full-motion video and replay channels on small hand-held devices as well as online, where viewers could watch programs broadcast earlier in the week. Similarly, TiVo and other digital services had already dealt a blow to scheduled "appointment" television. Some cable channels like the venerable MTV had developed programming networks, all linked to digital systems and interfaced with social networking sites online. For just under two decades, TV also made heavy use of the web for promotional purposes, advertising, and interactive connections with viewers. Television, as it had for decades, capitalized on digitization to once again improve its picture quality, sound, and reach. While some of the medium's digital strategy was somewhat accidental, there was no doubt that the anticipation of the great switchover of June 12, 2009, was a real impetus for thoughtful planning.

CULTURAL INFLUENCE OF TELEVISION

Television is a medium of enormous importance, power, and influence. Although radio still has larger audiences and greater reach worldwide, no one doubts the preeminent role of television as a *medium of communication*. Television is a *technology* and communication *platform*. It is also a *communication system* and an *industry*. It is a major force in the media economy as a conduit between audiences and advertisers, as well as a system of content. That content includes news and information, entertainment and sports, opinion programming, and, of course, advertising and other commercial content. Television thus delivers all the major functions of communication but is most often seen as a medium of entertainment. Perhaps because of this, many viewers have a more personal attachment and relationship with television than with any other medium. This is seen in the amount of time viewers spend with television and the immense popularity of particular programs. Additionally, TV images play a major role—popular culture and long-running shows reflect popular taste and preferences. As we will see in this chapter, the technology of television has been of critical importance from its early beginning as a mechanical invention, later as an electronic medium, and most recently as a digital medium. Invention and technology have played critical roles in television's development and in its ability to challenge, overtake, and eventually dominate other means of communication, from newspapers and magazines to radio and motion pictures.

In this and other chapters we will frequently refer to the enormous impact and influence of television on people's thinking, attitudes, and behavior. That impact continues to be a matter of discussion and debate usually focused on its role in the lives of children and in showcasing violence and antisocial behavior. Social scientists have studied this for years as have cultural critics who believe there is a link between the content of television and the images in society of women, people of color, gays, and others.

Television, like other twenty-first century media, is in the process of converging with other, newer media. Television has long been linked to Hollywood and the video production studio, and its owners often have other media and communication properties and interests. It is to some an old medium well established in the conventional media family, but it is also a cutting-edge, emerging digital medium, closely allied with such new media as cable, video-on-demand (VOD), wireless, and the web.

Cable was once a simple distribution system for existing television network stations and programs. Eventually, though, it took on a life if its own as a separable industry that generated its own original programming. Cable networks soon existed alongside terrestrial television broadcast networks. At one time cable was thought to hold the promise of being a great medium of the future, with fully interactive capacity and various service functions (such as voting in local and national elections via your home TV) but by the early 2000s, one critic lamented that "cable is just more TV," rather than a totally new medium with different functions, as had once been hoped. The satellite television industry also competes with and lives alongside over-the-air broadcast television. It can bring programming anywhere on earth, as well as originating its own programming and pay-per-view services. Television is a heavy user of websites and a source for them. There is truly a synergy between TV and the Internet as people follow their favorite programs online, including game shows, reality television, and others. Of course, TV networks, stations, and individual programs all have their own interactive websites.

In any consideration, television technology is vitally important today as the television, cable, satellite, and digital media industries compete, collaborate, interact, and integrate, as part of what analysts simply call "the television industries."

Television was born in controversy and remains controversial today. Some claim that it is the most important medium ever developed. Others believe that it is a harmful influence and a cause of many undesirable conditions in our society. Debates about television began early in its history with disputes as to who actually invented it. Following World War I, scientists in various parts of the world—England, Japan, Russia, and the United States—began experimenting with the idea of sending visual signals over the air using radio waves. Although the earliest television technology may not have been exclusively American, there is little doubt that in the United States it was developed swiftly as an enormously popular mass medium. Transmissions began as experiments in laboratories in the 1920s. By the late 1930s, it was a fledgling broadcast medium whose signals were being transmitted a few times a week in the New York City area to several hundred people using amateur-built receivers in their homes. Although its development was temporarily halted during World War II, by the end of the 1940s it was poised to sweep through society as a mass medium for home use. During the 1950s, it did just that. [3]

During its history, television has been a remarkably volatile medium. Its technology has steadily changed, its content has constantly evolved, its audiences have grown hugely, and large numbers of critics have continued a flow of condemnation because of its presumed effects. In spite of all that, TV quickly became and remains America's favorite, and arguably most influential, medium of entertainment and information, though some analysts think the Internet and World Wide Web might eventually claim this distinction.

At first, the typical factory-built receiver offered small black-and-white pictures about the size of a man's wallet. They were of poor quality by today's standards, but people were fascinated with the idea that moving pictures could be broadcast over the air and received in the home. Even the commercials seemed interesting because they *moved*. Before long, however, the novelty wore off, and audiences became more selective and demanding. They wanted larger screens, clearer pictures, more channels, and color.

Still later, they wanted greater control over what they viewed. This is something that digital television now offers.

As new technologies arrived to satisfy these wishes, Americans gleefully adopted them. Screens grew much bigger than the early versions. Better transmitters and receivers made the picture more stable. Cable brought more channels with greater choices of programs. Color made TV more pleasurable to watch. VCRs and DVDs transformed the TV set into a little movie screen in the living room. Hand-held remote controls, routinely supplied with new sets, enabled audiences to exorcise ruthlessly the bothersome commercials sandwiched between segments of programs. As we will see, this upset advertisers, who started to turn to alternative media, especially cable and the Internet, which reduced the earnings of the networks, eroded the income of advertising agencies, and generally threw the whole television industry into turmoil. Finally, direct signals from satellites and a transformation to digital technology brought change.

THE BIRTH OF TELEVISION

The history of television goes a lot further back than many people suppose. In 1884 Paul Nipkow, a German experimenter, developed a rotating disk with small holes arranged in a spiral pattern. It would be the basis of the earliest experiments. If a strong light was aimed at a picture or scene, it reflected patterns of light and dark back toward the disk. Those patterns of light passed through the holes in the rotating disk and were registered in light-sensitive electric vacuum tubes. This produced a very rapid scanning effect that was somewhat like the movement of a human eye scanning across a page. It was realized quite early that the perforated whirling disk could produce patterns of electrical impulses that could be sent along a wire so as to transmit pictures. Later, the same patterns would be transmitted by radio. The Nipkow disk became the central technology for further experimentation on the transmission of images, both by wire and later by radio waves. This scanning concept is at the heart of television, even today, although it is accomplished by electronic means rather than by a mechanical disk.[4]

Although the scanning disk was unique to early TV experiments, the entire histories of radio and television are closely intertwined. All the inventions and technologies that made radio broadcasting possible are also part of the history of television.

In addition, the social and economic organization of the television industry was set in place earlier by the development of radio. The medium is supported by advertising, as with radio. It is governed by the FCC, originally established to regulate radio. Its content is an extension of that developed in radio. The three major television networks that dominated early television were radio networks first. They were the same companies that pioneered commercial radio broadcasting.

Early in the 1920s, such corporations as General Electric and RCA allocated budgets for experiments with television, and other corporations soon followed. The idea seemed farfetched and futuristic to many in the industry, but television research was authorized in the hope that it would eventually pay off. General Electric employed an inventor, Ernst Alexanderson, to work exclusively on the problem, and within a short time he had developed a crude but workable system based on the Nipkow disk. However, his was not to be the system that the industry finally adopted.

Developing an Electronic System

Perhaps the most remarkable of the inventors who played a key role in developing the needed electronic technology was a skinny high school boy from an isolated part of the United States. Philo T. Farnsworth was a poor youngster from a large family in Rigby, Idaho, a small farm community. As a child he had started reading about electricity, and in 1922 he astounded his high school science teacher by showing him diagrams for electronic circuits that would make it possible to transmit and receive moving pictures over the air.

Philo had studied reports of television experiments based on the Nipkow disk. He correctly reasoned that such a system was primitive and clumsy. He had reached the conclusion that electronic devices were needed to sweep across a scene or picture rapidly in a series of horizontal lines and transform those variations into signals that could be broadcast over the air. Parallel electronic devices for reception and viewing were also needed. He had come up with designs of circuits for each transmission and reception apparatus and calculations as to how they could function. Philo's teacher enthusiastically encouraged him to try to perfect and patent the system.

During the same period, just after World War I, a talented Russian, Vladimir K. Zworykin, had come to the United States to work on radio research at Westinghouse. He had been a communication specialist in the army of Tsar Nicholas, where he had worked on early television experiments before the Russian Revolution. He asked for permission to continue development at Westinghouse. Directors of the huge corporation thought it was a long shot but decided to finance the work. Zworykin was also unimpressed with the mechanical disk approach and believed that electronic systems were needed for practical television transmission and reception. He set out to work on them with the full facilities of the great Westinghouse laboratories.

One of the inventors of television, Philo Farnsworth, conceived his idea when he was a high school student.

Meanwhile, a friend of Philo Farnsworth took him to California in 1925 and provided him with a place to work and funding for his experiments. There, on a shoestring budget and in great secrecy, Farnsworth transformed his circuits and drawings into a working apparatus, which he built in an apartment where he kept his blinds drawn. (The neighbors thought he was a bootlegger running a still, and he was raided by the police.) By 1927 Farnsworth began making actual transmissions. He showed his friend how his apparatus could broadcast and receive both fixed images and small scenes from motion pictures. It was a remarkable achievement.

Having created a working system, Farnsworth took his drawings to federal authorities and applied for the first electronic television patent. His application created an uproar. The great radio corporations, taken completely by surprise, were shocked and outraged that an obscure person had invented, built, and asked to patent a system that Westinghouse, RCA, and others had spent fortunes trying to develop and were themselves about to patent. They immediately contested the application.

After a great deal of controversy and legal maneuvering, Farnsworth won. To control the patent, RCA haggled with Farnsworth, who held out for a very profitable royalty settlement. Once a forgotten character in TV's development, Farnsworth was portrayed in a Broadway play in 2008 and the subject of a PBS documentary—and chronicled in several books, including *The Boy Who Invented Television* (Tanglewood Books, 2004). In 1983, he was depicted on a U.S. postage stamp. Although Farnsworth reached his solution before Zworykin, the latter invented some of

Early TV equipment and cameras were cumbersome and required heavy staffing.

Charles Van Doren (right) was at the center of a quiz show scandal in 1958 that rocked the industry.

the most critical components of television technology: the iconoscope (electronic picture tube) and the image orthicon camera. Meanwhile, Scottish engineer John Logie Baird invented a television system that was adopted by the BBC.

The Early Broadcasts

The earliest experimental television receivers had tiny screens made from cathode ray tubes about four inches in diameter. This picture tube, first invented in 1897, is a terminal or electrode of which electrons enter a system such as an electron tube. These bully tubes with their florescent screens documented TV until the sleeker flat panels appeared in the 1990s. Cameras were crude and required intense lighting to capture an image. People who appeared on the screen had to wear bizarre purple and green makeup to provide contrast for the picture. Nevertheless, in 1927, a picture of Herbert Hoover, then Secretary of Commerce, appeared on an experimental broadcast.

RCA set aside a million dollars to develop and demonstrate the new broadcast medium and by 1932 had built a TV station, complete with studio and transmitting facilities, in New York City's Empire State Building. In 1936, it began testing the system, broadcasting two programs of people moving around a studio or outside, once a week. By that time a few hundred enthusiasts in the New York area had constructed or obtained TV receivers and were able to pick up the transmissions in their homes. Meanwhile, the once federal government had developed procedures for awarding licenses to transmitters and had granted a limited number. By early 1941, the medium was set to take off. The demands of the economic depression and the coming of World War II caused delays in development.

However, the world was changing. Europe had been plunged into war as early as 1939. After the Japanese attack on Pearl Harbor in December 1941, America entered the war in Europe and the Pacific. This monumental war effort completely monopolized the attention of the country, and, along with almost every aspect of American life, the manufacture of television receivers was temporarily delayed. All the electronics manufacturers turned to producing equipment for the armed forces, and not until 1945 did these companies return to making products for the civilian market. In the immediate postwar years, however, television stations were quickly established in a number of major cities, and the public was ready to buy sets. TV was finally ready for home use.

THE PERIOD OF RAPID ADOPTION

By 1946, the FCC had issued twenty-four new licenses for television transmitters. The fledgling television networks, along with the advertising community eager to serve them, impatiently waited for the new medium to enter American homes. It seemed clear to all concerned that television might become a truly important broadcast medium, and there was a great scramble to take part.

The mass production and sale of home receivers began that same year. Although they were quite expensive, as sets became available, Americans rushed to buy them. In 1947, a set with a picture about six-by-seven inches cost around $400. That was more than a month's wages for many blue-collar working families, and it did not include the special antenna that had to be installed on the roof. A truly deluxe set, with a fancy wood cabinet and a mirror system for making the picture seem larger, sold for about one-fourth as much as a modest car. Thus in the early years of the new medium, only relatively affluent families could afford such a luxury, and so a TV set became a new kind of status symbol. Families who had receivers often invited their envious neighbors in to watch the transmissions (and to see visible evidence of their affluence). Stories circulated of people who put up an antenna to make their neighbors think they had a TV, when all they really had was an antenna—with no set hooked up below. In fact, TV was regarded as such a luxury that if a family receiving welfare was found to have a television set, it was regarded as a moral outrage.

One type of establishment that could often afford a set was the local tavern. By 1948, a television set was a central feature in almost every tavern in the country. Sports programs were the favorite, and big crowds would gather to watch the games. It is probably no exaggeration to say that the local tavern was a significant element in demonstrating and popularizing the new medium. Even today, people watch sports programming in bars and taverns, where they enjoy a communal medium as they discuss the game or watch with others.

An 8×10-inch screen television receiver with a clear glass cabinet attracted a great deal of attention at the 1939 New York World's Fair.

The Big Freeze

By the beginning of 1948, the FCC had issued approximately one hundred licenses. Some of the largest cities had two or even three stations, although most still had none. Soon, however, the same problems of signal proliferation and overlap that had troubled radio in its early years began bedeviling the television spectrum. The signals of one station sometimes interfered with those of another. This led the FCC to conclude that drastic action was needed to avoid upcoming difficulties. Beginning in 1948 and extending through 1952, the commission ordered a freeze on the issuance of new licenses and construction permits (although stations issued licenses prior to the freeze were allowed to start up). As a result, TV transmitters could not be built in many American communities until after the freeze was lifted. The FCC wanted to thoroughly study the technical aspects of television and related broadcasting so that it could allocate frequencies to TV, FM radio, and other kinds of transmissions appropriately.

During the freeze, the FCC developed a master plan (FCC Sixth Report and Order) that still governs TV over-the-air broadcasting today. The system prevents the signals of one television station from interfering with those of another, thus avoiding the chaos that characterized early radio broadcasting. When the freeze was lifted in 1952, television quickly spread throughout the United States, in accordance with the guidelines set forth by the FCC. Within a remarkably short time, it became so ubiquitous that most American families had a set. Social commentators began to speak of the "television generation" of Americans born after World War II who never knew a world without TV. The medium is presumed to have shaped their lives in significant ways.

Becoming a Nation of Television Viewers

Figure 8.1 shows how rapidly the American public adopted television. In 1950, less than 10% of American homes had a set. In 1960, only ten years later, nearly 90% had a receiver. By 1980, ownership of sets had virtually reached saturation levels in American

FIGURE 8.1

Curve of Adoption of Televisions per Household

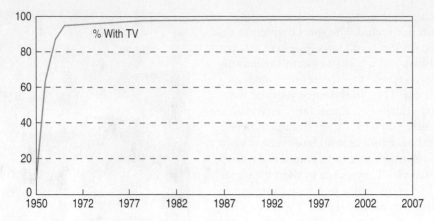

Source: VSS Communications Industry Forecast, 2008–2012, 22nd ed.

households. Today, it is very unusual to find a family without a television set, and most have more than one.

Another index of the popularity of television can be seen in terms of viewing time. The television set has been in use during an ever-growing number of hours per day for almost four decades. In 1950, those who owned sets had them on four- and- a- half-hours daily on average. That number rose sharply year after year to more than seven hours per day in recent years (see Figure 8.2). Today, it is becoming increasingly difficult to determine patterns of television viewing because TV sets can be used in so many

FIGURE 8.2

Household Hours of Television Viewing

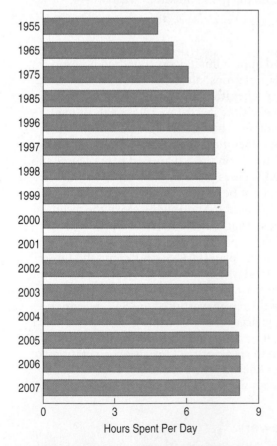

Sources: Veronis Suhler Stevenson, PO Media, Nielsen Media Research, Television Bureau of Advertising

ways. One can watch regular broadcasting, signals from satellites, cable channels, VCR cassettes or DVDs; play video games; or be connected to the Internet.

The Coming of Color

Color television got off to a slow start. Experiments had been performed with color test pictures as early as 1929, and there was much talk about commercial broadcasts in color even as early as 1940. There were problems, however, in settling on the best technology. By 1946, two separate color systems had been perfected. CBS had developed a system based on a rotating disk that actually gave very good results. However, it had one major problem: the FCC insisted that the system for color transmission be such that existing black-and-white television sets could still receive a picture (though not in color), and with the CBS system that was impossible. A new set was required. In 1953, the FCC approved a different system, developed by RCA. Although it produced less refined colors, it did allow existing black-and-white sets to receive programs.

For a variety of reasons, the networks exercised a great deal of caution in delivering color broadcasts. At first they transmitted only a few programs in color. By 1967, though, most network programs were in color, and even local stations began to produce programs in this mode. As a result, all the black-and-white cameras had to be phased out and new technicians trained. However, the industry made the transition to the new technology smoothly. Today almost all American homes have one or more color television sets.

BIG IDEAS: MEDIA THEORIES EXPLAINED

Social Expectations Theory

The term "socialization" refers to the process by which individuals learn how to take part in, or at least to understand, various kinds of groups in their society. Such groups range from the family and children's playmates early in life to increasingly complex groups as the person grows older. The individual goes on to school, then begins work, and generally must understand and deal with a remarkably wide variety of groups in his or her community and in the society.

Every human group has its own set of rules that must be followed. They include all of its customs and expectations for many kinds of social behavior. If the individual does not conform to these social expectations in a group, he or she risks social criticism and even rejection. Such expectations include *norms* (general rules for all members), *roles* (specialized parts for people in specific positions), *ranks* (defining who has more or less power, authority, or rewards), and *controls* (procedures used to reward or punish people for conformity or deviance).

But what are the sources from which we acquire our knowledge about the social expectations of others? The answer is that there are many. Obviously, we learn from our family, from peers, from school, and from the general community. But, in our modern world, there is another source from which we acquire a great deal of information about the social expectations of people who are members of various kinds of groups. That source is our mass media.

By watching television, going to a movie, or even by reading, one can learn the norms, roles, and other components of social expectations that make up the requirements of many kinds of groups. One can learn what is expected of a prisoner in a penitentiary, a father or a mother, a nurse in a hospital, or a corporation president conducting a board meeting. Or one can find out how to behave when at the horse races, in combat, gambling in a casino, or having dinner at an elegant restaurant (even if one has never been in such places).

continued

BIG IDEAS: MEDIA THEORIES EXPLAINED   *continued*

There is, in short, an almost endless parade of groups and social activities, with their behavioral rules, specialized roles, levels of power and prestige, and ways of controlling their members portrayed in the media. There is simply no way that the ordinary individual can actually participate in most of these groups, so as to learn by trial and error the appropriate forms of conduct. The media, then, provide broad if unwitting training in such social expectations.

This influence of the mass communicated lessons transmitted about such activities can be termed the *social expectations theory*. Its essential propositions can be summarized in the following terms:

1. Various kinds of content of the mass media often portray *social activities* and *group life*.
2. These portrayals are *representations* of reality that reflect—accurately or poorly—the nature of many kinds of groups in American society.
3. Individuals who are exposed to these representations receive *lessons* in the nature of norms, roles, social ranking, and social controls that prevail within many kinds of common groups.
4. The experience of exposure to portrayals of a particular kind of group results in *learning of behavior patterns* that are expected by others when acting within such a group.
5. **Therefore**, these learned expectations concerning appropriate behavior for self and others serve as *guides to action* when individuals actually encounter or try to understand such groups in real life.

Source: Robert Hornick, "Alternative Models of Behavior Change," Annenberg School for Communication, Working Paper 131, 1990, p. 5-6.

Television's First Golden Age

Two rather different periods are identified as "the golden age" of television, as cliché-ridden as that term has become. The first is the time when the medium was experiencing its most rapid period of growth—roughly from 1952 to around 1960. The second is a longer period, from about 1960 to around 1985, when network television had few competitors.

Those who identify with the earlier period do so not only because of the rapid growth of the medium but also on the basis of some of the programming. Some point to it as a golden era by noting the prevalence of dramatic programs of high quality, such as *Playhouse 90*. These were often sophisticated productions that seemed to fulfill some of the early claims that television would bring culture to the masses. Others noted that it was a time when family situation comedies, sports, and variety-vaudeville became new features of home viewing that had very wide appeal. Among the latter, Milton Berle's *Texaco Star Theater* and Ed Sullivan's *Toast of the Town* are often cited as examples of how great television programs were in those "good old days" and how the audience was united in their viewing.

Many younger people who view these programs today are at a loss to understand the glowing classifications. To them, the early shows can seem naïve and even dull. Whether the programming of the period should be regarded as "art," simple slapstick, or mindless and trivial pop culture of a particular era could be debated endlessly.

The Second Golden Age

On other grounds, the two decades between 1960 and 1985 can be regarded as a rather different kind of golden age of television. It may not have been so in some ideal sense of audience satisfaction or in terms of classic programming. On the contrary, at the time the public showed many signs of frustration and dissatisfaction with the medium. The period was one of turmoil in American society, beset by such emerging and divisive issues as civil rights, the Vietnam War, and increasing crime and violence. Many blamed TV for social ills, believing it to be a powerful medium that was eroding the moral standards and stability of the nation. As we will see later, such charges generated a great deal of interest in the social and psychological effects of television.

The same two decades spanned a time when the medium was dominated by three major networks (ABC, CBS, and NBC) with virtually no competition. Their profit margins were very high from advertising revenue, and they commanded the attention of virtually the entire viewing audience during prime time. Cable had yet to spread to more than a small proportion of American households, and there were no VCRs for home use. The networks competed with each other, but the three of them almost totally dominated the medium. If one wanted to watch TV during the period, there were very few alternatives to viewing network programming. A small proportion of Americans did view programs on educational stations and Public Broadcasting Service (PBS). Network television was widely criticized for broadcasting too much violence and for keeping the intellectual level of its programs low. Programs presented during the period were often designed with the tastes of the lower middle class in mind. Violence and fantasy were persistent themes. The lower-middle-class viewers in America were the ones who purchased the most beer, soap, detergent, soft drinks, and other nationally distributed products that could be advertised so effectively on television. The cumulative purchasing power of this vast majority was mind-boggling, and programming was directed toward that aggregate monetary bonanza. That translated into simple tastes and material at a relatively undemanding intellectual level. The majority of Americans loved that kind of TV content. At the same time, more sophisticated viewers understood that, in the words of Newton Minow (chairman of the FCC in 1961), network television was a "vast wasteland" of mindless comedy, unrealistic soap operas, staged wrestling, cartoons, spectator sports, quiz games, and shallow portrayals of family situations. Thirty years after his famed 1961 speech, Minow held to his assessment, arguing that TV had gotten even worse in spite of its growth and fragmentation.

Somehow, though, for both of the periods mentioned above, time has transformed what many critics regarded at the time as "trash" into the "good old days" of TV. That assessment may arise in large part from the fact that the content of the period was carefully designed to fit the limited tastes and intellectual preferences of the majority. Those same people are now older, but their tastes have not become noticeably elevated. Moreover, their children have similar tastes.[5] It is little wonder, then, that as they look back to the programs of the earlier periods they see classics, and the people who starred in those presentations as "significant performers." This makes us wonder whether some of the reality programming of the present will have nostalgic reruns twenty or thirty years from now. Much criticized programs like *The Jerry Springer Show,* which are regarded as vulgar, or others like *Survivor* or *American Idol,* which reflect the values of the period, might return long after they go off the air. With modern storage capacity, almost any image can be brought back or recycled. Indeed, financial analysts are counting on it as they assign values to "digital assets," that is, content stored digitally for possible future use.[6] Just as old movies have a long shelf life, so do old TV programs, as witnessed by the uncanny longevity of such favorites as *The Honeymooners, I Love Lucy, Murder She Wrote,* and others. The amazingly popular *Law & Order* and its various spin-offs are already rebroadcast across several channels and promise to continue to be broadcast long into the future.

ALTERNATIVES TO BROADCAST TELEVISION

Three technological advances have played a critical role in the reshaping of the American television industry. The first is the growth of cable television. The second is the widespread adoption of the VCR and DVD player. The third is the entry of direct satellite and digital broadcasting into the mix. All three are relatively recent events.

The Spread of Cable Systems

Cable TV began innocently enough. It was needed in certain locations because of the line-of-sight nature of the TV signal. For example, a community that is blocked by a large hill between it and the nearest television transmitter cannot receive the signal. The same is true for people who live in a valley or among a lot of tall buildings that block the signal transmission. Several local cable systems emerged at about the same time in the late 1940s and early 1950s in Pennsylvania, Oregon, and Arkansas. Some of the early pioneers and innovators were appliance store owners and sales people, although Milton Schapp, later governor of Pennsylvania, was credited for developing a master antenna so that all occupants of the same apartment house could receive cable signals. The Cable Center in Denver and Penn State University's cable museum keep alive the history of cable and recognize various early entrepreneurs and innovators who created this industry. At last count, no fewer than five hundred persons have been honored as cable pioneers.

In the 1950s, a number of local and very small systems were set up to overcome such obstacles. The solution was to put a large community antenna in a favorable location and to wire people's homes via coaxial cable to this central facility. Usually, the signal was amplified to make reception very clear. It worked fine and was especially attractive to people in rural areas and other hard-to-reach locations.

At first, the number of households that were "wired" in this way was very small (less than 2% of TV homes in 1960). It was actually a kind of "mom and pop" industry, with some 640 small systems each serving only several hundred to a few thousand clients. Then, the whole concept began to expand, largely because cable brought better pictures and more selection. This development angered the broadcasters, who saw the cable operator as a "parasite" who was pirating their programs off the air and selling them for a profit. Then, as the cable companies developed better technology, they began to offer their clients television signals that had originated in cities a long way off—effectively diminishing attention to local broadcasters. Even worse, some of the cable companies started originating their own programming!

Lawsuits were filed by many players from broadcasters and networks to local cable operators. Finally, it was resolved that the FCC had the right to regulate the cable companies, just as though they were broadcasting over the air. The broadcasters persuaded the FCC to impose stiff, complex regulations that effectively stopped the growth of more cable systems. By 1979, however, many of those restrictions were relaxed and local governments were given the right to grant franchises to private cable companies to provide service in the local community. Out of that came a great surge of development. In 1980, less than 20% of American homes were wired. By 2008, the proportion had soared to 98.2% as the adoption curve continued to rise.

FIGURE 8.3

Percent of U.S. Households with Cable TV

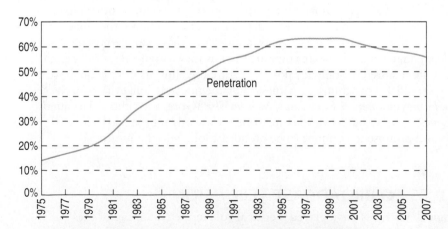

Sources: Subscribers: http://www.ncta.com/Statistic/Statistic/BasicSubs.aspx
Households: U.S. Census Bureau, Current Population Reports. From Statistical Abstract of the United States, 2008.

The increasing adoption of cable by American households has significantly altered the whole television industry. First, it has reduced the **market share** (proportion of the total television viewing audience) that watches regular network television. Indeed, the networks have suffered a slow but steady decline in market share for a number of years. Second, it has begun to segment the viewing public along the lines of their tastes and interests. With dozens of channels to choose from in a typical cable system, one no longer needs to view whatever the networks happen to be broadcasting at the moment. It is possible to find on most cable networks at any given time some form of program content that will fit almost anyone's interests. Thus, a pattern is developing much like that for magazines when the large general circulation periodicals gave way to the more focused specialized magazines. Advertisers follow these developments with keen interest. If one has a special product to advertise, it is more likely that a program that interests potential customers can be found in the cable TV lineup.

MEDIA LEADERS INSIGHTS: TELEVISION

CHRIS MCCUMBER

Executive Vice President

Marketing and Brand Strategy
USA Network

Among Chris McCumber's achievements at USA Network, where is a senior executive, was conceiving and executing its "Characters welcome" branding, which has given the cable programming service a clear identity in a competitive world. He is responsible for the overall strategic and creative vision for USA Network's marketing as well as overseeing "all expressions of the USA brand." Previously a senior vice president, he supervised campaigns that helped launch such popular shows as *Monk*, *The 4400*, and *Dead Zone*. He began his career as an associate producer at MTV Networks, moved on to a TV branding agency, and eventually joined Razorfish, a media and entertainment practice. He graduated from Lafayette College in Pennsylvania.

1. When and under what circumstances did you first realize the import of new media or the digital age?

   Back in the mid-'90s, I worked on the launch of MSNBC while at Lee Hunt Associates (a worldwide media branding agency). MSNBC at the time was billed as the "convergence of television news and the Internet." As we began to work on the campaign, I was struck by the fact that Microsoft's (the MS in the MSNBC) website would change the way in which viewers/consumers would be receiving news. If twenty-four-hour news networks like CNN had changed the way we view news, MSNBC would take that one step further and change the way we *consume* news. More than just twenty-four/seven access (like CNN), MSNBC had the ability to allow the viewer to receive any form of news, at any time, and ultimately in any place. Furthermore, you could have a "one-to-one" conversation with your viewer about your product, rather than the "scattershot shotgun" approach of television marketing. This is when we began to realize the power of digital media.

2. What impact did that experience have on you personally or professionally?

   It really changed the way in which I approached television branding because now there was a medium beyond television that could laser target my viewer and provided feedback from those viewers. There is also a lot of room for exploration and experimentation because the cost of delivering media via digital means is so low.

continued

MEDIA LEADERS INSIGHTS: TELEVISION *continued*

You can try something on your website, get viewer feedback, and adjust if necessary. It's a very efficient (and fun) way of doing business.

3. How has it influenced cable networks in the larger context of popular culture, media, and entertainment industries or within NBC Universal? You've rebranded USA Network in a very distinctive way, for example.

USA's slogan, "Characters welcome," is all about inviting the viewer to be a part of the brand. We celebrate both the characters on our air and the characters at home watching—so audience participation is a cornerstone of our brand. Digital media is the best way for our audience to be involved in USA. For example, back in 2004, we launched the first social networking site from a TV brand called ShowUsYourCharacter.com, where viewers could upload their own photos, videos, artwork—anything that "showed" their character. It has served as a "welcome mat" for USA viewers to join in on the brand.

4. What is the greatest challenge or benefit of the digital revolution for programming and advertising at USA Network?

As digital media disaggregates content and places it on multiple platforms, you have so many new ways for viewers to sample your content. From a marketing standpoint, that is a good thing. The trick is not to cannibalize your television audience, which is still the core of the business. We keep a constant eye on this and are very careful about the way in which we showcase our content.

5. Are you optimistic about the digital future?

I'm always optimistic about the future. While no one knows exactly how the digital future is going to play out, the one thing we do know is that the more access our audience has to our characters, the more they want to consume our content. Digital media has made our audience even more passionate for the shows we deliver. Great content plus a passionate audience equals a very bright future for USA Network.

6. What, if any, advice do you have for a person who aspires to a career in the cable industry?

Be willing to accept change. Be willing to question the way you operate, no matter how much success you've had. Be willing to take an honest look at mistakes you've made—and learn from them. Never, ever stop being creative. And, most of all, have fun. It's television, not brain surgery.

To the ordinary person, whether he or she views a program on true broadcast TV or on cable is of little interest or consequence, but in the industry the balance of power and great sums of money are determined by this. The major networks and their programming generally, though not always, trump cable networks for quality programming. One exception is the cable network HBO, which has produced such critically acclaimed programs as *The Sopranos, Six Feet Under,* and others.

While some critics complain about the redundancy and repetitiveness of some cable channels like Lifetime, others like USA Network have gotten traction with their "Characters welcome" brand and programs such as *Monk* and others. Some people complain that monthly cable fees are too high, there is too much advertising, and service is poor when a consumer calls the local cable operator. Only a few critics recall that cable was originally "paid TV" and was mostly ad-free, just as satellite radio is today.

THE VCR AND DVD

Like so many electronic devices, the VCR is an American invention and a Japanese success story. The Ampex Corporation in New York developed the original machine. In 1952, Charles Ginsberg, along with several other Ampex engineers, set out to develop a device that could be used to record television programs on a magnetic tape. Four years later, they had succeeded. The first videotape recorder was about the size of an upright piano and used large reels of two-inch-wide tape. It was quickly adopted by the TV industry as a means to record material for later broadcasting. Used in this way, it was very practical. No longer did everyone have to perform live. Programming errors could be edited or changes spliced in, allowing mistake-free programs at air time.

At the beginning of the 1970s, a number of American companies saw the potential of the device and set out to manufacture and market a small home version. However, they did not agree on the size and standards of the tape and other aspects of the system. By the middle of the decade, some five different standards were used in machines on the market. All were very expensive, and the prerecorded material available might or might not fit the machine purchased.

The Japanese stepped in. Indeed two competing Japanese systems led to a video format war between VHS (video home system, produced by the Victor Company) and Sony's Betamax, an alternative system. Although Betamax was regarded by many as superior with many advanced technical features, the VHS had longer playing time and ultimately triumphed. Ultimately, this standardized the systems and technology, brought prices down, and sold millions of the machines, and eventually more than two-thirds of American television households had a VCR. Figure 8.4 shows the pattern of adoption of the VCR for home use across nearly three decades. The device gave birth to a whole new industry but was soon challenged by the DVD (digital video disc). By 2006, 82.2% of U.S. households owned a DVD player while 79.2% were still using VCRs. Today, one can rent a movie for a very modest fee at a rental store or, increasingly, in supermarkets, convenience stores, or even gas stations. The popular NetFlix has also been a feeder for video content at home. To service this market, the movie industry has begun to produce films in these forms. A movie on DVD or cassette can generate enormous profits long after the film has exhausted its market at regular theaters. A host of other kinds of programs—ranging from exercise programs to bass fishing and home repair instruction tapes—have made the home video even more popular.

The proliferation of home videos was seen first as a threat by movie-makers, and broadcasters feared that people would record movies and programs off broadcast or cable TV, thus reducing video rentals and the effectiveness of TV advertising. That fear turned out to be unfounded. The tape technology at the heart of the VCR will soon be confined to the technology museum as DVDs have taken hold. Other, even more efficient, digital storage systems are under development.

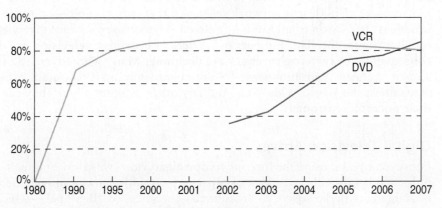

FIGURE 8.4
Curve of Adoption of VCRs and DVDs

Source: VSS Communications Industry Forecast, 2008–2012, 22nd ed.

Direct Broadcast Satellite

It has been possible to receive television signals from satellites for many years. Such reception required a large satellite "dish"—about the size of a barn door—stationed near the house. It had to be capable of being lined up and realigned on demand to point directly to the satellites from which the signals were being transmitted. The system was complex and awkward. Because of the complexity, appearance, size, and cost, few American families made use of this technology, although it did serve people in rural areas who were far from both regular television stations and cable systems.

In more recent years, a number of corporations have been marketing hardware and services that bring television signals from satellites directly into the home with the use of a dish about the size of a small pizza. In some cases, the equipment is purchased; in others, it is leased. In either case, the dish is permanently fixed on the roof, where it is pointed at the satellite and does not have to be moved or repositioned.

Unlike the older network broadcasts, these signals are not free. The system for making a profit for the services provided is essentially like that used by cable operators. The user pays a monthly subscription fee. A variety of "packages" are available. A "basic" package offers a bare-bones number of channels that are essentially similar to what a basic subscription to a cable system provides. The user can pay additional fees to add a number of movie, sports, or other special premium channels that contain programming of interest to the subscriber.

Direct broadcast satellite (DBS) systems are beginning a strong pattern of increasing adoption. They generally offer more viewing options—that is, a greater number of channels—and their signals produce a sharper picture on the typical TV set than is often the case with cable. The DTV transition of 2009 allows for more high-definition TV and better sound, thus leveling the technology playing field and at least one of the advantages of satellite TV. Once a struggling business with mostly rural and isolated customers, DBS (satellite TV) boomed too on new enthusiasm in the 1990s and early 2000s, touting its superior service, channel offerings, and other benefits. The industry also grew with the introduction of smaller dishes or earth stations, as well as from new financing for the DBS industry, which brought additional sports feeds and pay-per-view movies. By 2007 the industry had nearly 30.6 million subscribers. One respected assessment thought DBS might eventually achieve its earlier promise.[7] HDTV has been a driving force in both transmission production and new TV set production and sales, as viewers replace their old sets with HDTV-ready LCD and plasma TVs in the same way listeners replaced their record collections with CDs in the 1980s and 1990s.

Clearly, the DVD player, cable, and the hand-held remote control have made serious inroads into traditional broadcast television. The growing use of direct broadcast satellite systems and the shift to DVD movies will bring further inroads. We have seen the impact of new technology on existing media in previous chapters. Earlier, alternative sources for news brought a significant decline in newspaper subscriptions. The large-circulation general magazine was a victim of the shift to TV advertising. Television viewing almost destroyed radio, and it seriously displaced movie going. Today, it is network television that is in trouble—or, more precisely, broadcast television of all kinds—undercut by technologies that give viewers more of what they want. The numbers of viewers of broadcast television are down, and consequently advertising revenues are declining. Many who advertised their products almost exclusively on broadcast TV are now turning to direct mail, cable, specialty magazines, the World Wide Web, and any other medium where they can still reach their potential customers.

Digital Television Arrives

For several years, using the Internet to download video was slow and inefficient because of limited bandwidth and a lack of capacity to rapidly transmit moving images. All that is changing with the advent of broadband—the so-called "Big Pipe"—which is the largest communications conduit ever imagined. Although the actual methods by which the broadband revolution will be realized are not yet finalized, five separate industries are engaged in advanced broadband technology, something that will allow the consumer to combine video, phone, and data services with speedier access to the Internet. As communication expert Les Brown writes:

> Scarcely recognized is the effect of such great bandwidth on content and what impact that is likely to have on business and lifestyles. Content will differ markedly from what we have experienced...because digital broadband is interactive and can involve full motion video, multi-media, 3-D images and virtual reality.[8]

Although the five industries (cable, telephone, satellite, fixed wireless services and cellular) are not equally interested in the TV marketplace, several are, and the implications are enormous. Indeed broadband has been called "the third wiring of America," the first two being the telegraph and the telephone. In 2006, *The Economist* addressed the potential of telecom-TV convergence, declaring, "Your television is ringing" and noted that "telecoms firms are moving into television, but it may not be a license to print money" because of competition and lack of customer interest.[9]

As we mention elsewhere in this book, the migration from analog to digital is a key element in understanding the new digital television.[10] Digital is a method of signal representation with specific numerical values (1s and 0s) while analog has continuously fluctuating current or voltage. For television this technology is truly revolutionary. For the consumer it means high-definition television (better pictures) and CD-quality audio (better sound) but also interactive capacity (feedback and talkback). Much like the incremental development of color in earlier decades, digital TV had its beginnings in the 1980s but wasn't real to the public until 1998 when some TV stations in the United States started transmitting free over-the-air digital pictures and sound. In 1999, TV stations affiliated with four major networks were allowed to begin digital transmissions. While some quite expensive digital TV sets are on the market, other consumers are using conversion boxes and special antennas since the country moved slowly to fully digital television in 2009. In addition to the presumed benefits for consumers, digital television also has important implications for production, distribution, and transmission. New and more sophisticated cameras, switches, disc recorders, and other devices are involved.[11] The FCC maintains a detailed website explaining the implications of the digital transfer and answers consumer and industry questions.

If early TV meant only a few channels, and cable expanded the universe to one hundred or more, going digital means hundreds, even thousands, of new outlets and programming services. For broadcasters (TV stations and networks), it means more channel capacity, with each existing TV station getting up to six new twenty-four hour channels. As this is written, there is much debate and a myriad of unanswered questions about the changes heralded by digital television. Just what services the public will want and support; what kind of new programming is developed; and what the costs are for consumers, advertisers, and others are all factors that will help determine the future of this enhanced medium. Naturally, there are also political, regulatory, and private-sector concerns, not to mention international issues all to be worked out in the next few years. Whatever the outcome of these complicated and overlapping matters, change is once again coming for television. Former NBC News President Lawrence Grossman, who co-chairs a Carnegie Corporation initiative on digital television, sees also the promise of more social interests being served by the medium from ethnic and racial minorities to the older population, as well as many special interests and concerns.

TELEVISION AS A CONTEMPORARY MEDIUM

Like radio, from which it was derived, television is both a technology and a complex medium of communication. As its history amply demonstrates, it is also an economic system made up of communicators, advertisers, programs or content, and a large and diverse audience. It has become an omnipresent medium—the major form of mass communication preferred by the American public. On average, the television set is on more than seven hours a day in American households. At the same time, it is a medium that is little understood by its public. The majority of viewers know little about the behind-the-scenes dramas involving technology, ownership, or conflict among the individuals and groups that make up television systems.

The Economics of Competing Systems

Television signals are received from local stations over the air (or on cable). These local stations are still the backbone of the system. In mid-2008, there were 1,378 commercial and 410 educational television stations broadcasting in the nation. The five major networks are, of course, ABS, CBS, NBC, Fox, and CW. The Fox system is owned by Rupert Murdoch's News Corp., whose holdings (as noted in Chapter 3) also include a newspaper empire. In addition, there are programming services like CNN, now owned by Time Warner, and regional systems formed from local stations that banded together and share programming and promote advertising. The U.S. government operates a large television network overseas. Ostensibly for members of the armed forces, AFRTS (Armed Forces Radio and Television Service), as it is called, reaches into seventy countries and is seen not only by people in the armed forces but also by millions of U.S. and foreign civilians.

Over the years, the number of independent (not network-affiliated) stations has increased. This has given rise to **barter syndication**, which involves free programming with some ads already inserted. (The same structure exists for broadcasters.) Thus, a local station can get taped content from program syndicators who sell their wares to independent, non-network stations, creating what amounts to a series of small networks. Syndicated programming competes directly with network offerings. Much of the content of such syndicated programming consists of older reruns.

From the standpoint of a family viewing their TV set at home, the sources that deliver television programs can be a confusing jumble. What they see on their screen at any given time may originate from one of several networks, from an independent local station, from PBS, from their basic cable service (perhaps with an add-on subscription fee), via satellite, or by downloading online.

This variety in sources really makes little difference to viewers. A given movie provides the same viewing experience regardless of who delivers it. The same is true of a ball game, cartoon, or nature documentary. What do viewers care how it comes to them? Because it looks the same on the screen, regardless of what delivery system is being used, most families do not attach a great deal of importance to the various vendors and systems from which they can get their entertainment, sports programs, or even news. The main thing for them is that the programming they want to view is *there*.

However, for the players involved, what source viewers use is of *paramount* importance. It is the basis of consuming battles for profit and economic survival within the system. Thus, *competition* among the sources that deliver programming to audiences is the central factor in understanding the economics of contemporary television.

Competition has always existed among the various networks. Every year they vie for dominance in terms of commanding the largest audiences. And in fairly recent years competition arose between network television and its alternatives (cable TV and the VCR and DVD player) as these systems came online. That competition resulted in significant changes.

From the early days of TV up until the mid-1980s, regular broadcast television was very popular because of the relationship among networks, advertisers, those who produced TV content, and the audience—and because there was little alternative. Advertising revenues brought high earnings to the major networks, permitting them to produce expensive programs that were well received by audiences. Thus, a kind of reciprocal system was in place. Television advertising was very costly. However, because the commercial messages shown on the popular programs reached huge audiences, advertisers were willing to pay enormous fees for tiny segments of air time (like thirty seconds, or fifteen). And because of this great income, the networks were able to produce still more expensive programs with even greater appeal to the public. Thus, advertising revenues spiraled up and up, along with the size of the audience.

At the heart of this mutually profitable system is *audience attention*. The worst nightmare for both the advertiser and the television network executive is that people will not view the programs on which their wares are advertised. Various kinds of survey and polling techniques have been used to determine what kinds of people were viewing what kinds of television programs during what periods of time. For many years, the techniques used were rather simple; some were based on diaries kept at home by panels of carefully selected people or on verbal reports of audiences contacted by phone or mail about what they had been watching.

Those ratings, whatever their limitations, became *institutionalized*—that is, deeply established—as the ultimate measure of whether a given program would be kept on the air. They remain so today. Thus, what can be called the *law of large numbers* was the prevailing principle determining the television agenda presented by the major networks. The more eyes and ears a program attracts, the more valuable it is to an advertiser whose message is displayed during the transmission and to the broadcaster who profits from the sale of the time. If a program's ratings fell, even by a few points, it was in jeopardy. Many programs were simply dropped from the air if the ratings did not seem to justify what it cost to produce and broadcast them–especially if they did not draw enough advertisers to generate sufficient profits.

The use of such ratings as the ultimate criterion by which the networks assessed the worth of a particular program was just fine with the advertisers who supported the system. It ensured that the programs on the air, and the advertising commercials, commanded the attention of the largest possible number of potential customers. For several decades, this was how the system worked. Thus, in spite of competition among networks, the system as a whole remained rather stable and the networks continued to dominate television. The law of large numbers continues to prevail today but is being challenged because TV networks no longer have the massive share of the audience that they once did. With greater and greater fragmentation, TV networks still hold sway for some kinds of mass audiences, but market segmentation prevails elsewhere on cable channels, webcasting, and other competitors. It is also the case that simple measure of audience exposure to television are giving way to more sophisticated forms of audience analysis, which track how viewers experience messages and programs. While the long-standing Nielsen ratings still prevail, they are being challenged by advertisers, consumer groups, and scholars.

The Content Producers

Television networks (along with the studios and production houses owned by their parent corporations) produce much of the content that appears on television. Over time they have popularized the program genres of such entertainment fare as cop shows and lawyer shows, daytime drama (the soaps), sports, news, reality TV, and other forms. The ownership of these large corporations illustrates their natural alliances. For example, ABC is now owned by Disney, whose cable holdings include ESPN and is a giant owner of motion picture, broadcasting, cable, and other enterprises; NBC is owned by the General Electric Company; CW is owned by CBS and Warner Brothers, which is part of Time Warner; and, as mentioned earlier, Murdoch's News Corporation owns Fox.

Networks have extensive business (sales, marketing, and affiliate relations) and programming (news, sports, and entertainment) divisions. As economic entities, networks sell advertisers access to an audience. The news and sports divisions produce their own programming, while entertainment has a broad mandate that includes the daytime schedule (soaps, game shows, and talk shows), Saturday morning children's shows, late night programming, and prime-time programming.

TABLE 8.1

TOP TEN TV PROGRAMS—REGULARLY SCHEDULED

1. American Idol Tuesday (Fox)—15.5% of U.S. homes
2. American Idol Wednesday (Fox)—15.3%
3. Dancing with the Stars (ABC)—12.3%
4. Dancing with the Stars Results (ABC)—11.4%
5. The Mentalist (CBS)—10.0%
6. NBC Sunday Night Football (NBC)—10.0%
7. CSI (CBS)—8.1%
8. NCIS (CBS)—8.0%
9. 60 Minutes (CBS)—7.6%
10. Survivor: Gabon (CBS)—7.6%

Source: Nielsen's Top 10 List for 2008.

People often wonder how the fall schedule of a network actually evolves. It does so through a development cycle that begins with a concept, moves to script development, and then goes on to pilot production, to audience testing, and finally to an initial thirteen-week commitment as network executives breathlessly await the ratings. "The system is bizarre and makes absolutely no sense," says David Poltrack, executive vice president of CBS, Inc.[12] Poltrack notes that major investments and important decisions are made before there is any serious market research of systematic audience feedback. Much of TV programming is an intuitive process.

Perhaps for that reason, a few programs often make unexpected financial waves at the networks. The comedy show *Seinfeld,* for example, was the top earner for its network, NBC, for years before its star, Jerry Seinfeld, decided to terminate the show. An unlikely hit, *Who Wants to be a Millionaire?,* starring Regis Philbin, gained top ratings and had major earnings when it was introduced, as did the CBS reality program *Survivor* and later the runaway favorite *American Idol.* No one can predict just what program and program format will catch on with the public and garner high ratings—and a long, profitable life on the air.

Mad Men a critically acclaimed cable TV series on the AMC network in 2008 captured the values of and style of the advertising industry in the 1960s.

Television Content and Genres

Although television's content morphed out of radio, which also had news, situation comedies, soap operas, sports, and drama, it has found its own voice and draws on the unique characteristics of a visual medium from animated cartoons to computer graphics and high-definition pictures and sound. Early TV included children's programs like *Howdy Doody* and *Captain Kangaroo* and variety shows like *The Ed Sullivan Show* and *Milton Berle Show* or sitcoms like *I Love Lucy.* The *Tonight Show* was an early and longstanding entry in late-night programming. At the same time, news and sports attracted many eyeballs too.

Today, the main TV program formats, which also extend to cable, are:

News—Ranging from morning news shows to short midday breaks, headline news, and the more fulsome evening news programs between 5 and 7 p.m., depending on time zones, and late-night news. News programs in the morning are often friendlier and sometime less serious than those toward the end of the day. There is also twenty-four-hour news, pioneered by CNN but now seen on MSNBC, CNBC, Fox, and others.

News-Talk—These are largely commentary programs, interviews, and some of the politically charged programming mentioned earlier. This form often blends into entertainment-oriented programming where the issue of the moment is hyped to draw viewers.

Late Night/Variety Shows—These include *Late Show with David Letterman, The Tonight Show with Jay Leno,* and *Late Night with Conan O'Brien,* as well as others.

Daytime Programming—These are the so-called soap operas that dominate daytime and still carry household product ads from Proctor & Gamble as well as over the counter drugs and other personal products. Daytime includes the soap operas and also variety and talk shows like *The View* and *Oprah!*

Situation Comedies—This venerable form continues with such shows as *Monk, Ugly Betty,* and *Two & a Half Men* and features comedic themes. Sitcoms are among the longest lasting formats as old programs from decades past are still seen on cable channels.

30 Rock a popular and critically acclaimed TV series is an example of the situation comedy genre.

Dramatic Programs—These entertainment offerings include evening police shows, such as the *Law & Order* genre of programs, medical shows like *House,* and others, whether in a regular series or single programs. Dramatic programs follow trends and popular taste. In the 1950s, Westerns with cowboy themes were all the rage, as were medical shows and cop shows. Today, programs like *Boston Legal* and the several *CSI* shows continue this genre. Contemporary medical shows include *Scrubs, Nip/Tuck,* and *Grey's Anatomy.*

Reality Programs—These programs capture people in real or contrived "real-life" situations and generally feature ordinary people rather than actors. The first of these was *The Real World.* Other such offerings as *Survivor, The Fear Factor, The Bachelor, American Idol,* and *Dancing with the Stars* exemplify this genre.

Children's Programs—Mostly offered for young viewers in daytime hours or more commonly on Saturday mornings, these shows feature cartoons, fantasy series, science fiction, and even news and history.

Sports—Long a staple of TV on Monday nights or on Saturdays and Sundays, these programs originally followed the prescribed schedules of professional and college sports—basketball in winter, baseball in spring and summer, football in fall, and so on, but increasingly these sports plus hockey, golf, and others are played year-round. Still the granddaddy of sports programming is the much watched Super Bowl, played in January, which draws record audiences.

Documentaries and Docudramas—These are "real-life" treatments of famous people, historical events, or current affairs. Some use only actual footage of people and events, while others have dramatized sequences. Among the most heralded of this genre are the Ken Burns documentaries, which have included studies of the Civil War, baseball, and other topics. The History Channel and Biography are two important venues for this programming.

Movies—For decades now, TV has offered its viewers old or recently released movies as well as networks' own "made-for-TV" movies. Motion picture

Monk a cable series about a neurotic ex-detective is a situation comedy that exemplifies the U.S.A. network's slogan, "CHARACTERS WELCOME."

film libraries are sources for much programming on TCM and AMC cable channels, for example, and movies as well as sports are sources of video on demand.

Home Shopping—There are several twenty-four-hour home shopping channels on basic cable, including HSN (Home Shopping Network) and QVC, which feature such items as gemstones, jewelry, watches, electronics, beauty products, fashion, and other items that consumers can order by simply calling a 1-800 number or by logging in online. Hosts of these shows promote products in what is essentially an advertising and marketing channel.

Specials and Events—These include the Academy Awards, the Golden Globes, special holiday programs, celebrity interview shows such as *Barbara Walters Specials, The People's Choice Awards,* and others that track various events, awards programs, celebrations, and others.

Cultural Programs—Mostly on public television, these programs include *Great Performances,* featuring Broadway plays, operas, symphony orchestra presentations, and other examples of high and middle culture, usually telecast from concert halls. Some would also consider *Antiques Roadshow* a cultural program since it focuses on antique furniture, art works, and collectables and has something of an educational approach.

There are many other TV genres from religious programming to gay and lesbian programming, science fiction, and others. While we have focused here mostly on U.S. programming, it should be noted the TV program types attract audiences around the globe. There is a vast amount of global distribution of television programs, a cultural product, with much coming from the United States though there is also considerable locally produced and originated programming too.

Figure 8.5 shows the most frequently watched television types in five countries—Brazil, Mexico, the United States, Canada, and Japan. Some critics argue that TV programs are homogenized and can be sold like soap. Though some distinctive U.S. programs have another life in Africa and Asia, for example, but studies show that there are also differences in preferences between and among countries.

The Television Industry in Transition

Increasingly, television is a global industry with programming moving across national borders. What began as a technology for transmitting signals has become a major world economic institution. As we have pointed out, many U.S. television stations are owned by large corporations, although the number that a single owner can have is limited by law to twelve stations not covering more than 30% of the population of the country. Media ownership, along with that of many other business enterprises, is global. Although FCC regulations place limits on foreign ownership of broadcast properties, complex patterns of conglomerate ownership are common.

Television profits are a function of the total revenues of the whole industry— advertising sales, annual volume of advertising, network and station television billing, market ratings, and other indicators. The major players are networks, local stations, and barter syndicators who provide independent sources of programming. As mentioned earlier, the competition created by cable, VCR, satellite, and syndication services has brought a downturn in the economic fortunes of TV networks. But the networks nevertheless can still deliver impressive audiences, even though their share of total time spent with the medium is down.

In spite of the fact that a great deal is known about the social, cultural, and economic structure of the American population, one of the poorly charted aspects of television audiences is their actual composition. For example, TV industry market researchers give only superficial attention to the demographic characteristics of network television viewers. Cable services and public television sometimes claim to deliver "quality" or upscale audiences of viewers who are relatively well-educated and affluent in comparison with the general population. However, those claims are not backed with data from well-designed studies, and television as a whole does not conduct the precise and careful research on audiences in the same ways that marketers of many other products and services do.

Brazil (source: TGI Brasil)	Mexico (source: TGI Mexico)	USA (source: MARS)	Canada (source: PMB)	Japan (source: ACR)
70% National news	74% Local news	64% News	71% Movies	54% Weather
69% Local news	71% National news	51% Movies	58% News/current	53% Foreign movies
55% International	64% Action/adventure	47% Situation comedy	affairs	51% News
news	59% Comedy	41% Sports events	52% Comedies	48% Professional
54% Action/adventure	58% International	37% Drama	44% Sports	baseball
52% Comedy	news	36% Audience	43% Biographies	42% Travel
49% Domestic	55% Science fiction	participation/game	41% Suspense/crime	42% General drama
telenovelas	movies	33% News magazines	drama	40% Documentaries
46% Live sports	49% Horror	27% Talk/conversation	38% Game shows	40% Sports news
42% Weather	47% Recent	20% Music	34% Soap opera/serial	36% Entertainment
41% Sports news	Hollywood movies	19% Evening animation	drama	variety
38% Talk	46% Live sports	19% Award ceremony	32% Talk shows	35% Japanese
shows/interviews	44% Cartoons	19% Daytime drama	31% Family dramas	pop music
36% Cartoons	44% Classic	19% Reality-based	31% Nature shows	30% Family drama
33% Health &	Hollywood movies	show	29% Standup comedy	29% Comedy
medicine	43% Sport news	18% Science fiction	27% Science	28% Information
33% Nature & wildlife	43% Domestic	10% Daytime animation	fiction/fantasy drama	variety
32% Sports	telenovelas	9% Devotional/religious	27% Gardening/	26% Marathon
commentary	40% Drama	7% Sports anthology	home/cooking	25% Intellectual
32% Documentaries	38% Sports		25% Music videos	quiz/game
31% Drama	commentary		24% Children's	25% News commentary
30% Recent	35% Game		cartoons	24% Cartoons
Hollywood movies	shows/contests		23% Variety	24% Sumo wrestling
29% Musical shows	34% Weather		shows/specials	23% Samurai drama
27% Horror	33% Nature & wildlife			22% Hobby/utility
27% Science fiction	31% Music videos			20% Soccer
movies	30% Extreme sports			20% Japanese movies
25% Extreme sports	29% Talk			20% Entertainment
24% Music videos	shows/interviews			quiz/game
24% Game	26% Documentaries			
shows/contests	24% Variety shows			
21% Economy	24% Reality shows			
20% Reality shows	22% Health &			
20% Fashion & style	medicine			
20% Classical	22% Muisc concerts			
Hollywood movies	21% Economy			
	21% Science fiction			
	20% Science &			
	technology			

Source: TGI (Target Group Index), 2008, http://www.zonalatina.com/Zldata276.htm.

FIGURE 8.5

Most Frequently Watched Television Program Types (Top 20–30%)

An important concept of television stations is the *market* as an area. A **market** in this sense consists of a community and a contiguous area in which a substantial number of people live who can be reached by a station's signal. In practical terms this translates into a metropolitan area that includes a city. Some markets are relatively small, like that in which Little Rock, Arkansas, is located. Others are huge, such as that of Los Angeles or Philadelphia.

Emerging Trends in Television

In a digital age, terms like television and cable seem almost quaint, but they are the terms that have stuck with us to describe an ever complex and changing system. Increasingly television, cable, and satellite platforms are merging with digital, on-demand, and Internet platforms. Once the older technical platforms were the pipelines for programming to the home and dominated the media and entertainment landscape. But increasingly they are integrated and converging networks involving methods of distribution, program content, advertising, and storage of digital assets (also known as old programs). Internet sites like

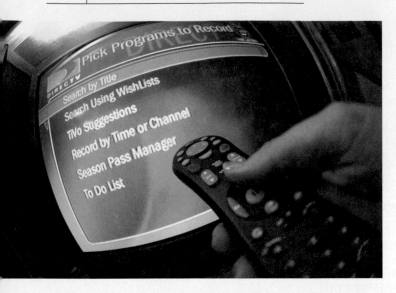

Tivo offered its subscribers TV-on-demand, not scheduled properly, thus freeing the viewer.

Hulu and NBC Rewind retrieve programming and allow it to be played on the home computer—or even the smart phone—at the viewer's convenience. This, as well as TiVo, discussed earlier, has moved viewers into a world of time-shifting. An entertainment conglomerate like Viacom, which controls CBS, also has cable networks like MTV, which also has some 40-plus networks of its own—and all are connected to scores of websites for networks, individual programs, talent, and others, which all court viewers.

On-demand digital programming services or so-called "personal TV" is expected to emerge around 2010 "ahead of an industry-wide shift between 2012 and 2018 when high-definition TV will also go mainstream with free-to-air channels," according to *The Economist's* "The World in 2009."[13] A premium television and video-on-demand service scheduled for late 2009, for example, was the result of collaborative effort that involved film giants Viacom, Paramount, MGM, and Lionsgate. There is much interest in the television advertising market, too, with companies like Microsoft and Google offering challenges.

The story of television today is one of connections and continuity—as well as new developments in technology, programming, and business models. And while much TV programming is in the world of entertainment and fantasies, it also dominates the news, as was evident in the 2008 presidential election in which the debates, convention speeches, and election itself drew massive and sustained audiences. Barack Obama's acceptance speech in November drew 78.6 million viewers, for example. Similarly, the Olympics and major sports events rely on TV as their primary platform and distribution system. TV is connecting itself effectively to the digital age and seeking advertising and other financial support by accentuating its mass audience offerings as well as those that appeal more to niche markets. Some commentators suggest that the TV and the PC will eventually merge into one seamless system. That will require massive and major reorganization of the structure of an industry that is now in its seventh decade.

CHAPTER REVIEW

- Pioneering experiments on sending pictures by radio began in several countries just after World War I. The earliest attempts made use of a revolving "Nipkow disk," a mechanical system that created a scanning effect when used with a beam of light. It was not until electronic scanning was developed that television became practical.
- The first patent for an electronic television system was awarded to Philo T. Farnsworth, an obscure inventor who had worked out the basic design while still a high school student. With minimal funding he built a working model in a small apartment in Los Angeles. Vladimir Zworykin, of Westinghouse laboratories, also invented an electronic system. Court battles resulted, but Farnsworth won.
- By 1932, a transmitter was installed in the Empire State Building in New York City. Regular transmissions began on a limited basis in 1936, with two broadcasts per week. A few hundred amateur enthusiasts who had built or purchased sets could receive the signals in the New York area. By 1940, television was capable of becoming mass media for home use. However, when World War II began in 1941, the need for war production temporarily halted the development of the new medium.

- The period of rapid adoption of home receivers began just after the war. Between 1950 and 1960, nearly 90% of American households acquired a television set. This rapid adoption happened in spite of a freeze on the licensing and construction of new television stations imposed by the FCC between 1948 and 1952.
- Television quickly became a part of family behavior patterns across the nation. The number of hours that sets are in use in homes climbed from about four and a half per day in 1950 to more than seven in recent years. During the 1970s, color sets all but completely replaced black and white.
- Two periods can be identified that might for different reasons be called television's golden age. One, based on the popularity of certain programming and television personalities, was roughly from the early 1950s to about 1960. The second, defined more in terms of the predominance and profitability of the television networks, was from 1960 to 1985.
- Alternative ways to use the TV set at home have now become a significant part of the total picture. Cable systems were not a major factor in the industry until the 1980s. During that decade, the proportion of American homes receiving cable transmissions increased sharply. The VCR was developed in the 1950s by an American company. Since the mid-1980s the Japanese have sold millions of the sets in the United States. Currently, digital television and especially direct satellite broadcasts may change the picture still further.
- As an industry, television broadcasting is undergoing a number of changes. New patterns of ownership are emerging. Large corporations and conglomerates are increasingly making TV stations and even networks part of their holdings. The result is changing patterns of competition within the industry. Also, the original networks have lost a large share of the market in terms of advertising dollars. Both cable and DVDs, which have replaced the VCR, are more widely used than ever before. Further changes lie ahead as this dynamic industry continues to evolve.
- Technological changes, convergences, and trends are in store for the medium in the near future. Digitally based HDTV will be available within a short number of years. It will change the format and clarity of the picture seen on the screen. Cable TV will be challenged by systems of delivery via phone wires, microwaves, or satellites. These technological improvements will offer more channels but are unlikely to create a revolution in the nature of television content.

STRATEGIC QUESTIONS

1. Tease out the meaning of the term "television," as a communications medium, technology, industry, and social force. How do these ideas work together to best describe and interpret what television is for people and society?
2. What delayed television's development as a major communications medium?
3. What were television's golden ages, and how does understanding them help understand TV's role today?
4. What has been the role of cable in the development of television as a medium—and social influence?
5. How is the digital revolution affecting television?
6. How has television's content and program types or genres changed over the years?

KEY CONCEPTS & TERMS

The Big Freeze   181
Color television   183
Cable TV   186
Television networks   185

Cable networks   186
Second golden age   184
Direct broadcast
   satellites   190

TV program types,
   genres   194
Reality TV   195
Home video   189

ENDNOTES

1. Jacques Steinberg, "Converters Signal a New Era for TVs," *New York Times*, June 7, 2007, p. C3. See also Stephen Bates, "The Day TV Died," *Wilson Quarterly,* Summer 2008.

2. Cliff Edwards, "Net TV: Coming into Focus," *BusinessWeek,* Sept. 10, 2007, p. 20. See also Douglas Gomery and Luke Jacobs, *Television Industries* (London: British Film Institute, 2008).

3. See "The Development of the Television Industry," Melvin L. DeFleur and Sandra Ball Rokeach, *Theories of Mass Communication,* 5th ed. (White Plains, NY: Longman, 1989), pp. 110–122.

4. For a thorough history of television up to the mid-1970s, see Eric Barnouw, *Tube of Plenty: The Evolution of American Television* (New York: Oxford University Press, 1975); Paul Schatzkin, *The Boy Who Invented Television* (Terre Haute, IN: Tanglewood Books, 2004); Evan I. Schwartz, *The Last Lone Inventor: A Tale of Genius, Deceit and the Birth of Television* (New York: HarperCollins, 2002).

5. John P. Murray, Ellen Wartella et al. *Children and Television: Fifty Years of Research,* (NJ: Lawrence Erlbaum & Associates, 2006).

6. Interview with Patrick Russo, The Salter Group, Sept. 19, 2007.

7. Benjamin M. Compaine and Benjamin Gomery, *Who Owns The Media?* 3rd ed. (Mahwah, NJ: Lawrence Erlbaum, 2000), pp. 266–270.

8. Les Brown, "The Nascent Age of Broadband," Fordham Center for Communications and The Broadband Forum, 1999, updated edition published by the Carnegie Corporation of New York, 2000, pp. 1, 4.

9. "A Survey of Telecoms Convergence," *The Economist,* Oct. 14, 2006, pp. 1, 14.

10. Tony Feldman, *An Introduction to Digital Media* (London: Routledge, 1997), pp.1–3. For some useful definitional material, see Wilson Dizard, Jr., *Old Media/New Media, Mass Communications in the Information Age* (New York: Longman, 2000).

11. Charles M. Firestone and Amy Korzick Garmer, eds., *Digital Broadcasting and the Public Interest* (Washington: The Aspen Institute, 1998), pp. vii, xi.

12. David Poltrack, executive vice president of CBS, Inc., in lecture February 7, 2006, Fordham Graduate School of Business, Lincoln Center, New York.

13. "The World in Figures: Industries" (media), *The World in 2009, The Economist,* Jan.–Mar. 2009.

News, Journalism, and Public Affairs

What impact, if any, is the digital age having on our conception of news and journalistic practice? Historically, news is news, regardless of the medium that delivers it. But, of course, from the era of the telegraph through communication satellites and the digital age, technologies have speeded up the transmission, pace, and delivery of news. As we've already discussed, news is now received on PCs, laptops, flat panels, and hand-held devices. And the news media include all the conventional sources plus search engines, social network sites, and other media forms. Now, with little effort, news consumers can bypass the so-called "appointment" media (those delivered on a specific schedule) and tune in to news and information on a continuous, twenty-four/seven basis, something that would have been impossible only a few years ago. The media have responded to the public's hunger for twenty-four/seven news with constant updating and round-the-clock online release of new information and new stories.[1] While CNN has championed twenty-four hour news for decades, in recent years, the mainstream news media—TV, magazines, and newspapers—have continually been changing websites, blogs, and podcasts, all offering news.

For the first time, there is now thought to be a generational divide in where people get their news. People in their teens and twenties prefer online news to that presented by the venerable, legacy media like newspapers and TV news. According to the Center for Digital Future, these age groups tend to accept the credibility of all kinds of online news, whether it carries the traditional brands (*New York Times* online edition) or not. Older adults are more skeptical and prefer to rely on traditional media and like to be sure much news retrieved via Google or other search sites is drawn from traditional media. Young people are also more open to **citizen journalism,** especially to reports from their peers and other ordinary individuals, rather than news gathered by professional reporters working for the media. For example, news reports posted by individuals on social networking sites like Facebook and MySpace are exceedingly popular with the younger news demographic. Sometimes news that is "cool" trumps the duller traditional reports. As *The State of the News Media 2008* put it, the major trends in news suggest a shift from news as a product "to becoming a service" that responds to citizen-consumers' query, "How can you help me, even empower me?" Other changes

I FIGURE 9.1

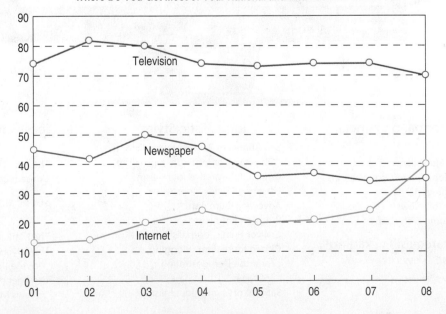

Where Do You Get Most of Your National and International News?

Internet Rivals TV as Main News Source for Young People*

Main source of news	Aug 2006	Sept 2007	Dec 2008	07–08 Change
	%	%	%	
Television	62	68	59	−11
Internet	32	34	59	+25
Newspapers	29	23	28	+5
Radio	16	13	18	+5
Magazines	1	*	4	+4
Other (Vol.)	3	5	6	+1

*Ages 18 to 29.
Figures add to more than 100% because multiple responses were allowed.

suggest that the niche market orientation of new media (narrow casting) means that the agenda of the news media in the United States continues to narrow, not broaden.[2]

These and other developments are radically altering the scope, topics, sources, and impact of news. Bloggers, most of them unpaid amateurs, can poke holes in a traditional news report and suddenly challenge news gathered by TV networks or other media. This impact can be great. In 2004 when then-CBS anchor Dan Rather reported on a controversial story about President George Bush's national guard service, bloggers took aim at unverified information and, eventually, Rather was forced to resign. The controversy over radio shock jock Don Imus, who made disparaging remarks about African American women on the Rutgers University basketball team, became a news story because of a web watchdog group that caught the Imus remark before 7 a.m. and transmitted it to the mainstream media, which picked it up several days later.[3] And repeatedly during the 2008 presidential campaign, bloggers unearthed embarrassing details about candidates and campaigns, which very quickly made it to the mainstream media. On occasion, a misleading blog report such as several involving President Obama's citizenship or the paternity of Sarah Palin's daughter's unborn child get picked up erroneously in traditional media. At the same time, the definition of news has not changed—nor have the purposes of journalism in the public arena—which involves surveillance of the environment for the citizenry. In this chapter, we review this vital function of the media.

NEWS: THE INFORMATION FUNCTION OF THE PRESS

From their inception, the news media have served as the "eyes and ears" of society. While originally referring only to newspapers, the term *news media* today includes all the print, broadcast, cable, and interactive media that bring news reports to the public. Through its monitoring of the social environment, the press gathers, processes, and disseminates the news. By attending to what is selected and presented, the public comes to comprehend, to a greater or lesser degree, a selected agenda of topics summarizing at least some of what happened in their community, region, nation, and the world.

Defining what is news can be complex. Hundreds of definitions have been advanced since scholars began writing about the topic. For our purposes, however, we can define news in a very simple way: *News is current or fresh knowledge about an event or subject that is gathered, processed, and disseminated via a medium to a significant number of interested people.*

Of critical importance for understanding the nature of news are the four key terms: *gathered, processed, disseminated,* and *public.* These four are the heart of the

news process—a series of steps by which accounts of events flow through news organizations and eventually reach the public. These steps consist of (1) gathering relevant facts or details selectively, (2) preparing them into stories judged to be newsworthy and suitably encoded for particular media, and (3) transmitting those accounts via a mass medium to an audience, which then (4) attends to and comprehends what has been presented to varying degrees. The news process may also be thought of as the "surveillance function of the media," in which it keeps an eye on what is going on for citizens and produces reliable reports about what appears to be important. Thus, citizens supposedly have trustworthy information enabling them to make informed decisions about events and issues that are of significance to them personally and to society at large. This idealized interpretation of the function of the press in our democracy is the justification for the special protections and privileges accorded the news media, and not extended to other kinds of profit-making businesses.

If the news process works well—that is, if the information presented is reasonably complete and accurate as a representation of reality—the public gets a valid picture of what is actually going on. This picture, at least presumably, creates a close correspondence between what the great public philosopher Walter Lippmann called the "world outside" and the "pictures in our heads." However, as this chapter will make clear, there are many reasons to believe that the news presented by the press has only a *limited* correspondence with what is actually happening in the real world.

Recognizing the limitations of the news process, as we do in this chapter, is not the same as condemning it. To show that the "pictures in our heads" that we create from the news media's presentations of "the world outside" are distorted is not to say that journalists or the media deliberately set out to mislead us. An alternative conclusion is that such distortions are an inevitable product of the forces, factors, and conditions within which the news media must operate to survive. At the same time the news media can and should be criticized—strongly in some cases—for policies and decisions that have been made by owners and managers. A major purpose of this chapter, therefore, is to examine the news process impartially so as to provide a better understanding of how well, or how poorly, it actually performs its surveillance function and why.

Categories for Surveillance

Reality, of course, is the ultimate source of all news. The problem is reality's mind-boggling complexity. In the words of the philosopher William James, the world is a great "blooming and buzzing confusion." Thus, the news is drawn from a reality made up of an enormous variety of issues, events, conflicts, trends, and a host of other happenings. Whatever the perplexing nature of reality, the first step in the news process is to observe, understand, interpret, and record it for public consumption.

To understand this initial stage of the news process, we need first to look at how practicing journalists reduce the complex world to a limited number of *categories* so as to divide up the task of surveillance. A brief look at each of these categories will help in understanding the initial stage of news-gathering.

Wall Street, the financial capital is an important news beat or territory that yields business and economic news.

1. Territories, Topics, and Organizations

These divisions have grown out of the practical experience of journalists over the years and have become deeply established by tradition.

They are shaped in part by journalists' conceptions of what will interest the public and in part by their beliefs that there are some things that the public should know about in a democratic society. One important set of categories is the natural division of geographic *territories*.[4] Thus, facts for news stories come from events that are *local, regional, national, or international*. Each of these rather imprecise territorial definitions refers to rather different types of facts that hold different levels of interest for particular segments of the public. Some in the audience are "cosmopolitans," who follow the international and national news avidly but who care little or nothing about what is happening locally. Others are "locals," who keep well informed about what is happening in their immediate community or region but have limited interest in national and international events.[5] These audience preferences have become well understood by professional journalists, who balance their news reports to meet the needs of these different kinds of people.

Within each territory there are additional well-understood classifications based on *specialized topics*. Typical of such topics are politics, the economy, science, health, education, sports, fashion, weather, entertainment, space, crime, and so on through a long list. These play a key role in structuring the nature of the surveillance engaged in by the various news media. In a digital world, the geographic boundaries of news merge with those that are topical or specialized, as it is possible now to reach people everywhere who are interested in a quite narrow subject. Territorial classification is somewhat less important today as more amateur media observers make fragmented comments such as Twitter tweets that are short comments on many newsworthy topics.

Still another broad category has to do with the *organizations* from which facts for developing news stories are often obtained. Thus, at a national level, reporters are specifically assigned to cover one or more institutions of government, such as the White House, the judiciary, the Pentagon, or Congress. Assignments at the local level may be to the police department, city hall, or the local university. Especially important today are "think tanks," policy research centers, and other non-governmental organizations (NGOs) as sources of news. These are often specialist organizations that are somewhat self-serving, but they are important and highly visible sources of news and information. Of course, there is some truth to the claim that virtually all news sources are self-serving or self-referential, though some are truly innocent news. Using these categories and subcategories as the basis for a division of labor in a news organization allows reporters to become specialized and thereby "experts" in one or more categories. Thus, some reporters confine themselves to international affairs or even to a particular area of the world. Others focus exclusively on a particular topic or kind of activity, such as fashion, science, or education. This kind of specialization helps reporters develop unique skills and perspectives in locating, understanding, and writing about the important facts that are central to the territory, activity, or organization over which they exercise surveillance.

2. Time as a Category

A rather different kind of distinction among news stories can be made, within any of the previously mentioned categories, on the basis of the *extension of the story through time*. Some news happenings are of short duration and essentially one-time events. For example, at the local level, a house may burn down or an explosion occurs. Such events provide **spot news**—a staple of the industry. Spot stories have no history. The event occurs, it provides facts for a news story, the account is prepared, it is disseminated to the public, and that is it. But, as we mentioned earlier, the concept of time has been greatly modified and expanded in the digital age, when twenty-four/seven news demands push for continual stories that are broken in pieces over a long stretch of time or repeated again and again with a numbing effect.

Other stories can be classified as *developing*. They occur in stages, like the acts of a play, and news stories are generated as the action or situation unfolds. Eventually, however, each story comes to an end and is no longer newsworthy to the same degree. An electoral campaign is a good example.

A rather different time-related category is *continuing* news. Here, there is a no clear beginning or end but only an ongoing series of related happenings. Each time some related event occurs, stories can be generated about the ongoing process. A good example is the

The U.S. Capitol in Washington is another news beat or territory that yields political and governmental news.

issue of abortion or gay rights. Protests, counter protests, court cases, and political debates about women's rights or the right to life have provided a continuing theme around which stories have been developed for decades. Gay rights and same-sex marriage have a similar story line. It is a story focus that is unlikely to come to an end. Other examples of continuing news are issues related to the use of drugs, nuclear waste dumps, development versus preservation of the environment, the disputes over Social Security, the death penalty, assisted suicide, and the American trade deficit.

3. Hard versus Soft News

Hard news is what most people ordinarily think of as news. Something actually happens on a particular day—a bank is robbed, a murder is committed, or a bridge collapses. Time is an important consideration in such stories. They are news precisely because they are today's fresh happenings and must be reported to the public as rapidly as possible. Hard news is news of crime, disaster, economics, politics, and public policy. **Soft news**, on the other hand, is not as time-critical. It focuses on situations, people, or events that have "human interest." Such stories are seldom based on events that are restricted to a particular day and can be used in the news whenever they are needed. Feature stories and coverage of lifestyles, popular culture, and the arts often qualify as soft news.

How Facts Become Distorted

To what sources do news gatherers turn to obtain facts, and what problems with each source can cause a story to depart from reality? In this section we identify a number of traditional sources and others that have come with the technological developments of our time, plus some of the ways facts from such sources can be unwittingly distorted.

Perhaps the source of news facts that most readily comes to mind is *direct observation*. Such "on-the-spot" covering of events or situations presumably gives the news gatherer the fullest access to the facts. A related source, which is very traditional in news-gathering, is the *reports of witnesses,* who themselves have observed an event and who in interviews can provide eyewitness accounts. Another related source is the *expert*, who may not have observed the particular event in question but who is knowledgeable about that general class of occurrences.

Many less personal sources are also used. One is the **news release**—a prepared handout provided to reporters in electronic form, video, or on paper by an organization (such as the Pentagon or a major corporation) to summarize the "official" version of an event or situation. A business will issue a news release to announce personnel changes or new products, for example. Another impersonal source of facts are the many published *documents* news gatherers use, such as reports of business, educational, or governmental groups; technical journals; census reports; or summaries of economic trends. These can be found in libraries or, in many cases,

These tabloids covering a story about trapped miners are an example of hard, breaking news headlines.

via online computerized databases. Finally, *public records*, such as court, tax agency, or property ownership records, are widely used as sources of facts. Once mostly paper records, these are now largely digitized.

Although professional standards prevailing among news gatherers demand a high degree of accuracy in observing and assembling facts, much evidence suggests that unwitting errors, biases, and misrepresentations of reality are inevitable when *any* of the previous sources are used. That is not to say that reporters or others in the news industries deliberately falsify the accounts they prepare. On the contrary, the majority try very hard to be factually meticulous. Nevertheless, for reasons that we will show, distortions always occur; it is largely a question of degree. Furthermore, some sources pose far more problems of this nature than others. And to be honest, facts can be deliberately distorted as in hoaxes and efforts to slant the news, which some ideologically oriented people do quite forthrightly. Blog hoaxes are quite common because it is easy to post a false, misleading or satirical report online—and even accompany it with a video. One example is the 2007 report that Facebook would shut down if individuals didn't respond to create a new group with at least one million people within seven days. One well-known site is Fake Steve Jobs, written by blogger Daniel Lyons, who pretends to be the Apple co-founder. Other hoaxes have included UFO sightings and fake earthquakes. Sometimes satire and humor in the news is also misunderstood and adds distortion when it is read as factual.

ENCODING STRATEGIES: PACKAGING THE NEWS

News stories don't create themselves. Whatever their medium of transmission, every story is broken into its component parts, arranged, composed, stored, and disseminated according to the particular style and practices demanded of the story and the medium. This process is known as **encoding**. Encoding is different for newspapers, magazines, radio, television, and the Internet. One encoding strategy is based on the need to emphasize certain *news values* in selecting stories, so as to make the report interesting enough to capture and hold the attention of the audience. Another encoding strategy is based on the need to *format* news stories, so as to organize the ways or sequences within which its facts are presented. Finally, encoding strategies must fit with the *journalistic style* preferred by a particular news organization or outlet. Each of these encoding strategies will be discussed in more detail.

A second consideration in encoding arises from the ways in which the newspapers, magazines, and broadcasters *organize their daily agenda* or list of stories actually printed or broadcast. Stories received from reporters are positioned in the paper or scheduled in the broadcast along with advertising and other content. That position may be more or less prominent or obscure—on the front page or back near the obituaries, at the beginning of a broadcast or following the weather report. All of these decisions influence the way people interpret a story and can erode the relationship between news reports and truth. As Walter Lippmann wrote:

> "Every newspaper when it reaches the reader is the result of a whole series of selections as to what items shall be printed, in what position they shall be printed, how much space each shall occupy, what emphasis each shall have. [Thus]...news and truth are not the same thing, and must be clearly distinguished."[6]

Lippmann's dictum aptly describes the news: *news and truth are not the same thing*. Editors, news directors, and others in the chain of command make many kinds of judgments about story size, content, location, and balance with other reports, ethical status, ideological slant, and general suitability for the particular medium. The end result of this processing by the organization is that the medium's news stories present versions of reality that are at least one generation removed from the events that actually happened. This does not imply a deliberate attempt to mislead the public. Such distortions result from the way in which news media function within our society.

Traditional News Values

A crucial requirement of any news story is that the account of what happened must be as interesting and understandable as possible. If the audience finds it either dull or too complex, communication will fail. This requirement determines a number of ways in which news accounts are encoded: Decisions have to be made about which stories will be selected, how they will be written, and where they will be positioned in the daily paper or broadcast. As these choices are made, they result in quite different versions of reality.

Journalists have developed convenient criteria for judging the "newsworthiness" (that is, potential interest level) of stories. These criteria are called **news values**, and the account prepared must incorporate as many of them as possible. Both print and broadcast journalists use a number of considerations to judge the general newsworthiness of a story. These criteria have been derived over a long period and represent a kind of historically distilled wisdom as to what the public wants to read, hear about, or view in news presentations. Such news values are of considerable importance to reporters when they initially decide what is worth covering and when they prepare their initial accounts of what happened. News values also guide editors and news directors in making final decisions about what to print, put on the air, or put on the Net. Citizen journalists, who are not news professionals per se, must also understand newsworthiness and cutting edge issues that will get their stories and reports the attention they seek.

At least seven major criteria can be applied in assessing a particular story as an attractive candidate for presentation to the public. Few stories fit all. Nevertheless, in a practical sense, these news values provide important guidelines for judging the newsworthiness of any particular story:

IMPACT.   This criterion refers to the number of people whose lives will be influenced in some way by the subject of the story, as well as to the degree of that influence. For example, if workers in a local bakery decided to strike, it may have only a minor impact on the majority of the community. There may be some inconvenience, but most people will be little affected. However, if a telephone system fails, almost everyone will feel its impact; thus, a news report about a bakery strike will have less impact than one about a telecommunications failure.

TIMELINESS.   One of the most important requirements of a news story is that it must be presented to the public while it is still fresh. News that is stale has little or no appeal. Thus, stories of recent events have higher news value than those about earlier happenings. Of particular value are the stories brought to the public ahead of the competition. An older term for such a story is "scoop." Journalists like to claim, "You read it (or heard it, or viewed it) here first."

PROMINENCE.   Stories about people who are in the public eye have much higher news value than those about obscure people, even if the occurrences are the same. Thus, a story about a well-known football or basketball star with a major problem would be more newsworthy than one about some unknown individual who had a similar difficulty.

PROXIMITY.   Stories about events and situations in one's home community are more newsworthy than events that take place far away. A rather grim hypothetical example often used by journalists to illustrate the point is to equate the news value of various numbers of deaths at various distances. If a thousand people drown in flood in a far-away country, the story has about the same news value as one describing how a hundred drowned in a distant part of the United States. That event, in turn, has about the same news value as a story concerning ten flood victims in one's own state. And, finally, a story about those ten has about the same value as a story describing a flood that drowns a single person in the local community.

THE BIZARRE.   An example that illustrates this criterion well is the oft-quoted definition of news attributed to John B. Bogart, who was the city editor of *The Sun* in New York during the 1880s: "When a dog bites a man," Bogart is purported to have said, "that's not news, because it happens so often. But if a man bites a dog, that is news." In the modern era, a bizarre shooting at a high school involving a single student will be of greater importance in the news than is the good behavior of millions of students. In any case, odd or peculiar events have always seemed more newsworthy than those of a routine nature. For that reason, the news media can usually be counted on to give space or time to sightings of UFOs, ghosts, or the likeness of Christ in an unlikely place.

CONFLICT.   The rule here is that consensus and harmony is generally dull, but strife is newsworthy. Stories that describe such events as messy divorces or child custody battles, rebellions, personal vendettas, and other kinds of clashes are high in news value. Thus, what transpired at a Quaker peace vigil might not make news, unless a fistfight broke out or someone attacked the peace demonstrators. That would make a good story.

CURRENCY.   More value is attributed to stories pertaining to issues or topics that are in the spotlight of public concern than to those about which people care less. Scandals of all kinds fit in this category.

Essentially, then, the news industry greatly prefers stories that their accumulated wisdom identifies as those in which public will be most interested. The cost of relying on such criteria to define newsworthiness is that many stories will be ignored that are in fact truly significant from other points of view. For example, discoveries in scientific research may be of historical importance, contribute to betterment of human condition, and advance the frontiers of knowledge. However, they may be judged as dull. If so, they are likely to be found in the back pages or in the last part of the newscast (if they appear at all). Thus, the human genome research gets less coverage than a celebrated murder or a sex scandal.

Story Formats

According to our second major encoding consideration, the story itself must be packaged in one of the *formats* that prevail in the relevant news medium in order to be understandable while maintaining or increasing its interest. Over many decades, journalists have worked out effective ways of organizing news stories that will accomplish those objectives. By tradition, one general format for a well-written newspaper story is that it tells *who* did *what, where, when,* and *why.* These "five W's" set forth the essential features of any good news story and are the basic format that every beginning journalism student learns. In large part, they encompass the way working print journalists package most of their stories. This inventory for story organization is also used in broadcast journalism. However, the requirements of radio, television, and the Internet are quite different from those of print and allow enhancements to the standard print format.

Using one or more of the five W's, news stories are organized in the so-called *inverted pyramid.* The basic idea is that the most important ideas should appear first. Journalists learned early that many people read only the headlines, and others read the "lead" sentence, or perhaps the first paragraph or two, and then go on to the next story.

This controversial cover of *The New Yorker* magazine satirizing Barrack and Michelle Obama as Muslim terrorists generated soft news coverage about race and ethnicity.

Thus, the important ideas need to be set forth at the beginning, and overall the account should both be interesting and make few intellectual demands. Journalists have little confidence in the willingness of the average citizen to linger over complex details or sophisticated analyses.

Electronic media reporters, of course, must also use formats. Radio and television news stories tend to follow the criteria of news values, the five W's, and the inverted pyramid. Remember that they are written for the ear—and for the eye through visuals. However, a radio or television newscast has much greater flexibility and can draw upon many variations to maintain audience interest. They organize to be seen or heard, rather than read. Radio news, for instance, can incorporate the "actualities" of sound effects, such as the noise of a log being sawed in a news report on a lumber mill. Television is even more flexible. The simplest format for TV newscast is the **word story**, where the anchorperson is shown behind a desk telling what happened. A variant is to provide a graphic that appears in the upper corner of the screen, with an identifying phrase keyed to the story. Another TV format is the **VO** (voice-over), in which the viewer first sees the anchorperson but is then switched to video with the anchor's voice over the ongoing picture. Still another is the **stand-up**, in which the anchor switches to a reporter in the field, who comments on the scene. The **stand-up with package** is similar, with a reporter interviewing someone at the scene. Several versions of such formats are regularly used in producing TV news in an effort to create audience interest and to provide richer information. All of these have the possibility of introducing meanings into a story that modify it in selective ways. And there are now scores of digital graphics techniques that aid the storytelling capacity of the electronic media, including linking them to digital, interactive websites.

JOURNALISTIC STYLES

While the ideals of fairness, objectivity, and accuracy currently hold sway within the news industry, this was not always the case, nor is it always the case even now. **Journalistic styles** are based on the idea that a particular set of facts can be combined into a news story in a variety of ways. A considerable number of such styles have emerged within journalism over the years. Some are far more widely used than others, but each has had its period of popularity, and each has left its mark on the contemporary news industries. Moreover, each presents the story within a different framework of meaning.

Sensational or Tabloid Journalism

This style characterized the press from the 1890s to about 1920, though it never really went away, as supermarket tabloids and some big city dailies with screaming headlines will attest. Sensationalism stresses shocking details, bizarre events, and sometimes appalling transgressions of the social norms. The newspapers in times of sensational issues thrived on implications of scandal and sin in high places. If a murder had been committed, the crime was described with special attention to the appearance of the corpse, the look of the blood, suggestions of illicit sex, and the insidious nature of the killer. Facts, in such accounts, were of secondary importance. The sensational style is alive and well in such tabloids as the *National Enquirer* and similar publications sold chiefly in supermarkets. And there are endless websites that celebrate sensationalism with lurid treatments of sex and violence. This form of journalism can be maddening, erratic, and not always reliable or useful.

"Objective" or Impartial Journalism

Sensationalism gave way to objectivity, which generally prevailed until about mid-century. In 1950, Alan Barth of the *Washington Post* wrote with pride, "The tradition of objectivity is one of the principal glories of American journalism."[7] In reality, that opinion was not universally held. As an examination of contemporary trade journals quickly shows objectivity had been under fire for generations. For a few years, however, there was almost complete consensus among journalists and consumers that objectivity was a vast improvement over the sensational journalism that characterized the earlier American press. Objectivity is a style that has traditionally been characterized by three aims: (1) separating *fact from opinion*, (2) presenting an *emotionally detached view* of the news, and (3) striving for *fairness and balance*, giving both sides an opportunity to reply in a way that provides full information to the audience. By world standards, American reporters have long been (and still are) relatively objective. That is, they are not ideological in a partisan political sense. For decades their aim has been to separate fact and opinion, keeping factual accounts in the news and opinion on the editorial page. However, beginning in the 1960s and continuing today, critics deny that this can actually be done, claiming that no human being is capable of complete objectivity. Instead, they tout "fairness" as an item of explanation. This form of journalism follows a regular and predictable pattern and delivers basic and predictable facts.

The challenge to objectivity occurred in part because critics had come to feel that American journalism was lifeless—unemotional and incapable of dealing with great social problems. There is much to be said for this view. For several decades now and heightened by the digital revolution, the news media are criticized with a vigor they had rarely encountered before. In this fate, they had much company; during the same period, most American institutions were challenged by widespread distrust and a search for new approaches. The outcome was that several alternative styles for presenting news stories emerged, and although they did revolutionize the press, they have influenced contemporary journalism. To understand how, we can examine a few of these alternatives more closely. They included the "new" journalism, along with *advocacy* and *precision* journalism. Today, objectivity—or, at least, fairness and balance—is still dominant. These newer styles are currently used to some extent in both print and broadcast media, although because of government regulation, most of them are more difficult to implement in broadcasting.

Critical, Interpretative Journalism

For years, the leaders and practitioners of the mainstream journalism that one finds in daily newspapers and television news argued that they were impartial observers, but, more recently, many media outlets are bluntly critical and interpretative when it comes to covering the news. Instead of just dutifully reporting what a source says, followed by one that might disagree or have another view, reporters take it upon themselves to search for more facts and to counter what they believe is false or misleading information. This is quite prevalent in political news coverage, when candidates often shade their achievements to appeal to the voters. So, when a candidate for president makes claims that a factual analysis can't support, reporters often say so—and quite critically. News reports once routinely avoided providing physical description of an individual. Now if a source seems angry, disheveled, or tired, that makes it into the story. And such reporters are not bashful about correcting sources and thus casting doubt on their credibility. Some critics say this reflects media bias—and it can. But in most cases, the critical reporter is not biased, ideologically driven, or prejudiced but simply providing a close analysis where he or she might see the source or subject matter differently from those promoting it. This is especially useful when self-serving individuals and institutions are trying to do "damage control" and cast the best possible light on the matter, whether it is a corporate scandal, disaster, or political controversy (something we cover in the chapter on public relations).

In these instances the critical reporter is more than a stenographer trying to dutifully report what an ordinary person can see, but tries to dig deeper and seek the truth. While news magazines like *Time, Newsweek,* and *U.S. News and World Report* have always been more descriptive and interpretative than newspaper or wire service reporters, this tendency has definitely made headway in traditional media like the *Washington Post, Chicago Tribune,* and *Los Angeles Times,* as well as such new media as Salon.com and the Huffington Post.[8]

Literary or "New" Journalism

This style was never an issue of great concern to the public, but it did alter the reigning definitions of news and writing forms within the profession. The first stirrings in the 1960s and 1970s of the new journalism came from three sources. One was journalists on newspapers and magazines who felt restricted by traditional formats such as the inverted pyramid. Another was literary figures, especially novelists, who were seeking a direct way to write about the nation's discontents. The third was broadcast journalists eager to explore less conventional sources and language. Some publications like *New York* magazine and its innovative editor Clay Felker pioneered this form with dramatic stories written by now well-known figures like Tom Wolfe and others. Journalists looking for change felt that traditional procedures were not effectively capturing the essence of the great social movements of the day or the changes in lifestyle. They felt that both the customary reliance on official sources (mainly public officials) and the conventional avoidance of rich description prevented them from capturing the tone of the great changes taking place then and later. Of course, as historians later proved, many official reports of the Vietnam period proved to be false or misleading. Governments often cover up mistakes and malfeasance, so there is good reason to be skeptical of official sources. As a result, they maintained, it was impossible to give the public the full story of what was happening. For example, the so-called "counterculture," which influenced millions of young people during the1960s and 1970s, was not considered to be presented fully in newspapers and newscasts because it was not tied to "authoritative" sources.

The result was that several young writers began experimenting with new journalistic techniques, such as *scene setting,* using many descriptive adjectives to give the reader a sense of being there. Another technique was *extended dialogue.* Rather than trying to be detached and objective, they also provided a *point of view,* sometimes allowing the attitudes or values of their sources to dominate their stories. To portray the thoughts of people who were news sources, as the sources reported them to the journalists, an *interior monologue* might be included. Finally, instead of quoting all sources by name, the new journalists sometimes created a *composite character* who brought together the characteristics of several people and stood for, say, the average prostitute or police officer.

All these devices are old tools of fiction writers. The new journalists claimed that these methods allowed them to offer a richer and truer portrait than the traditional news style permitted. One of the most famous examples was writer Truman Capote's *In Cold Blood,* a nonfiction novel. These new journalists were not necessarily political activists, but they wanted to observe and report on America's manners and morals in an exciting way instead of merely quoting official sources. The methods of fiction writers helped them to do so.

Despite controversy and criticism, the new journalism style continues to influence the conventions of the media generally. By the first decade of the twenty-first century, the new journalism's techniques were commonplace in radio and television documentaries, magazines, nonfiction novels, newspapers, and almost everywhere online, where length of story is not a barrier. For the most part, however, the influence of the new journalism has not been overwhelming or revolutionary but rather subtle and indirect.

Advocacy Journalism

Another alternative to objectivity is the **advocacy style**. Here, the reporter and the story identify with and "advocate"—that is, try to promote—a cause or position. Unlike editorial writing, advocacy journalism appears in news columns and not as a simple statement of opinion. In a sense, it is a kind of hybrid news story that promotes a particular point of view, departing from traditional journalism and investigative reporting, which we discuss in a later section.

Advocacy journalism appears mostly in magazines and on cable, radio, and endless websites. Some practitioners are known broadcast journalists and commentators such as Bill O'Reilly or Lou Dobbs, who are unabashed advocates, producing stories with a strong point of view that are not balanced or "fair" in the traditional sense of the word, though they would disagree. Dobbs, a controversial figure, aims his reports at immigrants and says he is a champion for the middle classes. O'Reilly, a TV journalist and commentator, was a pioneer in tabloid television. He says he operates a "no spin" zone and, like Dobbs, takes a populist perspective, though he is often seen as politically conservative. O'Reilly likes to berate judges who he believes coddle criminals, while Dobbs always looks for examples of government waste that hurts the middle class. Advocacy journalists see themselves as torchbearers for justice and pursue their mission knowing that plenty of people are promoting an opposite point of view. Critics see them as undisciplined mouthpieces for a single side of an issue. Advocacy reporting is not widely practiced, and most studies of journalists show that it is not particularly admired in the field.[9]

Precision Journalism

A very different style that is becoming increasingly important is **precision journalism**, most often called computer-assisted reporting or computer-assisted investigative reporting (CAR or CAIR). Essentially, it is a style of reporting and writing that makes use of some of the methods of the social sciences to gather and analyze quantitative information for the purposes of preparing news stories. It takes two forms: in active precision journalism, reporters actually conduct surveys or other research projects; in reactive precision journalism, they use reports already assembled by government agencies, universities, and private firms to develop stories around the provided data. The basic goal of these journalists is to present to the public understandable analyses based on quantitative information relevant to significant issues in the news. For example, let's suppose a town was proposing floating a bond issue to fund a new convention center. Traditional journalists would interview people selected casually or conveniently so as to give the impression of portraying the opinions of "people in the street." The precision journalist would interview a carefully chosen group of citizens selected according to the rules of scientific sampling, to obtain a more representative summary of the views shared in the community. The reported results might be the same; the method of arriving at them differed.

Civic or Public Journalism

This style of journalism, developed in the 1990s, often involves projects aimed at diagnosing and helping solve community problems. It is a journalistic effort to promote and achieve "civil society"—voluntary efforts that improve the quality of life for the public. While usually replete with facts, there is a fine line between advocacy journalism and civic journalism, though the latter is usually less ideological. It moves beyond simply relating the news into attempts to revive civic life and to improve public dialogue. Widely practiced by today's newspapers and some television stations, its goal is to keep the press grounded in the concerns of ordinary people, rather than in those of the elite. Essentially, this form of journalism identifies problems to be solved, such as high crime rates in the community, political corruption, or taxes that are imposed unevenly in different neighborhoods, and attempts to assist in their solution. The newspaper or TV station reports on citizens' meetings, assemblies, and other cooperative efforts where problems are aired, often taking sides in controversies.[10]

Promoters of this approach argue that traditional journalism is no longer trusted by the public and that this strategy can restore confidence. Journalism needs a rebirth, they maintain, as a more democratic profession concerned with the problems of ordinary people. Critics warn that it moves journalism away from its traditional impartial and

A citizen journalist uses a smart phone to photograph a soccer match and stream content from it.

disinterested stance to that of political activists pushing a particular agenda. They reject the notion that social problems can be fixed through journalism by having news columns take sides in local disputes. Such efforts are seen as inappropriate or even arrogant.

Citizen Journalism, Blogging, and the Demonstration of News

Unlike public journalism in which news is largely gathered by news media employees, though drawing on bottom-up information from ordinary persons, citizen journalism actually involves ordinary people, not professional journalists, producing news reports—as citizens participating in a democracy. As the *Online Journalism Review* puts it, citizen journalism includes audience participation, such as comments on news stories, blogs, podcasts, photos, and amateur video footage. It also includes independent bloggers such as media critic Todd Gitlin and others. Citizen journalism is usually delivered

FIGURE 9.3

Citizen Journalism: Top-Down News vs. Bottom-Up News

Broadcast: Top-Down News

Intercast: Bottom-Up News

Broadcast: Top-Down News
Model also called transmit, push. Characterized by media organization control.
All news is filtered through organization before getting to audience.

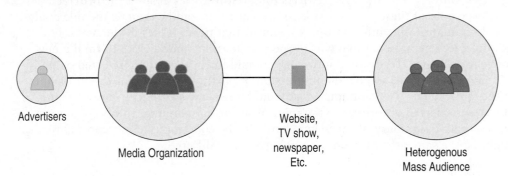

Intercast: Bottom-Up News
Also called peer-to-peer, social network. Participants are peers and have ability to change roles.
News is often unfiltered by a mediator before getting to its audience.

on a website and encourages interactivity and feedback. There is even a Center for Citizen Media, organized by Dan Gillmor, a former *San Jose Mercury News* reporter, who has become its champion. While citizen journalism could be delivered by newsletter and most any media form, it has truly accelerated as a result of digital technology, which makes interactivity easy.[11] Citizen journalism blurs together with blogs, both those from lone individuals seeking attention for their news and views and those created by big media organizations. There are also websites such as Blog News that aggregate news from hundreds, perhaps eventually thousands, of blogs. At the same time, much of the news on blogs and other online reports is taken from traditional sources, sometimes verbatim or otherwise commented upon or summarized. And traditional news sources pick up news tips and reports from blogs. The cycle is never ending.

It is argued that blogs and citizen journalism democratize the news, allowing more voices to be heard and thus reducing the powerlessness of ordinary people— whether they are citizens or not. In fact, citizen journalists often decry the term "news consumer" and prefer "citizen," which isn't always correct. The prevalence of blogs and other individual posts and reports is said to break the monopoly of big media, which dominates the news and is usually the source of most news and public affairs for the public.

Satirical or Humor Journalism

Sometimes called "fake news," humor journalism is a satirical take on the news "reported" by such figures as Jon Stewart, Stephen Colbert, and others on Comedy Central and elsewhere. Here, using a traditional news set, the anchor reports a supposed story with visuals and remains deadpan, even though it is often made up of fake quotes or quotes used out of context from TV news clips and other sources. Of course, the main source of stories for satirical journalism is authentic news taken from standard sources and presented with a humorous twist or tone. Some polls suggest that many people cite this form of journalism as a major source of news, though presumably they know they are dealing with something tongue in cheek. *The Onion* newspaper is also a source of this form as are the "news reports" on *Saturday Night Live*. Fake news has become so popular that major news sources, such as politicians, authors, and business leaders vie for interviews in these venues. This form is a major source of news for college students and young adults.

"Fake newscaster" Stephen Colbert on the popular *The Colbert Report* is a master of satirical or humor journalism.

SOCIAL AND CULTURAL INFLUENCES ON THE NEWS

Two sets of social and cultural factors play a significant part in shaping decisions as to what is finally transmitted to the public after specific news stories are passed from reporters to editors and news directors. First, influences arise from the *social organization of newsrooms*. These include a number of particular editorial and production roles within the teams that decide news policy and select the final assortment of stories that will make up the paper or the newscast. The second set of influences is broader, consisting of the cultural constraints on news organizations poised by the basic nature of private enterprise itself, as defined within our society. Both are important in shaping and reshaping the meaning of a news story.

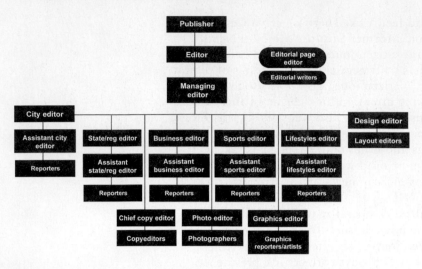

A traditional table of organization for a newspaper shows its employee-heavy demands.

The Social Organization of the Newsroom

Each news medium—online media, newspapers, magazines, radio, and television—has its own pattern of social organization. These patterns influence encoding decisions and therefore the nature of the news story as it is finally produced. At the top of the social structure are those who own the organization as a business enterprise. The owners, or their corporate representatives at the top, seldom exert direct control over specific news stories. (An exception to this is News Corp.'s Rupert Murdoch, who takes a personal interest in news coverage and who has been known to be heavy handed with his editor.) However, they do set broad guidelines as to which styles of journalism are to be emphasized and where the organization will locate itself along a liberal to conservative continuum.

Managers make up a second stratum. Upper-level managers are generally sensitive to the orientations of the owners. Theirs is the task of running the organization on a day-to-day basis, setting its more specific operating policies, and making certain that it achieves its goals. Below them are the middle managers—editors, directors, and producers whose daily task it is to assemble the content of a newspaper, get the magazine ready for the printer, or produce the news program in final form for broadcasting. Often, the personal preferences and values of these managers influence the ways in which news stories are finally shaped.

News stories or news services like AP or Bloomberg flow to the newsroom from reporters, stringers, freelancers, and the "wires." Here they are reviewed and reshaped by its hierarchy of editors and managers. At the core of this reshaping is the fact that so much is happening in the world, the nation, the state, and the local area that there is simply not enough time or space to bring it all to the attention of the public. In producing the daily newspaper, for example, the various ads and announcements that provide financial support must be accommodated first. What is left for editorial matter is called the *news hole*, and it is into that 20 to 40% of the paper that the news of the day must fit. Because there is always more news than space, only two kinds of decisions can be made to fit the news into the hole. They are to drop or to shrink the stories prepared by the reporters. The editor, often with a heavy hand, removes details that seem expendable—and again the gap widens between reality and its description in the news story. This is less true today as the infinite capacity of the Internet to store text allows editors to put long reports and documents online and link them to shorter news treatments.

To deal with the excessive number of stories that flow into the newsroom via the "wire" (including satellite and the Internet), wire editors read all the stories that accumulate up to a particular time and select the ones they view as important and suitable. Once again, through a process of selection, the gap widens between what happened in the "world outside" and what is reported in the newspaper.

These processes of selection and elimination of details or even entire stories are called **gatekeeping**. This complex process is a central part of all news editing and production systems. Individuals at different positions—editors, news directors, and others—have to make decisions about including or excluding material from news presentations. Obviously, gatekeeping significantly influences the selective construction of reality to be reported by the press. Again, some students of digital media argue that gatekeeping is no longer as important as it once was because virtually everything can be stored and news consumers can use search technologies to get what they want when they want it.

Consequences of the Profit Motive

Real people invest real dollars in newspapers, magazines, broadcasting stations, cable, and online systems. Logically enough, they expect to make real profits. What critics protest is not so much the idea that media owners make a return on investment, but *what the owners do* to maximize their profits. News is viewed as content—and as a commodity to bring in revenues.

Nowhere is the problem better illustrated than in the case of network television news. Three decades ago, news-gathering and broadcasting were supported by all of the other programming offered by the networks. The news programs themselves were not expected to show a profit. Their ratings were not as high as those of entertainment programming, and advertisers did not flock to news programs as a context for their commercials. Subsidizing the news was seen as similar to the system in newspapers. The news part of the paper is not expected to operate profitably

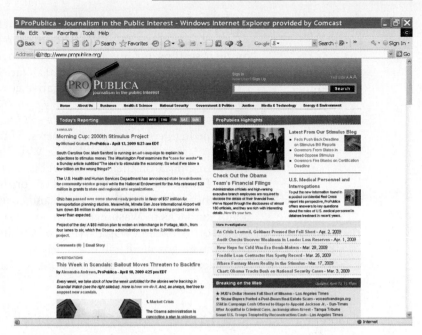

Pro Publica is a non-profit news service that produces long form journalism for various news outlets.

on its own. The revenues from the newspaper as a whole provide funding for news-gathering, editorial functions, printing, and the like. However, when cable and VCR usage began to eat into audience shares for network television, both corporate leadership and news policies changed significantly. The news policies declared that the news had to earn its own keep. It had to develop ways of offering the news that would increase ratings so as to make news broadcasts more attractive to advertisers. Under these new policies, the networks pared news teams down sharply to cut costs. Less funding was to be available for such frills as investigative reporting, on-the-spot coverage, and camera teams in foreign lands, or opinion and analysis. Even robotic cameras were employed to save labor costs.

Far more important, however, were corporate decisions to define news program content in different ways. It had to be more fun to watch, so as to bring in more viewers. New kinds of programming were designed, sometimes even "staging" or "re-creating" news events. The relationship of such programs to news in a traditional sense is remote. Indeed, critics used the term "trivialization" of the news to describe such programming. Out of these transformations of news substance came the concept of *infotainment*—a merging of information and entertainment—and now an important criterion for gatekeeping. From all that is available to news directors and editors, many selections appear to be made for their entertainment value, rather than because of their newsworthiness or their essential importance to society—for example, the excessive coverage of celebrities like Paris Hilton and Britney Spears. In greater or lesser degree, pressures toward trivialization exist in all of the news media, but it is a special problem for broadcast and cable networks. As the emphasis on infotainment has gradually become television standard, many thoughtful analysts feel that the nation is being poorly served. Indeed, the question can be raised as to whether the reasons for protecting TV news media with the First Amendment and various laws intended to shield or protect journalists make sense any more.

There are not-for-profit news operations including public radio and television, which rely on public pledge drives and grants from foundations and corporations. Efforts to promote nonprofit sources to produce better journalism and more investigative reporting have captured the imagination of various media foundations, which have underwritten experimental programs and news services. *Pro Publica,* a highly touted service, headed by Paul Steiger, longtime managing editor of the *Wall Street Journal,* was launched in 2008 to encourage long-form journalism and investigative reporting, which cost-conscious, profit-making media have downgraded in recent years. Steiger sees the service as a stopgap for news organizations that have cut back on their staffing for investigative reporting. *Pro Publica* offers its reporting to other media for that reason. There are also various regional and state news media services trying to encourage more investigative coverage.[12]

THE HIGH COST OF NEWS.   What *Pro Publica* and other nonprofit news efforts point out is the high cost of producing news. With declining profits for news organizations for several years and heightened by the Wall Street meltdown of 2008, news organizations are cutting back on their personnel budgets and reducing their newsroom and reporting staffs. Thousands of reporters and editors have been laid off, probably permanently; international bureaus have closed; and coverage is greatly diminished as evidenced in major cutbacks in Washington bureaus, even as a new administration with a highly newsworthy agenda was arriving in Washington in 2009. Whether new sources of news from the blogosphere will effectively supplement the content being lost in industry-wide cutbacks is a matter of debate as this is written.

SOCIAL AND CULTURAL FUNCTIONS OF THE NEWS

Individual newspapers and broadcasters vary in how they resolve the conflict between the obligation to inform the public fully and the need to be profitable. The choice involved can be very well illustrated by comparing two almost completely opposite prevailing conceptions of the nature and functions of news. These are the *marketing approach,* which avidly pursues the goal of maximizing profits by selling news as a product and sharply limiting public service, and the *adversarial approach,* which sees news as information needed by the public and which emphasizes the watchdog functions of the press, often at the expense of profits. That these strategies coexist in sharp contrast shows the two very different paths our nation's press may follow in carrying out its surveillance function in the future.

The Market Approach: News as a Product

A news organization that uses the market approach devotes considerable resources to the task of understanding what the audience wants to find in a news medium. Then it makes certain that it serves those interests. The idea is to market its product—that is, the news—in much the same way as any other commercial commodity, like beer, soap, or breakfast cereal is marketed.

This approach begins with extensive market research that assembles statistical data on the interests, media habits, and concerns of the audience. These data are then used as guidelines in determining what material will be offered and, especially, in what manner. Thus, both the content of news stories and the style in which they are offered to the public are selected on the basis of research findings that define what the audience wants most. *USA Today* offers users a marketing approach and has been criticized for giving the public what it says it *wants,* rather than what traditional editors think it *needs.*

Marketing the news is not a new idea. For many years, the marketing approach has been a staple for broadcasters. Newspapers were actually slow to adopt methods that broadcast stations had used routinely to calibrate their product to their audience. For example, the marketing approach has been applied to television news almost from its beginning, with changes in format and style made to attract a larger audience. For years, print journalists tended to treat these practices with contempt. But in the 1970s and 1980s, managers and owners of metropolitan daily newspapers were appalled by their declining circulation per household, and soon print journalists had their own "news doctors." There seemed to be many causes for the declining circulation; competition from television, the growth of the suburbs, new lifestyles, and a lack of relevance in the papers were all blamed. The newspapers responded with market research designed to diagnose the "ills" causing the decline. This concern continues today as firms like

Gannett promote useful news to their viewers, some of it aimed at moms, for example, to encourage greater involvement with news that is useful and compelling.

To end declines in newspaper circulation, the market researchers prescribed *change,* advising the newspapers to add new sections on topics such as lifestyles, entertainment, gardening, and housing—sections that help readers "use" their communities and their environment. Such sections are hardly "news." They are edited and written for audience interest and approval. In some ways, they represent extended and repackaged coverage of topics that have always been in the paper. For example, many newspapers covered real estate for years, but as a result of the marketing approach, some renamed the section "Shelter" or "Home" and began to treat the topic from the consumer's point of view, adding personal stories about how to find an apartment or remodel a house. Similarly, in their lifestyles sections, the newspapers print advice from "experts" on how people can solve their everyday problems—from how to get rid of stubborn stains to how to deal with a sullen child or a spouse's infidelity.

As mentioned earlier, the best-known example of a newspaper that relies heavily on the marketing approach is the nationally circulated *USA Today,* which was designed on the basis of market research and continues to make heavy use of research findings that indicate audience interests. *USA Today* not only selects its topics of coverage on the basis of guidelines from research but has also pioneered the use of color, new styles of graphic presentation, and brevity (some say superficiality) in writing. Many other newspapers have followed *USA Today's* style and approach.

Does the marketing approach serve readers better, or does it merely pander to the lowest tastes? Philip Meyer, a leader in the precision journalism movement, suggested that it helps newspapers obtain and respond to feedback from audiences and thus to communicate with them more effectively.[13] Others maintain that it leads to trivialization of the news, especially in broadcasting. Professional news consultants very often seem more concerned with the hairstyles of anchor people or the design of sets and computer graphics than with the substance of the stories. As this approach to news as a product has become increasingly commonplace, however, the definition of news itself has shifted further away from an emphasis on reports on public affairs and specific events, moving instead toward infotainment material that will gratify the audience.

The Adversarial Approach: Watchdogs of the Public Interest

The role of the press as an adversary of government is the one most honored in the traditions of journalism. In this capacity the press has sometimes been called the *fourth estate.* Thomas Carlyle (1795–1881) attributed the phrase to Edmund Burke (1729–1797), who called the reporters' gallery in the English Parliament "a Fourth Estate more important by far" than the other three estates of Parliament—the lords, bishops, and commons. It was because the right to speak out freely acted as a check on government, holding it accountable, that the American founders nurtured the principles of freedom of speech and protection of the right to public dissent. Today, the adversarial approach makes a critical contribution to society by increasing accountability and by exposing unsatisfactory conditions in both government and the private sector.

TRADITIONAL INVESTIGATIVE REPORTING.   Central to the adversarial approach is *investigative reporting.* This is a kind of news-gathering in which the reporter probes deeply into a situation and assembles evidence that discloses whether or not there is something unusual, unethical, illegal, or even outrageous going on. Although the fact gathering may be done by a single reporter or a team of individuals working together, the decision to undertake such an investigation is made by editors who must provide the financial support and be ready to disclose and defend reports on what is uncovered.[14]

The professional organization, Investigative Reporters and Editors (IRE), defines such reporting in the following terms: *It is reporting, through one's own work product and initiative, matters of importance that some persons or organizations wish to keep secret.* The three basic elements in this definition are that the investigation is made by someone else, that the subject of the story involves something of *reasonable importance* to the reader or viewer, and that others are attempting to *hide these matters* from the public.[15]

Investigative reporting started in the nineteenth century. Some view the first such investigation to have been conducted in the 1840s by James Gordon Bennett, the energetic publisher of the *New York Herald*. Dissatisfied with the usual ways of reporters covering the courts, he sought a way to provide more interesting accounts of serious crimes. Choosing the occasion of the spectacular murder of a young prostitute, he personally went to the "fancy house" where she worked, interviewed the "madam," poked through the victim's personal papers, and even examined the unfortunate girl's remains. The resulting story, rich in details about the place and the people involved, made very interesting reading.

Investigative reporting reached dramatic heights late in the nineteenth century. An adventurous young woman, "Nellie Bly" (a *nom de plume;* her name was actually Elizabeth Cochrane), became famous as a result of her investigative report of Blackwell's Island, an insane asylum in New York. In an elaborate scheme, she posed as a mentally ill person and was committed to the asylum. There, continuing the deception, she saw firsthand how patients were treated. The doctors and staff had no idea she was a reporter, and she received very bad treatment for about ten days. Fortunately, she had prearranged for her newspaper, Joseph Pulitzer's *New York World*, to extricate her. They did so, and her exposé of the hospital conditions gained worldwide attention.[16]

As Chapter 3 indicates, early in this century, the journalists of the muckraker tradition investigated many private and governmental institutions. They uncovered and exposed corruption, abuse, and crime that characterized both private industry and government at the time. The contribution of the muckrakers to American society was far more than just interesting reading material. Their exposés led to reform and legislation that still affect us today.[17]

American journalists have kept this great tradition alive. An extraordinary example of investigative reporting during the 1970s was the Watergate disclosures concerning the Nixon administration. A series of stories developed by investigative reporters Carl Bernstein and Robert Woodward of the *Washington Post* dominated American news media for months, exposing a conspiracy by the White House staff, the CIA, and others to cover up a number of covert illegal activities carried out by White House aides during the 1972 presidential election. The ensuing congressional investigation eventually implicated the president and led to his resignation. This has become an iconic example of investigative reporting so that aspects of the story—including the identity of the chief source, called "Deep Throat," continued to provoke comment for more than thirty years before that person, Mark Felt, revealed himself. He died in 2008. In the 1990s investigative reports in *Newsweek* and online in *The Drudge Report* played a key role in the investigation of President Clinton by special prosecutor Kenneth Starr and eventually led to an impeachment trial in the U.S. Senate. Investigative reporting is expensive and requires considerable time and other resources, and the practice has been reported to be on the wane in recent years. At the same time, some of the tools of the new media and digital applications do help reporters do their work faster and more thoroughly, although there is no substitute for what editors call "shoe leather" and personal interviews as well as the ability to travel widely. Magazine cover stories, one of the last vestiges

Bob Woodward and Carl Bernstein of *The Washington Post* broke the famous Watergate story that brought down a president and established them as exemplars of investigative reporting.

of in-depth investigative reporting, often take weeks or months to develop. Business magazines like *BusinessWeek* and *Fortune* are examples of this kind of thorough work, though their treatments are rarely sensational. Those are more likely to appear elsewhere, including magazines like *Vanity Fair*.

SEARCH ENGINES   Online data services, operated by commercial vendors, are especially valuable for obtaining background material for the development of a story or an investigation. At first they were used mainly for bibliographic retrieval, allowing a user to find out from a database who had published what in, say, scientific journals. Today, the thousands of different databases operating on a fee basis supply information ranging from stock market prices and airline schedules to complete files of scientific articles on every conceivable topic. Early online services were overtaken by now-common search engines and social networking sites. Google and Yahoo!, known to all, are the dominant ones.

The Agenda-Setting Function of the News Media

The final stage in constructing the daily news is deciding *which stories* to present to the public and the degree of *prominence* they deserve. Communications scholars refer to this final part of the news process as **agenda setting**. It means deciding on which positions within the newspaper or broadcast the stories of the day should appear. Some, it will be decided, should be prominent. These will be on the front page and have a large headline. They may have a photo or many column inches. Others, which seem less important, will have a smaller headline, be short, have no photo, and will be relegated to back sections of the paper. In the case of broadcast news, some stories can appear early in the presentation, perhaps be given more time, be accompanied by some background information, and have some video footage taken on the scene. Others can be presented in less dramatic and simpler form toward the end of the broadcast.

BIG IDEAS: MEDIA THEORIES EXPLAINED

The Agenda-Setting Theory of the Media

A theory concerning the influence of the press on peoples' beliefs and evaluations of the topics reported in the news was first developed by media scholars Maxwell McCombs and Donald Shaw. Their initial version of the theory explains how individuals come to regard some events and situations that they encounter via news reports in print and broadcast media as *more important* than others. Thus, the original agenda-setting theory implies a relationship between the prominence of the placement of a story in a news report in newspapers, on television, or in radio news and the *beliefs about its importance or significance* on the part of the news audience.

The theory came from a study of the presidential political campaign of 1968. Its authors observed how people decided which issues, among those receiving extended news attention, were important. As it turned out, the public developed a kind of ranking in their own minds about the importance of the different issues discussed in the news. The authors of the theory found a high level of correspondence between the amount and kind of attention paid to a particular political issue by the press and the level of importance assigned to that issue by people in the community who had received information about it in the press.

It was the press, therefore, that determined during a political campaign which issues people discussed among themselves and how much importance they attached to each. In other words, the press developed *its own agenda* concerning what issues were news and

continued

BIG IDEAS: MEDIA THEORIES EXPLAINED *continued*

how much space and prominence to give them. Then the agenda of the press became the agenda *of those who followed the news of the campaign*. This does not imply that the media tells people what they should *think* and decide about the issues. However, it does imply that the press tells people what they should *think about* and what issues are important enough so that they should develop an opinion.

Later, it was realized that such public opinion was a basis for policy decisions by leaders and politicians. Thus, both the public agenda and the public policy agenda were influenced by the press agenda. These basic ideas have been well verified by research. The theory is applicable mainly to the relationship between political issues and beliefs about their importance by those who follow campaigns in the news. Here are the theory's basic proportions:

1. The print, broadcast, and digital media select a number of issues, topics, and events from their daily surveillance of the political and social environment to process and report as "the news."

2. Because of limited space and time, and because of journalists' convictions as to what is "newsworthy," many issues and topics are *ignored* and do not become part of the news.

3. The press gives each of the selected news stories greater or lesser *prominence* in its reports by assigning it more or less space and a particular position (e.g., front page versus back page in a newspaper, or lead or late position with more or less time in the news broadcast). This forms the daily *news agenda* of the news media.

4. When the public attends to these reports, they will perceive the order of prominence assigned by the press in its agenda and will use it to decide their *personal rankings of importance* of the issues and topics that make up the news.

5. **Therefore**, as politicians become aware of the public's ranking of importance concerning these issues, that ranking can influence the *policy-making agenda* of leaders and legislators.

Source: Maxwell E. McCombs and Donald Lewis Shaw, "The Agenda-Setting Function of Mass Media," *Public Opinion Quarterly*, Vol. 36, No. 2, Summer 1972, pp. 176–187, and McCombs, "A Look at Agenda-Setting in the Mass Media: Past, Present, Future," *Journalism Studies* Vol. 6, 2005, pp. 543–557.

Whatever the medium, in the final setting of their agenda, those who make the decisions about content and prominence have already considered which news values to emphasize, what story or broadcasting formats will be used, and whether concerns over ethical, legal, or profit matters have been met. Thus, the final set of stories that appears in the newspaper or broadcast on any given day has undergone a very complex news process, beginning with the surveillance of the environment for story possibilities and ending with the decisions of what will be the actual content and positioning of each news story to be transmitted to the audience served by that particular medium.

Communication scholars and researchers have discovered that the agenda defined by news professionals, as just outlined, has a counterpart among the audiences that attend to their media. When people are asked about their personal ranking of importance of the news stories of the day, it has been found that their selection usually reflects the degree of prominence given to those same stories in newspapers and broadcasts. Simply put, people believe that a story is important if it is given a position of prominence by the press. This statement may hardly seem surprising, but it is an important issue.[18] What it means is that those who set the agenda of the press have significant influence on the public perception of what is important, including matters of politics, economics, law, and government. Thus, the agenda-setting function of the press is more than an interesting relationship uncovered by researchers. It can have profound influences on the direction the nation takes in developing new policies and laws.

CHAPTER REVIEW

- Digital Technologies have speeded up the transmission, pace, and delivery of news and have rendered obsolete much of the traditional "appointment" media, where the medium dictated when people read or viewed the news.
- News is now delivered twenty-four/seven across all channels from Internet websites and blogs to newspapers, magazines, radio, and TV stations, all of which harness the digital technologies even if they are technically daily, weekly, or even monthly publications in a time of continuous updating.
- The Internet and other technologies have altered the scope, topics, sources, and impact of news.
- News, the main commodity delivered by newspapers and other news media, is current or fresh information about an event or subject that is gathered, processed, and disseminated via a medium to a significant number of people.
- Certain social and human values influence and help structure the news. Among them are impact, timeliness, prominence, proximity, the bizarre, conflict, and currency.
- News is often packaged in a fashion that reflects journalistic styles, standards, and trends, ranging from sensational tabloid journalism to fact-based "objective" coverage.
- Among other innovations, the digital age has allowed for the development of citizen journalism, where any individual can go online, do reporting or question others' reports, and actually have an impact on the news across other channels as well.

STRATEGIC QUESTIONS

1. What is the role and function of news for individuals, the news media, and society? Do changes in media from early newspapers to the Internet have any discernible impact on news?
2. Compare professionally gathered and processed news with citizen journalism or blogging.
3. How are news beats, territories, or domains covered by the news media?
4. What is the role of time in a news story?
5. What benefits do different forms of journalism offer the public?
6. How has the digital revolution affected the gathering, processing, and dissemination of news?

KEY CONCEPTS & TERMS

Twenty-four/seven news 202
News process 203
Spot news 205
News values 208

Objectivity 211
Civic or public
   journalism 213

Investigative reporting 219
Agenda-setting 221

ENDNOTES

1. Deborah Potter, "The 24/7 News Cycle: News Never Stops in a Multi-Media World," *RTNDA Communicator,* Dec. 2006; on NewsLab.org; also see Pablo Boczkowski, *Digitizing the News, Innovations in Online Newspapers* (Cambridge, MA: MIT Press, 2004).
2. Project on Excellence in Journalism, *The State of the News Media 2008,* see major trends, www.stateofthenewsmedia.org/2008; also see, David T. Z. Mindich, *Tuned Out—Why Americans Under 40 Don't Follow the News* (New York: Oxford University Press, 2005).
3. Weston Kosova, "The Power That Was," *Newsweek,* August 23, 2007.
4. These classifications are based on a similar discussion in Gaye Tuchman, *Making the News: A Study in the Construction of Reality* (New York: Free Press, 1978), pp. 23–31.
5. The significance of this distinction between locals and cosmopolitans, and of their roles in the formation of media-related opinion in a community, can be found in the classic study by Robert K. Merton, "Types of Influentials: The Local and the Cosmopolitan," in his *Social Theory and Social Structure* (Glencoe, IL: Free Press, 1949), pp. 387-420.
6. Walter Lippmann, *Public Opinion* (New York: Harcourt, Brace, 1922), pp. 354–358.

7. Alan Barth, quoted in Herbert Brucker, "What's Wrong with Objectivity," *Saturday Review,* October 11, 1969, pp. 77.

8. Hamilton Nolan, "Salon.com Still Thriving as Brand Evolves," *PR Week,* Nov. 5, 2007.

9. Andrew Leonard, "How the World Works, In Defense of Lou Dobbs," Salon.com, Nov. 29, 2008. See also Paul Farhi, "Everybody Wins: Fox News Channel and CNN," *American Journalism Review,* Vol. 25, April 2003, passim.

10. For various views on civic journalism, see the following: Carl Session Stepp, "Public Journalism: Balancing the Scales," *American Journalism Review* (May 1996), pp. 28–40; Davis Merritt, *Public Journalism and Public Life: Why Telling the News Is Not Enough* (Mahwah, NJ: Lawrence Erlbaum Associates, 1995); Jay Rosen, *What Are Journalists For?* (New Haven, Yale University Press, 2000); and Everette E. Dennis and John C. Merrill, *Media Debates,* 4th ed. (Belmont, CA: Thompson/ Wadsworth, 2006).

11. Mark Glaser, "Dan Gillmor Finds His Center," MediaShift@www.pbs.org, January 31, 2006. See also Dan Gillmor, "Base Camp for Organizing Projects," July 4, 2008, citimedia.org/blog

12. See www.propublica.org; also comments by Paul Steiger at Reynolds Institute seminar, New York City, June 27, 2008.

13. Philip Meyer, "In Defense of the Marketing Approach," *Columbia Journalism Review* (January-February 1978), pp. 60–62 for a classic formulation of this concept, also treated in Meyer, *The Vanishing American Newspaper: Saving Journalism in the Information Age* (Columbia: University of Missouri Press, 2004).

14. See Margaret H. De Fleur, *Computer Assisted Investigative Reporting: Its Development and Methodology* (Mahwah, NJ: Lawrence Erlbaum Associates, 1997).

15. John Ullman and Steve Honeyman, eds. *The Reporter's Handbook: An Investigator's Guide to Documents and Techniques* (New York: Twayne Publishers, 1974), pp. 59–92.

16. Iris Noble, *Nellie Bly: First Woman Reporter* (New York: Julian Messner, 1956).

17. See "The History of the Standard Oil Company" in Mary E. Tompkins, *Ida M. Tarbell* (New York: Twayne Publishers, 1974), pp. 59–92.

18. The original study was: Maxwell E. McCombs and Donald Shaw, "The Agenda-Setting Function of Mass Media," *Public Opinion Quarterly,* 1972, pp.176–187.

CHAPTER 10

Popular Culture: Entertainment, Sports, and Music

Because popular culture is often equated with the tastes of the majority, successful media of communication are instantly an expression of popular culture and a platform for delivering it to the very public that will consume it. Thus the digital transformation of media has been a boon for popular culture and a very part of the popular culture itself. That is, pop culture is embraced by the masses; media brings pop culture to the masses, while digitization makes the media more efficient. Therefore, digitization brings more pop culture to more of the public. The forms and content of popular culture in a digital world are many and varied, from music file sharing and downloading to an almost infinite number of niche market cable channels and websites seeking instant popularity. As one critic wrote: "Consider the unending emergence of technology-fueled subcultures. Ham radio. Jazz. Beat poets. Personal computing. Hip-hop. Punk. Computer networking. Zines. Indie rock. Raves. Flash mobs. Alternate reality games. Virtual worlds."[1] Just when a cultural or social phenomenon enters the world of popular culture, sometimes called mass culture or mediated culture, is a matter of some debate, but technology has often played a role. The eminent sociologist Herbert J. Gans says, "One of the longest and lasting cultural struggles has pitted the educated practitioners of high culture against most of the rest of society, rich and poor, which prefers the mass or popular culture provided by the mass media and the consumer goods industry."[2]

The term **popular culture** is used loosely to mean many things from electronic games to theme parks to T-shirts with printed slogans. Sometimes popular culture seems to collide with and even devour itself. In 2007, for example, the hugely popular web-based social medium Second Life was at the center of a murder plot on three TV shows, *Law & Order: SVU, CSI: New York,* and *The Office.* Popular culture as expressed through the media is often ephemeral and quickly discarded. If, as often happens, it comes back years later, it is considered nostalgia or retro—and can again become the center of popular and media attention.

A once-famous photograph of two boys carrying a garbage can had this caption: "What are you throwing away that will be valuable tomorrow?" A visit to any antique or collectibles shop will quickly tell you what throwaway items of the past are now regarded as valuable. Items such as old signs and postcards, medicine bottles, calendars, medals, buttons, and comic books are part of that inventory. These and other "artifacts" or objects are cues to popular culture—what ordinary people enjoy, use, and consume. Cultural historian Richard Maltby writes that popular culture is "something you buy" as opposed to traditional folk culture (games, songs, crafts, etc.), which is "something you make."[3] The totality of popular social and artistic expression is usually referred to as popular culture, distinguishing it from elite or high culture, which is discussed later in this chapter.

THE NATURE AND IMPORTANCE OF POPULAR CULTURE

The mass media, from their inception, have been key players in the creation and promotion of popular culture. All "media products" are manufactured to be consumed, with some like music videos providing entertainment, while others like billboards, newspapers, and magazines are vehicles for advertisements that help sell goods and services. Eventually, much of the entertainment once offered only to small audiences expanded its reach through the use of the media. Thus, popular novels were also serialized in newspapers and magazines, while live drama eventually made its way into radio and television. Likewise, sports that began on the playing field quickly became fodder for newspaper stories, electronic media broadcasts, and podcasts.

The Media and Popular Culture

The content of popular culture was, by definition, aimed at large audiences of mainly middle and lower classes of varied education and income. Thus, there was an attempt to reach the *largest audience possible* with pleasurable, easily understood fare. Critics constantly complained that the popular culture offerings of the media debased and drove out so-called high culture or art.

Early in the debate between the defenders and critics of popular culture, the terms "lowbrow" and "highbrow" were coined. They were first used by the journalist and critic Will Irwin in a series of articles in the *New York Sun* in 1902 and 1903. The inevitable "middlebrow" came later. A lowbrow was a person of vulgar or uncultivated tastes, while a highbrow was said to aspire (or pretend to aspire) to "a high level of cultivation and learning." A "middlebrow" simply accepted and sometimes celebrated mediocre fare somewhere between the other two.[4]

Scholars, critics, journalists, and others have continued to debate and discuss these terms as they have assessed and examined both the content and effects of popular culture. For example, the respected critic John Storey in his *Cultural Theory and Popular Culture: An Introduction* argues that "popular culture is an empty conceptual category, one that can be filled in a wide variety of often conflicting ways depending on the context of use."[5] These concepts and others are explained later in the chapter, which discusses the entertainment function of the media. It focuses on media content in the forms of soap operas, comic strips, television sitcoms, advertising art, and play-by-play spectator sports. While considering both the content and supposed impact of such examples of popular culture, we also look at the "money connection" and the idea of consumption of cultural products. Popular culture is *big business* when it is distributed through new and traditional media. Much of the content of the mass media is popular culture that is being sold for a profit, and it is integral to the economics of the media. To be clear, media are the channels, and pop culture are the contents. Audiences are courted to consume popular culture, ranging from popular entertainment to sports and even pornography, that must be blunt and direct to be fully understood by its audience. People will probably argue forever about whether a given image or presentation is popular culture or not. So, too, will they debate the probable impact of such material: whether or not it is harmful and whether it drives out better-quality performance, higher caliber design, or more elegant writing.

An exuberant consumer after purchasing an iPhone in 2007 reflects the rapid adoption of smart phones, which are platforms for popular culture including music, videos and even motion pictures.

Defining Popular Culture

But just what is popular culture? Like many other topics of debate, it has been defined in many ways. Critic Ray Browne, who has written several books on the subject, broadly defines popular culture as "all those elements of life which are not narrowly intellectual or creatively elitist, and which are generally though not necessarily disseminated through the mass media."[6] Additional features are provided by scholar David Madden, who writes, "It is anything produced or disseminated by the mass media or mass production or transportation, either directly or indirectly and that reaches a majority of people."[7]

Even more inclusive definitions can be found. British historian Lord Asa Briggs wrote a book titled *Victorian Things*, treating such objects as tools, medals, hats, and other artifacts of popular culture.[8] In fact, campaign buttons or T-shirts are themselves expressions of popular culture. Gans has written musingly about T-shirts and the slogans and legends on them, indicating even that the messages and advertisements displayed on the ones worn by women tend to be different from those on the ones worn by men.[9]

Some students of popular culture study virtually anything that people use in everyday life—the lettering on cigar boxes, beer cans and wine labels, advertising in print and electronic media, billboards, and other messages that communicate effectively. The Newseum in Washington, D.C., a museum of news, exhibited a desk used by Mark Twain and a mangled car in which a reporter was killed by organized crime figures, among other artifacts, some of which are kitsch.

While all of these phenomena of everyday life hold their own fascination, in this chapter, we will not discuss in detail elements of popular culture that are not specifically part of the mass media—although some of them, such as fast food and clothing styles—do rely on the media for popularization. Somewhat arbitrarily, then, we can formulate a definition of popular culture as it will be discussed in the present text. Simply put: *It is mass-communicated messages that make limited intellectual and aesthetic demands—content that is designed to amuse and entertain media audiences.* Popular culture, in this sense, is disseminated by all of the print, broadcast, and digital media. Indeed, the term covers most of what they disseminate. Our focus, then, is on *media* popular culture, namely, media presentations such as reality programming, game shows, soap operas, spectator sports, crime drama, movies, popular music, the content of which can be classified as entertaining.

Sports heroes are central figures in popular culture, promoting the games they excel in and helping to sell products as well. LeBron James of the Cleveland Cavaliers relieves tension prior to a game with the Boston Celtics.

The Importance of Popular Culture

Debates over the value of the popular arts and the supposed superiority of high culture have gone on for decades, with the idea that much that is popular is unworthy junk. Thus, each generation seems to decry the reading habits, musical tastes, and other popular addictions of the next generation. One reason for all educated people to observe and understand popular culture is simply a matter *of keeping up with what is happening in society.* As musician Bob Dylan wrote in his "Ballad of a Thin Man," a response to attacks on popular culture: "You've been through all of F. Scott Fitzgerald's books/You're very well read, it's well known/But something is happening, and you don't know what it is, do you, Mr. Jones?" In recent years, much of the criticism of popular culture and its effect on media has centered on "dumbing down"; that is, media oversimplify the news and thus trivialize important issues and topics as well as themselves as social institutions.

There is much controversy about what to make of popular culture and how to sort it out. Theorist John Storey, mentioned earlier, argues for multiple dimensions of popular culture and decries a distinction between high and low culture. He says, for example, that these perspectives on popular culture point up the complexity of the debate:

■ *The Quantitative*—A literary work once in the purview of high culture, such as *Pride and Prejudice,* by Jane Austin, can be used to create movies, TV dramas, websites, and electronic games thus extending its reach. Children's books like the *Harry Potter* series can inspire mass sales, enormously popular movies, clothing, and other items.

- *The Left Overs*—The remnants of what was once of specialized or limited interest is reintroduced in a wave of nostalgia, harking to a glorious past. In the 1920s as Egyptian tombs were opened by explorers, there was a wave of Egypt mania with clothing, hairstyles, and even architecture, aping ancient designs, not to mention endless media fare, even in those pre-digital days. In the 1980s, the U.S. experienced King Tut mania again when the "Treasure of Tutankamen" travelled the U.S. and Steve Martin led a "Funky Tut" skit on *Saturday Night Live*.
- *The Mass Culture*—Quickly manufactured by greedy entrepreneurs for mass consumption, without regard to taste, quality, or anything else. Fads drive sales of the music of hyped stars of marginal talent such as those "manufactured" by the TV program *American Idol,* whose popularity tends to fade nearly as quickly as it grew.
- *The "Authentic"*—wherein anything that ordinary people create, use, or adopt becomes popular, such as the gangsta rap look or something as quaint as homemade quilts or food, such as retro comfort food of the 1950s coming back in 2009.
- *The Political*—In this view, popular culture is the result of the friction created when subordinated groups resist the interests of influential groups. Sometimes called hegemony theory, and always reflecting a struggle, political postmodernists don't recognize any distinction between high culture and popular culture.[10]

Japanese *sociologist* Hidetoshi Kato maintains that "the mass media can be seen as one of the most decisive factors shaping the populace of a society."[11] Kato says, "The belief systems and behavior patterns of the younger generation in many societies today are strongly affected by the messages they prefer to receive (or are forced to receive) either directly or indirectly through mass media." This kind of influence on audiences is what communications scholar Michael Real calls "mass-mediated culture." Real argues that, though it may be distasteful to some, there are good reasons for studying popular (or mass-mediated) culture.[12] These include:

1. It offers delight for everyone.
2. It reflects and influences human life.
3. It spreads specific ideas and ideology internationally.
4. It raises far-reaching policy questions, challenging education, and research.
5. It is us.

Although these reasons may seem self-evident to today's students, many universities have been reluctant in the recent past to allow the serious study of popular culture. At the University of Minnesota, for example, Arthur Asa Berger had a difficult time getting the approval of his PhD committee to let him write his dissertation on Al Capp's comic strip character "L'il Abner." In recent years Berger's early struggle resurfaced, as studies of *Seinfeld* and *The Simpsons* did win approval. Historically, few English departments in American universities were interested in having their students study pulp fiction or Gothic romances, although these books command far greater audiences than the most respected literary classics. Art history courses similarly were not much interested in advertising art, although it is produced by an impressively large labor force and consumed by millions. American history classes rarely take note of the meteoric rise of the fast-food industries, although firms like McDonald's have delivered enough sandwiches to their customers to form a line from Earth to the outer reaches of the solar system. In other words, the study of popular culture was long "tainted" in the eyes of many snobbish intellectuals, even though it influences us in many powerful ways. Today, studies of working-class culture and their cultural products are very much in vogue and widely studied. Studies of the Internet, the ultimate in popular culture, are encouraged, as are popular music and other forms.

Clearly, popular culture cannot be easily dismissed. The authors have long believed and have championed taking popular culture seriously in the study of communication because (1) it reaches almost all of the public in one form or another; (2) whether we like it or not, it influences the way we think, act, dress, and relate to others; (3) it has a tremendous economic impact on the media; and (4) it strongly influences almost all mass communication content.

Further, what is today's popular culture might become tomorrow's high culture. For example, editor Tad Friend, writing in *The New Republic,* maintains that "popular entertainment that outlasts its era gets re-examined by new critics, re-presented to a new audience, elevated and enshrined."[13] Some well-known examples include Matthew Brady's Civil War photographs, the movies of Charlie Chaplin and Buster Keaton, and the music of Patsy Cline and Jim Morrison. Also, even though many deplore it, historians today often study an era through its popular culture because it tells a great deal about what people liked and enjoyed. This accounts for the popularity of reruns of old TV shows, decades after they were introduced. Sirius and XM Satellite Radio have channels featuring the music of past decades.

Closely associated with popular culture studies are two kinds of media research. One is the study of *heroes;* the other focuses on *images.* The popular heroes of any period—athletes, rock stars, film sex goddesses, and even some of our military leaders and major politicians—are "products" of mass media portrayals. Similarly, one learns a great deal about a given culture by its media portrayals of the images of women in advertising, say, or the images of minority groups like African Americans, Latinos, and Native Americans in news photographs. The study of queer culture, for example, opens understanding of a part of society that was once considered to be deviant—in the socio-logical sense of the term. The frequency with which people appear in the media and the way they are depicted says a great deal about the values of a society and the decisions that media people make. In the early 1940s, for example, the *New York Times* and other newspapers mentioned African Americans mostly under the grisly topic of "lynching," rather than covering them for their achievements. Even earlier, many media stereotyped various ethnic groups in denigrating ways, again indicating the current social values of their popular culture. By the early 2000s, two New York City museums sponsored exhibitions of photos of lynching scenes—not as popular and grisly news this time but as historical and cultural artifacts.

Critiques of Popular Culture

As we indicated, the subject of popular culture has often erupted into a debate over its benefits and potential harm. That debate usually centers on the commercial nature of popular culture ("filthy lucre") and the tendency of "low-aiming" material to crowd out high-quality forms of literature, plays, and art. This is said to endanger high culture given the fact that the audience for information, entertainment, and cultural material is only so large and that the person who buys comic books might not also be buying serious literature. It is also said that too much consumption of popular culture, such as watching poor-quality television, has a negative effect on the viewers, creating a nation of couch potatoes. Indeed, childhood obesity has been linked to excessive TV watching by the American Academy of Pediatrics and others. An argument that begins with the negative effects of popular culture on individuals, in other words, is quickly extended to society. Some critics say that too much popular culture and kitsch dulls a person's sensibilities and, by extension, demeans society itself. Kitsch is an object or content that is thought to be sentimental, vulgar, or in bad taste. This is the "dumbing down" argument mentioned earlier, wherein people will have lower and lower standards. For example, movies aimed at preteens can drown out more sophisticated films that don't have the same audience appeal (that is, those with a limited attention span, as they are simply not receptive to better or more challenging content). Sometimes concerns about the negative effects of popular culture crosses borders. For example, Canadians have long been concerned about the cultural imperialism of U.S. media drowning out Canadian cultural products. The same criticism has been made globally, in what has been called media imperialism, where too much Western media and cultural content overwhelms the local fare in such locations as Africa, Latin America, and some parts of Asia.

Admittedly, kitsch and the arguments that support it are clearly laden with elitist and value judgments. However, many students of popular culture are more impartial and study such pop-culture works as romance novels with the same fervor that English professors give to Shakespeare, which is regarded as high culture.

POPULAR CULTURE AS ENTERTAINMENT

Most popular culture has an entertainment function, designed to amuse and serve as a pastime. However, some popular culture content, such as advertising or public relations, can be deadly serious about promoting a product or a point of view. And, at the same time that not all pop culture is entertainment, not all entertainment is associated with the media. An example is the circus, which is promoted and advertised in the media but stems from a circus tradition dating back to the Roman Empire. Today, however, the media are the most important delivery systems for most kinds of popular culture, which in many cases would not exist at all in the absence of mass communications.

Of the media we discuss in this book, it is the content of television and film that is most obviously concerned with entertainment. Newspapers, once a major source of entertainment, continue to provide utilitarian information. However, they do not carry a considerable amount of entertainment. When they do, they rely heavily on *feature syndicates* that bring in entertainment fare. Radio, once an important news medium, is now mainly devoted to entertainment, with its emphasis on music, talk shows, and sports broadcasts. Cable is both an entertainment and an information medium, but clearly entertainment is the dominant concern. Books, our oldest medium, also deliver both serious information and entertainment. The Internet has plenty of popular culture fare, but at present it is both information and entertainment driven, especially on social networking sites where-video clips and other videos can be seen. Today the online world is the major purveyor of popular culture.

Media Influences on Consumer Art

One of the most controversial—and most fascinating—social and cultural effects of the media is the constant invention and spread of popular songs, *gothic* romance paperbacks, *predictable* TV drama, *low-budget* TV and cable reality shows, *formulaic* film thrillers, comic strip characters, and other material deemed *unsophisticated* by critics. Such material reaches an enormous part of our population. People hum the latest popular tunes, suffer the latest problem of a soap opera heroine, exchange analyses of the latest big game based on news reports, and organize their activities around the weekly television schedule. In short, media output is at the heart of American popular culture. Like it or not, popular culture is beloved by millions. The development of well-articulated theories concerning both the sources and influences of popular culture represents a frontier of theory development that has been widely but not systematically explored. In the present section, we look at this area of mass communications and offer a tentative theory to explain why this type of content has become such a preoccupation of our media.

People have debated the artistic merits of media-produced culture and its impact on society for generations.[14] Media critics and defenders have disagreed hotly about whether deliberately manufactured mass "art" is blasphemy or blessing. These analyses of mass communication and its products

Campaign buttons are an artifact of popular culture, worn when they are new and part of current public discussion and later saved as a collectable or souvenir.

as art forms take place *outside the framework of science*. Media criticism is an arena of debate where conclusions are reached on the basis of personal opinions and values, rather than carefully assembled data subjected to the experimental scrutiny of the scientific method. Nevertheless, those who praise or condemn the content of mass communication perform an important service. They offer us contrasting sets of standards for judging the merits of media content. We may choose to accept or reject those standards, but by exercising some set of criteria we can reach our own conclusions about the merits of popular music, soap operas, or spectator sports.

Cultural Content and Taste Levels

In the sections that follow, we review a theory of mass-communicated (and mediated) popular culture induced from discussions of two issues: (1) the merits of various forms of popular culture manufactured and disseminated by the media and (2) the levels of cultural taste that characterize segments of the American population that are served by these media. These discussions are based on the *strong opinions, clear biases, and personal sets of values* of a number of critics. You may find these admittedly biased opinions consistent with your own views, or you may disagree violently. In either case, they illustrate the types of analyses found in debates over popular culture. (Hopefully, they will clarify your own thinking about popular culture.)

To understand how popular culture has become (and why it is) so ubiquitous as the prevailing content of the American media, we need to place it into a more general context of artistic products. Prior to the development of the mass media, critics tell us there were essentially two broad categories of art. These were *folk art* and *elite art*.[15] Today neither is seen as being of greater value than the other. However, there is an important relationship between the two, according to the popular culture theory we are developing.

FOLK ART.   This category of artistic products is developed out of the spontaneous effort of anonymous people. Such art is unsophisticated, localized, and natural. Its makers may be talented and creative and yet never receive recognition for their works. It is a grassroots type of art, created by its consumers and tied directly to the values and daily experiences of the maker. Thus, villages, regions, and nations develop characteristic furniture styles, music, dances, architectural forms, and decorative motifs for articles of everyday use. Folk art never takes guidelines from the elite of society but emerges as part of the traditions of ordinary people.

ELITE ART.   Products of elite art represent "high culture" deliberately produced by talented and creative individuals who often gain great personal recognition for their achievements. Elite art is technically and thematically complex. It is also highly individualistic, as its creators aim at discovering new ways of interpreting or representing their experience. Elite art includes the music, sculpture, dance, opera, and paintings that originated mainly in Europe and were given acclaim by sophisticates from all parts of the world. Although it has its great classics, it is marked by continuous innovation and is now produced in many countries. Novelists, composers, painters, and other creative artists constantly experiment with new forms and concepts.

KITSCH.   In modern times, many critics maintain, both folk and elite art are threatened by a tragically inferior category. The rise of privately owned, profit-oriented media linked to low-cost manufacturing has brought radical change and created a completely new kind of popular art. With the advent of cheap newspapers, magazines, paperback books, radio, movies, and television, this new form began catering to massive, relatively uneducated audiences with undeveloped aesthetic tastes.

The content of this new art form, say its critics, is unsophisticated, simplistic, and trivial. Unlike folk art, it is not intended as a genuine expression of local taste and culture but something mass manufactured and aimed at the lowest common denominator;

unlike high art, it is not intended to evoke a powerful aesthetic response in the individual. Instead, it imitates some aspect of a work of art, mass produces it cheaply, and sells it to consumers who want to be associated with the art it imitates. The term widely used to label such mass-mediated product is the German word *kitsch*. Similar in meaning to the English word "junk," it refers to trashy and garish items that are in bad taste and have no artistic merit. And, according to the popular culture theory we are here developing, it is the unrelenting demands of the media for entertainment content that produces the current deluge of kitsch, a term that dotes from a nineteenth-century critique of art in Germany.

CRITICISMS OF KITSCH.   Critics charge that, in manufacturing kitsch, those who produce it for the media often "mine" both folk and elite art for crass commercial purposes. They do so "the way improvident frontiersmen mine the soil, extracting its riches and putting back nothing."[16] The respected Clement Greenberg, a prominent mid-twentieth-century art critic, wrote:

> The precondition of kitsch...is the availability close at hand of a fully matured cultural tradition, whose discoveries, acquisitions, and perfected self-consciousness kitsch can take advantage of for its own ends.[17]

Why do critics see kitsch as such a problem? They maintain that the older separation between elite and folk art once corresponded to the distinction between aristocracy and common people. Although they do not necessarily approve of the aristocracy, they believe that it was critical to the existence of the most developed forms of art. Prior to the emergence of mass communication, according to the critics' claim, folk art and elite art could coexist because they had clearly defined constituencies.

Then came the dramatic spread of the media to all classes of society, geared to the largest numbers of consumers with purchasing power. The tastes of these consumers were not linked to either folk art or elite art—they were best satisfied with content characterized by low intellectual demand. The result was a deluge of inconsequential kitsch.

Kitsch affects all levels of society and art because it competes for the attention of everyone. Its constant presence and attention-grabbing qualities are the source of its popular appeal. Thus, critics conclude, people who earlier would have read Tolstoy now turn to one of a few dozen formula writers of mysteries and romances. Those who might have found entertainment at the symphony, ballet, or theater now tune in to Madonna or wrestling; those who would have gained political wisdom from modern versions of Lord Bryce and Alexis de Tocqueville now watch the latest "analyses" of Keith Olbermann or Rachel Maddow.

In other words, popular culture theory states that products in low artistic taste drive out elite art and higher culture, just as bad money drives out good money. In assessing the principal characteristics of popular culture, the critic Dwight MacDonald maintained that it is a debased, trivial culture that interferes with deeper understanding of both the realities (sex, death, failure, tragedy) and the simple, spontaneous pleasures. The masses, debauched by several generations of this sort of thing, in turn come to demand trivial and comfortable cultural products.[18]

Furthermore, the theory maintains, kitsch represents a double-barreled form of exploitation. Those who control the media not only rob citizens of a chance to acquire higher tastes by engulfing them with less demanding media products but also reap high profits from those whom they are depriving.

If true, this theory of popular culture leads to three major predictions: First, kitsch presumably diminishes both folk and elite art because it simplifies their content and, in using them, exhausts the sources of these arts. Second, it deprives its audiences of interest in developing tastes for more genuine art forms. Third, it is mainly a tool for economic exploitation of the masses.

These predictions represent serious charges. To try to see if this theory has merit, we can attempt to determine if at least one of the above conclusions is true. To do this, we can

Famed Olympic medalist Michael Phelps became a celebrity of popular culture through massive media coverage, which highlighted his great skill.

look at one aspect of popular culture—the heroes created by the media. Does the presence of media-created idols of kitsch tend to diminish the stature of genuine heroes as the theory predicts? Moreover, does a fascination with such media-created heroes lessen interest in meritorious accomplishments in real life? Furthermore, is economic exploitation a real factor?

HEROES OF THE MEDIA AS KITSCH. As is suggested above, one way of inferring whether our theory of popular culture has merit is to look at the kinds of heroes that our mass media have created. In early America, critics say, heroes and heroines were extraordinary individuals with rare personal qualities who performed admirable deeds. The list of heroes admired by the eighteenth- and nineteenth-century Americans included such notables as George Washington, Robert E. Lee, Sacajawea, Daniel Boone, Harriet Tubman, Geronimo, Davy Crockett, and Harriet Beecher Stowe. These men and women were real people who performed deeds that truly had a significant impact on history. They did not win acclaim because they were pretty or entertaining but because they had powerful determination to succeed in situations requiring courage, dedication, and self-sacrifice.

Even as the media arose in the twentieth century, the tradition of heroes lingered. Soldier Alvin York and pilot Eddie Rickenbacker emerged as the great heroes of World War I. But after that (following the rise of the new media) the number of real heroes known by their actual deeds began to thin out noticeably. Perhaps the last great hero, and one of the most acclaimed of all time, was Charles A. Lindbergh. His solitary 1927 flight across the vast Atlantic in a single-engine aircraft required steel nerves and an iron will. It was a feat that manifested all the qualities Americans admired in their heroes and made him the most acclaimed hero of the twentieth century—at least until the media of film and broadcasting came into their own. The astronauts of the late twentieth century, though now advanced in years, are also lionized by many for their bravery.

The change in our heroes that came with the full development of these media is the subject of a famous classic study. The sociologist Leo Lowenthal examined biographies in popular magazines, believing that ordinary people best understand history and contemporary affairs in terms of famous people. Looking at political, professional, and entertainment heroes, Lowenthal concluded that heroes are a product of the values and tastes of the time. For example, in the early years of the twentieth century, "idols of production" in fields like business, politics, and industry dominated magazine biography, but in recent decades with some exceptions the "idols of consumption"—persons from entertainment, sports, and the arts—have moved ahead in popular appeal.[19] However, in the present era, such business icons as Bill Gates, Warren Buffet, and even Donald Trump are much admired.

Hero study traces its origins back even earlier to an essay by the historian Thomas Carlyle published in 1885, which demonstrated how forceful personalities have shaped history. Although the "great man" or woman theory of history is now on the wane, scholars and media critics still find the study of heroes useful in examining people's attitudes and values. In effect, heroes become symbols for public hope and aspirations and, according to cultural critics, thus serve a positive social function.

Are the days of true or real-life heroes gone? Some people feel that they are. While such TV fare as the Biography Channel draws modest audiences, fictional heroes of comic book fame like Batman still have greater visibility and appeal. As the media assumed a greater presence, many critics maintain, a new *hero of kitsch* began to replace the hero and heroine of the *deed*. These new objects of public adulation are not individuals with extraordinary personal qualities. Instead, they are media-created idols known for their sex appeal, their alluring voices, or their athletic or other performance abilities.

It is greatly to the advantage of the media and those who create and supply popular culture to convince their audiences that the products they provide are *truly important*. One way that this is done is through highly publicized "competitions" in which a multitude of awards (Oscars, Tonys, Emmys, MTV Awards, Heisman trophies) are presented to the creators of kitsch, ever more frequently in highly publicized, televised ceremonies. These events powerfully reinforce the illusion that these are the people in our society that really "count." Yet, critics ask, are they simply modern versions of "The Lone Ranger," who was, as sociologist Richard Quinney noted, "nothing more than a creation of commercial enterprise"—a creature who had no real existence aside from images on film?

Thus, the view posed by popular culture theory is that most contemporary heroes are media creations of kitsch whose fame derives not from extraordinary acts that can inspire and benefit society but from images on the screen, sounds from CDs and tapes, or their ability to sell their words on paper. While some gain fame for their performances, others became notable as pure inventions—imaginary characters who have no real existence outside a movie, soap opera, or prime-time sitcom. There is ample reason to believe, say the critics, that in treating these illusions as though they are important, our society has merged fantasy with reality in a final commitment to kitsch. Of course, there will always be a debate about the relative merits of real-life versus fictional heroes.

There are several identifiable categories of such media-created heroes. First, there is the "hero of the ball and stick." Babe Ruth and Red Grange are among those who lead the long list of athletes who became celebrities through media attention followed by today's mega-stars Eli Manning and Michael Phelps. Clearly these individuals are superb athletes and have received extraordinary financial rewards. Yet critics find it difficult to account for their immense popularity on grounds other than the status conferred on them by the media.[20] Striking a ball skillfully with a bat, racket, or club contributes little to the national destiny. Athletic skill is scarcely the stuff of which advances in civilization are made.

Another significant category is the "hero of the titillating tune"—the singer instantly recognized by millions of fans. Few members of the older generation in the United States would fail to identify the voices of Bob Dylan or Tony Bennett. Today, the sounds of Beyonce and Kanye West command instant recognition. The musicians and songs made famous through the media constitute an important part of today's kitsch. Here popular culture shows its roots in folk and elite art since many songs that have made it to the top of the popularity lists are based on music from classical and American folk traditions, such as grassroots American ballads and the earliest jazz.

Of even greater interest are the "heroes of superhuman power." Characters of the imagination have long intrigued people. One could easily speculate, for example, that the various "supermen" of today's media are the counterparts of ancient mythological deities with fantastic powers who appeared in human form. There is a timeless attraction to fantasies of power and success that allows the entertainment of millions through the unusual deeds of a long list of fictional characters with superhuman capacities. Generations of readers have admired and coveted the powers of Superman, the Shadow, Wonder Woman, and Batman. Characters with superhuman strength, the ability to predict the future, or hear peoples' cries for help are often featured in TV shows and videos.

Other contemporary media characters have human limitations but are remarkably capable of combating the forces of evil. Here can be included the police "heroes of screeching tires," the cloak-and-dagger "heroes of international spydom," and the steely-eyed "private eye." The list would not be complete without the "heroes of legal ploy" and the venerable "heroes of suture and scalpel." These include the stars of medical shows like *ER* and *House* or *Law & Order* and its endless progeny. The capacities of real people in the real world are pale and flabby by comparison, although some modern heroes are, in fact, anti-heroes with many flaws, so much so that one cable network uses the slogan "Characters welcome."

Standing back, how can we assess the theory of popular culture and its application? The charge that popular culture draws attention away from elite culture can clearly be substantiated in many cases. However, whether popular culture should be *condemned* for doing so is an open question. The conclusion that the public is forced to pay for popular culture also seems correct, for the public ultimately pays the high salaries of media heroes and heroines that became part of the costs of advertising and marketing the products of sponsors. On the surface this does rather look like "economic exploitation of the masses," but the final assessment must be decided on the basis of one's personal values.

Finally, the charge that media heroes diminish interest in accomplishments in real life may be considered valid, when the significant achievements of "ordinary" people are moved into the back pages of the paper. The accomplishments of scientists, artists, and others who make significant contributions to our culture seldom receive much recognition, while gossip about celebrities often makes front-page headlines. Overall, then, the theory of popular culture makes important arguments. However, the degree to which these aspects of popular culture actually represent a *threat* to the public as a whole remains a matter of personal judgment.

"Taste Publics" as Markets for Media Presentations

The theory of popular culture makes important assumptions about taste levels among the public. Just what are the different levels of taste among those who the media serve, and how are these tastes linked to the production of kitsch? We will take a brief look at these issues in the present section. However, the analysis of "taste publics," like debates about the merits of popular culture, is also outside the framework of science, and it proceeds from individual opinions and standards. Judgments must be made about whether enjoying a particular artistic product represents "high" or "low" taste, or something in between, and judgments about "good" and "bad" taste depend on subjective values, not scientific criteria. Here the aim is only to focus our attention on significant factors in the basic support system of American media.

Because the task is difficult, and the risk that others will disagree strongly is great, not many scholars have analyzed what have come to be known as "taste publics" in the United States. Herbert Gans (mentioned earlier) has used the method of qualitative observation, however, to identify five major levels of taste in American society.[21] In the sections that follow, we describe these taste publics and the content they tend to prefer. Our description is based largely, but not exclusively, on Gans' analysis. Education seems most important in defining taste levels, but many other factors such as class, age, gender, and race are also involved.

The **high-culture taste public** likes the products of the "serious" writers, artists, and composers. High culture is found in the "little" magazines, in off-Broadway productions, in a few art-film theaters, and on rare occasions on public television. It values innovation and experimentation with form, substance, method, overt content, and covert symbolism. Styles tend to change often. Painting, art, and sculpture, for example, have been dominated at one time or another by expressionism, impressionism, abstraction, conceptual art, and so forth. In literary fiction, high culture has emphasized complex character development over plot. Modern high culture explores psychological and philosophical themes, among them alienation and conflict.

Clearly, this form of culture would have little appeal to the majority of the media's usual audience. For this reason, it is seldom found in mass communication. Members of the small segment of the public that prefers high culture consider themselves elite and their culture exclusive.

The **upper-middle taste public** is concentrated in the upper-middle socioeconomic class, which is composed mainly of professionals, executives, managers, and their families. These people are well educated and relatively affluent, but they are neither creators nor critics. For the most part they are consumers of literature, music, theater, and other art that is accepted as "good."

To characterize the upper-middle-class public, one might generalize that they prefer fiction that stresses plot over characters or issues and that this group favors stories about people like themselves who have successful careers and play important parts in significant affairs. They tend to like films and programs about likable upper-middle-class people in upper-middle-class settings. They read *Time* or *Newsweek* and enjoy the kind of new media fare that appears in *Wired*. They might well be familiar with classical music and opera but dislike contemporary or experimental compositions. They purchase hardcover trade books, support their local symphony orchestra, and occasionally attend the ballet. They subscribe to magazines like the *New Yorker, National Geographic,* and *Vanity Fair.* They follow blogs and websites that cater to their interests and were among the first to sign on to satellite radio. And they are typically early adopters of new technologies.

Although this group is fairly large, its influence on media content is actually quite limited. Some television dramas, public affairs programs, and FM radio represent the upper-middle level, but most media content is at the level below it. The reason is that, as a group, while they are relatively affluent, there is simply not enough of them for their aggregate purchasing power to add up to an impressive part of the total of the nation.

The **lower-middle taste public** is the dominant influence in mass communication for two reasons. First, the lower-middle taste public includes the largest number of Americans; second, it has sufficient income to purchase most media-advertised products. The people of this level tend to be white-collar workers (for example, public school teachers, lower-level managers, computer programmers, government bureaucrats, druggists, and higher-paid clerical workers). A substantial number are college-educated, many with degrees in technical subjects. This public often consciously rejects the culture preferred by the taste levels above it, but occasionally it appreciates and pursues some of their forms, especially once they have been transformed into popular culture.

The lower-middle public continues to support religion and its moral values. It tends to like books, films, and television drama in which old-fashioned virtues are rewarded and happy endings still occur. The lower-middle public likes unambiguous plots and heroes. They loved the late actor John Wayne, for instance, who espoused traditional virtues. They seek neither complexity of personality nor philosophical conflicts as dominant themes. People of lower-middle tastes commonly read romance novels, get their magazines online, and enjoy reality TV shows, situation comedies, cop-and-crook dramas, musical extravaganzas, soap operas, and quiz shows. In music, country and western is favored along with easy listening and golden oldies radio stations. Such music makes few intellectual demands from its listeners.

The **taste public for low culture** consists mainly of skilled and semi-skilled blue-collar workers in manufacturing and hands-on service occupations (factory-line workers, auto repair, furnace servicing, routine plumbing). Their education level tends to be at the vocational school level or less. Younger members of this category attend vocationally oriented community colleges. Although still numerically large, this taste public is shrinking. More blue-collar families are now sending their children to four-year colleges, and many manufacturing industries are rapidly being replaced.

The taste public for low culture likes action—often violent action—in film and television drama. It is to please this public that the media resists efforts to censor the portrayal of violence. This group enjoys simple police dramas, comedy shows, and western adventures. Popular with it are programs with a lot of slapstick, as well as *Wheel of Fortune,* wrestling, and country-western music. For reading, this group likes supermarket tabloids such as *National Enquirer,* confession magazines (for women), and *WWF All Star Wrestling* on TV.

The **quasi-folk taste public** is at the bottom of the socioeconomic ladder. It is composed mainly of people who are poor and have little education and few occupational skills. Many are on welfare or hold uncertain or unskilled jobs. A large portion are nonwhite and of rural or foreign origin. Although this group is numerous, it plays only a minor role in shaping media content, primarily because its aggregate purchasing power is so low.

The art appreciated at this bottom level of taste resembles that of the low culture level. These people tend to like simpler television shows, and in many urban areas foreign-language media cater to their needs. These people also preserve elements of their folk culture. For example, they may hold religious and ethnic festivals and social gatherings and display religious or ethnic artifacts and prints on the walls of their homes. Colorful murals adorn the streets of some urban ethnic neighborhoods.

The categories noted above are extremely elitist in their articulation, but they have some value in assessing media audiences and their tastes and choices.

In his classic book *Popular Culture and High Culture*, Gans points up the connection between culture and class, noting that poor and undereducated people often can't afford tickets to the opera and might not feel comfortable in tony art museums surrounded by affluent people. Of course, age, gender, and race also play key roles in popular cultural selections. Other scholars have introduced the term *omnivores* to account for people who make their taste choices from many menus cutting across popular and high culture. Of course, taste publics encompass a kind of shorthand for analyzing popular culture. Many people are *omnivores* with interests and tastes that run the gamut from dumbed-down and nearly mindless TV fare to complicated computer games to music and art of all kinds. The conflict between popular and high culture is very real in society, however, and often accounts for what we watch on TV or have access to in other media.

BIG IDEAS: MEDIA THEORIES EXPLAINED

Critical Cultural Theory

Media research and theoretical analyses in the United States have mainly been developed within a framework that has been derived from the *physical sciences* via the *social sciences*. The goal has been to examine the content of mass communication empirically to disclose undesirable influences of media content (violence and sex) that may have harmful influences on behavior. That goal, say critical cultural scholars, is not acceptable. What researchers should be doing is studying the exploitation of audiences within a framework of *power relationships* that explain how those who own and control the media use them to preserve the power.

The media, say the critics, are used by those in *control*. They deliberately encode messages into popular entertainment and news, maintaining people's beliefs that the society is just, admirable, and the most natural form of social order. This is false, the cultural critics state. In fact, most people receive meager rewards for their work. Only a few become wealthy or have great power in the capitalist system. However, those in control use the media to keep people believing it is the best of all systems. That is:

1. The Western industrial nations have a power structure based on *capitalism*, which includes both an economic and a political system.
2. The mass communication industries, which are designed to yield *profits* for their owners and are protected by a complex set of laws, are a central part of that power structure.
3. The content of mass communications provided to audiences is designed deliberately to support the values of that capitalist system and to *maintain the existing structure of power*.
4. Media audiences constantly receive lessons encoded into the messages they receive that make capitalism seem *attractive, proper,* and *fair*.
5. In fact, the capitalist system is *improper* and *unfair* because the majority of the people in the system receive relatively meager benefits compared with their contributions. Only a few, in positions of power, receive great benefits.
6. **Therefore**, those who control the media are deliberately or unwittingly *exploiting* audiences for their own benefit by using the media to reinforce the capitalist ideology—thereby keeping their audiences bound to the system and avoiding challenges to their power.

Implications of Popular Culture Theory

As the previous sections have made clear, popular culture as media content must be understood in terms of both the aggregate purchasing power and taste preferences of various segments of the public. Regardless of the protests, claims, and counterclaims of the critics, the media *must* continue to produce content that appeals to the largest taste publics, because that content attracts attention that the media sell to sponsors in order to stay in business. There is little likelihood, given these dependent relationships, that on their own the media will bring about a cultural revolution by emphasizing high or even upper-middle culture. The obvious prediction for the future is that lower-middle and lower tastes will continue to dominate American mass communication. Thus, no matter what the future holds in bigger screens, clearer pictures, more channels, or alternative modes of delivery, the taste of the lower-middle category will continue to drive and define much of the mass audience content. However, with millions of digital channels, high culture and intellectual or specialized content can flourish too.

ENTERTAINMENT MEDIA AND POPULAR CULTURE

As mentioned in Chapter 1, entertainment is one of the central functions of the media, and it is also a form of media content. Entertainment is defined by various dictionaries as "an activity to occupy one's time and attention agreeably, especially a public performance." In the debate over popular culture, entertainment is commonly regarded as "frivolous, superfluous, and unimportant" and is distinguished from the arts, which are supposed to challenge and enlighten the mind as "deeply moving the human spirit and permanently changing one's perspective on life." Of course, that is a somewhat overblown and idealized view, though it is often thought that, in media content, information is more important and more worthy than entertainment. This is probably true if one is comparing television coverage of a presidential election or of a war with, say, a light situation comedy. There are those who will argue that entertainment fare often has a deeper meaning and makes a statement about our culture. This is the notion that we are what we watch and read—or at least that it reflects our practices and values as individuals and as a society. Thus, the city of Baltimore, Maryland, proudly proclaims itself "The City That Reads," while no U.S. city brags that its residents watch more TV or play more video games than any other.

If there are some forms of media that can be considered purely entertaining, with little taint of information or news, they are motion pictures, recorded music, video games, and perhaps a few others. There is no truly pure entertainment that doesn't also transmit some information, though television, as we have learned in Chapter 8, is largely an entertainment medium when one totals the amount of time devoted to pure entertainment and sports programming as opposed to news and public affairs. The same is largely true of cable programming, which too often is simply regarded as more television, though technically it is not. Fiction books are entertainment media; even newspapers also have feature material, puzzles, comic strips, and other content that is pure entertainment.

Entertainment media are probably the best expressions of popular culture. Indeed they are usually devoted to popular culture content, although some high culture (concerts, operas, and ballets, for example) is also found there. However, contrary to the view expressed above, entertainment media are not

American Idol, one of the most popular TV shows in the United States, is part of the genre of reality TV and a showcase for amateur performers, some of whom achieve subsequent fame. The show's judges are themselves promoters of popular culture.

trivial or unimportant. They generate the lion's share of media revenues, though it is difficult to separate purely entertainment media from those devoted to information and opinion, since there is so much overlap and blurring. It is estimated, however, that entertainment media account for well over 60% of all media revenues, and that is probably a conservative figure.

Among the media industry activities that help us better understand popular culture are feature syndicates, among the earliest of these vehicles; sports media and content; as well as the recording industry.

Sports Media: Content and Culture

Sport is a form of popular culture deeply rooted in modern society. From neighborhood games to high school, college, and professional sports, it is so pervasive in our society that even presidential debates have to step aside rather than compete for public attention and approval. These days media and sports are inseparable. In fact, media are so influential that they heavily influence "how sport is played, organized, and thought about in society."[23] Although sports were first organized for local entertainment, their claim to fame comes through the media and through advertising. Without advertising and advertising sponsorships, the big money professional sports would be greatly diminished if not out of business altogether.

There is also a whole sports-culture industry, ranging from toys and games to cards, calendars, magazines, books, T-shirts, and clothing. The demand for such items is promoted by media coverage of sports and by advertising that features sports and sports figures. Sports have also been a major source for America's heroes. In baseball, figures like Babe Ruth, Lou Gehrig, Joe DiMaggio, and Mickey Mantle cast a long shadow across the sport and American life. In virtually every sport there have been great "heroes" such as Joe Louis and Muhammad Ali from the world of boxing. Whether it is hockey, tennis, golf, basketball, football, or baseball, each sport has its great figures, known by their athletic feats and by their personalities that Americans know far better than their national leaders or powerful figures from other fields.

If the amount of attention given to an aspect of popular culture is any indication of its importance, then sports heads the list of popular culture fare. Sports coverage in the media, whether in newspapers or on network, cable, and pay-per-view television, is dominant in terms of the time and space it occupies and the revenues it brings to media. Sports coverage occupies 20% of all newspaper space and 25% of television's weekend and special-event coverage, according to the *American Journalism Review*. Roughly 19% of all newspaper reporters cover sports, as do 21% of all consumer magazines. No other subject gets as much media attention.

Sports are a vital form of popular culture and have wide appeal. Images of winners and losers, success and failure, pain and pleasure are drawn from sports. Without muscular sports metaphors in the language, American businesses would probably not communicate at all. The most valuable and expensive advertising times on television are during the Super Bowl, the World Cup, and the Olympics.

The earliest sports journalism in the United States and elsewhere emphasized the pastimes of the wealthy, such as hunting and horse racing. Pastimes of the poor or common people received less attention. Though this has changed greatly over time, sports journalism today has a middle-class bias and covers mainly baseball, football, basketball, hockey, and a few other major sports. Upscale sports like skiing, golf, and tennis also get considerable coverage, while the down-home pastimes of less affluent people such as bass fishing, professional wrestling, and stock car racing are rarely covered in the sports pages.

In a very real sense, media industries and sports both date from the industrial revolution, when people began to have more leisure time. Newspapers at first paid little attention to sports, and some leading editors such as the legendary Horace Greeley of the *New York Tribune* seemed ambivalent about sports and its coverage. As historian John D. Stevens points out, Greeley once devoted six columns of coverage to a prizefight and a one-column editorial denouncing the brutality of the sport in the same issue. Still, sports and newspapers grew up together, and as the penny press of the 1830s developed, sports coverage helped draw ordinary people to these inexpensive, highly popular papers.

Henry Chadwick, an Englishman who came to America in 1824 at the age of 13, became America's first important sports writer and was especially influential in popularizing baseball. He wrote for the *New York Times*, Greeley's *New York Tribune*, the *Brooklyn Eagle*, and the *New York Clipper*, where he covered, promoted, criticized, and helped standardize the rules of baseball.

Although Chadwick did not invent baseball, he was known in his lifetime as the "Father of the Game." According to John Stevens, until the advent of baseball there was no uniformity to the games played across America. Baseball was at first an entirely amateur affair, but by the late 1860s players were being paid, sometimes under the table. The Cincinnati Red Stockings was the first team to admit having professional players, which came after a season of fifty-seven wins, no losses, and one tie.

Chadwick played an important role in covering and commenting on baseball during this period, and he published the first annual baseball guides. He noted that there was little agreement about the number of players on a team and the specific rules of the game. In his compilations, he summarized rules and helped to institutionalize baseball. People in distant places who had never seen the game played learned it from Chadwick's writings. This remarkable man urged the use of gloves and chest protectors for catchers, criticized team owners, and helped organize the first professional sportswriters organization. Chadwick is credited with helping to make baseball the national pastime, and he was one of the first non-players elected to the Baseball Hall of Fame in Cooperstown, New York.

Sports columns like those written by Chadwick became sports pages and eventually sports sections of newspapers. They were also the forerunners of sports magazines. As sports coverage spread over time, along the way other artifacts of popular culture such as sports books, baseball cards, and other materials appeared. With the advent of radio, actual coverage, including play-by-play action, was possible, and the dominant role of sports in the press, while still important, was never the same again. Television ushered in a new era of sports media fare and also a new era of media economics, wherein the rights to broadcast games of popular teams, the Olympics, and the Super Bowl generated huge revenues.

Sports broadcasting was largely invented and defined by two important events: David Sarnoff's coverage of the Dempsey-Carpentier championship boxing match in 1921 and the 1958 National Football League championship game between the Baltimore Colts and the New York Giants. Author Huntington Williams says the first event launched prizefighter Jack Dempsey, one of the most popular and mythic sports figures of all times, as a hero of popular culture, and established Sarnoff and his fledging National Broadcasting Company (NBC) as the leader of post–World War I radio (and eventually television). The NFL game coverage established professional football as the first money-sport of the television era.

The narrators of sports programs on radio and television became legends in their own time as well. In the 1920s Graham McNamee, who first covered the 1923 World Series, understood the game and communicated it well to the public, with a rich baritone voice and colorful play-by-play announcing. He was such a popular figure that he once received 50,000 letters during a World Series. And, of course, he and others who joined him in the broadcasting booths in stadiums all over America brought their listeners the heroic exploits of great teams and players, which themselves became legends of sport.

In the television era, ABC Sports, an independent company owned by the ABC network, did not treat sports as mere entertainment or as a subset of news but as a subject of its own. With live productions of sporting events, the network staged extravaganzas and harnessed new technology, dazzling the public with instant replays and other marvels of the electronic age. Under the leadership of Roone Arledge, one of the greatest programmers in modern broadcast history, and with the collaboration of engineer-technologist Julius Barnathan, ABC Sports harnessed satellites, employed minicams, and developed computer graphics long before they were used by other networks for sports, news, or entertainment. Most visible to the public through three decades of television's championing of sports was announcer Howard Cosell, sportscaster for "Monday Night Football." With a distinctive style and personality, Cosell became the most famous figure in television sports. He dominated the screen with his opinionated interviews, analyses, and play-by-play action. He even appeared in movies playing himself.

Television revenues took professional sports from a mostly local, modest enterprise to billion-dollar businesses. By the 1990s, as the television networks fell behind cable in the competition for the best sports fare, the sports industry was itself again in charge, and television was more of a vehicle for its distribution. The ESPN networks, twenty-four-hour, all-sports services on cable became a regular feature of most fans' TV diet.

There is no doubt that sports programming will remain as one of the most popular forms of popular culture. While there are significant segments of the population who have little interest in, or even detest, spectator sports, the ability of such content to attract attention makes it an advertiser's dream.

Sports and Their Significance

We have considered sports as media content, specific sports media, and the role of sports in our culture in this chapter. We have not specifically looked at the economic impact of sports on the media or as a part of the media industries, which is considerable. To do that requires considering the sports marketplace in the United States and globally. In the U.S. alone that includes national network programming, over-the-air advertising, national and regional cable networks, multi-channel video growth, and the increasing role of digital content on the Internet. The links between such U.S.-based companies as Rupert Murdoch's News Corp., which also owns Fox Sports, has an impact across Europe and Asia.

As media content, sports play a significant role, as mentioned earlier. It consumes larger shares of time and space in print and electronic media, and it accounts for large revenues. There is great audience appeal for the major sports like professional baseball, football, and basketball, for example, as well as golf, tennis, and, increasingly, soccer. There are studies examining this content, which is largely entertainment and promotional in nature.[24] It will likely be a staple in media fare for some time to come. Indeed, Internet entrepreneurs often refer to sports as one of the "killer apps" (for applications) of digital media, meaning that this content application is seen as a hot source of revenue. Other killer apps include health information, sex, and business.

Houston Rockets all-star Yao Ming uses his celebrity status to promote Ronald McDonald, a symbol for McDonald's charitable efforts for gravely ill children. This is sometimes called "noble hype," though the celebrity athletes are usually paid handsomely.

The specific sports media—TV, cable, radio, pay-per-view, magazines (print and online), as well as endless websites and blogs—are a part of larger media industries and live by their rules. For example, TV networks have sports divisions along with their entertainment and news divisions. At this writing, although there are hundreds of sports on the Internet, many are extensions of larger sports media enterprises such as ESPN, *Sports Illustrated,* and others. Amid all this there is a distinctive digital sports media industry evolving, one that sometimes makes end runs around traditional sports media and the sports establishment, opting instead to go directly to advertisers and the public. Virtually every sports media outlet these days is fully integrated with its Internet presence.[25] The sports digital media industry includes marketing efforts to sell tickets and sports souvenirs as well as websites (both official and fan-driven) for sports teams, famous athletes, and specific sports themselves. Sports management companies have extensive digital activities aimed at advancing the fame and fortune of their clients. There are also such groups as stadium managers and concessionaires who use the web and other digital outlets for their specific purposes. Sports content is packaged and repackaged for digital delivery as the 2008 Olympics proved. While originally broadcast in the U.S. on NBC, that network also sold rights to others including social networking sites for the redistribution and repurposing of sports content. There are digital sports media specialists and firms that specialize in this growing source of business and media activity.

Much has been written about the impact of sports on popular culture. The various taste publics favor different sports, for example, and the kind of sports that people engage in are reflective of cultural values and interests. Baseball was once called "the national pastime" in America, while the British favor cricket and soccer, and Canadians champion hockey. Increasingly, however, as media become more global, sports, too, take on a global presence, which is nowhere more evident than at the Olympic games, when the prowess of the athletes of different countries is celebrated and marketed through sports media, mainly television. In virtually every Olympics, the eyes of the world are on the selection of the site of the games (made years earlier) and the preparations made for their operations. Sometimes this has deeply political implications as in 2008 when the summer games were played in Beijing, China. Opposition to China's record on human rights, economic clout, and other issues surfaced in the months before the games, and the traditional running of the Olympic torch through various countries sparked controversy and near riots in some places.

Music Media Content and Culture

As mentioned earlier, music has always been one of the most distinct aspects of popular culture. Our images—visual and aural—of people and societies from the ancients to the present include music whether the ballads and songs of old or the continuing role of classical music and the coming of ragtime, jazz, rhythm and blues, doo-wop, rock and roll, hip hop, and other forms that reflect current tastes and preferences. Every generation of the modern era has had its own music, often scorned and discouraged by an older generation with memories of their own music from an earlier time.

Like sports, music is entertainment; it is also content for the music in its own right (as in video concerts and records) or as part of other media fare (such as the soundtracks of movies or themes for TV programs). Music in the media began in print with music publishers producing sheet music for sale, which they still do. But very early on, music had a link with electronic media, from early cylinders and discs to records, magnetic tape, videodiscs and CDs, as well as Internet music transmission. These technical inventions were employed by the music and recorded music industries and also used the medium of radio, television, and the Internet to reach masses and individual taste publics.

As a distinct industry that obviously works with other media industries and media platforms (notably the Internet, radio, television, and motion pictures), recorded music is "a producer of cultural goods, working in what may be the most uncertain, most volatile of media businesses," as Professors Eric Rothenbuhler and John Strick of the University of Iowa have written. They continue: "Consumer taste in recorded music is more ephemeral than consumer taste in newspapers, magazines, popular novels, TV shows, or movies and they also have more options for expressing that taste.... Yet the industry has succeeded, attracting consumer dollars and time at equivalent levels."[26] Another scholar, Geoffrey P. Hull explains succinctly:

> "In order to produce income, a record company usually referred to as a 'label' gains control over a master recording of a performance by an artist to sign an exclusive recording, then manufacturing and marketing copies...for producing a recording, then manufacturing and marketing copies ... for purchase by consumers. The label therefore has two basic functions that it must perform: acquire masters and market (them)."[27]

For years, the recorded music industry did just that, often acquiring and developing artists along the way, artists whose music and words reflected the interests and values of various taste publics. The rules included the copyright and ownership of music and payment of royalties and other fees to the labels, artists, and other professionals in the creative pipeline. This arrangement was dramatically challenged in the 1990s when the record industry found itself struggling against rampant unauthorized downloading of its music on the Internet. A court case in 2000 involving Napster, the Internet music directory service, brought the conflict of media to a head. While this decision by a federal court was a harbinger for resolving infringement of intellectual property issues, it signaled the changing nature of the recorded music industry and how people get their music.[28] Today, downloading music for a fee and also for free is commonplace.

Of course the Internet is a useful marketing tool for CDs and DVDs as well as other music products. New technologies are once again revolutionizing music distribution as music lovers can download the latest album by their favorite artists. Truly the Internet has conquered the music industry in the same way that radio, television, and the movies did in earlier times. Now the major labels work closely with social networking sites to promote and distribute their music.

MEDIA LEADERS INSIGHTS: MUSIC, MEDIA, AND POPULAR CULTURE

MICHAEL JOSELOFF

Vice President for Affiliate Relations and Marketing

MTV Networks

Witness to and participant in the transformation of MTV from music videos on cable to a vast storehouse of content delivered over many channels and through multiple platforms, Michael Joseloff connects the MTV Network's programming to audiences through various affiliates that range from massive cable systems and satellites to wireless devices and even hotel chains. He and his colleagues develop multiplatform marketing and advertising partnerships that embrace virtually all kinds of media. A graduate of the University of Rochester, he received an MBA from Fordham. Before coming to MTV Networks, he was a senior marketing strategist for a leading marketing company where he worked with clients ranging from Ethan Allen and Microsoft to HBO, Starbucks, and GE. At MTV he has crafted partnerships with major media companies like Comcast and Time Warner. He is part of an enterprise that is inventing and redefining the meaning of media "affiliate," once confined only to radio and TV stations.

1. When and under what circumstances did you first realize the import of new media or the digital age?

   The big energy during the first dot-com boom in the early 2000s seemed to be around ecommerce. Amazon.com roared across the country and threatened all kinds of business models and conventional ways of purchasing products. Suddenly, the confines of retail location seemed to disappear, and if you had a website you had the potential to reach every person connected to the web. As long as people could find their way to your site, you had the potential and the opportunity to convert them to customers or monetize their experiences. It was the beginning of an interactive one-to-one dialogue that now is taking the form of broad social communities and individualized marketing/communications, which are some of the tremendous benefits of the digital age.

2. What impact did that experience have on you personally or professionally?

   That time was all about potential, possibility, and opportunity. If you were not creating a web destination and making the appropriate digital land grab, you risked missing out on the future. Media companies and content creators were beginning to utilize the web in the same way because conventional distribution windows and pipelines did not limit exposure. A filmmaker shooting in her back yard in Omaha had the same potential to be seen by just as many people online as Spielberg. It was—and still is—about how to get an eyeball to your site, and as a marketer it was a time of learning, experiment, and a disregard to a conventional business model and plan. People would try anything as the priority was to make a bold splash in the marketplace and jumpstart traffic. Few businesses focused on core metrics, which ultimately ended up making and breaking many of the digital legends and brands of the time. At the end of the day, businesses need to make money no matter how great the hype or concept.

3. How has it influenced MTV Networks in the larger context of popular culture, media, and entertainment indutries?

MTV Networks is a leading content provider dedicated to serving its audiences wherever, whenever, and however they want it. Not only is the company a leader in distribution and delivering content in front of as broad an audience as possible, but also it is an innovator in the digital space by creating new ways to engage and dialogue with its audiences. In my opinion, the most radical element of the digital age is the dual ability to gain broad exposure to millions of potential audience members but still have the ability to have an individual experience with each and every one of them at any given time. Social communities, SEO (search engine optimization), behavioral marketing, and user generated content all provide tremendous new interactive opportunities to reinvent the traditional "push" media business model.

4. What is the greatest challenge or benefit of the digital revolution for advertising that drives music and programming at MTV?

The traditional mass-reach advertising model is an important revenue stream for the company though not its only stream. We are finding that digital enhances a broad array of revenue streams and facilitates broader touch points for our advertisers and partners to connect and engage with our audience. For examples, advertisers can have a more targeted dialogue with audiences that are engaged around strong brands. Reach and frequency and targeting can all be utilized in and around a variety of content. The digital world also enables diversification of revenues by facilitating additional ways to monetize distribution and provides additional opportunities with content, games, and products.

5. Are you optimistic about the digital future?

Ultimately, we are human beings. If digital continues to make our lives easier and fulfills basic human needs in the right way, then it will succeed. We still need social connections and interpersonal relationships. Our behaviors will still have us fall into the passive experience of watching TV on a big screen in a living room or trying on clothes in a store versus just ordering them online. However, the digital future opens up countless ways to make our lives easier, more fulfilling, and connected.

6. What, if any, advice do you have for a person who aspires to a career in a venue like MTV or other music/entertainment media?

Entertainment media is about reflecting, inspiring, connecting, and challenging your audience. One of the key measures of success is listening to and understanding what your stakeholders need, want, or desire. Every meeting or interaction is an opportunity to listen, and this is always an important first step in finding your place in the media industry.

Popular culture can be fickle because public attitudes toward a celebrity play a large role in their ability to get and keep commerical endorsements, as was the case when Beyonce Knowles replaced Britney Spears as spokesperson for Pepsi.

Music as Popular Culture

In assessing the recorded music industry, communication scholar Simon Frith wrote: "The history of the record industry is an aspect of the general history of the electrical goods industry, and has to be related to the development of radio, the cinema, and television. The new media had a profound effect on the social and economic organization of entertainment so that, for example, the rise of record companies meant the decline of the music publishing and piano-making empires, shifting roles for concert hall owners and live-music promoters."[29]

The Importance of Music

Volumes have been written on the impact and influence of music on the temper and tone of society and culture. Nowhere is the debate between high and popular culture more prevalent and pointed. Indeed, the kind of music offered by a medium largely signals the audience it seeks. Nowhere is this truer than with radio, wherein the programming formats use musical styles and preferences. Thus we have easy listening, hard rock, country and western, Latino, and other station formats. As stated earlier, music is a media industry of its own (recording labels and their parent companies, music publishers), but it is dependent on various old and new media outlets for distribution. Music can convey and influence people's attitudes and feelings as it both speaks to particular generations and also crosses generational lines. Music is another area where the *omnivores* are rampant—omnivores being people whose tastes embrace different forms of music and other popular culture. Obviously one can enjoy the classical music of the high culture taste public and any other musical styles that appeal to people in different class, racial, and ethnic groups.

Video Games in Popular Culture

As we've indicated, popular culture often manifests itself in certain media forms. Comic books, for example, are a classic articulation of popular culture, a distribution channel for stories and graphic forms that truly popularize material that might otherwise have been transmitted in a short story, novel, or film. In fact, cartoons and comic strips, as a popular culture form, provide content for print, electronic, and digital media. The Walt Disney Company with its long tradition producing animated movies, TV fare, and games is a vessel for popular culture.

In recent years one of the most dramatic and important entries in popular culture has been video games, a media force that now rivals motion picture production. Commentators consider video games to be popular culture just as comic books and graphic novels are. But they are more than that: they are a new multimedia culture based on digital computer technology. Thus, video games are a *platform* for popular culture, a *source of popular culture content* with its own following. They are also a distinct *media industry* and the *subject of analysis* in other media.

Much has happened since the introduction of early video games in the 1970s including Atari's *Pong* in arcades and Magnavox's *Odyssey,* a home system played on TV sets. Video games were made possible by computers (and such computing elements as sound cards, graphics cards, and CD-ROM drives) and were played in game arcades, on home computers, and on university mainframe computers. After a rush of badly designed games in the 1980s that resulted in an industry crash, video games came back as a robust media industry and had reached $10 billion in annual revenues by 2009. And further, their place in popular culture seemed assured. As the Canadian blogger and video game expert Ken Polsson has written, "gradually video games entered popular culture...[as] other media began making references to video games as popular arts just as they did

TABLE 10.1

BEST-SELLING VIDEO GAMES OF ALL TIME

Rank	Game	Release Date	Copies Sold
1	Pokémon Red, Blue, and Green	1996	20.08 million
2	Super Mario Bros. 3	1988	18 million
3	The Sims	2000	16 million
4	Nintendogs	2005	14.75 million
5	Pokémon Gold and Silver	2000	14.1 million
6	Super Mario Land	1989	14 million
7	Grand Theft Auto: Vice City	2003	13 million
8	Pokémon Ruby and Sapphire	2003	13 million
9	The Sims 2	2004	13 million
10	Grand Theft Auto: San Andreas	2004	12 million

Source: http://www.gunslot.com/blog/top-twenty-five-25-best-selling-video-games-all-time

television, music, and film." To assess their impact, Polsson documents all popular culture references from the early 1980s to the present in video games at http://www.islandnet.com/~kpolsson/ when:

- The medium itself is considered a popular part of past or current culture.
- The artist (creator/writer) specifically chose a video game when some other form of entertainment could have been used.
- The artist specifically chose a video game because of something special about video games.
- The product is targeted at the general public, not video game enthusiasts primarily.
- The reference is a minor or secondary part of the product, not the main focus.

The history of video games includes early arcade games, as mentioned, console gaming, the university mainframes (before the dawn of the PC), home computer, handheld devices, and various kinds of mobile devices.

At first, video games, invented by hobbyists and enthusiasts, were mostly played by students and young adults, but eventually they spread to children, all of whom became target groups for media industries, fashion, and music because of their purchasing power. The average age of video game players is 35, though a 2008 report noted that in the United States some 65 percent of American households play computer or video games (2008 Essential Facts, ESA). Another study noted that 60 percent of gamers are male, 40 percent female (2008 Essential Facts, ESA). According to the Entertainment Software Association, 25 percent of game players are under 18 years old, 49 percent are between 18–49 years old, and 26 percent are over 50 years old (http://www.theesa.com/facts/index.asp).

TABLE 10.2

BEST-SELLING VIDEO GAMES OF 2008

Rank	Game	Copies Sold
1	Mario Kart Wii	8.94 million
2	Wii Fit	8.31 million
3	Grand Theft Auto IV	7.29 million
4	Smash Bros. Brawl	6.32 million
5	Call of Duty: World at War	5.89 million

Source: http://news.gotgame.com/top-5-selling-video-games-for-2008/26021/

ESRB Rating Symbols

 EARLY CHILDHOOD

Titles rated **EC (Early Childhood)** have content that may be suitable for ages 3 and older. Contains no material that parents would find inappropriate.

 EVERYONE

Titles rated **E (Everyone)** have content that may be suitable for ages 6 and older. Titles in this category may contain minimal cartoon, fantasy or mild violence and/or infrequent use of mild language.

 EVERYONE 10+

Titles rated **E10+ (Everyone 10 and older)** have content that may be suitable for ages 10 and older. Titles in this category may contain more cartoon, fantasy or mild violence, mild language and/or minimal suggestive themes.

 **TEEN**

Titles rated **T (Teen)** have content that may be suitable for ages 13 and older. Titles in this category may contain violence, suggestive themes, crude humor, minimal blood, simulated gambling, and/or infrequent use of strong language.

 MATURE

Titles rated **M (Mature)** have content that may be suitable for persons ages 17 and older. Titles in this category may contain intense violence, blood and gore, sexual content and/or strong language.

 ADULTS ONLY

Titles rated **AO (Adults Only)** have content that should only be played by persons 18 years and older. Titles in this category may include prolonged scenes of intense violence and\or graphic sexual content and nudity.

 **CONTENT DESCRIPTORS**

Indicate elements in a game that may have triggered a particular rating and/or may be of interest or concern. They are found on the back of video game boxes.

The ESRB rating icons are registered trademarks of the Entertainment Software Association. The ESRB rating system applies to games sold in the United States and Canada. The Entertainment Software Rating Board provides ratings to video games using the following icons: "EC," "E," "E10+," "T," "M," "AO," and "RP."

Once cumbersome, the technology of video games have made them easier to use. As one scholar put it, "starting and playing electronic games has become easier in the last two decades. You don't need specific knowledge to use a *Game Boy* or a television-linked console—it is just plug and play."[31] Gaming and social networking are closely related as there are online and live local area network (LAN) gatherings. Key market segments are handheld and PC-based games.

Some early games were the outgrowth of TV programs like *The A-Team*, which inspired *Pac-Man* and *Hobby*. In the 1980s when the movie *War Games* opened in theaters, *Galaga* and *Ms. Pac-Man* made their debut in arcades. Later when *Ghostbusters II* was released, the popular *Super Mario Bros* (now several generations older) came on the market. There were games based on *Back to the Future* and *The Simpsons*. Games, of course, are linked to technologies so that the Wii console by Nintendo brought with it such games as *Wii Sports* and *Wii Fit* and many others. Various critics issue their annual best and worst lists of video games, and there are industry rankings for games as well. There are literally thousands of video games and various subcultures devoted to them. Video games have inspired a critical literature that assesses their beneficial and potentially hazardous effects. One can read a history of video games—there are several—get immersed in the technology of video games or study their role in popular culture, among other things. Those who prefer to consider video games as a distinct industry segment can do that—or assess them as part of the overall convergence (coming together, blurring and merging) of various media forms.

Video games are truly a worldwide force in popular culture, not only in their own right, but also in connection with film, video, TV, the Internet, social networking, and even search. Their growth has been phenomenal, and their economic impact is perhaps unprecedented among media. Even in an economic downturn in autumn 2008, industry analysts were asking whether the video game industry was recession-proof, especially when Blizzard Entertainment's *Wrath of the Lich*, then the latest version of the mega-hit *World of Warcraft*, broke the all-time record for PC game sales in a single day with 2.8 million units sold.[32] The earlier record of 2.4 million units was set in 2007 by the first WoW expansion, *The Burning Crusade*. The video-game industry was guardedly optimistic even in the face of record sales but was hoping that those positive earlier trends for movies and other entertainment fare in hard times would hold. Historically, according to the media merchant bank Veronis Suhler Stevenson, entertainment media, while not immune to economic downturns, usually fare well relative to ad-driven publishing and electronic media.

As popular culture, video games both draw on other media platforms and genres as well as contribute to them. Once the play things of "geeks" in computer labs, they are now part of everyday life as they fuel a distinct video game culture that contributes to the overall popular culture.

CHAPTER REVIEW

- A great need for popular culture was created by the Industrial Revolution of the nineteenth century. Factories with regular workdays defined and expanded people's leisure time. With larger blocks of free time available, the demand for amusement and entertainment expanded in the form of mass-communicated diversions, amusements, and entertainment.

- Much of the content of the mass media today is popular culture that is sold for a profit and integral to the economics of the media. Audiences are courted to consume popular culture, ranging from various forms of entertainment to sports and even pornography. People will probably argue forever about whether a given image or presentation is popular culture or not.

- Somewhat arbitrarily, for purposes of the present text, we can formulate a definition of popular culture. Simply put, it is mass-communicated messages that make limited intellectual and aesthetic demands—content that is designed to amuse and entertain media audiences.

- Some reasons for taking popular culture seriously in the study of communication are: (1) it reaches almost all of the public in one form or another; (2) whether we like it or not, it influences the way we think, act, dress, or relate to others; and (3) it has a tremendous economic impact on the media and strongly influences almost all mass communication content.

- People have debated the artistic merits of media-produced culture and its impact on society for generations. Media critics and defenders have disagreed hotly about whether deliberately manufactured mass "art" is blasphemy or blessing. These analyses take place *outside the framework of science*. Media criticism is an arena of debate where conclusions are reached on the basis of personal opinions and values, rather than carefully assembled data.

- Folk art consists of products that are developed spontaneously among anonymous people. It is unsophisticated, localized, and natural. It is produced by many unknown artists who are talented and creative but who receive no recognition for their contributions. It is a grassroots type of art created by its consumers and tied directly to their values and daily experiences.

- Elite art is deliberately produced by talented and creative individuals who often gain great personal recognition for their achievements. It is technically and thematically complex and often highly individualistic, as its creators aim at discovering new ways of interpreting or representing their experience.

- In modern times, many critics maintain, both folk and elite art are threatened by kitsch—a tragically inferior category. With the advent of cheap newspapers, magazines, paperback books, radio, movies, and television, this new form of art made its debut, catering to massive, relatively uneducated audiences with undeveloped aesthetic tastes.

- To assess the theory of popular culture, one form of mass communication provides evidence—the heroes created by the media. The presence of media-created idols of kitsch tends to diminish the stature of genuine heroes, as the theory states. Moreover, a fascination with such media-created heroes lessens interest in meritorious accomplishments in real life.

- The theory of popular culture makes important assumptions about taste levels among the public. Several different levels of taste exist among those whom the media serve. The largest is the lower-middle level, which has the greatest aggregate purchasing power, and therefore its preferences dominate the production of media content.

- One of the most durable of the delivery systems bringing entertainment content to the print media is that represented by the feature syndicates.
- Syndicates coordinate many people and tasks, including contracts between the creators of material, the syndicate itself, and contracts between the syndicate and subscribing newspapers. They also handle the flow of money from the newspaper to the syndicate and the payment of royalties to the writers and artists.
- Sports are a form of popular culture that is deeply rooted in modern society. From neighborhood games to high school, college, and professional sports, it is so pervasive in society that even presidential debates have to step aside rather than compete for public attention and approval.
- Music is a critical indicator of popular culture, expressing the values and references of different generations.
- If the amount of attention given to an aspect of popular culture is any indication of its importance, then sports heads the list of popular culture fare. Sports coverage occupies 20% of all newspaper space and 25% of television's weekend and special-event coverage. Roughly 19% of all newspaper reporters cover sports, as do 21% of all consumer magazines. No other subject gets as much media attention.

STRATEGIC QUESTIONS

1. Provide some examples of how media content draws on popular culture for television programs or advertising content.
2. If popular culture serves the tastes of the majority in society, how are the tastes of minorities and various niche audiences served?
3. What is cool or trendy in media content, and what is not? Offer two examples of each, and defend them.
4. How do taste levels affect the manufacture or creation of popular culture, sometimes called cultural content?
5. What is the role of heroes or celebrities in popular culture—for example, movie or rock stars? What accounts for their appeal, and how do they sustain it—if they do?
6. What role do sports and music play in popular culture?

KEY CONCEPTS & TERMS

Media products 226	Kitsch 233	High culture 236
Highbrow or lowbrow 227	Heroes of popular culture 234	Sports media 240
Mass-mediated culture 228	Taste publics 236	Music labels 243

ENDNOTES

1. Aaron Delwiche, "Defining Virtual Words: An Emerging Medium Collides With Popular Culture," Nov. 16, 2007, http://flowtv. org/?p=902.
2. Herbert Gans, *Popular Culture and High Culture* (New York: Basic Books, 1999).
3. Richard Maltby, *Passing Parade: A History of Popular Culture in the Twentieth Century* (New York: Oxford, 1989), p. 8. See also David Nasaw, *Going Out: The Rise of Public Amusements* (Cambridge, MA: Harvard University Press, 1999).
4. Maltby, *Passing Parade,* p. 8.
5. John Storey, *Cultural Theory and Popular Culture: An Introduction* (Athens: University of Georgia Press, 2002); also see Storey, *Cultural Theory and Popular Culture, A Reader* (Athens: University of Georgia Press, 2006).
6. William Morris, *Morris Dictionary of Word and Phrase Origins* (New York: Harper & Row, 1977), p. 101.
7. Ray B. Browne, "Popular Culture: Notes Toward a Definition," in Browne and David Madden, eds., *The Popular Culture Explosion* (Dubuque, Iowa: William C. Brown, 1973), p. 207.
8. David Madden, "Why Study Popular Culture?" in Ray B. Browne and Madden, eds., *The Popular Culture*

Explosion (Dubuque, Iowa: William C. Brown, 1973), p. 4.

9. Asa Briggs, *Victorian Things* (Chicago: University of Chicago Press, 1988).

10. Storey, op. cit.

11. Herbert J. Gans, "Bodies as Billboards," *New York Times,* Nov. 11, 1985, p. 29.

12. Hidetoshi Kato, *Essays in Comparative Popular Culture: Coffee, Comics, and Communication,* No. 13 (Honolulu, HI: Papers of the East-West Communication Institute, 1976).

13. See Michael R. Real, "The Significance of Mass-Mediated Culture," in Real, *Mass-Mediated Culture* (Englewood Cliffs, NJ: Prentice Hall, 1977).

14. Tad Friend, "The Case for Middlebrow," *The New Republic,* March 2, 1992, p. 24.

15. The term "culture" is being used here in an aesthetic sense rather than in the way anthropologists and sociologists use the term (and as it is used elsewhere in the present book). The reason is that in the literature on popular culture, the term is used consistently to refer to art, music, drama, and other aesthetic products.

16. Michael R. Real, *Mass-Mediated Culture* (Englewood Cliffs, NJ: Prentice Hall, 1977), pp. 6–7.

17. Clement Greenberg, "Avant Garde and Kitsch," *Partisan Review* (Fall 1939), p. 23.

18. Dwight MacDonald, "The Theory of Mass Culture," p. 14.

19. MacDonald, op. cit.

20. Leo Lowenthal, "Biographies in Popular Magazines," in Paul F. Lazarsfeld and Frank N. Stanton, *Radio Research,* 1942–1943 (New York: Duell, Sloan and Pearce, 1944), pp. 507–548.

21. Gans, op. cit.

23. Raymond Boyle and Richard Haynes, *Power Play: Sport, the Media and Popular Culture* (New York: Pearson Education, 2008).

24. Matthew Nicholson, *Sport and the Media* (New York: Elsevier, 2006) and Neil Blain, John Kinsella, Alina Bernstein, and McKenzie Wark, *Sport, Media, Culture* (London: Taylor & Francis Group, 2002).

25. Linda K. Fuller and Haworth Press, *Media-Mediated Relationships: Straight and Gay, Mainstream and Alternative Perspectives* (Binghampton, NY: Haworth Press, 1995).

26. Eric W. Rothenbuhler and John M. Streck, "The Economics of the Music Industry," in *Media Economics, Theory and Practice,* Alison Alexander et al., eds (Mahwah, NJ: Lawrence Erlbaum Associates, 1998), p. 219.

27. Geoffrey P. Hull, "The Structure of the Recorded Music Industry," in *The Media & Entertainment Industries,* Albert N. Greco, ed. (Boston: Allyn & Bacon, 2000), p. 76.

28. "Copyright in the Age of Napster," *New York Times,* July 29, 2000, p. A26 and Allen Weiss, "The New Jukebox, How the Internet Conquered the Music Industry," in Marshall (USC Business School), summer 1999.

29. Simon Frith, "Copyright and the Music Business," *Popular Music,* Vol. 7, 1987, pp. 57–75. Also see Simon Frith, *Performing Rites: On the Value of Popular Music* (Cambridge, MA: Harvard University Press, 1998).

30. NDP Group and Entertainment Software Assn., 2007.

31. Johannes Fromme, "Computer Games as Part of Children's Culture," *Game Studies,* Vol. 3, Issue 1, May 2003, see gamestudies.org.

32. Daniel Terdiman, "Is the Video Game Industry Recession-Proof?" news.cnet.com.

Advertising: Using Media in the Marketplace

Almost every aspect of advertising is touched by digital communication—and instead of being a bystander, as it has been with traditional media, advertising is now at the center of the action. Viral advertising, from annoying pop-up ads to streaming video, bombards consumers. They find advertising on search engines and as part of social networking sites, where advertisers even engage in promoting brand loyalty through "friending."[1] Global: Virtually every medium from books to television has a digital platform and seeks out advertising. The facilitating advertising agencies that have historically linked the advertiser (usually a product or service) with advertising media and thus, the public, have long ago adopted interactive thinking and interactive strategies. Some even call themselves "digital agencies," and at least one says it has created the first new advertising method or discipline, that of "connections planning,"[2] which, sure enough, makes heavy use of social networking. One critic mused that this technology is so integral to advertising that that the "ad power brokers of tomorrow meet across Facebook and Twitter rather than, or as well as, [New York's] Soho bars." The methods of measuring advertising and its impact are also under review with "new metrics appropriate to the twenty-first century being proposed and tested," says Randall Rothenberg, president of the Internet Advertising Bureau. He says the change will be revolutionary as agencies and media wonder, "Who needs old-fashioned 1957-style sampling technologies when we now have the whole universe of web visitors and users—and their every move—to guide us?"[3] Inside the advertising business, creative people and designers use computer graphics and create interactive websites with full-motion video and other eye-popping visuals. From the commercial world's desire to move goods and services with the help of advertising to advertising's actual contact with the consumer, all manner of digital tools are at work, marking the way "technology has fundamentally changed how brands and their audiences communicate... across all channels."[4]

The remarkable capacity of the Internet has also opened the way for new advertising ventures, previously impossible. For example, there are now ad networks that link the advertiser with potential customers without the benefit of ad agencies or traditional advertising media, while virtually cutting out two major players in the advertising supply chain in the process. In the same way, online real estate sites use digital media to link buyers and sellers, without benefit of the real estate salesperson or broker. This is called *disintermediation* and both simplifies and redefines the process of communication by eliminating the various facilitating functions and agencies in transmitting the ad message directly to the consumer. Advertising people speak of a multiple-media landscape and are concerned with digital media usage both separate from and integrated with conventional media of all kinds. And they still delight in a somewhat self-conscious desire to create digital strategies, thus bridging old and new media while hoping ultimately for integration. Already, people are saying that "digital advertising" will become a redundancy, as all advertising will be digital: a digital strategy will be no more common than an electricity strategy, which from the 1880s forward was very much in vogue as electricity (then called "the light fantastic") overtook gas lanterns and candles. The field of advertising, which we'll describe in detail later, has benefited from and contributed to the digital transition of media.

The way the economic and political institutions of the United States developed since the first Europeans settlers arrived more than four centuries ago make it almost impossible to imagine American business, industry, and the media without advertising. Our way of life today has as one of its truly unique features a dynamic advertising industry, which arguably can persuade consumers to buy the products and services that producers provide. Although many people deplore ads online or on TV, as well as billboards and other commercial signage, advertising is an engine that keeps the media economy going.

Within a media perspective, advertising is a critical part of the financial foundation on which rests our system of media and communication. It is one of two great streams of revenue that support American media industries. First, advertisers pay communications media well to present messages designed to market products and services. The second stream of revenue comes from individuals and families who buy magazines; subscribe to newspapers and cable services; and consume CDs, DVDs, and related media products. Thus, advertising revenues and those derived from subscriptions or user fees account for the largest share of financial resources for our communication system.

In some societies advertising plays no such role. Historically, this was the case in the former Soviet Union and the nations of central and Eastern Europe. Operating under a "command economy," rather than a commercial or capitalistic system, the media were both funded and controlled by the state or the ruling party. This changed after the collapse of communism, as local and international advertising appeared almost overnight. The Western model was almost immediately adopted or modified in those now-independent countries, as well as in China, which has embraced commercialism, even if guided by the government and communist party. Only in a few places today, such as North Korea, is commercial advertising virtually unknown. Nonetheless, even there, "ads" praising the country's leader are prevalent. From these considerations, an apparent principle can be derived: *Advertising is essential to any modern market economy.* There are no known instances in which there is a free market and an advertising-free society.

This chapter briefly looks at advertising's history and then reviews the organization of the advertising industry and the way its professional communicators develop their messages. This includes the advertising industry's attention to its strategies of persuasion, the types of media that are used, and the kinds of research that play an important role in the process. The chapter also discusses both criticisms of the industry and controls that are exercised over advertising.

ADVERTISING IN AMERICA: A BRIEF HISTORY

Archeologists have unearthed examples of advertising going back to the Greeks and Romans. Such artifacts, early symbols and identifying signs, called attention to the products of artisans who hand-produced products ranging from weapons to clothing. Although historians often date modern advertising to that period, the process and practice of advertising are actually much older than that. Some form of advertising, or what we now call branding, appeared in the earliest societies, as artifacts from the Native American pueblos and artifacts of human life in the European Middle Ages indicate. The watermarks of printers were also early and distinctive forms of advertising.

In colonial America, advertisers used many media. Coffee, chocolate, and tea, to name a few items, were hawked in messages on printed broadsides (pamphlets) and announced in simple ads in almanacs as well as in early newspapers and other periodicals. Early communications media thus were already factors in the marketplace for goods and services even before modern newspapers arrived. But advertising was not much of a source of revenue for colonial newspapers. They depended on subscriptions paid by readers and, in some cases, on government printing contracts for public announcements. Advertising in colonial times was very subdued—even primitive—by modern standards and rarely overshadowed the editorial content of the papers. But until recently, social historians have all but ignored advertising. Even most journalism histories seem oblivious to advertising's role in creating the modern mass media. One historical factor that does stand out to help explain why modern advertising took hold and developed quickly in the United States is *abundance*. It seems clear that, where resources are scarce, there is little or no need for manufacturers or producers to promote their wares. As economic historian David Potter wrote in a classic work:

> "It is when potential supply outstrips demand—that is when abundance prevails— that advertising begins to fulfill a really essential function. In this situation the producer knows that the limitation upon his operations and upon his growth

no longer lies, as it lay historically, in his productive capacity, for he can always produce as much as the market will absorb; the limitation has shifted to the market, and it is selling capacity which controls his growth."[5]

The Industrial Revolution

During the 1800s, advertising changed from primitive messages on simple printed handbills and crude outdoor announcements—such as signs painted on barns—to complex messages published in newspapers and magazines.

A number of colorful individuals stood out in the 1800s who understood the power of advertising. One was P.T. Barnum, whose circus (modestly characterized as "The Greatest Show on Earth!") became enormously popular. He grasped the principle that constant overblown claims, garish messages on posters or handbills, and colorful parades through towns prior to the performance brought in the public and its money.

PATENT MEDICINES.   Starting even before the Civil War, a number of hucksters—the proverbial "snake-oil" merchants—began to sell curious products that were (it was claimed) guaranteed to cure a long list of human ailments. While snake oil was an ancient Chinese medicine, unscrupulous medicine men travelled the United States in the nineteenth century falsely claiming they had a snake oil remedy for nearly all ailments. Although not strictly a product of the industrial revolution, in many ways these patent medicines led the way in demonstrating the huge financial benefits that could be achieved by advertising.

One of the most remarkable advertising successes of all times was achieved by a Quaker woman from Lynn, Massachusetts. On her kitchen stove she would occasionally cook up a mixture of herbs, seeds, and roots and give bottles of the stuff—well laced with alcohol—to her female friends. They reported that the mixture seemed to relieve what were delicately termed at the time "female complaints" (e.g., menstrual cramps, kidney discomfort, and others). In retrospect, it is little wonder that the women felt better. The strong alcohol base of the product could make almost anyone feel a bit better. In 1875, her two sons had the idea of promoting the mixture for sale by using pamphlets and eventually through an ad in the *Boston Herald*. They called it "Lydia Pinkham's Vegetable Compound." Almost immediately, they received a large number of orders from patent medicine wholesalers. When that happened, they began a systematic and nationwide advertising campaign, based in part on newspapers but also by using huge signs painted on barns, houses, and even large rocks. One of the most effective features of their ads was a picture of Lydia Pinkham herself: a dignified and rather elegant woman who had such a look of sincerity and honesty that few could doubt her claims.

But it was both expanding world trade and the industrial revolution, with its huge increase in the production of factory-made goods, that would make advertising so essential to the growing economy. All during the 1800s the need for advertising grew naturally as manufacturers, importers, and retailers wanted to market their expanding arrays of goods. As was noted in Chapter 3, as the nineteenth century progressed, advertising in newspapers accounted for an increasing proportion of their content and earnings. Newspapers were the ideal medium. The commercial announcements and notices of the time were mainly for locally marketed goods and services.

Actor Tom Mix plays a huckster of snake oil salesman in an early silent Western movie, about 1915, perhaps a forerunner of product placement in media.

THE DEVELOPMENT OF BRANDS.   Up until about the time of the Civil War, most of what was for sale at local stores was purchased in bulk. There were few "brands" as we know them today. The development of brands for packaged, bottled, and canned goods, as well as other products, was one of the most important developments in the history of advertising. A brand did two things: (1) It standardized the product, bringing "predictability" as to its characteristics for the consumer. If the purchaser was familiar with the brand, he or she knew just what it would be like when the package was opened. In fact, brands often ensured that the consumer would develop a kind of "loyalty" to the product, based on repeated satisfaction. (2) Brands also worked well for advertisers. They provided a clear identity for a product—the merits of which could be promoted in advertisements. Slogans were produced to reinforce the ideas of consistency and merit. With advertising, a bar of Ivory soap could be portrayed as being associated with a phrase such as "it floats." Or a brand of coffee could be promoted as "good to the last drop" or "mountain grown." These two ideas helped reinforce recognition of a brand name, such as Maxwell House and Folgers. Before brands, for example, crackers came in barrels and were sold by weight. The same was true for flour, beans, and rice. Household liquids, such as vinegar or syrup, were stored in tanks and were dispensed to customers in jugs or other containers that many brought with them. Buying foods like cheese followed a similar pattern: chunks were cut from a large round cheese and wrapped in cloth or even newspaper. There were no brand-labeled packages, boxes, or bottles of such products displayed on shelves from which the consumer could choose. A woman who wanted to buy soap would indicate to the storeowner the number of pounds she needed, and then that would be cut from a large slab. She would use that product not only to wash her family's laundry but also for her family's bath. The problem with such bulk-purchased goods was that there was no way to predict consistency of quality, taste, ingredients, or effectiveness.

Other changes came in the promotion of products through advertising. As early as 1851, a soap manufacturer named B.T. Babbitt introduced the preformed bar of soap, wrapped in its own paper cover. When the public was initially unresponsive to the product, Babbitt introduced a history-making innovation. He offered a *premium*. For every twenty-five empty soap wrappers a buyer presented, Babbitt promised a handsome colored picture in return. The lure attracted buyers by the thousands, and the idea of premiums took hold. We have been living with them ever since. For example, a major cigarette manufacturer currently offers 1 million prizes for coupons obtained by purchasing packs. These premiums range from a free package of cigarettes to T-shirts and even a free trip to an exotic place for two. Many public health authorities believe that this practice has been a factor in recent increases in teen smoking, which peaked in the mid-1990s and has been steadily declining ever since.[6]

By the end of the 1800s, the shift to brands was to open a whole new world of advertising. It took awhile for the innovation to catch on. Surpassing the successes of even the patent medicines was the creation of three major name-brand items—which were new in 1900. One was Royal Baking Powder—a simple mixture of bicarbonate of soda and a dry acid substance. When mixed with wet ingredients, the powder could be substituted for yeast—a rather considerable convenience for the housewife. Another successful brand was a soap made from vegetable oils (rather than the usual animal fats). This made it lighter than water, so a bar would float. It was said to be 99 and 44/100% pure (whatever that meant). The Procter family of Cincinnati marketed it as Ivory Soap. Still another was an inexpensive brand of footwear (Douglass Shoes) that was nationally marketed. Soon there were many manufacturers competing to produce and market a large variety of commonly used household and personal items under brand names, which would be packed in convenient cans, bottles, and boxes.[7] This competition made advertising even more essential.

FIGURE 11.1
This Kellogg's cereal ad featuring the famous British soccer player, Ian Wright, is one example of how celebrity endorsements are used to confer status to products.

NATIONALLY CIRCULATED GENERAL MAGAZINES.   In the late nineteenth century, a combination of improved transportation, cheap new postal rates favorable to regularly issued publications, and the desire of business for national markets stimulated the growth of national magazines. At first, the magazines were little interested in advertising and restricted it to a single page at the end of the periodical. Gradually, however, they began to follow the lead of Benjamin Day and his remarkably successful penny newspaper, the original *New York Sun*—that is, to depend significantly on advertising revenues to recover their costs and increase their profits. Soon, the idea caught on that the reader should be able to buy the magazine for a fraction of its actual production cost and that

A 1950s magazine advertisement promotes air-conditioned railroad travel by showing a female passenger in a seat that seems to float on air.

advertising should pay handsomely for advertising space. This turned out to be a very successful formula, and by the 1890s, magazines were inexpensive to buy and contained large amounts of advertising. Some had hundreds of thousands of subscribers and were a truly effective way of presenting products to consumers.

THE GENDERING OF CONSUMER CULTURE.   The nationally circulated magazines appealed greatly to women. As was explained in Chapter 5, many offered special sections of interest to women, such as child-rearing advice, fashion, plus serialized fiction. For the housewife, the profusion of goods advertised in these magazines offered a wondrous display of a life of abundance. They also taught women "their place" in society as both consumers and homemakers. One critic calls this "the gendering of consumer culture" and decries "the adman in the parlor," a function these magazines served. As advertisers increasingly defined women as their target audience, advertising-dependent magazines presented their women readers with fiction that encouraged them in their roles as consumers. This encouragement took different forms depending on the class of women addressed. Magazines addressed to cash-poor women presented ways to earn money to buy advertised goods and helped to justify their purchases, while suggesting that such consumption could be consistent with their values of thrift and moral responsibility. Magazines addressed to middle-class women, on the other hand, discouraged autonomous work and encouraged them to seek fulfillment in shopping and the care of their families.[8]

DEPARTMENT STORES.   Another consequence of the industrial revolution and the expansion of world trade in the late 1800s was the department store. One of the earliest and most successful was Wanamaker's in Philadelphia. By 1880, it had established itself a shopper's paradise. Establishments such as these in many cities soon displayed a dazzling array of goods never before assembled in such a way for examination and shopping convenience of consumers. Just walking through their floors and aisles and ogling the things that one might purchase was an adventure. Such shopping came to be a regular part of the weekly routines of many urban, middle-class women. However, to get women into the store and encourage them to purchase, it was necessary to advertise the goods and services that they would encounter when they arrived. Newspapers were the advertising medium of choice. Department stores were local, as were the newspapers themselves. Thus, before the age of the automobile, which currently accounts for a huge part of the revenues of newspaper advertisers, the department stores were steady and profitable purchasers of advertising space.

A second event contributing to the development of consumerism, and also based on the industrial revolution, was the establishment of mail-order department stores. Montgomery Ward and Sears, Roebuck & Co. began to retail an abundance of wares through their catalogues. Mail-order catalogue sales were made possible when Rural Free Delivery began, a new feature of the U.S. Postal Service that had come into being shortly after the Civil War. This was a blessing for rural Americans, who made up the majority of the population. Farm families, previously isolated from seeing the great abundance of goods available, because of their dispersion on farms, could now examine a dazzling array of goods in the catalogues and order them through the mail to be delivered by parcel post. Advertising such products under the brand names of the mail-order houses was a major development in retailing and a landmark in the history of advertising.

Establishing the Advertising Agency.   As the advertising industry grew, newspapers and magazines developed their own internal advertising departments catering to those commercial interests that wanted to buy their advertising space. Publications began to compete aggressively for the advertisers' business, especially in towns where there were competing media. Large retail organizations that purchased large amounts of advertising also began to establish their own advertising departments to plan and place their ads.

What was to come was an independent *agency* that worked neither for the media directly nor under the control of business that needed to advertise their wares. What emerged was an organization that coordinated the activities of both—and derived a profit from each. The idea was slow in catching on. The very first advertising agent using this strategy to open shop in the United States was Volney Parker. In 1848, he began soliciting orders for advertising for newspapers in Philadelphia. His customers produced their own copy that touted their wares. Volney bought large blocks of newspaper space cheaply and then sold it at a profit to those who wanted to advertise their products in the paper. Within a few years, others launched similar firms in Boston and New York City.[9]

During later decades in the 1800s, various kinds of intermediaries were facilitating the relationship between commercial enterprises and media organizations. As was the case with Volney, at first these intermediaries were merely space brokers who arranged for the placement of ads. Later, they expanded their operations to provide other kinds of services and became the world's first *advertising agencies*— organizations that specifically provided advertising copy, creative assistance, and management of advertising strategies to large numbers of clients. By 1910, a number of such agencies had been established in New York City, Boston, and other large cities. They had begun to provide their customers with full services in creating advertising messages and campaigns, as well as in buying media space in newspapers and magazines, which were likely to be read by audiences who would be interested in their products.

Advertising-Supported Modern Media

In the twentieth century, as new mass media were developed, the importance of advertising in promoting products accelerated greatly. Radio and television were ideal media to carry both national and local advertising, and they were especially effective. As we have seen in earlier chapters, the broadcast media very quickly became dependent on advertising revenues. One reason why they were effective was that their audiences paid nothing; a newspaper or magazine required the receiver to purchase a subscription or a copy of the publication. Broadcast messages were not only free but were also difficult to avoid. Thus, broadcasting for both local and national advertising was added to print as a major transmitter of persuasive messages.

Generally, then, as industrial society developed and matured during the nineteenth and twentieth centuries, a *symbiotic relationship* developed to provide the financial foundation of the American system of mass communication. Many would agree with David Potter, who in 1969 said that "Marconi may have invented the wireless and Henry Luce may have invented the news magazine, but it is advertising that has made both wireless and news magazines what they are in America today."[10]

Thus, the main features of the modern advertising industry were already in place by the 1950s. Its development both depended on and stimulated the growth of both the old and the new mass media. It could not have flowered without business eager to make profits, without the media eager to earn revenue by carrying their advertising messages, and without consumers ready to spend money—income earned from jobs in the great industrial growth that was taking place in the United States. Thus, advertising became a deeply established social institution linking our nation's productivity, our mass media, and our consuming public.

THE CONTEMPORARY ADVERTISING INDUSTRY

The advertising industry exists for the purpose of putting businesses (also known as the *advertisers*) that want to market and distribute goods and services in touch with consumers who want to buy and use them. Viewed in this way, the advertising industry today is a facilitator between the advertiser and the public. Components of the industry include: (1) *advertising agencies* of various kinds, (2) *media service organizations,* (3) *suppliers of supporting services* ranging from research to commercial art, and (4) *advertising media.* The last category includes print, electronic, digital, outdoor, specialty, direct mail, and a number of highly specialized or even exotic types of advertising. These are only the bare bones of the industry, and everything on the list comes in several versions, variations, and sizes. For example, there are massive national advertising agencies with offices in scores of cities in the United States and abroad, and there are small, local agencies with only a handful of employees and a few accounts.

Although the advertising industry is made up of a broad spectrum of independent business interests, and is by no means a tightly controlled national entity, various voluntary organizations and associations hold it together. There are, for example, associations of advertisers and advertising agencies. These include the important American Association of Advertising Agencies (or Four As), the American Advertising Federation (for ad professionals), and the Association of National Advertisers (the clients of agencies), as well as regional and state groups. There are also media associations concerned with advertising, including the Newspaper Advertising Bureau, the Outdoor Advertising Institute, the Television Bureau of Advertising, the Cable Advertising Bureau, and the Internet Advertising Bureau. Various publishers' associations are also greatly concerned with advertising, including the Newspaper Association of America, the National Association of Broadcasters, and the Online Publishers Association, to name a few.

MEDIA LEADERS INSIGHTS: ADVERTISING/NEW MEDIA

SEAN DUGGAN

Director, East Coast Sales

MySpace

Experience and an instinct for innovation has marked Sean Duggan's career even before he arrived at MySpace.com, the number one consumer site in the U.S. Media Metrix. Starting out in financial services, he made a transition to media and "has never regretted it."

At MySpace, he manages national advertising sales for the popular social networking site, which is now owned by Rupert Murdoch's News Corp. He has worked in and across several media platforms, beginning with public radio, where he helped create new revenue streams for WFUV-FM, in New York, one of the nation's most listened to public stations. From there he went to ABC/ESPN Radio Networks, where he helped define advertising in digital radio space. That led him him to the cable giant Comcast Corp, where he managed interactive advertising sales for ITV, VOD (video on demand), and online content. He has an MBA from Fordham's Graduate School of Business.

1. When and under what circumstances did you first realize the import of new media or the digital age?

   My first job after college in 1993 was with the PC Financial Network. PCFN was an early pioneer in the online brokerage industry and was eventually by E*Trade. It was during this period that I started to realize the world was going to be reshaped by the e-commerece and the Internet.

2. What impact did that experience have on you personally or professionally?

   After becoming immersed in the online world at work, I started becoming a user of the Internet in 1994 at home for communication, news, and entertainment. I began to realize there was a tremendous opportunity for me professionally if I could learn how the Internet can be leveraged properly for advertising and combined with traditional media.

3. When did you start using social networking?

   I first started using MySpace in 2004 to check out the profiles of bands and artists. I loved the ability to stream music for free, view videos, and get updates on new music and tour dates.

4. What is the greatest challenge or benefit of social networking for users?

   The greatest benefit for social networking users is the ability to connect, discover, and share their passion/enthusiasms with a wide group of friends quickly and easily.

5. Are you optimistic about the digital future?

   I'm very optimistic about the digital future and particularly social networking. At MySpace we are continuing to innovate and respond to the needs of our 75 million unique users.

6. What, if any, advice do you have for a person who aspires to a career in online advertising or social networking?

   Use and explore new online publishers and social networking websites. It is also important to follow wider trends in media usage—this is invaluable for understanding how people consume media and will facilitate an understanding into *the next big thing*.

These organizations and others produce regular publications that carry news of the advertising industry. Some are general-interest periodicals and websites for advertising (like *Advertising Age*), whereas others are very specific (like *Folio,* which deals with magazine marketing). Each category of advertising (direct mail, outdoor signs, packaging, and so on) has its own publications.

All this adds up to a huge industry with a substantial economic impact. In the late 1990s, American businesses spent more than $126 billion per year on advertising, including that conveyed by the media and such other approaches as direct-mail marketing. By 2006, this number reached at least $265 billion across all media. (See Table 11.1.)[11] These statistics when followed over time note the rise and fall of various media as new competitors come into the market. Some media economists have argued that there is a "constancy hypothesis" at work, wherein the amount of spending on information and entertainment as a share of individual or family expenditures doesn't grow much but does get redistributed. This is especially evident today, with Internet-advertising spending now making inroads on older forms, though this is hard to chart because so much advertising across all media is now digital. Newspapers, for example, are a troubled medium with declining circulations and market penetration, which has led to social networking and search sites like MySpace and Google to usurp their advertising revenues.

Of the total amount of advertising spending at the beginning of the twenty-first century, media were getting about 60%, with the rest going to such activities as sales promotion, direct marketing, package design, and the like. It was estimated that the top one hundred advertising agencies—the principal facilitators between advertisers, the media, and the public—were getting about 36% of this amount, which represented a slight but noticeable decline from earlier decades. It has also

TABLE 11.1

U.S. AD SPENDING TOTALS BY MEDIA

From Robert J. Coen's Universal McCann U.S. Volume Report as reported in 100 Leading National Advertisers (AA, June, 27, 2005). This table shows advertising totals by media. Ad spending figures are for calendar 2004 in billions and include all commissions as well as art, mechanical and production expenses. *Includes network, spot, syndicated and Spanish-language TV.

RANK	MEDIUM	U.S AD SPENDING	% OF TOTAL
1	Direct mail	$52.19	19.8
2	Newspaper	46.61	17.7
3	Broadcast TV*	46.26	17.5
4	Cable TV	21.53	8.2
5	Radio	19.58	7.4
6	Yellow Pages	14.00	5.3
7	Consumer magazine	12.25	4.6
8	Internet	6.85	2.6
9	Out of home	5.77	2.2
10	Business publication	4.07	1.5
	All other	34.65	13.2
	Total	263.77	

been estimated that some 460,000 persons are employed in advertising and public relations, the two being combined by the U.S. Bureau of Labor Statistics because so many PR firms are owned by advertising holding companies. One estimate suggested about five-sixths of the total, or 385,000, were working in advertising; about half of that number work in advertising agencies as opposed to ad media and other places. The U.S. Bureau of the Census currently estimates that there are nearly 40,000 advertising firms.[12]

The trend toward concentration of ownership that we have seen elsewhere in the communication industry has also characterized advertising. A handful of multinational holding companies own most ad and PR agencies as well as other marketing and specialized communication channels. The big four are the Interpublic Group of Companies, WPP Group, Publicis Groupe, and Omnicom Group, which together account for nearly 48% of the industry. The remaining 52% is spread across hundreds—if not thousands—of smaller firms, some of them employing a single person. The top-grossing agencies owned by the big companies, making up only a tiny fraction of the total number of such firms, handle about one-third of all of the nation's advertising business. For example, J. Walter Thompson (JWT), the top U.S. agency, and Young and Rubicam, the largest agency in the United States, which are both owned by Britain's WPP Group, had U.S. billings of $476 million in 2006 while WPP's revenues were more than $9 billion worldwide. Omnicom's worldwide revenues were $9.75 billion. There are multifaceted full-service agencies as well as multicultural agencies serving Latinos, African and Asian Americans, media specialists firms, and interactive agencies while others cater to specialized fields like health care or financial services.[13]

The various elements of the advertising industry noted above are interrelated parts of a dynamic system that is very competitive. The images of the harried advertising account executive often presented in movies and television may be an overstatement, but advertising is a field marked by intense energy and fervent competition as agencies and firms do battle for accounts. A fascinating, if dated, image of ad agencies in the 1960s when their iconic images were formed in popular culture was seen in the 2008

AMC series "Mad Men," which was lauded as an accurate portrayal of the time, if laced with sexism and ethnic bias.

Types of Advertising Agencies

At one time, most major advertising agencies and the bulk of the advertising business were based in New York City—mainly in and around Madison Avenue. The fascination with Madison Avenue still continues with the popular portrayals in the media as noted earlier. While there were strong regional centers like Chicago, Boston, Los Angeles, and a few others, serious national advertisers usually looked to New York for big-time agencies. In the 1990s and beyond, with the advance of Internet technologies, many local and regional agencies in smaller cities like Atlanta, Minneapolis, Seattle, Portland, and Kansas City began to pick up major national accounts outside of their own regions.

With storyboards and preliminary designs, a team of advertising agency designers discuss a campaign.

The industry is still firmly planted in New York, which remains the capital of virtually all of the mass communications industries. But observers are closely watching these regional developments.

Advertising agencies have come a long way since the nineteenth century, when they were essentially space brokers. Today, there are several different types. One is the *full-service agency*, which performs virtually every aspect of the advertising process for its clients. Another is the *creative boutique*, which is much smaller and is focused on providing creative ideas for ads and on execution of those ideas. Still another is the *specialist agency*, which focuses on particular products or services, such as foods, women's products, or financial services. A fourth is the *in-house agency* or *department*, which serves a single industry, chain of stores, large manufacturer, or other business. The role played by each is reviewed briefly.

FULL-SERVICE AGENCY. The full-service agency employs writers, artists, media experts, researchers, television producers, account executives, and others as part of the organization. Advertising scholar William Arens has identified three main functions of the full-service advertising agency:[14]

1. *Planning.* The agency must know its client, its product, the competition, and the market well enough to recommend plans for advertising.
2. *Creation and execution.* The agency creates the advertisements and contacts the media that will present them to the intended audience.
3. *Coordination.* The agency works with salespeople, distributors, researchers, and retailers to see that the advertising works.[15]

As noted earlier, an innovative digital agency called Anomaly NYC says it has pioneered "connections planning," which especially employs social networking and other digital strategies across all media.[16]

Within the full-service agency are several major functions and groups that work as a team to accomplish their overall goals. These can be summarized in the following terms:

1. *Account management.* The account executive and his or her staff provide services to a firm or product. An account management director is responsible for relations between the agency and the client.

2. *The creative department.* The creative director supervises writers, directors, artists, and producers who write and design the ads, including video production and Internet applications.
3. *Media selection.* A media director heads a department in which the specific media to be used for particular ads are chosen.
4. *The research department.* Advertising messages are pretested and data are gathered to help the creative staff fashion a specific design and message. The research director supervises in-house research and hires outside research firms for more extensive national and regional studies.
5. *Internal control.* The administrative operations of the agency, including public relations, are concentrated in one department.

An administrative director runs the agency. Of course, large agencies have a board of directors, top executives, and senior management as well as and the usual trappings of any big business.

An advertising agency offers *service,* and it is confidence in that service that brings the client to pay a significant percentage of its total billings (costs of its advertising efforts) to the ad agency. The exact amounts can differ, but 15% would be typical. Just what happens from the time of the initial contact between an agency and a client to the finished advertising campaign varies considerably, depending on the size of the agency and the nature of the account. But essentially this is how it works.

To establish a relationship with a client, the *account management director* either contacts a business—say, a local company that manufactures solar heating devices—or someone from the business contacts the advertising agency. Indeed, the company may contact several agencies and ask all of them for ad proposals—with the understanding that only one will receive the account. The account management director then selects an *account executive* from within the agency, who arranges a meeting among *company executives* from the solar heating firm, his or her boss (the account management director), and other appropriate people from the agency. They discuss potential advertising objectives, the budget, and the timetable. In many ways, the strategy can be compared with that used to plan a military operation or campaign. The first step is *intelligence-gathering.* In a process called "situations analysis," every conceivable set of facts about the product, its consumers, as well as the expectations of the client is reviewed before any attempt is undertaken to design ads or a campaign. Questions are asked, such as: Exactly what does this device do? What kinds of people use it and for what purpose? How is it better than its competitors? Who are likely future customers for the device? What advertising has been done in the past with what media, what appeals, and what results? What medium will best reach the likely customers? What persuasive strategies and appeals are likely to be effective in a new campaign?

Once the full set of background information and facts about the product are understood, the account executive goes to work inside the agency. The *research department* conducts studies or assembles information to answer some of the questions about potential consumers. The agency's *creative department* holds brainstorming sessions, discussing ideas for a potential campaign. *Artists* and *writers,* who have been informed of all background facts and research results, create sample ads. These may be rough sketches of newspaper or magazine advertisements, broadcast storyboards for television (which are a series of drawings on a panel indicating each step of a commercial), or other preliminary versions of ads being prepared for other media. Depending on how complex and detailed the campaign will be, a variety of other specialists may be involved, such as sound engineers, graphic artists, lighting experts, and actors.

The results of all this creative activity are the *preliminary versions of ads* from which the final versions will be chosen. These ad candidates are then *pretested* on potential consumers. The agency's research department conducts or supervises this pretesting and suggests which of several approaches would probably work best for the client. In recent years, copy-testing research has grown in importance, wherein all elements of a print ad or broadcast commercial are tested carefully for consumer reactions. This process removes some of the financial risks of advertising and generally pleases the client. Research also guides the agency and client in deciding what media to use. Various options are print, broadcast, the Internet, outdoor advertising, on matchbook covers and subways, and so on.

The account executive then gathers this information and, along with other agency personnel, conducts a *presentation* for the client company. Potential costs are clearly laid out so that the company can evaluate the proposal. This type of presentation is often elaborate, with PowerPoint and video presentations and sample ads. Research and creative personnel discuss various features of the ads, and members from the media department discuss the advantages and disadvantages of using particular media for the campaign. Now the ball is in the client company's court: The client's executives either accept or reject the agency's proposal. Their acceptance may, of course, be conditional on various modifications they prefer.

Once the go-ahead is given, the account executive coordinates activity within the agency to produce the actual ads. He or she works with the *media* department to contact the appropriate media and arrange for the advertising campaign to reach the public. The research department prepares its strategy to *evaluate* the campaign so that the agency can present evidence about whom the campaign has actually reached and with what results. It also pre-tests ads and client messages with focus groups, surveys, and ethnographic qualitative research. Hopefully, these will ensure that the account will be renewed in the future.

Finally, the advertisement reaches the *consumer* as he or she reads a newspaper or magazine, watches TV, listens to the radio, surfs the Internet, or uses some other medium. This is, of course, the "bottom line," where "the rubber hits the road." Brand building is a critical goal, but the ultimate test of the effectiveness of any advertisement or campaign is not whether the client likes the ads but whether the ads bring about an increase in the sales of the product or service. The goal, after all, is to motivate an ample number of consumers to head toward a local store to buy the product or use the service. Some ads fail this test; others succeed.

CREATIVE BOUTIQUES.　A boutique agency, unlike its full-service counterpart, has more limited goals and offers fewer services. It is essentially a *creative department* and may hire other agencies and independent groups to provide other kinds of advertising services for particular clients and products or services. Often boutiques work closely with in-house agencies—that is, a small ad group or department formed by a business to handle its own products. Most boutiques are small agencies established by people who once worked for full-service agencies.

SPECIALIST AGENCY.　Obviously, to reach just the right target audience, the advertisement must be placed in appropriate media. Space or time has to be arranged so that the ad can appear in those media. Specialist agencies, which are sometimes called *media service organizations,* exist to provide an important service for advertisers. They buy space in the media at reasonable rates. They then negotiate with advertising agencies that need to use that space or time. Many people in these media service organizations also once worked for the advertising agencies.

A graphic designer examines an ad that features spheres floating over a grid.

IN-HOUSE AGENCY OR DEPARTMENT.　Whole industries, as well as large department stores or other businesses, sometimes have their own internal agencies or advertising departments. Unlike advertising agencies, which are independent "middlemen" serving several accounts or businesses, the advertising department of a business works exclusively with that firm's products or services and is part of its staff. This department has an intimate knowledge of the business or industry and makes proposals for advertising plans and strategies. Its main concern is the final outcome—increasing sales or heightening the awareness of a particular product or service. Advertising departments work closely with independent advertising agencies, which compete for their business and present alternative proposals for an advertising campaign. Some retail advertising departments are organized and function just like a small advertising agency and place advertising directly with local media. For more complicated transactions that involve research and other specialties, however, they are likely to look to independent agencies for assistance.

Advertising Networks

Advertising networks make end runs around the traditional advertising agencies, whether full service or boutique, as they go directly to advertisers and seek out their own platforms (or media) for delivery of their ad messages. Their argument is that ad agencies—with their complex billing system and tiers of specialists—are a waste of money, and advertising networks offer to do that work directly. Part of their pitch is that they rarely use the traditional ad media (newspapers, TV, cable), instead concentrating their messages on YouTube or Facebook to network with the younger audiences that advertisers want, using all the tools and techniques of the web. One ad network executive, Edmund Carey, formerly a managing director for advertising at the *New York Times,* argues that ad networks are "the future of advertising since they are fast, efficient and cost-effective."[17] Carey argues that many specialty services of the ad agency are omitted and replaced by more cost-effective, web-based tools. This often results in significant cost savings, he says. Others believe the ad networks lack the professionalism and finesse of the traditional ad food chain—from advertiser to consumer via ad agencies and ad media. Some say ad networks could be subsumed by digital agencies already acquainted with the Internet ad space.

Advertising networks grew up as *interactive agencies,* many of them before traditional agencies began to seriously exploit digital tools. Some began as *search engine agencies,* which combined Search Engine Marketing (SEM) and Search Engine Optimization (SEO) that use websites to promote purchase of products online. Some critics like the Tribble Ad Agency say that many big ad agency holding companies are actually misusing the term "digital" by offering only Flash and Photoshop when "the client is asking for SEO and SMO."[18] The term "digital agency" is something of a catch-all term that some critics think may eventually disappear as advertising and the advertising industry defuses itself more carefully. Some digital agencies use only digital tools and platforms for their work while digital (sometimes called *tradigital*), services within full-service ad agencies offer broader services and play new media/digital solutions off the whole range of media platforms available to their clients. There is much quibbling about the terminology, but the message is clear—aggressive young digital agencies are vying for their place in the advertising world in a cost-effective way while older agencies with their expansive and often bureaucratic services are scrambling to compete.

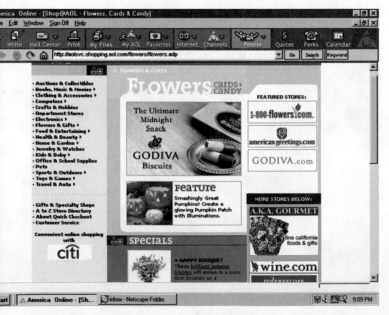

This AOL website is an advertising network that promotes candy, flowers, wine, and other products.

Advertising Media

All of the standard mass media are, of course, advertising vehicles. Indeed as the media researcher and guru Leo Bogart pointed out in his book *Commercial Culture* and

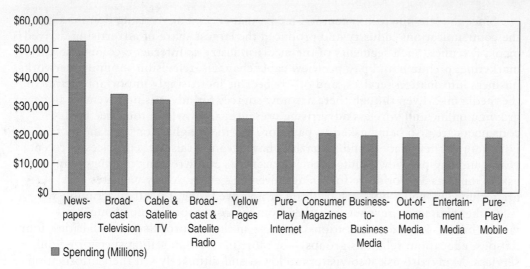

FIGURE 11.2
U.S. Ad Spending by
Medium, 2007

Spending (Millions)

Source: Veronis Suhler Stevenson (VSS) Communications Industry Forecast, 2008–2012, 22nd ed.

other places, the term "media" was invented by the early twentieth-century ad agencies.[19] Bogart, not incidentally, spent most of his illustrious and prolific career at the Newspaper Advertising Bureau. Newspapers, magazines, television and radio stations, cable companies, the Internet, and other media are all involved. Some have advertising departments. At both the national and the local level, the media compete vigorously for advertising dollars. Each of the major media has some kind of national advertising association that gathers data and tries to show that its medium is the "best buy" for reaching particular audiences. At the local level, advertising salespeople who work for media organizations—such as newspapers or radio or TV stations—sell space or time, either directly to a business or to a business through an advertising agency or media service organization.

In selecting a medium, the business or advertising agency considers what target audience is to be reached, the cost of advertising, and the effectiveness of a medium for reaching the desired consumers. While various sources report slightly different data, it is clear that newspapers get the largest share of the advertising dollar among the traditional mass media—currently just under one-fifth (17.7%). This is followed closely by broadcast television, with 17.5%, which when combined with cable (8.2%) is arguably the most important advertising medium. Ad spending as Table 11.1 indicates is now dominated by direct mail (19.8%), which has risen sharply as advertisers use fliers and catalogs to hawk their products.

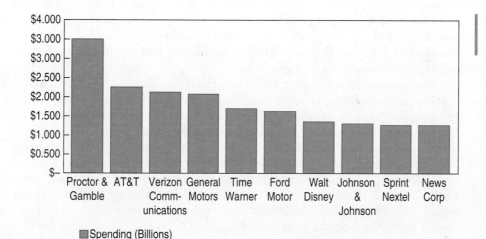

FIGURE 11.3
Top 10 Advertisers,
2007

Spending (Billions)

Source: Veronis Suhler Stevenson (VSS) Communications Industry Forecast, 2008–2012, 22nd ed.

Since the late nineteenth century, media that carried advertising dominated the communications industry and produced the largest share of advertising-derived media revenues. Such segments of the media industry as Internet e-commerce and marketing, premium and pay-per-view cable channels, television shopping networks, business information services, and others became increasingly important factors in the media mix. Even though there are now sources for advertising revenues and a growing online and wireless advertising presence, all of which tout free media, consumers are also being asked to pay more of "the freight" for their media fare. For example, newspapers and magazines have steadily raised their prices in recent years, and pay-per-view events such as prizefights and wrestling matches may ask as much as $50 or more for a single evening's event. Many websites that are technically media outlets have little or no advertising, thus they scramble to find other sources of revenue, whether from their sponsors in the commercial world (businesses and corporations) or those in the nonprofit sector (charities, foundations, education, religious groups)—or more likely from selling specialized online services. Many also ask web visitors to log in and ultimately sell their information to various sources that want databases for commercial or even political purposes. Advertising may or may not be central to such media. In such a climate, it is probable that advertising will play a slightly less significant role than in the past, and certainly the idea that people pay little or nothing for their media because of advertising will no longer be true.[20] Increasingly, though websites and even independent bloggers are eager to attract advertising, companies are realizing that keeping these media operational does require money. Companies hawking their products online also create advertising messages. In mid-year 2008, the Internet Advertising Bureau, which represents interactive companies and media, reported that digital ad revenues had jumped from less than $500 million in 1997 to $5.8 billion. With its nimble approach and low costs, interactive advertising is likely to continue to grow, though cyclical changes in the economy, especially in 2008 and 2009, could have a significant impact on that.[21] Just as the *Wall Street Journal Online* secured nearly fully paying customers, the paper's new ownership decided this highly successful and much praised "subscription model" was less effective than a pure advertising model based on the notion that a free *Wall Street Journal* would drive more visitors to the website and thus create a greater demand for advertising.

The "other types" of advertising media include *retail signs* and *displays* in stores; *specialty advertising,* as on pens, calendars, and similar items; *outdoor advertising* on billboards and other large surfaces; *transit advertising* in the form of placards on buses and other vehicles; and *business-site* advertising in such settings as trade shows. There are even rather exotic forms, such as electronic headline advertising in taxicabs and even commercial messages posted in public restrooms. But this list gives only a hint of the diverse media for advertising. There are even firms that specialize in skywriting and towing of banners by aircraft or messages on blimps.

Not to be overlooked as a major advertising medium is direct mail and telemarketing (via the telephone), much of this now orchestrated digitally. Both are growing very rapidly. Direct mail began with low rates offered by the post office for deliveries of catalogues, brochures, broadsides, and other materials. Advanced technologies are now being used to call potential customers on the telephone (e.g., automated dialing). As further advances are made in communications technologies, it is virtually certain that they will be added to the list of "advertising media." One of those, mentioned earlier, is search marketing and advertising, which is developing as a whole field into itself—in a convergence context of course. Search firms like Google, Yahoo!, Ask.com, AOL, and MSN account for 40% of all online advertising and is regarded as "an ever-more-important driver of traffic across the web."[22]

BIG IDEAS: MEDIA THEORIES EXPLAINED

Media Information Utility Theory

People in societies such as ours rely on the media to provide them with many lids of information. They read books, newspapers, and magazines. They go to the movies, watch TV, surf the Internet, rent films for their DVD players, and listen to the radio in their cars. In many cases they do this because media content is entertaining, fulfilling deep-seated needs, and providing complex psychological gratifications.

However, people in modern society also have come to rely heavily on mass communications for many other kinds of information (unrelated to entertainment) that they use for routine purposes. For example, they have to find out where they can purchase a car, clothing, food, or other things at the best price; to locate suitable housing, a job, or the latest fashions; or sometimes to meet someone to date or even marry. In short, people are *dependent* on the media to provide many kinds of utilitarian information that has little to do with fulfillment of deep-seated needs or providing complex psychological gratification.

At an earlier time, when modern media did not exist, word-of-mouth communication was the source for such information. People had networks of families and friends from which they obtained the information they needed for routine matters. Populations of similar cultural backgrounds lived together in small communities, generation after generation. Thus, social ties between people were both extensive and deep.

In modern life, and especially in urban areas, those networks are much more difficult to establish and maintain. People of many diverse backgrounds live in physical proximity to each other. However, they often differ from each other in terms of ethnicity, race, education, income, religion, political affiliation, and other characteristics. Such social and cultural differences pose many *barriers* to open communication through word-of-mouth channels. This tends to inhibit contacts and the free exchange of ideas between people, leading them to turn to other channels, less personal sources, to get the information that they require.

Today, the mass media provide that information. In their news, advertisements, syndicated columns, and even in their entertainment content, they provide a great deal of practical information that people use. That is, the media provide a constant flow of advice, interpretations, information, instruction, and role models that people use as a basis for making choices. Thus, they become dependent on this kind of mass-communicated information. Stated formally:

1. People in all societies need to make *decisions* about routine and practical matters, such as obtaining food, shelter, clothing, transportation, entertainment, and other aspects of daily life.
2. In traditional societies people were linked together in well-established networks of friends and family. It was through those networks that they obtained by *word of mouth* the practical information that they used for such decisions.
3. In urban-industrial societies, composed of unlike people brought together, populations are *greatly differentiated* by race, ethnicity, income, education, occupation, religion, and social class.
4. Because of such social diversity, urban industrial populations have *fewer effective word-of-mouth channels* based on deeply established social networks through which they can obtain the practical information they routinely need.
5. **Therefore**, people in urban-industrial societies become *dependent on mass media* to obtain the utilitarian information that they require to make many kinds of routine daily decisions.

From London's Piccadilly Circus, outdoor advertising for electronic products, beer and hamburgers attest public attention in a very busy urban setting.

ADVERTISING AS PERSUASIVE COMMUNICATION

The idea of *persuasion* has ancient roots. Centuries before mass communication became available, when the human voice was the only medium that could be used, *rhetoric* was used as a strategy for influencing the beliefs and actions of people. It was a time when the words used in a speech, the ways in which arguments were presented, and the elegance of composition of messages were the only means available to sway the judgments and conduct of listeners. In that sense, rhetoric is as important today in the world of advertising, political campaigns, and fundraising as it was when Mark Antony delivered his classic speech eulogizing the death of Julius Caesar. In any promotional message devised today, the message must be constructed with exquisite care if it is to achieve its goal. Words have to be carefully selected, arguments explaining why people should take the recommended actions must be skillfully organized, and the overall composition of the message must fit easily into the cultural habits of the target audience.

In recent decades, social scientists have studied various strategies that have been used to persuade populations to believe or behave in a host of different ways.[23] The process of persuasion lies at the heart of such widely studied activities as *propaganda*—using media to sway peoples' commitments to such matters as loyalty to a particular leader, acceptance of a specific political system, willingness to make personal sacrifices in times of war, and so on. Persuasion also is the basic process of the *political campaign* in countries within which ordinary citizens can play a role in selecting their leaders as they compete in elections. It is also fundamental to shaping or changing *public opinion* as legislators need to seek popular support for particular social programs or economic policies.

In such contexts, a very large body of research and theory has accumulated, revealing the *persuasive strategies* that communicators have used in seeking to accomplish their goals. Such strategies are based on underlying psychological and sociological assumptions about how human beings can be motivated to adopt particular beliefs or to take actions that are desired by the communicator.

Humor is sometimes used in advertising as with this spoof of the well-known brand White Castle, seen here as Fright Castle, which was produced by Topps bubble gum company in the 1970s.

Not all advertising focuses on a specific product, such as diapers, oatmeal, or soap. Such ads are the mainstay of the industry, and the goal is to motivate purchases. Another form of advertising, called *institutional advertising,* is much less direct. For example, many firms want to embrace the green revolution to demonstrate their social consciousness. The housing industry promotes environmentally safe products, and a company that makes paper and other forest-related products presents a television commercial or website extolling the virtues of a beautiful, well-managed forest, showing cute animals but saying nothing about its specific product, providing only the corporation's name. The goal is, of course, to get the public to associate the corporation with the "selfless" ad and lovely images—fostering beliefs that here is a company that "really cares."

One of the basic issues in designing any form of persuasive message, regardless of the strategy employed, is to define exactly what the message is expected to accomplish. There are at least two ways to define success in terms of persuasion. One would be that some *personal orientation* has been changed—as in the institutional example above—in which some opinion, belief, feeling, or attitude of members of a target audience have been altered in ways desired by the communicator. A more demanding definition would be that a particular form of *overt behavior* on the part of audience members has been triggered. This means that a person actually buys the product, votes for the candidate, gives a donation, or engages in some other form of action that the message is intended to motivate. Both of these outcomes can be important, often for different types of clients, but the underlying strategies on which they are based may have much in common.

Basic Strategies for Constructing Persuasive Messages

What basic strategies are available for the persuasive communicator who wants either to alter personal orientations or to motivate an audience to engage in specific overt action? While there are many strategies that can be used, there are two that are basic. One

New York's Time Square, once called "The Great White Way," is awash with massive electronic and digital advertisements.

that is very widely used in advertising is based on the assumption that both personal orientations and overt actions are based on *individual psychological factors*—either emotional or rational—that determine how a person will behave in a particular context. Persuasive communicators who develop their messages based on this idea are using a *psychodynamic strategy.* Another approach is to assume that people's beliefs and their overt actions are shaped by the context of social rules and shared cultural expectations of people around them. Here, messages are designed to convince the receiver that a particular form of belief or action is required by that context. Communicators using this set of assumptions make use of *sociocultural strategy* for constructing their persuasive messages.[24]

THE PSYCHODYNAMIC STRATEGY.   Modern advertising messages often use either emotional appeals or those based on reason (a cognitive approach) to persuade members of a target audience to purchase a particular product. An example of the use of reason would be an ad for a car that stresses economy of purchase and operation—claiming that the [brand of car] is the choice anyone who wants the best possible price, the best gas mileage available, a high trade-in value, and a favorable record of repairs. Not all products lend themselves to this approach. Far more common is the use of *appeals,* which are more likely to be based on emotional needs, desires, and wants than on reason or rationality. Here, ads are based on such inducements as appeals to status—suggesting that purchasing this product will give you greater status. Also common are sexual themes—indicating that using this product will make you more attractive to others and that purchasing it will bring you more opportunities for engaging the behavior that you desire. Other commonly used appeals are based on greed, humor, fear, pride, envy, or other psychological states that presumably can be aroused by the message.

A simple interpretation of how such advertisements work is that the persuasive message arouses some sort of *feeling* or emotional state within the individual's psychological functioning, and this increases the receiver's motivation to behave in the manner desired by the advertiser. It is an old idea, but it does illustrate the psychodynamic strategy. As advertising scholar John Jones explains this rather elementary theory:

> To understand how advertising works, we need to know the order of events.... The earliest theory was based on a simple chain of causality described by Charles Raymond as *"learn, feel, do."* In this theory, people receive factual knowledge about a brand. As a result, their [feelings] toward the brand change and they develop a preference for it. Then they buy it.[25]

Fluid advertising in billboards and posters can promote a product as "cool" as with these series of Apple iPod posters.

THE SOCIOCULTURAL STRATEGY. It is obvious that the culture within which an individual makes decisions about action's is profoundly important in shaping his or her behavior. Simply put, cultures shape actions, even though to someone looking on from outside some actions may seem bizarre or even irrational. In traditional India, for example, the culturally approved practice of *suttee* dictated that when a woman's husband died it was the duty of a faithful wife to kill herself by throwing herself on his funeral pyre. This practice and others involving mutilations have ignited much opposition among human rights groups, which also use advertising media and various persuasive methods to change behavior and some traditional cultural practices.

In the United States, culture also dictates action. Strong cultural norms, role definitions, requirements of social ranking, and the existence of many forms of social controls (rewards and punishments) are deeply understood by the majority—and compliance is routine. Advertisements that call attention to these cultural requirements and urge the purchase of particular products or try to persuade people to engage in other kinds of actions to conform are based on a sociocultural strategy. This was precisely the strategy used in a recent Massachusetts antismoking campaign in which a series of ads was aimed at youths. As researchers Michael Siegal of Boston University and Lois Biener of the University of Massachusetts reported, "The advertisements aimed to denormalize tobacco use by showing youths that smoking by their peers was not the *norm.*"[26] In the commercial world, an example would be an ad that urges the use of a particular mouthwash or a brand of deodorant. In such cases, the risk of offending accepted norms about bad breath or body smells provides a motivation for purchasing the product. Other ads may be based on *role definitions,* such as a mother's duty to provide certain nostrums to her child suffering from a cold or flu. *Ranking* is used in ads that show some high-ranking celebrity endorsing a product—assuming that the consumer wants to be like that prestigious person. In the case of *social controls,* advertisements for greeting cards are based on the culturally accepted concept that sending such missives is a sort of moral requirement on birthdays, anniversaries, Valentine's Day, and so on. Many of these practices, which are largely commercially driven, push people toward certain behaviors because violation of these norms might risk criticism or even rejection (social control). There is perpetual criticism of these practices, especially around Christmas (and other religious holidays), where gift giving is deemed essential. More recently, parties for small children are a source for considerable commercial activity to supply parties, gift bags, and other new conventions of contemporary parents and children.

Thus, the basic approach used in the sociocultural strategy is straightforward: A persuasive message defines a cultural requirement. It indicates the consequences of failing to conform. It shows that use of the product will allow the consumer to avoid those negative consequences. In contrast to the simple *learn-feel-do* formula of the psychodynamic strategy, it is based on a *conform-or-be-punished* approach.

There are obviously many other ways in which persuasive messages can be designed. Advertisers are quite possibly the most creative professionals in the American labor force today. They constantly invent new ways to advertise and promote the wares of their clients. Some of them work enormously well and become part of the popular culture. Others are less effective, and some are simply duds. But whatever strategy is being used, advertisers are following in the steps of ancient orators like Cicero, Socrates, Aristotle, and others who couched their arguments in persuasive rhetoric to try to get people to adopt their ideas.

Cutting Through the Clutter: The Problem of Gaining Attention

If an advertisement is not seen and understood by members of the target audience, it is just so much wasted effort. Therefore, one of the most precious commodities for the advertiser is *attention*. For that reason, those who create the content of ads strive for compositions of words, colors, images, and sounds that capture and focus the attention of the TV viewer, the magazine or newspaper reader, the Internet surfer, or the radio listener. A major problem is the sheer volume of media content that exists today. Quite obviously there are limitations on the time that people can spend during any twenty-four hours attending to the media. Therefore, it is essential that advertisers understand in depth the exact nature of their target audience, the kinds of media to which they attend, and the pattern of interests and tastes that will bring such people to attend to a particular advertisement positioned among dozens, even hundreds, of competitors. An ad's ability to break through the clutter (of competing messages) and gain the attention of the right consumers, then, is a critical matter that can spell success or failure for any particular ad.

Creating ads that can do this, and at the same time retaining the persuasive appeals that will sell the product or service, is one of the most creative challenges that exist in the contemporary communications world. If an agency does not have the kinds of individuals who can visualize ways in which their advertisements can capture the right attention of the right people, it will soon go out of business.

There has been a constant flow of advertising styles and content over the years in an effort to attract attention. In the 1890s, advertising styles included ornate and highly decorated soap and cosmetic ads. By the 1920s, these were gone and were replaced by the clean lines of the art deco designs. These gave way to psychedelic poster-like ads of the 1960s and early 1970s. More recently, during the 1990s, the clean and orderly Swiss Gothic look yielded to the more traditional and formal design, including that regarded as "retro, harkening back to another era, even though present consumers did not experience that time at all." It is, say design experts, all a matter of coordinating art and typography with content. Advertising that works is therefore an index of popular culture. That was recognized as far back as 1917, when writer Norman Douglas claimed, "You can tell the ideals of a nation by its advertisements."[27] Thus, changes in advertising over the years have been closely tied to changes in American society as a whole.

Digital Advertising Challenges

Throughout this chapter we make mention of the implications of the digital age for advertising and the various uses of viral or digital media in delivering advertising messages. Digital advertising, once called Internet advertising, began simply as static website ads or the more annoying pop-ups. Later came streaming video and various computer graphic features that exceeded what traditional ad media like newspapers, magazines, television, and radio could then do. In the era of Web 1.0, which was mainly a communication network where the sender was in the driver's seat and there was minimal interaction with the end user, ads were embedded around content— or marketing messages. Subsequently, in the era of social networking and the highly interactive Web 2.0, advertisers now have much greater capacity to reach individuals and audiences with addressable, targeted messages tailored to the specific

From its headquarters in Santa Clara, California, Google revolutionized the world of online search. The company says its mission is to organize the world's information and to make it universally accessible.

consumer. The many benefits of digital media, however, are also confronted by problems such as:

- Fragmentation—There is an ever-growing array of media outlets using the Internet and wireless communication to bombard consumers. There are an infinite number of websites and blogs growing by the minute, and at the same time both new media and traditional media are aggressively using their digital capacities to promote ideas, sell goods and services, and otherwise persuade those who pay attention.
- Clutter—Within the digital media, which now encompasses all the traditional media and many new non-media outlets such as pure marketing sites, there is remarkable clutter—an endless stream of material from competing sources seeking end user attention. Sorting out and navigating the web and web-based media is a challenge in itself, partly aided by search engines but also confounded by users who don't want to do their own assessment of so many choices and brands. It is as though the supermarket expanded its offerings 100 million times and constantly asked the consumer to make choices.
- Ad skipping—From the time that the *remote* was invented for television, viewers could skip ads by moving to another channel or by pressing the mute button. More recently, TiVo and other digital-recording systems allow viewers to remove advertising from programming. And there are many other end-run methods for consumers to avoid ads, the very ads that advertisers pay handsomely to reach. Increasingly, audience research factors in ad skipping to the detriment of the media studies.
- Endless changes—Advertisers, advertising agencies, and others who promote and value advertising as a vital revenue source for free media worry that an endless array of new handheld devices, video products, software, and other innovations are coming too fast for consumers to effectively adapt, and thus any decisions about advertising platforms that work best must be re-evaluated constantly. There is, of course, a digital divide among so-called *"digital natives,"* those who grew up with the Internet and digital media, and *"digital immigrants,"* the vast majority of the population that struggles to adapt to and understand the shifting ground of digital media.
- Audience economics—Once the impact and influence of advertising was confined to media use and exposure. This included TV ratings like Nielsen or radio ratings like Arbitron as a measure of how many people watched. Now students of media economics and market research leaders argue that simple *exposure* is not enough but that *experience* with media is the more vital factor. Experience, however, is harder to measure and assess because it involves how people use the media messages they get—if they get them at all in an era of decreasing attention spans.

As a result of these and other conditions, the *field of advertising* and the *advertising process* is being redefined by technological change and how people are reacting to it. This has meant an onslaught of web entrepreneurs creating their own advertising networks and digital agencies while old-line *advertising agencies* struggled to catch up and master the tools of the digital age. *Advertising media* (traditional and new) have also accommodated the changes as they connected their online activities with those of traditional publishing or electronic media. *Advertisers* themselves—those commercial and nonprofit clients seeking a market for their goods, services, and ideas—have also had to learn about the digital space to get the most for their money and fulfill their commercial or cultural objectives. Finally, *the consumer,* the ultimate target of advertising, needs to be reached by the advertisers on the one hand and to be protected from advertising on the other. We take up these and other issues later in the chapter.

THE ROLE OF ADVERTISING RESEARCH

The advertising industry is a great generator of research. The reason is that those who pay for advertising are increasingly demanding *accountability*. They are not content with airy assurances from the advertising agency that "of course our ads for you are working—they are so clever that there can be no other conclusion." Clients are demanding hard evidence that the ads will be effective even before they get released to the media. This is due, in part, to the vast array of media outlets and platforms and the difficulty clients have knowing and believing which is best in an era of interactivity and citizen media. After the ads have been presented to the public, clients want data that show whether or not they are achieving their goals. Therefore, each of the advertising media hires research firms, rating services, and other groups to gather data showing the pulling power of that medium. To meet the goal of accountability, then, agencies conduct or contract for research on potential ad designs and actual effectiveness of the ads they prepare in terms of people's awareness of their clients' products and responses to them. In addition, academics—including sociologists, psychologists, and anthropologists—conduct research on the industry and its effects. Various types of researchers study topics such as marketing strategies, persuasive appeals, the psychology of consumer decisions, the effectiveness of different media, and every aspect of consumer behavior.

The results of certain kinds of research can be found in trade publications and academic periodicals, such as the *Journal of Advertising* and the *Journal of Advertising Research*. Some associations and groups will provide copies of research reports (for example, on the ability of magazines to sell a particular product, such as whiskey) to anyone who asks for them. Much of the research on the effectiveness of advertising, however, is *proprietary*. That is, the results are the intellectual property of those who produce or pay for them for their own use, and then they hide the results from the public. Some proprietary results are gathered by research firms and then sold to the highest bidder. Such research may be conducted by a specific company for its own use or by agencies for particular clients. Much proprietary research is self-serving, designed to demonstrate that a consumer or advertising agency or business has been wise to take a certain action. As a result, there are always questions as to its objectivity. Businesses sometimes hire consultants to help them sort out the various claims of these kinds of researchers. The digital age has spawned various new measurement firms that promote new methods of gathering data about Internet use patterns versus those of other media. And as noted earlier, the Internet, with its massive storage capacity and ability to log in and track all users, offers an enormous treasure trove of data for analysis that is far more complete and accurate than anything gathered heretofore. Major research suppliers and polling firms, for example, are making use of interactive media to conduct surveys or assessments with the whole population that has purchased a given product or that subscribes to a magazine. Now it is possible to have something more sophisticated than card inserts or earlier, cruder efforts at consumer feedback. The former Louis Harris Associates, which conducts the Harris Poll, for example, has been renamed Harris Interactive. It should be noted that, while digital researchers make great claims about the accuracy and completeness of their work, others disagree. Some media outlets, such as ABC News, are wary of online polls, arguing that they are not really scientific. ABC News pollster Gary Langer, for example, says the Internet is a source of considerable mischief about public opinion.[28]

At the same time that there are cogent arguments about the quality of quantitative social science research, there has been a rise of ethnographic research, especially involving advertising and media studies. Here, observational data about how people actually use a product, and other issues, are probed by researchers who go into the field, visiting individuals in their homes or offices. In addition, the tried and much-tested focus group is still alive and well. A focus group is a small number of people (between four and fifteen, but often about eight) selected from the larger population and in which a moderator stimulates a conversation and seeks questions to sample public opinions.

Studying the Effects of Advertising

If conducted systematically, research can reveal whether a particular ad or campaign actually has the effects hoped for by those who have designed it. Earlier we mentioned an example of persuasive advertising based on a sociocultural strategy—urging youths to refrain from smoking. It was a $54 million television campaign sponsored by the Massachusetts Department of Public Health. The goal of the campaign was to reduce the number of teenagers in the state who took up smoking. Funded by the state agency, the investigators followed a sample of six hundred of the state's teenagers for four years. None were smokers at the beginning of the study (although a few had experimented with cigarettes). The research focused on the effects on those who had been systematically exposed to a series of antismoking TV messages aired over several years in the state. The question was whether the ads were effective in preventing teenagers from becoming habitual smokers. Each of the ads showed a devastating health effect on a habitual smoker. Typical was a woman who appeared to be ill, shown lying on a hospital bed breathing through an oxygen tube. In the ad she explained that she had been a heavy smoker for many years and that her resulting emphysema was now so advanced that it was probably going to be fatal. These were moving messages showing real people with real health problems. The ads stressed that smoking was not normative among young people. The results indicated that, among children twelve to fourteen years old who had attended to the ads, taking up smoking had been cut in half (compared with similar youths who did not see the ads). This was a dramatic and very clear effect. However, among somewhat older children, whose orientations to smoking had already been formed before exposure, the normative strategy used in the ads had little effect.[29]

Advertising researchers may use surveys, panel studies, or experiments. Briefly, in panel studies (such as the smoking study discussed above), researchers may take a group of subjects and analyze their beliefs or behavior over time. In experiments, they may set up "treatment" and "control" groups to determine the effects of advertising messages. But whatever the method used, Russell Colley claims, good research on advertising effectiveness must make "a systematic evaluation of the degree to which the advertising succeeded in accomplishing predetermined goals."[30]

What are these goals? If advertising is successful, says Colley, it results in a sale, and to do that it must carry consumers through four levels of understanding: (1) *awareness* of a brand or company, (2) *comprehension* of the product and what it will do for them, (3) a *conviction* that they should buy the product, and (4) *action*—that is, buying the product.[31] Colley urges advertisers to use precise research, including the following types, to evaluate whether an advertisement has succeeded: (1) *Audience research*—this involves gathering basic data on the audience to be reached, including the number of people in various groups (based on age, sex, religion, and so on) who see and respond to advertising. (2) *Media research*—media research involves studying the particular characteristics of each medium and what it can do, including comparisons of the pulling power and persuasiveness of various media. (3) *Copy research*—this means making comparisons of reactions of typical target audience members to particular advertisements. For example, researchers might compare the effectiveness of ads using a sexual appeal with those that arouse fear, humor, or some other reaction.

A videographer captures a focus group through a two-way mirror in an advertising agency.

Consumer and Lifestyle Research

A more general type of research focuses on consumer behavior. Much of this is also privately funded, proprietary, and hidden from public view. From the studies of consumers, researchers help businesses and ad agencies learn who their most likely consumers are and what kinds of advertising are most likely to reach them. They might study how needs, drives, and motives affect consumers' buying, how perception of an advertisement might vary among different categories of consumers, and what opinions, attitudes, beliefs, and prejudices should be taken into account in fashioning a particular message.[32] Some researchers focus on a clearly defined category, such as children. These specialists might examine children at different stages of their development and then predict what kinds of things kids tend to like at certain ages and how they may influence their parents' purchases of toys, food, and so on. Advertising agencies may then use this information to prepare particular kinds of commercials, such as those for Saturday morning cartoon shows.

Another area of study is *lifestyle research,* which grew out of surveys studying trends in American living patterns and buying behavior. These studies inform advertisers about the changing attitudes and lifestyles that characterize potential consumers at different ages and stages—information that can be immensely helpful in fashioning an advertising campaign. For example, research shows that many older people today are moving out of larger houses, where they raised families, into smaller new condos and apartments where they live alone. If they are interested in simplifying their domestic tasks so they can have more free time, then they are new potential consumers for several specific types of goods. These would include such items as single-serving frozen food dishes, microwave ovens, and airline tickets.[33] It would be worthwhile, then, for companies producing these items to use ads and media that are likely to reach that target audience.

Generally, then, advertising research has *applied* objectives. Its purpose is not to uncover basic concepts and theories that explain human behavior. Rather, it is to help stimulate sales of specific products or services to specific categories of consumers. Not surprisingly, this use of research, aimed at discovering how to manipulate people, has aroused considerable criticism. Although the research tries to demonstrate the effectiveness of particular advertisements and campaigns, critics claim that no scientific cause-and-effect relationship can be established between a given ad and the product or service it seeks to sell. Many social scientists believe that there are just too many uncontrollable variables in almost any situation to prove that particular ads actually work. In spite of these criticisms, however, those preparing or funding ads *believe* that advertising works—and they are the ones making decisions to spend millions of dollars to promote products and services.

Qualitative Research on Advertising

There is considerable research that focuses on how advertising employs qualitative or ethnographic methods, some of them derived from critical studies of media as cultural products. Some of this research focuses on gender and racial stereotypes or antisocial concerns, including some that take up the negative impact of advertising on children. Studies have looked at the iconic (whether good or bad) commercial products, from the SUV to Starbucks, examining how they did their branding and their origins and likely social effect. Through observation and a good deal of content study, conclusions are drawn about the impact of media commercialism on people, institutions, and society itself. This is a growing area and sometimes constitutes a basis for critiques of advertising that the industry hears and heeds, while some of it is mostly published in academic journals, where it has an audience of like-minded critics. Recent critiques of the sexual exploitation of women or children in advertising has been informed by this

A female survey-research worker interviews a man on the street using a market research questionnaire.

From this observation lab, market researchers observe young children playing with new toys.

research. For example, the clothing firm of Abercrombie & Fitch is famous for catalogs of scantily clad teenagers, which have been scorned by cultural critics.

Assessing Target Audiences in an Age of Market Segmentation

Although advertisers would like to sell their wares to everyone, they know that is not possible or perhaps even desirable, and so after careful research they go after a particular *segment* of the market. That segment may be defined by age, income, gender, education, race, and so on. At one time, most advertising was *product-oriented;* that is, the content was mainly concerned with a persuasive message about the attributes of the product. Now most advertising is *user-oriented,* with messages aimed at the specific needs, interests, and desires of particular consumers. As historian Daniel Pope put it:

> Segmentation campaigns are user-focused and concentrate on consumer benefits rather than product attributes. They show people with whom the target audience can identify; people who represent a credible source of authority for them or who express their latent desires and dreams. Marketing hones in on consumers whose lifestyles and personalities have been carefully profiled.[34]

This new emphasis also suggests problems for the ethical presentation of advertising. It is much easier to apply a "truth in advertising" standard to statements about the qualities of a product than to apply indirect appeals to the desires of a segment of the audience. The trend toward market segmentation has also led to some specialization in advertising agencies and promoted the growth of media that appeal to a specific rather than a general audience. There is, of course, a body of law governing advertising as well as Federal Trade Commission rules. Also, laws and regulations related to misrepresentation and fraud can apply.

Increasingly, a considerable yield of research evidence is emerging from what John Phelan of Fordham University calls "noble hype," that is, information campaigns aimed at good causes, such as the prevention of HIV/AIDS, heart disease, and other problems that affect society. A considerable amount of money has been poured into information campaign studies that use direct advertising strategies and messages to achieve such goals. The dramatic success of AIDS advertising—which is credited, in part, for the decrease in sexual activity likely to spread the disease—seems in a preliminary way to bode well for advertising effectiveness. At the same time, other researchers and critics say that AIDS is a special case that does not apply generally.

CRITICISM AND CONTROL OF ADVERTISING

Few people doubt that advertising has a significant impact or that it plays an important role in America. Most would agree that it reflects the culture and ideals of America—although many people also find that idea disturbing. Noting its importance, however, is very different from granting approval, and advertising has been criticized on many grounds. Some disparage advertising in general for its economic and social effects. Others criticize the content of some ads or their effects on some groups. These criticisms, as we shall see, have led to attempts to *regulate* advertising.

Economic and Social Criticisms

A favorable view of advertising claims that it stimulates competition, which is good for the economy, and that it encourages the development of new products, which is good for consumers. Proof of the pudding, defenders say, is that people choose to buy the new products. And consumers are happier because they can achieve the good life and the fruits of capitalism—the "American dream."

However, critics have many answers to these comments. First, a great deal of advertising has nothing at all to do with objective information and does not help consumers make wise choices. Yet, even though they do not benefit, people must pay for advertising because its cost raises the price of the goods they buy. Therefore, say such critics, advertising is wasteful.

What is more, faultfinders say, rather than stimulating competition, advertising contributes to monopoly. Large firms can easily afford to invest in expensive national advertising, whereas smaller firms cannot. Larger firms can then perpetuate and even expand their hold on the market. For example, there are few local brands of cola that effectively compete in the marketplace alongside Coca-Cola and Pepsi. Even in the absence of an actual monopoly, some economists see advertising as hindering the development of perfect competition and leading to the condition known as imperfect competition. Several consequences may follow, including, according to critic Neil Borden, "improper allocation of capital investment," "underutilization of productive capacity and underemployment," "relatively rigid prices," and increasingly severe cyclical fluctuations in business, from inflation to recession and back again.[35]

According to Borden, even the diversity of goods stimulated by advertising is not beneficial. Anyone who has visited the breakfast cereal aisle of a large supermarket will understand that comment. Consumers, writes Borden, "are confused by the large number of meaningless product differentiations and consequently do not make wise choices."[36] Other critics point to more general supposed effects of advertising on individuals and society. Advertising is often believed to be manipulative and deceptive. By creating new wants and desires, advertising is also said to distance people from their "true selves, contributing to their alienation and dissatisfaction, and making like an unending and hopeless quest for trivial goods or for the perfect image."

We certainly cannot evaluate point by point either the economic or social analyses advanced by advertising's critics, and we have stated their complaints rather briefly. But note that advertising is a form of mass communication, and the principles we will review in Chapter 14, regarding the media's influence on individuals and society, apply in general to advertising as well. That is, we should not think of advertising messages as "magic bullets" that cause uniform effects among all who receive them. Moreover, we would be ill-advised to consider the people seeing or hearing the messages to be passive automatons receiving them helplessly, whether they want to or not. Nor should we think of advertising as a single, isolated cause of behavior, such as a decision to purchase a product. Reaction to advertising messages is locked into complex causes and influences that prevail among media audiences. Only a great deal of careful research will reveal the answers to whether the long list of criticisms of advertising is valid.

Discerning students who have taken a course in economics may recall how textbooks in that field devote little attention to advertising. The distinguished Harvard economist John Kenneth Galbraith once remarked there is a good reason why such texts downplay its importance. Economists like to believe that consumer wants are held deeply within the human psyche. They subscribe to the idea of consumer sovereignty. But Galbraith once wrote:

> So long as wants are original with the consumer, their satisfaction serves the highest of human purposes. Specifically, an original, inherent need is being satisfied. And economics as a subject matter or science thus becomes basic to the highest human service. But [this] holds only if wants cannot be created, cultivated, shaped, deepened or otherwise induced. Heaven forbid that wants should have their source in the producer of the product of service as aided and guided by his advertising agency.[37]

Other pro-advertising commentators argue that advertising can't work effectively unless it speaks to consumer interests, needs, and wants. They say consumers are capable of taking care of themselves.

Thus, it would downgrade some of the most basic principles of economics if it were true that consumer wants were actually generated by advertising and not by human nature itself.

The Issue of Children and Advertising

Few aspects of advertising have generated more concern or research than advertising directed at children, specifically television commercials. Critics fear that children's advertising creates wants that cannot be fulfilled and that it prompts them to ask their parents for innumerable things that they cannot afford. Thus, children's advertising may generate tension and conflict in the family and teach many lessons that are simply wrong because children mistake advertisements for realistic portrayals of the world. In defense of such advertising, supporters maintain that it helps children learn to be consumers, a role that is vital to our economy.

Any evaluation of advertising's effect on children required answers to several questions, including the following: (1) To what extent do children pay attention to commercials? (2) What, if any, effects do commercials have on children's thinking processes? (3) Can they, for example, distinguish between fact and fantasy in a commercial? (4) What, if any, influence do children exert on their parents' buying as a result of commercials?

Government, foundations, ad agencies, and other businesses have spent a lot of money to answer these and similar questions. Research by advertisers and ad agencies, however, is devoted understandably to one purpose: to determine how to make better and more persuasive messages. Although their results are usually kept secret, we are beginning to get some answers to these questions from outside researchers. There is now a corpus of some 50 years of rigorous research on children and advertising that offers guidance for scholars, parents, and advertisers.[38]

To date, the findings suggest that the younger the child, the fuller the attention he or she pays to commercials. However, their trust in commercials declines with age.[39] Very young children do not know the difference between TV commercials and programs. They pay a good deal of attention even to commercials that would seem to be irrelevant to them, such as ads for beer or household cleaning products. Perhaps they are simply using the commercial to learn about what is unfamiliar to them. As they get older, children pay less and less attention to commercials, and by the time they are adolescents they usually scorn them. The evidence so far indicates that children do pressure their parents to buy the products they have seen advertised. Overall, however, we do not yet know enough about advertising's effects on children, and many questions have yet to be explored in depth.

Meanwhile, critics such as parent groups are taking their concerns to the government and seeking controls on advertising. In the controversy over advertising appeals to children, particular media (such as television) have debated with consumer groups and government. The *Wall Street Journal* has noted that, while network television had high standards for children's advertising, independent stations usually did not. While the networks barred the over-glamorization of a product or the use of exhortative language such as "Ask Mom to buy...," independent stations were quite lax on these and other points. As criticism mounted, the Better Business Bureau continued to urge local TV stations to be more vigilant, and eventually the board of the Association of Independent Television Stations endorsed guidelines for children's advertising. Finally, the U.S. Senate passed legislation to limit the number of commercials aired during children's programs.[40] Several important research centers have been developed where issues involving children's media and media use are probed extensively. Since mid-2005, two of them, the Joan Ganz Cooney Center for Children and Television in New York (named for the founder of Sesame Street) and the Fred Rogers Center for Early

Childhood Education and Children's Media, in Latrobe, Pennsylvania (named for the iconic "Mr. Rogers"), have organized vigorous research and policy programs.

Sources of Control

Whatever the general effects of advertising, the content of many advertisements has often been attacked for being in poor taste, making exaggerated claims, and using annoying hucksterisms. As a result of these specific sins, some controls on American advertising have developed. Shabby practices led to a gradual erosion of the ancient principle of *caveat emptor* ("let the buyer beware") toward one of *caveat venditor* ("let the seller beware")—that is, toward regulation. Advertisers today live with certain constraints, some imposed by the government and some by the industry itself.

REGULATION BY GOVERNMENT.   As early as 1911, *Printer's Ink*, an industry magazine, called for greater attention to ethics in advertising and proposed a model statute that made fraudulent and misleading advertising a misdemeanor. Before long, with a strong push from the Better Business Bureau, most states enacted it as law. Although there is doubt about its effectiveness, the statute was a statement on advertising ethics as well as being a standard-setter. A few years later, in 1914, the Federal Trade Commission (FTC) also set up some ground rules for advertising. In administrative rulings over the years, the FTC has written rules related to puffery, taste, and guarantees in advertising claims. At times the FTC has demanded "effective relief" for those wronged by misleading advertising and has levied fines against companies engaging in unfair, misleading, and otherwise deceptive advertising.

The Federal Communications Commission also scrutinizes advertising. In addition, several other federal agencies, including the Food and Drug Administration, the U.S. Postal Service, the Securities and Exchange Commission, and the Alcohol and Tobacco Tax Division of the Internal Revenue Service, influence advertising. State and local governments have passed laws on advertising for lotteries, obscenity in ads, occupational advertising, and other matters. Government controls over advertising relaxed considerably in the era of industry deregulation for some thirty years, since the late 1980s.

INDUSTRY CODES OF ETHICS.   In the private sector, various advertising organizations and individual industries have developed codes of ethics to govern advertising. The broadcasting industry, for example, has codes that set standards for the total amount of non-program material and commercial interruptions per time period. (However, a long-standing limit controlling the amount of time commercials could air for each hour of programming for adults was relaxed considerably during the deregulation of broadcasting.) In fact, say some critics, today some programs are, in fact, hour-long paid advertisements. Most of these air late at night and promote business-success schemes, real-estate deals, "classic" record collections, and other products and schemes. In many states, local industry organizations such as advertising review committees and fair-advertising groups promote truth in advertising. The National Advertising Review Council promotes ethical advertising and fights deception, and the Better Business Bureau prepares reports of particular firms and their advertising.

COURT RULINGS.   In recent years, both the public and private sectors have followed closely various court decisions regarding whether or to what degree the First Amendment's guarantee of freedom of speech and the press extends to advertising. To date, the courts have distinguished between advertising that promotes one's views, which is *protected* by the First Amendment, and advertising that is designed only for commercial gain, which is *not*—although at times it is difficult to separate the two. This is being modified, however, as a doctrine of commercial speech has developed in the courts, which has defined the rights of businesses to communicate their views. Typically, courts have stoutly defended what they call "political speech," or expression that promotes public discussion of public affairs. The courts have until recently been less kind to "commercial speech," which is aimed at selling products. Now all of that is changing as commentators recognize that separating public and private speech is difficult at best. These lines have been somewhat blurred, however, and courts, especially when dealing with advertising that promotes special interests and causes, have been quite permissive.

CONSUMER GROUPS.   In addition, many consumer groups monitor advertising and protest when they object to particular content. These groups range from the Action for Children's Television, which opposes much of the advertising aimed at children, to religious groups that object to newspaper ads soliciting sex.

Advertisers have in the past responded to public criticism, and advertising itself has undergone constant change. For example, for many years radio and television commercials included very few African Americans, Latinos, and others. When they did appear, they were often shown in trivial or demeaning roles. But by the late 1960s, advertisements began to portray people of color more frequently and more realistically. Today, minorities are frequently seen in all forms of advertising. Similar changes have begun to take place in the portrayals of women, who have typically been shown in domestic situations or in sexually suggestive portrayals. The same is true of older people, who are the objects of overt ageism.[41] This has attracted greater interest as the baby boomer generation (born between 1946 and 1964) grew older, with many now in their sixties. The United States is rapidly approaching a time when some 20% of the population will be over sixty-five, as people live longer. Some critics have called this "the singular demographic of our time," thus underscoring the ageist concerns.[42]

It is likely that the debate over ethnic, sexual, and ageist stereotyping in advertising will continue for a long time. Many advertisers appeal blatantly to sexual desire, and much of what they put before the public is clearly sexist. Occasionally various groups representing women, religion, and other social forces protest and even boycott particular products. Because advertisers almost always want to avoid controversy—after all, they want to sell products, not enrage consumers—some of these protests have worked.

Once, sex appeal in advertising was largely aimed at men and exploited women in the process; yet this has changed in recent years as suggestive poses of men are now commonly featured, displaying males as sex objects appealing to gay male audiences, as well as to women. Just how influential sexual portrayals are is a matter of debate. Some argue that they affect consumer behavior, especially in clothing, hairstyles, and grooming products, but it is possible, of course, that advertising does not influence people as much as its critics claim. Sociologist Michael Schudson argues that advertising rarely has a chance to create consumer wants but instead reinforces those that already exist. In assessing the role of advertising in American society, Schudson asserts that:

1. Advertising serves a useful informational function that will not and should not be abandoned.
2. Advertising probably has a socially democratizing influence, but it is one with an ultimate egalitarian outcome.
3. Some advertising promotes dangerous products or promotes potentially dangerous products to groups unlikely to be able to use them wisely.
4. Non-price advertising often promotes bad values, whether it effectively sells products or not.
5. Advertising could survive and sell goods without promoting values as bad as those it favors now.
6. Advertising is but one factor among many in shaping consumer choice and human values.[43]

Critics who object not to specific aspects of some advertisements but to advertising's broader effects on individuals, society, and the economy will not see the changes they desire any time soon. Government is unlikely to impose stringent controls. Advertisers are likely to continue to appeal to our desires to be attractive, liked, and somehow better than our neighbors—in short, to have more or better or just about anything, whatever may be the psychological, cultural, or economic effects of these appeals so long as they think the messages work. Furthermore, advertisers are likely to continue to engulf us with their messages unless there are monumental changes in the economy and society.

All of the above considerations lead to a reaffirmation of our central thesis: The media, the economy, advertising, and the population as consumers are inextricably linked in a deeply institutionalized way. Thus, advertising is a central social institution in our society.

CHAPTER REVIEW

- Advertising is involved in virtually all aspects of digital communication in its creation, development, and distribution.
- Advertising agencies make heavy use of digital media, and there are even digital agencies.
- Social networking and search advertising are highly touted and growing in the midst of virtually all media integrating digital technologies.
- Advertising is a form of controlled communication about a particular product (or service), which attempts to persuade an appropriate audience, through the use of a variety of appeals and strategies, to adopt a belief or to make a decision to perform an action, such as to buy or use a product or service.
- Advertising is essential to both the nation's economy and to its mass media, for which it is the media's principal source of revenue. Without that revenue, American's would not have their current great variety of mass communication content from which to choose.
- Advertising began long ago, but it expanded greatly as the industrial revolution came with its expansion of consumer goods. Advertising for such products as patent medicines led the way and proved how successful it could be. Advertising product brands has an even larger place in the economy. The development of department stores and nationally circulated magazines were important milestones in the field's history.
- As the need for advertising grew, agencies were developed to provide services to both the media of the time and to those who wanted to market their products. Today, there are three major types of such groups: large and small "creative boutique" advertising agencies, media service organizations (also called specialist agencies), and in-house advertising departments.
- Today, advertising agencies are composed of managers, writers, artists, researchers, and other specialists. Boutique agencies and various media service organizations offer more limited, specialized services.
- Advertising researchers study various categories of consumers, focusing on their lifestyles and the characteristics that can lead them to purchase specific products. They also investigate the influences of specific advertising campaigns and test which ads might be most effective.
- Virtually any medium via which a persuasive message can be brought to the attention of some segment of the public can be used to transmit advertising messages. These include the usual mass media as well as many kinds of specialized forms—such as matchbook covers, billboards, blimps, subway posters, and many others.
- Advertisers use both psychodynamic strategies, with both rational and emotional appeals, and sociocultural strategies, based on conforming to cultural requirements to develop persuasive messages. Cutting through the clutter and gaining attention is one of the advertisers' most difficult tasks.

STRATEGIC QUESTIONS

1. What influence and impact does advertising have in modern society? What is its major function, and is that changing?
2. What impact is the digital revolution having on the advertising industry?
3. What are advertising media, and which are the most important ones today?
4. What is the function of advertising agencies, and how do they work?
5. What are the benefits and disadvantages of advertising for individuals and society? What do scholars and critics say? What do you think?
6. Does the public require protection from advertisers and advertising? How so?

KEY CONCEPTS & TERMS

ENDNOTES

1. Joe Plummer, Steve Rappaport, et al. *Online Advertising Playbook* (New York: John Wiley & Sons, 2007), Julius Wieldelmann, *Advertising Now, Online* (Cologne, Germany: Taschen, 2006), see also World Digital Media Trends at www.wan-press.org.

2. See www.anomalynyc.com/people for a discussion on Anomaly digital advertising agency and CEO Carl Johnson; see also John Michelet, et al., *Advertising Industry in Peril* (Chicago: Olympian Publishing, Inc. 2006).

3. Randall Rothenberg, Reynolds Journalism Institute seminar on "Imagining The Future of News", ILC-USA, June 27, 2008.

4. Interactive Advertising Trends, "Ten Trends in Digital Advertising for 2008," http://interactivemarketingtrends. blogspot.com.

5. David M. Potter, *People of Plenty*, 2nd ed. (Chicago: University of Chicago Press, 1969), p. 172.

6. Jane E. Brody, "In Adolescents, Addiction to Alcohol Comes Easy," *New York Times*, Feb. 12, 2008, www.nytimes.com/ 2008/02/12/health

7. Stephen Fox, *The Mirror Makers: A History of American Advertising and Its Creators* (New York: Morrow, 1984), pp. 13–39.

8. Ellen Gruber Garvey, *The Adman in the Parlor: Magazines and the Gendering of Consumer Culture, 1880s to 1910* (New York: Oxford University Press, 1996), p. 8.

9. The historical examples discussed in these sections are drawn from Fox, *The Mirror Makers*, pp. 13–39.

10. Potter, *People of Plenty*, p. 168. For an excellent cultural critique of advertising, see, "Advertising and Culture," in Robin Anderson and Lance Strate, eds., *Critical Studies in Media Commercialism* (New York: Oxford University Press, 2000).

11. *2006 Fact Pack, 4th Annual Guide to Advertising & Marketing* (New York: Crain Communications, Inc. 2006), p. 11.

12. U.S. Department of Labor, Bureau of Labor Statistics, Advertising and Public Relations Services, www.bls.gov, see pp. 1–2.

13. *2006 Fact Pack,* op cit, passim.

14. William F. Arens, *Advertising*, 6th ed. (Chicago: Irwin, 1996), pp. 76-80; Al Ries and Laura Ries, *The Fall of Advertising and the Rise of PR* (New York: Harper Business, 2002).

15. John S. Wright, et al. *Advertising*, 5th ed. (New York: McGraw-Hill), 1982, pp. 161–162; for a more contemporary treatment of the industry, see William D. Wells, John Burnett, and Sandra Moriarty, *Advertising: Principles and Practice*, 6th ed. (Englewood Cliffs, NJ: Prentice Hall, 2002).

16. Anomalynyc.com, op. cit.

17. Edmund Carey, presentation at Fordham Graduate School of Business, New York City, March 26, 2008, and subsequent conversation/interview.

18. "Define Digital Advertising for 2009," Jan. 1, 2009, at www.tribbleagency. com/?=3682.

19. Leo Bogart, *Commercial Culture, The Media System and the Public Interest* (New York: Oxford University Press, 1994).

20. *Media Private Market Value Estimates,* Paul Kagan Associates, Inc., 1992.

21. Internet Advertising Bureau, June 17, 2008, www.iab.net.

22. *Search Marketing Fact Pack 2007* (New York: Crain Communications, Inc., 2007).

23. Gerald R. Miller, "Persuasion," in Charles R. Berger and Steven H. Chafee, *Handbook of Communication Science* (Newbury Park, CA: Sage Publications, 1987), pp. 446-483; see also B. D. Till and D. W. Baack, "Recall and Persuasion: Does Creative Advertising Matter? *Journal of Advertising,* 2005, 34 (3), 47-57.

24. Melvin L. DeFleur and Sandra Ball Rokeach, "Theoretical Strategies for Persuasion," *Theories of Mass Communication,* 5th ed. (White Plains, NY: Longman, 1989), pp. 272–293.

25. John Phillip Jones, *What's in a Name: Advertising and the Concepts of Brands* (Lexington, MA: Lexington Books, 1986), p. 141.

26. Michael Siegal and Lois Biener, "The Impact of an Anti-Smoking Media Campaign on Progression to Established Smoking:

A Longitudinal Study," *The American Journal of Public Health,* 90, 2000, p. 384.

27. Norman Douglas, *South Wind* (1917), in *Bartlett's Familiar Quotations,* 13th ed., (Boston: Little, Brown and Company, 1968), p. 840.

28. Gary Langer, ABC News, presentation at Age Boom Academy, Harvard Club of New York, June 5, 2008.

29. Siegal and Biener, "The Impact of an Anti-Smoking Media Campaign," pp. 47–48.

30. Russell H. Colley, *Defining Advertising Goals for Measured Advertising Results* (New York: Association of National Manufacturers, 1961), p. 35.

31. Colley, *Defining Advertising Goals,* p. 38.

32. Wright, et al., *Advertising,* p. 392.

33. Otto Kleppner, *Advertising Procedure,* 7th ed. (Englewood Cliffs, NJ: Prentice Hall, 1985), pp. 301-302.

34. Daniel Pope, *The Making of Advertising* (New York: Basic Books, 1983), pp. 289–290; see also Kim B. Rotzoll and James E. Haefner, *Advertising in Contemporary Society* (Cincinnati: South-Western, 1986).

35. John S. Wright and John E. Mertes, *Advertising's Role in Society* (St. Paul, MN: West, 1974), pp. vii-viii.

36. Wright and Mertes, *Advertising's Role,* pp. vii-viii.

37. John Kenneth Galbraith, "Economics and Advertising: Exercise in Denial," *Advertising Age,* Nov. 9, 1988, p. 81.

38. Norma Pecora, John Marray, and Ellen Wartella, *Children & Television: Fifty Years of Research* (Mahwah, NJ: Lawrence Erlbaum Associates, 2006).

39. For an extended discussion of research evidence on television advertising and children, see Pecora, Murray, and Wartella, op. cit, 2006, and Robert M. Liebert, Joyce N. Sprafkin, and Emily S. Davidson, *The Early Window: Effects of Television on Children and Youth,* 2nd ed. (New York: Pergamon Press, 1982), pp. 142-159.

40. Joanne Lipman, "Double Standard for Kids' TV Ads," *Wall Street Journal,* June 10, 1988, sec. 2, p. 1. See also "Congress Approves Limiting TV Ads Aimed at Children," *Wall Street Journal,* Oct. 20, 1988, sec. 2, p. 6.

41. *Ageism in America* (New York: International Longevity Center, 2006).

42. Robert N. Butler, *The Longevity Revolution* (New York: Public Affairs, 2008).

43. Michael Schudson, *Advertising, The Uneasy Persuasion: Its Dubious Impact on American Society* (New York: Basic Books, 1984), pp. 239–241.

Public Relations: Influencing Beliefs, Attitudes, and Actions

The changes in media and society linked to digital communication are having a profound effect on the public relations field. When modern PR firms and their practitioners are asked to specify their "practice areas," they often list digital public relations as a specialty along with corporate reputation, marketing communications, or corporate social responsibility. Up close, public relations professionals and the organizations they work for, which we'll discuss later, engage in Internet strategy audits, digital PR campaigns, online media use, building online communities, setting up virtual pressrooms, or placing Internet advertising. A 2007 report on the state of the public relations industry declared, "Digital and social media spending presents a major opportunity for public relations firms."[1] A survey of PR professionals ranked the "proliferation of new media communication channels: including text messaging, MySpace, etc." as highest among six industry trends examined, ranking it at 4.51 on a 5-point scale.[2] While digital connections are now very much on the radar screen for people in the public relations field, with some arguing that considering it a separate practice area makes no more sense than trying to separate digital media from media generally, it is still acknowledged that "most public relations firms are not there yet," though social media is "the biggest single driver of revenue growth."[3] Commentators have argued recently that "if advertising is the wind, PR is the sun," and they say that, in the balance and integration between these two related fields, we are experiencing "the fall of advertising and the rise of PR," though this is somewhat overstated, as we'll explain later in this chapter, which introduces public relations as a concept and social influence as well as an industry and a profession. Its integral relationship with the media is also explored from its early history to the present day.

Digital PR strategies usually involve search engine optimization (getting one's message on Google and other search sites), blogging/blogger relations (getting the message on key blogs), and social media (using Facebook, MySpace, and other platforms for messages). One firm, Bliss PR, says its PR digital strategy engages its digital team to help clients enter the digital dialogue and to:

- Monitor and evaluate relevant online media conversations.
- Engage with key influencers in the blogosphere.
- Develop corporate blogs, social network sites, and multimedia tools.
- Plan the design and develop the content for corporate websites.
- Optimize communications for effective distribution in the digital space.[4]

One organization that received an award for its digital PR strategy was Scouting for Girls, a British organization, that used its website to set up live "Wolfclubs" for members and offered audio, video, blogs, and even a photo gallery—all interactive. The site was meant to connect scouts and their families but also to recruit others and establish a strong image as a "cool" space for girls to network about music, vote in MTV contests, and hook up with scouts in other places, such as Berlin.

For centuries those in power have sought ways to influence the beliefs, attitudes, and actions of their followers by using effective communication strategies. Almost universally, their goal was to inspire awe and respect on the part of their supporters and fear on the part of their enemies. Today, the purposes behind many public pronouncements and displays of power are for reasons of *publicity*—expanding the number of people who are aware of some person, policy, or program. Public relations is also often associated with **propaganda**, that is persuasive communications designed to gain people's approval—or, as we might say today, to capture their hearts and minds—concerning some action taken or planned, some individual, or some decision that has been made. (The term "propaganda" originally referred to the Roman Catholic Church's efforts to "propagate the faith" through the communication efforts of missionaries, which in many respects was a kind of public relations campaign.) As we will explain later, public relations today is far more than publicity and propaganda, but that is clearly where it began. The U.S. Department of Labor, for example, acknowledges the importance of public relations, stating, "An organization's reputation, profitability, and even its continued existence can depend on the degree to which its targeted 'publics' support its goals and policies."[5]

Publicity and propaganda are time-honored objectives. Certainly both played major roles in the American colonies before the Revolution, when "committees of correspondence" (patriots advocating separation from England) sought to win the support of the public. Also, many American presidents have had a need to sway public opinion in a direction favorable for their policies. Abraham Lincoln, for example, had a definite "public relations problem" with his Emancipation Proclamation of 1862. It freed all slaves in states and territories at war with the Union but not in those fighting on the northern side. Several states not in the Confederacy were reluctant to give up the idea of slavery, and Lincoln had a "hard sell." If he had been able to use public opinion polls at the time (they did not exist) he might never have issued his Proclamation until he prepared the population for it with public relations efforts. Similarly, in 1939 President Franklin D. Roosevelt began (unsuccessfully at first) to convince the American people that it was in the country's best interests to come to the aid of the British in their fight against Adolf Hitler. By 1941, he had begun to turn the situation around with his speeches and policies. However, the need was eliminated after the Japanese bombed the Pacific fleet at Pearl Harbor. After another surprise attack on U.S. soil on September 11, 2001, President George W. Bush's approval ratings soared and set the stage for the Iraq War, which later lost public favor. During the twentieth century, other national leaders such as Gandhi, Martin Luther King, John F. Kennedy, and Ronald Reagan became masters of communications designed to promote approval of their political and policy goals. During his impeachment crisis in the 1990s, Bill Clinton's masterful public relations kept his approval ratings high, even as his reputation in Congress plummeted. Thus, throughout both ancient and recent times, efforts to change public beliefs, attitudes, and behaviors through the use of effective communication strategies have been a part of human society.

THE DEVELOPMENT OF PUBLIC RELATIONS

As a professional field, public relations (using that actual term) has a much briefer history. It grew out of reactions to the "public be damned" attitude that characterized American big business at the turn of the twentieth century. As the 1900s began, the "captains of industry" who ran the nation's corporations did as they pleased regardless of what people thought. Eventually, however, the public became aroused over their excesses—especially after many of their practices were exposed by the "muckraker" journalists of the time. To counter this negative trend, many of the large corporations began to use public relations in one form or another to head off confrontations.[6]

MEDIA LEADERS INSIGHTS: PUBLIC RELATIONS

REBECCA LOWELL EDWARDS

Group Senior Vice President

Ruder Finn

With a career that included newspaper reporting, public relations, and the nonprofit sector, Rebacca Lowell Edwards leads the Branding Practice at Ruder Finn, a leading public relations firm where she focuses on communication strategies and specializes in corporater reputation and corporate social responsibility. Building on earlier experience as a reporter at the *Wall Street Journal* and Dow Jones News Service, she worked several years for Ruder Finn, left to join a PR firm that specialized in health and religion, and also served as senior communications officer for a foundation. She was recruited back to Ruder Finn, which elevated her to senior vice president, acknowledging her work on such award-winning and long-lasting PR campaigns as "Start Healthy, Stay Healthy," for the Gerber account. A graduate of Georgetown's School of Foreign Service, she also has an MBA from Fordham.

1. When and under what circumstances did you first realize the import of new media or the digital age?

   In early 1997, my husband joined the staff of TheStreet.com as a reporter. The idea of a news organization that existed solely on the Web was a real eye-opener for me. Of course, I was skeptical at first, but the fact that the operation was attraction seasoned journalists and promising and (ultimately) delivering high-quality analysis and information made me realize that we were on the brink a real paradigm shift in media.

2. What impact did that experience have on you personally or professionally?

   At that time, I was working at the Dow Jones News Service, a wire whose value proposition is providing news and information in real time. So, personally I was acutely aware of the competitive concerns of another outlet that was threatening to scoop me on stories. Additionally, I was in graduate school at Fordham studying the business of media. Therefore, I was intensely curious about what a low-cost provider of news would do to the previously stable field of competitors (Bloomberg, Dow Jones, Reuters). Of course, I could have never predicted the tremendous impact that digital media would have more broadly on traditional media beyond wires services.

3. How has it influenced the public relations field generally, especially agencies likle Ruder Finn?

   Being a communication consultant has always required a continuing-education approach. As people evolve in the way they communicate, we have to consider how best to tab into the latest topics and trends. However, the innovation possible through digital media seems to grow exponentially. Therefore, It's incredibly exciting but also very challenging to keep up. And you cannot sit on the sidelines and expect to gain an appreciation and understanding for it. Certainly, agencies like Ruder Finn that have always encouraged a mingling of personal and professional creativity are better positioned to meet these opportunities.

4. To what extent is digital PR separate from or integrated into agencies and other public relations activities and services?

   I think agencies are reallyl struggling with how to integrate public relations through digital media and traditional media activities. Some have appointed heads of digital or social media who work in isolation from the traditional media spectialists. I believe, as do my colleagues at RF, that you cannot separate the two. When considering how to carry a message to a particular audience, you have to consider both the type of content and the desired recipient. How best will the message be carried and received? Therefore, It's ideal to look at the full continuum of possibilities from traditional print and broadcast to newer social and digital media channels. Of course, when it comes to implementing a strategy, it is helpful to rely on experts who understand specifically how to execute in one form or the other.

5. Are you optimistic about the digital future?

   I am extremely optimistic about the digital future. Already, we've seen impact of digital media in making communication from one to many and many to many extremely efficient and accessible. In the U.S., it has changed the political process by allowing grassroots mobilization to take place swiftly. Of course, it's a bit painful to watch what

continued

it's doing to the traditional print media. Yet considering the mission of journalism to provide the public with news, information, and analysis, it seems clear that journalism and digital media should enjoy a symbiotic relationship.

6. What, if any, advice do you have for a person who aspires to a career in the public relations or corporate relations fields?

Don't become a one-trick pony. Sure, you should follow your interests far enough to develop a particular area of expertise. However, it is better to think of your expertise as a window or framework for understanding the big picture. There are subject-matter, industry, and communications-area experts. Yet those who succeed know how to draw upon that expertise to develop insights and perspectives on issues beyond their comfort zone.

Birth of the Public Relations Agency

A forerunner of the modern public relations *agency* was the Publicity Bureau of Boston, founded in 1900 by three former newspapermen. They established an important pattern in the way that public relations services were provided for clients. For a fee they would promote a company's causes and business interests by getting favorable stories in the newspapers and by other forms of *managed communication*. The bureau's early clients included AT&T, Harvard University, Fore River Shipyard, and Boston Elevated (trolley lines).

By 1911 the Bureau had died, but other public relations and press agencies quickly formed. For example, publicist and former journalist Ivy Lee, after working for political candidates and the Pennsylvania Railroad, recognized the value for businesses of a positive public image and the possibilities of creating such an image systematically through favorable publicity. He set up a firm providing services that we would now call public relations activities to help businesses communicate with the public. His clients eventually included what was perhaps the most famous of all "captains of industry," John D. Rockefeller, Jr., and his infamous Standard Oil Company. Among his famous PR coups was softening the company's image after the infamous Ludlow massacre in Colorado, where hired guards attacked union protesters. Another early publicist was Pendleton Dudley, who at Lee's urging opened an office on Wall Street. According to Scott Cutlip, Dudley denied that early public relations efforts were in direct response to the muckraking journalists.

During these early days, public relations specialists were called "publicity men," or sometimes "press agents." In 1919, the newspapers of New York took a census of the number who worked regularly in that capacity in the city and found that there were about twelve hundred actively employed.[7] Furthermore, their functions were well understood by that time. Journalism scholar Walter Lippmann noted that it was their task to use the media (mainly newspapers at the time) to provide the public with "interpretations" of events related to their clients:

> The development of the publicity man is a clear sign that the facts of modern life do not spontaneously take a shape in which they can be known. They must be given a shape by somebody, and since in the daily routine reporters cannot give a shape to facts, and since there is little disinterested organization of intelligence, the need for some formulation is being met by [press agents and publicity people].[8]

Thus, there was a thriving public relations industry by the time of World War I. Its professional communicators performed the same services as their modern counterparts. However, these communicators had only the print media with which to work as they attempted to create favorable meanings and images among the public for those they represented.

Today, the field of public relations has grown into a sophisticated and complex occupational field, with a large part of the work carried out either by relatively large agencies mostly owned by international holding companies or by public relations departments in many kinds of corporations, government agencies, or non-profits. However, some old-fashioned publicity agents (still using that name) continue to work, especially in New York City, serving the needs of people and groups in such high-visibility fields as the entertainment and fashion industries. Increasingly, though, celebrities, once the main clients for publicity agents, work with large talent management firms, which have a range of services to offer.

Defining Public Relations Today

Although it is a complex field, it is not difficult to define the basic nature of public relations in terms of what its practitioners actually do. Public relations is an organized communication process, conducted by people who make a living as professional communicators. It can be defined in terms of conducting the following activities:

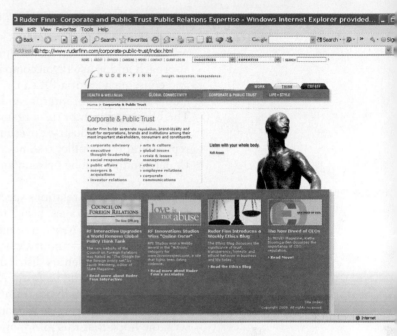

The public relations firm Ruder Finn maintains an inviting website, using the technology of web 2.0.

Paid professional practitioners design and transmit messages, for behalf of a client, via a variety of media to relevant and targeted audiences in an attempt to influence their beliefs, attitudes, or even actions regarding some person, organization, policy, situation, or event.

While this is a complex definition, it sets forth the basics of what practitioners actually do. However, it does not provide enough details so that non-specialists can actually understand the field in greater depth. Taking each of the ideas in the definition and explaining them more fully will help. Adding texture here, the U.S. Department of Labor says "public relations specialists—also referred to as communications specialists and media specialists, among other titles—serve as advocates for businesses, nonprofit associations, universities, hospitals, and other organizations" as they "build and maintain relationships with the public."[9]

PRACTITIONERS. Professional public relations practitioners are usually people whose education and perhaps prior employment has been in a field in which writing and producing other forms of messages have been major focuses. The best route has been a college degree in public relations, journalism, or other communications-related field. Such practitioners serve many types of clients. They may work in an agency that contracts for services, or they may be salaried employees of a corporation, government agency, or nonprofit group. They may have such titles as communications specialist, media specialist, information officer, press secretary, and even the unlikely term "evangelist" in the high-tech fields, but their activities are similar regardless of the setting in which they work or the clients they serve.

STRATEGIES. Increasingly, public relations firms and their personnel need to fashion a broad vision as they

Press Kits prepared by public relations firms—usually available online too—brief reporters and other media personnel on events, activities and issues.

think strategically about the public or stakeholders whom they will connect with on behalf of their clients. This means scoping out the role, image, and vision that the client wants to achieve—and marshaling the resources to make it happen. This is the overall approach and is usually accompanied with an evaluation plan through which the results and consequences of a PR campaign or overall PR services can be assessed. A strategy employs methods of internal and external communication to reach the various publics. The PR strategy embraces organizational functions such as outreach to media, community, consumer, industry, government relations, politics and elections, interest group representation, conflict resolution or mediation, and investor and employee relations. Understanding public opinion and attitudes of various stakeholders is crucial.[10]

MESSAGES.   Public relations specialists develop communication strategies and prepare many kinds of messages, using many kinds of media—including news releases and information campaigns. Most messages are of a routine nature. Examples are brochures that provide information about a corporation, government agency, or nonprofit group. Other examples are newsletters distributed to various "stakeholders," such as alumni, employees, stockholders, and so forth. An annual report on the status, finances, activities, and accomplishments of an organization is still another example. Public relations specialists also assist in preparing news stories and other information to be released to the press with the hope that this information will appear on the web or in the paper or news broadcast.

CLIENTS.   There are almost as many kinds of clients served by public relations practitioners as there are individuals and groups in the United States that produce materials and services for the public. These include corporations and industries that manufacture goods; local, state, and federal government agencies; the military; institutions that provide health-care services; investment firms; banks; schools, college; and universities; organized charities; religious groups; and so on. To this comprehensive list could be added public personalities, such as prominent actors, singers, politicians, preachers, and musicians who need a constant flow of publicity in order to foster beliefs about their importance on the part of the public.

MEDIA.   Virtually every kind of medium used for communication today plays some part in the activities of public relations specialists. Information is prepared and transmitted using newspapers, magazines, radio and television, and the Internet, where blogs, podcasts, and social networking operations are common. Increasingly, information about their client or employer is prepared for distribution via the Internet or through a virtual newsroom open to all media and the public. In addition, practitioners design special events, such as trade show displays and formal presentations of new products. They write speeches and magazine articles for their employers or clients. They provide briefings and talking points and hold practice interviews. They help prepare clients and employers for formal speeches, public appearances, and meetings with the press. In addition, their clients or employers may sponsor sports events—ranging from golf competitions to bass fishing contests—which are designed for public relations purposes.

In some cases, they prepare messages intended to achieve **damage control**. If an airplane crashes, a train derails, an oil tanker spills, or a scandal occurs, public relations specialists help to design messages aimed at limiting the negative consequences for their client. That does not mean that the public relations specialists either avoid responsibility or misrepresent the situation (which can happen in some cases). More often, they help design information releases or help management focus on steps that the public sees as meeting their responsibilities. Serious mistakes are made by those who try to cover up, deny, or lie about a bad situation.

One of the most famous cases of successful damage control was the Tylenol crisis of 1982, in which seven people in the Chicago area died after ingesting an Extra Strength Tylenol capsule laced with poisonous cyanide. The product had been contaminated after leaving the Johnson & Johnson plant where it was manufactured. In a now legendary PR response, the company alerted the public and exhibited complete candor as it recalled the product and told consumers not to use any Tylenol product until there was a full investigation and a plan for fail-safe product safety. Although it averted a nationwide panic, since Tylenol was the leading aspirin alternative with 37% of the market, Johnson & Johnson then had to plan a comeback for its product. It did so only because of its extraordinary openness with the news media, including full access to the company's top executives, and extensive advertising aimed at restoring public confidence. The PR plan included work with pharmacies and other stakeholders. The J&J response was almost universally praised for its thoroughness, speed of response, and integrity. This was a thoughtful, well-planned damage control public relations plan, was led by top management, and carried out by the company's public relations department with help from leading PR firms. Ultimately, the media were not only a conduit for the messages but a validator of them as well. This contrasts with other firms that have tried, at first, to cover up damaging or embarrassing messages only to be found out by consumers or the media.

During the 2008 presidential campaign, then-Senator Barack Obama faced a crisis that threatened to derail his bid for the presidency. Rev. Jeremiah Wright, Obama's fiery Chicago pastor, was the subject of a series of news reports portraying him as a dangerous radical with un-American proclivities, including a video clip repeated again and again on TV, cable, and YouTube crying out "God damn America." In a classic case of guilt-by-association, Obama's critics and rivals seized on his longtime relationship with the pastor suggesting he was thus unfit to be president. The issue involved race—Obama's and Wright's and the highly emotional style of the black church. It was believed this would turn off white voters and thus crush Obama's chances for the presidency. At first, Obama and his staff tried to explain that the charges against the pastor and the senator were unfair and unrepresentative. He then tried to distance himself from the pastor to no avail as Fox News and conservative news outlets hammered away. News about the pastor and old video clips were everywhere. Since the issue was race, a topic Obama had previously downplayed, he and his aides developed a damage control strategy to address race head on. He did so in a widely covered speech in Philadelphia, considered one of his best, which put racial issues in context and both offered an explanation for Wright's rhetoric as the product of his civil rights generation and separated Obama from it. The speech drew large audiences across the media and was part of Obama's successful use of social networking as well with information about it reaching supporters, campaign volunteers, funders, and others—as well as much of the general public. Before that, race had rarely been mentioned by Obama, who was to become the nation's first African American president, and he put the topic on the public agenda in a dramatic and reassuring way. Even though Rev. Wright was apparently angered by the speech and made speeches critical of Obama, crisis was averted. The Obama response to prejudice, distrust, and fear, even if unfair, was important to his winning subsequent primaries and caucuses, where race was often an unspoken issue. The speech became the template for what was a well-planned and executed public relations campaign.

AUDIENCES.   The messages developed and transmitted by public relations specialists are prepared for many different categories of people. Obviously, some are broadly defined and are intended to be read or viewed by the public at large—as in a news release prepared for the readers of a local newspaper or an interview designed as a TV news story. Beyond that are more narrowly defined groups, such as the constituents of an office holder, the employees of a large company, or the personnel of a major military organization. Another group might be the investors who hold stock in a large corporation. Sometimes the intended audience is very narrowly defined. For example, information may be prepared specifically for the surviving family members of an air crash or a military accident. In any of these cases, the public relations practitioner must understand the nature of that audience and the impression that will be made on them after receiving the specific information that is being prepared. Here polls, online surveys, focus groups, and other sources of intelligence—much of it online and readily available—are employed.

INFLUENCES.   The bottom line in public relations is to have the messages that are transmitted accomplish the purposes for which they were designed. There are many such purposes, and each depends on the complexities of the situation. For example, a long-range public relations campaign may be designed to alter the behavior of the public regarding some form of action that has national significance. Campaigns to prevent HIV/AIDs, combat childhood obesity, or conserve fuel are examples of usually transparent and quite direct public relations efforts, often associated with building a brand for the organization or product.

Many public relations messages have less dramatic goals. Many are designed to turn the public around regarding some person, issue, or event that has taken a negative turn. Historically, some corporations had deservedly bad reputations due to their ruthlessness or lack of concern for people. A strategy to change this image began with carefully articulated donations to charities or other philanthropic activity. Names like Carnegie, Rockefeller, and Nobel once had very bad reputations but today are associated with foundations or awards programs. In recent times Microsoft's Bill Gates, who had a reputation as a brilliant but cutthroat operator, greatly softened his image by creating the Bill and Melinda Gates Foundation. While substantive in nature, the act also had a PR effect. Even in the midst of controversy swirling around Microsoft, the Gates Foundation, the world's largest, has developed such a good reputation that when the financier Warren Buffet decided to give away his billions in 2007, he designated the Gates Foundation to dispense the funds.

The majority of PR messages are quite ordinary, often prepared to inform as well as to set a positive, persuasive tone. They may consist of a news story concerning a new CEO taking over the reins of a corporation, the release of a new model of a product, an explanation of a new policy by a government official, or a briefing about a campaign by a military spokesperson.

PR–Media Interplay

Too much cannot be said about the interplay between the media and public relations. On the one hand, public relations is a communications process, closely related to the lessons of communication theory; on the other, it is also a practical reality—and media are among its chief platforms for delivering messages, as we've discussed earlier in the chapter. But the relationship between media and public relations is symbiotic, each depending on the other. Without news, entertainment, and opinion media, public relations would have little chance of reaching large masses and smaller specialized audiences with its persuasive messages. And by the same token, the media depend on PR for news, information, and data that become the sources of content. Strip away all the material in the media that has either come from or been facilitated by public relations and there would be very little content left.

When people consider the interplay between the media and PR, they typically think of the conventional news media—newspapers, magazines, radio, TV, cable, and even books. But the digital world, as we have explained, is playing an increasingly important role in public relations through email and instant messages to tweets from Twittering to websites, blogs, and social networking. At the same time, PR agencies on behalf of their clients also work with entertainment media, including television productions and movies, trying to push positive images and portrayals. There has been much effort over the years to advance women's rights, as well as racial, ethnic, and sexual orientation equality. In the health-care field, PR officers and consultants try to reach Hollywood screenwriters, for example. And, quite naturally, PR people assist their clients in meeting with newspaper and magazine editorial boards or the producers of politically charged radio and cable talk shows. PR has certainly mastered media relations from the oldest to the newest form of media.

Public Relations versus Advertising

The above discussion may make public relations and advertising seem somewhat alike. Like advertising, public relations is a controlled communication process in a sense that it is planned and organized and depends in large part on the mass media to convey its messages. But unlike advertising, which makes use of *purchased slots of media space and time,* public relations does not have such easy access to mass communications. Some critics call advertising space "captive media," because an advertiser buys and uses it according to his or her own discretion. Public relations messages, on the other hand, do not use space or time purchased so that messages will appear in the media. Instead, the messages are offered persuasively to editors, news directors, and others who then determine whether that information is worth including in their agenda. Of course, advertising and PR can play off each other. As Al and Laura Ries have written in a provocative book, "PR has credibility. Advertising does not. PR provides the positive perceptions that an advertising campaign, if properly directed, can exploit."[11]

Although some public relations campaigns involve advertisements, such as those that promote tourism or the general integrity of a corporation like Pfizer, the pharmaceutical giant, public relations specialists often use more indirect, persuasive means to build a favorable climate of opinion or achieve other goals. Moreover, public relations efforts are not always identifiable. We know an advertisement when we see it on television or in a magazine, but we do not always know the source of a news article or the staging of a golf tournament, bowling contest, or other public event—even though these events may be a part of a carefully planned public relations campaign. Rarely do public relations people announce exactly what they are doing or for what purposes. Thus, while public relations personnel may use advertising as part of their overall activities, they are much more involved than advertisers in the total process of communication, from initiating the message to getting feedback from the public.

In summary, public relations is a complex professional field in which paid communicators design and distribute messages for a great variety of purposes. Overall, it is a field representing a very broad spectrum of communication activities. Some activities are clearly essential for the adequate functioning of the society. Others are less significant, except to the people involved. In either case, public relations is deeply dependent on the mass media. Through the activities of its practitioners, much of what is learned by the public about people, activities, and organizations in their society is generated to accomplish one or more of its goals. In the final analysis, then, public relations is a set of strategies for *deliberately manipulating meanings* in ways that are not always apparent to the target audience, so as to influence the audience's interpretations of a person, group, or policy represented by the communicator. This does not necessarily mean, however, that such manipulation is deceptive or unethical.

PUBLIC RELATIONS SETTINGS AND ACTIVITIES

Public relations professionals go by many names and are found virtually everywhere—in the private sector in business, industry, charities, churches, labor unions, and so on. In the public sector they are in all levels of government from the White House to the local school or fire station. The number of people employed in public relations is impressive. The U.S. Department of Labor estimated in 1970 that there were some 76,000 public relations specialists in the United States. By 2004, this had grown to 188,000 jobs. This is a very low estimate because the figures include only the rather narrow category of "public relations specialists" and does not necessary include a whole range of other people associated with the public relations function both within and outside of business. In contrast, the U.S. Bureau of the Census reports that more than half a million persons are currently engaged in various forms of public relations work.

Conventions and corporate trade shows and exhibitions are a major public relations and promotional tool. People come together to advance their cause and meet others in their field at these events. These events have exhibitions halls, like this one at the Taipei World Trade Centreon which held the "Information Technology Month," where vendors display products.

The Public Relations Industry

As a business, public relations had humble beginnings, with a single practitioner and sometimes an assistant. In modern times, it has expanded into large international holding companies that have advertising agencies and PR firms under the same roof. Four major multinational players have emerged. These are Omnicom Group, WPP Group, Interpublic Group of Companies, and Publicis Groupe. Each has some well-known international PR firms under its roof, including:

- **WPP** – Burson-Marsteller, Cohn & Wolfe, GCI Group, Hill & Knowlton, and Ogilvy Public Relations Worldwide.
- **Omnicom** – Brodeur Pleon, Fleischman-Hillard, Ketchum, and Porter Novelli.
- **Interpublic** – GolinHarris, WeberShadwick, and IMG's Constituency Management Group.
- Other important players include Edelman, Inc., the world's largest independent PR firm, and Ruder Finn.[12]

Public relations activities are conducted in a variety of organized ways. Most are carried out as team efforts by various kinds of groups. Perhaps most common is the *public relations counselor* or *agency*. This person or organization operates much like an advertising agency or law firm, taking on clients and representing them by conducting public relations activities on their behalf. The client may be an individual who wants better understanding from the public or a large company that wants an experienced firm that can provide special services. These services may include conducting research and designing publications to help the company's own in-house public relations staff. Agencies represent only a relatively small part of this labor force.

Somewhat related is the *public relations department* within particular businesses, industries, or other settings. These departments act as part of the overall management team and attempt to interpret the firm to the public and internal constituents. A public relations department will also provide channels for feedback from the public to management. In the industry, these departments are expected to contribute to the firm's profits by helping it achieve its overall business goals. The public relations department of General Motors, for example, sets communication goals to support and enhance the corporation's economic achievements. Public relations departments of a similar nature also exist within nonprofit or educational institutions. Publicity for organizations such as colleges and labor unions usually involves a range of internal and external activities, from publications to fund drives.

Public relations departments also provide services within governmental agencies. This can be at the federal, state, or even local level. In government, the terms "public information" and "public affairs" refer to any activity that communicates the purposes and work of an agency to the general public or to users of the agency's services. For example, welfare recipients need to know about the policies of the state social services department, and taxpayers need to know how their money is being spent. Similarly, a metropolitan police department typically has a "public affairs" department to provide information about its services and accomplishments to citizens.

Other individuals who carry out organized public relations activities are *specialized consultants*. These people range from political advisors who work exclusively on public relations problems during election campaigns to information specialists who are experts in communications in a specific field such as health, transportation, or insurance.

Movie favorite Reese Witherspoon takes part in the Avon Walk for Breast Cancer, which reflects the cosmetics firm's corporate social responsibility.

Policy consultants provide a related form of organized public relations activity. These specialists suggest and design courses of action to public and private institutions that want to develop a policy for the use of information resources. These types of institutions may want to influence the policies of Congress or the Federal Communications Commission, or develop an early warning system to assess and trace the influences of a particular issue or program on corporate clients. This is a new area of public relations that has expanded considerably, sometimes in PR firms, sometimes in lobbying organizations, whose sole purpose is to influence public officials.

Finally, the field includes communication specialists in *technical areas*. For example, in Chapter 7 we discussed television consultants who try to improve the ratings of a radio station's news programs. Others include specialized firms that work with corporate clients to help them better understand and work with television, training programs for company presidents who serve as spokespersons, and placement services that get corporate clients on the air in various cities. Technical specialists also include graphics practitioners who provide full-service publication assistance, producing publicity messages that fit into an organization's overall public relations plan.

As in any dynamic industry, new ways of accomplishing goals constantly emerge. For example, a number of advertising agencies have recently acquired many established public relations firms or have set up new ones within their own organizations. Many public relations practitioners and media critics fear that public relations, if it becomes a branch of advertising, will become a servant of product promotion and not maintain ethical practices. They assert that the credibility of an independent public relations agency is greater than that of a public relations program under an advertising agency.

Recent changes in the communication industry have complicated the world of public relations. Independent public relations agencies are becoming less common as advertising agencies acquire and subject them to the corporate requirements of the parent company. It is too early to predict whether this trend within the industry will continue and what it will mean for public relations practice.

Major Practice Areas

Public relations firms have increasingly organized themselves into industry sectors and practice areas reflecting the needs and interests of their clients. Industry sectors include: consumer, industrial, health, technology, financial services, government, and nonprofit. While overlapping, these are sometimes further organized around consumers, business to business, corporations, finance, public affairs, crisis communications, and employee relations. So-called practice areas also include reputation management, content management, and others. When asked in a 2007 study about the outlook for the various practice areas, PR professionals surveyed gave these responses when asked where they expected the greatest growth:[13]

Two Wal-Mart employees hold a giant check reflecting the company's charitable contribution to a non profit in San Antonio, Texas.

- Corporate Reputation — 62.6%
- Digital public relations — 43.8
- Marketing communications — 34.5
- Social responsibility — 27.1
- Public affairs — 17.7
- Investor relations — 14.8
- Word-of-mouth — 10.1
- Employee communications — 9.4

In recent years the concept of corporate social responsibility (CSR) has also taken hold, and some PR firms have separate departments or divisions to service this interest. CSR programs involve working with communities and nonprofits and linking corporations to them—for mutually beneficial purposes. For example, Edelman Health, a division of the PR firm Edelman, Inc., worked with nonprofits in the aging field with support from Pfizer to create a ten-country alliance in Europe that promoted policy solutions to health problems and issues. This resulted in "thought leadership," that is promoting ideas, which was shaped and fostered by Edelman and its clients. Edelman's clients were the International Longevity Center, nonprofit think tanks in the United States, UK, and France. In a project largely funded by Pfizer, Inc., a well-crafted campaign was devised that involved policy research on health indicators across Europe, country by country. Understanding what policies lead to the best health practices based on scholarly and professional evidence was accompanied by high-profile conferences and meetings involving top public officials, scientists, corporate leaders, economists, and others. This was connected to a campaign that reached out to government agencies and institutions, professional associations, and others through direct contact, websites, and media coverage to alert the public to health policies and practices that would extend life and make for a healthier society. One feature of the campaign was life guides on topics ranging from cognitive health to vision, hearing, and balance produced in the form of brochures—and digitally on the web. These showed how people's health decisions at young ages influence their health at young, middle, and old ages. It told what to do at what age including such mundane but important prompters as wearing ear plugs at rock concerts and sunglasses on the beach. This was an extensive effort that involved a genuine partnership between a corporate funder, three nonprofit research policy centers, and a public relations firm to a common end: public awareness of critical health issues across the life span—and support for government policies both within individual countries and in the European Union.

Typical Tasks and Work Assignments

As the above discussion suggests, the actual tasks and work assignments of public relations practitioners vary widely from one professional setting to another. Much depends, of course, on the position of the practitioner within the power hierarchy of the agency. In some businesses, the vice president for public relations is a high-ranking person who is involved in all major corporate decisions and is a part of the policy-making team. In other firms, the public relations officer has less power and is brought in only to provide "damage control" through publicity. Still others are the drones of public relations— entry-level or low-ranking employees who do the many day-to-day tasks that are necessary in public relations campaigns. Thus, at the top end of the organization are those who engage in tactical and strategic planning while those lower levels perform more routine tasks involved in implementing such plans.

Top-level policy makers set long-tem objectives and usually agree on some realistic expectations for results. This somewhat abstract agreement is then channeled into specific approaches, using publicity tools ranging from sponsored events to television presentations and press conferences to websites and information pamphlets. Thus, the complete public relations process involves planning and implementation—both in the overall thinking and in the precise technical work that makes achievement of the goals possible.

Lone practitioners, or people in small firms, usually do everything—from designing strategy and tactics to writing copy for press releases. In any case, there are a number of specific tasks that must be accomplished in implementing a campaign. In larger firms with a significant division of labor, the work assignments may be highly specialized. For example, a particular specialist may spend most of his or her time writing news releases for a political candidate. Another may specialize in communicating new, high-tech information to nurses or engineers. In smaller firms, personnel will handle a wider range of duties. However, regardless of the size of a public relations agency or department, certain categories of work assignments are common. One leading text lists common tasks and specific forms of work:

1. *Writing:* producing news releases aimed at the general media and drafting copy for specialized publications, brochures, posters, catalogues, and other pieces intended for distribution to the public
2. *Editing:* revising and checking text of speeches, company magazines, newsletters, and electronic bulletin boards
3. *Media relations and placement:* getting clients in the newspaper and on the air and coordinating media coverage of events
4. *Special events:* organizing media events such as anniversaries of organizations, openings of new programs, sponsored performances, donations of money, dedications of new facilities, and similar ceremonies
5. *Speaking:* writing and delivering speeches to various groups on behalf of the client organization
6. *Production:* working with designers, typesetters, editors, and producers to present material in printed or visual form
7. *Research:* evaluating programs, developing questionnaires for surveys, and analyzing media coverage of an event or issue
8. *Programming and counseling:* developing a plan for the client or department and giving advice about how to handle a particular event or limit negative publicity
9. *Training and management:* providing training services to employees, advising them on how to set a proper climate in a firm, and coordinating employees of varied skills and backgrounds to ensure the success of a program[14]

In addition to being able to perform the above kinds of work, effective public relations practitioners usually must have certain personal qualities. Publicists usually have excellent written and oral communication skills; are at ease socially; have a thorough knowledge of the media, management, and business; and possess the ability to function both as problem-solvers and decision-makers. Other common qualities are stability, common sense, intellectual curiosity, and a tolerance for frustration.

Public Relations Campaigns

Public relations practitioners or agencies work in systematic ways. Typical of their activities on behalf of clients is the *public relations campaign.* This is an organized way of communicating carefully designed messages with specific meanings to targeted audiences that are important to the client. In contrast to a single news release, speech, or television interview, a campaign orchestrates many kinds of messages that are presented in many different ways, making use of a number of media to achieve its goals.

Public relations campaigns become necessary for businesses and other organizations under many kinds of circumstances. Some have positive goals in mind; others may not. Some examples are as follows: (1) A business has been causing industrial pollution and is gaining a bad reputation. The firm now wants to convince the public that it is dedicated to protection of the environment. (2) A health-maintenance organization (HMO) wants to erase the stigma of being too profit-oriented to the detriment of the quality of healthcare provided. (3) An educational institution has experienced a bad sports scandal with consequent

Even the fire department engages in public relations activity as indicated by this tour of a fire house by school children in Alameda, California.

negative publicity. Enrollments have dropped, and it now wants to attract students and get alumni donations to resume. (4) A government agency promoting prenatal child care for the poor wants women to make better use of its services. All of these groups achieve their goals with public relations campaigns.

The first and most obvious task of the specialist designing a public relations campaign is to meet with the client at length to go over exactly what goals are being sought. Those goals must be clearly understood and agreed upon by all parties. These sessions must include full disclosure of what efforts have been made in the past, by whom, and using what strategies; and what worked and what did not. Another obvious problem is money. What, precisely, is the budget that is being allocated by the client to the campaign? A timetable needs to be established, and decisions must be made as to the specific indicators that will be used to decide whether the goal of the campaign was accomplished or not.

According to public relations scholars Scott Cutlip, Allen Center, and Glenn Broom, any effective public relations campaign must be designed around four basic stages or steps:

1. *Fact-finding and feedback*. This stage involves background research on the desired audience. This research is in the scientific tradition as well as impressionistic observations by knowledgeable observers and careful studies of public opinion. The public relations practitioner uses this information to define the problem and to identify the audience to be reached.
2. *Planning and programming*. The publicist uses the information from the fact-finding stage and plans a broad strategy for the entire public relations program. This strategy includes a timetable, media, budgets, and possible targets for the message.
3. *Action and communication*. In this stage the publicist initiates the actual communication process using the media and the appropriate publicity tools. Pamphlets are distributed, speeches are given, events are sponsored, and news releases are sent to media organizations.
4. *Evaluation*. After the program is initiated and carried out, it is assessed in several ways: by measuring changes in beliefs, attitudes, and opinions among particular publics; by counting the number of news clippings or reports on radio and television to evaluate the effectiveness of contacts with the news media; or by interviewing key opinion leaders. If carried to its logical conclusion, evaluation should affect future public relations activities, depending on what worked and what did not.[15]

To illustrate how these steps would be implemented in practice, a typical public relations campaign can be reviewed. As indicated, it begins with the recognition of a problem or the perceived need for an image change of some sort. One such effort was a 2009 PR campaign carried out by Ogilvy Public Relations Worldwide for the Lance Armstrong Foundation to expand public awareness of cancer. The campaign builds on a decade-old effort of the foundation called LiveStrong, which wanted the effort to have a global presence. The *fact-finding and feedback* phase with the client involved date about public knowledge of and attitudes toward cancer—as well as health practices. That led to *planning and programming* for a global campaign, including using champion cyclist Armstrong's own global schedule as a template for the effort. As for *action and communication,* the two-year LiveStrong Global Cancer Campaign was launched in Australia with an event aimed at nongovernmental organizations (NGOs) and Australian policy makers (government officials, legislators). There were media availabilities (appearances) and reach out for Armstrong and his aides as well as such digital efforts as an Australian website for the effort. Similar activities were planned for other countries but with each tailored to local circumstances because attitudes toward cancer differ and there is a great stigma attached to cancer in some countries. The Ogilvy firm engaged local advocates leveraging their events and they developed market research, press materials, and public service announcements. The purpose of the campaign was to increase awareness of the need for cancer screening and treatment.

Evaluation of the effort is linked to public opinion data and the actual impact of the campaign, as far as it can be measured and isolated, on increases in cancer screening and eventually more and better treatment. As is true with all PR campaigns, they live in a social environment where there are many contributing factors. In this instance an international celebrity hires a PR firm to direct a campaign conducted in concert with already existing cancer awareness efforts across the globe. Thus actual credit for the end results of this campaign, and others, may have many drivers and influences. The Ogilvy campaign, however, was unique when announced as the first time a nonprofit hired a PR firm to conduct a global campaign, something that giant commercial companies do all the time. This shows the effective reach of PR in both the corporate and nonprofit sectors.

Leaders in public relations are quick to point out that their work involves much more than mass communication. Sometimes they distinguish *internal* from *external* communication. Internal communication is communication within an organization directed to its members. For example, a labor union communicates to its members through newsletters, meetings, bulletin boards, and other internal media. This kind of communication is aimed at a discrete group of people, not at the general public through mass media. In contrast, external communication transmits messages via the mass media to a large, diverse audience or to particular segments of the population outside the organization.

Managing Elections

A kind of organized public relations work that has expanded greatly in recent years is managing election campaigns. Today, public relations consultants often serve as the strategists and managers of such campaigns during elections. In particular, they key their efforts to opinion polls and results of focus groups. Although they usually stay out of the public eye, such consultants occasionally appear on CNN and various network talk shows to speak on behalf of their clients. Typically, however, they avoid the limelight and engage in a kind of guerrilla warfare, by plotting strategy, designing modes of attack, and coaching defensive responses for their clients when they are under fire. This kind of organized activity brings together public opinion research, strategic planning, and more traditional public relations. According to Jerry Hagstrom of the *National Journal,* who is an expert on this new form of public relations, there is an elite corps of these Washington, D.C.-based polling and media firms that play a profound role in national presidential campaigns and other races. Similar firms exist across the country and typically serve the Republican and Democratic parties. And, although national campaigns are the most prestigious races, Hagstrom observes that the most elite consultants usually center their efforts on statewide campaigns because they are more financially lucrative. One of the most famous is James Carville, who represents Democratic candidates and was long associated with Bill and Hillary Clinton. His wife, Mary Matalin, is an equally famous Republican consultant.

Part of managing elections is strategic personal appearances by candidates like President Obama.

Hagstrom states that this cadre of consultants has virtually replaced state and local political bosses and party chairpersons as behind-the-scenes power brokers. What was once done intuitively by political operatives is now in the task of consultants. In dealing with the media, public relations campaign managers often engage in what has come to be called "spin control" (a term from billiards, where a left or right spin can be put on a ball, making it curve to one side or the other as it moves across the table). They do so with carefully controlled use of language. If a political figure has unintentionally made an error in reporting the use of campaign funds, a political *spinmeister* may advise his or her client to attack the opponent by characterizing the situation as a "disgraceful scandal" and claim that "people who violate decent standards of behavior should never be allowed to hold public office." Spin control from the other side will claim "unintentional mistakes are being escalated out of control by my opponent using wild claims in a political vendetta."

Carefully orchestrated spin control measures during election campaigns can make a difference. For example, during the 2008 presidential and congressional elections, advisors to both parties crafted messages to highlight their differences in both positive and negative ways. Trying to connect talking points (or emphasis areas) with public opinion on terrorism and the Iraq War, health care, energy, immigration, and climate change gave both parties and their surrogates much material for factual and highly distorted claims. The role of political consultants, celebrity consultants and those less well known is often debated, but their role is undisputed. In the 2008 campaign, the most famous of these (and ultimately the most successful) was David Axelrod, who was top adviser to the Democratic presidential campaign, crafted the campaign's strategy, and ended up as President Obama's senior advisor in the White House with an office close to the president. Senator John McCain's campaign in 2007 and 2008 had flagged and was on the downslide when a blue-chip panel of advisors was engaged, and he went on to win the crucial New Hampshire primary and eventually the Republican nomination for president. There is no one single definition for political consultants. They are a mix of managers, pollsters, advertising experts, and media advisors who either develop a consistent campaign that works and adjust it along the way or are engaged to make mid-course corrections to rescue a campaign that is thought to be in trouble.

Over the years these advisors have included Karl Rove, once called "Bush's Brain" in a documentary, and earlier stars like Lee Atwater, said to be the architect of strategies for a conservative Republican resurgence. Others like Pat Caddell, a pollster, worked for Jimmy Carter and Paul Begalla, who worked for Bill Clinton, became staples of TV and cable political talk shows.

Political campaigning, then, has become a battleground of public relations managers who are experts of assessing public opinion and desires and who can design messages that resonate with voters. Many critics complain that this has shifted the democratic process of election campaigning from a more traditional one in which candidates make their principles and plans clear to one in which they shift from one position to another as advisors use polls to manage their messages.

BIG IDEAS: MEDIA THEORIES EXPLAINED

Two-Step Flow of Communication Theory

While most people get their news and other kinds of information directly from the mass media, stories are often transmitted to additional receivers by word of mouth. Thus, even in our sophisticated "information" society, with its satellites, computers, and digital media with worldwide reach, word-of-mouth communication is still a part of the mass-communication process.

In a now-classic study of the role of the mass media in the 1940 presidential campaign of Franklin D. Roosevelt versus Wendell Wilkie, communication researchers Paul Lazarsfeld, Bernard Berelson, and Hazel Gaudet rediscovered the importance of the diffusion of information through interpersonal communication. To their surprise, they found that many of the people they were interviewing did not get their information about the issues and candidates directly from the media at all but *from other people* who had read about the campaign in the newspapers or who had listened to the broadcast speeches of the candidates on the radio.

The researchers found that such "opinion leaders" passed on information to other people who had much less contact with the media. As they did so, they had an *influence* on the way the information was interpreted. Thus, the term "opinion leaders" described not only their activity of word-of-mouth transmission but also their role in providing personal interpretations.

Out of that famous research project came a theory that has come to be called the "two-step flow of communication." It is important in understanding the word-of-mouth transmission of news to a larger audience than just those who are initially exposed. The two-step flow of communication process has been widely studied since it was first formulated in the 1940s.

Most of us can recall learning of some major news event this way, but modern research on word-of-mouth transmission of news has shown that it is not a very reliable or accurate system for moving complex information that includes many details. Still the commentators say that the two-step flow anticipated social networking sites like YouTube and MySpace sixty years early.

Such word-of-mouth diffusion of news stories works best for short messages of a dramatic nature, such as "the space shuttle blew up," "the president has been shot," or "we won the big game." But the theory has been well verified, and it can be summarized in the following set of assumptions and their predictions:

1. The mass media present a constant *flow of information* about a great variety of topics of interest and importance to people in contemporary society, but most people attend only selectively.
2. Some people, at all levels of society, *attend fully* to the media than others and become more knowledgeable than their families, friends, or neighbors in certain areas of media content.
3. Among those who attend more fully are people who become identified by others as *opinion leaders*—persons like themselves but who are especially knowledgeable and trustworthy as sources of information and interpretation about certain areas of media content.
4. Such opinion leaders often pass on, *by word of mouth, information about specialized topics* that they obtain from the media to others who have turned to them to obtain news and interpretations about those topics.
5. **Therefore**, mass communications often move *in two distinct stages*—from the media to opinion leaders, who attend directly to media presentations about selected topics, and then by word of mouth to other people whom they influence with their information and interpretations.

PUBLIC RELATIONS AND THE MEDIA

We noted that there is an important difference between advertising messages and most of the messages that are prepared by public relations practitioners. Advertisers simply purchase the time or space in print or broadcast media and place their messages where they want. Public relations practitioners can do this, of course, but they are far more likely to try to get the media to accept (without cost) news releases, interviews, and other messages favorable to their clients (but which are not easily seen as public relations efforts).

Individuals or interests that want to achieve a positive public image by using the mass media in this way face at least two barriers: First, the media are independent entities with their own goals—which may *conflict* with those of the publicity seekers. For example, a politician's desire for positive coverage on the evening news obviously would conflict with the local television station's intention to disclose the same politician's alleged wrongdoing. Second, there is great *competition* for limited space and time in the media and other public forums, and many worthy individuals and causes simply cannot receive the media attention and public exposure they desire. Of course, the web and various blogs welcome an infinite number of posts and comments from those who follow them, thus negating the constraints of time and space. For this reason, newspapers, magazines, and electronic media news have websites where interactive comments and critique are welcomed.

Mascots such as "Chipper," who represents California highway patrol, are useful public relations devices.

The Gatekeeping Process

An important theory explaining how the media select only a limited number of news stories to print or air in a particular edition or broadcast is the *gatekeeping theory*. While there may be infinite outlets with no constraints on space or time in a digital world, there is still a scarcity of reader and viewer attention span, and thus it becomes important for PR professionals to get through the fog of bombarding and competing messages to gain support for their clients. Gatekeeping is thus still important. This theory is important in understanding the complex relationship between public relations and the media. It states that those who select the content for the daily newspaper, news broadcast, or online news site do so by using a number of criteria to decide what is "newsworthy." They realize full well that there is only a limited amount of time or space that they have available. Only those stories judged to be most important, or in which their audience will be most interested, will be given priority. Those that meet these criteria will be selected from the abundance of stories that is available to them from reporters, wire services, and the like. The latest news release from a public relations agency, press secretary, or political consultant may not survive this test. Indeed, unless it has some special quality that the editors and news directors feel is important, it is likely to get ignored.

On the other hand, public relations practitioners know this full well. They have no illusions that editors will eagerly accept and make public any kind of news release or other information handouts that they prepare. To help in opening the channels, a public relations practitioner will try to become acquainted with those who make news decisions. An effective public relations specialist will establish *good personal relationships*—intended to generate and maintain confidence and credibility—with reporters, editors, and news directors. However, journalists often remain wary and are not likely to trust just any public relations person who approaches them with information.

Philanthropy can provide a public relations platform that softens and improves the image of an individual or corporation such as the Bill and Melinda Gates Foundation, which got a major infusion of money from investor Warren Buffett thus creating the world's largest foundation aimed at eradicating disease and solving social problems.

A Relationship of Mutual Dependency

Adding to this complex relationship between public relations and journalism is the fact that these two groups *need* each other. They live in a *state of mutual dependency*. A careful examination of a daily newspaper or a television news broadcast will reveal that a very large proportion of what appears in the news has its origin in someone's news conference, news release, or other form of material originally prepared by a public relations or public affairs specialist and then released to the press. This does not mean that the press blindly makes public whatever practitioners provide. Reporters follow up, interview people with other points of view, and so on. Nevertheless, much of the agenda in the daily press has its start with public relations specialists.

To illustrate: If a plane crashes, public money is misappropriated, or a corporation is caught harassing women or mistreating minorities, some spokesperson for the relevant organization (airline, government agency, corporation) will hold a news conference. The purpose in appearing before reporters is not just to provide information. It is to put the best possible interpretation (spin) on what happened, how the situation could not have been foreseen, what the corporation, for example, is doing about it, and so on. Such press conferences are not casual appearances. Most such presentations are *carefully rehearsed* ahead of time with the aid of public relations specialists—who warn of damaging questions that are likely to be asked and who develop ways of deflecting ones that are likely to create harm to the agency or authorities.

The reporters, on the other hand, *need news*. On a typical day, there may be little going on that is actually newsworthy. While some minor events might be made interesting by clever writing (a pie-eating contest, a dog that falls through the ice on the pond, or another service-station robbery), it is often the case that these do not provide enough copy to fill out the day's news agenda. In such cases, journalists have to make use of what public relations people supply because *something* has to appear in the paper for subscribers to read or on the newscast for viewers to see. The reporters must meet deadlines and have very little time to generate alternatives to what the practitioners are providing. About all they can do is to flesh out the provided story with a few quotes from experts or from individuals who represent contrary points of view and with some background information.

Another example of the dependent relationship between public relations and journalism is the video news release (VNR)—a self-serving promotion of a person or organization presented on videotape or simply downloaded on a website. These are especially important for television news broadcasts. Originally used by companies to promote their general image or to respond to a crisis are now increasingly used by political candidates as well. Media organizations are then free to use the material verbatim, edit it heavily, or identify it as a statement from those appearing therein. An ethical problem associated with this kind of communication concerns identification of the source. When television stations do not identify the VNR as such, they do their viewers a disservice. Yet stations do not always give the public due warning that self-serving VNR material is produced by the candidate or company represented and was not subject to usual journalistic checks for accuracy. VNRs are now mostly delivered as email attachments with full-motion videos, rather than by mail or messenger.

Lobbying is an instrument of public relations that uses many media platforms to achieve its goal. This health-care industry lobbyist speaks on a cell phone while reading from a news release.

Thus, in spite of their basic distrust of each other, public relations practitioners and journalists live in a state of mutual dependency. Even a casual examination of the agenda produced by a daily paper or a newscast will reveal that many stories— often the majority—are products of routine happenings in business, government, entertainment industries, education, politics, and so on. Here, reporters clearly rely on those who speak for politicians, personalities, corporations, and other special interests in the society. Thus, it is out of such complex interactions and exchanges that much of the daily news is generated and shaped.

LOBBYING AS PUBLIC RELATIONS

A special form of public relations is **lobbying**, although some experts would not see it as part of the field. Notwithstanding, lobbying has many similarities to the kinds of activities we have described as constituting public relations. Lobbyists are defined as persons employed "to influence legislators to introduce or vote for measures favorable to the interests they represent."[16]

A healthcare-industry lobbyist uses his cell phone standing in front of the U.S. Capitol during a Congressional session.

To achieve their influence, lobbyists rely mainly on *interpersonal communication* and *informal contacts* with those whom they try to influence. Nevertheless, lobbyists are persons or groups paid to engage in efforts to influence the beliefs, attitudes, and actions of specifically defined target individuals through the use of deliberately designed messages. Defined in this way, they fit quite well within the broad definition of public relations provided earlier. The main differences are that they seldom use the mass media, and they focus their influence attempts narrowly on legislators.

Where did the name come from? When they were first identified in the nineteenth century as a distinct group of influence peddlers in Washington, D.C., they stood in the lobby of the venerable Willard Hotel in that city. The hotel still stands only a short walk from the White House and a few blocks from the Capitol building. Many politicians walked to the hotel to have lunch or an evening meal. When office holders came through the long, narrow lobby, those wanting to influence them would clutch at their sleeves and try to get their attention (much as influence-seekers at the centers of power had done since organized government began). In time, they came to be called "lobbyists." Even today, the Westin Willard Hotel proudly tells its guests that the name was born right there.

Lobbyists represent a great variety of groups and interests. These include trade associations, veteran's groups, labor unions, political action committees, consumer advocates, professional associations, churches, foreign governments, and many more. There are literally tens of thousands of organizations and individuals who want to influence the legislative process. A lobbyist might be a lawyer, public relations practitioner, or policy expert who has been hired to influence the work of Congress. Not all work at the federal level; some represent clients at state and even local centers of government.

Federal law requires that lobbyists register with the Records and Registration Division of the Capitol Hill Lobbying Office. Just how many lobbyists actually exist in Washington D.C. is anybody's guess with one public service organization claiming about 15,000 and the *Washington Post* reporting official figures that put it at 34,000. Some of the groups identify themselves as lobbying specialists. Others are public relations agencies, law firms, and "think tanks" (various mission-oriented institutes and centers).

Lobbying and lobbyists have always been a subject of controversy. Some critics regard them with deep suspicion. The topic was alive and well in the 2008 campaign when both candidates decried lobbyists and both had to dismiss key staffers who had been lobbyists for controversial cases, unrelated to the candidate. A move by any person between lobbying and government, or the reverse, illustrates a continuing focus of criticism. There is a constant rotation of individuals between government service and private influence-seeking roles. The problem that many people see is that former government officials or employees, when they return to or take jobs in lobbying, will use their inside knowledge and contacts to give the special interests that they represent an unfair advantage. There are now laws that prevent them from doing so for several years after they leave office.

For a number of years, the two largest lobbying and public relations firms in Washington, D.C., have been Hill & Knowlton, Inc., and Burson-Marstellar, Inc., each of which has ties to advertising and public relations groups on a worldwide basis. Clients pay huge fees to be represented by such groups, and their annual billings are in the millions of dollars. Such firms use every conceivable tool and process to promote, change or impede legislation pending before Congress that can have an influence on their clients. Sometimes even getting a single word changed in a bill (e.g., from "shall" to "may" or from "never" to "seldom") passing through a committee can mean millions to a client. Similar to the work of more traditional public relations, these types of lobbying and public relations firms organize events, perform research, develop communication strategies, or sometimes shape news on behalf of their clients. Lobbyists at both federal and state levels write articles, make speeches, designs campaigns, buy advertising, influence journalists, and try to guide public officials.

While many critics deplore all lobbying and lobbyists, others point out that they have a legitimate role in the process of government. They do bring a great deal of information to the attention of office-holders, which should be taken into account as laws are formed or modified. They bring together those who have legitimate interests with those who can have powerful influences on those interests. Often, legislators need to know who will be affected by the outcome of bills under consideration. The downside comes when special interests gain an advantage over the public good and scandals arise. Fortunately, consumer groups, the press, and our government constantly monitor lobbyists for ethical and other kinds of violations.

PUBLIC RELATIONS AS AN EMERGING PROFESSION

The term "professional" is an ancient one, going back to the Middle Ages, when there were only three basic "learned professions"—divinity, law, and medicine. What set them apart from other vocational pursuits were these major criteria: (1) Each had an extensive *body of sophisticated knowledge* requiring long periods of formal study to learn and master. (2) Their practitioners used that body of knowledge on behalf of the public *within a set of ethical norms*. And (3) their practitioners *monitored each other* to ensure compliance with the norms, rejecting from their ranks those who engaged in unethical practices. To some extent, that prestigious interpretation of "profession" has survived, and many people want their particular type of vocational activity to be regarded as such. Among those are public relations practitioners. Today, there is a strong movement in public relations to develop the field as a profession.

Earlier, when the field was being established, no particular credentials were required to become a public relations specialist. Indeed, many of the earliest practitioners were simply ex-journalists who had an understanding of the workings of the press and who knew how to get stories about their clients into the pages of the newspapers. Today other media play a serious role, including social network. Moreover, it was all done by the "seat of the pants." That is, there was no body of concepts and principles that had been developed by systematic research. It was a field in which intuition, creativity, insights, and lore held sway. Often the guesses and inspirations of practitioners led to success—just as often they did not.

The label "professional" is now widely applied by the public to designate virtually any specialized occupational group. Thus, we hear of "professional" hair dressers, prize-fighters, bartenders, and even dog-groomers. However, it is the traditional meaning of the term, and its prestige, to which public relations practitioners and educators aspire, and there is evidence that at least some progress is being made. Today, two major factors are playing a central role in the evolution of public relations as a professional field. One is the increasing establishment and acceptance of *courses and degree programs in higher education*—meeting the criterion of formal study. The other is *systematic research and scholarly inquiry* aimed directly at the second criterion, developing a complex body of knowledge. This body of knowledge consists of a growing accumulation of concepts, principles, theories, and practical solutions that are used in the practice of public relations.

A very important question concerns the third criterion of what constitutes a profession in the classical case. This is whether the field's practitioners use that knowledge for the benefit of the public within an ethical framework. Furthermore, whether they monitor each other and reject those who transgress the ethical norms is something else altogether. That certainly is the case in the law, in medicine, and (perhaps less clearly) in the clergy. In the section that follows, we focus on public relations within the framework of the three formal criteria of a true profession.

Public Relations Education

Public relations has been taught in universities since 1923, when Edward Bernays organized the first course at New York University. Early on, it was taught mostly in journalism schools, which were largely newspaper-oriented and not always hospitable to the inclusion of public relations in the curriculum. This prejudice toward public relations has faded over the years, although a few journalism schools still bar it from the curriculum. The first formal undergraduate degree program in public relations was established at Boston University in 1947. In more recent times, departments of speech-communication also have added public relations programs, as have many comprehensive communication schools and colleges. In addition, there are individual courses in public relations at community colleges and industry trade schools.

Today, public relations has not only developed into a rapidly growing field of study in higher education, but it also has taken other important steps to establish itself as a profession. For example, the organization that periodically examines and approves of journalism and mass communication curricula in the United States also reviews public relations course work in specific institutions to determine if it qualifies as an "accredited" sequence. (Other regularly reviewed areas of study are news-editorial, magazine, and radio-television news.)

There are several hundred professors of public relations offering courses in schools or departments of journalism and communications and in speech communication programs in the United States, and every year thousands of students major in the field. Student internships are available with public relations firms, businesses, government agencies, and professional associations. Dozens of textbooks and a number of technical journals reporting research results are devoted to the field. Public relations practitioners also have their own national organization called the Public Relations Society of America (PRSA) with student chapters on many campuses as well.

A formal curriculum in public relations at the undergraduate level usually includes substantial work in the liberal arts and sciences. Typically, a public relations major takes an overview course on public relations as a communication field, an advanced course in public relations methods, and other specific courses of instruction in various aspects of the field, depending on the size and sophistication of the program. Public relations curricula at the graduate level usually involve formal communication theory courses and (science-based) research training as well as instruction in the field's areas of specialization. Over the last three decades, public relations has become one of the most popular communication majors as students in the information age realize the importance of the field and of other media-consulting activities. The fact that the field pays more than most other media-related industries is an added attraction.

The purpose of public relations education is to promote the field as a professional communications activity, to produce a well-educated workforce, and to foster research. However, this does not mean that people who aspire to work in public relations must major in public relations at a university or college. Although there is a great and growing demand for people formally educated in public relations, many still get into the field by working for newspapers or other media. Some people come into public relations as specialists—for example, they may have a background in public health and take up a public relations assignment in that area. Thus, there are many pathways to a public relations career. At the same time, most university-based public relations programs have the advantage of having close links with the industry and are better positioned to help their students get jobs in the field.

Public Relations Research

A second significant area of development in public relations is research. This, too, represents an effort to gain full professional status by fulfilling the first criterion of having an extensive body of specialized knowledge. However, as will be made clear, in many ways that body remains to be developed.

Much of the research done in the field stems from practical rather than theoretical considerations. Clients want to see what kind of "bang" they have received for their "buck." This means that "research" consists mainly of assessing the results of a particular campaign or determining the needs of a client in order to develop an appropriate strategy. Although public relations was once carried out with little formal evaluation, businesses and governmental departments increasingly require that public relations practitioners document expenditures and provide reliable evidence that some kinds of benefits flow from those costs.

Much of the body of more sophisticated knowledge relevant to the impact and influence of public relations continues to be derived from basic media and communication research conducted by social scientists and academic media scholars. Thus, research probes on such topics as the process of persuasion, how media agenda setting take place, the nature of attitudes and their links to behavior, and how public opinion is formed, influenced, and translated into policy shifts as well as the behavior of specific categories of citizens.

At the same time, a growing field of applied research—more specifically focused on problems and practices in public relations—has also emerged. Some public relations agencies and departments conduct in-house assessment studies simply to take stock of their activities. Other applied research is done in universities by public relations professors. This type of academic research is broader in scope and less parochial than that typically done by public relations practitioners. University research typically aims at establishing general concepts, patterned relationships, and theories that help explain processes and effects in the field. Thus, this research makes important contributions to the growing body of knowledge that is developing in the field.

Public relations scholar John V. Pavlik has identified at least three general reasons for conducting basic public relations research: One is understanding public relations *as communication*, which involves building communication theory and studying the effects of public relations activity on the individual, group, and society. A second is *solving practical problems* in the field, including monitoring the public relations environment, measuring social performance, and auditing communication and public relations. A third motivation stems from the need to *monitor the profession,* by taking stock of how public relations practitioners, individually and collectively, are performing technically and ethically.[17]

At the practitioner level, much of the in-house public relations research done by agencies gives clients feedback and helps them improve communication with their constituencies. Some critics say that such research is manipulative, but defenders say it is simply intelligent, systematic information that can make the client more sensitive to the desired audience. How public relations people use such information is up to them— hopefully most will use it ethically.

The state of *proprietary* public relations research (yielding results that are kept secret by an agency or practitioner) and its actual use by people in the field is difficult to ascertain. The largest and most powerful public relations firms and government departments spend a considerable amount of time and money testing their messages and monitoring campaigns for evidence that they are having some effect. At the same time, many small public relations firms and individual practitioners make limited use of research in their work. Some publicists do not use research at all, preferring an intuitive "seat of the pants" approach. General usage on a day-to-day basis of the kinds of public relations research typically reported in academic journals is limited. Yet such research contributes to that much-needed body of knowledge that can help imaginative and thoughtful practitioners and planners move toward professional status.

Ethical Issues and Criticisms

As public relations continues its struggle to be recognized as a profession, one of its major problems lies in the *public image* of the field and in developing and enforcing a meaningful *code of ethics*. This is a bit ironic, of course, but like the shoemaker's children who didn't have shoes, PR has wrestled with its own public image for decades.

Although it is generally acknowledged as an essential (and useful) enterprise and is done best when honesty and integrity prevail, PR has never fully shaken off allegations of deception and misleading information, unfair as this generally may be. As we noted earlier, almost from its beginnings public relations has had its detractors. Critics charge that public relations activity is manipulative, self-serving, and often unethical. They maintain that it distorts and blurs issues in its attempts to persuade the public, and that publicists will use just about any means to ensure a favorable image for their clients.

Such charges are not without foundation. There are unscrupulous people in public relations. The same is true of physicians, lawyers, and any other profession. However, in public relations, questionable or unethical practices become especially visible because of the nature of what practitioners do. Unlike the botched surgery or the ineptly handled legal case, the products of public relations practitioners are open to scrutiny. Public-spirited groups and the news media make special efforts try to ferret out deceptive activities. As a result, public relations practitioners who transgress norms almost immediately receive unfavorable press coverage. In addition, even if not detected immediately, unethical practices sometimes backfire and at a later time harm the image that public relations is meant to polish. Sometimes those transgressions are inadvertent. For example, a representative of Ketchum public relations, a large agency, was in Memphis in 2000 working on an account for its client FedEx when he made what the company called a "lapse in judgment" by sending a tweet (a message transmitted on Twitter) saying that "I'm in one of those towns where I scratch my head and say, 'I would die if I had to live here.'" This slur on Memphis got the attention of executives at FedEx and at Ketchum, who apologized. In public relations, as in medicine, the first rule of professionalism is do no harm.[18]

To its credit, the field makes extensive efforts to reduce poor practices. To be accredited by the Public Relations Society of America, a practitioner working professionally in the field must pass tests of communication skills and agree to abide by a code of good practice. The Universal Accreditation Board accredits PR specialists who belong to PRSA and take (and pass) a rigorous exam plus have at least five years of experience in the field. They then earn an accredited in public relations (APR) designation.

In spite of these efforts, those who criticize the basic task of public relations focus on a more fundamental problem: They raise the question as to whether there is something less than honorable in a business devoted to enhancing the image of a corporation or individual by suppressing truths that would bring criticism and emphasizing only favorable meanings. To the critics this is a serious charge, and it is this aspect of the basic mission of many public relations campaigns that is most troublesome. Defenders say that a corporation or individual has every right to put on the best face possible before the public. Moreover, public relations practitioners do provide useful information to people in an increasingly complex and bureaucratic world—although most would agree that in an ideal world such information should be balanced with information from more objective sources.

As efforts toward professionalization of the field continue, such negative views of the field may change. One reason is that, during the past twenty years, "public accountability" is an important concept that has found increasing favor among public relations specialists. This idea has received much attention and has been integrated into public relations education, thinking, and practice. The accountability concept is tied to the idea of corporate social responsibility, which stipulates that a business ought to contribute as much to the common good as to its own economic success.

THE FUTURE OF THE FIELD

While many efforts are being made by public relations to be identified as a "profession" in the traditional sense, it is clear that the field has a way to go. The current status of the field can be assessed against the three criteria discussed previously: Progress is clearly being made on the first criterion. That is, the field is assembling through research and scholarship a *body of complex knowledge*. Moreover, that accumulated knowledge is now being taught in formal courses and degree sequences in colleges and universities. There is less certainty as to how well the second criterion is being met. That is, it could be hotly debated whether public relations practitioners *serve the public* with their knowledge. In some ways they do, but there are grounds for concluding that for the most part they serve only those well-heeled clients who can afford their fees. Indeed, many critics believe that public relations campaigns often deliberately fool the public by suppressing damaging information and emphasizing only positive messages about their clients. Finally, there is as of yet no codified set of ethical norms to which public relations practitioners universally subscribe, and there certainly is no way in which those who cross the line on ethical standards can be drummed out of the profession. Therefore, it will be interesting to see, in the years ahead, if the field can resolve these problems and gain the public trust that has largely failed to develop over the years thus far.

One way in which public relations will continue to change in the future is through the development of new strategies to reach relevant publics. That is not to "serve" the public—the benefits go to clients who pay the bills. In any case, practitioners seek ways to make use of technological advances in communication systems within the United States and all over the world. With digital strategies and digital media now available, public relations specialists have been able to craft new approaches using social networking sites and other efforts that enhance community building for their clients and thus help make relations with publics truly interactive.

Today public relations messages compete with other kinds of information for public attention in an environment that includes many kinds of media and a great variety of sources. Increasingly important are personal computers connected to the Internet and its World Wide Web. Many millions of people worldwide access a vast array of specialized information via this medium. Email, IMs and, truets as well as file-sharing services like Flickr enable people, both within and between groups, to transmit and receive information of many kinds. Similarly, teleconferencing brings small groups together for discussions, even though they may be at sites remote from each other. Public relations agencies, consultants, and individual practitioners make use of all of these media for a variety of purposes. For example, Web 2.0 sites feature blogs and full-motion video. Digital media truly enhance the capacity of public relations in every aspect of that field's goals.

As we've noted in earlier chapters, the evolving world of digital media does not diminish traditional mass media or other longstanding venues for messages and communication from conferences and meetings to kiosks. More than ever, PR can use digital media to reach out to specific individuals, within both established groups and new constituencies. The digital medium offers a more precise way of reaching a desired audience than, say, the special interest magazine. In fact, the most specialized publication probably has a more diverse readership than the audiences currently being targeted by new data services. There is also a considerable online news industry now undergoing a pattern of increasingly rapid use. Special interest newsletters, often transmitted electronically, reach every conceivable category of the public, from chocolate lovers to travelers of exotic countries to fans of professional wrestling. Thus, many "publics" that desire highly specific information can be reached with new media. This has inspired some commentators and critics to call for a "new PR," which would involve (a) a reconsideration of the role played by PR professionals moving well beyond the concerns of business to those of consumers and citizens, (2) a new code of conduct for online communicators, (3) new tools for PR professionals including relationship portals; and (4) new paradigms, players, and resources by considering the various socio-technical shifts affecting media and the public.[19]

In a basic sense, the future of public relations is not difficult to predict. It is a field that has developed rapidly over the last century, and, regardless of its critics, there is no doubt that it will continue to be an essential part of our complex society in the future. Organizations that produce goods and services that are important to the public need public relations to maintain goodwill and favorable attitudes on the part of those who consume their products. The public, on the other hand, benefits when such organizations continue to function—employing people, providing products and services, and conducting activities that the society requires.

As explained, there is a relationship of dependency between public relations and journalism. Reporters, editors, and news directors need information that public relations supply because it makes up a large part of what journalists report to the public. Increasingly, though, as we've pointed out in Chapter 9, traditional journalism is coping with citizen journalism for better or worse, and PR must incorporate that development into its work plans. In turn, public relations practitioners are dependent on the news media to transmit many of their announcements, campaigns, and releases to their audiences. Thus, public relations will remain a field intricately interwoven into the major media, activities, and affairs of the society. It is completely unrealistic to assume that its importance will diminish in the years ahead.

CHAPTER REVIEW

- Public relations has been greatly benefited by the digital media and have developed digital media practice areas, though it is imagined that these might eventually be integrated with other PR practice areas.
- Demands on PR are shifting as digital strategies become more necessary at a time when virtually all media are going digital with interactive involvement of many new stakeholders.
- Public relations can be defined as the work and outcomes of paid professional practitioners who design and transmit messages, on behalf of a client, via a variety of media to relevant and targeted audiences in an attempt to influence their beliefs, attitudes, or even actions regarding some person, organization, policy, situation, or event.
- Many of the communication strategies used today in public relations have ancient origins. An example is the sun-god strategy used by Hammurabi to characterize his laws. That dates back four thousand years. However, the field's more modern origins lie in the "publicity agents," "press agents," and agencies that developed in New York City early in the twentieth century. Their task was, much as it is today, to improve the image of clients.
- Most, but not all, public relations efforts make extensive use of media of all kinds. Practitioners constantly try to draw attention to their clients by information transmitted by the media in news reports, talk shows, or in any form of print, online, or broadcast content that can show their client in a favorable light.
- An uneasy relationship exists between the field of public relations and the media—more specifically, journalism. Each is dependent upon the other. Much of what appears in the news has origins in events or information released by public relations practitioners. At the same time, such practitioners are deeply dependent on the media as a means of transmitting their messages to their desired audiences.
- Lobbying can be considered as a special, if controversial, form of public relations. Lobbyists use a variety of interpersonal and other communication techniques to try to influence legislators as they initiate, modify, and pass laws that can have an influence on their clients.
- Today, there is a strong movement among its practitioners and educators to try to transform public relations into a *profession*. Whether this will be successful or not depends on how well the field meets three major criteria: (1) developing a body of sophisticated knowledge, (2) using that knowledge for the public good within a system of ethical norms, and (3) ensuring compliance to those norms by monitoring practitioners.

STRATEGIC QUESTIONS

1. How does public relations differ from advertising? Connect this answer with free and paid media.
2. Discuss the concept of public relations and how public relations agencies and public relations practitioners in such institutions as business, government, and education embrace it.
3. What do the major practice areas of public relations tell you about trends in the industry?

4. How is a public relations campaign conceived and executed? How are its results and impact determined—or measured?

5. How and to what extent are public relations and the news media "mutually dependent"? Is this a good or bad thing, and how is the public protected in the process?

6. What impact is the digital revolution having on the public relations industry and field?

KEY CONCEPTS & TERMS

PR agency 290
Public relations specialists 307
PR clients 292
Lobbying 305
Public Relations Society of America accreditation 308

"Public relations solution" 294
News release and video news release 303
Social networking media 311

Damage control 292
Propaganda 287
Persuasion 294

ENDNOTES

1. Paul A. Holmes, editor, *The State of the Public Relations Industry,* June 2007 (for Huntsworth plc), p. 1., see also Internet Advocacy Center, www.internetadvoacycenter.com.

2. Public Relations Society of America, *2006 State of the PR Profession Opinion Survey* (Bacon's Information Service, 2007), p. 5.

3. Holmes Report, p. 23.

4. http://blisspr.com, 2008.

5. U.S. Department of Labor, Bureau of Labor Statistics, "Public Relations Specialists," www.bls.gov/oco/ocos086.htm.

6. Scott M. Cutlip, Allen H. Center, and Glenn M. Broom, *Effective Public Relations,* 6th ed. (Englewood Cliffs, NJ: Prentice-Hall, 1985), pp. 138-230. See also Cutlip, Center, and Broom, *Effective Public Relations,* 9thed. (Englewood Cliffs: Prentice-Hall, 2005).

7. Frank Cobb, *The New Republic,* Dec. 31, 1919, p. 44. For a critical assessment of PR history, see Larry Tye, *The Father of the Spin: Edward L. Bernays and the Birth of Public Relations* (New York: Crown, 1998) and Stewart Ewan, *PR—A Social History of Spin* (New York: Basic Books, 1998).

8. Walter Lippman, *Public Opinion* (New York: Harcourt, Brace and Company, 1922), p. 345.

9. U.S. Department of Labor, op. cit.

10. Ronald D. Smith, *Strategic Planning for Public Relations,* 2d. ed. (Mahwah, NJ: Lawrence Erlbaum, 2004).

11. Al Ries and Laura Ries, *The Fall of Advertising and the Rise of PR* (New York: Harper Business, 2002), xi.

12. Holmes Report, pp. 5-6.

13. Holmes Report, p. 17.

14. Lippman, *Public Opinion,* p. 64. See also James E. Grunig and Todd Hunt, *Managing Public Relations* (New York: Holt, 1984), Chapter 5. A useful text is Dennis L. Wilcox, Philip Ault, Warren K. Asee, and Glen T. Cameron, *Public Relations: Strategies and Tactics,* 6th ed. (New York: Longman, 2000). See also Scott M. Cutlip, Allen H. Center, and Glenn M. Broom, *Effective Public Relations,* 8th ed. (Englewood Cliffs, NJ: Prentice-Hall, 1999).

15. Cutlip, op. cit.

16. *American Heritage Dictionary of the English Language* (Boston: Houghton Mifflin, 1970). See also Clarke L. Caywood, ed., *The Handbook of Strategic Public Relations and Integrated Communications* (New York: McGraw Hill, 1996).

17. John V. Pavlik, *Public Relations: What Research Tells Us* (Beverly Hills: Sage Publications, 1987).

18. Tonya Garcia, "Ketchum Employee's Tweet Causes Client Controversy," *PR Week,* Jan. 16, 2009, at http://www.prweekus.com/Ketchum-employees-Tweet-causes-client-controversy/article/126079/.

19. Global PR Blog Week 1.0, "The New PR—A Call to Action," www.globalproblogweek.com.

Social Forces: Economics, Technology, and Policy

We cannot really understand media in a digital age unless we first know about the swirling and interacting social forces that influence and shape communication in and around the larger society. Digital media are the product of these powerful forces. In other chapters, we have traced the impact and interplay of digital media on conventional media, as a process of change. But if we view the full media scene from 30,000 feet, as business leaders say, we learn the true backstory. At first, the digital revolution evolved incrementally, but then it swept onto the scene with great impact and force. It was and is the product of the media economy (and the general economy, of course), technological innovation, and interface with the social, political, and policy spheres.

Some analysts say that the economy, first and foremost, creates a climate for innovation, but new developments only occur when creative individuals invent new systems and devices (computers, the World Wide Web, and the Internet, for starters) usually thought of as hardware and software. At the same time the regulatory hand of government can either encourage or erect barriers to the implementation and use of new media. And sometimes old media also create impediments to change. For example, the greatest enemy of the telecommunication companies that ultimately helped harness the Internet for the use of ordinary people was the newspaper industry, which feared the death of its classified advertising, realizing as it did that online ads with their interactive capabilities would quickly render obsolete those in the ink-on-paper newsprint. Today newspapers, although belatedly, embrace digital communication and have worked feverishly to implement it in their own enterprises.

New media propelled by the forces we have just mentioned have already gone through at least three phases of development: as we noted in Chapter 2, each dramatic and impactful in its own way.

- The Beginnings. There was the period of early development resulting from the creation of the World Wide Web and articulation of the Internet as a massive information, storage, and retrieval network, indeed a network of networks. From the 1970s forward, when early renditions of this new platform was largely in the realm of the military and educational institutions, relatively few people knew about it or thought they'd ever use it.[1]
- Boom and Bust. From 1994 forward, the new platform blossomed as the personal computer won wide adoption, not just in offices and businesses, but at home too. Around 1998 or 1999 the Internet bubble began, and new businesses (called dot-coms) soared as tens of thousands of websites blossomed, and a powerful new media economy with billions of dollars at stake emerged. On paper, thousands of new multimillionaires (many in their twenties) triumphed as they created a web industry attended by early search engines and social networking activities. Big media entered the picture creating new enterprises, the most celebrated being the merger of Time-Warner, the publishing and electronic media company, with a relative newcomer, America Online (AOL). Overheated stocks, slow-speed Internet, and other factors brought about the dot-com crash in 2000 and 2001.[2] But the new platform and all that it represented was not to be counted out.
- Rebirth. By 2002 and 2003 there was a comeback with new media companies evolving and old media, some who had not been involved in the dot-com revolution, cautiously entering the fray. With high-speed Internet, flat-panel computer devices, cell phones, and other activity that connected old-line media with the new media of the Internet, broadband, wireless and satellite communication, and digital communication got a new lease on life.[3] This happened because of new economic conditions, easing government restrictions, the deregulation of some old media industries, and other factors.[4] And it should be noted that nothing is static. Once-powerful financial

barriers to entry kept ordinary people from setting up media companies, but that changed with the Internet. And with this powerful force unleashed, the traditional media felt the bite and came to realize that their old business models (with advertising and user fees in a corporate structure) no longer sufficed and called for new approaches, all driven by the digital revolution. It was the connection and interplay that led to a new era for digital media, sometimes called Web 2.0, which involves greater interactivity, better visual and audio capacity, high-speed Internet, and more. Compare websites and Internet media from the late 1990s to those of 2009 and beyond, and one sees a radical change. And no doubt other changes will ensue, driven by the great social forces that guide, influence, and sometimes direct what happens to institutions, organizations, and individuals. It is the interplay of economic and technological forces that influence and stimulate policy—an institutional force that opens pathways for development or sets limits on them. As this was written, the recession of 2008 and 2009 was challenging new media as never before.

Less visible are the ideas and concepts behind the digital media, such as convergence, which we introduced in Chapter 1, and others like connectivity, the digital commons, and networking, which were first the brainchildren of *thinkers* before the *doers* entered the scene. This, not coincidentally, is a case for studying communication theory and other big-idea intelligence. People who studied cybernetics and systems theory in the 1960s got a thirty-year advance look at what would become the Internet. Thoughtful observers of media today often wonder what big ideas are going to shape the communication world of tomorrow and whether digital media is simply another transition on the way to yet another new media revolution.

AN INTERPLAY OF FORCES

The mass media must exist within a particular economic system with all its realities, harsh and happy, and must also cope with government within a particular political system. In a global society with multinational companies, this becomes much more complex, often involving relations between and among countries, global and regional agreements that live within the rules of individual countries, as well as international law and convention. Like other social institutions, the media wind their way through the economic and political systems. A new technology is often the driving force that influences what media do and how they do it.

In this chapter we deal with *communication policy,* usually in the realm of law and regulation, that affects media industries and eventually media audiences. But it also includes the powerful role of the media economy in what is largely a *commercial* communication system in the United States. We look first at political protections and constraints in the context of the role of government and then touch on economic factors. We have dealt repeatedly with the media economy in chapters on individual media and in our discussions of the historical development of communication industries as well as the role of advertising. In our view, **communication policy** is more than governmental rules. It includes the interplay of many factors and forces involving cultural values and traditions; politics and government; economic trends and patterns; and with new media, of course, the march of technology, which has been a driving force. Some commentators prefer to organize all outside influences that affect media under public policy and the mantra of policy that has many and conflicting meanings. Here we prefer to consider communication policy as an integral part of public policy—the organizing framework, formal and informal, of the public and private sectors in play as they cope with social development and change.

For the media sector, communication policy once was mostly associated with the telecommunications industry, a highly regulated entity. The actions that various regulatory agencies take (notably for media, the Federal Communications Communication) result in public policy in the form or regulations, rule-making, and their implementation.

In more recent times, communication policy has taken on a broader interpretation, including electronic media regulation, the digital strategies of corporations, and much more. Always, though, policy is a formulated response to change, sometimes incremental, sometimes radical. Policy also means politics and a political-governmental interface that assesses and adjudicates disputes involving people and institutions. At the time of a new administration in Washington, various study groups, foundations, and others can be counted on to draft manifestos of their policy preferences—and urge the new administration to consider and act on them. When President Obama arrived in the Oval Office on January 20, 2009, there was a stack of such proposals touching on digital television, universal broadband and media ownership, among others.

In the United States, even as media are becoming more global, they are beset with apparent confusions and contradictions. For example, the media in the U.S. enjoy extensive freedoms embodied in the First Amendment to the Constitution of the United States and envied around the globe, which prohibit government interference with freedom of speech and press and which have generally been applied to the modern media system. "No law means no law," the great First Amendment absolutist Justice Hugo Black used to thunder, meaning that freedom of the press meant that government, including all of its branches, should keep "hands off" the free media. However, there are libraries full of court decisions, statutes, and other evidence of a communication law in the United States, some of it promulgated by the very Congress prohibited from doing so in the First Amendment. Lurking below such noble talk is the fact that the U.S. system, linked as it is to commercialization and capitalism, also makes it easy for firms to make money, and often individual rights and property rights are debated by legislative bodies and the courts. As the great broadcaster Fred Friendly once said, "When they say it's not about the money, it's about the money."

It is also curious that government still, to some degree, regulates a media system that is mostly commercial, living within a market economy. This is especially true for broadcasting and some other electronic media. In such a system there is a continuous debate about just what the **public interest**—something required and mandated by government in various communications acts—is and how it is to be expressed and accounted for. The assumption here and in much of the literature of communication law and history is that media get enormous freedoms on behalf of the public as part of a democratic system. What they give back to the public—their **public duty**—is presumably information, entertainment, opinion, and a platform for goods and services. But just how they do this, and whether the public has any say in the matter, is often a case for discussion and sometimes government action.

SEARCHING FOR THE PUBLIC INTEREST

When it reopened its doors in spring 2008, the Newseum, a news museum, underwritten by the media foundation Freedom Forum with contributions from other media companies and philantrophies, its massive façade carried the words of the First Amendment to the U.S. Constitution, thus enshrining them on the Washington Mall not far from the Capitol and the White House. Over the years, media people, scholars, and jurists have raised the question "media freedom for whom?" One Supreme Court justice, Potter Stewart, asked whether this freedom was an *individual right* to be exercised by any criteria or an *institutional right*. With another First Amendment right, that of *religion*, this question is rarely raised. Anyone can exercise freedom of religion, and at the same time organized religion also claims rights as an institution guaranteeing religious freedom. Until the Internet came along, it was difficult to argue that individuals could easily exercise freedom of the press, except as members of the audience. The Internet and World Wide Web allowed anyone who was online to communicate widely and speedily with others most everywhere. This led some critics to say that freedom of the press belongs to those who own a press or broadcast station. Not unreasonably, then, the conflict that exists between government and the media has involved the free flow of information, the content of communication, the ownership of the media, and other matters.

As noted earlier, the print media have been relatively unregulated in form and number (if not in content) because, theoretically, there is no limit on the number of publications that can be produced. This became even more evident when the Internet exploded onto the scene. Electronic media, on the other hand, have had to live with a limited broadcast spectrum that led to government regulation of radio, television, telecommunications, and some aspects of cable. In these instances government has been both traffic cop and an evaluator of the performance of the broadcast system. Unlike many European countries, broadcasting in the United States opted for a commercial approach mainly supported by advertising, instead of a public service system. (This distinction is less important today, however, as electronic media around the world are moving closer to the market model.) In contrast, the Internet operates for the most part with little government restraint. Some regimes, such as China, have demonstrated, though, that it is possible to block some websites the government dislikes.

The issue of diversity of voices in the *marketplace of ideas*—the objective of the laws under which U.S. broadcasting have traditionally operated—is less relevant in a digital era, when almost anyone can have a website and attempt to communicate with others: from a few acquaintances to large numbers of people anywhere in the world. How effectively and with what impact is another issue, but technically what was once impossible in a broadcast system with limited spectrum space is now a reality, for example, to those who post videos on YouTube.

For years, defining *the public interest* was mostly conceived in economic terms. Whatever interested the public was deemed to be *of public interest*. Whether it met a more subtle test that separated matters of public interest from those truly *in the public interest* is another consideration that requires much study and analysis. However, for decades broadcast regulators in the United States tried to enforce a *public interest standard* by requiring public affairs programs, minority hiring, and equal time for political candidates. The idea was to ensure that broadcasters would use the public airwaves to render service to the audience and the community.

DENYING THE BUSINESS OF MEDIA

We treat media economics in this chapter as a force influencing the nature and shape of communications, closely linked to the legal and regulatory framework in what we regard as a capitalistic or free-market economy. There are plenty of media critics, mentioned in earlier chapters, who decry this system, with its emphasis on economic profit, as they worry about the concentration of ownership, biased cultural and political content, the dumbing down of entertainment, and other factors. That said, there has long been a bias against business among many media people, who, while recognizing advertising as "a necessary evil," would have preferred a system where money was not a factor in media operations. That is not the case, however, and the power, role, and emergence of the media as big business is a fact of life in a modern world where the fuel that runs the media machine (advertising and subscriptions) is no longer an adequate explanation for what is happening. The mythology about the news media not being constrained by budgets and spending what they needed to do the job is and was pure fantasy. Someone always paid the bill, and from very early times, in the view of the hardened entrepreneur, the purpose of the media was to deliver audiences to advertisers, though many beneficent owners did believe in the public interest and that they were, in effect, operating a quasi-public institution dedicated to serving their communities or audiences.

While critics today decry the use of the term "media consumer," preferring "citizen" or "person," the fact is that both apply, and both are useful in underscoring the dual role of the media—as a citizen of its community and as a profit-making business. Even the nonprofit media—such as public broadcasting and educational and religious media—require

A playful campaign to oppose media monopolies through a change in communication policy.

commercial discipline and in recent years have also acknowledged that they too operate with a "business model," or means of sustaining their activity with financial resources. If at one time it was unusual to have MBAs in the media, that is no longer the case: they are working not only in the business operations and advertising but also in editorial and programming units. In the best of circumstances, people with creative interests and a desire to write, direct, edit, or produce work alongside those who obtain financing, sell advertising, and scope out new business opportunities. Of course, this reality also has its share of conflicts and the endless debate about who's in charge and whether the media can be truly independent. One of the beauties of the U.S. media scene is a deeply held belief in independent media where there is a firewall or "church-state" relationship between economic interests and professionally developed content, whether news and opinion or entertainment. Once the news media claimed to separate fact from opinion—say, distinguishing news content from editorials and columns—and television separated ads from programming. This is much more difficult in a digital age when bloggers blur information and opinion and are often part and parcel of commercial and advertising interests. At a time when digital media aggregate material from many sources (many from traditional media) and contribute little of their own original work, navigating between factual information and the arguments of advocates is difficult indeed when bloggers blur information and opinion and are often part and parcel of commercial and advertising interests. It is a continuing challenge.

ENTER MEDIA ECONOMICS

Economists and media scholars once gave little attention to the economic role of the media, except as that of another business or industry sector, in the same way that the auto or sport shoe industry is a subset of the larger economic system. That changed in recent decades, when the field of media economics emerged, first from serious study of individual media, such as the economics of the newspaper or the cable industry, and moving on to larger macroeconomic concerns. Media economics gained traction as a field of study from the 1980s forward and was defined by the pioneering media economist Robert Picard as the study of "how media operators meet the information and entertainment wants and needs of audiences, advertisers and society with available resources. It deals with factors influencing production of media goods and services and with the allocation of those products for consumption."[5] As media and entertainment industries and other information industries became more important, their financial earnings attracted greater interest. When media companies, including movie studios, television networks, and newspaper groups, became publicly traded companies with shareholders, as opposed to privately owned (often family) firms, their economic role stimulated important questions by critics, scholars, and policy makers, such as:

- Who owns the media?
- Who supports the media?
- How are media companies financed?
- What are the financial drivers of media firms?
- What accounts for profits and losses?
- What inspires innovation?
- What is the role of technology?

Nestle Corporation products have occasionally been at the center of controversy in disputes with consumer advocates and advocates for developing countries.

As the German media economist Marc M. Treutler put it in a 2004 paper: "Media in general fulfill many, often taken for granted, functions within society. Without media, modern societies would lack communication infrastructure, as well as the political power of the fourth estate, and the wide range from trivial to sophisticated information, not to mention the entertainment provided by media. This importance of media in combination with the outstanding developments within media technology in the last century has made the study of media more popular and significant."[6] Philip Napoli, who studies media policy and economics, says there is another reason: people simply spend more time with the media than they typically do with other products or industries and thus have a greater interest—and stake.[7] That's at the heart of the connection between media economics and communication policy, which we'll discuss later in the chapter.

Media economics is usually paired with media management, or how media companies and enterprises are organized, led, and managed. Commentators study media companies large and small, media leaders, and the so-called moguls, or media barons who own or head large media companies. There are studies of their leadership styles, traits, and passions including biographies of such figures as Oprah Winfrey, Martha Stewart, Ted Turner, Sumner Redstone, Rupert Murdoch, and others as well as studies of their companies. There are endless "how to" management books ranging from how to start and monetize a website to how to create a new magazine or a low-power radio station.

Thus it is clear that the economics of media industries are integrally connected with the overall economic system. The system is largely commercial but not exclusively. Exceptions to the economic profit model are publicly supported media such as the PBS system, National Public Radio, and the U.S. Government Printing Office.

Government and public opinion does, however, play a role in regulating and legitimizing some media transactions. For example, in 1999 and 2000, when two massive media mergers were announced—Viacom's acquisition of CBS and AOL's of TimeWarner—these transactions had to wind their way through the political and regulatory system. There were hearings in Congress and at the Federal Communications Commission since it was necessary to get approval for these corporate marriages. In a country where monopolies are usually forbidden by federal law, these four firms had to make their case in Washington before their deals on Wall Street were fully consummated.[8]

Government regulating the media economy waxes and wanes, depending on public support and ultimate policy. For several decades, there was a tendency toward deregulation of media and a hands-off attitude, but this is always subject to change with political currents and public support.

In the context of controls and driving forces that shape, influence, and guide the media, there is nothing more potent or more powerful than the economy. If the media were once small players in the overall national or world economy, that is no longer true as the big media and telecommunication mergers of recent years have indicated. Whether the issue is Microsoft trying to buy Yahoo!, Google making deals with media companies seeking a larger distribution network, or News Corp. acquiring MySpace after sitting out the first dot-com revolution, new media–old media mashups are likely and continuing. Similarly, the media once lived mostly behind national borders and relied on local and national economic factors to garner their audiences and produce their revenues. Today, global companies produce global media for global audiences, thus crossing national borders in more than a physical sense but economically as well.

Media and the Digital Economy

In a real sense, the media industries bridge the so-called sea changes in the economy, what some call the paradigm change in communication and entertainment industries. The media were a product of the industrial revolution as they produced a product (newspaper, magazines, books, and the like) that was manufactured and sold. The media industries produced cultural objects that they sold to audiences, sometimes with intermediaries involved such as theater owners, bookshops, etc. But a part of manufacturing and extractive industries they were. Even news was a commodity for sale to readers, listeners, and viewers. To some extent radio and television changed that equation. Their products were programs and content sold to stations that subsequently garnered audiences and sold that audience access to advertisers. The motion pictures were also a manufacturing entity producing films and later videos for rental to audiences. With the coming of digitally driven computer communication, the media became a part of the information revolution and its digital economy, which is made up of firms that sell information, interactive relationships, and digital access to various products through **e-commerce** (for electronic).

When AOL announced at the dawn of the twenty-first century that it was acquiring the media giant TimeWarner, the news shocked the world. Highly valued shares of the Internet portal and information company (AOL) made that firm more valuable than TimeWarner even though TimeWarner had tangible assets—subscribers, buildings, employees, etc.—and AOL was more of a virtual company whose main assets were information storage and retrieval—and a sound rating on Wall Street, where investor confidence reigns. Now there are consulting firms that fix values for "digital assets," whether those are old TV programs or news content, much in the way that film libraries are bought, sold, and traded. For a time, all this was enhanced by fact that the media sector was one of the fastest growing segments of the U.S. and world economy on stock exchanges around the world.

The American media system and that of much of the rest of the world now takes two forms, what scholar Wilson Dizard calls "big media/little media."[9] **Big media** are the giant communication companies and conglomerates like Sony, AOL-TimeWarner, and Viacom. They also include major media groups such as newspaper companies, magazine publishers, book publishing groups, broadcast groups, multisystem operators (cable), and others. Some of big media may be a single entity such as an independent broadcast station or newspaper while others represent many "media properties," as the individual units are called, and some cut across industry lines. For example, a firm may have both print and electronic media operations.

At the same time, there are **little media** startups or entrepreneurs, sometimes begun by a single individual with a website and operated with little overhead to a targeted audience. These firms are found almost anywhere these days, not simply in such locales as the Silicon Valley of California, New York City's "Silicon Alley," and Boston's Route 128 electronic corridor. Sometimes these startups are the handiwork of rugged individualists not unlike the pioneering printers of Colonial America. They and their colleagues seek financing through venture capital and other sources of funds. If they are successful in taking their privately held firms to the initial public offering (IPO) stage on the stock market, they have created a publicly held company of which people can buy shares.

Media companies, and thus the media economy, traditionally have had two fundamental sources of revenue or income—advertising and user fees. There are some others such as syndication rights, but even they rely mainly on their "sales" to advertisers of audiences and their revenues from subscriptions; newsstand sales; and monthly cable, Internet, and other fees.[10] The digital revolution has inspired considerable thought about how media business models are changing and modes for explaining them. One such development is "the Long Tail," a term used to explain the **niche strategies** of such firms as Amazon.com, eBay, and Netflix, known for selling a large number of unique items in very small quantities, thus challenging the notion that small inventories trump large ones. The term first appeared in *Wired* magazine in 2004 in the article "Power Laws, Weblogs and Inequality," by Chris Anderson,[11] and was later expanded into a book. He observed that a very few websites had a lot of hits going into them, but millions have only a handful of hits, thus resulting in a frequency distribution with a long tail. Or, as he quoted an Amazon employee, "We sold more books today that didn't sell at all yesterday than we sold today of all the books that did sell yesterday."[12] This explains that the term "the Long Tail" was inspired by a long-known statistical concept but gained popularity by its obvious application to digital media economics. The theory was disputed in a *Harvard Business Review* study in spring/summer 2008 because it did not always work out in practice. Tests on the theory are still ongoing.

BIG IDEAS: MEDIA THEORIES EXPLAINED

The Long Tail Theory

The Long Tail is truly an economic theory for the digital age born in the pages of *Wired* in a 2004 article written by a business journalist named Chris Anderson, but it is based on statistical models that date at least back to 1946. It is based on a power law graph that is used to rank the popularity of specific items. In the movie industry, for example, a few blockbuster films will account for the greatest number of movie admissions and thus revenues, while many films rarely get noticed and have historically disappeared quickly, sometimes the first weekend after their release. The Long Tail explains how businesses with a huge inventory that sell items in small quantities can survive and succeed. A visit to a digital jukebox company called Ecast inspired Anderson to write his article to explain the "business model" for new media companies like eBay, Amazon, and Netflix, which seemed to defy the way businesses, including media businesses, usually work. Typically, they observe the 80/20 rule, in which 20% of the products generate 80% of the revenue. Ecast, by contrast, was not based on the blockbuster principle of the motion pictures, book publishing, and other industries in which there are large sales of a very few items. Anderson noticed that Ecast and other new media companies had niche strategies in which a handful of links could connect up with millions of web logs.

A key factor in the utility of the Long Tail Theory for digital media is storage capacity. If old brick and mortar businesses only allowed for a limited inventory, digital media companies from music labels to cable and financial information services had an almost infinite "shelf space" in cyberspace for their products. This explains why as late as 2008, the twenty-five best-selling albums in American history all had been released before the year 2000. Or as Anderson put it in his book *The Long Tail: Why the Future of Business Is Selling Less for More* (Hyperion, 2006), the "emerging digital entertainment economy is going to be radically different from today's mass market. If the twentieth century entertainment was about *hits,* the twenty-first will be equally about *niches.*" An Amazon employee puts it in practical terms: "we sold more books today that didn't sell yesterday than we sold today of all the books that did sell yesterday." The Long Tail has gained considerable currency in media industries, online business, and viral marketing, for example. Named and popularized by a journalist rather than a scholar, the theory nonetheless draws on early work in mathematical statistics and studies by such scholars as Erik Brynjolfsson, Yu Hu, Michael D. Smith, and others who have used a log-linear curve on an XY graph. There is now considerable research documenting the impact and influence of the Long Tail, but at least one researcher argues that the theory may be a compelling idea—that there is more money to be made in niche products than in blockbusters—but that data sometimes tell a different story (Anita Elberse, *Harvard Business Review,* July-August 2008).

Expressed simply, the theory posits that:

1. With search and social networking sites, a vast array of items and products to select from is no longer a constraint, and online channels can change the shape of the demand curve because people want highly individualized niche products.
2. A lot of small sales add up to something big, collectively outdistancing the traditional blockbusters because digital storage allows for the accumulation of digital assets (or media content) that can be repurposed and resold.
3. Drivers of the Long Tail are affordable computer hardware, high-speed broadband, and "such elaborate filters as search engines, blogs, and online reviews," which help coordinate supply and demand. (See John Cassidy, "Going Long," *The New Yorker,* July 10, 2006.)
4. A glitch in the Long Tail Theory is the continued popularity of blockbuster movies and books (like *Harry Potter*), which Anderson says won't vanish altogether but will gradually decline.
5. **Therefore**, the Long Tail Theory is a useful construct for new media entrepreneurs seeking financing and a framework for new economic measures for the media industries that will validate today's niche strategies—or sink them.

Corporate Cultures and Revenue Models

While media companies originally based their business plans on the **law of large numbers**, in which they delivered larger and larger audiences to advertisers, they are increasingly involved with the **law of right numbers**—specific demographics of audience or even their psychological preferences. Newspapers, magazines, radio, and television were masters of the large numbers. They found advertisers who paid for much, if not all, of the costs of production. Then they gave their audiences a bargain—a newspaper or magazine for a fraction of the amount it really cost to produce. A single copy of a newspaper that might cost $5 to produce, say, was sold for $1. Television, of course, is the master of large numbers, delivering massive audiences for the Super Bowl or Olympics or a celebrated trial, all paid for by advertisers, as the viewing public paid only for their television set and the electricity needed to power it.

The "right numbers" connects audience demographics with specific content. A "right numbers" model, as opposed to "large numbers," offers a smaller audience but one that is targeted—by age, gender, income, education, location, interests, and other demographic factors—specifically to the content of the message. Thus, a skier would pay a premium for a glossy specialized magazine that was only partly paid for by advertising. Cable programming followed this model as well by offering programs like MTV and VH1 for young audiences or Lifetime for female viewers. Some program fare also aimed at lifestyle or "psychographic" characteristics, such as people who want luxury goods and famous brand names, even though they might not be in the highest income bracket.

As for their structure, media and media firms range from small entrepreneurs to large corporations or conglomerates. In the family business model (a kind of mom-and-pop operation) a single individual or family owns and controls the enterprise. Some of these privately held operations, like the Hearst Corporation or the *Forbes* magazine group, often associated with founding families, can get quite large. Other media follow the corporate model with financing from various sources and executives who work for a board of directors. There are also media industry groups, such as a large publishing firm that produces scores of magazine titles, or a newspaper group (sometimes called a chain) with papers (a.k.a. "properties") in several cities and countries. Media groups might own print, broadcast, and electronic media enterprises as well as integrated digital operations from many entry points and seek what they call "synergy" when they can work together and benefit from corporate cooperation. Conglomerates most often own a variety of firms such as communication media and other enterprises like hotels, pharmaceuticals, and the like.

New Business Models for Media

Although some new media business models have seemingly evolved naturally (like "the Long Tail," which was not in the mind of founders of eBay), others are more self-conscious and are inspired by changes in the economy. For example, the digital revolution has displaced some of the major media, such as newspapers, magazines, and television as well as ad agencies. The reason: more competition, new platforms, and less revenue for some firms. Thus the displacement between traditional and new media has spurred remarkable job loss as tens of thousands of employees have been fired. The newspaper industry, especially hard hit, began to cut its reporting staffs, especially investigative reporting and foreign correspondence, both of which are expensive. This inspired nonprofit enterprises, usually foundation funded, aimed at filling the gap. At the same time, advertising and subscription losses across other media have given rise to a national conversation on new business models (terms once unknown to most journalists and media professionals) to fund media that no longer seem to compete well in a ruthless economy where a few firms dominate. Some of the new models are:

- *Philanthropic Funding*—A generous donor or foundation decides to underwrite a new project, such as ProPublica, an investigative reporting service, led by the former managing editor of the *Wall Street Journal,* or the Knight Foundation's innovative new media initiatives that fund start-up projects and help incubate creative efforts to provide community coverage.

■ *Foundation Model*—A media firm simply incorporates as a foundation or as a 501(c)(3) tax exempt nonprofit and leaves behind the commercial model by getting grants or contributions that give donors a tax exemption. Advertising can be accepted if all proceeds go back into the company and no profits are made—or taken. Harper's magazine follows this model, as does the *St. Petersburg Times,* which is owned by a foundation, the Poynter Institute.

■ *Membership Model*—a media enterprise supported by member dues, rather than advertising. One example of this type of model is *National Geographic,* where subscribers become members of the National Geographic Society, a scientific organization. Another example is *consumer Reports,* published by the 501 (c) (3) tax-exempt nonprofit Consumers Union of United States, Inc., which also does not accept advertising, and its members are the paid subscribers of *Consumer Reports* and ConsumerReports.org. One of the most successful membership organizations that produces media is AARP, which publishes the largest magazine in America. Some public broadcasting stations are also member-supported.

■ *Employee Ownership Model*—Employees of a media company finance the establishment or purchase of media outlets, with stock assigned accordingly and used as an incentive along with salary increases. This has been tried before in newspapers—and currently is the model for the book publisher W.W. Norton and might work again.

■ *Government Subsidy Model*—More common in Europe, where government subsidies to newspapers have a long tradition to keep diversity of voices alive, in the United States there are various tax-exempt benefits media derive from government, and some local communities have provided new Internet businesses with free rent, tax exemptions, and other benefits to promote job growth. The U.S. government also has prohibited sales tax on Internet businesses to promote their development. There have been various conferences[13] and seminars—ranging from universities to media reform groups—on the notion of new business models, both to save dying old media forms and valued media services that no longer seem commercially feasible. Another impetus is diversity of voices. An important book by law professor C. Edwin Baker, *Media Concentration and Democracy* (2007),[14] mentioned tax exemptions and subsidies as a possible solution to media concentration. And, of course, there have been postal subsidies for distributing media products from the beginning of the postal service. New media models, however, are really not new. In the nineteenth century, editor Horace Greeley urged and then created an employee-ownership model at his *New York Tribune,* and for many years the *Kansas City Star* and *Milwaukee Journal* were employee-owned. In the 1930s, in his classic work, *Lords of the Press*, the press critic George Seldes urged labor unions, universities, and foundations to establish general interest newspapers (instead of simply covering their own concerns), but this idea never took off.

A test lab at *Consumer Reports* assesses the effectiveness of a computer gadget that will be reported in an article in the magazine, which is an example of the membership model for media businesses.

Free Markets and Regulatory Controls

There is much written about the motives, corporate cultures, and long-term effects of the media environment of which we are now a part.[15] The wild card will be the role of the digital communication, including the Internet, where many firms have sometimes had high stock values, but few have achieved sustained profits. As noted previously, the Internet economic model is still largely unsettled, although it seems to be settling into one that is advertising-based. Most of the content and information offerings of the Internet are free for the user and paid for by advertisers, special interests, or product manufacturers.

A few media firms do charge for subscriptions and encrypt their content. However, one of the most successful paid Internet publications, the Wall Street Journal Online, changed its model when Rupert Murdoch bought it in 2007 as he argued paid advertising paired with free content was preferable. The Internet offers both the "right audience" of highly specialized and specific individuals as well as potentially massive cumulative audiences. It combines the best of the large circulation and narrowly oriented audience segment. It is both "broadcasting" in the sense of reaching millions or even billions and "narrowcasting" to small, segmented audiences. Of course, it also has the advantage of interactivity. At the same time, the Internet, unlike television, does not yet reach everyone, but the "digital divide" mentioned earlier is closing. By 2010 it is anticipated that only a few—among them older people, the poor, and homeless—will be without Internet service.

In recent years many traditional media have refined and modified the "large numbers" model, including newspapers with business plans that carefully segment their markets, seeking upscale readers instead of serving the general interest reader as they once did. This is disturbing to many critics who fear that communication for the common person, pioneered in America and transmitted to the world, may be in jeopardy. Others say that the world will soon be fully connected, and nearly universal communication will be possible.

So it is clear that the world of traditional and new media traverse both the old economy of manufacturing and hard goods as well as the virtual economy of digital communication. At the moment these operate with only modest government intervention and oversight. That could change, of course, since politics and policy are creatures of economic trends. In good times, regulation, and control usually decline, but when depressions, recessions, and other downturns come, the role of regulation accelerates as the media economy lives on a continuum between optimum freedom, even near absolute freedom, and control by government and the public sector.

Thus, the economic, technological, and policy considerations in understanding media truly commingle and interface as they become more or less important depending on circumstances. Public policy, of course, is the beneficiary of all of them connecting together since policy is a political, governmental, or private sector articulation in changing the course of the media industries and functions as well as a problem solver—and sometimes a troublemaker too. The media must traverse very human forces that greatly influence and sometimes direct the societal factors that ultimately determine media's future for citizens, institutions, and society itself.

INDEPENDENCE WITH CONTROLS

Communication Policy

Communication policy is variously described as government interface with media institutions on behalf of the public, to a more complex formulation that involves the private sector, other social institutions, and interests.[16] It grew out of the legal and regulatory regime that originally governed broadcasting, although the scholar Daniel Lacy once observed that all communication policy in the United States starts with the First Amendment. Still, in a society that regards its media system as independent, with guarantees of press freedom enshrined in the Constitution, a discussion of media policy or "controls" on the media may seem curious. Control, after all, is at the other end of the continuum from freedom; where there is complete and authoritarian control, there can be little, if any, freedom. In the American context, however, controls are in fact merely constraints, such as regulations with a public policy purpose that allow the balancing of various individual and social interests with those of the media. Such controls include communication policies that set standards and allow for resolution of disputes as well as the political activity that shaped those policies in the first place.

Controlling Objectionable Content

In colonial America, people feared royal charters that licensed the media and could shut them down. Today, Americans and citizens of other countries are concerned about potential controls or constraints on cyberspace and the free flow of information. Well-meaning efforts to fight cyber crime, for example, can have the unintended effect of constraining freedom and even fostering censorship. While technical limitations may make censorship difficult on the Internet, there have been efforts to block pornography and political material in the United States and Germany, for example, and to stop political dissidents in China. Because of its capacity to store and manipulate information, the Internet poses new challenges for those who invest in and own media. It is a widely held belief that Internet content should be free. Some go so far as to consider it a right.

Not all controls involve government. While **censorship** is an official act of a government to block communication, individual merchants have the right to censor by refusing to stock certain objectionable CDs, videos, books, or magazines. The giant firm Wal-Mart, for example, has refused to sell some music, books, and magazines it objects to, even though their content is not illegal in any sense. Media owners can decide to carry a cable channel or pay-per-view offering—or not. Influence on advertisers from economic, religious, educational, and other interests can also play a role in the communications process. A business that gets a critical article can pull its advertising. Thus, there are very real influences of policy and politics that shape our media system, operations, and content.

Controlling Political Communication

In any discussion of the political conditions that confront the mass media in America, it is critical to distinguish between the media as "the press," or news media—which include both publishing and electronic media with all their digital incarnations—and other forms of communication whose efforts are mainly directed toward entertainment or advertising, for which there have traditionally been different standards. While the lines between all media are blurring, converging, and merging, the legal system still deals with news and entertainment/advertising differently, though this will likely change in time. Of course, all media are part of an integrated system, and all are affected by the entire complex of political factors that relate media and government in the American society.

Against a worldwide standard, American media, whether delivering news or entertainment, are separate from government; they operate independently and are not reliant on government funds or supervision. At the same time, it should be said that media systems in Latin America, Asia, and Russia, once tightly controlled by government, are moving toward full democratization. At the same time there remain government-owned satellite and television channels in the Middle East. Still there has been enough change in Latin America and Asia, for example, that it is fair to say they are liberalizing, and the once stark contrasts with the United States no longer exist. However, exceptions remain in totalitarian states such as Cuba, Myanmar, and North Korea. And it should be said that the media in Russia, while technically free, face considerable government restraint.

That said, looking at media through a country-by-country comparison is no longer very useful. There is now a global media system with global media companies that must live within the laws of various nations in an internationally acceptable manner. The rather permissive media laws and traditions of the United States do not always apply abroad, and naturally this reality is shaping what media companies can do. In a world of

Political advertising, a part of political communication, uses many platforms and platforms within platforms, such as this human rights demonstration where T-shirts and signs are used.

cross-border communication, there are some international agreements about the Internet, intellectual property (copyright), and satellite transmissions, but there is also much that is yet undefined. The flip side of this issue is that piracy of intellectual property is a fact of life in some countries, where media outlets simply appropriate content from U.S. sources. This includes movies, TV shows, books, video games, and other material. And as we mention later in connection with libel, some individuals, companies, and governments go "forum shopping," finding a place where they can sue U.S. media on grounds that no American court would accept. Similarly, governments like Russia and Singapore have expelled media outlets and correspondents when they did not please the local regime in spite of whatever First Amendment rights might exist back home.

Protecting the Public Interest

By deeply established tradition, the news media in the United States are expected to provide information, debate, and opinion to the public and are often described as "trustees" or "representatives" of the people. However, there is no legal requirement for them to do so. They have been variously labeled the "watchdogs of the public interest," and even as the "**fourth estate**," implying that they act almost as a branch of government. Quite often, this role puts the press in conflict with the government. There is typically conflict between the media and virtually every American president, most often involving the control of information—and embarrassing revelations. During the Bush administration, for example, revelations about CIA domestic spying by intercepting phone calls on citizens in the name of national security sparked controversies.

The press and government often are at odds during wartime, which has caused historians to remark that "the first casualty" in war is the truth. This has been the case in the United States from the American Revolution and through the Iraq and Afghanistan wars of the twenty-first century. Similarly, the War on Terrorism, which began after the attacks on the World Trade Center and the Pentagon in September 2001, has brought much wrangling between the media and government over transparency of information. Historically, in most conflicts, the government not only controlled the conduct of troops, but it also attempted to control information about the war, especially those related to national security. The news media, in their desire to deliver information and form opinion on this important public concern, naturally resisted and even resented that control. In the Iraq War, which began in 2003, reporters were "embedded" with military units but had limitations on what they wrote and observed.

Sometimes conflict between press and government centers on particular individuals, for example by focusing on the alleged sexual or financial misconduct of members of Congress or the executive branch.

Covering Electoral Politics

Another area of conflict between government and the press is the coverage of elections, especially presidential elections. In presidential campaigns, the candidates and their campaigns are often sharply critical of the press, charging bias and unfair portrayals.[17] In the 2008 presidential campaign, the old pattern was there from the primaries forward, with the campaigns complaining loudly about press bias or, in the case of Senator Hillary Clinton, who eventually lost the Democratic nomination to then-Senator Barack Obama, that the press was unnecessarily snide and sexist. Senator John McCain's campaign likewise accused the press of being a conduit for ageist attacks. Such criticism has inspired media critiques, ad watches, and other efforts at media accountability. In other countries, disputes with the press during elections have often led to censorship of a harsh nature. This has notably been true in some African and Middle Eastern countries in recent years. This has not happened in the United States, though candidates are sometimes wary because the public often has a negative view of the media. In fact, one recent survey suggested that if the public could reconsider the Bill of Rights in the U.S. Constitution, it would not grant so much latitude and freedom to the press.

To survive in our system, the mass media perform two major functions:

■ First, the media provide a forum of communication for the nation, a *commonality of interest*. The daily agenda for public discussion is set by the press, and this provides a sort of list of topics and issues to talk about. That agenda allows public opinion to form and emerge as people discuss its topics within the information provided by the press.

■ Second, the media serve both as *advocates* and *intermediaries* for the citizenry as they debate the topics on the news agenda from the standpoint of various social, economic, and political institutions.

The first function leads to consensus and cooperation, whereas the latter may lead to conflict. One allows the media to be a central nervous system for the nation, while the other is a correcting device that represents the people when other institutions need an independent evaluation. For example, a government agency that is performing poorly will not announce its shortcomings to the public, which deserves to know them. It is the responsibility of the press as watchdog of the public interest to report them.

Thus our news media exist in an atmosphere of both consensus and conflict. The balance between the two is closely related to the ability of the press to adjust to the political and governmental climate at the time. The news media both report on the activities of government and occasionally participate in it as petitioners in court or as supporters (or opponents) of candidates for public office.

To understand our press fully, it is vital to realize that, for the most part, *they* see themselves as non-ideological entities, or as instruments of fairness and impartiality in a world of self-serving politicians and government officials. Some citizens, especially those who are criticized by the news media, obviously have a different view. But in comparison with news systems that openly declare partisan political allegiances, such as exist in Britain and France, our press is to a large extent politically independent and generally nonpartisan. Occasionally the press may endorse political candidates, but the media are not part of any political party or funded directly by the government—the hallmarks of media in other countries.

POLITICAL PROTECTIONS: THE CONSTITUTIONAL FRAMEWORK

Political as well as economic considerations place limitations on media in all democratic systems. In Great Britain, for example, although newspapers are privately owned, it is a crime to publish anything from public documents unless prior authorization is obtained. Reporters are allowed to report only what is said at a trial, nothing more. Pretrial publicity is not permitted.

The political environment of the American media has two fundamental elements:

■ First, a guarantee of freedom of the press is *clearly embodied* in the U.S. Constitution.
■ Second, that freedom is *not absolute*. As it has come into conflict with other rights and freedoms, legal limitations on freedom of the press have been established.

We begin an examination of these limitations by looking at the constitutional guarantee of a free press that arose from America's colonial experience.

The Free Press: A Historical Legacy

Prior to the Revolution, the American colonies were ruled by England. Governors representing the Crown were appointed for each colony to ensure that English laws and English policies prevailed. With English law came a specific set of legal relationships between the press and the government. One principle embedded in those laws was that of **prior restraint**; that is, the government could not only punish those responsible for illegal publications but also prevent the publication of material it did not like. The government, in short, could censor publication.

In England, the Crown had not enforced its prior restraint laws for many decades before the Revolution, although as noted in Chapters 3 and 4, it had jailed or fined some individuals whose publications it did not like. English pamphleteers and newspaper writers in the eighteenth century often criticized the government without reprisal. But in the colonies, where rebellions were an ever-present possibility, the Crown's governors sometimes required that any comment on the government's activities be reviewed and approved before publication. As detailed in our history of the newspaper, the governors would occasionally decide to crack down, as in the case of Ben Franklin's brother, James, who was jailed and later forced to give up his paper for criticizing the government, and the celebrated case of John Peter Zenger, publisher of the *New York Weekly Journal*.

Zenger was charged with seditious libel, that is, libel against the government or state—for defaming the Crown and its governor. At his lawyer's urging, the jury found him not guilty because what he had published, although critical of government, was true. The jury's verdict thus asserted the right of citizens to speak out against the government. The Zenger case did not change the laws regarding libel, but it did put public opinion firmly behind the idea that newspapers should be allowed to print the truth even if it was contrary to the wishes of the government. All during the remaining time of English rule, the principle of prior restraint remained a part of the legal system for many years, but it was seldom enforced.

In the first great freedom of expression case in the American colonies, learned lawyer Andrew Hamilton defends printer John Peter Zenger.

The First Amendment

Curiously enough, despite the key role played by newspapers, pamphlets, and broadsides in mobilizing support for the Revolution, the framers of the U.S. Constitution did not mention freedom of the press in the original document. For one thing, they could neither agree on what the concept meant in practical terms nor see how such a provision could be enforced. In addition, some of the members of the constitutional convention argued that there was no need to guarantee such freedoms.

Before the Constitution was finally ratified, however, several states insisted on several amendments that guaranteed a list of freedoms. These ten amendments were accepted and known as the Bill of Rights. Pre-eminent among these is the **First Amendment**, which states, "Congress shall make no law...abridging the freedom of speech, or of the press." These words are known as the free speech and free press *clause* of the First Amendment. (The amendment also includes guarantees of freedom of religion and freedom of assembly). At first glance, the clause seems clear and unambiguous. Yet through the years, as additional media have come into being, the press and the government have become enmeshed in a tangle of issues that have confused the public, perplexed the most able jurists, and placed a variety of constraints on those who operate the mass media.

How could such confusion occur? At the outset, we should recognize that even in the first days of the republic, many of the founders had mixed feelings about the merits of a "free press" and the extent to which it should be unfettered. Some had qualms because it seemed obvious that newspapers were instruments of political power. For example, newspaper enthusiasts today are fond of quoting Thomas Jefferson, who wrote, "Were

New York Times journalist Judith Miller was jailed for refusing to reveal her sources who identified and unmasked a CIA operative.

The Newseum in Washington, D.C. promotes and defends First Amendment values through exhibits and public programs. The words of the First Amendment are on the left face of the building on the Washington Mall.

it left to me to decide whether we should have a government without newspapers, or newspapers without government, I should not hesitate a moment to prefer the latter." Less frequently quoted is the qualifying sentence that followed in the language of the day: "But I should mean that *every man should receive those papers and be capable of reading them*." And almost never quoted are the disillusioned remarks of Jefferson after being opposed frequently by the press. He bitterly noted, "The man who never looks into a newspaper is better informed than he who reads them, inasmuch as he who knows nothing is nearer to the truth than he whose mind is filled with falsehoods and errors."

Almost all Americans will nod vigorously in agreement if asked whether they believe in freedom of the press. It ranks with freedom, the family, and the American flag as a source of national esteem. But when pressed on some specific case—such as pornography, criticism of their favorite public figure, or unfavorable stories about themselves—their assent to a free press is likely to vanish. Generally, then, support of freedom of the press is often based not on the idea that the government simply has no right to control the press but on the belief that a free press is the best method for ensuring a well-informed public and a stable democracy. When the press appears to be doing a poor job of informing the public, support for its freedom is likely to diminish.

The issue of freedom of the press (media in general) is complicated by issues related to libel, offensive material (e.g., sacrilegious films, pornography), technical needs to control the airwaves, secrets during wartime, and many other issues. It is further complicated by jurisdictional boundaries between various courts. For example, over the years, most libel cases were fought in the state courts under state statutes. Federal courts rarely intervened to broaden press freedom until well into the twentieth century. By then, the debate over freedom of the press had become more complicated with the appearance of film and the broadcast media.

PROTECTED VS. UNPROTECTED SPEECH   Are the movies, soap operas, and radio programs forms of "speech" and "the press," and therefore protected by the First Amendment? As long ago as 1915 the Supreme Court ruled that cinema was a "business, pure and simple, originated and conducted for profit" (*Mutual Film Company v. Ohio*). Therefore, the Court continued, it was not protected by constitutional guarantees of free speech and a free press. But in 1952, the Supreme Court reversed this decision, after the state of New York forbade the screening of an Italian film (*The Miracle*) in the state because it was "sacrilegious." When the case was appealed in the Supreme Court, it ruled that the state had no power to censor films on religious grounds.[18] The effect was that films were granted the protection of the First Amendment.

Radio and television present a more complicated situation. Whereas in principle there are no limits to the number of newspapers that can be published, or films produced, because of technical limitations, the number of frequencies that can be used for broadcasting has been severely restricted although liberalized in recent years. This difference between broadcasting and print has provided the basis for a host of government regulations regarding broadcasting. In other words, broadcast regulation has been justified by the scarcity of channels. Therefore, government regulates the owners of broadcast stations by granting and renewing broadcast licenses, as well as by regulating content to some extent. Regulations regarding broadcasting are generally compromised between the principle that "the public owns the airwaves" and the Constitution's guarantee of freedom of speech.

TECHNOLOGICAL CHALLENGES TO REGULATION   As the media developed, and especially with multiple cable channels, digital television, and Internet broadcasts or bloggers' posts, the idea of a scarcity of channels became obsolete. New technologies have greatly expanded the means by which messages can be transmitted to audiences. For example, with the advent of cable television and direct broadcast satellite transmission, as well as such emerging technologies as broadband, we are entering a period not of broadcast scarcity but of *abundance*. While this has led to a certain amount of deregulation, some of the old regulatory regime still reigns. Perhaps the greatest source of conflict over the right to a free press comes from the fact that it is only one among many other important rights. The right to a free press sometimes conflicts with society's right to maintain order and security. For example, the media's exercise of its freedom may conflict with the ability of the police and courts to do their jobs, or with the government's ability to maintain secrets it deems necessary for national security. Freedom of the press may also conflict with the rights of individuals, such as the right to privacy and the right to a fair trial. As a result of these conflicts, the courts have frequently ruled against the press's right to publish anything it pleases. The most important limitations on the press imposed by the courts concern *libel, coverage of trials, obscene material, and government secrets.*

As we noted in Chapter 8, television is in the midst of yet another revolution—that of a conversion from conventional *analog* to *digital* transmission. For years critics fretted about this, arguing that large numbers of people would be disenfranchised by the change, but when it was scheduled to occur in 2009, about 10 million U.S. households were not getting cable or satellite service and thus had the option of buying a simple transmission box with the help of a government coupon and still use their old TV set. This does point up the underlying discussion, much of which centers on how the public interest can best be served in a digital era when technology has pushed aside many of the guidelines that have protected the public in the past. And while there will be more and more abundance of TV and other wireless and electronic options for people, there are still many aspects of the communication system that are regulated by the government. As Charles Firestone and Amy Korzick Garmer of the Aspen Institute have written, "quite simply, the move to digital broadcasting will likely change the very nature of the most powerful and important medium of communication in the world."[19]

Technology's Place in Regulation: From Printing to Cyberspace

Government policies or controls have often focused on technology as a way of encouraging access to information or blocking it. From early printing presses, which were licensed, to cyberspace, which was the subject of official law in the United States and other countries, governments acting as agents for citizens (or for leaders or both) have always played a role. Without a royal license in many European and Asian societies, printers were not allowed to make copies of their works for distribution. Because absolute monarchs believed that they should control all communication—and thus have a clear sense of what was being said and by whom—they guarded this authority jealously. The right to freely print and distribute news, information, and opinions was central to revolutions in the United States, France, and other nations, and often still is, as undemocratic regimes are replaced. In the 1980s and 1990s, as communism fell in the former U.S.S.R and its satellites, military regimes were toppling in Latin America, and Asia was charged by new economic progress, though some governments had policies that were hardly friendly to the media. Although media freedom is usually guaranteed by law or encouraged by enlightened regimes, even in the freest of societies government agencies act as traffic cops to assign broadcast frequencies; register copyrights; prevent advertising practices; or other social, community, or citizen functions.

Much of the activity of government and other institutions trying to monitor, administer, or influence communication has been driven by technology. To prevent a kind of broadcast anarchy, it was necessary to assign frequencies and channels for radio and television. Later, cable systems were "franchised" in local communities that were given to a cable operator to develop since it was believed that only a monopoly system would be economically feasible. Telecommunication or telephone systems also benefited from the same kind of monopoly, much of which has been subsequently broken. Federal agencies evolved to administer communications, trade, and other arenas where monitoring and adjudicating disputes was believed to be essential. While regulation often seems to come down on the negative side, limiting the choices of media operators and enforcing rules, that's not really the case. Historically in the United States, media regulation has been mostly a hands-off policy by the government. If anything, government has encouraged the development of radio, TV, cable, telecommunications, and broadband by minimizing regulation as compared with regimes in Latin America and Asia, for example. Internet businesses were tax-exempt to encourage the development of the medium and to foster job creation. A major indicator of the "regulation light" policy of several administrations in Washington beginning with the Carter presidency and continuing through Reagan, Bush I, Clinton, and Bush II rarely resulted in fines for media operators, loss of broadcast licenses—or approval of mergers that created larger and larger media firms.

In the 1990s, as various media industries (telephone, cable, broadcast, motion pictures, newspapers) vied for control of new media enterprises, old regulatory schemes were scrapped for a new one. The Telecommunications Reform Act of 1996 was passed by Congress and signed into law. It permitted various business connections between media industries that previously would have been in restraint of trade and subject to antitrust laws, which exist to break up monopolies. The legislation also relaxed the rules for media ownership and content. For most observers, the new act was profoundly important. To many in industry it deregulated a once highly regulated industry and allowed for more competition. To other critics the new law was the handiwork of big media companies and was a "license to make money" unconnected to the public interest. It was argued that the new law was a tradeoff that freed broadcasters and other media industries from regulation in return for providing business growth and new jobs. And there was also the hope that the law would spur the growth of the Internet and make it more widely available to school children in the classroom and all citizens at home. This happened with amazing speed.

INDECENCY AND REGULATION   One part of the Telecommunications Reform Act that drew considerable controversy was the Communications Decency Act, which banned indecent or patently offensive speech. The act imposed criminal sanctions for content that was deemed obscene or indecent that was transmitted over the Internet. The act made it a crime to use an "interactive computer service" to send minors "any comment, request, suggestion, proposal, image or other communication that, in context, depicts or describes, in terms patently offensive as measured by contemporary community standards, sexual or excretory activities or organs."[20] Although signed into law by President Clinton, many civil liberties and cyberspace groups objected, saying that any control over the Internet would "criminalize" speech and curtail the free and open system for which the Internet is known. The case was reviewed in the courts and struck down by a federal court in Philadelphia; the Supreme Court of the United States subsequently upheld a free and open Internet. The Internet and other forms of digital communication may have increased access to communication, but they have not ended government interest in monitoring and controlling. It is inevitable that every new technology will bring legal and other government control interests. Sometimes these reflect citizen interests, for example, parents in the case of the Internet or specific industries trying to block new competition. In all disputes over technology, both sides cite the public interest rationale for their actions. Even the highly favorable exemption of e-commerce from sales taxes is a government control, although a favorable one.

LINCHPINS OF COMMUNICATION LAW

Against the backdrop of communication policy issues in Washington and various efforts to encourage or constrain digital communication, the old world of media law still exists. It includes defamation—libel and slander (written and spoken defamation)—which protects reputations; privacy, the "right" to be let alone and to enjoy one's personal freedom; copyright, the protection of intellectual property; obscenity and pornography, linked to changing concepts of decency and morality; advertising law; and other aspects especially related to digital conflicts. Other concerns of the media that have gotten considerable attention include reporters' privilege, involving protection of reporters' sources, and fair trial–free press concerns, which involve the balance between First Amendment freedom of the press and the right to "a fair and speedy trial," guaranteed by the Sixth Amendment to the U.S. Constitution. For the most part media law is handled in the state courts in the United States and only gets into the federal system in the rare cases of espionage law, copyright (guaranteed in the Constitution), or electronic media regulation. Thousands of cases move through the courts every year, and occasionally crises or various issues rise to a higher plane. For example, a pattern of large libel judgments might be seen as eroding freedom of the press and undermining investigative reporting, or privacy judgments may suggest that we are gaining on or losing privacy. In the digital age, all of the legal standards that applied to the old media are still applicable, though many people don't believe this or wish it were not so. A person can be libeled on a blog or have his or her privacy intruded on. Copyright or intellectual property is often a major concern as downloading and file sharing makes copying very easy. In one dispute, the media giant Viacom, which owns MTV Networks and other media properties, sued Google because clips from its shows had been uploaded by users of Google's YouTube website. Although this dispute was eventually settled, it is exemplary of the kinds of conflict likely to occur when one person's (or company's) unconstrained freedom bumps into another's rights—or property.[21]

The Libel Conundrum

Injunctions against making false, defamatory statements about others have ancient origins. Among the Ten Commandments is the injunction "Thou shalt not bear false witness against thy neighbor." In ancient Norman law it was written that "a man who falsely called another a thief or manslayer must pay damages, and holding his nose with his fingers, must publicly confess himself a liar."[22] The idea that a person whose reputation had been damaged by another's untrue public statements is entitled to compensation was passed on to the American colonies and on into our contemporary legal system through English law. Today, libel laws not only protect the reputations of individuals but also those of corporations and businesses. With the development of media with huge audiences, it became possible to "bear false witness" and damage reputations on a very large scale, with very serious economic consequences.

Libel Laws and the Media

Every year, libel suits are brought against newspapers, magazines, book publishers, broadcast stations, cable companies, and Internet firms. They constantly test the principle of freedom of the press. The courts must weigh the right of the press to publish freely against the right of people to preserve their privacy, reputation, and peace of mind. The situation is complicated in the absence of any federal statutes concerning libel. It is a matter of state law, and each has its own statutes.

State laws usually give news reporters and the news media some protection against libel suits. They usually allow publication of public records and "fair comment and criticism" of both public figures and public officials. Unfortunately, it is not entirely clear who qualifies as either under the laws of the various states. However, various court cases have defined *public figures* essentially as persons who are well known. Examples are prominent sports stars, entertainment personalities, widely read novelists, or even well-known scientists.

Constitutional protection of the media in libel suits is well established. In a landmark 1964 case, *The New York Times v. Sullivan,* the Supreme Court considered for the first time whether state laws regarding libel might be overturned on the grounds that they violate the First Amendment to the Constitution. During the height of the civil rights conflict in the South, the *Times* had published an advertisement that indirectly attacked the Birmingham,

Alabama, commissioner of public safety. An Alabama jury ruled that the *Times* had to pay $500,000 in damages because the advertisement included some misstatements of fact. But the Supreme Court overruled the Alabama jury, holding that its decision violated freedom of the press. Essentially, the Supreme Court held that a full and robust discussion of public issues, including criticism of public officials, was too important to allow the states to restrain the press through their libel laws. After this case and into the twenty-first century, it is very difficult for public officials to claim libel damages. According to the Supreme Court, only when public officials could prove that the press had shown "malice," "reckless disregard of the truth," or "knowing falsehood" could they sue for libel.

By no means was the libel issue decided once and for all in *Times v. Sullivan*. Since that time courts have repeatedly redefined who is and who is not a public official or a public figure.

Multimillion-Dollar Libel Suits

While the Supreme Court did not radically rewrite the law of libel between the 1980s and the first decade of the twenty-first century, other conditions—mainly economic ones—called attention to the importance of libel as a constraint on freedom of the press. There have been scores of mega-buck libel suits involving business leaders, entertainers, even members of organized crime families; sometime they win, but most often they lose. In recent years, Russian business moguls and Saudi oil interests have engaged in "libel tourism," whereby they sue U.S. media in countries like the U.K., where libel laws are harsher than they are in the United States. Today U.S. courts have not enforced these judgements. Whatever their outcome, the suits are costly for all parties, whether there is a judgment or not. The rising cost of libel trials involves not only those judgments of the courts that penalize the media but also legal fees and increasing libel insurance premiums.

Some critics cite an increasingly conservative judiciary as one of the reasons for increasing libel costs, although David Anderson, a law professor at the University of Texas, argues that the media win nearly as many cases as they lose in the courts.[23] Still, win or lose, the legal costs are substantial. Some observers say that increasing costs have been responsible for diminishing investigative reporting (the so-called "chilling effect"), while others say that the costs check the growing power of the media in necessary ways. It should be noted that many large libel judgments are greatly reduced on appeal or by judges. Almost all knowledgeable observers agree, however, that the cost of libel is having a significant effect.[24]

Libel law and libel cases always bear watching because the law in that area is complex, and it is relatively easy to bring a suit. It should be noted that, although the media often win libel cases or have them thrown out of court, there is still a great cost due to legal fees that can be especially harmful to small publications and broadcasters. One legal scholar, Donald M. Gillmor, sees public officials and celebrities as the culprits in many libel suits and proposes to deny protection to those with "high visibility and the resources to communicate with broad sections of the public," saving the tougher provisions of libel law for ordinary citizens who are genuinely damaged by the media with little ability to fight back.[25] Over the years there have been efforts to mount a libel reform movement. Interest in libel reform typically comes from the media after major cases are lost, but to date it has had little public support. More importantly, the legal profession has little enthusiasm for reform, perhaps because lawyers would stand to lose huge fees under any such plan.

Other proposals have been made to circumvent libel and other media-public confrontations. One such proposal has been advanced by the late Robert Chandler, an Oregon publisher, who called for community complaint councils that would have less authority than press councils but would still offer a safety valve for public feedback.[26] The durable Minnesota News Council, mentioned elsewhere in this book, has also taken up cases on a trial basis in other states and has proposed a modest "nationalization" of their efforts. In Washington State, a news council also thrives. Various public interest groups and foundations have supported press councils and media assessment projects, but only a few have taken hold.

TRIAL BY MEDIA

The Constitution guarantees freedom of the press, but in the Sixth Amendment it also guarantees a fair and speedy trial to defendants. Sometimes publicity about a crime and the suspected criminal seems to make a fair trial impossible. Examples of trial by publicity have been played out many times in high-profile court cases. At one time cameras were barred from courtrooms, but in recent years television and cable coverage of celebrated trials is almost continuous, as in the famous case of O.J. Simpson. Indeed the cable channel Court TV owes its existence to the public's fascination with sensational trials involving celebrities and others. Such cable commentators as Nancy Grace and others offer highly opinionated coverage of leading trials, and there are many legal experts and attorneys eager to be on-the-air sources, giving their views even in the midst of trials.

Various efforts to promote fair trial–free press standards have been proposed over the years. The original rule barring cameras (then mostly still and motion picture) from courtrooms was inspired by the Lindbergh kidnapping case in the 1930s, when the infant son of the country's most famous hero, the flyer Charles A. Lindbergh, was killed. Later the messy murder trial in Ohio involving Dr. Sam Sheppard, and cited as a case of "trial by media," as well as the behavior of the media in their coverage of President John F. Kennedy's alleged assassin, Lee Harvey Oswald, the American Bar Association took action to protect defendants against unnecessary publicity before trial by convening a national commission to establish better rules for the protection of defendants. Led by Justice Paul Reardon of the Massachusetts Supreme Court, the ABA commission suggested rules to restrict the release of prejudicial information. For judges, court officers, attorneys, juries, prosecutors, and the police, these rules carried the weight of law once they were adopted by federal and state courts.

For the press, the Reardon guidelines were voluntary. Nevertheless, in more than thirty states, for more than two decades, "fair trial–free press" committees charged with promoting recommended "codes of conduct" were set up. The guidelines were even issued on little cards for reporters, and for the most part they worked well. Then, in a Washington state case in the late 1970s, a judge used the voluntary guidelines as the basis to restrict press coverage of a murder trial. The fear that this could happen elsewhere quickly unraveled many, though not all, of the codes of the state committees. This illustrates the fragility of the First Amendment, which can be employed to stop even a seemingly beneficial measure like this one, if it could possibly impair press freedom.

Today, few reporters use the Reardon guidelines as such, and there is renewed discussion of the need for some voluntary curbs in a period when television, more often than newspapers, has become more sensational, a phenomenon journalism historian John D. Stevens has called "wretched excess."[27] However, screaming newspaper headlines that might be considered prejudicial are not a thing of the past. In covering many celebrated trials in recent years, supermarket tabloids like the *National Enquirer* or the *Star,* as well as big-city tabloids such as the *New York Post* or *Boston Herald,* have featured accusatory headlines about such highly visible defendants in murder cases. Today most sensational coverage occurs on the 24-hour cable news channels, where ideological programming abounds and "screaming heads" run fast and loose with legal cases and all kinds of political matters and issues.

YouTube co-founders Steven Chen and Chad Hurley learned quickly that they had to deal with changes in copyright infringement, a key issue for digital media. Viacom is suing YouTube and its parent company Google for more than $1 billion.

Google CEO Eric Schmidt created one of the world's largest and most successful digital media companies.

MORAL VALUES: OBSCENITY AND PORNOGRAPHY

Do parents have the right to protect their children from seeing advertisements on the street for pornographic movies or from seeing pornographic magazines displayed at the local drugstore? Many Americans would answer yes, but the Supreme Court's answers have been ambiguous. The most emotional issue in recent times has been child pornography: magazines and films depicting young children engaged in explicit sexual acts with adults and with each other. Public pressure prompts Congress to hold hearings on the subject with some regularity, usually resulting in various laws to curtail the distribution of such material. As a result, the media are virtually forbidden to produce, distribute, or sell child pornography. This issue has accelerated in the age of the Internet.

Two very different conceptions of the role of government underlie debates about regulation of obscene material. Some First Amendment *absolutists* deplore censorship of such material, arguing that government should not attempt in any way to regulate the moral behavior of its citizens as long as the people involved are consenting adults. On the other hand, others take a more moderate line and are inclined to see censorship of obscenity as the proper duty of local or even national government. They tend to feel that a safe society can be maintained only through government regulation of personal behavior, such as sexual activity or the use of alcohol and drugs.

Over the years, the media have received strange and convoluted signals concerning pornography and obscenity: The Supreme Court seemed to side with the conservatives in 1957 when it announced "Obscenity is not within the area of constitutionally protected speech or press" (*Roth v. United States*). That may seem clear enough, but it has not been easy to determine what is or is not obscene. In the 1960s, material could not be declared obscene if it had "any redeeming social value" whatsoever. Then in 1973 the Court made it easier to ban materials by relaxing this standard. Moreover, it stated that material should be judged by local authorities according to standards that "prevail in a given community" (*Miller v. California*). Thus, what is considered obscene in one community may not be obscene in another. But since this decision, the Court has overturned some efforts by local governments to ban materials. What can and cannot be censored on obscenity grounds remains far from clear. In the face of public pressure, the media have censored themselves to some extent. Various industry associations have drawn up codes limiting the treatment of material related to sex. A classic example is the self-regulation of the movie industry in the 1930s, when the self-imposed Motion Picture Producers and Distributors Code became so puritanical that at one point not even butterflies could be shown mating. Later in the 1950s the comic book industry voluntarily (if grumpily) curtailed production of horror comics in response to a public outcry. (Congressional hearings were actually held to determine whether such comic books were harmful to children.) In recent times, electronic games have also had their place at the Congressional witness table as have television and movie producers on occasions when Congress gets agitated about sex or violence.

Today, the National Association of Broadcasters forbids (rather unsuccessfully) the use of "dirty" words and explicit sexual content. The relative purity of broadcasting, however, is also a result of the Federal Communications Commission's enforcement of the Federal Communication Act's strict rules against obscenity. Although we have been dealing here with moral values as they are embodied in the law, the role of the media as a moral teacher and "enforcer" of values, too, has come up repeatedly in recent years. Arguing that the media are not taking on the role once filled by the family, church, or school, critics urge more

Moral values are often an issue in media portrayals, as was the case with singer and actress Miley Cyrus when she appeared in a suggestive photo (not the one here).

care and accountability among media professionals. However, this is strictly a voluntary matter, not something that can be enforced by the courts or other authorities.[28] A whole raft of parents' groups and other monitoring organizations actively pursue what they regard as off-color or suggestive TV programs and even print advertising, especially that with teenagers and younger children in sexually provocative poses. Media too, pick up the scent, as in 2008 when the fifteen-year-old Miley Cyrus, who plays "Hannah Montana," was featured partially clothed in a *Vanity Fair* photo spread. A cable program on MSNBC, *To Catch a Predator,* tracks pedophiles who use the Internet to lure underage children into sexual encounters. Indeed, whatever the old media's transgressions as willing or unwitting transmission belts for suggestive material, the Internet has trumped them ten thousand-fold. There is an endless number provocative websites that are targets for law enforcement agencies probing cyber crime, often aided by bloggers and citizen groups.

THE GOVERNMENT'S SECRETS DURING NATIONAL CRISES

Although the Patriot Act—passed in 2002 as a direct response to the 9-11 attacks—was not aimed at the media per se, it did open a longstanding discussion of what measure a government might take to protect its citizenry in times of national emergencies. This can sometimes mean, for better or worse, a lack of transparency and openness with regard to information about the government and its actions. Certainly this was the case in the administration of George W. Bush, who frequently denied access to information to the media and, according to his press secretary Scott McClellan in a controversial 2008 book,[29] actually misled the media and the public on matters related to the Iraq War and other issues. This is nothing new, however, as most presidents have been at odds with the media over the flow of information, most notably in times of war or other crises.

Recognizing the increased security risks, Americans have generally accepted some form of censorship during wars and politically sensitive periods, including Red scares in the 1950s, the Cold War, and others. Espionage is frequently an issue whether there is a war or not. Even many fervent civil libertarians agree that the government deserves and requires protection during wartime. But such censorship obviously contradicts the guarantee of a free press and limits the public's right to know.

In peace and war, government secrecy has led to many controversies. When Iraq invaded Kuwait in 1991 and the United States sent troops to the Middle East, media access again became an issue. The Iraq War of 2003 revisited the conflict between press and government. One controversial issue was the photo and video coverage of the Abu Ghraib prison.

Direct Censorship in Wartime

In past wars, the government has been able to use various indirect methods to protect its secrets. One of the earliest indirect ways used to control information was to deny access to telegraph, cable, and similar facilities. Reporters then either had to let military censors screen their copy or try to transmit it in some other way. For example, when the battleship *Maine* blew up in the harbor of Havana, Cuba, in 1898, the U.S. government immediately closed the Havana cable to reporters. Similarly, at the outbreak of World War I, the British immediately severed the cables between Germany and the United States. American reporters had to use the English-controlled cables between Europe and the United States and submit their copy to rigid British censorship.

Former CBS (now CNN) correspondent John Roberts was embedded with U.S. Troops in the Iraq War, a practice later criticized.

LIVE

WITH
USMC
1ST
MARINE
DIVISION

JOHN ROBERTS
SOUTHERN IRAQ

"Th' hell with it . . . I ain't standin' up till he does."

"Th' hell with it . . . I ain't standin' up till he does," Joe says to Willie in a panel from the legendary World War II Willie & Joe cartoon series by Bill Mauldin.

The government has also imposed censorship through codes, regulations and guidelines. During World War I, the Espionage Act of 1917 stipulated fines and prison terms for anyone interfering with the war effort in any way. For example, criticism of arms manufacturers was said to be unpatriotic. This enraged newspaper publishers, and legal battles over the issue went all the way to the Supreme Court. Such censorship was later declared unconstitutional, but Congress passed new, even stricter laws to control information. The Sedition Act of 1918 made it a crime to publish anything that abused, scorned, or showed contempt for the government of the United States, its flag, or even the uniforms of its armed forces. As a way to enforce the law, such publications could be banned from the mail. In World War II, only a few days after the Japanese attack on Pearl Harbor, President Roosevelt created the U.S. Office of Censorship and charged it with reviewing all communications entering or leaving the United States for the duration of the war. At the peak of its activity, the office employed more than 10,000 people. Its main objective was to review all mail, cables, and radiograms. A Code of Wartime Practices for the American Press was also issued to newspapers requesting voluntary cooperation from the nation's editors and publishers. Its purpose was to deny the Axis powers any information concerning military matters, production, supplies, armaments, weather, and so on.

Even in peacetime, the media have sometimes censored themselves to protect the national interest. In 1960, for example, the Soviet Union shot down an American U2 spy plane. The incident temporarily ended attempts to improve Soviet-American relations. For a year before the plane was shot down, however, James Reston of the *New York Times* had known that American spy planes were flying over the Soviet Union, but "the *New York Times* did not publish this fact until one of the planes was shot down in 1960."[30] Later, as a favor to President John Kennedy, Reston withheld information about the planned U.S. invasion of Cuba at the Bay of Pigs. Historians and press experts today regard this as a mistake—and subsequent efforts by the White House to get the media to withhold information have usually been rejected.

Challenges to Government Secrecy

While the press often engages in voluntary censorship, there are many examples when the media and the government have been locked in conflict, disputing the government's right to censor the news. Because our shared belief in the need for freedom of the press became such a tradition very early in the life of the nation, any effort by the government to limit that freedom has always met with hostility.

During the Civil War, for example, the 57th Article of War stipulated a court martial and possible death sentence for anyone, civilian and military alike, who gave military information to the enemy. However, newspapers were an indirect source of military information, and Confederate leaders went to great lengths to obtain copies of major Northern papers because they often revealed the whereabouts of military units and naval vessels. As a result, the U.S. War Department tried to prevent newspapers from publishing any stories that described the movements of troops or ships. Editors generally ignored these orders. Even after the war, General Sherman refused to shake hands with Horace Greeley, publisher of the *New York Tribune*, maintaining that Greeley's paper had caused a heavy loss of life by revealing troop movements to the enemy.[31]

Thus, even in wartime Americans have questioned censorship, asking what kind of controls should be imposed and by whom. Clearly, the government has the need to protect itself and a duty to protect the nation. But the press claims a right to inform the public of what government is doing, and the news media maintain that the public has the right to know. Therefore, an inherent conflict exists between the right to a free press and the need to control information that would be damaging to the government.[32]

During the Johnson administration, the Defense Department put together a forty-seven-volume history of American involvement in Vietnam from 1945 to 1967, including secret cables, memos, and other documents. The history, which came to be known as the Pentagon Papers, was classified as *top secret*. In 1971, Daniel Ellsberg, who had worked on the papers but later opposed the war, leaked them to the *New York Times*, hoping that their release would turn public opinion against the war and help bring about its end. Although the papers were both stolen and classified, the *Times* began publishing a series of articles summarizing the contents and some of the documents themselves.

The Nixon administration went to court to stop the *Times* (and later other newspapers) from printing additional articles on the papers, arguing that their publication would endanger national security. In response, the courts issued a temporary restraining order stopping the *Times* from continuing its planned series on the papers. In effect, the courts imposed prior restraint.

Eventually, the case went to the Supreme Court, which ruled against the government. The government had failed to convince the Court that publication of the Pentagon Papers constituted a danger severe enough to warrant suspending freedom of the press. Relieved and triumphant, the newspapers resumed their articles. (Ellsberg was later tried for stealing the documents.) Yet the Court's decision in the Pentagon Papers case is still regarded as controversial, and it resolved little of the debate between government and the press. Conflict continues over the press's right to publish, the public's right to know, and the government's need to protect the secrecy of some activities.

During the 1980s, the Reagan administration engaged in a contentious tug of war with the press over access to government information. President Reagan proposed sweeping changes in the Freedom of Information Act, which provides public access to the various departments and agencies of government, and issued executive orders making access to information about agencies like the FBI and CIA more difficult. Professional groups like the Society of Professional Journalists and the American Society of Newspaper Editors campaigned vigorously against these restrictions. In this instance, there was profound disagreement between the government, which claimed it acted in the best interest of the people by limiting access, and the press, which said the public was better served by the free flow of information. During the administrations of both President Bushes (George H. W. and George W.) as well as President Clinton skirmishes over information release with the media were not uncommon.

POLITICAL CONSTRAINTS: THE AGENTS OF CONTROL

We have discussed several specific areas in which freedom of the press as guaranteed by the Constitution is limited, not absolute. But in practice, freedom of the press depends not only on this abstract constitutional framework but also on the daily decisions of courts, bureaucrats, and politicians.[33]The constitutional framework itself continues to evolve as specific problems and conflicts arise. Moreover, in particular cases the actual freedom of the press may differ from its theoretical freedom. Therefore, we look next at the various agents of political control of the media, including the courts, legislatures, White House, bureaucrats, and even private citizens. These groups may exert both formal controls on the media and informal influence on the flow of information.

Often, the Supreme Court's interpretations of either prevailing laws or the Constitution itself have broken new ground and established new policies. Over the years, the Court has ruled on a long list of issues affecting the media, including newsroom searches, libel, confidentiality of journalists' sources, regulation of advertising, and other matters. It is all a matter of "rights in conflict," as journalist Anthony Lewis once wrote:

> We have libel suits because we think a civilized society should take account of an interest besides freedom to criticize. In other words, individuals have rights too; sometimes they conflict with the rights of the press. It is not uncommon to find rights in conflict; that's why we have judges. But sometimes the press sounds as though the Constitution considers only its interests. If a network or a newspaper loses a case, "That's it, the Constitution is gone; Big Brother has taken over." Well, I don't think life is so simple. The interest of the press may not be the only one of constitutional dimension when there are conflicts.[34]

As a social institution, the media pay more than passing attention to personnel changes at the Supreme Court. Since every presidential election reminds us that presidents do make Supreme Court (and other judicial appointments) subject to Senate confirmation, people speculate about how liberal, moderate, or conservative justices might vote on matters involving press freedom or communication policy. According to media scholar David Anderson, however, press defendants appearing before the Court, from its beginning two hundred years ago to the present, have generally fared worse than other defendants.[35]

The Regulatory Agencies

The Federal Communications Commission (FCC) makes and enforces rules and policies that govern all kinds of communication industries, from telephone companies to television networks. The FCC's rulings have the status of law and can be overturned only by the federal courts or by congressional action. Its rules govern advertising, ownership of broadcasting stations, obscenity, and a number of special circumstances. For example, the FCC and the courts legislated a personal attack law, which gives individuals who are attacked by a broadcast station airtime to respond. The FCC also enforces the equal-time rule for political candidates, which states: "If a licensee shall permit any person who is a legally qualified candidate for any public office to use a broadcasting station, he shall afford equal opportunities to all other such candidates for that office in the use of such broadcasting station." Based on the equal-time rule, the commission later formed the fairness doctrine, which grants equal time to people representing issues and causes. Subsequently in the 1980s, the FCC dropped the fairness doctrine ruling, stating that it penalized the media and had outlived its usefulness in an era when abundance replaced scarcity of broadcast signals. Some members of Congress maintained that the fairness doctrine inhibited speech on the part of the media and the public, whereas most disagreed and reinstated the doctrine, only to have it vetoed by then-President Reagan. This convoluted series of changes, and other aspects of broadcast regulation, are frequently debated by media people, legal scholars, and legislators. Debates over the fairness doctrine are still heard, especially on radio talk shows. Much of the FCC's attention is given to interpreting its own rules as it resolves disputes between various interests. In some instances, these rules are very specific, as is the equal-time rule. But in other instances they are vague, and the commission frequently wrangles over terms like "the public interest," trying to determine just what it is in each circumstance.

The FCC also handles the issuance and renewal of broadcast licenses granted to radio and television stations. It has the power to revoke licenses, but it rarely does so. In recent years the government has greatly simplified procedures for license renewal and diminished its demands for detailed information from broadcasters. Still, the FCC is charged with seeing whether and how well a broadcast station is serving the public's interest, convenience, and necessity. Although broadcasters often complain of the heavy hand of government, the FCC has been remarkably lenient in renewing licenses. In fact, one critic compared the relationship between the FCC and the industry to a wrestling match wherein "the grunts and groans resound through the land, but no permanent injury seems to result."[36]

A case in point is the FCC's handling of obscenity. The Federal Communications Act gives the commission the power to revoke the licenses of stations broadcasting obscene or indecent material over the airwaves. Although there have been numerous instances of stations running pornographic films and comedy routines in the past, the maximum penalty usually imposed by the FCC is a fine.

The deregulation of broadcasting, discussed in earlier chapters, has altered the role of the FCC in recent years. Although the commission has had a major economic impact, its rules on media content, children's programming, advertising, and even obscenity have relaxed considerably. However, major debates over diversity in the marketplace, competition, localism, and universal service are very much on the agenda. Still, the very existence of a government agency regulating the entire communications industry is widely viewed as a constraint on broadcasting. Even with much less rigorous rules today, compared with earlier years, many broadcasters still complain that the FCC is a bureaucratic nuisance. However, the notion that broadcasters are obliged to fulfill the public trust by accepting a government license makes them markedly different from other media. Former Chief Justice Warren Burger as a federal appeals court judge once stated:

> A broadcaster seeks and is granted the free and exclusive use of a limited and valued part of the public domain; when he accepts that franchise it is burdened by enforceable public obligations. A newspaper can be operated by the whim or caprice of its owners; a broadcast station cannot.[37]

Controls by the Federal Trade Commission

Over the years the Federal Trade Commission (FTC) has conducted hearings to determine whether the growing concentration of ownership in the media influenced the flow of information. Although the hearings generated no definitive answers, media owners denounced the FTC for its potential interference. Those hearings reflect only a small part of the FTC's interest in mass communication and other industries. Like the FCC, the FTC is an independent regulatory agency of the federal government that exists for the purpose of preventing unfair competition. In relation to the media, this task generally translates into the regulation of advertising.

Since its inception in 1914, the FTC has viewed deceptive advertising as unfair competition. Both the FTC and the FCC have brought suits against manufacturers and the media for false claims or misrepresentations. Consumer protection is usually the key concern. The most famous consumer protection case, however, came not from the FCC or the FTC but from Congress, which banned cigarette advertising from television and required manufacturers to label each package with a warning to users that cigarette smoking could endanger their health. Although the FTC directs its actions mainly against individual advertisers, it has a strong indirect effect on the mass media,

FIGURE 13.1
The complex interfaces
of social media—or social
networking media—offer
challenges on intellectual
property issues, among
others.

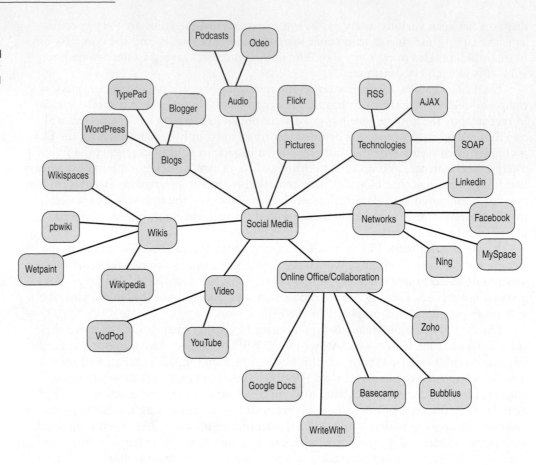

which are the channels for advertising. The FTC issues warnings before moving to formal orders. Some of these orders have the effect of law, and the commission can and has levied punitive fines on manufacturers, sometimes for hundreds of thousands of dollars.

Decisions by the FTC have defined the scope of deception in advertising, discussed the concept of truth in advertising, and denounced puffery, or exaggerated claims. The FTC also legislates rules, holds conferences on trade practices, issues guides for advertising and labeling practices, and hands down advisory opinions for advertisers requesting advance comments about advertisements. In recent years, the FTC has frequently called on communications researchers to help examine issues such as the effects of television commercials aimed at children.

Deregulation and Outside Pressures

Underlying deregulation has been the assumption that competition in the marketplace is the best way to conduct business in America and that government rules, even if intended to protect the public, are an intrusion. Recently, both the FCC and the FTC have been more lenient in regulating the communication industry. This reflects the general trend toward deregulation of various industries, which we discussed in previous chapters with regard to newspaper and broadcast ownership. By the early 1990s, there was again a call for more government regulation of television. In 1991, former FCC chairman Newton Minow declared in a speech that revisited his famous "Vast Wasteland" speech thirty years earlier:

> I reject the view of an FCC chairman in the early 1980s who said that "a television set is merely a toaster with pictures." I reject this ideological view that the marketplace will regulate itself and give us perfection.[38]

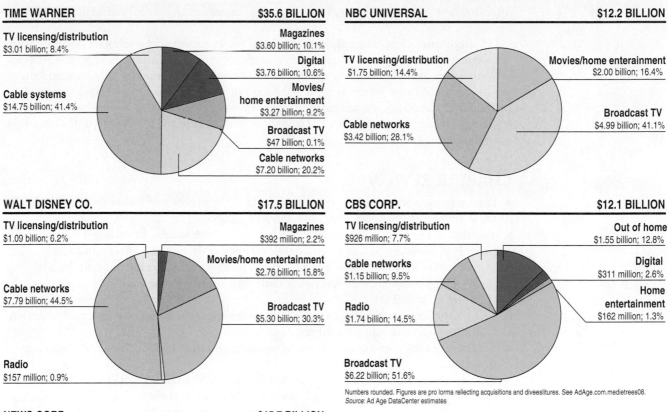

TIME WARNER — **$35.6 BILLION**

TV licensing/distribution $3.01 billion; 8.4%
Cable systems $14.75 billion; 41.4%
Magazines $3.60 billion; 10.1%
Digital $3.76 billion; 10.6%
Movies/home entertainment $3.27 billion; 9.2%
Broadcast TV $47 billion; 0.1%
Cable networks $7.20 billion; 20.2%

NBC UNIVERSAL — **$12.2 BILLION**

TV licensing/distribution $1.75 billion; 14.4%
Cable networks $3.42 billion; 28.1%
Movies/home enterainment $2.00 billion; 16.4%
Broadcast TV $4.99 billion; 41.1%

WALT DISNEY CO. — **$17.5 BILLION**

TV licensing/distribution $1.09 billion; 6.2%
Cable networks $7.79 billion; 44.5%
Radio $157 million; 0.9%
Magazines $392 million; 2.2%
Movies/home entertainment $2.76 billion; 15.8%
Broadcast TV $5.30 billion; 30.3%

CBS CORP. — **$12.1 BILLION**

TV licensing/distribution $926 million; 7.7%
Cable networks $1.15 billion; 9.5%
Radio $1.74 billion; 14.5%
Broadcast TV $6.22 billion; 51.6%
Out of home $1.55 billion; 12.8%
Digital $311 million; 2.6%
Home entertainment $162 million; 1.3%

Numbers rounded. Figures are pro lorma rellecting acquisitions and diveeslitures. See AdAge.com.medietrees08.
Source: Ad Age DataCenter estimates

NEWS CORP. — **$15.7 BILLION**

Free-standing inserts $614 million; 3.9%
TV licensing/distribution $932 million; 5.9%
Cable networks $4.18 billion; 26.6%
Broadcast TV $4.91 billion; 31.3%
Newspapers $1.50 billion; 9.6%
Digital $642 million; 4.1%
Movies/home entertainment $2.91 billion; 18.6%

| **FIGURE 13.2**

Overall, regulation of the media by the FCC and FTC is a complex arena that is constantly evolving. Regulation policies and implementation are shaped by many views, and the uneasy relationship between these government agencies and the media will continue to generate debate.

Political influences and pressures on the media do not exist either in isolation or in the narrow confines of a government agency. Private lobbyists and special interest groups attempt to influence the media for their own purposes. Congressional committees sometimes provide them with a forum and allow testimony in favor of or against a piece of legislation affecting broadcasting and the print media. Over the past few years, lobbies and other special interest groups have tried to influence such matters as the amount of violence on television, hiring policies in the media (especially with regard to women and minorities), election coverage before the polls close, the screening of sexually explicit movies in local theaters, and a variety of other issues. These issues change, but one thing is sure: major public concern about the media will often become a political issue, because public concerns shape government legislation and agendas.

The complexity of communication-related issues causes some scholars and critics to ponder whether the United States needs a more coherent communication policy. At present our policy, if there is one, is spread among various governmental branches and the private sector. As new issues arise, it is difficult to know whether they should be resolved by the FCC, Congress, the executive branch, or others. Some even argue that many policy issues are simply resolved by the private sector because the government does not take enough interest.

CHAPTER REVIEW

- Digital integration and impact on the media is the product of social forces—especially those involving economics, technology, and policy.
- The digital revolution has gone through at least three stages, including 1970s to early 1990s—invention and early development involving the military and educational institutions; 1994 to 2000—Internet comes to home and heralds dot-com boom; 2001—dot-com bust and regrouping with high-speed Internet and new strategies resulting in Web 2.0.
- The public interest is at the center of all communication law and policy and is drawn from the First Amendment and regulatory rules.
- Media revenues come mainly from advertising and user fees, such as cable subscriptions, etc.
- Broadcasting and narrowcasting coexist in the modern media world, although *interactivity* and *digital* communication is changing the stakes.
- A "law of large numbers" in media economics lives alongside a "law of right numbers," one aiming for the biggest possible audience, the other seeking targeted, segmented portions of the audience.
- Although most Americans approve of a free press and believe we have one, the mass media in the United States operate in a complex web of limitations arising from politics and government.
- The First Amendment forbids Congress to make laws restricting the freedom of the press, but that freedom often conflicts with other rights, such as the right to privacy and the right to a fair trial.
- Libel laws are intended to protect people from false and damaging statements made about them, and libel suits today can result in awards of millions of dollars.
- The courts have sometimes placed restrictions on the press to try to limit publicity that might prejudice juries, but generally efforts in this area have centered on voluntary cooperation from the press.
- Obscene material is not clearly under the protection of the First Amendment. Although the courts take action to prevent the publication or broadcast of material deemed obscene, debate continues over what exactly constitutes obscenity and how far it should be controlled.
- Reporters claim a right to keep their sources confidential. Some have been willing to go to jail rather than identify their sources when ordered to do so by the courts.
- The courts are frequently referees when the right to a free press and other rights conflict. Legislatures and the executive branch also influence the press, both through formal powers and informal influence over the flow of information. Both bureaucrats and politicians through informal influence can introduce bias in what is reported.
- The FCC has the power to regulate many aspects of broadcasting but is sometimes less than vigorous in doing so. Groups of private citizens as well as public opinion exert other pressures on the press.

- The media are largely *commercial* enterprises and live within the rules of the larger economy.
- The digital economy of the present day is partly driven by technology and communication (or media industries).
- The digital revolution has caused all media to seek innovative and alternative business models.

STRATEGIC QUESTIONS

1. How do such strategic drivers as economics and policy influence the media?
2. What is communication policy, and how does it evolve? How is the public interest in media and communication defended and protected?
3. Why are the economics (and business) of media often controversial? What are the sources of the controversies, and how are they resolved?
4. Alternative models to the traditional business model of media (economic profit) have not always been successful. Why is that so, and is there hope that this might change?
5. What are the constitutional/political protections for the media, and how well do they work?
6. Does media in cyberspace raise new questions about social forces affecting the media? How and why?

KEY CONCEPTS & TERMS

Media economics   319
Communication policy   316
The public interest   317
The law of right
    numbers   323

Employee ownership
    model   324
Media regulation   326
Libel law   333

Government secrecy   337
Federal Communications
    Commission   340

ENDNOTES

1. Katie Hafner and Matthew Lyon, *Where Wizards Stay Up Late* (New York: Simon & Schuster, 1996).
2. John Montavalli, *Bamboozled at the Revolution* (New York: Viking, 2002); Everette E. Dennis and John C. Merrill, "Concentration of Media Ownership," in Dennis and Merrill, *Media Debates, Great Issues for the Digital Age* (Belmont, CA: Wadsworth 2006), pp. 44–53. Also see James M. Citrin, *Zoom, How 12 Exceptional Companies Are Navigating the Road to the Next Economy* (New York: Doubleday, 2002).
3. Gillian Doyle, *Understanding Media Economics* (London: Paul Chapman Pub., 2009) and Lawrence Lessig, *The Future of Ideas* (New York: Random House, 2001).
4. Louise Story, "$1 Billion Suit Aims to Counter Threat by YouTube," *New York Times*, March 19, 2007, p. C1. For an excellent treatment mass media law, including new digital applicants, see Don R. Pember and Clay Calvert, *Mass Media Law* (New York: McGraw-Hill College, 2006) and

T. Barton Carter, Juliet Lushbough Dee, and Harvey L. Zuckerman, *Communication Law in a Nutshell* (S. Paul: Thompson West, 2007).
5. Robert G. Picard, *Media Economics, Concepts and Issues* (Newbury Park, CA: Sage Publications, 1989), p. 1; also see Picard, *Media Firms: Structures, Operations, Performance* (NJ: Lawrence Erlbaum), 2002.
6. Marc M. Treutler, "Media Economics: A Media Theoretical Approach," presentation to the North Group, Washington University, St. Louis, Mo, Oct. 11, 2004, pp. 1, 3.
7. Philip M. Napoli, *Audience Economics: Media Institutions and the Audience Marketplace* (New York: Columbia University Press, 2003). Also see Napoli, *Foundations of Communication Policy* (Cresskill, NJ: Hampton Press, 2001).
8. Peter Huber, "The Death of Old Media," and Michael J. Wolf, "And the Triumph of Broadband," *Wall Street Journal*, Jan. 11, 2000, p. A22 and Reuven Frank, "A Slight Case of Merger," *The New*

Leader, Oct. 18, 1999, pp. 20–21. Another useful background source is Alison Alexander, et al., *Media Economics, Theory and Practice* (Mahwah, NJ: Lawrence Erlbaum Associates, 1998).

9. Wilson Dizard, *Old Media, New Media,* 3rd ed. (New York: Longman, 2000).

10. Ken Auletta, "Ten Rules of the Information Age," *At Random,* spring/summer 1997, and Albert Greco, ed., *Media and Entertainment Industries* (Boston: Allyn & Bacon, 2000).

11. Chris Anderson, *The Long Tail: Why the Future of Business Is Selling Less of More* (New York: Hyperion, 2006).

12. Anderson, *The Long Tail,* Final Round, op. cit.

13. *News in the Public Interest, A Free and Subsidized Press,* The Breaux Symposium, 2004 (Baton Rouge: Louisiana State University Press, 2004); also see Everette E. Dennis, "A Free and Subsidized Press?—The European Experience with Newspaper Subsidies and Other Government Interventions," Breaux Symposium, March 19, 2004.

14. C. Edwin Baker, *Media Concentration and Democracy: Why Ownership Matters* (New York, NY: Cambridge University Press, 2007).

15. Benjamin M. Compaine and Douglas Gomery, *Who Owns the Media? Competition and Concentration in the Mass Media Industries,* 3rd ed. (Mahwah, NJ: Lawrence Erlbaum Associates, 2000). See also Susan Tifft and Alex S. Jones, *The Trust* (New York: Random House, 2000) for a textured discussion of "family" ownership at the *New York Times.*

16. Napoli, *Communication Policy,* op cit.

17. Everette E. Dennis, "Liberal reporters, yes; liberal slant, no," *American Editor,* January/February 1997, pp. 4–9. An excellent source on the politics and ideology of journalists is David Weaver and G. Cleveland Wilhoit, *The American Journalist* (Bloomington: Indiana University Press, 1996).

18. John L. Hulting and Roy P. Nelson, *The Fourth Estate,* 2nd ed. (New York: Harper & Row, 1983), p. 9.

19. Charles Firestone and Amy K. Garmer, *Digital Broadcasting and the Public Interest* (Washington, DC: The Aspen Institute, 1998).

20. "Government Enjoined from Enforcing Indecency Law," in *The News Media and the Law,* summer 1996, p. 19.

21. Joe Nocera, "Awaiting Compromise on YouTube," *New York Times,* March 17, 2007, p. C1.

22. William S. Holdsworth, "Defamation in the Sixteenth and Seventeenth Centuries," *Law Quarterly Review* 40, 1924, pp. 302–304.

23. David Anderson, "The Legal Model: Finding the Right Mix," in *Media Freedom and Accountability,* Everette E. Dennis, Donald M. illmor, and Theodore Glasser, eds. (Westport, CT: Greenwood Press, 1989).

24. Everette E. Dennis and Eli M. Noam, eds., *The Cost of Libel: Economic and Policy Considerations* (New York: Columbia University Press), 1989.

25. Donald M. Gillmor, *Power, Publicity, and the Abuse of Libel Law* (New York: Oxford University Press), 1989.

26. Robert W. Chandler, "Controlling Conflict: Working Proposal for Settling Disputes Between Newspapers and Those Who Feel Harmed by Them," working paper from the Gannett Center for Media Studies, New York, 1989.

27. *John D. Stevens, Wretched Excess* (New York: Columbia University Press, 1990).

28. John C. Merrill, *The Dialectic in Journalism: Toward a Responsible Use of Press Freedom* (Baton Rouge: Louisiana State University Press, 1989). See also Everette E. Dennis and John Merrill, *Media Debates: Great Issues for the Digital Age,* 4th ed. (Belmont, CA: Wadsworth Publishers, 2006).

29. Scott McClellan, *What Happened: Inside the Bush White House and Washington's Culture of Deception* (New York: Public Affairs, 2008).

30. James Reston, *The Artillery of the Press* (New York: Harper & Row, 1996), p. 20.

31. Frank Luther Mott, *American Journalism,* 3rd ed. (New York: Macmillan, 1962), pp. 336–338.

32. Hunting and Nelson, The Fourth Estate, p. 9. See also Everette E. Dennis and Robert Snyder, eds. *Covering Congress* (New Brunswick, NJ: Transaction, 1998).

33. J. Herbert Altschull, *From Milton to McLuhan: Ideas and American Journalism* (White Plains, NY: Longman, 1989).

34. Anthony Lewis, "Life Isn't So Simple as the Press Would Have It," *ASNE Bulletin,* September 1983, p. 34.

35. David A. Anderson, "Media Success in the Supreme Court," working paper from the Gannett Center for Media Studies, New York, 1987.

36. R. H. Coase, "Economics of Broadcasting and Government," *American Economic Review, Papers and Proceedings,* May 1966, p. 442. See also Roger G. Noll and

Monroe E. Price, eds., *A Communications Cornucopia, Essays on Information Policy* (Washington, DC: Brookings Institution Press, 1998). See also Philip M. Napoli, *Foundations of Communication Policy* (Cresskill, NJ: Hampton Press, 2001).

37. *United Church of Christ v. the Federal Communications Commission,* 349 F2d 994 (D.C. Cir. 1966).

38. Newton H. Minow, "How Vast the Wasteland Now?" Gannett Foundation Media Center public lecture, New York, May 1991.

Media Effects: The Processes and Influences of Mass Communication

The social and behavioral impact of digital technologies on media of all kinds are often overlooked as people scramble to keep pace with changing tools and applications in a communications environment that is faster and more complex than any before it in human history. The need to know just what impact and influence both traditional and new web-based media have on individuals, institutions, society, and culture is greater than ever. Almost everyone wants to know how communication works in the digital world, and what exactly the multiple and converged media channels and platforms can do—short term and long term—both for us and to us. It is not uncommon for digital media enthusiasts to attribute great new capacity, influence, and power to new media platforms, assuming them to have exceeded anything that older media forms were ever able to do. Some people can't imagine (or remember) a world before the Internet or that a web-based network and system has much to learn from traditional media, whether that involves the newspaper, radio, or television. Studies of media effects across several decades and different disciplines (media studies, the social sciences, journalism, etc.) have led to unifying theories that explain the processes, effects, and impact of media of all kinds, including digital media. This was clearly evident at a 2008 symposium at the University of North Carolina that asked what was the Internet's impact on existing theories of mass communication, as it reviewed these "big idea" theories that have explained media influence for almost as long as it has been studied. These included several that were mentioned previously in this book—like agenda setting, minimal effects, cultivation, gatekeeping, diffusion theory, uses and gratifications, and the two-step flow.[1]

Recently the Internet Advertising Bureau paid tribute to two of media effects study's founding fathers, declaring them to be "Facebook's Grandfathers (& MySpace's Too!)"[2] and noting that the careful assessment of media influence and power made by scholars had never reached those who work in the media, whether they are advertising copywriters or anchormen and -women. Many ordinary citizens assume that the media possess great powers to shape opinion and thus voting or buying; however, the most thoughtful students of the media, who search out short- and long-term impact, aren't so sure and always ask for evidence. It is critical to understand the difference between people who work in media and those who study them. Just as news or journalism is said to be "history in a hurry," and often wrong when viewed years later, so does today's audience and impact research (which traces whether anyone is reading an online ad or watching a video on YouTube) benefit by knowing more about the work of the thought leaders who have been watching media effects for generations.[3]

Thus, understanding media and communication requires more than a walking tour through the media industries, as fascinating as that may be. It also requires knowledge of the efforts of media scholars and researchers today, and for more than a century, who have developed explanations in the form of theories of how the process of mass communication takes place and the kinds of influences that media content has on audiences. A number of these theories have already been referred to in previous chapters. The goal of this chapter to extend that effort by showing how our current theories of the process and effects of mass communication were developed by scientists, media researchers, and other scholars. Several major theories were developed as those investigators and scholars conducted a variety of research efforts now regarded as classics. The results of those studies led to a constant process of formulating, testing, and revising those theories that now permit detailed understanding of many features of the process and effects of "mass communication," a term that, as we explained in Chapter 1, has grown ever more complex, to the point that, though it is still the one most commonly used, scholars now wonder whether a new and better nomenclature should be sought.

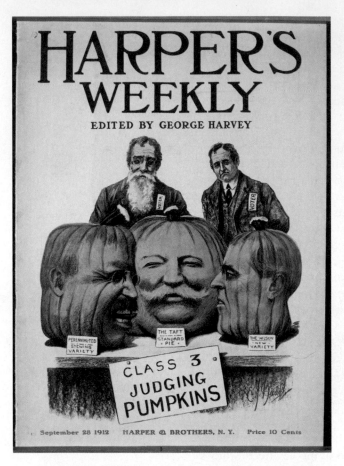

Stereotypes are the lifeblood of cartoonists as this treatment of three American presidents—Theodore Roosevelt, William Howard Taft and Woodrow Wilson—on the cover of Harper's weekly in 1912 demonstrate.

EARLY VIEWS OF MEDIA INFLUENCES

Almost as soon as the penny press started producing daily newspapers for ordinary citizens, there were thoughtful observers and writers who were concerned about their influences. Some scholars of the time saw them as having great benefits for the population; others saw them doing great harm. However, there was only speculation because there were no media researchers who actively sought to assess the influences and effects of the print media available at the time using scientific methods. One respected writer believed that the cheap newspapers would *reduce individuality* and *create similarity* in the population. Alexis de Tocqueville was a French scholar who traveled widely in the United States from 1835 to 1840, when modern newspapers had recently been invented and were starting to be widely adopted. He wrote extensively about the nature of the American democracy and its people. Specifically, de Tocqueville proposed that increased communication among members of a population, such as took place via the new type of newspaper, would lead to a severe loss of individuality. He subscribed to what came to be called the *dead-level theory*. This theory states that if everyone is exposed to the same flow of ideas, then they will be influenced in a uniform manner. This exposure and influence will lead them to be very similar to each other in what they know about, think about, and (inevitably) in the ways in which they act.

This theory was widely believed for many years by intellectuals. For example, many decades later, writing in *Harper's Magazine* in 1904, journalist John Burroughs explained that if all the people in a society are exposed to the same topics and ideas, they become very similar in their thoughts and ideas. As he put it:

> Constant inter-communication, [as takes place when everyone reads the same newspapers] makes us all alike; we are as it were, all pebbles on the same shore, washed by the same waves.[4]

Other writers were more positive about the effects of newspapers. One of the founders of modern sociology was Charles Horton Cooley, an American scholar who wrote extensively about the influences of both interpersonal and mass communication processes on human nature and the social order. While he didn't use those exact terms, he clearly distinguished the interpersonal from larger social media. Writing in 1907, Cooley proposed that the existence of modern newspapers *expanded the awareness* of people about other parts of the world, creating a much more extended mentality. He pointed out that before they existed, with their daily editions and wire services bringing news from afar, people knew little about what went on beyond their local area:

> Public consciousness of any active kind was confined to small localities. Travel was slow, uncomfortable, costly [and dangerous]. The newspapers appearing weekly in the larger towns were entirely lacking what we would call news....People are far more alive today to what is going on in China, if it happens to interest them that they were to events a hundred miles away.[5]

Moreover, Cooley wrote, newspapers and the other new forms of communication he saw (such as the telegraph and telephone) were developing diversity and differences among people. He explained this beneficial influence of mass communications with a *theory of individuality*. The newspapers, he pointed out, were bringing a remarkable variety of ideas to their readers—information about almost anything one could conceive of. With such an abundance of specialized topics to choose from, a person could pursue virtually any kind of interest. Anyone, he wrote, "having a [specific interest] should be more able to find influences to nourish it. If he has a turn, say for entomology, he can read through journals, correspondence and meetings, get in touch with a group of men similarly inclined and with a congenial tradition."[6] In other words, as people developed such specialized interests and pursued them through modern means of communication, it had the result of making people different from one another—thus creating *diversity* and *individuality* in the population.

By the beginning of the 1900s, then, and on into the early decades of the twentieth century, there remained a variety of views as to the effects of mass communication. Some claimed that they were of great benefit to humankind, expanding awareness and understanding of events beyond the local government. Others pronounced they were a menace—creating a dulling uniformity in the thinking and actions of the majority. All sides of the debate, however, believed that *newspapers had great power* over individuals and that they played a major role in shaping public opinion, moral norms, and patterns of overt behavior in modern society. Similarly, as film and broadcasting arrived in subsequent decades, people became deeply concerned about the problems for society that these even newer media were presumably creating.

Eventually, the uniform influence theory first advocated by Tocqueville and elaborated by others seemed to dominate. A major factor supporting this view, and what came to be called the *magic bullet theory,* was the extensive and very successful use made of propaganda by both sides (the Axis and Allied powers) during World War I (1914–1918).

The stakes were enormous, and governments on both sides felt justified in sending stories (even fake ones) to their press about the brutality and evil deeds of their enemy. They did so to motivate their civilian populations—to keep them working enthusiastically in factories and on farms to supply the arms, food, and fiber needed by their militaries. They also had to convince parents, who were sending their young men to the awful slaughter of trench warfare, that their cause was just, that the enemies were inhuman brutes, and that God was on their side.

It worked! Almost any story about the war was avidly read. Moreover, there was no reason to believe that the newspapers of the time would lie. The result was that entire populations were trained to hate their enemy, to work long hours for the cause, and to accept the sacrifices that military service required. The consequence was that the media (newspapers, magazines, and to a limited extent film) were seen by scholars as well as by the public as having *great power*. It seemed clear that their messages reached everyone and that they influenced all members of their audiences equally, causing them to respond in much the same way. Essentially, then, following World War I, people in our society shared a set of assumptions that our mass media have *immediate, uniform, and powerful effects*. It was this set of assumptions that was fundamental to what came to be called the *magic bullet theory*. Although never formulated systematically at the time, its basic ideas were at the center stage just before systematic research on mass communications got its start.

MEDIA EFFECTS RESEARCH BEGINS

A critical issue for understanding mass communications today is whether—as many citizens assume—the "magic bullet" assumptions *still* provide a valid perspective for assessing the influences of our media. In spite of decades of research, many people have a quite simplistic view of media impact and influence. That is, as the twenty-first century begins, do mass communications have powerful, uniform, and often negative effects, such as *eroding*

Comedian and commentator George Carlin stirred controversy with his sometimes profane and unique form of social comedy performed live and on film and video.

our moral standards by depicting unacceptable sexual conduct or by *stimulating aggression* among children and adults by portraying violence? Do they *degrade our language* by an increasing use of coarse and vulgar words? Do they present and get people to believe in *misleading images* (whether positive and negative) of the character and actions of our leaders? Do their misrepresentations *limit our ability* to make intelligent political decisions? Are mass media messages used as *insidious instruments of persuasion,* shaping what we think we need and what we want to buy? More generally, do they shape *how we conduct our lives?*

A National Dilemma

Questions of this kind point to a potentially serious challenge to basic democratic values posed by our mass media. If the answer is "yes" to any of them, it follows logically that the broad concept of "freedom of the press" (and the right to portray social life in movies and on TV in any way producers want) may not be a very good idea. That is, allowing anyone who controls a medium to print, broadcast, or display any content that they wish, for any purpose that they wish, may not be in the best interests of our society as a whole. Recall that, with the new ease of entry into the media market in the digital age, anyone can be a web publisher or a blogger. If some kinds of mass communications unfairly cause *unacceptable conduct* or significantly *mislead* large numbers of people, it would seem logical to conclude that the content of the media should be closely controlled. That is, it should be *censored* so as to eliminate those forms of content that create unacceptable effects. This argument has a certain potency when one considers the dark side of the Internet, which is a natural portal for cyber crime, misrepresentation, fraud, and other antisocial behavior. Of course, one can argue that the telephone did the same thing, though it lacked the massive reach and interactive capability of social networking sites. Thus, many proposals for control and censoring some Internet content have emerged. The proposition is that censorship for the right reasons is acceptable. But is it?

The difficulty with such a conclusion is that the cure may be worse than the problem. Most Americans would find such controls completely unacceptable; obviously, this issue goes to the heart of the issue of freedom of expression and our cherished constitutional guarantees. Therefore, it is little wonder that debates about effects of mass communications are conducted with such vigor.

A central problem, if such a censorship policy were to be adopted, is *how to decide* whether a particular medium or form of mass communication has effects that are personally or socially destructive. Some in society who speak out on this issue would use the teachings of religion or the assumptions of a particular (liberal or conservative) political ideology to reach their decisions as to what should be allowed to be transmitted to the public. One example of an effort to clean up websites resulted in a library removing the word "breast" from text, assuming that would catch sexually explicit material, inappropriate for young audiences. However, it was discovered that material on "breast cancer" was also blocked.

Many scholars who study the media take the position that, among the alternatives for understanding the effects of mass communication, *research conducted within a systematic perspective,* whether relying on quantitative or qualitative methods (or both) provides the most trustworthy answers. That means considering earlier research with consistency and finding the most pertinent evidence. No one would claim that research findings are always right. Studies can be done poorly, or they can pursue the wrong questions. However, *in the long run,* scientific investigation seems to be the most effective way to gain reliable information to make decisions about complex and perplexing questions, such as those that concern the influences of mass communications.

The Nature and Functions of Research

Quantitative studies of the process and effects of mass communication make use of the research methods of the social sciences. These include using the logical designs of the *experiment*, the systematic sampling and measurement techniques of *surveys* (similar to opinion polls), and the formal procedures of *content analysis* (careful inspection and statistical analysis of existing messages in print, film, or broadcast format). Each of these depends on a set of techniques, methods, and practices that have been derived from the research methodology originally developed in the physical sciences. Over decades, they have been adapted and refined for the study of communication issues and questions. Obviously, mass communication research does not use microscopes, test tubes, or other devices used in physics, chemistry, or biology, but it does make use of the same underlying logic for making decisions as to whether the results that are observed in a particular study are merely products of chance or the products of influence of communication factors that bring about certain outcomes or consequences. Using such research methods, specific hypotheses can be tested and conclusions can be reached that help to decide the merits of various kinds of theories that have been advanced.

Other kinds of studies are done on a qualitative rather than quantitative basis. For example, the quantitative scholar may use statistical data while the qualitative scholar may look for patterns and trends that cannot be measured directly, only intuitively observed. Most social scientists use qualitative measures while historians and other humanists find other kinds of evidence. Often these are *long-term studies* of factors that cannot easily be observed by an opinion-poll-type survey completed in a day or two or by conducting some kind of short-term experiment. In other words, carefully observing trends and changes in a society over extended periods of time can sometimes yield important information about media influences that cannot be discovered in any other way.

DISTINCTIVE RESEARCH GOALS.   There are many kinds of mass communication research, using many different strategies, conducted for a variety of purposes. Some studies are designed to determine in a preliminary way if a theory can be formulated that can explain a particular kind of influence or effect that can be observed in a population. Other studies can indicate whether a particular theory that has already been formulated—and which may seem to be valid—can accurately describe and explain a particular type of media process or effect. These applications of scientific methods are often called *basic* research—seeking explanations, rather than practical ways.

Another category is called *applied research*. This consists of studies undertaken for various kinds of clients who have some problem related to communication. The goal may be to compare two possible advertising messages to see which appeals most to potential consumers. Or a goal may be to determine the best campaign strategy for a person running for political office. Still other applied projects may be conducted to assess how well a public relations campaign is working to shape or change the attitudes of some segment of the public toward a personality, a corporation, or a government's policy.

While applied research is an important part of commercial, governmental, and non-profit enterprises in the United States, we are concerned in this chapter with more *basic scholarly research* aimed at developing and assessing theory. The goal here is to try to describe and explain the processes and effects of mass communication so that the ways in which these take place can be better understood. However, the distinction between applied and scientific research is not always clear. Often, the one contributes to the other. Findings from basic research can inform applied research, which in turn can clarify a theory.

RESEARCH MOVES THE CUTTING EDGE FORWARD.   In this chapter, we will review a number of investigations completed during various periods of media history. Our reason for this approach is that these studies have become "milestones" in the search for trustworthy theories that help explain the processes of mass communication or its influences on individuals and the society as a whole. During the nearly seven decades since this type of research began, literally tens of thousands of additional studies were published—testing, expanding, and modifying our knowledge of the process and effects of mass communication. It is not possible in a single chapter to summarize such a large body of research results. It is for that reason that the focus in this chapter is on the classic studies. As we've noted earlier, they are still much debated, and their application and relevance is frequently confirmed and underscored. Of course, the digital landscape has made this even more complex.

The story of research efforts is similar to what happens in all branches of scientific endeavor. That is, while some yielded conclusions that were and still are still quite *correct*, others were *inconsistent*. Still others (seen in hindsight) were just plain *wrong*. However, we will see that, as the ability to conduct research on the influences of the media improved, additional understandings were provided by each new investigation. Thus, scientific research is "self-policing." As the "cutting edge" of research moves forward, incorrect conclusions are gradually eliminated and replaced with alternatives that more adequately describe the realities of mass communications and their influences. It is this *self-corrective* feature of science that makes it an attractive means of gaining trustworthy knowledge in the long run.

Generally, then, it is the larger picture that counts. There is little doubt that in the early studies, the research methods used were crude and often inadequate. The theories developed from them were quite simple, and some are now obviously invalid. However—and this is a major point—during the nearly seven decades represented by these studies, *there has been a slow but steady accumulation of valid knowledge* about how our media function and what they do and do not do to individuals and our society. That kind of development is exactly what research is all about.

Early Support for the Magic Bullet Theory

Scientific research on the effects of mass communication lagged far behind the development of the media themselves. Large-scale studies did not begin until the late 1920s. The reason for the delay was that the necessary statistical tests, research strategies, and measurement techniques required to conduct such investigations—using the logic and methods of science—were not available. By the 1920s, research procedures were sufficiently developed within the social sciences—mainly psychology and sociology—for investigation of the effects of mass communication to become possible. As we follow the story of media research during the subsequent decades, we need to understand (1) *the basic theories* that researchers developed over the years, (2) how they used *increasingly sophisticated* research methods for studying the effects of mass communication, and (3) how new findings sometimes forced them to *change or even to abandon* some theories.

THE PAYNE FUND CONSIDERS MOVIES AND KIDS.   Social scientists interested in large-scale research on the effects of mass communication first focused on the movies. There were clear reasons for this choice. During the first decade of the twentieth century, movies were a novelty. During the second decade, they became the principal medium for family entertainment. By the end of the 1920s, feature-length films with soundtracks had become standard, and the practice of going to the movies for entertainment at least once a week had been deeply established.

Meanwhile, the public had become uneasy about the influence of the movies on children. In 1929 alone, an estimated 40 million minors, including more than 17 million children under the age of fourteen, went to the movies weekly.[7] Critics raised alarming questions about their effects. Were the new picture shows destroying parents' control over their children? Were they teaching immorality? Films with unwholesome themes—horror, crime, immoral relationships, and the illegal use of alcohol (during Prohibition)—were especially troubling.

No government agency existed to give money to investigators who wanted to assess the impact of films on children, but a private group (the Motion Picture Research Council) decided to seek research data in order to develop a national policy concerning standards in the production of motion pictures. This council called together a group of social scientists to plan large-scale studies to probe the effects of motion pictures on youth. A private foundation called the Payne Fund was persuaded to supply the necessary money.

The overall results of the Payne Fund studies seemed to confirm the charges of the critics of the movies and the worst fears of parents. Their results indicated *widespread and significant influences* on children's ideas and behavior. When its thirteen reports were finally published in the early 1930s, the Payne Fund studies were the best available evaluation of the impact of motion pictures on children. The assumptions and predictions of the magic bullet theory seemed to have been confirmed, and parents were deeply concerned.

These researchers used approaches that included collecting and interpreting anecdotes about responses to movies, conducting experiments that measured attitudes and behavior, analyzing responses to survey questionnaires, and performing systematic analyses of the content of films. By today's standards of research, many of these studies now seem quaint and naïve.

THE "INVASION FROM MARS."   On October 30, 1938, horrible creatures from Mars invaded the United States and killed millions of people with death rays. At least, that was the firm belief of many of the 6 million people who were listening to the CBS show "Mercury Theater of the Air" that evening. The broadcast was only a radio play—a clever adaptation of H.G. Wells' science-fiction novel *War of the Worlds*. But it was so realistically presented, in a "newscast" format, that the many listeners who tuned in late missed the information that it was only a play. They thought that Martian monsters were really taking over.

If there had been any doubt that a mass medium could have a powerful impact on its audience, that doubt was dispelled as soon as the next day. Among those who believed the show was a real news report, large numbers panicked. They saw the invasion as a direct threat to their values, property, and lives—and literally the end of their world. Terrified people prayed, hid, cried, or fled. A high school girl later reported:

> I was writing a history theme. The girl upstairs came and made me go up to her place. Everybody was so excited I felt as [if] I was going crazy and kept on saying, "What can we do, what difference does it make whether we die sooner or later?" We were holding each other. Everything seemed unimportant in the face of death. I was afraid to die, just kept on listening.[8]

Among those who believed that the Martians were destroying everything and that nothing could be done to stop them, many simply abandoned all hope:

> I became terribly frightened and got it in the car and started for the priest so I could make peace with God before dying. Then I began to think that perhaps it might have been a story, but discounted that because of the introduction as a special news broadcast. While en route to my destination, a curve loomed up and traveling at between seventy-five and eighty miles per hour, I knew I couldn't make it though as I recall it didn't greatly concern me either. To die one way or another, it made no

One of the iconic examples of a media effect was actor Orson Welles' production of *War of the Worlds* on radio in 1938, which caused thousands of listeners to panic fearing that there was an invasion from Mars.

difference as death was inevitable. After turning over twice the car landed upright and I got out, looked at the car, thought that it didn't matter that it wasn't my car or that it was wrecked as the owner would have no more use for it.[9]

In fact, the Mercury Theater and the actors had no intention of deceiving people. The script was written and the program was presented in the tradition of telling "spook stories" for Halloween. It was clearly identified as a play before and after the broadcast and in newspaper schedules.[10] But the newscast style, the powerful directing, and the talented performances of the actors conspired to make the presentation seem very real. The result was one of the most remarkable media events of all time. And it has been the subject of several motion pictures drawing on the "War of the Worlds," the most recent one starring Tom Cruise.

INCONSISTENCIES IN THE MAGIC BULLET THEORY.   Immediately after the broadcast, social psychologist Hadley Cantril hastily began a research study to uncover the causes of panic in a general sense, as well as reactions to the radio broadcast. More specifically, he sought to discover the psychological conditions and the circumstances that led people to believe that the invasion was real. Although the scope of the investigation was limited and its flaws numerous, the Cantril study became one of the milestones of mass media research.[11] The researchers concluded that "critical ability" was the most significant variable related to the response people made to the broadcast. Critical ability was defined generally as *the capacity to make intelligent decisions*. Those who were low in critical ability tended to accept the invasion as real and failed to make reliable checks on the broadcast or listen to other stations, for thousands of people did call or try to call the authorities, though they knew no more than ordinary citizens did. Especially low in critical ability were those with strong religious beliefs, who thought the invasion was an act of God and that it was the end of the world. Some thought a mad scientist was responsible. Those high in critical ability tended not to believe the broadcast was real. They were more likely to be able to sort out the situation, even if they tuned in late. These people tended to be more educated than those low in critical ability. In fact, statistical data obtained from CBS revealed that amount of education was the single best factor in predicting whether people would check the broadcast against other sources of information. The conclusions derived from the Cantril study posed a *dilemma*. In some ways, the magic bullet theory was supported, but in other ways it was not. For example, it was clear that the radio broadcast brought about some very powerful effects. Yet, *they were not the same for everyone*. This was not consistent with the magic bullet theory. To be consistent, the broadcast should have had about the same effect on everyone who heard it. But the Cantril study isolated individual characteristics of listeners that strongly influenced their response: critical ability and amount of education. For the public, the *War of the Worlds* broadcast seemed to reinforce a belief in the great power of the media, but many researchers saw that that magic bullet theory had flaws.

BEYOND THE MAGIC BULLET: SELECTIVE AND LIMITED EFFECTS

We next review two classic studies that were milestones in *replacing* the magic bullet theory. One examined soldiers in training during World War II, and the second analyzed the presidential election of 1940. Both studies helped build new ways of understanding how and to what extent mass communications have the power to influence ideas, opinions, and behavior.

The "Why We Fight" Film Experiments

By the time of World War II, social scientists had developed fairly sophisticated techniques of experimentation, measurement, and statistical analysis. The military therefore felt that these techniques could contribute to the war effort. In one project, the Army formed a special team of social psychologists to study the effectiveness of a set of films that had been designed to teach recruits about the background of the war and to influence their opinions and to motivate them.[12]

When America entered the war in 1941, many young men were ill-informed about all the reasons for America's participation. It was a society that was without television—our main source for news today—and people were both less educated and less informed. Everyone knew about Japan's attack on Pearl Harbor, but not everyone knew about the rise of fascism, Hitler's conquest of Europe, his alliance with Mussolini, or the consequences of militarism in Japan. Moreover, the United States was (and still is) a nation with diverse regions, subcultures, and ethnic groups. The newly drafted soldiers included men from such unlike categories as farmers from Tennessee; ethnic men from big-city slums; small-town, middle-class youths; and young men from the ranches of the West. All were plunged into basic training, but many understood only dimly what it was all about.

World War II, dramatically illustrated in the Japanese attack on Pearl Harbor, ushered in research on selective and limited media effects through the "Why We Fight" film experiments.

GOALS AND CONDUCT OF THE EXPERIMENTS. The Army chief of staff, General George C. Marshall, had decided that the troops needed to be told *why* they had to fight, *what* their enemies had done, *who* their allies were, and *why* achieving victory would be a tough job. They had to learn that the war had to be continued until the Axis Powers agreed to unconditional surrender. Since no one (not even Marshall) knew about the atom bomb being built, which would ultimately end the war in Japan, everyone thought that the terrible conflict would drag on for several additional years after Hitler was defeated. General Marshall believed that special orientation *films* could give the diverse and poorly informed recruits the necessary explanations of the causes of the war and provide an understanding of why it would not end soon. He hoped that it would also result in more positive attitudes toward American allies (Great Britain and France) and generally create higher morale.

A top Hollywood director, Frank Capra, was hired to produce seven films—a series called *Why We Fight*. The U.S. Army gave the job of studying their effectiveness to social psychologists in the Army's Research Branch of the Information and Education Division. The basic plan was to see if exposure to such a film would result in measurable influences on the understandings and orientations of the soldiers. These included a firm belief in the *right of the American cause;* a realization *that the job would be tough;* plus confidence in *our side's ability to win.* The U.S. Army officials also hoped that, by presenting the facts, the films would create *resentment of Germany and Japan* for making the fight necessary. Finally, they anticipated that seeing the films would foster a belief that through military victory the political achievement of *a better world order* would be possible.

We can summarize the procedures used rather simply: Four of Capra's *Why We Fight* films were used in a series of well-conducted *experiments*. Great control over the experimental conditions was possible because the subjects were under orders to participate in the experiments. The soldiers were under the watchful eyes of tough sergeants who saw to it that they took the research seriously and that none "goofed off." (Few experimenters today could match this!) Under such conditions, several hundred men who were undergoing training were given a "before" questionnaire that measured understanding of facts, various kinds of opinions, and overall attitudes. These questionnaires were carefully pre-tested on at least two hundred soldiers in order to minimize ambiguities in their language. Then the men were divided (by company units of about a hundred men each) into *experimental groups* and a *control group*. Each company that was designated as an experimental group saw one of the four films from the *Why We Fight* series. The control group saw a neutral film that did not deal with the war.

After they had seen the film, all subjects answered an "after" questionnaire. It measured the same variables as the first questionnaire, but the questions were rephrased so that repeated exposure to the test could not account for changes in responses. Thus, by comparing the amount of change in each experimental group with that of the control group, the effect of the films could be assessed. The researchers were surprised when no dramatic results were obtained! The films produced only minor changes in their audiences. Thus the effects were very limited.

IMPLICATIONS: MEDIA HAVE LIMITED EFFECTS.   Generally, the researchers concluded that the *Why We Fight* films—with powerful propaganda messages—were modestly successful in teaching soldiers facts about events leading up to war. They were also modestly effective in altering a *few specific opinions* related to the facts covered. But they clearly had no great power to fire soldiers with enthusiasm for the war, to create lasting hatred of the enemy, or to establish confidence in the Allies. Moreover, the effects were different for soldiers with low, medium, and high levels of education. Generally, soldiers with more education learned more from the films, although their attitudes were little influenced. These results certainly did not confirm earlier beliefs in all-powerful media. And the finding that variations in education modified the effects flatly contradicted the old notion that communications were *magic bullets* penetrating every eye and ear in the same way, creating similar effects in every receiver. For all intents and purposes, the older theory of uniform influences and powerful effects died at this point. Even today, the U.S. Army film studies are seen as models of careful research. They left no room for doubt about either the precision of their methods or the validity of their conclusions.

Effects of the Media in a Presidential Campaign

One the most famous and influential studies was conducted in 1940, though it wasn't published until several years later; it focused on a presidential election campaign. Sociologists Paul Lazarsfeld, Bernard Berelson, and Hazel Gaudet probed the web of influences within which voters made up their minds as a result of mass media coverage in a presidential campaign. In a now-classic work called *The People's Choice,* and based on the 1940 election when Franklin D. Roosevelt was elected to a third term, the researchers studied the role of mass communications as influences on voters.[13] This study is a landmark for two reasons. First, its scale was large and its methodology sophisticated. In fact, even today, few studies have rivaled it in these respects. Second, the findings revealed completely new perspectives on both the process and the effects of mass communication.

President-elect Barack Obama addressing a crowd in Chicago on election night 2008 when he became the first African-American elected to the presidency. His skillful use of all forms of media has been widely noted.

GREAT IMPROVEMENTS IN RESEARCH METHODS.   Lazarsfeld and his colleagues interviewed some three thousand people from both urban and rural areas of Erie County, Ohio. It was an area that had voted in presidential elections much like the entire nation for decades. Interviewing began in May 1940 and ended in November of the same year, when Roosevelt defeated challenger Wendell Wilkie. All three thousand subjects were interviewed in May, and they agreed to give further monthly interviews as the election campaign progressed. The research strategy used was new at the time and very clever: A random sample of six hundred was selected from the three thousand interviewed and designated as the *main panel*. The remaining twenty-four hundred were randomly divided into four additional panels of six hundred each. Those in the main panel were interviewed each month from May to November for a total of seven interviews. The other four groups served as *control* panels, and each was to be interviewed only one more time. One of the four control panels was given a second interview in July, another in August, and another in October. At each point, the results of these interviews were compared with those of the main panel. This procedure allowed researchers to see how *repeated interviews* were affecting the main panel compared with each fresh panel. After three such comparisons they found that the repeated interviews were having *no measurable cumulative effect,* and they decided that using the fourth panel was not necessary. Thus, the researchers were confident that their findings were meaningful and were not an artificial result of their multiple interviews of the main panel.

Some respondents decided early for whom to vote; some decided late. Some shifted from one candidate to another; some who had firmly decided fell back into indecision. Always the interviewers tried to find out why the voters made these changes. They also focused on the social categories into which the subject could be classified. Rural and urban dwellers were compared. People at various income levels were contrasted. The same was true of people of different religious backgrounds, political party affiliations, and habits of using the media. Using complex methods, the researchers found that these category memberships could be used with fair success to *predict* voting intentions and actual voting behavior. Thus, rigorous methods were employed to generate new knowledge.

MEDIA AS PART OF A WEB OF INFLUENCES.   Then, and even more so now, much of a political campaign is waged in the media through both news reports and paid advertising. But Lazarsfeld and his colleagues did not find all-powerful media controlling voters' minds. Instead, the media were *just one part of a web of influences on voters*. People's personal characteristics, social category memberships, families, friends, and associates as well as the media all helped them to make up their minds. Furthermore, the media did not influence all voters in the same way. When the media did have an effect, three kinds of influences were found. The researchers called these influences *activation, reinforcement, and conversion*.

Activation is the process of getting people to do what they are "predisposed" to do by their social category memberships—pushing people along in ways they are headed anyway. For example, for almost fifty years in Erie County most well-to-do Protestants had voted Democratic. Indeed, all across the country, many voters tend to have certain socially based predispositions for and against each of the main political parties. Yet, even though many voters in Erie County said they were undecided as the campaign progressed, the media helped activate voters to *follow their predispositions*.

Reinforcement is a different process. Fully half of the people studied already knew in May for whom they would vote in November. They made up their minds early and never wavered. Does this mean that the media had no effect on such voters? Not at all. The media were important in such cases because they strengthened the voters' intentions. Political parties can ill afford to concentrate only on attracting new followers. The intentions of the party faithful must constantly be reinforced through communications that show that they have made the right choice. The media campaign is used to provide this reassurance. Clearly, reinforcement is not a dramatic effect, but it is a critical one. It keeps people doing what they already are doing.

Finally, conversion was rare. The presidential campaign presented in the mass media did move a few voters from one party to the other in Erie County, but

President Obama's 2008 campaign ad and his slogan, "Yes, we can," was widely featured on Internet social networking sites, using the form of music video. Obama's use of the Internet was notable in this campaign and subsequent presidency.

Yes We Can - Barack Obama Music Video

0:21 / 4:30

Rate: ★★★★★   Views: 8,513,777

the number was small indeed. Most people either made up their minds in May, went with the party they were predisposed toward, or paid attention only to the campaign of their own party. Conversion took place among a very small number who had only weak party affiliation to begin with. Perhaps the major conclusion emerging from this study is that the media had not only *selective* but *limited* influences.

THE TWO-STEP FLOW.   One unexpected but extremely important finding emerged from *The People's Choice*. It was a two-step process of communication that described both the flow of *personal influence* in interpreting the campaign and the word-of-mouth *diffusion of the news*. Its discovery occurred almost by accident, in a way that scientists call "serendipitous." About halfway through the Erie County study, the researchers began to realize that in addition to the mass media (radio, newspapers, and magazines at the time) another major source of information and influence for voters was the *other people*. The researchers found that many individuals did not learn about the election from the media. Instead, they turned to family, friends, and acquaintances to obtain information about the candidates and the issues. Inevitably, those who provided the information also provided *interpretation*. Thus, the two-step flow of information between people also included a flow of influence. (The researchers called this *personal influence* in contrast with *media influence*.) Those who served most often as sources of information and influence had two important characteristics: (1) they had given great *attention* to the media campaign, and (2) their socioeconomic status was similar to that of those whom they influenced. In other words, voters were turning for information and influence to people who were *like themselves* but whom they regarded as *knowledgeable*. Thus, in the two-step flow, content moves *from the mass media to opinion leaders*, who then *pass it on to others* whom they inevitably influence. Since *The People's Choice* was published, hundreds of other studies have tried to understand the nature and implications of the two-step flow theory and the personal influence of opinion leaders as part of mass communication. In popular literature, some of writer Malcolm Gladwell's work connects social science theories and research with understanding of contemporary human behavior, such as his 2008 book, *The Outliers,* which explains human success.

IMPLICATIONS: MEDIA HAVE SELECTIVE AND LIMITED INFLUENCES.   It was overwhelmingly clear by this time that the old magic bullet theory was completely inadequate and had to be totally abandoned. Meanwhile, as the century progressed, the social and behavioral sciences made great advances in understanding the nature of human beings, both individually and collectively. These discoveries would prove to be important in understanding the process and effects of mass communication. Later, psychologists had discovered the importance of learning in human beings. The older idea of uniform inherited instincts as guides to conduct was abandoned. They developed numerous theories and explanations of how the learning process played a part in shaping the organization and functioning of the human psyche. It was clear that people varied greatly in their learned beliefs, attitudes, interests, values, and other psychological attributes. The key idea was that individual differences in what people learned led to *great interpersonal diversity*. It became clear that no two human beings were organized psychologically in exactly the same way. Each person, as a result of learning in his or her unique personal environment, had a different psychological organization—through which the individual perceived and interpreted the world. It was obvious that those individual psychological differences contributed to the patterns of selectivity with which people attended to the media. Even earlier, sociologists and anthropologists, who had studied the emerging urban-industrial society intensively, also found a picture of *great social diversity*. In this case, it was based on the numerous *social categories* into which people could be classified. Societies had complex social class structures, based on such factors as income, education, and occupational prestige. People were grouped into other categories by their race, gender, ethnicity, political preference, and religion. Within each category *distinct subcultures* developed, bringing people within a given category to share many beliefs, attitudes, and forms of behavior. These also played a part in shaping the ways in which people attended to the media and were influenced by them.

Also important, social scientists found that people did not live socially isolated lives in a "lonely crowd" existence. In rural areas and even in big cities, they still maintained *social relationships* with family, friends, and acquaintances. These had truly significant influences on their interpretations and actions toward the world in which they lived. These social ties were also a significant factor influencing people to attend to mass communication in specific ways.

In summary, then, it came to be understood that these sources of diversity—individual psychological differences, social category subcultures, and patterns of social relationships—all had powerful influences on the mass communications behavior of individuals. *The People's Choice* research on the presidential election had truly been a breakthrough in revealing the foundations for a new general theory of the *selective and limited effects* of mass communication based on such considerations. While the authors of that study did not actually set forth that general theory, its basic ideas were widely understood, and it came to be the central way to explain the process and effects of mass communication. During the decades that followed, the theory received wide support from literally hundreds of research studies of the ways in which people attended to and were influenced by the mass media. Today, the basic assumptions of the theory that replaced the magic bullet formulation can be summarized as selective and limited effects. This classic work inspired many subsequent studies, including one titled "Impersonal Influence," which argued for continued research in the digital age that connects interpersonal and organizational communication with mass communication.[14] Of course, today's narrowcasting with its capacity to achieve market segmentation takes us back to the two-step flow, though it involved large, undifferentiated audiences.[15] This is the other side of the coin.

AUDIENCES USE MEDIA CONTENT TO OBTAIN GRATIFICATIONS

In the mid-twentieth century, before television reached that critical 50% mark noted in Chapter 1, several leading scholars tried to go beyond the mere recognition that people were selective in what they tuned to in the daily flood of media messages. They wanted to understand what psychological factors motivated their choices. That is, they wanted to understand what *gratifications* resulted (what needs were fulfilled and satisfactions obtained) when audiences selected and attended to media content. Soon, studies began to provide answers, and an explanation was developed. It was called the *"uses and gratification theory."* In retrospect, because of the focus on satisfaction and need-fulfillment, a better name is "uses *for* gratification," and that will be the phrase used to identify this theory in the present text.

This new focus of research did not seek an explanation of the "effects" of mass communications. Instead, it sought to understand and explain a part of the "process" by which specific messages from specific media selectively reached specific segments of the audience. It sought to explain various kinds of gratifications that the content of the media provided once it had been selected by members of an audience. In that sense, it extended the factor of selectively by addressing audience motivation underlying the selective and limited influences theory.

Eventually, a new theory was developed. It portrayed the audience as *active* in freely choosing and selectively consuming message content, rather than as *passive* and "acted upon" by the media—as had been the case with the magic bullet theory. That is, it stated that because of a variety of psychological needs, people sought out content to provide satisfactions that they desired to obtain from the available media.

Gratifications Found in Media Content

In one of the first studies of uses for gratification in the 1940s, Herta Herzog interviewed women who listened to radio's daytime serials (soap operas), the forerunner of today's daytime television. She found that they listened for a variety of reasons.[16] Some found satisfaction in *identifying* with the heroes or heroines of the dramas who suffered many problems. (The term "identifying" implies that a person is *like,* or *wants to be like,* a person who is portrayed, such as a lead character in a soap opera.) By doing this, they said, they could understand their own woes better. Others did so to obtain *emotional release.* For example, they could cry when tragedies befell their favorite person depicted in a drama or could feel rewarded when something good happened to that character. Still others engaged in *wishful thinking* about the adventures of soap opera characters who had interesting experiences. In addition, many felt that the serials were a source of *valuable advice* about how to handle their own family difficulties, for example how to deal with ungrateful children or a straying husband.

In another classic study of uses for gratification, sociologist Bernard Berelson conducted an exploratory survey of people's reactions to a two-week-long strike by those who delivered New York City's newspapers.[17] He found that, when people had been deprived of their newspapers for many days, they missed them "intensely." However, when the researcher probed more deeply into exactly what they missed, only a third said it was "serious" news presented by the paper—most kept up with that via radio. Actually, in response to detailed probing, "different people read different parts of the newspapers for different reasons at different times."[18] Some did miss information about public affairs. Others felt deprived because they could not read the comics or the sports pages daily. All of these categories of newspaper content filled needs and provided gratifications that went unfulfilled during the strike. Other gratifications were obtained by following the news so as to gain social prestige by seeming knowledgeable. Still other satisfactions came from personal-advice columns, human-interest stories, and vicarious participation in the lives of the rich and famous. As television evolved and was almost universally adopted, this new theory would play a role in guiding research on why people viewed the programs. In fact, as we will see below, one of the largest studies of children and television ever conducted was based on the theoretical perspective of uses for gratifications.

Children and Television

As television reached almost every family, the same concerns about its impact and influence on children emerged once again, as they had previously with movies. What was this new medium doing to them? And, most of all, what was it doing to their children? A trickle of early research did little to quiet the public's fears. It showed that when a family acquired a TV set it changed the lives of its children in a number of ways. It reduced the time they spent playing, postponed their bedtime, and modified what they did in their free time. Children with TV spent less time attending movies, reading, and listening to the radio.[19] But no one knew whether television viewing limited or broadened children's knowledge, raised or lowered their aesthetic tastes, changed their values, created passivity, or stimulated aggression. Research was urgently needed to clarify such issues.

Today, there are thousands of studies conducted over a fifty-year period, and summarized in a 2006 study, that probe the impact of television on children, but three early investigations stand out as landmarks. The first was comparison of television viewers and nonviewers. The second was a series of studies on the relationship between portrayals of violence and aggressive conduct by children. The third was not a single investigation but a synthesis of the findings of several hundreds of studies conducted over a ten-year period.

Television aimed at children has been the subject of much criticism—and praise as in the instance of the warm-hearted Fred Rogers, who presided over *Mister Rogers' Neighborhood,* one of the most popular children's programs of all time, known for its music, puppets and credo, "I like you just the way you are."

In 1960, Wilbur Schramm, Jack Lyle, and Edwin Parker published the first large-scale American investigation of children's uses of television.[20] The study was concerned not with what television does *to* children but with what children do *with* television. In that sense, it was in the tradition of the uses for gratification theory. The researchers looked at the content of television shows, the personalities of young viewers, and the social setting of television viewing. In eleven studies, conducted in both the United States and Canada, they interviewed nearly six thousand children, along with fifteen hundred parents and a number of teachers and school officials. They used in-depth interviews and standardized questionnaires, with statistical analyses of the results. In the end, they had an impressive mass of quantitative data, plus detailed insights about children's viewing patterns and their uses of television.

PATTERNS OF VIEWING.   Very early in the life of the children studied, television emerged as the most attended to mass medium (it remains so for children today). By age three, children were watching about forty-five minutes per weekday, and their viewing increased rapidly with each additional year. By the time children were five years old, they watched television an average of two hours per weekday, and by age eight the average viewing time had risen to three hours. In fact, it startles Americans to learn that from ages three to sixteen, in any given year, their children spent more time watching than they spent in school! Only sleep and perhaps play took up as much or more of their time. Children's tastes in television programs varied with their age, gender, and intelligence, but their families were the chief influence on taste. Middle-class children tended to watch realistic, self-betterment programs. Working-class children viewed more programs that provided sheer entertainment or fantasy.

GRATIFICATIONS OBTAINED FROM THE PROGRAMS.   For several reasons, *fantasy* was one of the most important pleasures obtained from TV. This type of gratification was derived from being entertained, from identifying with exciting and attractive people, and from getting away from real-life pressures. In other words, television provided a pleasurable experience that was free from the constraining limitations of daily living. Thus, fantasy provided both escape and wish fulfillment.

One important finding was that children often turned to television for *diversion*, but in fact they often received *instruction*. This teaching was neither formal nor planned, nor did the youthful viewers *intend* to learn anything. Such unplanned, unintentional education is called *incidental learning*. This is a very important concept that continues to help us understand the influence of television on children even today. What is learned is related, of course, to the child's abilities, needs, preferences, and patterns of viewing. The incidental lessons taught by television are not necessarily objective or correct. TV sometimes portrays reality realistically, sometimes falsely. But whatever their validity, such lessons are a significant source of instructions for young viewers.

BASIC FINDING: VIEWING TELEVISION SEEMED TO POSE FEW DANGERS.   Overall, the results from this massive study did not reveal truly dramatic problems for children arising from television. Indeed, the effects of the medium on this audience were selective and limited. Although the researchers found that children were preoccupied with viewing, they did not find that they were passive receivers of evil influences from it. Instead the selective effects of television depended on factors such as the child's family, mental ability, group ties, age, gender, needs, and general personality.

Although the study had some flaws in its methods, its findings remain important. It offered further evidence of the validity of the selective and limited influences theory. It showed that TV's influences vary among children with different individual characteristics and among those of one social category of children to another. Furthermore, the research evidence supported the central thesis of the uses for gratifications theory, explaining why programming choices were made. Essentially, children actively selected what they viewed, and that content fulfilled many needs and provided a variety of satisfactions.

Two boys imitate violent TV programming, which has stirred critics and social scientists to assess the influence of televised and video violence on behavior.

Since that time scholars have looked carefully at the cognitive impact of TV on children's thinking and perception, as well as such important concerns as learning how to buy (consumer behavior) and political socialization of media (learning one's politics and how to vote).[21]

TELEVISION AND YOUTH VIOLENCE

Fear of harmful effects resulting from viewing television was the motivation for conducting the largest single research program ever aimed at understanding media effects. It has been the case in American society that, as each new medium appears, vocal critics pronounce it to be the cause of society's mounting ills. The fact that these ills are rooted in the long-term trends of migration, urbanization, industrialization, and poverty is not readily accepted by most of the public. They want simpler answers. The media are visible targets to blame. Thus, it is not surprising that many people once saw television as the cause of the nation's rising rates of delinquency and crime, drug use, and juvenile violence as well as deteriorating moral values. In recent times, scholars have also worried about the impact of TV aimed at children on childhood obesity because poor eating habits are promoted in ads for sodas, candies, and the like. Other studies probe the negative effects of video games on children as well as the dangers of exposure to adult fare on websites and cable programming.

The Report to the Surgeon General

As fears of the medium grew, public concern brought pressure on Congress to "do something." In March 1969, Senator John Pastore said on the floor of Congress that he was:

> Exceedingly troubled by the lack of definitive information which would help resolve the question of whether there is a causal connection between televised...violence and antisocial behavior by individuals, especially children.

With Pastore's urging, Congress quickly appropriated $1 million to conduct research into the effects of television. The National Institute of Mental Health (NIMH) became the agency responsible for managing the program. NIMH appointed a committee of distinguished communication researchers to design the projects and a staff to do the routine administration and to prepare a final report. Those on the committee, however, first had to be "approved" by the television networks—which is somewhat like asking the fox to designate who will watch the chickens! Some researchers who had published negative opinions about networks were actually blacklisted from participation. Needless to say, many highly qualified investigators thought that such exclusions were unethical and simply refused to play any part in the project.

In any case, the Surgeon General of the United States charged the committee with two goals: (1) to review what was already known about television's effects, and (2) to launch new studies on the subject. Eventually, some sixty studies, plus reviews of hundreds of prior investigations, were published in five volumes and a sixth summary volume.[22] Many issues were addressed, including the influence of advertising, activities displaced by television, and the information learned from television. A major focus, however, was on *televised violence* and its *influence on children*. We can review briefly some of the main findings on this topic.

NETWORK TELEVISION'S VIOLENT CONTENT.   Just how violent were network television shows at the time of the study? Volume one of the research report presented some striking answers. For example, one researcher studied a full week of primetime television. He found that eight of every ten programs contained violence. Even more striking, the hours during which children viewed most were the most violent of all. What kind of people were shown as aggressive? Violence was carried out on the screen mostly by men who were free of family responsibilities. About three-fourths of all leading characters were males who engaged in violence. They were American, middle or upper class, unmarried, and in the prime of life. Killings occurred between strangers or slight acquaintances, and a few women were violent. (In real life most killings involve family members or people who know each other.) Overall, then, television's portrayals of violence were very *frequent* and very *unrealistic*.

SOCIAL LEARNING FROM MODELS FOR BEHAVIOR.   Television content clearly presents large amounts of violence. But do such portrayals provide *models* that children imitate that cause them to become more aggressive? In an attempt to answer this question, one volume of the report to the surgeon general reviewed all the research that had been published on what psychologists call *observational learning*. This kind of learning is just what the term implies. As a result of seeing the actions of someone else, the observer adopts the modeled beliefs, attitudes, or behavior.

Findings from earlier research on modeling behavior (not part of the surgeon general's project) are important to the issue of whether portrayals of violence on television can provide models that stimulate aggression among children. The most widely know studies of modeling at that time were those done by psychologist Albert Bandura and his associates.[23] Bandura had children watch a live (or sometimes a filmed) human model strike a large inflated "Bobo" doll (a large clown-like figure that always springs back upright if punched or hit). In one experimental condition children saw the model *rewarded* for this aggressive behavior (punching the doll). In a second condition, children saw the human model receive *no consequences* for such aggression. In a third experimental condition, the subjects observed the model being *punished* for punching the Bobo.

Each group of children who had received these "treatments" were then left in a room full of toys—including a Bobo doll like the one the model had beaten. The children who had seen the model rewarded or receive no consequences for aggressive behavior showed a great deal of *direct imitation*. They too beat up the Bobo doll. Those who had observed the model being punished for aggression *were much less likely* to be violent toward the doll. It seemed clear that children copied or did not copy the behavior of the model, depending on whether or not aggressive behavior was punished.

Later, to check to see if the subjects had understood the actions of the human models, the children in all three groups were asked to show the experimenter what the model had done. They were able to do so without difficulty. In other words, *observational learning* had taken place regardless of whether the model had been rewarded or punished. The children knew full well that the model had beaten the doll. However, whether the children imitated that behavior depended on what experimental condition they had been in—on what they had observed to be the consequences of being aggressive.

What do such experiments mean? There is no doubt that children often imitate what they see others doing, and most psychologists believe that such modeling is an important factor in personality development. But does that mean that children blindly imitate violence portrayed on television? There are no clear answers. Modeling influences in experiments may be very different than the effects of mass communication in "real life," where family controls are in place. Nevertheless, the results of these experiments, along with an accumulation of subsequent research, led to the formulation of *modeling theory*.

BIG IDEAS: MEDIA THEORIES EXPLAINED

Modeling Theory

The American mass media, especially television and movies, present many depictions of people acting out patterns of behavior in various ways. These can be ways of speaking, smoking, relating to members of the opposite sex, dressing, walking, or virtually any form of meaningful action. These depictions can serve as "models" of behavior that can be imitated, and people who see such actions depicted may adopt them as part of their own behavioral repertoire.

One explanation of how and why this can take place is *modeling theory*. It was derived from a more general perspective called "social learning theory," originally formulated by psychologist Albert Bandura. Social learning theory provides explanations of the ways in which individuals acquire certain forms of behavior by seeing them performed by someone else, whether the media are involved or not. When applied to adopting forms of action portrayed by actors and depictions observed in the media, it is called "modeling theory."

The reason why modeling theory is particularly relevant to television programs and motion pictures is that they actually show actions performed by persons (models). That is, in the course of various kinds of dramas or other content, models can be seen acting out, in various kinds of social settings, the behavior that an observer may find attractive. Thus, the modeled behavior is depicted more realistically than if it were only described and heard in verbal terms, as in radio, or if it were read in print form.

Modeling theory does not imply any *intentions* on the part of the media, the model, or even on the part of the viewer. The adoption of a form of action after seeing it portrayed in the media may be entirely *unplanned* and *unwitting*. Certainly there is no implication that those who designed or performed the media depiction *intended* them as models for others to adopt (with the exception of behavior modeled in advertisements). Thus, viewers may imitate a behavior pattern, whether or not the people who created the portrayal intended it to serve as a guide, and the effects of viewing a model can be completely unrecognized on the part of the imitating party.

In the modeling process, the receiver first *encounters* a media presentation of the model depicting the behavior. If the person *identifies* with the model, he or she may *reproduce* the form of action portrayed by the model. But, before permanently adopting it, it must have some positive *benefit* for the observer. If so, the behavior may be tried out, and if adopting it *solves some problem* for the person, it may be used again and again in similar circumstances.

Stated more formally, modeling theory can be summarized briefly in terms of the following set of assumptions and their predictive preposition:

1. An individual *encounters a form of action* portrayed by a person (who models the behavior) in a media presentation.
2. The individual *identifies with the model*; that is, the viewer believes that he or she is like (or wants to be like) the model.
3. The individual *remembers and reproduces* (imitates) the actions of the model in some later situation.
4. Performing the reproduced activity *solves some problem* or *results in some reward* for the individual (provides positive reinforcement).
5. **Therefore,** receiving positive reinforcement increases the probability that the person will *use the reproduced activity repeatedly* as a means of responding to similar situations in the future.

TELEVISION AND TEENAGE AGGRESSION.   Other studies that were a part of the *Report to the Surgeon General* did look at attitudes and behaviors in real-life settings. In the volume titled *Television and Adolescent Aggression*, eight projects are reported that attempted to (1) measure adolescent use of television, (2) measure adolescent aggressiveness, and (3) relate use of television to violent behavior.[24]

Perhaps the most interesting of these studies is one by Monroe Lefkowitz and his associates. This ten-year *longitudinal* project covered one set of subjects over a period of a full decade—unusual in communication research. Some 436 children in Columbia County, New York, were tested while in the third grade and again ten years later. The children were asked to rate themselves and each other on such characteristics as popularity and aggression. The researchers also interviewed the parents. The ratings and interviews revealed that a child who was unpopular in the third grade tended both to watch television more and to become more aggressive as they got older. Thus, frequency of viewing violence portrayed on television was related to actual levels of aggression in the group studied, and the effects of viewing television violence were greatest for those who viewed most often. This seemed to confirm the role of TV in stimulating aggression.

Violent images on television have inspired regulatory rules and scientific studies, especially in relationship to their impact on children.

Overall, the studies of adolescent aggression found that specific kinds of youths were more likely both to watch televised violence and to be aggressive. The youths studied were males, younger adolescents, those of lesser intelligence, and those in lower socioeconomic levels. Thus, among youths in these social categories, viewing violence on television and aggressiveness went together. At the same time, the relationship between these behaviors was not strong enough to imply that television *flatly caused* the aggressiveness. This is an important point in interpreting such research. To show that two things tend to occur together is not the same as showing that one of those things actually causes the other.

OVERALL FINDINGS: VIEWING VIOLENCE ON TELEVISION MAY CAUSE AGGRESSION. The final report of the advisory committee, titled *Television and Growing Up,* contains a summary of the findings of the above and a number of additional studies. It makes recommendations concerning further research and public policy. Finally, it offers a statement about the relationship between televised violence and aggressive behavior. After reviewing the entire body of evidence, the Scientific Advisory Committee concluded that televised portrayals of violence *could be harmful to some children.* As they put it, the issue posed a potential public health problem:

> Thus the two sets of findings (laboratory and survey) converge in three respects: a preliminary and tentative indication of a casual relation between viewing violence on television and aggressive behavior, an indication that any such causal relation operated only on some children (who are predisposed to be aggressive), and an indication that it operated only in some environmental contexts. Such tentative and limited conclusions are not very satisfying [yet] they represent substantially more knowledge than we had two years ago.[25]

The committee's conclusions from the research findings created a storm of controversy. Senate hearings were held to explore what it all meant. The public, disregarding all the hedges, limitations, and qualifications of the scientists, focused on the idea that *television causes kids to be aggressive.* The television industry, seizing mainly on the shortcomings of the research and the tentative nature of the conclusions, declared the findings to be of *little importance.* Many media critics were outraged; a number of the researchers charged that their work had been misrepresented. Perhaps the final word went to Surgeon General J. L. Steinfield:

> These studies—and scores of similar ones—make it clear to me that the relationship between televised violence and anti-social behavior is sufficiently proved to warrant immediate remedial action. Indeed the time has come to be blunt: we can no longer tolerate the present high level of violence that is put before children in American homes.[26]

In effect, then, the Surgeon General of the United States concluded that *televised violence may be dangerous to your child's health!* However, that conclusion was still hedged with caveats that only certain kinds of children were influenced under certain kinds of conditions.

Perhaps most interesting of all is the clear contradiction between the implications of the findings from the studies of Schramm and his associates, a decade earlier, and those of the *Report to the Surgeon General*. The first suggested that television posed no danger to children, while the second suggested that, for some, the medium could be dangerous. Here, then, is the classic situation that often confronts a scientific community. Which one is the correct interpretation? As we indicated earlier, the answer always lies in further research leading to theories that more closely portray reality.

The Second Report to the Surgeon General

By 1980, the pace of research on the effects of television had increased sharply. In fact, 90% of *all* research ever done on the effects of viewing television on behavior (up to that time) was done between 1971 and 1980—the decade following the publication of the first *Report to the Surgeon General*. So many research findings were available that it was difficult to grasp their overall meaning. Additionally, the *Report to the Surgeon General,* on children and violence, had created many controversies and left many questions unanswered. Because of these two factors, Julius Richard, then the surgeon general, asked the National Institute of Mental Health to undertake a *synthesis* and *evaluation* of the mass of research evidence that was then available. Thus, in 1982, a decade after the first report, a second was published.

THE INCREASED PACE OF RESEARCH.   The new *Report to the Surgeon General,* titled, *Television and Behavior: Ten Years of Scientific Progress and Implications for the Eighties,* was not based on new research sponsored by the government.[27] Instead, it was a compilation of the main findings of more than twenty-five hundred studies of the influence of television on behavior, most of which had been published since the first report.

Overall, this was an enormously valuable synthesis and evaluation of thousands of research studies on television, showing how the medium influenced a number of forms of behavior. Seven broad areas of influence were reviewed. These included (1) television and health, (2) violence and aggression, (3) prosocial behavior, (4) cognitive and affective aspects of viewing, (5) the family and interpersonal relations, (6) social beliefs and social behavior, and (7) television's effects on American society.

It is not possible to summarize in a few paragraphs the nature of the thousands of studies and details of findings of so massive an amount of material. We can, however, focus on that part of the report devoted to studies of violence and aggression. The report noted that television had been and remained devoted to showing violence. By the time of the publication (in the early 1980s), the portrayal of violence on television had continued unabated since the 1950s, with only a few minor fluctuations. In fact, over the decade covered in the report, there had been an *increase* in violence in children's weekend programs, which by the end of the period had become more violent than primetime television.

CONFIRMING FINDINGS: VIEWING OF TELEVISED VIOLENCE BY CHILDREN CLEARLY DOES CAUSE AGGRESSION.   A major difference in conclusion between the first and second *Report to the Surgeon General* was that there was no longer any question whether a relationship existed between exposure to violent television programs and increased tendencies toward aggressive behavior among *some categories* of children and youths viewing such content. However, as is the case in the association between smoking and cancer, one cannot predict on an individual basis. That is, it is not clear whether violent programs will cause a particular person to become more aggressive. However, the totality of evidence for inferring that viewing violent programs raises *rates* of aggression among those children who are heavy viewers was even clearer than it was in the earlier *Report to the Surgeon General*.

LONG-TERM INFLUENCES ON SOCIETY AND CULTURE

Those who study and evaluate the process and effects of mass communications in modern society have long been troubled by a perplexing and recurrent contradiction. When they try to understand the influence of mass communications in our society, two *opposite conclusions* can be reached. Both are clearly based on trustworthy sources of information. And—compounding the problem—both of those conclusions seem to be correct!

The contradiction is this: Looking at the research findings that have been produced over a number of decades leads to a clear conclusion that the media have only *selective and limited influence* on most people's beliefs, attitudes, and behavior. However, anyone who has even an elementary acquaintance with recent American history must reach the quite different conclusion that, frequently, the media have had very powerful influences on a number of social and cultural situations, trends, and processes within our society. The perplexing dilemma has to be resolved. Did the research reveal a false picture of minimal effects? If so, that would contradict our earlier claim that science reveals trustworthy knowledge. Or is our reading of recent history faulty when it seems to show that mass communications often have powerful effects on our society and culture? To resolve that dilemma, we will show in the present chapter that *both conclusions are correct*. That is, the media do have weak effects, but they also have powerful effects. That may sound like impossible double talk. However, the key to understanding this seemingly irreconcilable puzzle lies in recognizing the difference between short-term effects on individuals and long-term influences on a population's shared beliefs, attitudes, and behaviors that can change cultural norms and social institutions in the society at large. One problem with developing such long-range theories is that they go beyond what can currently be confirmed by easily observable research evidence. That is, they deal with influences and effects of mass communications that cannot be readily uncovered by short-term scientific experiments or on-time surveys. Yet these theories are more than just opinions and guesses. Powerful media effects can be revealed by careful observation of historical events and trends over long periods of time.

Campaigns for AIDS prevention have heightened awareness of the disease and have championed methods to promote safe sex and combat excessive drinking.

Accumulating Media Effects and Social Expectations

It is not difficult to show that mass communications can play a vital role in stimulating social and cultural change. In this section we will look at two theories explaining ways in which the media can be instrumental in promoting long-term changes within the society. The first, *theory of the accumulation of minimal effects,* helps in understanding how changes in public opinion and other shared beliefs in a population can take place.[28] Examples of such changes are public support for and beliefs in reducing pollution, limiting access to guns by juveniles, getting drunken drivers off the road, or reducing smoking by the young. The second, *social expectations theory*, explains long-term media influences on people as they slowly acquire clearer and clearer conceptions of the organization, functions, and consequences of key groups within a society—groups in which they personally play no part but that they understand quite well.

Accumulation Theory: The "Adding Up" of Minimal Effects

One way to understand long-term media influences is to identify the factors that must be present before minimal effects can "add up." This can show how the media often have a great deal of influence in shaping people's ideas and interpretations of a situation, even though any particular message they present to any one individual probably will have quite limited effects in a short-term sense.

There are three factors that must be present in a situation before accumulation theory can explain how significant changes occur over a long period. First, the media must focus *repeatedly* on a particular issue; second, they must be relatively *consistent* in presenting a more-or-less uniform interpretation; and third, the major media (newspapers, radio, television, and magazines) must *corroborate* each other with parallel content.

But what evidence is there that powerful media effects are brought about under such conditions? Clearly, no such evidence can be derived from either short-term experiments or from surveys completed at a particular point in time. However, *historical analyses* can supply examples that show the theory in action. We can identify very obvious examples of accumulative effects by looking at changing patterns of public response to certain events that have occurred in recent decades where media played a decisive role.

In recent years, the United States has engaged in armed interventions in several countries, most notably since 2002 and 2003 in Afghanistan and Iraq as well as other places earlier. Just what role communication plays in these conflicts is worthy of considerable research. These armed interventions in our recent history show very clearly the dramatic consequences to society that can result from *consistent, persistent,* and *corroborative* media attention to human tragedies. However, to show that these actions were not something totally unique, we will also briefly examine several additional examples.

ARMED INTERVENTIONS.   Sending military forces of the United States to invade a foreign country is a drastic step in international affairs—and one with great consequences, as the wars in Iraq and Afghanistan have demonstrated since 2002. But such interventions do happen, whether as in the Persian Gulf War of 1991, the Iraq War of 2003, or earlier conflicts in Central America, the Caribbean, or in Central Europe (Bosnia and Serbia), sometimes with international approval and support, sometimes not. Since war always has a profound and tragic impact, studying its origins in public support and public policy within a media framework is useful.

In the case of Iraq, the Bush administration built its case around two assumptions: (1) that regime change and the end of Saddam Hussein's rule was necessary and (2) that there were weapons of mass destruction that threatened the region and the world. These themes were repeated over time and won wide public support, even though there was initial opposition to the Iraq War since there was already a war in Afghanistan aimed at Al-Qaida and those responsible for 9/11. Even though there was no direct link between the Iraqi leadership and the terrorist leaders of Al-Qaida, people eventually thought there was, as polls later indicated. Just how does this happen, when details in news reports and other sources of intelligence offer contrary evidence and raise profound questions? Accumulation theory provides one answer. Months of repetitious TV coverage, a search for weapons of mass destruction (WMDs), as well as the demonizing of Hussein, clearly an odious tyrant but not significantly different from other antidemocratic leaders elsewhere. Portrayals in all of the media were *consistent, persistent, and corroborative.* As a result, public sentiment built up to a point that President George Bush was able, initially with a high level of approval, to take the extraordinary step of invading another country. The issue was alive and well in the presidential campaign in 2008.

Earlier, during the first Clinton administration, the media had played much the same role by providing a constant flow of accounts and images of suffering in Haiti and in Bosnia. Similarly, dreadful television pictures, magazine stories, and newspaper accounts of "ethnic cleansing" in Kosovo preceded bombing campaigns in that area, and, in the case of Serbia, much the same occurred. In both of these cases, public support for military action was strong. That is not to say that mass communications *caused* these interventions, but such policies would never have been supported without cumulative changes that took place among the public as a result of repeated, consistent, and corroborative media content.

SMOKING AND HEALTH.   A second example of the accumulation of minimal effects is the twenty-five-year campaign against smoking—waged largely in the media. The continuous, consistent, and corroborated portrayal of smoking as harmful to health in news and public-service campaigns slowly but surely brought about a significant change in the thinking and actions of large segments of the public. Eventually, the public supported a variety of new laws concerning that habit.

Additional examples could be cited, showing ways in which effects slowly accumulate when consistent messages about a topic are persistently presented and corroborated across media. They would include our current emphasis on living "green," avoiding wasting energy with improved light bulbs; fighting childhood and adult obesity by staving off fast foods; an increasing preoccupation with exercise; and our shared concerns about the dangers of using drugs and alcohol. At one time the messages from the media concerning drugs were mixed. Now the media have placed the negative aspects of these problems high on their agenda and have brought them sharply into focus for the public. Finally, in the same general category, there is an impressive role of the media in helping to define the dangers of HIV/AIDS through the use of condoms and "safe sex." This is done across virtually all media functions in informative articles and reports; in opinion media that make a direct, persuasive appeal in entertainment programs; and in advertising.

TWO GOOD REASONS TO GET AN HIV TEST.

1 IF YOU'RE INFECTED, YOU CAN GET TREATMENT THAT MAY HELP YOU LIVE A LONGER, HEALTHIER LIFE.

2 IF YOU'RE NOT, YOU CAN LEARN HOW TO STAY THAT WAY.

CALL 1-800-541-AIDS

Health concerns like HIV/AIDS are often the source of public-interest campaigns that underscore assumptions about the impact and influence of advertising on people's attitudes and behavior.

Social Expectations Theory: Learning Group Requirements

Another way of looking at long-term influences on media audiences is to note how, over time, people learn the rules and requirements for acting out parts within various kinds of groups by seeing them portrayed in media content. Here, the focus is not on isolated specific acts that are acquired from mediated models but on developing an understanding over time of the pattern of customs and routines of behavior expected within specific groups by seeing their portrayals in the media. More specifically, what is it that must be learned by a particular individual for effective participation in a group or for being accepted in any kind of social setting? In every human group there is a complex set of understandings of what behavior is expected. Those expectations must be acquired before the individual can act effectively in such circumstances.

To understand this process we can begin by noting the essential features of any human group, large or small. First, groups are made up of people who come together to accomplish a *goal* that they deem important—and which cannot effectively be accomplished by the same number of individuals acting alone. Thus, it is the *coordination* of their actions into an organized "team-like" pattern that gives the advantage to the group over solitary action.

It is the rules of that team-like coordinated behavior—often called the group's *social organization*—that set it apart from actions taken by individuals alone. Without such a pattern of social organization, learned and followed by each member of the group, their collective actions would be chaos. Thus, groups—from the smallest family to the largest government agency or corporation—have rules and expectations that define and govern the activities of each of their members if their collective goal is to be accomplished.

What are the major components of such a shared pattern of social organization, and how do human beings acquire their personal knowledge of such requirements? Briefly stated, social organization can be defined as *that pattern of general group norms, specialized roles, ranking positions, and the set of social controls used by the group to ensure reasonable conformity to its requirements.* Each of these components of organized social activities is important in stabilizing a group and getting its members to work effectively for whatever goals brought its members together in the first place.[29]

Group *norms* is an easy idea to understand. Every group has a set of general rules that all members of a particular group are expected to follow. These may have to do with the way people dress, use certain specialized language, greet each other, and so on through literally hundreds of activities that make up the behavior performed in the group. They differ greatly according to the type of group. The norms of army life are very different from those of a religious order, and both are very different from the norms followed by members of a local labor union. Nevertheless, all such groups have some set of general norms that all members must learn, understand, and follow to a reasonable degree. Social roles is also a basic concept. These are more specialized rules that apply to persons playing particular parts or defined positions in the group. Such definitions of expected behavior must be understood, not only by the person performing a particular role, but also by those who must relate their own roles to it. For example, imagine a baseball team in which the batter, pitcher, and each other player understands only what he or she is to do in his or her position but not what each of the other players are supposed to do under various circumstances. It would be chaos, and the goal of winning could never be accomplished. Thus, the key ideas regarding roles are both *specialization* and *interdependence.* That is, in most groups, the role requirements for each position in the group are not only different (specialized), but they are also interlinked with the specialized activities of other members. It is this feature of a coordinated "division of labor" that makes groups far more efficient than the same number of uncoordinated individuals.

Again, how do people in a society of interdependence gain knowledge of the roles of others with whom they never have personal contact? A key idea in social organization is *ranking.* There are few groups, if any, in which every member has precisely the same level of authority, power, status, and rewards. Even in informal groups of friends, some members are leaders and are looked up to, while others are followers and command less prestige. In large and complex groups, many ranking layers exist. People at different levels have varying amounts of power and authority, and they receive different amounts of respect and rewards. Such differences in ranking arise from many sources. Generally speaking, those at the top take the greatest responsibility, they possess scarce but critical skills, they have had extensive experience, and they are not easily replaced. Those with opposite characteristics tend to remain at the bottom. However, most people can identify the basic social ranking of many categories of people. How do they acquire such knowledge?

Finally, every human group makes use of *social controls.* Maintaining the stability of a group takes place through the use of some combination of rewards and punishments. These are used by a group to prevent excessive deviation from, and to reward conformity to, its social expectations. They can range from mild sanctions, such a words or gestures of approval and disapproval, to really significant actions of control, ranging from awarding medals to those who perform in a significantly positive way to executing those whose deviations are too great to tolerate. Most groups allow limited deviation from norms, some personal variability in the manner in which people fulfill role requirements, or even some disregard for rank. However, there are always limits beyond which sanctions will be invoked.

People in societies without media learn these social requirements by a slow process. Older members in the society teach the young, or they acquire the needed knowledge by a process of trial and error, which can sometimes be painful. In a media society, however, an enormous variety of groups and social activities are *portrayed in communications media.* People from childhood forward learn about politics and voting from television, the Internet, and advertising just as they learn about consumer behavior from media portrayals and advertising.

An important caution is that the way that various groups are portrayed in media—in movies, television programs, or even in print—may be misleading, inconsistent, or just plain wrong. There is a long history of prejudice against women, people of color, gays and lesbians, and virtually every ethnic group that has been carried and underscored by the media, whether intentionally or unintentionally.

Implications of Long-Term Theories

Both accumulation theory and social expectations theory aid in resolving the contradiction that we posed earlier. It remains entirely true that from a short-term perspective mass communications have very limited and very selective influences on individuals. There is every reason to be confident in that conclusion. However, repeated exposure to a consistent message can change people. It still may be less than dramatic for any particular person, but it does happen, and such changes add up. Eventually, among large populations repeatedly exposed to relatively consistent interpretations presented and corroborated across media, an accumulation of individual influences eventually results in significant change.

It must be recognized that the existence of such long-term influences has not been supported as yet by systematic research that fits the requirements of science. Methods for making clear, quantitative, and unambiguous observations of media influences on long-term changes in individuals or on society and culture have yet to be developed. Accumulation theory and social expectations theory, therefore, are relatively new and remain to be checked against reality through systematic research. On the other hand, looking at long-term trends and changes in a society and trying to see if they are possibly a product of the accumulation of small changes appears to be a promising strategy. Many such changes have taken place in the United States in which the mass media may indeed have played a part. This includes the present-day "green" movement, civic engagement, and concern for older people, as well as the great civil rights and women's movements of earlier times, which continue to be felt today in education, voting, employment, housing, and many other areas of daily life. Television played a remarkable role in these social movements and concerns, but today the Internet has taken on a major role because of widespread access, ease of communication, and interactivity. Clearly, both the earlier and current focal points for public priorities underscore the value of long-term perspectives that avoid the limitations of short-term research, but they also do not always fit the model of social science. Much more systematic strategies and methods are needed for controlled observations and various forms of ethnographic study to truly pay off. Scholars from the cultural studies and critical theory tradition, as we've noted earlier, champion qualitative analysis and assessment, drawing on assumptions about ideology, power, and the social contract. Some of this seeps into the media in commentaries but is rarely seen by media analysts, strategists, and researchers who are more comfortable with quantitative methods and what they call "real numbers," whether gathered with precision or not.

While we've made no effort here to be exhaustive, we have drawn on the most influential and widely tested theories. A major conclusion that may be drawn from what has been presented in this chapter is this: Using the logic and methods of social science or humanistic analysis—suitably adapted for the study of mass communications—requires the following strategy. (1) conducting research that yields findings from which theories can be derived; (2) conducting further research that tests out in realistic settings the validity of the derived explanations; (3) modifying such explanations if new data show that they need change (or abandon them if necessary); and (4) using such theories, when supported, as the best available explanations of how mass communications influence people.

What are the alternatives? Essentially, they are (1) reaching conclusions on the basis of preconceived political or religious ideologies and qualitative observations, (2) using personal hunches or speculations to decide on the truth, or (3) reaching conclusions based on the dictates of a philosophical commitment on the role of the media or other set of *priori* (previously accepted) conceptions of reality. For most scholars, intellectuals, and researchers who study the processes and effects of mass communication, these alternatives do not seem as attractive as the use of scientific research in seeking answers. There are plenty of commentators who believe that evidence about media impact has to agree with their political or social view, rather than seeking a more value-neutral perspective from which to assess the many forces and factors that influence media and that media, in turn, also influence. Some of this work was explored in Chapter 10.

CHAPTER REVIEW

- Digital media developments like those in conventional media benefit from long-term, theoretical study and research.
- All media including digital media are part of a process of communication that is better understood through sense-making theories based on evidence.
- Before modern research methods were developed, many scholars speculated about the influence of mass press on audiences. Lacking objectively assembled facts and relying on hunches and opinions, each came to different and often contradictory views.
- The earliest research was guided by the assumptions of the magic bullet theory, later abandoned, which said the media have immediate, powerful, and universal effects. The findings of studies, such as those on influences of the movies on youth, seemed to support that idea.
- Further research, such as that on women and daytime media, revealed that audience members with different psychological and social characteristics actively select from available media content that will gratify needs or provide satisfactions.
- In a study of a presidential election campaign, it was found that media messages and influences often flow in a two-step process, first to opinion leaders who attend first-hand and then to others in the population. In election campaigns, media messages can activate voters and reinforce prior predispositions, but they seldom convert people from one party or position to another.
- Studies of televised violence do not support the idea that the medium routinely sends youths into the streets to become aggressive after attending to depictions of violence. Aggressive behavior is more closely linked to the personal and social characteristics of individuals. However, televised violence may raise the probability of aggressive acts among certain categories of youths.
- Theories, now supported by research, aid in understanding such processes as modeling of behavior that is depicted in the media, in which the actions performed by persons in media content serve as sources for adoption of particular forms of behavior.
- If a particular idea or situation is portrayed repeatedly, consistently, and uniformly by several media, both traditional and digital, it can have a long-term accumulated influence on individuals and the society as a whole.
- Another long-term influence is learning the social expectations regarding norms, roles, ranks, and controls in groups within which an individual plays no part but to which the person is linked in a web of mutual social dependencies.

STRATEGIC QUESTIONS

1. How does understanding the process and effects of mass communication help us understand the impact and effects of media on individuals, organizations, and society itself?
2. What did early media effects research reveal about the media? How did that hold up over time?
3. Why do we need scholarly or scientific research on media to understand their influence and power?
4. Historically, what kinds of social concerns and issues have prompted media research? Has that research, aimed at answering questions about major problems, been applicable to everyday life too?
5. How well do research findings on media effects hold up in the digital age?
6. Are media research and theory that probe media effect more important for short-term considerations or longer term explanations? Draw your conclusion from the evidence in this chapter.

KEY CONCEPTS & TERMS

ENDNOTES

1. "Raising the Ante: The Internet's Impact on Journalism Education and Existing Theories of Mass Communication," a symposium in honor of Philip Meyer, University of North Carolina, March 27–28, 2008; see discussion of Internet and community use, agenda-setting, cultivation theory, minimal effects, gatekeeping, two-step flow, uses and gratifications, and diffusion theory, http://jomc.unc.edu/raisingtheante.

2. "Facebook's Grandfathers (& MySpace too)," in *I, A Bee,* buzz and pollination from the Internet Advertising Bureau, at www.randallrothenberg.com.

3. David Holmes, *Communication Theory: Media, Technology and Society* (Thousand Oaks, CA: Sage Publications, 2005).

4. John Burroughs, "Some Natural History Doubts and Conclusions," *Harper's Monthly Magazine,* August 1904, pp. 360–364.

5. Charles Horton Cooley, *Social Organization* (New York: Charles Scribner's Sons, 1909), p. 82.

6. Cooley, *Social Organization,* p. 91.

7. Edgar Dale, *Children's Attendance at Motion Pictures* (New York: Arno Press, 1970), p. 73; originally published in 1935.

8. Hadley Cantrill, *The Invasion from Mars: A Study in the Psychology of Panic* (Princeton, NJ: Princeton University Press), p. 96.

9. Cantril, *The Invasion from Mars,* p. 98.

10. Howard Koch, *The Panic Broadcast: Portrait of an Event* (Boston: Little Brown, 1970).

11. The full account of the study and its findings can be found in Cantril, *The Invasion from Mars.*

12. C. J. Hovland, A. A. Lumsdaine, and F. D. Sheffield, *Experiments on Mass Communication,* Vol. III of *Studies of Social Psychology in World War II* (New York: John Wiley & Sons, 1965).

13. Paul Lazarsfeld, Bernard Berelson, and Hazel Gaudet, *The People's Choice* (New York: Columbia University Press, 1948). See also Jefferson Pooley, "Fifteen Pages That Shook the Field: Personal Influence, Edward Shils, and the Remembered History of Mass Communication Research," *Annals of the American Academy of Political and Social Science* Vol. 608 (2006), pp. 130, 131.

14. Diana C. Mutz, *Interpersonal Influence, How Perceptions of Mass Collectives Affect Political Attitudes* (New York: Cambridge University Press, 1998), xvii; pp. 4–5.

15. Everette E. Dennis, "The Two-Step Flow and the Internet Age," see Raising the Ante, op cit.

16. Herta Herzog, "What Do We Really Know About Daytime Serial Listeners," in Paul F. Lazarsfeld and Frank N. Stanton, *Radio Research,* 1942–1943 (New York: Duell, Sloan & Pierce, 1944), pp. 3–33.

17. Bernard Berelson, "What Missing the Newspaper Means," in Paul F. Lazarsfeld and Frank N. Stanton, *Communications Research,* 1948–1949 (New York: Harper and Brothers, 1949), pp. 111–129.

18. Berelson, "What Missing the Newspaper Means," p. 116.

19. Eleonor E. Maccoby, "Television: Its Impact on School Children," Public Opinion Quarterly (1951), pp. 421–444; also Paul I. Lyness, "The Place of Mass Media in the Lives of Boys and Girls," *Journalism Quarterly,* 29 (1952), pp. 43–54.

20. Wilbur Schramm, Jack Lyle, and Edwin Parker, *Television in the Lives of Our Children* (Palo Alto, CA: Stanford University Press, 1961).

21. Norma Pecora, John Murray, and Ellen Wartella, *Children & Television: Fifty Years of Research* (Mahwah, NJ: Lawrence Erlbaum Associates, 2006).

22. Each volume has this title with a different subtitle; the subtitles are *Media Content and Control* (Volume 1), *Television and Social Learning* (Volume 2), *Television and Adolescent Aggression* (Volume 3), *Television in Day-to-Day Life: Patterns of Use* (Volume 4), and *Television's Effects: Further Explorations* (Volume 5). The various reports were prepared by George A. Comstock, John P. Murray, and Eli A. Rubenstein. They were published by the Government Printing Office, Washington, D.C., in 1971. The summary volume, *Television and Growing Up,* appeared in 1972.

23. A. Bandura and S. A. Ross, "Transmission of Aggression Through Imitation of Aggressive Models," *Journal of Abnormal and Social Psychology,* 63 (1961), pp. 575–582.

24. *Television and Growing Up,* p. 11.
25. Surgeon General's Scientific Advisory Committee on Television and Social Behavior, *Television and Growing Up: The Impact of Televised Violence.* Report to the Surgeon General, United States Public Health Service (Washington, DC: U.S. Government Printing Office, 1971), p. 11.
26. J. L. Steinfeld, "TV Violence is Harmful," *The Reader's Digest,* April 1973, pp. 34–40.
27. *Television and Behavior: Ten Years of Scientific Progress and Implications for the Eighties* (Rockville, MD: National Institute of Mental Health, 1982).
28. This particular theory has been developed for the purposes of this text, and it does not appear by this name in the theory literature.
29. For an extended treatment of these features of social organization and how they shape behavior for the members of human groups, see "Social Organization," in Melvin L. DeFleur, et al., *Sociology: Human Society* (New York: Random House, 1984), pp. 72–104.

Ethics: Assessing Content and Behavior of the Media

Ethics, a branch of philosophy, is concerned with morals and moral choices. Media ethics is concerned with the content of media and the behavior of those who lead, manage, and work with media. Digital media, with their unparalleled speed, worldwide instantaneous reach, and virtually unlimited storage capacity, raise all kinds of questions for those interested in an ethical, morally correct media in an increasingly complex and fragmented society. If simple honesty, fairness, and transparency are hallmarks of ethical media, then digital media are, on one level, no different from conventional media. But that's only part of the story, as they do pose quite new, different, and multidimensional challenges. First and foremost, the open and instantaneous nature of digital media means many of the traditional functions of media—news, information, advocacy, entertainment, and advertising—are becoming blurred across the digital platforms. In the language of media scholars, they are said to be *converging*. The firewalls that old media championed are gone, as opinionated bloggers claim to "cover the news" and actually affect it as critics and provocateurs. People download music and movies, copy them for their friends, and are puzzled when asked whether this is ethical or even legal behavior. A persistent argument between free and paid media ensues, as do new questions about privacy in an era when "friending" and other forms of social networking reveal the personal aspects of people's lives as never before. And there is endless cyber crime enabled by new tools and technologies. At the same time, the capacity to do good, to expand freedom of expression, and to make end runs around once closed systems of old media are encouraging. Media people drill down and produce remarkable, multimedia websites with much substance and depth alongside sensational media that is unchecked and runs amok. At a time of great fragmentation and true redefinition of media convergence, media ethics remains a dilemma in search of answers.[1]

Media ethics are usually associated with media professionals, from high-level executives and owners to middle managers and even entry-level employees, and their behavior, as well as the character of the content they produce. Some critics complain that media ethics most often focuses on individual behavior and seeks to find out who is responsible or accountable. A transgressing editor or producer sometimes becomes a scapegoat for what is, in fact, a systemic institutional problem. One dramatic example of this was the 2003 case of Jayson Blair, a falsifying and plagiarizing reporter at the *New York Times* whose transgressions were so extreme that the paper ran pages of apologies and re-reported articles when the case was revealed. Initially, Blair was fired and the newspaper organized a task force (with respected outside members) to get to the bottom of the scandal.[2] Their report pointed to systemic problems at the newspaper and called for reforms, including naming an ombudsman, or public editor, to head off such problems in the future. However, this did not put an end to both public and internal criticism; eventually, the paper's two top editors were held to be responsible and were fired.[3]

Another notable example of a de facto ethics "symposium" occurred in 2007, when media baron Rupert Murdoch made a bid for, and eventually succeeded in buying, the *Wall Street Journal*. For weeks, critics, analysts, and policy makers debated Murdoch's performance as a media owner, his commitment to journalistic integrity, and other issues. When he did eventually buy the paper from the Bancroft family, which had owned it for more than a century, he felt obliged to set up a review board with outside members to assure critics and the public of the continued independence and integrity of the newspaper. Murdoch's history as a media owner, especially involving his ethics and integrity, was very much at issue.

Some modern-day, digital media ethics issues are less grand than high-level maneuvering among elites at America's most important newspapers but instead involve ordinary individuals and, ultimately, the media industries themselves. For example, in 2008 when blogger Ed Bott on his *Microsoft Report* asked, "Where do you stand on digital media ethics?" he was asking something more basic. He asked eleven questions in an online poll, to wit:

- Do you think it is proper to buy a CD, rip it to your hard drive, and then make copies for your own personal use on multiple devices and computers?
- Do you think it is proper to buy a CD, rip it off your hard drive, and then trade the CD at your local used-media store or online?
- Is it OK to borrow a CD from a friend and rip it to your hard drive? Is it proper to buy a CD and make a copy for a friend?
- If you buy a DRM-protected track from an online music or video store like iTunes, is it proper to strip the DRM and make an unprotected backup copy?
- If you rent a DVD from Netflix or Blockbuster, it is OK to make a copy before you return it?
- If you miss an episode of your favorite TV program from a broadcast network, is it OK to download it from BitTorrent or a file-sharing network? Does it make a difference if it's a program form a subscription-only channel like HBO? What about if the same program is available for free with ads from an official website or for a charge from an online service?[4]

Not incidentally, the answers respondents gave to the first question were Yes, 96%; No, 2%; and Sometimes/It Depends, 2%. It is clear that individual consumer choices have had a massive impact on the media and entertainment industries (especially music and movies) as well as stimulating much discussion. At the same time, litigation about intellectual property, piracy, and other topics has had consequences far beyond an individual's personal choices. Some commentators say these issues, as we've noted earlier, are possibly generational. Many people have a kind of digital faith that all things digital should be free and widely shared, while others see some of them as commercial properties that deserve compensation for their producers, songwriters, authors, or investors. There is a yawning gap between those who adhere to a "you get what you pay for" philosophy and those who believe in free-form networking and open-source sharing. This debate is at the heart of any distinction between digital media ethics and more generic media ethics. There are clearly generational differences involving attitudes and values. Some distinguish between so-called digital immigrants (those who did not grow up with the Internet) and those who did—the digital natives whether these differences on privacy and free content will hold is anybody's guess. Some say technology trumps old-school values, while others disagree. Today's college students and their parents often disagree on these issues. (Perhaps their professors are in between). And there are efforts to reach younger children in the classroom where one website, Cable in the Classroom, simply states, "Digital ethics is all about teaching ethical, courteous, and productive behavior while using digital media."[5] The site especially focuses on plagiarism and copyright issues while urging courteous online behavior. A K-12 school district in Lee's Summit, Missouri, tries to teach digital ethics through a series of interactive questions, such as:

May I download and use music? Is it OK to copy and use a poem from a textbook? May I use video clips from a television show? What is ethical behavior in the digital age? How is plagiarism defined? How can it be detected?[6]

As we'll see later, some of these queries are a matter of values and judgment, while others skirt the law and can lead to civil penalties and fines. This may be trivial in kindergarten, but as these practices escalate later on in life and careers, they can be serious matters indeed.

Many commentators, like those at the Poynter Institute for Media Ethics, have drafted codes of online journalism ethics[7] and argue that ethics is platform-neutral, suggesting that the role of journalism in a digital age is no different (except in degree) than it was with earlier technologies, though they admit it is certainly harder. Still, accuracy, credibility, and transparency are desirable hallmarks of ethical media content whether one is producing a small newsletter, a television newscast, or an online newspaper.

Of course, accuracy, and therefore *credibility,* is very important to journalists and others in the media industries. Indeed, it is the single-most vital factor for the survival and success of the communications industry. As our previous chapters have shown, those who present the news, public relations campaigns, advertising, and other media content want the public to believe that they are telling the truth and that they are transmitting their messages within ethical bounds. After all, professional communicators know only too well that if the information, opinion, and even entertainment they present to the public lacked believability, it would quickly erode public confidence and they would lose their audience. Communications in a civilized society must not only be competent but also credible to be valuable to people. Thus, ethics is more than an arcane topic that is debated by religious authorities, do-gooders, and philosophers. It is a deeply practical concern across all of the communications industries. When ethical norms are violated, it upsets most professional communicators because it threatens their livelihood. In the interactive, digital era this continues to be important. Still, digital communication has a capacity to manipulate images and information so that its use overall and the specific portrayals and the patterns of behavior it enables can be both morally elevating and troubling.

MEDIA-WIDE ETHICS WATCH

While much of the concern about media ethics is directed to the *content* of communication (whether the accuracy of a newspaper or magazine report, the selective editing of a television program or podcast, or a questionable photograph) or the *behavior* of communicators, especially journalists (whether they exercised professional standards or not), this is only a small part of the ethics dilemma for media industries. First, ethics is a vital matter for all of the communication functions—information, opinion, entertainment, and advertising/marketing. Second, all media industries confront the ethics issue, though some are noisier than others about it. This being said, most material on media ethics is associated with news, information, and journalism since they have a great importance to the functioning of the society and the ability of people to communicate effectively with each other. However, unethical content and behavior in motion pictures, on Internet websites, or in the practice of public relations and advertising can have great impact in direct and indirect ways.[8] However, some people argue that all users of media, especially digital media, ought not be expected to adhere to the same standard. For example, do personal communications, like IMs, Twitter messages, emails, or texts, that are designed to be communicated between and among a few people (though potentially millions could be included) have the same obligation as professional media aimed at massive and or discrete audiences? Perhaps here the analogy is between a telephone call and a broadcast, though ethicists differ on this. Today in the digital age, the question grows even more complex because interactivity extends access and reach and thus may create new and more serious ethical dilemmas and breaches.

To be sure, ethics is relevant to people across the media industries, not just information gatherers and purveyors. It makes a difference whether advertising sales people represent themselves with honesty and integrity. The same is true for the heads of television networks, book publishing firms, news services, video production companies, and others. Whether the "media person" is an entry-level employee, a middle manager, or the chairman and chief executive, ethical behavior and ethical breaches can and do become matters of public concern. Easy (and deserving) targets are high-profile television hosts like Jerry Springer, Bill O'Reilly, and others whose controversial TV and cable programs can be tasteless and grotesque. These hosts have found themselves in the heat of controversy when guests on their shows who felt wronged subsequently committed murder and other antisocial acts said by some to be linked with the show. No less a media luminary than Rupert Murdoch has been criticized for advancing the tabloid cause and cheapening media content. The publisher of the *Los Angeles Times* was accused of blending journalistic and advertising functions, breaking what some believe should be a "church-state" division in a profit-sharing venture with a convention center. As mentioned earlier, the venerated *New York Times* unwittingly allowed a reporter to fabricate stories and sources for several years before he was caught. The same thing happened at *The New Republic,* where an unethical writer also produced stories entirely made up before he too was caught and fired. In both instances the two wrote books, one of which even became a motion picture, titled *Shattered Glass* (the writer's name was Stephen Glass). Think of ways the various media industries get involved in ethical disputes and controversies.

- Motion Pictures—Often rapped for distorting reality when treating real-life and historical figures in films, such as Oliver Stone's movies about JFK and Nixon, which blurred fact and fiction.
- Book Publishers—Deciding to cancel a publishing contact because of outside pressures or a case of plagiarism or misrepresentation like flawed books unknowingly promoted by Oprah Winfrey.
- Advertising—Exploiting the sexuality of children to move products such as Abercrombie & Fitch ads with sexy teen poses.
- Internet Websites—Engaging in plagiarism and misuse of others' intellectual property while running fast and loose with the facts, including several that have fabricated news items.
- Public Relations—Misrepresenting a client's background and record or crossing the damage-control threshold in representing a reprehensible or dishonest client.
- Television—Sensationalizing and distorting events and issues, or misleading the public.
- Music—Files are downloaded, thus depriving artists and labels of revenues, or an artist steals a tune from another performer without arbitration.

There are many more good and bad examples, of course, and as we later note, there is a great public and professional preoccupation with ethics that has led to many ethical codes, standard-setting, and professional groups eager to enhance media ethics.[9]

The issue of ethics affects not only mass communications but also everyone who is in public life. It is involved in matters of personal morality, campaign financing, and various conflicts of interest and other matters. Concern over ethics is also a lively one across American society. It is not uncommon for charges of breaches of ethics to be front-page news, whether the charge involves government, business, other institutions, or individuals in our society. In recent years, critics worried about Internet privacy, copyright violation, outright plagiarism, Wall Street greed, government corruption, and hypocrisy in the lives of politicians, sports heroes, televangelists, and other public people.

Of course, scandals and other incidents that are spurred by ethics issues are rarely simple. It is not just a matter of right and wrong but also discovery of the questionable act and public exposure. Sometimes that is the work of "whistleblowers," people inside an organization who make revelations, often at great risk. Sometimes they do it for a noble cause, such as serving the public interest; other times they are angry and disgruntled employees who want to get back at their bosses. In other instances, ethics violations are made public by political enemies of the people under fire.

While public interest in ethics varies over time, it has been exceptionally high for more than a decade, especially in the face of corruption in high places, profiteering, and political misrepresentation. It seems, in fact, that there is no field that is exempt from ethical concerns, as various conferences and seminars have pointed out. Ethical conduct is on the docket in businesses, churches, schools, and other institutions. It is not unusual for a newsmagazine, like *Time, U.S. News & World Report,* or *Newsweek* to cover ethics as a beat and even to feature ethics as a cover story. And there are endless digital ethics blogs. And perhaps even more importantly bloggers who monitor media can have a profound impact as they point out errors and misrepresentations or simply catch embarrassing gaffes. They do this across society, of course, not just in their media watches, but their assessment in other realms often makes news, as in the 2008 presidential campaign when embarrassing comments and claims by candidates and their handlers led to public revelations. Hillary Clinton falsely claimed to have come under enemy fire on an international trip, and John Edwards lied about an affair and fathering a child out of wedlock.

While public preoccupation with ethical issues across so many fields is rare, media ethics has long been a subject of public discussion. Some critics ridicule the idea that competitive and profit-driven media can operate within an ethical framework. But most knowledgeable people disagree, saying that no media system can exist very long without public confidence, and that requires accurate, honest, and believable communication. As we have made clear in previous chapters, this does not mean that the media industries are always reliable or that all of them share the same values or ethical standards.[10]

NEW TECHNOLOGY CHALLENGES

From their beginnings, every new media platform or technology, from the telegraph to the Internet, has been gathering places for human interchange and interaction. Traditional, non-interactive media follow a command-and-control model, in which owners and their employees control the messages and their distribution. With the high-speed Internet and the interactive character of new media on social networking sites, it is common for the end user to initiate messages, often creating the problems and challenges that ensue. While YouTube, MySpace, Friendster, and other social networking portals provide a channel for all kinds of social interaction and personal media development of a positive nature, they are also platforms for mischief when unscrupulous people use them inappropriately, for everything from misrepresenting their age and intent to hawking nonexistent products. The 3D virtual world "Second Life," with its own monetary system and infinite capacity for community creation and social networking, offers additional opportunities for ethical challenges. In "Second Life" people use avatars, cartoonish characters that can provide people with new (and sometimes multiple) identities. On one level this is entertainment, a game, but on another level people take it quite seriously and sometimes spend an inordinate amount of time online in the game, well outside of their real life on Earth. Much has been written about peoples' new identities in "Second Life," which can be a source of great personal pleasure and endless creativity. At the same time, there is a darker side of "Second Life," which Jeffrey Cole, director of the Center for the Digital Future, says "can be a very unpleasant place to be in the midst of crime and other antisocial activity."[11] All this raises ethical dilemmas about assuming different identities, misrepresenting and confusing one's real self with one's "Second Life" avatar—and sometime balancing several avatars in relationships with other players of the game who are also real people. Whether virtual worlds will survive depends on whether people ultimately are willing to pay for them. Both MTV and VH1 created virtual worlds in connection with some of their own shows, such as "Virtual Hills." This is part of the landscape of modern-day gaming, including electronic games that pose ethical dilemmas for their players—and in the case of very young players, their parents. Technologies and software systems that facilitate anonymous communication can be a problem when misused. Of course, misrepresentation in some forms is a legal offense, as is misuse of false identity, something that the Internet facilitates nicely.[12]

DIMENSIONS OF ETHICS FOR THE MEDIA

Typically, media ethics have centered on three major issues: (1) *accuracy* and *fairness* in reporting and other activities; (2) the *behavior of reporters,* especially in relation to their sources; and (3) avoidance of *conflicts of interest.*

Accuracy and Fairness

It is often said that the first rule of journalism is "accuracy, accuracy, accuracy." Burton Benjamin, a longtime producer at CBS News, got caught up in an accuracy and fair-play conflict when CBS was accused of deliberately distorting information about the Vietnam War and General William Westmoreland in a news documentary. Criticism from outside circles as well as media people themselves was so fierce that CBS executives commissioned Benjamin to investigate the charges and deliver a report. He found his network colleagues guilty of violating their own stated (and written) news standards and later wrote a book about the incident, titled *Fair Play*.[13]

Reports like Benjamin's (which are rare) and other critiques of media performance, good and bad, constitute a kind of common law of ethics. For almost every ethical dilemma in the press, there is a history and context, but unfortunately the press has little "institutional memory" and often ignores the past or reinvents the wheel.

The unnatural and intrusive nature of celebrity news coverage is seen in this field of photographers stalking a political candidate.

The Behavior of Reporters

The second area of ethical concern, the behavior of reporters, has to do with an important aspect of professionalism—whether reporters and other media personnel conduct themselves honestly and with integrity. This usually means being honest and aboveboard to *sources* about the purposes of gathering information. For many years, it was thought to be unethical to misrepresent oneself deliberately to obtain information—for example by claiming to be someone else such as a lawyer or police officer. Yet the precise relationship that should exist between journalists and sources has never been fully understood or established. In a now famous article in *The New Yorker*, Janet Malcolm blasted her fellow journalist Joe McGinniss for misleading a famous news source, Dr. Jeffrey MacDonald, who was convicted of murdering his wife and children. As Malcolm wrote:

> Every journalist who is not too stupid or too full of himself to notice what is going on knows that what he does is morally indefensible. He is a kind of confidence man, preying on people's vanity, ignorance, or loneliness, gaining their trust and betraying them without remorse. Like the credulous widow who wakes up one day to find the charming young man and all her savings gone, so the consenting subject of a piece of nonfiction writing learns—when the article or book appears—his hard lesson. Journalists justify their treachery in various ways according to their temperaments. The more pompous talk about freedom of speech and "the public's right to know"; the least talented talk about Art; the seemliest murmur about earning a living.[14]

The cause for Malcolm's agitation was that she felt McGinniss had convinced Dr. MacDonald that he was his friend and would actually do a book that was beneficial for his case. The issue of whether a journalist seeking full cooperation from a news source is prone to deceiving the source was widely discussed at the time. People joined from all sides, some condemning McGinniss and others accusing Malcolm of having committed in the past similar breaches herself. Malcolm's observations led to a lively nationwide debate in the journalistic community wherein the obligations, if any, of reporters to sources were thoroughly discussed. However, there was no clear resolution.

Paparazzi surround celebrity Lindsay Lohan whose life and antics are the stuff on which tabloids feed.

Conflict of Interest

Conflict of interest is a third area of ethical concern. The term typically refers to engaging in activity that compromises one's integrity in the performance of one's professional or public duties. It is, for example, difficult to be engaged in partisan politics while writing impartially about politics. By the same token, media people have been urged to avoid cronyism, nepotism, and other conflicts that can compromise their integrity or give the appearance of such compromise. A closely related area has been *checkbook journalism,* wherein news organizations pay sources to give interviews. This is a violation of journalistic norms, although there are times when media people do it and defend the practice. In the case of news people, conflict of interest usually involves a reporter or editor covering a topic in which he or she has a personal stake—a family member may be involved, the reporter may do work on the side for a company being scrutinized, and so forth. This sort of thing is strongly discouraged, even to the point where some reporters are fired for conflict of interest.

DISTINGUISHING ETHICS AND LAW

Some people wonder why ethical breaches are not illegal and therefore punishable by censure, fines, or prison sentences. The answer is that many questionable practices and apparent deceptions are not necessarily illegal. There are whole categories of criminal acts prohibited by law, including murder, robbery, theft, and many others. There are also various civil offenses and torts (or hurtful acts) that are also unlawful, because legislation was enacted so defining them, and courts (including juries and judges) make determinations in cases involving individuals who are sued by someone claiming damages. A moral code evolves based on social custom but does not necessarily cross the legal line where blame can be assessed. For example, it may be unpleasant if your neighbor is repeatedly shunning you and being rude and inconsiderate. This may hurt your feelings, but in most instances that's tough and you have no legal course of action to say otherwise. If, on the other hand, your neighbor posts a large sign denouncing you and accusing you of a crime you did not commit, you can sue for libel and, if you win your case, collect damages.

For the media, there are some acts that are clearly illegal, such as breaking into an office to steal papers, committing deliberate misrepresentation by claiming to be someone else, engaging in insider trading in the stock market, and performing other acts that are usually frowned upon by courts in gathering the news. Sometimes such instances lead to ethical disputes too. For example, a few years ago, the *Chicago Sun-Times* bought a bar called "The Mirage" and operated it to have a window on various city inspectors receiving payoffs and committing other criminal acts. The newspaper, in fact, misrepresented itself to gather news. A blogger interviewing former President Clinton in the 2008 presidential campaign misrepresented herself as an ordinary citizen with a question about the role of race in politics, when she intended to use his comments on a blog. Senators Barack Obama and John McCain were also caught short by unidentified bloggers covering private campaign meetings. Some say anything a high-profile public person says is fair game; others argue that identifying oneself as a reporter is the ethical thing to do. In an era of citizen journalism and cell phones that are cameras, almost anything goes, as Britney Spears learned when she was photographed in her cell while serving a sentence for a hit-and-run incident and driving without a valid license.

Long before digital issues were prevalent, a perplexing case that led to spirited debates about media ethics was that of Richard Jewell, a security guard accused in the 1996 Olympic bombing in Atlanta. Jewell was a suspect fingered by the FBI and other law enforcement officials who also tipped off the press. While never formally accused of the crime, he was hounded by the media and law enforcement officials and subject to a flood of negative publicity. Eventually, charges against him were dropped, and he sorrowfully asked, "How can I recover my reputation?" Constitutional lawyers doubted that Jewell had much of a case against the press, which based their reports on police and FBI tips, but nevertheless most people in various surveys believed that Jewell was wronged. Eventually, NBC News and CNN settled out of court with the suspect. Other litigation went on for years.

In the Jewell case, wide publicity given to apparently wrong accusations was the issue and whether the press acted too zealously and recklessly in emphasizing the suspicion against the security guard without also balancing such claims against his rights—and consistent denials. The media, according to Lawrence Grossman, a former president of NBC News, have trouble "saying they are sorry for much of anything. Reporters just don't like to admit that they are wrong—even when they are shown to be so after the fact."[15] The Jewell case was especially illustrative because, initially, Jewell was thought to be a hero whose bravery was trumpeted in news stories and interviews. Then, when he was suspected of the bombing, press coverage emphasized the accusation and "hounded him like an animal," in his words. Jewell and his mother couldn't leave their Atlanta home without encountering a sea of cameras and microphones and shouting reporters.

Whether the Jewell case represented a breach of ethics has been the subject of many seminars, articles, and television debates, with no clear answers.

GROWING CONCERN OVER MEDIA ETHICS

As a general field, ethics is a branch of philosophy that tries to promote good values and goodwill, as opposed to mean-spirited or venal behavior. Some critics feel that the issue of media ethics is too broad and elusive to have much meaning. For example, no unified field of media ethics offers rules or standards that apply to all media platforms. What is taboo for a newspaper reporter may be business as usual for an advertising salesperson from the same organization. Ethics, say critics, is simply a matter of personal integrity. This ties the question of ethics for the media and media organizations to personal standards of forthright, honest, and competent behavior.

Others say that ethics is a collective concept and that corporations, networks, and newspaper publishing chains have a responsibility to see that they are honest and competent. The value of this may seem obvious, but in a society where business is often described as "dog eat dog," the idea that the media industry should be socially responsible and a good corporate citizen to the public might be dismissed as platitudinous. Indeed, some argue that the phrase "media ethics" is an oxymoron—a contradiction in terms. The reason it should not be is that media organizations and their people clearly have self-interest in being ethical, especially in the sense of being moral and credible.

Moral lapses by celebrities often generate excessive media coverage and raise concern about media ethics.

Ethical behavior in a general sense is not hard to define. It simply means that people should not lie, steal, cheat, or commit other antisocial acts. Ethics is doing what is "right," but the problem is that "right" is defined differently by different people. Thus, the need exists for serious attention to media ethics in a society increasingly concerned about the ethics of all occupational groups and professionals, whether they are lawyers, doctors, architects, or journalists. A commitment to basic ethical standards is what binds us together as a society, distinguishing us as socially responsible as opposed to self-serving individuals.

All of the media and their supporting systems—including the news, book publishing, movies, cable, newsletters, advertising, public relations, and other enterprises—are governed by general business ethics. Moreover, most of them also have codes of ethics, standards of conduct, and good ethical practices for their employees.

Most people who work in the media, ranging from financial writers to videographers, agree to abide by certain standards or rules that embody ethical values. Most, however, include few explicit ethical values beyond those taught generally in the family, churches, or schools.[16]

At one time, some areas of communication were virtually exempt from ethics. For example, people did not apply the same standards of fact and verification to advertising and public relations that they did to newspapers and magazines, arguing that advocates should have license to make the case for their clients to the point of exaggeration. Whether justified or not, people tended to discount a "public relations approach" or self-serving political or ideological appeals. Similarly, religious observers proclaiming their faith were not necessarily expected to be fair and impartial.

Now that is changing, partly because of the blurring and merging of the various functions of the media. For example, it is no longer possible to distinguish easily between informational news and entertainment. News programs increasingly use entertainment devices, dramatic language, and simulations of probable events, even if they didn't occur that way. A good story sometimes carries the day, even if it isn't true. Thus, ethics are sometimes a casualty in the competitive struggle for a good story.

Sometimes, careless attention to ethics brings confusion as to just what constitutes news. For at least two decades, electronic media executives and critics worried about the injection of entertainment values into the news, especially as tabloid TV shows won viewer allegiance. At the same time, a respected poll indicated that many Americans had trouble distinguishing news and entertainment fare on television.

Similarly, it is difficult to sort out when a particular article or program is news, entertainment, opinion, or even advertising. The blurring of lines between the traditional functions of the media is creating an ethical dilemma. Under conventional "rules" there are clear ethical definitions of what news is supposed to be. It is clearly to be separated from opinion. Opinion has great latitude to do and say what it will, though there is typically a standard of "intellectual honesty" applied. Entertainment fare also has wide latitude and may engage in almost any kind of fiction. As these forms merge, the role and function of ethics appears to get lost in the confusion.

Comic artists and editorial cartoonists have often faced the problem of crossing the line between information and entertainment. Comic strips like *Doonesbury* have so enraged some people such as the late Frank Sinatra that lawsuits have been filed to protest humorous commentary. Such fare has increasingly been subject to libel suits, although ridicule is the basis for even offensive humor.

As new media industries evolve, ranging from business information services to pay-per-view TV fare and home-shopping services, the question of what is ethical often arises. Former CNN financial commentator Lou Dobbs was criticized for appearing in a promotional tape for a brokerage house. Some critics believed that Dobbs violated the public trust he had as a financial commentator and newscaster on the cable network. This was the tip of the iceberg about the extent to which reporters should mix their roles. In the film *The People vs. Larry Flynt,* Donna Hanover, a New York television anchor and commentator who was married to New York Mayor Rudolph Giuliani, appeared in the film, which was said by some to undermine family values by glorifying Flynt, the controversial publisher of *Hustler* magazine. Other questions about reporters' ethics and independence arose in articles in *The New Yorker* by media critic Ken Auletta and in a celebrated book by author and editor James Fallows. At issue: celebrity reporters taking large speaking fees from businesses, trade associations, colleges and universities, and others. To Auletta and Fallows, the practice is clearly wrong and needs public exposure. Others say that as long as the reporter's employer knows, there is no problem. The question, as we will see later in this chapter, has to do with conflicts of interest. Does a reporter breach his or her credibility by taking fees on the side as a celebrity and public speaker while still maintaining a position of independence in covering the news? Some say yes; others say no, not unless there is a clear conflict of interest—that is, say, a reporter speaking for a fee at a trade association meeting and then covering news about that same group later. Some highly compensated reporters who are on the lecture circuit maintain that they never cover the organizations they speak for, but others aren't so sure, arguing that many issues these days are commingled and hard to separate out.

Special Privileges, Special Responsibilities

Are we being unreasonable when we demand that our press be fair and act ethically? The answer to that question is less clear than many might suppose. By consulting legal authorities, one may learn a good deal about the range and scope of the *rights* of news organizations and the people who work for them. First, there is the general franchise for press freedom laid out in the Bill of Rights, specifically the First Amendment. Then there are rights set out in state constitutions, statutes, and various court decisions that have been described and celebrated in various books. Far less common is the discussion of the *duties* and *responsibilities* of our protected press and mass media. In fact, in 1947, when the famed Hutchins Commission on Freedom of the Press suggested that the press has such obligations, the press protested strongly and denounced the Commission's report.

The Hutchins Commission was a privately financed effort to look carefully at freedom of the press in America, especially in the years immediately following World War II. The Commission, made up of philosophers, legal scholars, and other intellectual and cultural leaders, wanted publicly to encourage a system of expression that was responsible to society at large yet free to practice without constraints. It made recommendations for the government, the press, and the public, none of them binding but all intriguing as statements of social criticism and as a plea for ethically sensitive media. Among other things, the Commission proposed *press councils* made up of responsible citizens that would monitor the press and provide for feedback to the media and other mass communication agencies. Over the years, the Hutchins Commission's report has gained respect and is now regarded as one of the most important documents in the history of American media. At the same time, it has no official standing.

Under the First Amendment to the Constitution of the United States, which guarantees press freedom, there is no requirement that the media be fair, responsible, or accurate. The courts have stated this quite explicitly, yet increasingly there is a higher standard of media performance evident in libel cases and other legal action against the mass and specialized media. It is not uncommon these days for those suing the press to bring expert witnesses into court to testify that a particular story or program did or did not meet "normal professional standards." Although there is no accepted norm for such standards, courts have looked to witnesses for guidance. In fact, some feel that they may write an ethical code for media institutions, perhaps without constitutional authority.

Beyond the First Amendment

If the mass media derive their legal authority from the First Amendment, they derive their moral authority from holding the public trust. From the beginning, the media have claimed to play two roles: that of the *social conscience* of society or a representative of the people in a non-legalistic sense, and that of a *profit-making* business that needs to survive to fulfill its first obligation. Newspapers have long cultivated this kind of self-image. In contrast, because of government regulation, broadcasting and other electronic media have been regarded as less free than the print media and therefore required to serve the public "interest, convenience and necessity" as stated in the Federal Communications Act. However, just where legal requirements end and ethical ones begin is not clear.

Other media institutions, such as advertising and public relations, have also laid claim to moral authority and assert that they pursue ethical ends in their work, although this claim may rest on shaky ground and is often disputed. Media support services like wire services and syndicates have generally been guided by the standards of the news media. Their value is in the quality of the work they produce, whether it is accurate news reports

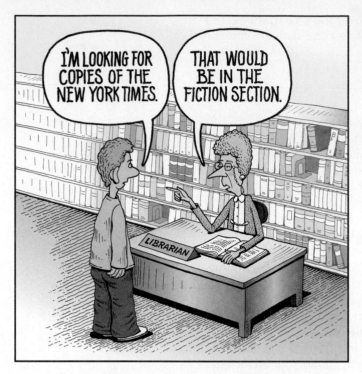

Even the most established newspapers are subject to media criticism as is the case with *The New York Times,* whose conservative critics often accuse it of biased or fictional treatments of the news.

or entertainment matter such as comics, columns, and puzzles. Some media institutions, such as newspapers and newsmagazines, regard themselves as having more elevated ethical standards and concerns than their advertising agencies or political public relations consultants.

The Long Struggle for Professionalism

Institutional media ethics have evolved considerably since the press of the nation's early years—a time sometimes called the dark ages of American journalism. In Chapter 3 we saw that the early press was often scurrilous, making unwarranted partisan attacks on political figures with little regard for truth or accuracy. Later, a sensational press played on the public's morbid curiosity to stir up the audience and attract readers. The press was known to run hoaxes and engage in deliberate deception. For example, even Benjamin Franklin, sometimes with tongue-in-cheek, made up interesting characters to illuminate the columns of his newspaper. We mentioned the famous "moon hoax" of 1835, in which the *New York Sun* claimed that a Scottish astronomer had observed lifelike creatures on the moon through his telescope.

Hoaxes continue to the present day and are sometimes transmitted on the Internet, where instant communication is not always checked carefully.

As the press became more responsible in the late nineteenth century, editors urged a dedication to the public interest and proclaimed statements of noble purpose. Although some of these statements were platitudes that would have been hard to enforce, they did establish the tradition of a public-spirited rather than self-serving press. Eventually it was generally believed that the newspaper and magazine press had obligations of fairness and impartiality that went far beyond those of typical businesses. While there was no enforcement clause for such assumptions, they were later supported by codes of ethics and books extolling the idea of a virtuous press crusading to rectify wrongs in a world where corruption and foul play were rampant. Journalism organizations ranging from publishers' and editors' societies to education groups also proclaimed concern for ethics and public accountability.

The Rise of Mixed Media Culture

Two leading commentators, Bill Kovach and Tom Rosenstiel, have argued that the examples cited above are only the beginning of a blurring and merging of media functions, thus creating a new mixed media culture. Arguing that beginning with the massive coverage of O. J. Simpson's double murder trial and continuing through the Monica Lewinsky–Bill Clinton scandal, there was a convergence of longstanding media trends involving commercial exploitation and sensationalism. As they put it in their book *Warp Speed: America in the Age of Mixed Media,* the media culture is:

> A newly diversified mass media in which the cultures of entertainment, infotainment, argument, analysis, tabloid and mainstream press not only work side by side but intermingle and merge. It is a culture in which Matt Drudge sits alongside William Safire on "Meet the Press" and Ted Koppel talks about the nuances of oral sex, in which "Hard Copy" and CBS News jostle for camera position outside the federal grand jury to hear from a special prosecutor.[17]

Although these observations are hardly new, these commentators and others feel that big media with its commercial interests in promoting movies alongside books and newspapers are drivers for this effect. For example, when NBC News gives extensive coverage to a film produced by its parent, the conglomerate NBC Universal, questions arise about conflict of interest. So many major media companies including News Corp., which owns the Fox networks, commingle their commercial interests with their news interests, which illustrates the natural hazards of a mixed media culture. Knowing who owns or is behind a message—and the motivation of those delivering it, whether innocent or malevolent—makes for considerable controversy. Critics also worry that the media are cheapened in the public mind when newscasters advertise products or onetime spin doctors and spokespeople are subsequently employed as news analysts and commentators. For example, George Stephanopoulos, President Clinton's onetime communications director, and Karl Rove, President Bush's White House communications guru, landed top assignments with television networks (ABC and Fox), thus crossing the line between media manipulation and media practitioner.

Sexual scandals are fodder for tabloid journalism as was the case in revelations about former President Bill Clinton's relationships with women outside his marriage, one of which led to his impeachment by the House of Representatives, though he was acquitted in the U.S. Senate.

This again is nothing new, as political figures and media people have often moved back and forth. The difference now is that the public gets cynical about matters of credibility. However, when the beloved *Meet the Press* anchor Tim Russert died suddenly in 2008, his knowledge of politics as an aide for a Democratic senator and governor was cited as beneficial.

The new mixed media culture is said to have five characteristics:[18]

- A Never-Ending News Cycle Makes Journalism Less Complete—the twenty-four hour demands of cable, television, and websites often lead to sloppy and incomplete reporting, fragments rather than whole stories.
- Sources Are Gaining Power over Journalists—People with self-interests and axes to grind offer more information with strings attached, and media rush to publicize rumors, leads, etc.
- There Are No More Gatekeepers—This is a bit of an exaggeration, but there is less editing and fact checking than was formerly the case, and web reports often have none.
- Argument Is Overwhelming Reporting—An argument culture has emerged and often drowns out factual information on various cable news programs and commentaries that are more shouting matches than reasoned presentations.
- The "Blockbuster Mentality"—The media love big stories that dominate the news for days, even weeks and months, whether the death of Anna Nicole Smith and the subsequent custody trial for her baby daughter; the fall from grace of New York's governor, Elliott Spitzer; or the Clinton scandals. This massive over-coverage again drowns out other legitimate news. It seems there is an endless supply of public officials—Senator Larry Craig of Idaho comes to mind—who get caught in scandals, triggered by their own behavior.

The implications of these and other factors on news the U.S. and globally are significant. There is a tendency to do "made for TV" fictional movies that often run head on into public life and public affairs. One such example was a TV movie in 2008 about the 2000 presidential election stalemate in Florida that played fast and loose with its depiction of some real-life characters. Famous trials and controversies are quickly fictionalized and exploited, thus confusing the public and raising questions about the role of communication media in society. There are many points of view in play on these topics from critics who scold media owners for their callous exploitation to others who believe this is just the price of freedom of expression.

The Poynter Institute which promotes media ethics and training here offers historical information about the original Ponzi schemer, Charles Ponzi.

ETHICAL CHALLENGES TO MIXED-MEDIA CULTURE. Ethical expectations and demands are crossing national boundaries as a result of the international concern about honesty, ethics, and accurate information. For example, although China's political news remains highly suspect, its financial information is now more accurate, for the international market expects and demands it, and no market economy can function on unreliable information. This being the case, the issue of ethics is not only here to stay but will probably play a greater role in all kinds of media—and not only in conventional news media but also in new media that under earlier standards might not have been held accountable.

To many commentators, media ethics really refers to journalistic ethics, or the moral conduct and behavior of journalists doing their work as news gatherers, editors, and disseminators of information for the larger society. Journalists are expected to produce reliable and believable information gathered under scrupulously honest conditions and checked along the way for accuracy. On occasion, an ethical breach in journalism receives publicity. For example, *TV Guide* once deliberately printed a misleading photograph of Oprah Winfrey's head on actress Ann Margaret's body. Realizing that misrepresentation and deception are almost universally regarded as unethical behavior and that the photo might jeopardize *TV Guide's* credibility as a serious and respected publication, the magazine later recanted.

In the 1990s, at the outset of the O. J. Simpson case, *Time* magazine doctored a photo of Simpson by darkening his skin color apparently to make him look more sinister. The result was a debate over whether this visual alteration was an act of racism, something always unethical, if not illegal. This is what journalism professor Paul Lester calls "images that injure," pictorial stereotypes in the media. In a book by the same name, Lester and several contributors decry racial, gender, age, physical, and sexual orientation stereotypes that cause psychological pain, ridicule, or embarrassment to individuals and groups.[19] Often, allegations of racism or sexism are at the root of many ethical dilemmas for the media. Here perception is often deemed more important than the motivation of the communicator. Thoughtlessness is more often a greater culprit than recklessness or deliberate efforts to denigrate others through images—still photos, moving images, cartoons, line drawings, and others. This ethical concern often runs head on into satire and humor, however. Some depictions—visual and verbal—by cartoonists, humorists, and others are meant to be funny or ironic, but still have the potential of offending someone sometime.

Closely connected to this debate is the complex and continuing controversy over what is called "political correctness," an idea that suggests there are appropriate ideas acceptable to most of society. This suggests that attacks on people for their race, gender, sexual orientation, disability, or other characteristics are out of line. The existence of sexism, racism, homophobia, and ageism in the media is well documented. Sometimes it is inadvertent and at other times quite deliberate. And, of course, the media carry the antisocial remarks of celebrities and other public people, which sometimes leads to a national conversation on the matter. As we pointed out in Chapter 7, shock jock Don Imus' racial slurs led to swift social disapproval—and even, for a time, the loss of his job and place on the air. Some argue that, carried to the extreme, this view thwarts free speech, however hurtful or inappropriate that speech may be. Another view suggests that political correctness carried to an extreme is counterproductive for a free society. Richard Bernstein, a *New York Times* reporter, in his book *Dictatorship of Virtue* argues that multiculturalism often insists on adherence to one view "with truth or fairness often falling victim to the demands of ethnic or racial self-esteem."[20]

As the foregoing examples illustrate, and as we have shown elsewhere in this book, certain controls influence what the media do and how they do it. These controls include economic, political, and legal factors, but they also include cultural and philosophical forces. Media ethics is one such force.[21] The manner and method the various media of communication use to conduct their business and carry on discourse with the rest of society are often under scrutiny.

Here the media do not stand alone but are seen in the context of social responsibility in general. Concern with ethics and ethical behavior has focused on business, government, religion, news media, and other institutions. Generally, then, some of the growing concern over media ethics has come from outside critics. However, some has also come from internal sources who want to elevate and advance the work of newspapers, magazines, radio, television and cable, databases, advertising agencies, public relations firms, and other media organizations or support services.

As our discussion has shown, media ethics is not an obscure or irrelevant topic but something that arises daily as citizens observe, the way media institutions relate to their communities as participants, observers, and critics. Ethical dilemmas also arise over the content of the media—whether it is entertainment, news, opinion, or advertising—as well as over the behavior of media people. In a simple sense, ethical choices are between right and wrong, good and bad, matters that are genuinely in the public interest or harmful to the common good.

Complicating the problem of examining and understanding media ethics is the fact that as simple as choices may seem at first, they typically are not. Ethical decisions involve complex human relationships and often pit values cherished by the media against those preferred by other people. The media are concerned with communicating to the rest of society, whether in news stories that emphasize conflict, in opinion journals that feature debates, or on entertainment programs that often promote consensus and reinforce values. Different media obviously have different purposes, yet most want to be considered ethical. Sometimes, though, public exposure involves information about a person or organization that has heretofore been protected from outside scrutiny. In such instances a person's right to privacy conflicts with the media's interest in public disclosure. There is often no legal issue here but an ethical issue—a matter of personal choice between doing what is good for society versus what is good for an individual.

MEDIA CRITICISM AND MEDIA ETHICS

If there has been a consistent thread promoting media ethics over the years, it has been media *criticism,* which dates back to the nineteenth century. Critics typically charged the press with violating common decency and obscuring the truth. Many American presidents have criticized the press for what they regarded as irresponsible reporting. For example, during the period of muckraking (Chapter 3), magazine journalists just after the turn of the century crusaded to clean up sweatshops and reform corrupt businesses and governments. Soon afterward, the press confronted considerable criticism led by President Theodore Roosevelt, who thought muckraking journalism was far too negative and bad for the nation. Press critics such as Upton Sinclair began to censure the press for its internal inconsistencies and conflicts of interest and even went so far as to claim that the press itself was corrupt and deliberately poisoning information. Much of this reproach concerned ethics, for rarely was it suggested that the transgressions of the press were illegal, only unethical.

Journalism schools established in the years before World War I often had professional practice courses

The news media are a conduit for coverage of ethics, including business ethics, as was the case in revelations about Ponzi schemer Bernard Madoff who cheated investors out of tens of billions of dollars. He got a 150-year jail sentence in 2009.

that promoted ideal or ethical behavior. The public outcry over ethics also led to a variety of codes and voluntary guidelines for the media. (The "Printer's Ink" statutes aimed at deceptive advertising mentioned in Chapter 11 were one set.) The American Society of Newspaper Editors issued the "Canons of Journalism" in 1923. This was followed by similar codes promulgated by the Newspaper Association of America, the Associated Press Managing Editors, various broadcast organizations and stations including the CBS network, and public relations organizations. Over a fifty-year period from the 1920s to the 1970s, then, the bulk of American media developed ethical codes. Most were strictly voluntary, but some were part of the work rules of media organizations. Employees who violate the codes of their organization today may be disciplined or even fired.

A Double Standard

Media criticism that centers on institutional, individual, or content-related ethics generally distinguishes between the editorial and business functions of the media. Editorial employees were once expected to avoid conflicts of interest, check their work for accuracy, and act as professionals at all times. Typically, this meant keeping distance from such newsmakers as politicians and not mixing one's personal views with the news. On the other hand, publishers and other business-side personnel faced no such prohibitions. They could seek public office and otherwise participate in community affairs without being considered guilty of conflict of interest or unprofessional behavior.

This situation would later be challenged, largely unsuccessfully, by such scholar-critics as Philip Meyer, whose book *Ethical Journalism* urged an institutional model for media ethics wherein all employees would have the same high standards. To Meyer, it was unthinkable that reporters and editors should be held to one standard for conflict of interest, while advertising managers, publishers, and others were not.[22]

As noted earlier, most of what is written about media ethics has to do with the behavior of media people or the content they produce. On occasion, the owners of the media also come under fire. That was the basis of much of the criticism of media critic George Seldes, who from the 1920s to the 1990s railed against corrupt ownership. The ethics of a media baron was at issue when a controversy arose over a $5 million book advance offered to former House Speaker Newt Gingrich by a publisher owned by Rupert Murdoch, who was lobbying Congress in connection with reform of the Communications Act. Gingrich eventually turned down the advance as criticism mounted. The Hutchins Commission Report specifically pointed to the transgressions of owners like William Randolph Hearst and Frank Gannett. Other critics have critiqued Congress in its supervision of communication legislation, foundations that try to influence the media and others outside the behavior-content circle of media people.

At times virtually all media functions are scrutinized for ethical breaches, whether this involves a movie that misrepresents or overstates (for example, Oliver Stone's *JFK* and *Nixon* films); a radio talk show host who is accused of lying; a rock video that panders to sexual misbehavior; a novelist who appropriates the work of others, or an Internet hacker who perpetuates a cruel hoax.

The Link to Individuals and Content

Media ethics is rarely concerned with abstract institutional behavior but is instead tied to the "blood and guts" of daily decision making and various disputes that later come to the attention of the public. Although journalistic inventions and fakery are not unknown in our history, the public was shocked in 1980 when it learned that *Washington Post* reporter Janet Cooke had faked a gripping story about "little Jimmy," an eight-year-old heroin addict in Washington's African-American community. No such person existed. Cooke claimed that it was a "composite." To its considerable embarrassment, the *Post* (which won a Pulitzer Prize for the story) had to admit the deception. The prize was returned, and the newspaper, to its credit, launched a major internal investigation of the ruse and released its findings to the public.

Later, the then-existing National News Council, with a grant from the Twentieth Century Fund, produced a book about the "little Jimmy" controversy and its impact on American journalism and journalistic ethics in general. The deception shook the roots of American journalism as people worried about the accuracy of stories in the press and the ethical standards of reporters. Commentators scrutinized the press's institutional responsibility to prevent this kind of behavior in the future, calling for routine personnel procedures and checking of resumes (which had also been faked in part).

The same issue of public deception arose years later when ABC News aired a piece of news footage allegedly showing a U.S. diplomat passing secrets to the Russians. The grainy and authentic-looking footage was actually staged and featured actors as reporters. The story was based on allegations in news reports, but anchor Peter Jennings later apologized to the American people for the newscast, which was a deliberate deception. By the 1990s simulations on network news were mostly a thing of the past, though they are still common on other TV shows, especially in tabloid fare.

Of course, the fakery of Benjamin Franklin differs greatly from that of ABC News or Matt Drudge, because news standards and social values have changed since the age of the printing press. The press was a primitive instrument in Franklin's day; now it is a large and powerful enterprise that has considerable influence over all of its information, opinion, and entertainment functions.

ALTERNATIVE APPROACHES TO ETHICS

Standardized codes of media ethics are difficult to establish because there are few ethical imperatives that work in all situations. Also, most codes of ethics and guidelines are so general that they are not always applicable to specific circumstances. For these reasons and others, a system of *situational ethics* has long been advocated for the media.

Situational Ethics

In a situation covered by situational ethics, each decision is made not with respect to a universal or "one-size-fits-all" code but within the context of a specific situation. In other words, it is argued, a decision about ethics "depends" on many time- and place-specific situations. Within this perspective, media ethics, like all other ethical considerations, is linked to human choices that involve doing the right thing at the right time. For example, in following up on a report on a political candidate's secret sex life, a reporter may invoke "the people's right to know" (about the character of their public servants) as an ethical reason for violating privacy and digging deeply into the individual's private affairs. In the case of a private citizen with similar secrets, however, that standard may not make sense. Publicizing details about such a person's private life may simply be unethical snooping.

The *American Journalism Review* and other journalism magazines and websites regularly assess media performance from an ethical perspective.

The Continuing Search

The search for alternative answers has been a topic of lively debate among journalists for a long time. One thing is certain: the issue of media ethics remains on the agenda and is often discussed both within and outside the communications industry. Many industry seminars probe ethical issues and dilemmas; television series and regular PBS and CNN programs are devoted to the media ethics. Journalism schools have taught journalistic ethics intermittently since the 1920s and have established scores of new courses. One—the University of Oregon—even gives an annual ethics award to media firms, individuals, and students. There are at least ten relatively new texts on the topic. Various study centers and think tanks are working on media ethics issues, and some are single-mindedly devoted to this topic. There is a *Journal of Media Ethics,* which takes up important issues and seeks resolution as well as several ethics websites. In fact, there are scores if not hundreds of websites that make it their business to monitor media, looking for inconsistencies, distortions, and outright lies. And they are not reluctant to share this information far and wide, thus providing a new force for media ethics in this digital age.

Most of the efforts to encourage media ethics have been less intellectual and more action-oriented. Earlier we mentioned press councils—small groups of responsible citizens organized at the local, state, and national levels as feedback mechanisms. While only partially successful, these efforts nonetheless represent models for accountability and ethical pursuit.

In one form or another, various codes of ethics have spread to virtually every part of the communications industry. Once mainly in the purview of journalism, there are now formalized ethical standards in advertising, public relations, opinion polling, market research, sports writing, and other areas. The fact that they exist, however, does not mean that they will be followed. These are generalized documents and not usually enforceable, but they still represent a serious concern for ethics.

Credibility Studies and Market Research

Perhaps the most important efforts to promote media ethics have been *credibility studies,* which probe public attitudes about the news media and dredge up concerns and problems ranging from sensationalism to reporter rudeness. A media credibility movement emerged in the 1980s because it was felt that news organizations in particular were losing ground as believable and trustworthy agencies. This probably stemmed from worry that a loss of credibility would both impair the media's moral authority and undermine their economic might. At a time of feverish competition among print and broadcast media for audiences and advertising, there was real reason to deal with matters of credibility and ethics. Today, the Pew Center on People and the Press continues the tradition of monitoring public attitudes toward the media through regular surveys and widely distributed reports. The Annenberg Public Policy Center has also commissioned reports that assess people's impressions of media, including whether they regard opinion commentators as journalists.

Market research is also a force that perhaps unwittingly promotes media ethics. Market and audience research provides media organizations and others in the communications industry with certain kinds of feedback about public tastes, preferences, and concerns. Often this feedback centers on matters that have an ethical connection and are therefore appropriate for discussion.

As we suggested, a concern with ethics now stretches across all media fields. Opinion makers—whether talk show hosts, media consultants, advertising executives, or entertainment producers—have standards and codes of conduct. Authors have ethical concerns and so do those who produce and manufacture their work. It is still most common to tie ethics to professional rather than to technical functions, but even that distinction has broken down. Television camera operators had better have ethical standards, or the work they direct will be tainted. The same is true with printers, operators of desktop publishing systems, cartoonists, and others. It is true that the ethics of each of these categories of people may differ, reflecting varied concerns and values, but, to be sure, they are all connected in some way with the current media ethics debate.

Ethics, Technology, and the Future

New technologies of communication, especially in the past ten years, have raised a variety of ethical questions and controversies. With the manipulative capacity of digital media, false reports and false images can and have been transmitted. Sometimes they are caught, sometimes not.

Ethical breaches using technology are often linked to privacy, including hidden cameras and microphones and the use of databases to mine personal information about individuals. For example, through distant sensing cameras it is easy to "spy" on news sources. Various audio and video recorders make this even easier. Some Internet sites have sought and misused personal information like Social Security numbers.

Satellite communication allows for easy movement over national boundaries and into the midst of world crises and conflicts. This can result in ethical chaos.

Because it is now so easy to capture newsworthy, scandalous, and embarrassing video on cell phones or other hand-held devices, this material makes it to the major media, sometimes via YouTube, which is famous for its file-sharing distribution of video of all kinds. Citizen journalism also empowers people everywhere to enter the fray for better or worse. There are also more professional freelancers inundating TV and cable programs with footage. Determining the veracity of this material, let alone the qualifications and proficiency of the person who presents it is not easy. Indeed this is the age of the amateur, when everyone is a communicator.

These are many examples of ethical problems raised by new communications technologies. The speed of these new tools and their reach makes them both liberating and dangerous devices that warrant discussion. Again, they affect virtually all aspects of the media industries and much of society. Yet, in the first decade of the twenty-first century, much of the discussion of media ethics is still locked firmly in the matrix of the past. However, it is also clear that much of the debate charts new ground and moves beyond established rules. Considerable thought, therefore, must go into determining (1) what should be codified as a lasting part of institutional and individual rules carried over from the past, (2) what should be left to the imagination of situational decision making in order to maximize freedom of expression, and (3) how ethical considerations need to be re-evaluated to take into account the technologies of the future. Whatever those decisions, any system of accountability, no matter how modest, always impinges on freedom of choice. Of course, sometimes that infringement is warranted and even desirable.[23]

An important principle for the future is that voluntary methods of resolving ethical dilemmas are typically preferable to those that eventually end up in the courts. Although many ethical matters are not immediately legal concerns, in our litigious society one might guess that if they are not they soon might be. To date most of the impetus for media ethics has come internally from the media industries themselves and from communications education. This might not always be the case. It is easy to imagine courts or legislative bodies mandating a system of ethics that would be onerous, especially during a period of unpopularity for the media. In fact, the idea of licensing journalists and giving them a required code of ethics has actually been proposed. It was quickly dismissed, however, because of the seeming violation of the First Amendment.

Today, media ethics is something of a cottage industry and the subject of scores of professional seminars held for journalists, broadcasters, public relations people, and others. Many universities now offer courses in media ethics and have a rich literature on which to draw—not only many treatises, books, and articles but also case studies that point to the dilemmas and decisions that people must make in a modern society, many of them coping directly with ethics.

That cottage industry may be leading to significant changes in media ethics. Communications law scholar Donald Gillmor has written that such changes come in cycles. In the 1920s there was an ethics movement in the media, which waned and later resurfaced. Perhaps with a continually improving system of information storage and retrieval, that will not happen again. Ethical dilemmas abound, and they seem to compel enough human attention both from media professionals and from the consumers of communication that we can likely look forward to a period of maturation and development for this new and still uncharted territory.

CHAPTER REVIEW

- Some critics ridicule the idea that competitive and profit-driven media can operate within an ethical framework. But most people disagree, saying that no media system can exist very long without public confidence, and that requires accurate, honest, and believable communication.

- Ethical behavior in a general sense simply means that people should not lie, steal, cheat, or commit other antisocial acts. Ethics is doing what is "right," but the problem is that "right" is defined differently by different people. Thus, the need exists for serious attention to media ethics in a society increasingly concerned about the ethics of all occupational groups and professionals.

- Technology opens up new avenues for ethical concerns, and the digital media have great capacity both for good works and mischief.

- Media ethics is not an obscure or irrelevant topic but something that arises daily as citizens observe the way media institutions relate to their communities as participants, observers, and critics. Ethical dilemmas also arise over the content of the media—whether it is entertainment, news, opinion, or advertising—as well as over the behavior of media people.

- Under the First Amendment to the Constitution of the United States, there is no requirement that the media be fair, responsible, or accurate. The courts have stated this quite explicitly, yet increasingly there is a higher standard of media performance evident in libel cases and other legal action against the mass and specialized media.

- Institutional media ethics have evolved considerably since the press of the early years of American journalism. During that time the press was often scurrilous, making unwarranted partisan attacks on political figures with little regard for truth or accuracy. Later, a sensational press played on the public's morbid curiosity to stir up the audience and attract readers.

- A consistent thread promoting media ethics over the years has been media *criticism*, which dates back to the nineteenth century. Critics typically charged the press with violating common decency and obscuring the truth. This has kept public attention focused on the need for ethical standards.

- Typically, media ethics have centered on three major issues: (1) accuracy and fairness in reporting and other activities; (2) the behavior of reporters, especially in relation to their sources; and (3) avoidance of conflicts of interest.

- Standardized codes of media ethics are difficult to establish because there are few ethical imperatives that work in all situations. Also, most codes of ethics and guidelines are so general that they are not always applicable to specific circumstances. For these reasons and others, a system of *situational ethics* has long been advocated for the media.

- In one form or another, various codes of ethics have spread to virtually every part of the communications industry. Once mainly in the purview of journalism, there are now formalized ethical standards in advertising, public relations, opinion polling, market research, sports writing, and other areas. The fact that they exist, however, does not mean that they will be followed.

- New technologies of communication, especially in the past ten years, have raised a variety of ethical questions and controversies. The speed of these new tools and their reach makes them both liberating and dangerous devices that warrant discussion. They affect virtually all aspects of the media industries and much of society.

- An important principle for the future is that voluntary methods of resolving ethical dilemmas are typically preferable to those that eventually end up in the courts. To date most of the impetus for media ethics has come internally from the media industries themselves and from communications education. This might not always be the case.

STRATEGIC QUESTIONS

1. Should media and journalistic ethics apply to all media—traditional and new media—or do the digital media present special problems and issues?
2. Should media ethics focus on the content of communication or the behavior of communicators—or both? Explain why each matters, if they do.
3. Most writings on media ethics focus on news and journalism, but should the concern be broader and include all media functions and operations, including the business of media?
4. How is the public interest in media determined? Should being of public interest (audiences eager for information and news) be equated with being "in the public interest"?
5. How does new technology in media affect media ethics?
6. Discuss the relationships and differences between media law and media ethics. Where are they different? Where do they overlap?

KEY CONCEPTS & TERMS

Accuracy and credibility   380
Digital ethics   379
Doing what is right   385
Hutchins Commission on
    Freedom of the Press   387

Professionalism   388
Fictional news
    portrayals/hoaxes   388
Conflict of interest   384

Checkbook journalism   384
Situational ethics   393
Creditability studies   394
Codes of ethics   393

ENDNOTES

1. Celia Friend and Jane B. Singer, *Online Journalism Ethics: Traditions and Transitions* (Armonk, NY: M.E. Sharpe, 2007); also see *Ed Bott's Microsoft Report,* Oct. 9, 2007, "Where Do You Stand on Digital Ethics," ZDNet.com, and *Digital Media Report,* see min.com, and Ed Bott, "Digital Media Ethics: Its Personal," Oct. 17, 2007.

2. Seth Mnookin, *Hard News, the Scandals at the New York Times and Their Meaning for American Media* (New York: Random House, 2004).

3. "Assertions of Ethical Decision-Making in Digital Media," August 2006, *Online Journalism Ethics,* poynter.org.

4. "Will the Last One Out of Second Life Please Turn Off the Digital Lights?" *Digital Media Report,* June 25, 2008, p. 1, min.com.

5. "Digital Ethics," Cable in the Classroom, www.ciconline.org/digital ethics.

6. "Digital Ethics," Lee's Summit R-7 School District, http://leessummit.k12.mo.us/digitalethic.htm.

7. *Digital Media Report,* June 25, 2008, op cit.

8. Claude-Jean Bertrand, *Media Ethics and Accountability Systems* (New Brunswick, NJ: Transaction Books, 2000). Also see Everette E. Dennis and Robert Snyder, eds., *Media and Public Life* (New Brunswick, NJ: Transaction Books, 1997) and Louis A. Day, *Ethics in Mass Communication: Cases and Controversies* (Belmont, CA: Wadsworth Publishing, 1999).

9. David Pritchard, ed., *Holding the Media Accountable: Citizens, Ethics, and the Law* (Bloomington, IN: Indiana University Press, 2000).

10. Mark Fitzgerald, "Why They Do It—Desperation? Kleptomania? Stupidity? or Just Plain Lazy," *Editor & Publisher*, Aug. 7, 2000, p. 23, offers a discussion of recent plagiarism cases in the media and why they happened. A useful and standard text that offers context for this and other ethical dilemmas is Clifford G. Christians, et al., *Media Ethics: Cases and Moral Reasoning,* 6th ed. (New York: Longman, 2000).

11. Interview with Jeffrey Cole, director, Center for the Digital Future, USC Annenberg School, in New York, April 4, 2008.

12. *Digital Media Report,* June 25, 2008, op cit.

13. Burton Benjamin, *Fair Play* (New York: Harper & Row, 1988).

14. Janet Malcolm's work appeared in *The New Yorker,* March 13 and March 20, 1989. It was later published as *The Journalist and the Murderer* (New York: Knopf, 1990).

15. Lawrence K. Grossman, "To Err is Human, to Admit it is Divine," *Columbia Journalism Review* (March/April 1997), p. 16.

16. Everette E. Dennis, Donald M. Gillmor, and Theodore Glasser, eds., *Media Freedom and Accountability* (Westport, CT: Greenwood, 1990).

17. Bill Kovach and Tom Rosenstiel, *Warp Speed: America in the Age of Mixed Media* (New York: Century Foundation, 1999). See also Colin Sparks, et al., *Tabloid Tales: Global Debates Over Media Standards* (London: Rowman and Littlefield, 2000).

18. Kovach and Rosenteil supplied the characteristics, but the explanation and examples are those of the authors.
19. Paul K. Lester, ed., *Images That Injure, Pictorial Stereotypes in the Media* (Westport, CT: Praeger, 1996).
20. Richard Bernstein, *Dictatorship of Virtue, Multiculturism and the Battle for America's Future* (New York: Knopf, 1994).
21. Edmund B. Lamberth, *Committed Journalism: An Ethic for the Profession* (Bloomington, IN: Indiana State University Press, 1986).
22. Philip Meyer, *Ethical Journalism* (White Plains, NY: Longman, 1987).
23. John C. Merrill, *The Dialectic in Journalism: Toward a Responsible Use of Press Freedom* (Baton Rouge, Louisiana State University Press, 1989). Also see John C. Merrill, *Journalism Ethics, Philosophical Foundations for News Media* (New York: St. Martin's Press, 1997).

PHOTO CREDITS

TEXT CREDITS

T 1.1: John Carey as compiled from Electronic Industry Association, U.S. Department of Commerce, Dataquest; Fig. 1.1 and Fig. 1.2: Significant Transitions in Human Communication; Fig. 2.1: World Internet Penetration Rates by Geographic Regions. Source: Internet World Stats: www.internetworldstats.com/stats.htm Copyright © 2008, Miniwatts Marketing Group; Fig. 2.2: "Consumer Adoption of New Technologies–Consumption Spreads Faster Today." Source: New York Times Week in Review, Feb. 10, 2008, p. 14; see also W Michael Coz and Richard Alm, "You are What You Spend," also p. 14; Fig. 2.4: "Global Media Giants." Source: Modified from WGBH Educational Foundation, "Frontline-Merchants of Cool-Media Giants PBS; T. 2.1: "Top 25 Global Media Companies." Source: Datamonitor ComputerWire–Top 25 Global Media Companies." Source: Datamonitor ComputerWire—Top 25 Global Media Companies. http://www.computerwire.com/companies/lists/list/?ID=95032661-E4CB-4E36-B785-2EEF835DEFB1; Fig. 3.1: U.S. Census Bureau Abstracts of the U.S. by year; and http://www.bowker.com; T. 3.2: Datus C. Smith Jr., GUIDE TO BOOK PUBLISHING (1989), pp. 128–129; used by permission of University of Washington Press; Fig. 3.3: Veronis Suhler Stevenson, Communication Industries Forecast, 2008–2012; Fig. 3.4: Dr. John Miller, President, Central Connecticut State University, is the author of this study. Research for this edition of AMLC was conducted in collaboration with the Center for Public Policy and Social Research at CCSU; Fig. 4.1: The Curve of Adoption of Daily Newspapers in the U.S., 1850–2000; Fig. 4.2: Editor and Publisher, NA; T 5.1: AP, "Farm Population Lowest Since 1850s," New York Times, July 20, 1988 and USDA; T. 5.3: Samir Husni's Guide to New Consumer Magazines, 2008; T. 5.4: MRI Fall, 2007, National Directory of Magazines, 2008, Oxbridge Communications; T.5.5: Harrington Associates, 1999, 2008; T. 5.6: Oxbridge Communications,2008; P 138: Propositions (1–5) from Martin, Brian, "The Selective Usefulness of Game Theory," *Social Studies of Science* Vol. 8, 1978,pp. 85–110; P 158: Propositions (1–5) from Raacke, J. and Jennifer Bonds-Raacke, "MySpace and Facebook: Applying the Uses and Gratifications Theory to Exploring Friend-Networking Sites," *Cyberpsychology & Behavior*, Vol. 11, Number 2, 2008 (New Rochelle, NY: Mary Ann Liebert, Inc.); T. 7.1: BIAfn Media Access Pro,PEJ Research, December 2007; T. 7.2: 2008 Arbitron, Inc.; Fig. 7.1: U.S. Bureau of the Census; Radio Advertising Bureau Report; Fig.7.2: http://www.fcc.gov/mb/audio/totals/; Fig. 7.3: BIA Financial Network, PEJ Research; Fig. 7.4: Toby Sheets / Rio Grande Mud Media as found on http://www.facebook.com/l/; http://www.riograndemud.com/clockwheel/index.htm. Used with permission; P 184: Propositions (1–5) from Hornick, Robert, "Alternative Models of Behavior Change," Annenberg School for Communication, Working Paper 131, 1990, p. 5/6; Fig. 8.1: VSS Communications Industry Forecast, 2008–2012, 22nd ed.; Fig. 8.2: Veronis Suhler Stevenson, PQ Media, Nielsen media Research, Television Bureau of Advertising; Fig.8.3: Subsribers: http://www.ncta.com/Statistic/BasicSubs.aspx. Households: Source: U.S. Census Bureau, Current Population Reports. From Statistical Abstract of the United States, 2008; Fig.8.4: VSS Communications Industry Forecast, 2008–2012, 22nd ed.; Fig. 8.5: TGI (Target Group Index), 2008, http://www.zonalatina.com/Zldata276.htm; P 222: Propositions (1–5) from Maxwell E. McCombs and Donald Lewis Shaw, "The Agenda-Setting Function of Mass Media, *Public Opinion Quarterly*, Vol. 36, No. 2, Summer 1972, pp. 176–187, and McCombs, "A Look at Agenda-Setting in the Mass Media: Past, Present, Future, *Journalism Studies* (2005), 6: 543–557; Fig. 9.3: Citizen Journalism: Top-down news vs. bottom-up news (Fig. 1.1) http://www.hypergene.net/wemedia/images/uploads/compare1.gif) . Used with permission; T. 10.1: http://www.gunslot.com/blog/top-twenty-five-25-best-selling-video-games-all-time; T 10.2: http://news.gotgame.com/top-5-selling-video-games-for-2008/26021/; Fig. 11.1: The Coca-Cola Company, 2008, all rights reserved; Fig. 13.1: From: http://lgnewmedia.net/blog/wp-content/uploads/2007/05/bubblus-social-media.jpg. Used with permission; Fig 13.2: "100 Leading Media Companies." Advertising Age, September 29, 2008. Reprinted with permission from the Sept. 29, 2008 issue of *Advertising Age*. Copyright, Crain Communications Inc. 2008.

Godey's Lady Book, 95
Going Long, 322
Golden age, 71, 93, 122, 157–159, 175, 184
Golden Globe Awards, 142, 196
Goldwyn, Samuel, 132
Golf, 101–102
GolinHarris, 296
Good Housekeeping, 101–102
Google, 3, 21, 27–28, 44, 111, 198, 202, 221, 261, 268, 287, 320
Gourmet, 103
Government secrecy, 337–339
Government subsidy model, 324
Grammar, 7, 9, 51, 61, 127
Grange, Red, 235
Great Britain, 155, 328, 357
Great Depression, 130, 159
Great Performances, 196
Great Train Robbery, The, 196
Greeley, Horace, 68, 240, 324, 339
Grey Gardens, 130
Grey's Anatomy, 195
Grierson, John, 129
Griffith, D. W., 127
Grossman, Lawrence, 191, 385
Group norms, 372
Gucci, 109
Gulf & Western, 372
Gutenberg, Johannes, 32–43, 63, 66, 130

Hachette, 31
Hachette Book Group, 44
Hadden, Briton, 98
Hagstrom, Jerry, 301
Haiti, 370
Ham radio, 226
Hammurabi (Babylonian King), 40
Hannah Montana, 337
Hannity, Sean, 170
Hanover, Donna, 386
Hard Copy, 388
Hard news, 80, 206
HarperCollins, 53
Harper's Magazine, 101–102, 324, 350
Harper's Weekly, 96, 350
Harris, Benjamin, 64
Harris, John P., 120
Harris Interactive, 275
Harry Potter, 228, 322
Harvard Business Review, 3, 321–322
Harvard Lampoon, 102–103
Harvard Magazine, 99
Harvard University, 290
Havana, Cuba, 337
Hays Code, 137, 139–140
Hays, Will H., 188, 244, 379
HBO, 188, 244, 379
HD Radio, 170–171
HDTV, 190
Hearst Corporation, 103–104, 323
Hearst, William Randolph, 70–76, 392
Heart of Minds, 130
Henry VIII of England, 38
Henry, Joseph, 149
Hertz, Heinrich, 150
Herzog, Herta, 361
Hiawatha, 48

Hieroglyphic, 12, 39
High definition, 126, 171, 190–191, 194, 198
High speed internet, 22–24, 176, 315–316, 382
Highbrow, 227
High-culture taste public. *See* Taste publics
Hill & Knowlton, Inc., 296, 306
Hilton, Paris, 217
Hip-hop, 226
Hitler, Adolf, 159, 288, 357
HIV/AIDs campaign, 294, 371
Hobby, 248
Hollywood
  movies, 21, 30, 116–117
  history, 121, 128, 132
  political censorship, 140–141
  awards, 142
  TV link, 177
  screenwriters, 294
Holtzbrinck Publishing Holdings, 53
Home shopping, 196, 386
Home video, 123–126, 189
Homo erectus, 2
Homo habilis, 2
Homo sapiens sapiens, 2
Honeymooners, The, 185
Hoover, Herbert, 155–156, 180
House, 195, 235
House Un-American Activities Committee, 140–141
Howard, Scripps, 74
Howdy Doody, 194
Hu, Yu, 322
Hucksters, 255
Huffington Post, 212
Hull, Geoffrey P., 243
Hulu, 198
Humor journalism, 215
Humor magazines, 102–103
Hurricane Katrina, 49
Hustler, 100, 386
Hutchins Commission, 387, 392

I Love Lucy, 185, 194
IM, 14
Imdb.com, 130
IMG's Constituency Management Group, 296
Impartial journalism. *See* Objective journalism
Imus, Don, 169–170, 203, 390
In Cold Blood, 212
Indie rock, 226
Infinity, 166
Information age, 22, 26, 163, 308
Information exchange, 39
Information society, 22, 302
Infotainment, 22, 26, 163, 308
In-house agency or department, 263, 265–266
INS, 73
Institute of the Press, 83
Institutional advertising, 156, 270
Intellectual magazines, 101–102
Interactive agencies, 262, 266
Internet blogger, 169
Intermediaries, 259, 320, 328
Intermediate communication, 26
Internal communication, 301

Internal Revenue Service, 281
International Association of Theatrical and Stage Employees, 131
International Boat Industry, 99
International Longevity Center, 298
International News Service. *See* INS
Internet, 21–26, 30–31
  advertising, 253–275
  books, 21–26, 30–31, 43–46
  magazines, 88, 106–112
  movies, 116, 126, 142
  news source, 202–203
  newspapers, 59–60, 79–84
  radio, 146, 165–172
  television, 176–183, 190–191, 197
Internet Advertising Bureau, 2, 253, 260, 268, 349
Internet bubble, 315
Internet penetration, 22–23
Internet radio, 165, 167, 171
Interpretative journalism, 211
Interpublic Group of Companies, 262, 296
Inverted pyramid, 210, 212
Investigative reporters, 82, 220
Investigative Reporters and Editors (IRE), 162, 219
Investigative reporting, 76, 89, 96–97, 213, 217–221, 323
iPhone, 3, 6, 227
IPO, 321
Iraq war, 40, 288, 302, 327, 337, 370
Irwin, Will, 227
ITV, 260

James, William, 204
Jayson Blair, 378
Jazz Singer, The, 122
Jerry Springer Show, The, 16, 185, 380
Jewell, Richard, 370, 384–385
Joan Ganz Cooney Center for Children and Television in New York, 280
Johnson & Johnson, 267, 293
Johnson, Samuel, 91
Jolie, Angelina, 116
Jolson, Al, 122
Joseloff, Michael, 244
Journal of Advertising, 275
Journal of Advertising Research, 275
Journal of Media Ethics, 394
Judaism, 40

Kansas City Star, 324
Kanye West. *See* West, Kanye
Karp, Jonathan, 44, 55
Kato, Hidetoshi, 229
KDKA, 153
Kean University, 124
Keaton, Buster, 127, 230
Kennedy, Edward, 44
Kennedy, John F., 288
Ketchum, 296, 310
Kindle, 46, 105, 112
Kinetescope, 119
King Charles II, 64
King, Martin Luther. *See* Martin Luther King
Kinney National, 132